THE CRIME AND DISORDER ACT 1998

THE CRIME AND DISORDER ACT 1998

Richard Card LLB, LLM, FRSA
Professor of Law and Chairman of the School of Law
De Montfort University, Leicester

Richard Ward LLB, Solicitor
Professor of Public Law and Head of the
Department of Law
De Montfort University, Leicester

JORDANS
1998

Published by
Jordan Publishing Limited
21 St Thomas Street
Bristol BS1 6JS

British Library Cataloguing-in-Publication Data
A catalogue record for this book is available from the British Library.

ISBN 0 85308 490 4

Typeset by Mendip Communications Ltd, Frome, Somerset
Printed by MPG Books Ltd, Bodmin, Cornwall

PREFACE

The Crime and Disorder Act 1998 is the latest legislative intervention in the criminal justice process, and the first such intervention introduced by the Blair administration. It contains a wide variety of provisions, most of which implement a substantial number of commitments in the Labour Party's 1997 manifesto.

The book is primarily concerned with providing for practitioners a guide to the provisions of the new Act and their implications. It is not intended to provide a critique of the policies that underpin them.

Needless to say, we owe thanks to those who have assisted in the preparation of this book, in particular to Rachel Card, who spent many hours helping in the production at all its stages, and to Kathleen Williamson and Liz Steward in the School of Law, who assisted in the preparation of the manuscript. Thanks are also due to Stephen Honey, Mollie Dickenson and others at Jordans for their support and speedy production of the book.

The law is stated as at 1 August 1998, although we have been able to add at proof stage references to the two Commencement Orders which have been published at the time this Preface was written.

Richard Card
Richard Ward
September 1998

CONTENTS

TABLE OF CASES

References are to paragraph numbers. *Italic* references are to Appendix page numbers.

TABLE OF STATUTES

References are to paragraph numbers. *Italic* **references are to Appendix page numbers. Underlined** *italic* **references refer to page numbers where statutory matter is set out in annotations to the Act.**

TABLE OF STATUTORY INSTRUMENTS AND CODES ETC

References are to paragraph numbers. *Italic* **references are to Appendix page numbers. Underlined** *italic* **references refer to page numbers where statutory instrument matter is set out in annotations to the Act.**

TABLE OF EUROPEAN MATERIALS

References are to paragraph numbers.

Chapter 1

INTRODUCTION

1.1 This book is concerned with those provisions in the Crime and Disorder Act 1998 which apply to England and Wales.[1] It is divided into two parts: a narrative, followed by the Crime and Disorder Act 1998 with annotations thereto. The narrative and the annotated statute have different purposes. The narrative is intended to set out, explain and comment on the provisions of the Act, to give the reasons for them and to set them in the context of the current law. Generally, the text eschews detailed definitions of terms used in the Act, or detailed accounts of provisions referred to by it, which are not essential to a basic understanding of the Act and its operation. The purpose of the annotations is to deal with those matters of detail excluded from the narrative and also to provide, where necessary, some explanation of various legal rules underlying particular provisions.

In both the narrative and the annotations, references to other statutory provisions are to those provisions as amended by legislation other than the new Act. For the sake of simplicity, the amending legislation has not been referred to unless this has been essential to explain the point being made.

---

1 Section 121 prescribes the extent of the Act.

1.2 References are made occasionally to the date on which this book went to press. That date is 30 September 1998. References in this book to 'the Act', to 'the new Act', to 'the 1998 Act' or to any section are to the Crime and Disorder Act 1998 or to a section of it, unless the contrary is indicated.

1.3 In both parts of this book, references are made to the Parliamentary debates on the Crime and Disorder Bill. The Parliamentary progress of the Bill was as follows:

HOUSE OF LORDS
First reading: HL Deb, vol 583, 2 December 1997, cols 1245–1246.
Second reading: HL Deb, vol 584, 16 December 1997, cols 532–599.
Committee: HL Deb, vol 585, 3 February 1998, cols 508–518, 533–580, 597–634; HL Deb, vol 585, 10 February 1998, cols 1000–1009, 1021–1130; HL Deb, vol 585, 12 February 1998, cols 1265–1325, 1340–1382; HL Deb, vol 586, 24 February 1998, cols 548–559, 573–618, 634–674; HL Deb, vol 586, 3 March 1998, cols 1097–1186.

Where column numbers are duplicated, references to column numbers are followed by the date of the debate.

Report: HL Deb, vol 587, 17 March 1998, cols 575–640,
                              657–708, 822–862, 873–887, 890–950.
Third reading: HL Deb, vol 588, 31 March 1998, cols 154–264.

HOUSE OF COMMONS
First reading: 1 April 1998.
Second reading: HC Deb, vol 310, 8 April 1998, cols 370–452.
Standing Committee B: The Committee met 22 times between 28 April and
                              11 June 1998. Its deliberations are recorded in cols
                              1–874 of the Official Report.
Report: HC Deb, vol 314, 22 June 1998, cols 708–812, and 23
                              June, cols 842–938.
Third reading: HC Deb, vol 314, 23 June 1998, cols 938–957.

HOUSE OF LORDS
Consideration of Commons' amendments: HL Deb, vol 592, 22 July 1998, cols
918–976 and 990–1030.

HOUSE OF COMMONS
Consideration of Lords' disagreement (with Commons' amendment to reduce
age of consent to certain sexual acts): HC Deb, vol 317, 28 July 1998, cols
176–211.

ROYAL ASSENT
31 July 1998.

COMMENCEMENT

1.4   The Act comes into force on such days as are appointed by the Secretary
of State (s 121(2)). Different days may be appointed for different purposes or
different areas (s 121(2)). A commencement order may make such transitional
provisions and savings as appear to the Secretary of State necessary or
expedient (s 121(3)). A commencement order must be made by statutory
instrument (s 114(1)(a)).

Because quite a number of the Act's provisions are to be piloted, some of the
initial commencements will be limited in their extent. The pilot trials will
enable the Government to learn from experience the most effective way to
implement the measures in question. They will also enable the Government to
make accurate estimates of the costs and savings which will result when the
piloted provisions are fully in force, and so will help to inform decisions over
the timing of national implementation.[1] Where regulations have to be made to
implement a provision, they can be refined in the light of experience before
being extended nationally.

When this book went to press, two commencement orders[2] had been made
under the Act. They have brought into force various implementatory provisions

(including s 114, referred to above), the general interpretation section and (in whole or in part) most of the Act's substantive provisions. The details are set out at the relevant point in the text and Appendix II. Where the anticipated commencement dates for other provisions are known, they have been referred to at the appropriate point in the text. To facilitate exposition, however, this book is written on the basis that it is fully operative.

1 *No More Excuses – A New Approach to Tackling Youth Crime in England and Wales*, Cm 3809 (1997), para 10.3.
2 Crime and Disorder Act 1998 (Commencement No 1) Order 1998, SI 1998/1883; Crime and Disorder Act 1998 (Commencement No 2 and Transitional Provisions) Order 1998, SI 1998/2327.

1.5   There is nothing in the Act to rebut the presumption of interpretation that statutes do not operate retrospectively.[1] Thus, the various offences introduced by the Act do not apply to conduct occurring before they came into force. In addition, where the Act repeals a statutory provision governing an offence, this does not affect the institution or continuation of a prosecution in respect of offences alleged to have been committed before the date of the repeal,[2] because no contrary intention appears in the Act. On the other hand, unless the contrary is indicated, any procedural or evidential provisions created by the Act are applicable after they come into force to conduct occurring before then.[1].

1 *L'Office Cherifien des Phosphates v Yamashita-Shinnihon Steamship Co Ltd* [1994] 1 AC 486, [1994] 1 All ER 20 (HL).
2 Interpretation Act 1978, s 16(1).

OUTLINE OF THE ACT

1.6   The Act is yet another legislative attempt to tackle crime and disorder, although the first by the present Government. It implements 12 of the Labour Party's manifesto commitments and might be viewed as delivering that party's pledge to be 'Tough on crime; tough on the causes of crime'. It does so by introducing measures designed to modify, modernise and improve the criminal justice system.

'Tough on the causes of crime' receives some recognition in the Act, in terms, for example, of obliging local authorities and the police, working with other partners, to formulate and implement strategies for the reduction of crime and disorder in their particular area. However, the emphasis of the Act is on 'tough on crime', by widening the reach of the law and strengthening the criminal justice process against juveniles.[1]

1 See Rutherford *A Bill to be Tough on Crime* (1998) 148 NLJ 13.

1.7   The Bill was not preceded by principled discussion or detailed analysis. This is true of the discussion paper prepared in 1996 when the Government was

in opposition, of the consultation papers issued by the Government in 1997[1]
(for which there were very short time-limits for consultation) and of the White
Paper *No More Excuses – A New Approach to Tackling Youth Crime in England and
Wales* published in November 1997.[2]

---

1 The following are the relevant consultation papers, published by the Home Office:
  – *Racial Violence and Harassment*;
  – *Tackling Youth Crime*;
  – *Tackling Delays in the Youth Justice System*;
  – *New National and Local Focus on Youth Crime*;
  – *Getting to Grips with Crime: A New Framework for Local Action*;
  – *Community Safety Orders*;
  – *Preventing Children Offending*.
2 Cm 3809.

1.8   Like other Criminal Justice Acts, the Act contains a miscellany of
provisions dealing with a wide range of matters, but the overwhelming majority
of them fall within one of the following six main themes:

(1) tackling youth crime;
(2) combating anti-social behaviour and promoting local action against crime
     and disorder;
(3) reducing delay in the criminal justice system;
(4) tackling racist crime;
(5) protecting the public from sexual, violent and drug-misusing offenders;
(6) providing greater consistency and clarity in sentencing.

Tackling youth crime

1.9   The Act implements a number of measures put forward in the White
Paper *No More Excuses*.[1] Youth justice measures permeate the Act. Indeed, they
appear in every Part.

It is difficult to estimate how many offences juveniles commit. Much crime is
unreported. A substantial amount of reported crime is not cleared up, and
therefore an offender is not identified.

The best indicator is the number of known offenders, ie those cautioned by the
police or convicted by the courts. These figures show that, despite a fall since
the mid-1980s (the reasons for which are not fully understood), there were in
England and Wales in 1995 142,000 known male offenders aged 10 to 17 and
37,000 female offenders, and that increases have occurred for offences of
violence against the person, robbery and drug offences.[2] The fall in the
offending rate was reversed in 1993, since when there has been a small rise.[2]

Home Office research estimates that 26% of known offenders are under 18 and
that 3% of young offenders commit 26% of youth crime.[3] This small hard core
of persistent offenders causes the Government particular concern.

According to Home Office research, persistent school truancy and associating
with offenders are two important influences in youth offending, but the most

important factor is the quality of a young person's home life, including parental supervision.[3] Another research study lists such factors as one of a number of major risk factors, such as early child-bearing, personality, educational attainment, parental conflict, social and economic deprivation and social influences.[4] Many of these factors coincide.

1 *No More Excuses – A New Approach to Tackling Youth Crime in England and Wales*, Cm 3809 (1997).
2 *Aspects of Crime: Young Offenders, 1995* (Home Office, 1997). A Home Office self-report study, *Young People and Crime* (Home Office Research Study no 145, 1995), found that the ratio of 14- to 17-year-old males to females who admitted that they had ever committed an offence was nearly 1:1.
3 *Young People and Crime: Research Findings No 24* (Home Office, 1995).
4 Farrington *Understanding and Preventing Youth Crime: Research Findings 93* (Joseph Rowntree Foundation, 1996).

1.10   The focus of the youth justice provisions in the Act is on:

–   Providing a clear strategy to prevent offending and re-offending by juveniles. In addition to providing for local partnerships to combat local problems of crime and disorder, which will not, of course, be solely concerned with youth crime, the Act does the following:
  –   It places a duty on youth justice agencies to have regard to the need to prevent offending by young people.
  –   It states that the prevention of offending by children and young persons is the principal aim of the youth justice system.
  We deal with these matters in Chapter 2.
–   Establishment of a framework for agencies to deliver local youth justice systems through youth offending teams. A Youth Justice Board for England and Wales, expected to be in operation by October 1998, will help Ministers to set standards and monitor performance of the system. We deal with these matters in Chapter 2.
–   Early intervention with children and young persons to stop them being drawn into crime – since those who start committing offences at an early age are more likely to become serious and persistent offenders[1] – and, if they are drawn in, to halt their offending before it escalates.
  –   The Act introduces child safety orders, and powers for local authorities to establish local child curfews.
  –   It replaces cautioning for juveniles with a statutory final warning and reprimand scheme. This will address the need to involve the juvenile offender and his family in making changes which will reduce the risks of further criminal activity.
  –   It provides a power for a police officer to remove a truanting child from a public place.
  We deal with these matters in Chapter 3.
–   Reinforcing the responsibility of the child and of the parent for their actions.
  –   The Act abolishes the presumption of doli incapax in respect of children aged 10–13. This is dealt with in Chapter 9.

- It introduces new reparation and action plan orders to bring young offenders face to face with the human consequences of their conduct and require them to make amends to their victim. We deal with these orders in Chapter 4.
- It introduces parenting orders in an attempt to help parents and guardians to control their children's unacceptable behaviour. We deal with this in Chapter 3.
- Speeding up the youth justice process. The various provisions which are concerned with this are dealt with in Chapter 6.
- The Act makes a number of other changes in respect of dealing with young offenders. These are dealt with in Chapters 4 and 9.

---

1 See *No More Excuses – A New Approach to Tackling Youth Crime in England and Wales*, Cm 3809 (1997), para 1.13.

Combating anti-social behaviour and promoting local action against crime and disorder

1.11 As we explain in Chapter 5, Part I of the Act creates a new anti-social behaviour order. This new civil order is one of the more controversial provisions in the Act, and will prohibit behaviour which is likely to cause harassment, alarm or distress. Breach of an order is made an offence.

Part I also places a joint responsibility on local authorities and the police to develop and implement local strategies to reduce crime and disorder. Local authorities will also be placed under a duty to consider the crime and disorder implications of their policies. These matters are dealt with in Chapter 2.

Improving the speed and efficiency of the criminal justice system

1.12 Part III of the Act is concerned with this. Much of Part III implements a number of recommendations made by the Narey Report: *Review of Delay in the Criminal Justice System*,[1] published in February 1997. Among the relevant sections are provisions to abolish committal proceedings in respect of adults charged with offences triable only on indictment, provisions to improve the management of the prosecution process and the management of cases in the magistrates' courts, and provisions tightening up, and extending, the regime of time limits for criminal cases, enabling more exacting limits to be set in respect of juveniles – especially persistent juvenile offenders. We deal with all these matters in Chapter 6.

---

1 Home Office.

Tackling racist crime

1.13 The whole of Chapter 8 deals with this. Part II of the Act introduces new racially-aggravated offences parallel to various existing offences involving violence, assault, criminal damage, public disorder or harassment. For each

new offence there will be a greater maximum penalty than for the corresponding existing offence. In addition, s 82 in Part IV puts on a statutory footing the
judgment in *A-G's Reference (Nos 29, 30 and 31 of 1994)*[1] to the effect that, in
general, racial aggravation in connection with an offence is an aggravating
factor in sentencing.

---

1 (1995) 16 Cr App Rep (S) 698 (CA).

Protecting the public against sexual, violent and drug-misusing offenders

1.14   Sections 2 and 3 in Part I of the Act provide for sex offender orders,
which we describe in Chapter 5. This new civil order gives power to forbid the
majority of known sex offenders from specified conduct which poses a risk of
serious harm. Breach of an order is made a criminal offence. An order will carry
with it a requirement to be listed on the sex offenders register.

Part IV contains sections (ss 58 and 59) which provide for extended supervision
after release of certain adult and juvenile violent offenders. Released offenders
who break their licence will be liable to recall by the Parole Board. Section 61
provides for a new drug treatment and testing order. This will require the
courts to take an active role in monitoring the progress of drug-misusing
offenders who agree to undergo drug treatment as part of their sentence. We
deal with these matters in Chapter 7.

Promoting greater clarity and consistency in sentencing

1.15   Section 80 of the Act places a duty on the Court of Appeal (Criminal
Division) to consider producing sentencing guidelines for the main offences. It
is intended that these guidelines will take account of the need for consistency
and the need to secure public confidence in the criminal justice system. They
will help sentencers to determine offence-seriousness and to decide the weight
to be given to the offender's previous convictions and response to previous
sentences.

Section 81 provides for the establishment by the Lord Chancellor of a
Sentencing Advisory Panel. The Panel will advise the Lord Chancellor on
sentencing, and may suggest that the Court of Appeal produce guidelines for a
given category of offence. Sections 80 and 81 are dealt with in Chapter 7.

Other provisions

1.16   Apart from these main themes, there is a miscellany of other
provisions, for example, the abolition of the death penalty for treason and
piracy and early release on home detention curfews for short-term prisoners.

In addition, the Government clearly envisages the introduction of long-
overdue consolidating legislation in respect of sentencing. As part of the
preparation for that consolidation, the new Act introduces a variety of changes,
often of a drafting or tidying-up nature.

1.17   Section 115 deals with the disclosure of information. Clearly, effective
work with children and offenders requires that agencies with relevant
information should share that information with other agencies. That is, after
all, the fundamental nature of working in partnership in the way envisaged by
the new Act.[1] In particular, assessment of risk in respect of sex offenders[2]
necessitates information being shared, albeit subject to safeguards contained
in protocols established locally.

However, some public bodies may not until now have had the power to disclose
that information to the police. It is to remedy that possible gap that s 115 of the
new Act provides a new power. Any person who, apart from s 115(1), would not
have power to disclose information:

(a)   to a relevant authority; or
(b)   to a person acting on behalf of such an authority;

now has the power to do so in any case where the disclosure is necessary or
expedient for the purposes of any provision of the new Act.

The use of the term 'expedient' ensures that the power has the widest possible
application.

'Relevant authority' is defined by s 115(2) in such a way as to authorise
disclosure of information to any police force or police authority, a district or
county council, London borough council, the Common Council of the City of
London or (in Wales) a county borough council, a probation committee or a
health authority. Perhaps surprisingly, given the role in child protection
performed by organisations such as the NSPCC, disclosure of information to
such an organisation does not fall within the terms of s 115.

Section 115 came into force on 30 September 1998: see Appendix II.

---

1 See para **2.3**.
2 See para **5.72**.

Chapter 2

MANAGING CRIMINAL JUSTICE

Crime and disorder strategies – Reform of youth justice – Structural change to the youth justice system – Youth offending teams – The Youth Justice Board

2.1   The new Act makes significant changes to the management of the criminal justice process. It does so by creating a new framework for the development and management of crime and disorder strategies, and through a new system for managing the youth justice system. Through these two initiatives, the Government is seeking to develop an approach to the prevention of crime, and the management of crime, based on inter-agency initiatives and co-operation. Further, a new duty is imposed on local authorities, requiring them to take account of the crime and disorder implications of their actions and of the need to do all that they can to prevent crime and disorder in their areas.

The new Act also introduces new mechanisms to deal with consistency of sentencing and sentencing strategies. This is dealt with in Chapter 7.

CRIME AND DISORDER STRATEGIES

Introduction

2.2   In 1997 the Government strategy in respect of the fight against crime became clear, with the publication of its Consultation Paper, *Getting to Grips with Crime: A New Framework for Local Action*.[1] This Consultation Paper identified the fact that there is a realisation generally that the police cannot be expected to fight crime alone, and identified a wide range of partnership arrangements currently operating up and down the country, involving different agencies from the public and voluntary sectors at all levels. These range from multi-agency umbrella groups covering whole police force areas, to close collaboration between a beat officer and local Neighbourhood Watch groups.[2]

This approach is very much based on the recommendations of the Morgan Report, which was published in 1991.[3] Much of the current thinking on the importance of inter-agency partnership and on the most effective mechanisms for delivering it stems from the publication of that report, which was the work of an independent working group convened by the then Home Office Standing Conference on Crime Prevention.

1 See para **1.7**.
2 See para **2.3**.
3 *Safer Communities: the Local Delivery of Crime Prevention through the Partnership Approach* (Home
  Office, 1991).

2.3   The Morgan Committee examined in detail the opportunities and
problems which existed for those wanting to work in partnerships to prevent
and reduce crime. The Report underlined the need for broadly based,
multi-agency approaches to crime prevention and crime reduction, within
which agencies could co-operate as well as deliver their own contribution. It
highlighted the importance of involving the voluntary and business sectors as
partners in this work; it identified structural barriers to success such as differing
operational areas between police service, local authority and probation service
boundaries; and expressed the view that a factual analysis of local problems was
an essential first step in the development of a successful local crime prevention
partnership.

Getting to Grips with Crime identified the fact that the police and local authorities
have embraced the concept of multi-agency work and set out the results of a
survey of local authorities.[1] Some 90% of authorities which participated in the
survey recognised community safety as an area of work relevant to them, and
84% had reported on it to the relevant committee within the two preceding
years; 62% of authorities were engaged in independent multi-agency partnerships, with 32% also involved in other types of partnership; 62% undertook
local crime pattern analysis, and over one-third of authorities did crime audits;
51% had a separate budget for community safety; 37% have appointed their
own community safety officer; and 67% run diversionary holiday schemes for
young people.

There were also some less encouraging findings. Various factors restricting
further development of the work were identified, including the attitude of
central government, the internal priority attached to the subject and the effects
of local government re-organisation. One of the biggest barriers to progress was
seen as the lack of a statutory role for local authorities.

1 See *Survey of Community Safety Activities in Local Government in England and Wales* (Home Office,
  1996).

2.4   *Getting to Grips with Crime* identified the fact that appropriate action by
local authorities can have significant effects on crime prevention. It costs
nothing for a local authority to make crime one of the many factors which is
routinely considered when, say, new policies for the delivery of social services
are planned, or new housing estates are built – but it can be very expensive
indeed to later put right the problems which often flow from omitting this
important stage. As the Consultation Paper observes, 'The crime and disorder
reduction implications of all decisions made by local authorities should be
considered by elected members and council officials as routinely as, say, the
financial or equal opportunities implications are today'.[1]

It is for this reason that the Government, in the new Act, has sought to create a new duty, and new mechanisms, to harness effectively the initiatives that are occurring informally and, often, on a voluntary basis. Local authorities are to be 'equal stakeholders' with the police in crime and disorder strategies. Crime and disorder strategies are to be developed on a joint and equal partnership basis. The duty imposed on these bodies would require them to come together in a group to establish the mechanism by which their obligations could be fulfilled, through the performance of specific tasks. It is also recognised that a wide variety of other bodies, whether local or voluntary groups or organisations, from the private sector or from the public sector have legitimate interests in making inputs to solutions and decision-making on a partnership basis.

Through these mechanisms, planning is to occur to set targets, and to secure achievement of those targets. It is not intended that it should be planning for planning sake. Thus the strategy to achieve objectives set, and the monitoring of that achievement, is as important as the setting of the objectives themselves. Such planning, and monitoring, is also intended to go hand-in-hand with planning which occurs in different contexts, but which nevertheless interrelate. Examples of this include the annual policing plan, and plans prepared under the Education Act 1996.

---

1 *Getting to Grips with Crime: A New Framework for Local Action*; see para **1.7**.

The new statutory framework[1]

2.5   The functions which are conferred on local authorities by the new Act are exercisable in relation to each local government area[2] by the responsible authorities. The 'responsible authorities' are the council for the area (ie the district council, London borough council or other unitary authority; in the case of a district council the county council is also a responsible authority) (s 5(1)(a)). This should be contrasted with the organisational structure in respect of youth justice where the obligation is placed on county councils or unitary authorities, but not non-unitary district councils. The intention is that crime and disorder functions should be primarily taken forward by bodies that have responsibility for the immediate locality. The responsible authority also includes the chief officer of police[3] any part of whose police area lies within the local authority area.

---

1 The relevant provisions came into force on 30 September 1998: see Appendix II.
2 'Local government area' means: (a) in relation to England, each district or London borough, the City of London, the Isle of Wight and the Isles of Scilly; (b) in relation to Wales each county or county borough (s 5(4)).
3 Which means the Chief Constable of each force maintained under the Police Act 1996, s 2, together with the Commissioner of Police for the Metropolis and the Commissioner of the City of London police: see s 18, and annotations thereto.

2.6   The responsible local authorities and the responsible chief officers of police are under a duty to act in co-operation with others (s 5(2)). Whilst, of course, there is no reason why the responsible authorities should not act in co-operation with anybody, the *duty* extends to certain stated persons or bodies. These are specified by s 5(2) as:

(a) every police authority any part of whose police area lies within the area;
(b) every probation committee or health authority any part of whose area lies within the area; and
(c) every person or body of a description which is for the time being prescribed by order of the Home Secretary under s 5(2).

It is the duty of those persons and bodies to co-operate in the exercise by the responsible authorities of those functions (s 5(2)). The Home Secretary may also specify persons or bodies of particular types or descriptions. If he does so, the responsible authority must invite the participation in the exercise of the functions of at least one person or body of each description.

2.7   The responsible authorities are under a duty to formulate and implement, for each relevant period, a strategy for the reduction of crime and disorder in the area (s 6(1)).

Before they do so, the responsible authorities must:

(a) carry out a review of the levels and patterns of crime and disorder in the area (taking due account of the knowledge and experience of persons in the area);
(b) prepare an analysis of the results of that review;
(c) publish in the area a report of that analysis; and
(d) obtain the views on that report of persons or bodies in the area (including those of a description prescribed by order under s 5(3)), whether by holding public meetings or otherwise.

In formulating a strategy, the responsible authorities must have regard to the analysis prepared and the views obtained under s 6(2).

What must the strategy include?

2.8   This is dealt with by s 6(4). It must include the following:

(a) objectives to be pursued by the responsible authorities, by co-operating persons or bodies or, under agreements with the responsible authorities, by other persons or bodies; and
(b) long-term and short-term performance targets for measuring the extent to which such objectives are achieved.

Dissemination of the strategy

2.9   The results must be contained in a document published in the area, and include details of:

(a) co-operating persons and bodies;
(b) the review carried out under s 6(2);
(c) the report published under s 6(2); and
(d) the strategy, including in particular the objectives and performance targets set.

While implementing a strategy, the responsible authorities must keep it under review with a view to monitoring its effectiveness and making any changes to it that appear necessary or expedient.

The period the strategy covers

2.10   The strategy must be kept under review (s 6(6)). However, it has a life of three years beginning with such day as the Home Secretary may by order appoint; and it must be replaced and updated by a new plan every three years.

DUTY TO CONSIDER CRIME AND DISORDER IMPLICATIONS

2.11   The other side of this approach has already been identified, namely, the duty of local authorities to consider the crime and disorder implications of what they do. Section 17[1] requires each authority to which it applies to exercise its various functions with due regard to the likely effect of the exercise of those functions on crime and disorder in its area and the need to do all that it reasonably can to prevent crime and disorder there (s 17(1)).

Section 17 applies to:

(a)   a county council, a district council, a London borough council, the Common Council of the City of London and a parish council (in England);
(b)   a county council, county borough council or community council (in Wales);
(c)   a joint authority for fire and civil defence in Metropolitan counties, the London Fire and Civil Defence authority, and a Metropolitan county passenger transport authority;
(d)   a police authority;
(e)   a National Parks authority; and
(f)   the Broads Authority (s 17(2)).

The Home Secretary is the Police Authority for the Metropolitan Police. Arrangements have been agreed under which the Home Secretary will ask the Metropolitan Police Committee to undertake any necessary liaison on his behalf.[2]

The application of s 17 to joint authorities seems surprising, and its application to National Park authorities and to the Broads Authority even more so. The role of the latter two types of authority is essentially a planning one, which seems to have little impact on crime and disorder. However, the application of s 17 to them was defended in the House of Lords on the ground that planning decisions can sometimes have significant implications for crime and disorder and should be made after due regard for such implications, and on the further ground in the case of the Broads Authority that it has byelaw-making powers about the way in which craft are used in its area.[3]

1 Came into force on 30 September 1998: see Appendix II.
2 Lord Williams of Mostyn, Parliamentary Under-Secretary, Home Office, HL Committee, col 105.
3 Lord Williams of Mostyn and Viscount Colville of Culross, HL Committee, cols 1057 and 1058.

STRUCTURAL CHANGE TO THE YOUTH JUSTICE SYSTEM

2.12 These provisions, contained mainly in Part III of the new Act, implement Government proposals to improve the delivery or work with young offenders in the community. They form part of a wider strategy, identified by the Morgan Report,[1] which underlined the need for broadly based, multi-agency approaches to crime prevention and reduction, with agencies co-operating in partnership as well as delivering their own contribution.[2] The Report highlighted the importance of involving the voluntary and business sectors as partners, and identified structural barriers to success. Local authorities have a key role to play in crime prevention, as do agencies working in partnership. The Government's Consultation Paper, *Getting to Grips with Crime* identified the growth over the last few years of partnership schemes between agencies, and outlined its strategies to create 'a sympathetic and helpful new framework within which partnerships to reduce crime and insecurity can develop'.[2] Sections 6 and 7 seek to create this framework. They require district councils, and chief officers of police, to create crime and disorder strategies, in consultation with other relevant authorities, organisations and persons.[3] Such local strategies will include strategies in respect of the content, and delivery, of youth services.

The provisions of s 41(3), relating to the membership of the Youth Justice Board, came into effect on 1 August 1998. The other parts of s 41, and the remaining provisions relating to the youth justice arrangements came into force on 30 September 1998: see Appendix II. The Youth Offending Team provisions are being piloted (see para **2.19**).[4]

1 See paras **2.2–2.3**.
2 See para **2.2**.
3 See paras **2.3–2.4**.
4 See Crime and Disorder Act 1998 (Commencement No 1) Order 1998, SI 1998/1883 and Appendix II.

2.13 This inter-agency approach is particularly important in the context of the delivery of youth justice. The Criminal Justice Act 1991, and Home Office Circular 30/1992, both encouraged joint initiatives in relation to 16 and 17-year-old offenders.[1] Existing responsibility for such offenders is split between local authority social service departments, who generally have prime responsibility for offenders aged under 16, and for those aged 16 known to them, and the probation service which generally deals with offenders aged 17, but also some offenders aged 16 and a few younger offenders.[2] The details of this division of responsibility are a matter for local negotiation and agreement. Some parts of England and Wales have inter-agency teams which deal with young offenders, but the precise arrangements vary widely and are not consistent.[3] The rationale for change was explained in a consultation paper[4] as follows:

> 'The Government believes that action is needed to bring about greater consistency in the approach to work with young offenders in the community and to ensure that all the relevant local agencies play a full part. Such action will need to be built on the best of existing work but, to ensure that youth justice is given proper priority by the relevant agencies and is clearly focused on challenging offending behaviour, the Government believes that a more structured approach is required. This will involve clear and specific duties on those agencies and greater openness and accountability concerning the way in which those duties are discharged.'

It is for that reason that the new Act seeks to define the general aim of the youth justice system.

---

1 *New National and Local Focus on Youth Crime: A Consultation Paper* (Home Office, 1997), paras 11–14.
2 See general annotations.
3 *New National and Local Focus on Youth Crime*, op cit, para 13.
4 Ibid, para 14.

The aim of the youth justice system

2.14   Section 37(1) states that the principal aim of the youth justice system is to prevent offending by children and young persons. It is the duty of all persons and bodies carrying out functions in relation to the youth justice system to have regard to that aim (s 37(2)). This approach, of stating an overall aim, is not new: a particularly relevant example of another such provision is s 44 of the Children and Young Persons Act 1933, which requires a court, in fulfilling its duties, to take account of the welfare of the child or young person before the court. By contrast, the aim stated by s 37(1) does not individualise the aim to the individual offender before the court. Thus an individual young offender may, quite legitimately within the principal aim stated by s 37(1), be dealt with in a way which will prevent offending generally by children and young persons, even if it does not have that effect individually.

The new duty will apply to all those working within the context of the youth justice system, including local authorities, health authorities, probation services, voluntary agencies, the police and the courts. A police officer in determining whether or not to issue a reprimand or final warning[1] will be required to have regard to this general duty; the Crown Prosecution Service will need to have regard to s 37 when determining whether a prosecution should be undertaken. A sentencing court will likewise have, as a principal aim, the prevention of re-offending. The duty will extend to defence solicitors and barristers. It does not follow from that that such bodies will be required to give effect in their decisions to that aim irrespective of other considerations. The phrase 'principal aim' identifies the overall aim of the system: individuals working within it are required to have regard to that aim, but not to the exclusion of other legitimate aims or objectives, such as the protection of the public or their own professional obligations. Thus the general duty does not detract from the duty a lawyer owes to his client, or of a Crown Prosecutor to have regard to the Code for Crown Prosecutors. If the means by which offending by an individual, or by other individuals, can be prevented, is by the imposition of a custodial order then nothing in s 37 prevents that.

1 See the examples given by Alun Michael, MP, Minister of State, Home Office, HC Committee, cols 371–372.

2.15   The general duty could be described as a statement of how issues relating to youth offenders should be addressed. Its purpose was explained by the Minister of State, as follows:[1]

> 'Many debates have taken place about the balance between considering the welfare of a child before the court, determining the appropriate punishment and preventing re-offending. That long-standing debate has sometimes contributed to muddled decisions by practitioners in the youth justice system. [Section 37] provides a clear statement that the principal aim of the youth justice system should be to prevent re-offending by the children and young people with whom it deals. It clarifies the main aim of those who work within the criminal justice system. The clause is intended to end both the uncertainty about what is expected of those who work for youth justice agencies, and the confusion about balancing the interests of the offender, the victim and the community. That confusion has been apparent for some time and has undermined public confidence in the youth justice system.'

It therefore is intended to achieve clarity of purpose and focus. The welfare of the individual offender (to which the court must have regard)[2] is not the prime purpose of the criminal justice system, although almost always the welfare of the offender will be promoted by the preventing of re-offending, and a failure to address the offending behaviour might be regarded as contrary to the welfare principle.[3] For this reason, arguments put in mitigation that an offender should not be made the subject of a particular custodial order, because it might increase, rather than decrease, the potential for re-offending, are unlikely to be justifiable by reference to the general duty imposed by s 37.

1 Alun Michael, MP, Minister of State, Home Office, HC Committee, cols 375–376.
2 Children and Young Persons Act 1933, s 44: see para **2.14**.
3 Alun Michael, MP, Minister of State, Home Offfice, HC Committee, col 375.

The duty imposed on local authorities

2.16   Each local authority[1] is under a duty to secure that, to such extent as is appropriate for its area, all youth justice services are available there (s 38(1)).

These services will have to be provided in accordance with national standards drawn up by the newly created Youth Justice Board.[2] The duty is to be performed in co-operation with the appropriate chief constable and police authorities,[3] probation committee and health authority (s 38(1),(2)), and such bodies are under a statutory duty to co-operate in the discharge of that duty by the local authority. National guidance in respect of such co-operation arrangements will be issued in due course by the Government.

'Youth justice services' are defined by s 38(4) as any of the following:

(a) the provision of persons to act as appropriate adults[4] to safeguard the interests of children and young persons detained or questioned by police officers;

(b) the assessment of children and young persons, and the provision for them of rehabilitation programmes for the purposes of the provisions of s 66 (reprimands and warnings);[5]

(c) the provision of support for children and young persons remanded or committed on bail while awaiting trial or sentence;

(d) the placement in local authority accommodation of children and young persons remanded or committed to such accommodation under s 23 of the Children and Young Persons Act;[6]

(e) the provision of reports and other information required by courts in criminal proceedings against children and young persons;

(f) the provision of persons to act as responsible officers in relation to parenting orders, child safety orders, reparation orders and action plan orders;[7]

(g) the supervision of young persons sentenced to a probation order, a community service order or a combination order;

(h) the supervision of young persons sentenced to a detention and training order[8] or a supervision order;[9]

(i) the post-release supervision of children and young persons under s 37(4A) or s 65 of the Criminal Justice Act 1991, or s 31 of the Crime (Sentences) Act 1997;[10]

(j) the performance of functions under s 71 of the new Act (supervision of person subject to detention and training order).[8]

The Home Secretary may from time to time amend this definition so as to extend, restrict or otherwise alter it, by order (s 38(5)).

---

1 A local authority is defined widely for this purpose to include county councils, district councils (where the district does not form part of an area that has a county council), London borough councils or the Common Council of the City of London or, in relation to Wales, a county council or borough council (s 42(1)).

2 *New National and Local Focus on Youth Crime*, op cit, p 3.

3 Ibid, p 3.

4 See annotation to s 65.

5 See paras **3.66–3.75**.

6 See annotations to s 97.

7 See paras **3.32**, **3.17**, **4.2** and **4.24**.

8 See paras **4.49** et seq.
9 See paras **4.34–4.41**.
10 See annotations to s 38.

Youth justice plans

2.17   Each local authority will, each year, formulate and implement a youth justice plan. This plan, which will be published, will set out (s 40(1)):

(a) how youth justice services in their area are to be provided and funded; and
(b) how the youth offending team(s), referred to below, are to be composed and funded, how they are to operate and what functions they are to carry out.

These provisions are similar to other statutory provisions. As already noted,[1] s 6 of the new Act imposes a duty on a local authority (which is usually a different local authority from that under a duty to publish a youth justice plan)[2] to prepare a community safety and crime reduction strategy. The Children Act 1989 imposes a duty on a local authority to produce a children's services plan. Police authorities are under a duty, imposed by s 8 of the Police Act 1996, to produce an annual policing plan. Section 9 of the Education Act 1997 requires the publication of a plan setting out the proposed arrangements for dealing with pupils with behavioural difficulties, including persistent non-attenders and excluded pupils. Clearly, a measure of coordination and dialogue is required if plans are not to end up being contradictory, but each of these plans will have different overall objectives. That of the youth justice plan is to prevent re-offending by children and young persons.

The youth justice plan will identify the local infrastructure of youth justice services, and provides the context in which youth offending teams will work. The plan will include[3] appropriate arrangements for bail supervision and support, arrangements for supervision work in support of the final warning system created by the new Act,[4] arrangements for the supervision of the range of community sentences available in respect of young offenders, and for the management of parenting and child safety orders. The plan will not concern itself with the operation or administration of the courts: that said, it is intended that such plans should address the timeliness and efficiency of the court process, and can include provisions for 'fast tracking' persistent young offenders, for the preparation of pre-sentence and other reports, and liaison with the Crown Prosecution Service.

1 See paras **2.5–2.10**.
2 See s 5(4), which defines a local authority for the purposes of s 5.
3 *New National and Local Focus on Youth Crime*, op cit, para 32.
4 See paras **3.66–3.75**.

2.18   Youth justice provision, and youth justice teams, will be funded by local authorities. However, a local authority and other agencies can create a common fund out of which payments for youth justice services can be met (s 39(4)). In such a case, accountability will rest with the local authority.

Youth offending teams

2.19   Central to the provision of youth justice services will be youth offending teams. The concept of multi-agency teams takes forward in a practical form the broad objectives identified by the Morgan Committee, and discussed earlier.[1] The new Act introduces youth offending teams. Following initial pilots, it is intended to introduce the new teams nationwide during 1999–2000.[2]

These youth justice teams will be under a duty to coordinate the provision of youth justice services within the local authority area, and to carry out such functions as are assigned to the team in the local authority's youth justice plan made under s 40 (s 39(7)). The Government's intention is that such teams 'should pull together all the relevant local agencies in delivering community-based interventions with, and supervision of, young offenders'.[3] The right local infrastructure should exist on which youth offending teams can draw, and the courts should have access to appropriate bail support arrangements in dealing with young people. Not all functions will necessarily be performed by the youth offending teams themselves: their work may in fact draw on programmes and activities provided by local agencies or by the voluntary sector. One detailed example of this is the fact that whilst wider preventative and family support work might be undertaken by the local authority social services department, it may be appropriate in some instances for orders such as parenting orders[4] to be supervised by members of the team (eg where the order is imposed on the parents of a young offender). Again, a team might supervise a child safety order if the team was involved locally in preventative work or if the family concerned was known to it.[5]

It will be crucial, however, that the team does not lose sight of its criminal justice objectives. Thus the primary functions are likely to be the assessment and intervention work in support of the final warning (including work with the offender to bring about behavioural change, reparation work with victims, supervised leisure activities and work with parents), supervision of community sentences (if appropriate drawing on agencies and projects outside the team), ensuring that there is an 'appropriate adult'[6] service available for police interviews, provision of bail information to assist the courts in making decisions about juveniles, bail supervision and support, the placement of young people in open or secure accommodation, remand fostering or approved accommodation, court work and the preparation of reports, and through-care during, and undertaking post-release supervision following, a custodial sentence. The Government also proposes a role for youth offending teams in relation to parenting and child safety orders.[7]

---

1 See paras **2.3** and **2.4**.
2 *No More Excuses*, op cit, para 10.5. The pilot areas for Youth Offending Teams are Hammersmith and Fulham, Kensington and Chelsea, and Westminister (jointly); Lewisham; Hampshire, Southampton, Portsmouth and the Isle of Wight (jointly); Devon; Sheffield; St Helens; Wolverhampton; Blackburn with Darwen; and Luton and Bedfordshire (jointly). The pilot areas are the same as for those for s 38 (see para **2.12**) and s 40 (see para **2.17**), and in some of them ss 65 and 66 (reprimands and warnings) will also be piloted: see Appendix II.
3 Ibid, para 15.
4 See paras **3.31–3.41**.
5 *New National and Local Focus on Youth Crime*, op cit, para 20.

6 See annotations to s 65.
7 See paras **3.20** and **3.33**.

Composition

2.20   Each local authority must establish at least one youth offending team, in co-operation with relevant police authorities, probation committees and health authorities (s 39(1), (3)). Two or more authorities may choose to act together to establish one or more youth offending teams for their areas: the Act entitles them to do so (s 39(2)). Each team will include at least one probation officer, local authority social worker, police officer, nominee of a health authority and of the local education authority (s 39(5)). The Government does not intend to prescribe the precise composition of teams or the roles of individual members.[1] Nor is the list in s 39(5) intended to be exhaustive. After consultation with the police authority, probation committee and health authority, the local authority may include on the youth offending team such other person as it thinks appropriate (s 39(6)). The key consideration in determining the composition of each of them will be the need for the work of such teams to be clearly directed towards tackling offending behaviour and to challenge young offenders to change behaviour and attitudes.[2] The composition should be such as to reflect this key objective. Clearly, social workers will be key members of the team. The young offender, or his family, may be known to social services or receiving support or other social services intervention. The young offender may be, or have been, in care. Probation officers will likewise be key players, and it is intended that their expertise be made available potentially to a wider range of offenders. Currently, the law restricts (although does not totally prohibit) the supervision by probation officers of 10–12-year-olds.[3] That restriction is removed by the new Act.[4] In future, the supervisor of a young person under a supervision order will be a member of a youth offending team within whose area it appears to a court that the supervised person resides or will reside. This change is made to facilitate the new 'mixed economy' envisaged by the new scheme.[5] In future, it will be the most appropriate person who will supervise the offender.

---

1 *New National and Local Focus on Youth Crime*, op cit, para 33.
2 Ibid, para 34.
3 Children and Young Persons Act 1969, s 13(2).
4 Schedule 8, para 19. See also s 71(5) for the selection of supervision for supervision orders.
5 *New National and Local Focus on Youth Crime*, op cit, para 37.

2.21   Other participants in the youth offending team include police officers, the local authority education department and health authority staff. Police officers will be expected to ensure good liaison with police colleagues dealing with the final warning under s 65,[1] expected to highlight to the offender the consequences of offending on victims and of a criminal record, to help supervise more persistent young offenders (eg by checking curfews and attendance at projects) and to promote wider community safety and crime reduction schemes (eg supervised leisure activities). Local authority education department workers will be able to ensure that educational and training issues and needs are addressed, and be involved in work with truants or excluded pupils. Health authority staff will be able to liaise in respect of local alcohol and drug misuse and psychiatric provision, feeding in, perhaps, to the rehabilitation programme that accompanies the final warning envisaged by s 66. Whether all or any such individuals need to be full-time members of the youth offending team will be a matter for local decision. Individuals from other agencies and organisations, such as the local authority youth service, or voluntary agencies, may be involved directly, or more indirectly through partnership arrangements. So too may representatives from the business community.

1 See paras **3.66–3.75**.

The Youth Justice Board

2.22   Section 41(1) creates a new body corporate, the Youth Justice Board. This will comprise 10, 11 or 12 members, appointed by the Home Secretary, who will include persons with extensive recent experience of the youth justice system (s 41(3), (4)). In particular, persons with experience of the courts in dealing with young offenders and with experience of services for victims are among the areas of expertise which will be sought.[1]

Detailed provisions relating to membership, procedure and financial arrangements are contained in Sch 2. An individual will be appointed for a fixed period no longer than five years, and may be re-appointed (even more than once) provided his total length of service does not exceed 10 years (Sch 2, para 2(5)). A member may be removed from membership where the conditions of appointment so permit, where there has been a failure (without reasonable excuse) to discharge functions for a continuous period of three months beginning not earlier than six months before the removal, upon conviction for a criminal offence, the making of a bankruptcy or similar order, or where the individual is unfit to discharge the functions of a member (Sch 2, para 2(9)). Members may be paid, in accordance with terms set out by the Home Secretary. The Board will be chaired by one member appointed by the Home Secretary as chairman (Sch 2, para 1), and will determine its own procedure (Sch 2, para 7). The Board is under a duty to publish an Annual Report and accounts (Sch 2, para 8).

1 Alun Michael, MP, Minister of State, Home Office, HC Committee, col 393.

2.23   The functions of the Board are set out in s 41(5), as follows:

(a) to monitor the operation of the youth justice system and the provision of youth justice services;
(b) to advise the Home Secretary on the following matters, namely:
     (i)   the operation of that system and the provision of such services;
     (ii) how the principal aim of that system might most effectively be pursued;

    (iii) the content of any national standards he may see fit to set with respect to the provision of such services, or the accommodation in which children and young persons are kept in custody; and

    (iv) the steps which might be taken to prevent offending by children and young persons;

(c) to monitor the extent to which that aim is being achieved and any such standards met;

(d) for the purposes of paragraphs (a), (b) and (c), to obtain information from relevant authorities;

(e) to publish information so obtained;

(f) to identify, to make known and to promote good practice in the following matters, namely:

    (i) the operation of the youth justice system and the provision of youth justice services;

    (ii) the prevention of offending by children and young persons; and

    (iii) working with children and young persons who are or are at risk of becoming offenders;

(g) to make grants, with the approval of the Home Secretary, to local authorities or other bodies for them to develop such practice, or to commission research in connection with such practice; and

(h) itself to commission research in connection with such practice.

The work of the Board will thus provide the framework, context and information base within, and upon, which local authorities and youth offending teams will operate. One important aspect of this will be to advise the Government on the drawing up of new National Standards for the work of youth offending teams and the provision of youth justice services, focusing on the particular needs and objectives of work with young people. The existing National Standards for the Supervision of Offenders in the Community are primarily focused on adult offenders. The new National Standards will provide benchmarks for the work of the various inspectorates that oversee, or might oversee, the work of the youth offending teams.

Chapter 3

CHILDREN AND YOUNG PERSONS: EARLY INTERVENTION AND PARENTAL RESPONSIBILITY

Local child curfew schemes – Child safety orders – Parenting orders – Removal of truants to schools or designated premises – Reprimands and warnings

3.1 Two ways in which the Act seeks to deal with youth crime are its provisions aimed at early intervention to stop juveniles, especially those under the age of criminal responsibility, drifting into a criminal culture and its provisions aimed at reinforcing parental responsibility.

The provisions about parenting orders dealt with in this chapter are aimed at reinforcing parental responsibility; the others at early intervention.

LOCAL CHILD CURFEW SCHEMES

3.2 The background to these schemes was given by the then Solicitor-General in the House of Lords as follows:

'Everyone knows that some neighbourhoods are troubled by the criminal and anti-social activities of unsupervised young children. Gathered in public places at night they can cause real alarm and misery to the local community. They can also encourage each other into anti-social and criminal habits. To address such concerns we believe that local councils, following consultation with local communities, should have the option of using local child curfews as a response to a particular identified problem. Local child curfews will form one part of a wider community safety strategy.'[1]

Police in Kent and parts of London have already imposed child curfews on problem housing estates,[2] but the Act puts child curfews on a statutory basis.

---

1 HL Committee, col 1107 (10 February).
2 (1997) *Guardian*, 4 October.

What is a local child curfew scheme?

3.3 Section 14 provides powers for local authorities to set up local child curfew schemes for children aged under 10. Contrary to earlier indications,[1] the provisions for local child curfews will not be piloted before being introduced generally.[2] They came into force on 30 September 1998.[2]

The following example of how a local child curfew would work (which assumes the existence of a local child curfew scheme) was given in *No More Excuses*:

> 'For example, if young children were regularly congregating at night in the public spaces of a housing estate making residents' lives intolerable through vandalism, pilfering and abusive behaviour, local residents might seek the help of the police. If normal policing methods did not work the local authority, after consultation, might decide to introduce a local child curfew for a ninety day period.'[3]

Section 14(1) and (2) defines a local child curfew scheme as a scheme made by a local authority which enables the authority to give a notice imposing, for a specified period, a ban on children of specified ages[4] (under 10) being in a public place within a specified area:

(a) during specified hours (between 9pm and 6am);[5] and

(b) otherwise than under the effective control of a parent (of whatever age) or of a responsible person aged 18[4] or over.

The following local authorities may make a curfew scheme: the council of a district (including a unitary authority), a London borough council, the Common Council of the City of London, the Council of the Isle of Wight or the Council of the Isles of Scilly (in England) or a county or county borough council (in Wales) (s 14(8)). A 'public place' has the same meaning in this context as in Part II of the Public Order Act 1986 (s 14(8)), viz 'any highway and any place to which at the material time the public or any section of the public has access, on payment or otherwise, as of right or by virtue of express or implied permission'.[5] Streets, shops, the communal areas of blocks of flats, shopping centres, local authority parks and recreation grounds, and amusement arcades, all fall within this definition.

---

1 *Tackling Youth Crime: A Consultation Paper* (Home Office, 1997), para 123.
2 See Appendix II.
3 Ibid, para 5.8.
4 See general annotations.
5 See annotations to s 14.

3.4   The age of 10 has been chosen as the upper age-limit for those to whom a curfew notice can be made to apply, on the ground that anti-social behaviour orders under s 1 are available in respect of those of 10 or over. Such an order can include in certain cases the imposition of a curfew in respect of anyone named in the order. In addition, there will be available the range of offences and supporting police powers in respect of those aged 10 or more.[1]

In terms of anti-social behaviour orders there is this interesting comparison. Such an order can only be made in respect of an individual who has been proved to have acted in an 'anti-social manner', whereas a curfew notice will apply to children in general under the age specified in it who are not proved to have done anything wrong and whose parents are not proved to have done so either.

---

1 Lord Falconer of Thoroton, Solicitor-General, HL Committee, cols 1113–1114 (10 February).

Procedure for making a local child curfew scheme

3.5   Before making a scheme, a local authority must consult:

(a) every chief constable (or Commissioner of Police) any part of whose area lies within its area;[1] and

(b) such other persons or bodies as it thinks appropriate (s 14(3)), such as social services departments, voluntary agencies and the local community (eg residents' groups).[2]

A scheme must be made under the common seal of the local authority. It does not have effect until confirmed by the Home Secretary (s 14(4)). The Home Secretary:

(a) may confirm, or refuse to confirm, a scheme; and

(b) may fix the date on which it is to come into operation (s 14(5)).

If no date is fixed, the scheme will come into operation at the end of one month[1] beginning with the date of its confirmation (ibid).

The Home Secretary's role in giving approval does not include varying a scheme once it is submitted. He is responsible for ensuring that the applicant authority has complied with the terms of the legislation, particularly in relation to consultation. Guidance is to be given by the Home Office as to the kind of information required by the Home Secretary before confirming a scheme. Draft guidance was issued in August 1998.

In order to be approved, the scheme will need to specify the arrangements for consulting the local police and residents in the area to which a curfew notice is proposed to be applied and the arrangements for making local residents and others aware of it when it is brought into force.[3]

---

1 See annotations to s 14.

2 *No More Excuses – A New Approach to Tackling Youth Crime in England and Wales*, Cm 3809 (1997), para 5.6; Lord Falconer of Thoroton, Solicitor-General, HL Committee, cols 1115 and 1119 (10 February).

3 *Tackling Youth Crime: A Consultation Paper* (Home Office, 1997), para 118.

Curfew notice

When can it be given?

3.6   A local authority may only give a notice imposing a curfew:

(a) subject to and in accordance with the provisions of the local curfew scheme; and

(b) if, after such consultation as is required by the scheme, the authority considers it necessary for the purpose of maintaining order (s 14(1)).

The only criterion for giving a notice making the order is that the local authority must consider that it is necessary for the purpose of maintaining order (s 14(1)). The fact that the making of schemes, and of notices under them, is a matter for the local authority is liable to lead to variation in practice from one authority to another.

Consultation

3.7   Given that the approval mechanism for a curfew scheme will play particular regard to the adequacy of consultation and to the local authority's response to it, defects in the consultative process are more likely to be challenged in respect of the requirement for consultation before a curfew notice is given.

An authoritative statement of what consultation requires was given by Webster J in *Secretary of State for Social Services, ex parte Association of Metropolitan Authorities:*[1]

> 'The essence of consultation is the communication of a genuine invitation to give advice and a genuine consideration of that advice. ... To achieve consultation sufficient information must be supplied by the consulting to the consulted party to enable it to tender helpful advice. Sufficient time must be given by the consulting to the consulted party to enable it to do that, and sufficient time must be available for such advice to be considered by the consulting party. Sufficient, in that context, does not mean ample, but at least enough to enable the relevant purpose to be fulfilled. By helpful advice, in this context, I mean sufficiently informed and considered information or advice about aspects of the form or substance of the proposals, or their implications for the consulted party, being aspects material to the implementation of the proposal as to which the [consulting party] might not be fully informed or advised and as to which the party consulted might have relevant information or advice to offer.'

A failure to consult (at all or properly) as required would be likely to lead a court to hold on an application by a person entitled to be consulted that there had been a breach of a mandatory procedural requirement, rendering the scheme or notice (as the case may be) invalid and of no effect.[2] On the other hand, if the local authority failed to heed the views put forward during proper consultation, this would not in itself affect the validity of the notice. The local authority's statutory duty is to consult and to be receptive to what consultees say. It is not a duty to be dictated to by them. Serious views carefully advanced by consultees must not simply be ignored, but the weight to be given to them, balanced against all the other relevant factors, is for the local authority to decide. However, if its conclusions are so unreasonable that no reasonable local authority could ever have come to them, the courts could interfere under the *Wednesbury* principle[3] in an application for judicial review.

---

1 [1986] 1 All ER 164 at 167.

2 *Agricultural, Horticultural and Forestry Industry Training Board v Aylesbury Mushrooms Ltd* [1972] 1 All ER 200 (DC). Failure to consult in breach of a duty to do so will not necessarily lead a court to hold that the provision in question is invalid and of no effect. If the court concludes that there is a broad public interest in not upsetting the provision, in order, for example, to avoid consequential uncertainty, it may simply grant a declaration that the provision-maker has failed to comply with the duty to consult: see *Secretary of State for Social Services, Ex parte Association of Metropolitan Authorities* [1986] 1 All ER 164 (DC).

3 *Associated Provincial Picture Houses Ltd v Wednesbury Corpn* [1948] 1 KB 223, [1947] 2 All ER 680 (CA).

Specification of different hours

3.8   A notice given under a curfew scheme (a 'curfew notice') may specify different hours in relation to children of different ages (s 14(6)). The mind boggles at the problems of enforcement that there will be if a notice is of an age-differential nature. It is going to be difficult enough sorting out the under 10s from the 10 or overs.

Publicity

3.9   A curfew notice is required to be given:

(a) by posting it in some conspicuous place or places within the specified area; and
(b) in such other manner, if any, as appears to the local authority to be desirable for giving publicity to the notice (s 14(7)).

The requirement in (a) would seem to be a mandatory requirement, with the result that, if a notice is not posted in at least one conspicuous place in the specified area, notice is not given and a curfew is not imposed.

Duration

3.10   The maximum duration of a curfew which may be specified by a curfew notice is 90 days (s 14(1)).[1] If the local authority wants an extension beyond the specified period it will have to consult again and go through the rest of the procedure set out above.

A number of local authorities have expressed concern at the maximum of 90 days, taking the view that the effort of setting up a scheme, including obtaining approval, and then making a curfew notice makes it questionable whether it would be worth the trouble, even if a curfew was needed in an area.[2]

The Government explained the maximum time limit for a notice, and the procedural requirements for making a scheme or notice, on the ground that there has to be a proper balance between the human rights aspects and the public protection and child safety aspects.[3]

---

1 See general annotations.
2 Baroness Anelay of St Johns, HL Committee, cols 1111–1112 (10 February).
3 Lord Williams of Mostyn, Parliamentary Under-Secretary, Home Office, HL Committee, col 1112 (10 February).

Contravention

3.11   A curfew notice may be broken by conduct which would otherwise not be a cause for concern. For example, if there is a notice in force in the area, a group of nine-year-olds playing football in a park near their home soon after 9pm would be in breach of the order. If some of the footballers are 10 there will not be a breach vis-à-vis them. This is liable to cause problems in terms of identifying the under 10s. Although the police powers mentioned in the next paragraph apply to any child whom the police officer has reasonable cause to believe is under 10, they cannot be used if he does not have such a belief or actually knows the child is 10 or over; he will have to leave that child and pick out the others.

Other examples of breach of a curfew notice by being in a public place during the curfew hours specified in a notice are riding bicycles with friends, posting a letter and carol singing, unaccompanied in each case by a parent or a responsible adult.[1] Another example would be where a nine-year-old child is brought back from his grandparents by his 17-year-old brother or sister.[2]

There may be problems in enforcing a curfew notice where a gang of children break it.

---

1 These were quoted from a letter from a member of the public by Lord Thomas of Gresford, HL Report, col 635.
2 This example was given by Lord Goodhart, HL 2nd Reading, col 587.

3.12   Where a police officer has reasonable cause to believe[1] that a child is in a public place, unaccompanied, in contravention of a ban imposed by a curfew notice, the officer may remove the child to the child's place of residence unless he has reasonable cause to believe that the child would, if removed there, be likely to suffer significant harm (s 15(1) and (3)). The officer is not required to be in uniform. The question of what force, if any, the officer may use to remove a child gives rise to similar issues to those involved in the power to remove truants; they are dealt with in para **3.63**.

It may be noted that there is no requirement to take the child home. The decision whether or not to do so is left to the police officer. In making that decision, the officer must also answer the question whether there is reasonable cause to believe that taking the child home would expose the child to the likelihood of suffering significant harm. This is the same question as has to be asked by a police officer before exercising the power under s 46(1) of the Children Act 1989[2] to remove a child to suitable accommodation. The officer will normally have knowledge of the area; he may know the child's family and home circumstances. If, for example, he knows that there is a history of child abuse or neglect, he may well conclude that he should not take the child home because there are reasonable grounds to believe that otherwise the child would suffer significant harm and, the threshold criteria being the same, decide to remove the child to suitable accommodation under s 46(1) of the 1989 Act.

If the officer does decide to take the child home, he is not required to hand the child over to a responsible person. While it is a bar to the removal of the child in the first instance to the child's place of residence that there is reasonable cause to believe that the child's removal is likely to cause that child significant harm, discovery of the absence there of a responsible person is not in itself a bar to the child being left there. However, it is likely that, if there is no responsible person there to look after the child, or that person is likely to abuse the child, the officer will use his power under s 46(1) of the Children Act 1989 to remove the child to other suitable accommodation on the ground that otherwise the child would be likely to suffer significant harm.

---

1 See general annotations.
2 Under the 1989 Act, s 31(9), 'harm' means ill-treatment or the impairment of health or development, and 'ill-treatment' is defined as including sexual abuse and non-physical forms of ill-treatment.

3.13   The suitable accommodation to which a police officer will take a child in a breach-of-curfew situation will be a matter for discussion between the relevant agencies prior to the imposition of a curfew notice, so that appropriate arrangements will be in force during the curfew.[1] The matter will be covered in the guidance to be issued by the Home Office.[1]

A child in respect of whom a police officer exercises the power of removal under s 46(1) of the 1989 Act is referred to as 'having been taken into police protection' (1989 Act, s 46(2)).

As soon as is reasonably practicable[2] after taking a child into police protection, the police officer concerned is required to:

(a) inform the local authority (as defined later) within whose area the child was found of the steps that have been, and are proposed to be, taken with respect to the child under s 46 of the 1989 Act and the reasons for taking them;

(b) give details to the local authority (as defined later) within whose area the child is ordinarily resident ('the appropriate authority') of the place at which the child is being accommodated;

(c) inform the child (if he appears capable of understanding):
     (i)   of the steps that have been taken with respect to him under s 46 of the 1989 Act and of the reasons for taking them; and
     (ii) of the further steps that may be taken with respect to him under this section;

(d) take such steps as are reasonably practicable[2] to discover the child's wishes and feelings; and

(e) secure that the case is inquired into by an officer designated for the purposes of this section by the chief officer of the police area concerned (1989 Act, s 46(3)).

As soon as is reasonably practicable[2] after taking a child into police protection, the police officer concerned must take such steps as are reasonably practicable to inform:

(a) the child's parents;

(b) every person who is not a parent of his but who has parental responsibility for him; and

(c) any other person with whom the child was living immediately before being taken into police protection, of the steps that he has taken under s 46 of the 1989 Act with respect to the child, the reasons for taking them and the further steps that may be taken with respect to him under that section (ibid, s 46(4)).

On completing any inquiry referred to above, the officer conducting it must release the child from police protection unless he considers that there is still reasonable cause for believing[2] that the child would be likely to suffer significant harm if released (ibid, s 46(5)).

No child may be kept in police protection for more than 72 hours (ibid, s 46(6)). While a child is being kept in police protection, the designated officer may apply on behalf of the appropriate authority for an emergency protection order[3] to be made under s 44 of the 1989 Act with respect to the child (ibid, s 46(7)). The maximum duration of such an order is eight days, excluding Sundays and public holidays (ibid, s 45(1) and (2)). An order can be extended by seven days in certain circumstances (ibid, s 45(4) and (5)).

Where a child has been taken into police protection, the designated officer (or the appropriate authority if the child is in its accommodation) must allow:

(a) the child's parents;
(b) any person who is not a parent of the child but who has parental responsibility for him;
(c) any person with whom the child was living immediately before he was taken into police protection;
(d) any person in whose favour a contact order is in force with respect to the child;
(e) any person who is allowed to have contact with the child by a court order; and
(f) any person acting on behalf of any of those persons,

to have such contact (if any) with the child as, in the opinion of the designated officer, is both reasonable and in the child's best interests (ibid, s 46(10) and (11)).

The references to 'local authority' in this paragraph and in the next (para **3.14**) are to a somewhat different list than the list of local authorities which can make a local child curfew scheme (and give notice under it) – see para **3.3**. In particular, for the purposes of the Children Act 1989, a 'local authority' includes a county council but not a district council.[4] This difference between the list of authorities who can impose local child curfews and those involved if a child is found in breach of such a curfew is an unhappy one.

---

1 Lord Williams of Mostyn, Parliamentary Under-Secretary, Home Office, HL Report, col 658.
2 See general annotations.
3 An emergency protection order, inter alia, gives the applicant parental responsibility (Children Act 1989, s 44(5)).
4 In the Children Act 1989, 'local authority' means, in relation to England, the council of a county [including a unitary authority], a metropolitan district, a London borough or the

Common Council of the City of London, and in relation to Wales, the council of a county or a county borough (1989 Act, s 105(1)).

3.14   Where a police officer has reasonable cause to believe[1] that a child is in a public place, unaccompanied, in contravention of a curfew notice, the officer must also, as soon as practicable[1] inform the local authority which made the notice that the child has contravened it, however minor the contravention (s 15(1) and (2)).The local authority will then send a social worker to the child's family to see why the child was in breach of the curfew and then to decide whether further action is necessary to prevent any repetition.[2] The local authority is required to do so by s 47(1) of the Children Act 1989, as amended by s 15(4). As amended, s 47(1) provides that where a local authority is informed that a child who lives, or is found, in its area has contravened a ban imposed by a curfew notice, it must make, or cause to be made, such enquiries as it considers necessary to enable it to decide whether it should take any action to safeguard or promote the child's welfare. In addition, as amended, s 47(1) of the 1989 Act requires that enquiries shall be commenced as soon as practicable[1] and, in any event, within 48 hours of the authority receiving the information.

The local authority will have the option to apply for an emergency protection order or to begin welfare proceedings under the Children Act 1989 or to apply for a child safety order, because breach of a curfew notice is a ground for such an order.[3]

---

1 See general annotations.
2 Lord Williams of Mostyn, Parliamentary Under-Secretary, Home Office, HL Committee, col 1127 (10 February).
3 See para **3.25**.

Challenging local child curfews

3.15   A local child curfew scheme or a notice under one is, of course, judicially reviewable on normal judicial review grounds, including that of unreasonableness under the *Wednesbury* principle, ie was the decision to make the scheme or give the notice so unreasonable that no reasonable local authority could ever have come to it?[1]

Another way of challenging a local child curfew scheme or notice would be by alleging that it contravened art 8 of the European Convention on Human Rights, since there must be doubts as to the compatibility of the provisions as to child curfews with that provision. Article 8 provides that the State can interfere with a person's private and family life only if it is necessary in a democratic society in the interests of national security, public safety or the economic well-being of the country, for the prevention of disorder or crime, for the protection of health or morals, or for the protection of the rights and freedom of others. Can the misconduct (actual or potential) of those under 10 ever be so serious as to justify a *blanket* curfew in an area in a democratic society, particularly when there are already powers under the Children Act 1989 to deal with problematic individuals?

The concept of proportionality, embryonic in our administrative law, is important in the context of the European Convention on Human Rights. The Human Rights Bill 1998, when in force, will require a court to have regard to the Convention, and to the jurisprudence of the Court of Human Rights. Thus, restrictions or prohibitions which interfere with otherwise lawful acts of an individual must be proportionate to the harm that is sought to be prevented. Extreme curfew schemes or notices would need the highest level of justification. A court will need to consider the effect of the proposed prohibition, and balance the effect of that prohibition on children caught by it against the danger of harm to the public.

---

1 See, for example, *Garner's Administrative Law* (8th edn) ch 8, esp pp 231–236.

CHILD SAFETY ORDERS

3.16　　　In *No More Excuses* the Government expressed the view that more needed to be done to help prevent children under 10 from turning to crime.[1] A Home Office research study[2] showed that peer pressure can exercise very strong influence over children and young people. It indicated that association with delinquent peers increased the odds of a young person offending by a factor of three.

The child safety order is intended to help young people break away from negative peer pressure.[3] This new type of order enables a court to impose requirements on a child under 10 who is at risk of becoming involved in crime, for example because he is wandering the streets unsupervised at night or is truanting. The relevant provisions are contained in ss 11–13.

---

1 *No More Excuses – A New Approach to Tackling Youth Crime in England and Wales*, Cm 3809 (1997), para 5.2.
2 *Young People and Crime* (Home Office Research Study no 145, 1995).
3 *Tackling Youth Crime: A Consultation Paper* (Home Office, 1997), paras 98–112; *No More Excuses*, op cit, para 5.4.

What is a child safety order?

3.17　　　By s 11(1), it is an order which:

(a) places a child, for a period specified in the order, under the supervision of the responsible officer; and
(b) requires the child to comply with such requirements as are so specified.

3.18　　　Section 11(4) specifies a permitted maximum period of supervision for the purposes of s 11(1). It is three months,[1] unless the court is satisfied that the circumstances of the case are exceptional (in which case it is 12 months).

The norm of a maximum of three months seems low in terms of the effectiveness of such a short period of supervision and the trouble and expense involved in making the order.

---

1 See general annotations.

3.19　　The requirements that may be specified under s 11(1)(b) are those which the court considers desirable in the interests of:

(a) securing that the child receives appropriate care, protection and support and is subject to proper control; or
(b) preventing any repetition of the kind of behaviour which led to the child safety order being made (s 11(5)).

Examples of such requirements are that the child is at home at specified times or stays away from certain places or people. Another requirement would be one prohibiting truanting from school.[1] The following example was given in *No More Excuses*:[2]

> '[A]n 8 year old girl found shoplifting with a group of older girls in the local shopping centre might be referred by the police to social services. The local authority could apply to the court for a child safety order. The order might require her to stay away from the shopping centre, not mix with the older girls and (with the agreement of the organisers) attend a local youth programme to make constructive use of her leisure time.'

As far as practicable,[3] the requirements in a child safety order must be such as to avoid:

(a) any conflict with the parent's (sic) religious belief; and
(b) any interference with the times, if any, at which the child normally attends school (s 12(3)).

The reference here to 'parent' as opposed to 'parent or guardian' in the previous subsection (s 12(2)), described in para **3.26**, is striking. It is not clear why there is no requirement to avoid conflict with a guardian's religious belief (such as that of a grandparent with care of a child).

---

1 *No More Excuses – A New Approach to Tackling Youth Crime*, Cm 3809 (1997), para 5.5.
2 Ibid.
3 See general annotations.

3.20　　The main responsibility of the responsible officer will be to the child and paramount to that will be the need to supervise the child and to ensure full compliance with the requirements of the order.[1] However, the officer will also have an important role to play in relation to the child's family circumstances.[1]

The 'responsible officer' will be one of the following who is specified in the order:

(a) a social worker of a local authority social services department; and
(b) a member of a youth offending team.[1]

The social worker or member must be a social worker of, or a member of a youth offending team established by, the local authority within whose area it appears to the court that the child resides or will reside (s 18(4)).

In most cases, the court will no doubt specify a local authority social worker as the responsible officer in respect of a child safety order, because the various factors which it will consider (such as the child's age and previous involvement with the child and/or his family) will point in the direction of a member of the local authority social services department. However, the alternative of appointing a member of a youth offending team was inserted because it may be appropriate to have someone else,[2] as, for example, might be the case where the team was involved locally in preventative work or if the family concerned was known to it.[3] Involving a youth offending team member with the supervision of a child under 10 is perhaps not the best alternative because of the cultural differences between members of a youth offending team and people like local authority social workers.

---

1 Section 11(8). As to 'local authority' see annotations to s 11. As to 'youth offending team', see paras **2.19–2.21**.
2 Lord Falconer of Thoroton, Solicitor-General, HL Committee, col 1100 (10 February).
3 These examples were given in *Getting to Grips with Crime: A New Framework For Local Action: A Consultation Paper* (Home Office, 1997), para 20.

3.21   The child safety order is directed to the child and requires or prohibits conduct specified in it. Where it is linked with a parenting order that order could make associated requirements of the parent. For example, if the child safety order requires a child to be home by 7pm, the associated parenting order could require the parent to ensure that the child is home by then.

Child safety orders will sit alongside options under the Children Act 1989, such as supervision orders under that Act which may be more appropriate in particular cases. The main distinction between the child safety order (and, indeed, the local curfew notice and the parenting order) and orders under the Children Act is that the former are aimed at, and involve, protecting both the child and the community; the latter are concerned essentially with the protection of the child.[1]

---

1 This distinction was drawn by Mike O'Brien, MP, Parliamentary Under-Secretary, Home Office, HC Committee, col 272.

3.22   Child safety orders are being piloted for 18 months commencing 30 September 1998.[1] Consequently, a court must not make an order unless it has been notified by the Home Secretary that arrangements for implementing such orders are available in the area in which it appears that the child resides or will reside and the notice has not been withdrawn (s 11(2)). Nine areas have been selected for the piloting of child safety orders: Hammersmith and Fulham, Kensington and Chelsea, and Westminster (jointly); Lewisham; Hampshire, Southampton, Portsmouth and the Isle of Wight (jointly); Wolverhampton; Sheffield; Luton and Bedfordshire (jointly); Devon; St Helens; and parts of Sunderland.[2]

The estimated annual cost to local authority social services departments and youth offending teams of child safety orders, once fully in operation, is £250,000, as opposed to £3.75 million for parenting orders.[3] The Government's expectation that the latter orders will be much more frequently made is open to question.

---

1 See Appendix II; Mike O'Brien, MP, Parliamentary Under-Secretary, Home Office, HC Committee, col 272; *No More Excuses – A New Approach to Youth Crime in England and Wales*, Cm 3809 (1997), para 10.5.
2 HC Deb, vol 313, col WA 219.
3 Alun Michael, MP, Minister of State, Home Office, HC Committee, col 217.

Who can make an order?

3.23   Child safety orders will be made by magistrates' courts sitting as family proceedings courts.[1] As a result, unless the court otherwise directs, only the officers of the court, the parties to the case and their legal representatives, witnesses and news reporters may attend the proceedings.[2] Another result is that there are strict limitations on the particulars which may be published in a news report of proceedings for a child safety order.[3]

Under Sch 11, para 2, to the Children Act 1989, the Lord Chancellor may make an order providing for the transfer of family proceedings from one magistrates' court to another (horizontal transfer) or from a magistrates' court to a county court with the potential for transfer to the High Court (vertical transfer). The Children (Allocation of Proceedings) Order 1991[4] makes such provision, but it applies only to those family proceedings which existed before the new Act. However, the new Act assumes[5] that provision for transfer of child safety order proceedings will be made. This will probably be done by an amendment to the 1991 order. When the Lord Chancellor has made the necessary change, family proceedings in respect of a child safety order will only be transferable for the purpose of consolidating them with other proceedings in another court under the Children Act 1989 or for wardship or (albeit unlikely) adoption proceedings.

---

1 This is the effect of s 11(6); see annotations to s 11.
2 Magistrates' Courts Act 1980, s 69.
3 Ibid, s 70.
4 SI 1991/1677.
5 See para **3.27**.

When can an order be made?

3.24   A child safety order cannot be made without an application by a local
authority (s 11(1)), ie a council of a county (including a unitary authority), a
metropolitan district or London borough council or the Common Council of
the City of London (in England) or a county or county borough council (in
Wales).[1]

---

1 Section 11(7). Where a local authority:
  (a) is informed that a child who lives, or is found in its area –
     (i) is the subject of an emergency protection order; or
     (ii) is in police protection; or
     (iii) has contravened a ban imposed by a curfew notice; or
  (b) has reasonable cause to suspect that a child who lives, or is found, in its area is suffering,
    or is likely to suffer significant harm,
the authority is required to make, or cause to be made, such enquiries as it considers
necessary to enable it to decide whether it should take action to safeguard or promote the
child's welfare (Children Act 1989, s 47(1), as amended by s 15(4)). The enquiries must, in
particular, be directed towards establishing, inter alia, whether the authority should apply to
the court, or exercise any of its other powers under the Children Act 1989 or s 11 of the new
Act, with respect to the child (Children Act 1989, s 47(3), as amended by Sch 8, para 69).

3.25   By s 11(1) and (3), a family proceedings court can make an order only
if it is convinced that, with respect to a child under 10,[1] one or more of the
following conditions is satisfied:

(a) that the child has committed an act which, if he had been 10 or over, would
    have constituted an offence. This comes close to criminalising the conduct
    of children under 10. The requirement of the commission of an act 'which
    would have constituted an offence' if the child had been 10 or over raises
    questions about proof of mens rea. Generally, conduct is not in itself an
    offence; surrounding circumstances and/or resulting consequences and a
    requisite mental element (mens rea) must also be proved. If mens rea is
    required, the younger the child the harder it will be to prove it.
    Consequently, the reference to 'an act' is odd. The view put forward by a
    Home Office Minister in the House of Commons, that 'We do not need to
    go into all the circumstances of proving mens rea and actus reus that does
    not arise (sic)',[2] is unacceptable, and cannot be correct. It is also odd in
    that some offences consist not of an act but of an omission or of an event
    (state of affairs). Possession of a controlled drug is, for example, an event
    crime. It is not inconceivable that a child of eight or nine could be in
    possession of such a drug. The wording of the present condition would
    seem not to be satisfied, nor any of the other conditions in such a case;

(b) that a child safety order is necessary to prevent the child committing such
    an act. This likewise raises questions about mens rea and the use of the
    word 'act';

(c) that the child has contravened a ban imposed by a curfew notice.[3] It does
    not have to be proved that a child safety order is necessary to prevent a
    further breach of the curfew notice; or

(d) that the child has acted in a manner that caused or was likely to cause harassment, alarm or distress to one or more persons not of the same household[4] as himself. As discussed in paras **5.24** to **5.26**, harassment, alarm or distress are wide terms. They are liable to be satisfied by boisterous children.

The standard of proof in proceedings under s 11 is the civil standard, ie proof on the balance of probabilities (s 11(6)).[5] There is no minimum age for an order, only a maximum one.

It would seem that, in relation to conditions (a), (c) or (d), it is enough that the child was under 10 at the time when the conduct which satisfies the conditions occurred and that it is irrelevant that he is aged 10 when he appears in court or when the court makes its determination. The words of the provision can be interpreted in this way. It would be unfortunate, especially in respect of (a), if the contrary interpretation was taken because, the child being under the age of criminal responsibility at the time of his conduct in question, he could not be convicted of an offence in respect of it. This can hardly be intended by an Act specifically designed to crack down on young delinquents.

On the other hand, the wording of the provisions makes it clear that the child must be under 10 at the time when an order based solely on (b) is made.

---

1 See general annotations.
2 Mike O'Brien, MP, Parliamentary Under-Secretary, Home Office, HC Committee, col 279.
3 See paras **3.7–3.10**.
4 See annotations to s 1.
5 See annotations to s 11, and para **5.41**.

Procedural requirements

3.26   Before making a child safety order, the court must obtain and consider information about the child's family circumstances and the likely effect of the order on those circumstances (s 12(1)). Although the Act itself does not require a parent or guardian to attend court, s 34A(1) of the Children and Young Persons Act 1933 obliges a court, including a family proceedings court, before whom a child or young person under 16 is brought to require a parent or guardian of his to attend at the court during all the stages of the proceedings, unless and to the extent that the court is satisfied that it would be unreasonable to require such attendance, having regard to the circumstances of the case. On the other hand, there is no requirement in this or any other Act for the child to be present in court. However, the child can be permitted to attend. Whether or not he is will depend on the circumstances. It may be appropriate for a child to attend, particularly if it is necessary to emphasise to him that the issue was serious. In other cases, the court may feel it inappropriate, as where distress might be caused to the child because of his family circumstances.[1]

In addition, before making the order, the court must explain to the parent(s) or guardian(s) of the child in ordinary language:

(a) the effect of the order and of the requirements proposed to be included in it;

(b) the consequences which may follow if the child fails to comply with any of those requirements; and

(c) that the court has power to review the order on the application either of the parent or guardian or of the responsible officer (s 12(2)).

A 'parent' effectively means a biological parent;[2] a 'guardian' means any person who in the opinion of the court has for the time being care of the child (s 117(1)).

---

1 These examples were given by Mike O'Brien, MP, Parliamentary Under-Secretary, Home Office, HC Committee, col 270.
2 Family Law Reform Act 1987, s 1.

Appeal

3.27 Appeal lies to the High Court against the making of a child safety order by a family proceedings court (s 13(1)). There is no appeal against a refusal to make an order. In such a case, an application may be made by the local authority for judicial review if there is an appropriate ground.

The Act does not say who has locus standi to make an appeal against the making of a child safety order. Presumably, it is a parent or guardian just as it is in respect of an application for variation or discharge of a child safety order.[1] It would seem that the appeal will be heard by a single judge of the Family Division, as are appeals against the making or refusal of an order under the Children Act 1989 by a magistrates' court sitting as a family proceedings court.[2]

On an appeal the High Court:

(a) may make such orders as may be necessary to give effect to its determination of the appeal; and

(b) may also make such incidental or consequential orders as appear to it to be just (s 13(1)).

Besides an order directing that an application be re-heard by a family proceedings court, any order of the High Court made on appeal is, for the purposes of the provisions (below) relating to variation, discharge or breach of an order, treated as if it were an order of the family proceedings court from whom the appeal was brought and not an order of the High Court (s 13(2)).

As stated above, Sch 11, para 2 to the Children Act 1989 gives the Lord Chancellor power to make orders concerning the transfer of civil cases involving children. The Lord Chancellor has not yet made any order in respect of the transfer of child safety orders. If he does, the question of an appeal against a transfer or proposed transfer will arise. Section 13(3), which had not come into force when this book went to press, deals with this. It empowers the Lord Chancellor to make, by order, provision as to the circumstances in which appeals may be made against decisions taken by courts on questions arising in connection with the transfer, or proposed transfer, of proceedings by virtue of any order under Sch 11, para 2 to the Children Act 1989. Save to the extent provided for in any order, no appeal lies against such a decision (ibid). An order under s 13(3) must be made by statutory instrument and is subject to annulment in pursuance of a resolution of either House of Parliament (s 114(2)).

---

1 See para **3.28**.
2 Children Act 1989, s 94; Family Proceedings Rules 1991, SI 1991/1247, r 4.22; *Practice Direction (Children Act 1989: Appeals from Magistrates' Courts)* [1992] 1 All ER 864.

Discharge and variation

3.28   The responsible officer, or a parent or guardian of the child, may apply to the court which made the order for the discharge or variation of a child safety order (s 12(4)). The court may order a discharge or variation only if it appears to it appropriate to do so (ibid). Variation may be made either by cancelling any provision in the order, or by inserting in it (either by addition or by substitution) any provision that could have been included in the order if the court then had power to make it and were exercising the power (ibid).

An application for discharge or variation may be made only to the court which made the order. The court has no power to discharge or vary a child safety order of its own motion, although it could in other proceedings invite an application for discharge or variation of the order.

Where an application for discharge is dismissed, no further application for discharge may be made by any person (not just the previous applicant) except with the consent of the court which made the child safety order (s 12(5)). There is no such bar where an application for variation has been dismissed.

Breach of a child safety order

3.29   The 'responsible officer' will have the responsibility for supervising the operation of the order. Proceedings for breach of a child safety order must be brought by the responsible officer (s 12(6)). Unlike an application for discharge or variation, an application in respect of a breach of a child safety order need not be heard by the same court as made the order; it can also be heard by another magistrates' court sitting as a family proceedings court (s 11(6)) for the same petty sessions area.[1]

If on such an application it is proved on the balance of probabilities[2] that the child has failed to comply with any requirement in the order, the magistrates' court which made it or any other such court sitting as a family proceedings court in the same petty sessions area:[1]

(a) may discharge the order and of its own motion make in respect of the child a care order under s 31(1)(a) of the Children Act 1989;[2] or
(b) may make an order varying the order in the same way as on a variation after an application for discharge (s 12(6)).[3]

Perhaps surprisingly, these powers are not qualified by a requirement that the child's failure be 'without reasonable excuse', but the existence of a factor which could constitute such an excuse would be a relevant matter when it came to deciding whether to make any order at all if an application was made following a breach. For no apparent reason, s 12(6) requires that the child safety order be in force when the failure to comply is established. This prevents the court from taking any action under s 12(6) where the order has expired by effluxion of time before the matter can be brought before the court, albeit the failure occurred when the order was in force.

Breach of a child safety order may also result in the making of a parenting order; it is one of the triggers of such an order.

---

1 See general annotations.
2 See annotations to s 12.
3 See para **3.28**.

3.30   With respect to the making of a care order as a sanction for breach of a child safety order, this is a second route into care additional to the existing one under s 31 of the Children Act 1989 whereby a local authority or authorised person may apply direct to a family proceedings court for a care order. As the reference by s 12 to s 31(1)(a) of the 1989 Act indicates, a care order made as a sanction for breach of a child safety order will be the same as one obtained by the other route, viz an order placing the child in the care of a designated local authority.

In deciding whether or not to make a care order, the court must be guided by the child's welfare. Section 1 of the Children Act 1989 provides that:

'when a court determines any question with respect to –

(a) the upbringing of a child, ...
(b) the child's welfare shall be the court's paramount consideration.'[1]

On the other hand, the conditions in s 31(2) of the 1989 Act, which apply to the existing route to a care order, and which refer to the court being satisfied that the child is suffering, or is at risk of suffering, from significant harm and that this is attributable to the care that the child is receiving, or is likely to receive, not being what it would be reasonable to expect a parent to give him, or attributable to the child being beyond parental control, do not apply (s 12(7)).

One might have expected the court also to have power to make a supervision order under s 31 of the 1989 Act in response to breach of a child safety order, particularly because breach of a child safety order may indicate that a longer period of supervision[2] is necessary than can be provided under a child safety order. There is, however, nothing to stop a local authority or authorised person (eg the NSPCC) applying for a supervision order in the ordinary way under s 31 of the 1989 Act, although it would then have to prove the conditions in s 31(2) of the 1989 Act, set out above, which also apply to an application for a supervision order under s 31.

1 This was confirmed by Alun Michael, MP, Minister of State, Home Office, HC Committee, cols 289–290.
2 The duration of a supervision order is one year, but it may be extended up to a maximum of three years: Children Act 1989, Sch 3, part II, para 6.

PARENTING ORDERS

3.31   Home Office research has shown that 42% of juveniles who had a low or medium level of parental supervision had offended whereas, for juveniles who had experienced high levels of parental supervision, the figure was 20%. The same research showed that the quality of the relationship between parent and child is absolutely crucial in predicting whether or not a juvenile is likely to offend, and that parents who are harsh and erratic are twice as likely to have children who offend.[1] The Government believed that more help should be given to parents to change their children's behaviour. The Act seeks to do this by means of the parenting order.

1 *Young People and Crime* (Home Office Research Study no 145, 1995).

What is a parenting order?

3.32   A parenting order[1] is a court order requiring 'the parent' of a child (ie someone under 14)[2] or young person (ie someone of 14 or over but under 18):[2]

(a) to comply, for up to 12 months,[3] with such requirements as are specified in the order; and
(b) to attend, for a concurrent period not exceeding three months,[3] and not more than once in any week,[4] such counselling and guidance sessions as may be specified in directions given by the responsible officer (s 8(4)).

Requirements specified in, and directions given under, a parenting order must, as far as practicable, be such as to avoid:

(i) any conflict with the parent's religious beliefs; and
(ii) any interference with the times, if any, at which the parent normally works or attends an educational establishment (s 9(4)).

1 The potential confusion between a 'parenting order', 'parental order' in favour of a husband and wife, one or both of whom are donors in surrogacy cases, under the Human Embryology and Fertilisation Act 1990, s 30, and a 'parental responsibility order' available to an unmarried father under the Children Act 1989, s 4, was pointed out by Richard White *Clutching at Straw's* (1997) 147 NLJ 1556.
2 Section 117(1).
3 See general annotations.
4 Ie a period of seven days (see general annotations) beginning with a Sunday (s 8(4)).

Requirement to attend counselling and guidance sessions

3.33   At the sessions referred to in (b) (above), a parent would receive counselling and guidance about, for example, how to set and enforce consistent standards of behaviour and how to respond more effectively to changing adolescent demands.[1] A parenting order need not include a counselling and guidance-session requirement under (b) if the parent has previously been made subject to such an order, although it may do so (s 8(5)). Apart from this, an order must contain such a requirement, although it need not contain any requirements under (a). This seems somewhat inflexible. Suppose, for example, that a court wishes to impose requirements under (a) (eg to keep a child in at night) on a parent who has already begun to attend on a voluntary basis a parenting skill course. If the parent has not previously been subject to a parenting order, a requirement to attend such counselling or guidance sessions as may be specified by the responsible officer must be made. There is no guarantee that the officer would specify the voluntary sessions, quite apart from the possible negative effect of making attendance compulsory.

The reference in (b) to 'the responsible officer' who is to specify the counselling or guidance sessions to be attended is to one of the following, who is to be specified in the order:

(a)   a probation officer;[2]
(b)   a social worker of a local authority social services department; and
(c)   a member of a youth offending team (s 8(8)).[3]

It seems that it will not be common for a member of a youth offending team to supervise a parenting order. A case where it might be appropriate would be where the team is already, or has been, involved in providing or arranging guidance or counselling for the parents of a young offender who is, or has been, subject to a final warning.[4]

In order to give a direction, a probation officer must be an officer appointed for or assigned to the petty sessions area[5] within which it appears to the court that the child or, as the case may be, the parent resides or will reside (s 18(3)).

Where directions under a parenting order are to be given by:

(a)   a local authority social worker; or
(b)   a member of a youth offending team,

the social worker or member must be a social worker of, or a member of a youth offending team established by, the local authority within whose area it appears to the court that the child, or, as the case may be, the parent resides or will reside (s 18(4)).

The responsible officer's role is also to ensure that parents attend whatever sessions are specified in his directions[6] and to ensure compliance with the order and any requirements under it.[7]

---

1 Alun Michael, MP, Minister of State, Home Office, HC Committee, col 255.
2 See s 18 and annotations thereto.
3 See s 39; paras **2.19–2.21**.
4 This example was given in *Getting to Grips with Crime: A New Framework for Local Action: A Consultation Paper* (Home Office, 1997), para 20. Oddly, in *Tackling Youth Crime: A*

Consultation Paper (Home Office), published in the same month, it was said (para 38) without further explanation: 'Normally the responsible officer [in respect of a parenting order] will be a member of the Youth Offender (sic) Team'.

5 See general annotations.

6 Alun Michael, MP, Minister of State, Home Office, HC Committee, col 252.

7 Ibid, cols 255–256.

Other requirements specified in the order

3.34   The requirements which may be specified under (a) above are those which the court considers desirable in the interest of preventing any repetition of the kind of conduct which 'triggers' the making of a parenting order or (as the case may be) the commission of any further offence of the type which is a 'trigger' (s 8(7)). We describe such conduct and offences in para **3.38**.

Examples of requirements which can be made under (a) are a requirement to ensure that the child is escorted to school every day by a responsible adult, a requirement to exercise control over him and a requirement to ensure that he is home by a certain time of night. Section 8 does not lay down any direct limitations on the requirements which may be made, but the facts that s 8(2) permits an order to be made only if 'the relevant condition' is satisfied, and that the various relevant conditions are defined in s 8(6) in terms of the parenting order being desirable in the interests of preventing particular consequences, seem to indicate that a requirement must be directed at such prevention, otherwise it can be overturned on appeal or challenged by judicial review (if made by an inferior court, as will normally be the case).

The power to make a requirement under (a) was aimed by the Government at parents who are wilfully negligent in controlling their children.[1] Where a child safety order has already been made or is made alongside a parenting order the requirement which could be made in the parenting order will doubtless already be contained in the child safety order. Although a parenting order itself is not intended to apportion blame to a parent, or to punish a parent, for a child's wrongdoing, a criminal sanction is available for those in breach of an order.

1 Alun Michael, MP, Minister of State, Home Office, HC Committee, col 256.

3.35   The provisions relating to parenting orders are being piloted for 18 months commencing 30 September 1998 in certain areas (where voluntary parental training and guidance provision is already available); the areas chosen are the same as those in which child safety orders are to be piloted (see para **3.22**).[1] As with other aspects of Part I, parenting orders are going to involve additional resources. The estimated annual cost to local authority social service departments, the probation service and youth offending teams, of parenting orders when fully in operation, is £3.75m.[2] Will the additional resources be available?

1 HC Deb, vol 313, col WA 219.

2 Alun Michael, MP, Minister of State, Home Office, HC Committee, col 251.

Against whom can a parenting order be made?

3.36   A parenting order may be made against various people depending on
the context. First, it may be made against one or both 'parents', ie biological
parents.[1] It is not necessary that a parent should have parental responsibility.
Thus an order can be made against the father of a child or young person, who
was not married to the mother when the child was born and who has not
acquired parental responsibility under s 4 of the Children Act 1989.

The court is not obliged to make a parenting order against both parents. This is
sensible. Otherwise there could be problems where one of the parents has
never had or has lost contact with the child (and in similar cases) or is working
abroad. It may be desirable to make a parenting order against the other parent
but quite pointless in relation to the parent just referred to (and merely set in
train the prospect at the outset of proceedings for breach of the parenting
order).

Another consequence of the drafting of the present provision is that an order
can be made against the parent or parents even though the child is in local
authority care or under local authority supervision. In such a case, the child
may well be living at home with his parents. However, he may be living with local
authority foster-parents or in local authority accommodation. Although the
potentiality of a parenting order against the actual parent(s) in such a case may
seem absurd, there may be cases where it could make sense. The court may
conclude that counselling and guidance could lead to the eventual return of
the child to his parents.

A parenting order may also be made against a person who is a guardian of a
child or young person (s 8(2)).[2] Guardians are defined here as any person who
in the opinion of the court has for the time being the care of a child or young
person (s 117(1)); in effect anyone in loco parentis at the time the order is
made. This would include someone looking after a child or young person on a
temporary basis. *Hereafter, the term 'the parent' is used to cover these other people.*

The wording of the provisions is such that a parenting order can be made
against the parent(s) of a young person who is him or herself married and/or a
parent. In practice, such an order would be most unlikely.

---

1 Family Law Reform Act 1987, s 1(1).
2 Section 8(2) says that an order can also be made against a parent or other person with
   parental responsibilities or care for the child who has been convicted of an offence under
   s 443 or s 444 of the Education Act 1996 in respect of a child or young person's non-
   attendance at school, but this provision is strictly unnecessary because such a person
   inevitably falls within the definition of 'parent or guardian'.

When can an order be made?

3.37   A court must not make a parenting order unless it has been notified by
the Home Secretary that arrangements for implementing such orders are

available in the area in which it appears to the court that the parent resides or will reside (s 8(3)).

3.38   Subject to s 8(2), parenting orders may be made in any court proceedings where:

(a)   a child safety order is made in respect of a child;
(b)   an anti-social behaviour order or sex offender order is made in respect of a child or young person (ie someone aged under 18);[1]
(c)   a child or young person is convicted of an offence; or
(d)   a person is convicted of an offence under s 443 (failure to comply with a school attendance order) or s 444 (failure to secure regular attendance at school of a registered pupil) of the Education Act 1996 (s 8(1)).[2]

By the nature of these conditions, an order under (a) will be made by a magistrates' court, sitting as a family proceedings court; an order under (b) or (d) by a magistrates' court; and an order under (c) by a youth court or (where the conviction is in the Crown Court) the Crown Court. In the case of an acquittal of an offence in the circumstances set out under (c) or (d) in a magistrates' court followed by an appeal by the prosecutor to a divisional court of the Queen's Bench Division, it is within that court's power to replace the acquittal with a conviction. In such a case, the divisional court could make a parenting order.

---

1 Section 117(1).
2 See annotations to s 8.

3.39   Point (c) at para **3.38** is over and above two other provisions which continue to apply to the parents of a juvenile offender. The first is under s 55 of the Children and Young Persons Act 1933 whereby a parent or guardian of a juvenile offender must (juvenile under 16) or can (juvenile aged 16 or 17) be made to pay fines. The second is s 58 of the Criminal Justice Act 1991 for binding-over a parent or guardian to take proper care of and exercise proper control over a child or young person who is convicted of an offence.

These powers are ineffective to improve the behaviour of the juvenile where the parents have no control over him. The idea is that the provision of a continuing programme of support will stand a greater chance of being effective.

The power to bind over under the 1991 Act is infrequently used. The Government intends to reconsider the case for retaining it in the light of the experience of piloting the parenting order.[1]

Point (d) at para **3.38** was prompted by the well-known links between the slide into criminality and truancy and poor educational achievements. It is arguably unnecessary. A family proceedings court has power under the Children Act 1989[2] to make an education supervision order where it is satisfied that a child of compulsory school age is not being properly educated. A parent who unreasonably and persistently fails to comply with such an order commits an offence and is liable to a fine not exceeding level 3 on the standard scale, the same fine as for breach of a parenting order.[3]

It was argued in the House of Lords by Baroness Kennedy of The Shaws[4] that 'Many of those involved in youth-justice and penal affairs believe that matters relating to education and home/school liaison are essentially civil, and should remain under the auspices of the family proceedings court rather than the criminal courts'. This, however, is an attack better directed at the non-attendance at school offences under ss 443 and 444 of the Education Act 1996, which criminalise the parents of truants, rather than the new provisions which simply add another sentencing option (and a positive one in that it is intended to help to deal with a parent's inability to ensure school-attendance by his child).

---

1 *Tackling Youth Crime: A Consultation Paper* (Home Office, 1997), para 45.
2 1989 Act, s 36 and Sch 3.
3 See para **3.49**.
4 HL Committee, cols 1068–1069 (10 February).

3.40   If the court is satisfied that 'the relevant condition' is fulfilled, it may make a parenting order in respect of a person who is the parent or guardian[1] of the child or young person (s 8(2)).

The 'relevant condition' is that the parenting order would be desirable in the interests of preventing:

(a)   in a case falling within s 8(1)(a) or (b), any repetition of the kind of behaviour which led to the child safety order, anti-social behaviour[2] or sex offender order[2] being made;
(b)   in a case falling within s 8(1)(c), the commission of any further offence by the child or young person;
(c)   in a case falling within s 8(1)(d), the commission of any further offence under s 443 or s 444 of the Education Act 1996.

'Desirable in the interests of' is an unusual piece of legislative phraseology. It is not clear whether the requirement made by it can be satisfied where the object in question is desirable but it is clear that the parent will have no effect in relation to the child's behaviour.

The Government's view that:

> 'It [a parenting order] will be ordered by the magistrates' court when that court believes it can help the parents both by giving them guidance and by making it clear to them that they have a responsibility for their children's offending behaviour',[3]

is not necessarily supported by the words of the legislation.

---

1 Or the person convicted of an offence under the Education Act 1996, ss 443 or 444; in effect the 'parent or guardian': see para **3.36**, n 2.
2 See Chapter 5.

3 Lord Falconer of Thoroton, Solicitor-General, HL 2nd Reading, col 596.

Where an order must normally be made

3.41   A court is not normally obliged to make a parenting order if one of the four conditions in s 8(1) is proved; it simply has the power to do so. There is one exception: s 9(1) provides a statutory presumption in favour of making a parenting order where the relevant condition is point (c) at para **3.38** – conviction of an offence – and the offender is under 16 at the time of conviction. It provides:

'Where a person under the age[1] of 16 is convicted of an offence, the court by or before which he is so convicted –

(a) if it is satisfied that the relevant condition (ie that under s 8(1)(c)) is fulfilled, shall make a parenting order; and

(b) if it is not so satisfied, shall state in open court[2] that it is not and why it is not.'

This presumption is liable to lead to the making of orders in cases where involvement in voluntary schemes is already ongoing or is being or could be arranged. It is also liable to lead to orders being made as part of the sentence in circumstances which are inappropriate.

The reason for the distinction between offenders under 16 and those aged 16 or 17 was given as follows by Lord Williams of Mostyn, Parliamentary Under-Secretary, Home Office:

'[J]uveniles aged 16 and 17 are quite different in their development from younger children. They are at a transitional stage between childhood and adulthood and should have different considerations given to them. The emotional, intellectual and physical development of 16 and 17-year-olds will vary greatly. Some will have left school, they may be at work, they may be living independently. They may even in these days have family responsibilities of their own. Others may be living fully dependent upon their parents at home in full-time education.

We believe that when children under 16 go to court in criminal proceedings, the parents must be involved. Subsection (1) [of s 9], therefore, puts a duty on the court to make a parenting order where a child or young person under the age of 16 is convicted of a criminal offence – and this is the important matter – when the condition is met – that is, it is desirable in the interests of preventing a further commission of an offence by that child or young person.

For older juveniles, we believe that the situation is somewhat different. It will often be right for parents of 16 and 17-year-olds, to be involved, but in some circumstances it may not be. We therefore put the duty on the courts to involve the parents of children and young people under 16. For 16 to 17-year-olds, we say that should be a power. We believe that that reflects what occurs in real life because 16 and 17-year-olds are at a different stage of development.'[3]

1 See general annotations.
2 See annotations to s 9.
3 HL Committee, cols 1076–1077 (10 February).

Procedural requirements

3.42   Before making a parenting order:

(a) in a case falling within s 8(1)(a) (order in tandem with a child safety order);

(b) in a case falling within s 8(1)(b) or (c) (order in tandem with an anti-social behaviour or sex offender order[1] made in respect of a child or young person or order made on conviction of a child or young person), where the person concerned is under 16; or

(c) in a case falling within s 8(1)(d) (order made on conviction in respect of pupil's non-attendance at school), where the person to whom the offence related is under 16,

a court must obtain and consider information about the person's family circumstances and the likely effect of the order on those circumstances (s 9(2)). By virtue of this last provision, a court would have to consider, for example, an adverse effect that a parenting order would have on a juvenile's attendance at school or any conflict with the child's religious beliefs. This provision mirrors the rule which applies in respect of the making of supervision orders[2] or curfew orders[3] against juveniles under 16.

In addition, whatever the age of the juvenile concerned, before making a parenting order, a court must explain to the parent in ordinary language:

(a) the effect of the order and of the requirements proposed to be included in it;

(b) the consequences which may follow (see para **3.49**) if he fails to comply with any of those requirements; and

(c) that the court has power to review the order on the application either of the parent or of the responsible officer (s 9(3)).

---

1 See Chapter 5.
2 Children and Young Persons Act 1969, s 12A(6).
3 Criminal Justice Act 1991, s 12(6A).

Appeal

3.43   Section 10 provides for an appeal against the making of a parenting order. Such an appeal includes an appeal against the terms of an order. The relevant route depends on the subsection of s 8(1) by virtue of which the order was made.

3.44   Where the order is made by virtue of s 8(1)(a) (order in tandem with a child safety order) appeal lies to the High Court (s 10(1)(a)). Where the order is made by virtue of s 8(1)(b) (order in tandem with an anti-social behaviour order or sex offender order in respect of child or young person) appeal lies to the Crown Court (s 10(1)(b)). On an appeal, the High Court or the Crown Court:

(a) may make such orders as may be necessary to give effect to its determination of the appeal; and

(b) may also make such incidental or consequential orders as appear to it to be just (s 10(2)).

Any order made on the appeal (other than one directing that an application be re-heard by a magistrates' court) is, for the purposes of the provisions (below) relating to variation, discharge or breach of an order, treated as if it were an order of the court from which the appeal was brought and not an order of the High Court or Crown Court (s 10(3)).

3.45   Where the parenting order is made by virtue of s 8(1)(c) (child or young person convicted of an offence), a person in respect of whom it is made has the same right of appeal against the making of it as if:

(a) the offence leading to the making of the order was an offence committed by him; and

(b) the order was a sentence passed on him for the offence (s 10(4)).

Consequently, for example, if an order is made by a youth court by virtue of the conviction of a child aged 13, the person subject to the order may appeal to the Crown Court or by case stated on a point of law or jurisdiction to a divisional court of the Queen's Bench Division.[1]

---

1 Magistrates' Courts Act 1980, ss 108 and 110.

3.46   Where a parenting order is made by virtue of s 8(1)(d) (offence under s 443 or s 444 of the Education Act 1996), a person in respect of whom the order is made has the same right of appeal against the making of the order as if the order were a sentence passed on him for the offence that led to the making of the order (s 10(5)). The above offences are summary only[1] and therefore appeal lies from a magistrates' court in which the person was convicted either to the Crown Court or by case stated on a point of law or jurisdiction to a divisional court of the Queen's Bench Division.[2]

---

1 Education Act 1996, ss 443(4) and 444(8).
2 Magistrates' Courts Act 1980, ss 108 and 110.

3.47   We have already indicated that a child safety order, whose making is one of the triggers for a parenting order, is made by a magistrates' court sitting as a family proceedings court, a civil court, and that the Lord Chancellor has power to make orders concerning the horizontal or vertical transfer of family proceedings in certain circumstances. The Lord Chancellor has not yet made any order in respect of the transfer of child safety orders. If he does, the question of an appeal against a transfer or proposed transfer will arise.

Section 10(6) provides that the Lord Chancellor may by order make provision as to the circumstances in which appeals against a parenting order made by virtue of s 8(1)(a) (making of a child safety order) may be made against decisions taken by courts on questions arising in connection with the transfer, or proposed transfer, of proceedings by virtue of any order under Sch 11, para 2 to the 1989 Act. Except to the extent provided in such an order, no appeal may be made against decisions in respect of the transfer or proposed transfer of a case (s 10(7)). Any order under s 10(6) must be made by statutory instrument and is subject to annulment in pursuance of a resolution of either House of Parliament (s 114(2)). Section 10(6) and (7) had not come into force when this book went to press.

Discharge or variation

3.48 The responsible officer or the parent may apply for the discharge or variation of a parenting order (s 9(5)). The court can order a discharge or variation only if it appears that it is appropriate to do so (ibid). Variation may be made:

(a) by cancelling any provision included in the order; or
(b) by inserting in it (either in addition to or in substitution for any of its provisions) any provision that could have been included in the order if the court had then had power to make it and was exercising the power (ibid).

An order for discharge or variation can be made only by the court which made the parenting order (s 9(5)). The court has no power to discharge or vary a parenting order of its own motion.

Where an application for the discharge of a parenting order is dismissed, no further application for its discharge may be made by any person (not just the previous applicant) except with the consent of the court which made the order (s 9(6)).

Breach

3.49 As long as a parenting order is in force, it is a summary offence for a parent to fail without reasonable excuse to comply with any requirement included in a parenting order, or specified in directions given by the responsible officer (s 9(7)). The offence is not punishable with imprisonment but is punishable with a fine not exceeding level 3 on the standard scale[1] (s 9(7)).

---

1 See general annotations.

3.50 Section 9 does not say who is responsible for instituting proceedings, nor in which magistrates' court proceedings are to be brought. Leaving aside the theoretical possibility of a private prosecution, the process envisaged by the Government is that the responsible officer will report to the police an alleged breach of a parenting order. The police will investigate the allegation, taking statements etc and give the results of their investigation to the Crown Prosecution Service. It will then be for the CPS to determine whether or not a prosecution should be brought, applying the usual test of public interest.

This can be contrasted with breach of a probation or community service order where it is the Probation Service which brings proceedings and conducts them.

3.51   In order to constitute an offence under s 9(7) the failure must be a failure to comply with any requirement in an order, or specified in directions given by the responsible officer. Thus, if a requirement is to ensure that a child attends school it will be non-compliance with it if the child does not so attend, whereas if a requirement is to take reasonable steps to ensure that the child attends school, and the child does not attend despite the parent taking reasonable steps to ensure that he does, there will not be non-compliance with the requirement and cannot be an offence of failing.

It is not inconceivable that a parent may fail to comply with a direction which has been inadequately communicated or understood. This raises the question of whether or not the offence is one of strict liability. The approach of the courts to this question does not make one particularly optimistic that the courts will imply a mens rea requirement.[1]

While there may be no objection to making deliberate breach of a parenting order an offence, there may be reservations to imposing criminal liability in the case of parents, perhaps a single parent mother, where the juvenile who is the basis for the order is beyond control (and possibly physically intimidating), especially if that parent lacks the means to pay a fine.

---

1 In relation to the issue of strict liability and the interpretation of a criminal statute in this respect, see Card, Cross and Jones *Criminal Law* (14th edn), ch 5.

3.52   The burden of proof of establishing the offence is, of course, on the prosecution. The prosecution will need to establish that a parenting order was made and its terms. This will be done by producing to the court a copy of the order. The prosecution will also need to prove that there has been a breach of the order, by the accused failing to comply with the order (with knowledge of this failure, if mens rea is required). In many cases that may be by an admission through a plea of guilty, or a formal admission under s 9 of the Criminal Justice Act 1967. If there is not a formal admission or a plea of guilty, the breach will be proved in the normal way through admissible evidence. These being criminal proceedings the relevant rules of evidence governing hearsay evidence (including documentary evidence)[1] will apply.

---

1 See, in particular, Criminal Justice Act 1991, ss 23–26.

3.53   In the context of other offences, it has been held that whether there is a reasonable excuse depends on whether a reasonable person would think the excuse reasonable in the circumstances,[1] but as a matter of law there are limitations (imposed by the courts) as to what a reasonable person might think.[2] This is likely to be the approach taken by the courts in relation to the present provision (and others in the Act where 'without reasonable excuse' appears).

In terms of other offences of 'failing', the limits of what a reasonable person would think a reasonable excuse have been particularly well developed in respect of offences of failing to supply a specimen under the drink-drive legislation. We think that the case-law there can be applied by analogy to other offences of 'failing' such as the present one. According to that case-law, a reasonable person would not think it a reasonable excuse that the accused mistakenly believed that the requirement or direction was invalid.[3] On the other hand, the fact that the accused was physically or mentally incapable of complying (or there is a substantial risk to his health or safety if he complies) with any requirement in the order, or specified in the direction given by the responsible officer is capable of amounting to a reasonable excuse.[4] This would, for example, cover cases where he is confined to bed by illness or injury. Likewise, if the offence is construed as one of strict liability, it would seem that the fact that the accused is mentally incapable of understanding that a direction is being made to him or what he is being required to do (as where he is a recent immigrant with little understanding of English) can amount to a reasonable excuse.[5]

It remains to be seen whether there could be a reasonable excuse if the failure was due to difficulty in complying or the disruptive effect of complying, as when one of the accused's children or parents was ill. No doubt, if such a story was regarded as bona fide, the case would not be reported or, if it was, would not be prosecuted. As a matter of practice, the decision on any social work project to recommend that proceedings be brought for breach is taken as a last resort, ie when the person has demonstrated a determined failure not to comply. Thus, the point may never be tested.

It would seem that, since s 9(4) assumes that an order, or directions under it, can be made despite conflicting with the parent's religious beliefs or interfering with attendance at work or an educational establishment, such conflict or interference would not be a reasonable excuse for failing to comply with a requirement in an order or a direction under it. Subject to this, it is arguable that there is a reasonable excuse for a failure to comply with an unreasonable direction.

---

1 *Bryan v Mott* (1975) 62 Cr App Rep 71 (DC).
2 Ibid; *Evans v Hughes* [1972] 3 All ER 412 (DC).
3 *Reid* [1973] 3 All ER 1020 (CA); *McGrath v Vipas* (1984) 48 JP 405 (DC).
4 *Lennard* [1973] 2 All ER 831 (CA).
5 *Chief Constable of Avon and Somerset Constabulary v Singh* [1988] RTR 107 (DC). An alleged linguistic difficulty must be scrutinised very carefully: *DPP v Whalley* [1991] Crim LR 211 (DC). Cf *Densu* [1998] Crim LR 345 (DC) (strict liability offence of possessing offensive weapon in a public place without lawful authority or reasonable excuse; held ignorance that the thing is an offensive weapon cannot amount to a reasonable excuse).

3.54   Clearly, an evidential burden of establishing reasonable excuse is placed on the accused. But on whom is the legal burden? This is unclear. Unlike some statutory provisions,[1] no express burden of proof is placed on the accused. The question therefore is whether the terms of s 101 of the Magistrates' Courts Act 1980 have that same effect.

Section 101 provides a major statutory exception to this principle.[2] The question to be determined is whether the words in a statutory provision alleged to constitute an exception to the general rule are an integral part of the constituent elements of the offence, or a true exception to it. In *Polychronakis v Richards and Jerrom Ltd*[3] it was stated that, where 'reasonable excuse' is a defence, it is not for the accused to prove it unless the specific statutory provision so requires. This is in line with other authority,[4] although not all.[5] In *Hunt*,[6] it was stressed by the House of Lords that each case turns on the construction of the particular legislation, but that a court should be slow to infer that Parliament intended to impose an onerous duty of the defendant to prove his innocence. On the other hand, the fact that a matter was within the knowledge of the accused, and could be most easily established by him was a relevant factor which might justify the burden being placed on the accused. It is unclear whether this is such a case. All that the prosecution can do is to establish a breach of the order. The prosecution cannot know the circumstances that may excuse non-compliance with the order: it is the accused who can best explain why he failed to comply. However, the balance of authority suggests that the accused bears no more than an evidential burden, and it is submitted that the better view is that this is what will be decided when the matter comes up for authoritative decision.

If the burden of proof is indeed on the prosecution, the absence of reasonable excuse will have to be proved beyond reasonable doubt. If, by contrast, the burden of showing that reasonable excuse existed is on the accused, it is to the standard of the balance of probabilities.[7]

---

1 See eg Prevention of Crime Act 1953, s 1.
2 Section 101 provides as follows: 'Where the defendant to an information or complaint relies for his defence on any exception, exemption, proviso, excuse or qualification, whether or not it accompanies the description of the offence or matter of complaint in the enactment creating the offence or on which the complaint is founded, the burden of proving the exception, exemption, proviso, excuse or qualification shall be on him; and this notwithstanding that the information or complaint contains an allegation negativing the exception, exemption, proviso, excuse or qualification'.
3 (1997) *The Times*, 16 November (DC).
4 *Mallows v Harris* [1979] RTR 404 (DC); *O'Boyle* [1973] RTR 445 (CA); *Briggs* [1987] Crim LR 708 (CA).
5 See *Gatland v Metropolitan Police Commissioner* [1968] 2 QB 279, [1968] 2 All ER 100 (DC).
6 [1987] AC 352, [1987] 1 All ER 1 (HL).
7 *Islington LBC v Panico* [1973] 3 All ER 485 (DC).

Legal aid

3.55   The normal rules relating to legal aid will apply to proceedings for a parenting order. The assistance by way of representation rules (ABWOR) will be amended so as to apply to civil proceedings for an order.[1]

Where a person is charged with breach of a parenting order, the normal rules as to criminal legal aid apply.

1 Mike O'Brien, MP, Parliamentary Under-Secretary, Home Office, HC Committee, col 266.

Effectiveness

3.56   Reinforcing parental responsibility and control is regarded as an important aspect of tackling youth crime. Voluntary parenting skills courses are already run by a number of bodies, such as the NSPCC, and are intended to contribute to such reinforcement. They can help to improve parenting and reduce family break-up, the taking of children into care and the likelihood of offending, truancy and anti-social behaviour by juveniles.[1]

So far, voluntary parenting skills courses in this country have not been subjected to detailed, independent evaluation, although some projects have been regarded as 'promising' in leading to a reduced delinquency level.[2] A programme which has been extensively evaluated is in the United States, at the Oregon Social Learning Centre. Work there with 'uncontrollable children' shows that parent training is likely to prove most effective with children aged under 10.[3]

1 NACRO, Briefing for the HL 2nd Reading (1997).
2 *Reducing Criminality Among Young People: A Sample of Relevant Programmes in the United Kingdom* (Home Office Research Study no 161, 1997).
3 *Crime and the Family* (Occasional Paper no 16, Family Policy Studies Centre, London, 1993).

3.57   Nevertheless, the effectiveness of a parenting order is open to doubt. By definition, the child concerned will already have proved to be a problem child and the parents may be unwilling to co-operate; guidance and counselling are likely to be more effective when undertaken voluntarily by a parent rather than under the coercion of a court order, which may be counter-productive. Groups such as Barnardo's and the Children's Society expressed the view that compulsory attendance at guidance and counselling sessions is likely to exacerbate tension between parent and child, and, in some instances, lead to excessive physical punishment and/or result in family breakdown and admissions to care.[1] More useful would be to make more widely available voluntary training programmes in parenting skills, particularly for parents of younger children, something which appears to be likely under the Government's 'Sure Start' programme announced in July 1998. Failure to co-operate with an order will be punishable with a fine. The threat of financial penalties to parents who are often already poor, inadequate and sometimes in despair may be unlikely to achieve very much that is positive. Doubtless, in some cases a fine will not be paid and imprisonment for non-payment will follow, which will only worsen relationships in a malfunctioning family. Nevertheless, the Government's thinking was that, although voluntary schemes are preferable, a compulsory scheme of guidance and counselling may be of assistance for those 'who do not wish it, who are perhaps afraid of it' and is better than doing nothing.[2] This suggests that parenting orders are unlikely to be made unless a parent is unwilling to attend a course on a voluntary basis.

1 Damian Green, MP, HC 2nd Reading, col 427.
2 Lord Williams of Mostyn, Parliamentary Under-Secretary, Home Office, HL Committee, cols 1077 and 1080 (10 February).

REMOVAL OF TRUANTS TO SCHOOLS OR DESIGNATED PREMISES

3.58   Truancy is a significant contemporary problem. At least one million children take at least one half day off from school a year without authority. According to one survey, nearly one in ten 15-year-olds truant at least once a week. Truancy is closely associated with crime. A quarter of school-age offenders have truanted significantly. In the Metropolitan police area, 5% of offences are committed by children in school hours.[1]

1 These figures were given by Mike O'Brien, MP, Parliamentary Under-Secretary, Home Office, HC Committee, col 778. For a detailed study of truancy, see *Wasted Youth* (Institute of Public Policy Research, 1998).

3.59   In some areas, the police have already worked closely with schools on truancy reduction schemes; such schemes have been effective, in the immediate and the long term, but they have lacked a legal basis and the police have lacked explicit powers to do anything when a truanting child has been found.[1]

Section 16 provides a means by which the police can deal with truants. Its provisions are intended to be part of a multi-agency approach to the problem of truancy, in which the police, schools and local education authorities will identify and discuss local problems and draw up strategies to deal with them.[2]

Section 16 will come into force on 1 December 1998: see Appendix II.

1 Mike O'Brien, op cit, cols 778 and 780.
2 Ibid, col 784; Lord Williams of Mostyn, Parliamentary Under-Secretary, Home Office, Lords Consideration of Commons' Amendments, col 931.

The new power

3.60   Section 16 provides that, where a direction has been given under s 16(2), a police officer may remove a juvenile of compulsory school age[1] whom he has reasonable cause to believe to be truanting to designated premises or to the juvenile's school.

1 See annotations to s 16.

3.61   In order for a direction to be given under s 16(2), a local authority,[1] which in this context means the local education authority, must have designated premises to which children and young persons of compulsory school age may be removed under s 16, and notified the chief constable for the police area concerned (or the Metropolitan or City of London Police Commissioner, as the case may be) of the designation (s 16(1)). The designated place could be a social services department or it could be a school where there are suitable facilities and staff able to deal with children who may have come from other schools. It is not anticipated that it would be a police station.[2] It was not intended by the Government that local education authorities would have to make constant provision for a designated place. It was envisaged that the new power would not be used frequently, but only for particular periods.

It is noteworthy that the operation of the new truancy provisions has to be triggered by the local education authority designating premises, since the provisions can apply to truanting from any school, grant-maintained or private, as well as to a school maintained by the local education authority.

---

1 Ie, in England, a county council, a district council whose district does not form part of a
  county council's area (ie a unitary authority), a London borough council or the Common
  Council of the City of London; in Wales, a county council or county borough council
  (s 16(5)).
2 Mike O'Brien, MP, Parliamentary Under-Secretary, Home Office, HC Committee, col 784.

Direction for exercise of power
3.62   Where premises have been designated in a police area under s 16(1), a police officer of, or above, the rank of superintendent may direct that the powers conferred on a police officer under s 16(3), see para **3.63**, are to be exercisable as respects any area falling within the police area,[1] which is specified in the direction (s 16(2)(a)). The powers will be exercisable only during the period specified in the direction (s 16(2)(b)). The Act does not specify a minimum or maximum period, despite the Government's intention that the power would be exercisable for only a specified period and in a specified area.[2] Failure to specify the period and/or area of a direction will render it invalid because the powers under s 16(3) can only be exercised in an area, and for a duration, specified in the direction. It is a moot point whether a direction which states that the powers under s 16(3) are to be exercisable 'until further notice' or 'until this direction be revoked' would specify 'a period'.

No criteria are laid down to govern the making of a direction. The direction is not required to be made in writing, although doubtless in practice it will be.

A direction will probably be made only after discussions between a school and the police about a perceived truanting problem.[3]

---

1 See s 18(1) and annotations thereto.
2 Mike O'Brien, MP, Parliamentary Under-Secretary, Home Office, HC Committee, col 785.
3 Ibid, col 784.

Exercise of the power

3.63   Section 16(3) provides that, where a police officer has reasonable cause to believe[1] that a child or young person found by him in a public place in a specified area during a specified period:

(a) is of compulsory school age;[2] and
(b) is absent from a school[2] without lawful authority,

he may remove the child or young person to designated premises, or to the school[2] from which he is so absent. Surprisingly, the constable does not have to be in uniform. The child must be 'found in a public place' by a police officer. There is no power to enter private premises (eg the child's home) nor to remove a truant found on private premises on which the police officer is already lawfully present. 'Public place' has the same meaning as in s 14 (s 16(5)).[3] Streets, shopping centres, local authority parks, recreation grounds and swimming pools, and amusement arcades, in many of which truanting children tend to congregate and make a nuisance of themselves are all 'public places' within this definition.

For the purpose of the requirement of a reasonable belief in the juvenile's absence from a school without lawful authority, a child's absence is deemed to be without lawful authority unless it is absent with leave, or because attendance at school is prevented by sickness or any unavoidable cause, or because the absence is on a day exclusively set aside for religious observance by the religious body to which his parent belongs (s 16(4)).[2] A child proceeding from a lesson at one site of a school to a lesson at another site would be absent with leave. A child who is being educated at home, and does not have a school, cannot be absent from a school. It will not always be easy for a police officer to have a reasonable cause to believe the relevant things.

Although the power under s 16 is not described as a power of arrest, the power of removal must have inherent in it the power to deprive a juvenile of his liberty, and to use reasonable force to do so, despite the fact that the juvenile has neither committed an offence nor attempted to do so. This was certainly the Government's view in Parliament:

> 'The police officer would be entitled to use such reasonable force as was necessary in all the circumstances. The force would have to be proportionate to the child's power and behaviour. Resistance with violence would constitute an offence of assault, and other powers would come into play. The provision establishes a clear authority for police action, without the disadvantage of criminalising truancy. The reasonable force should be proportionate to the circumstances, and in practice a court would be very unlikely to regard, say, the use of handcuffs as reasonable. Existing guidance to the police about handcuffs is not normally to use them on juveniles in any event.'[4]

If it transpired that the police officer did not have the necessary reasonable belief, or the child was not found in a public place, any force used by the officer would be unlawful and he would not be acting in the execution of his duty.[5]

1 See general annotations.
2 See annotations to s 16. 'Parent' in this context includes a person who is not a parent but
   who has parental responsibility or care for the child (Education Act 1996, s 576).
3 See annotations to s 14.
4 Mike O'Brien, MP, Parliamentary Under-Secretary, Home Office, HC Committee, col 784.
5 See, for example, *Waterfield* [1964] 1 QB 164, [1963] 3 All ER 659 (CA); *Piddington v Bates*
   [1960] 3 All ER 660 (DC).

3.64   If a child is removed, not to his school, but to designated premises he
will not be detained there; he will be there in the same way as a child at school. If
he seeks to leave, he will be dealt with in the same way.

How long a child stays at the designated premises will be a matter for the local
education authority; in many cases it will wish to get the child back to his own
school as soon as possible. Where there are special problems the authority can
resort to its powers under the Children Act 1989. If a child absconds from the
premises, the authority would be in the same position, and have the same
powers, as a head teacher has over a child who absconds from school.
Moreover, the police would seem to be able to exercise the power of removal
under s 16 because the child would again be absent from a school without
lawful authority.

Effectiveness

3.65   How effective will the new provisions be? They impose yet another task
on the police but no extra resources have been promised; if they are effective
the police will be freed from dealing with reports of truant-generated crime
and detecting the offenders which would release resources elsewhere. The new
provisions are unlikely to be effective in the case of determined truants, but
experience so far shows that they are likely to succeed with those who are
drifting into truancy and to have a powerful deterrent effect on those who
might.

The Home Office and the Department for Education and Employment will,
after consulting local education authorities and others, issue guidance to the
police and local authorities about the operation of s 16. No doubt this will
include guidance as to when truants should be removed to designated premises
and when they should be taken back to their schools.

REPRIMANDS AND WARNINGS FOR YOUNG OFFENDERS

3.66   Section 65 introduces a system of reprimands and warnings for young
offenders. It replaces the current system of police cautions for young offenders.

The practice of formal cautioning of offenders, which can be traced back to
1929, has been governed by Home Office Circular No 18/94, which stated,

inter alia, that there was to be a presumption in favour of the cautioning of juveniles, and a high probability of a caution for young adults aged 17 to 20. The Circular aimed to achieve not only greater consistency of practice in the use of cautions[1] but also a greater degree of flexibility as to when they were used. Despite the changes made to the Home Office Guidance, juvenile offenders were still more likely to be cautioned than adults. The Royal Commission on Criminal Justice[2] considered the use of cautions, and one of its recommendations was that consideration should be given to combining cautions with other support, through social services or the probation service. It also recognised that a failure to prosecute an individual can itself damage confidence in the criminal justice system.

The rationale for the change made by s 65 is two-fold. First, research shows that those children who show signs of criminal behaviour at an early age are most likely to end up as serious or persistent offenders.[3] Early intervention may prevent this occurring. The Government believes that 'many young people can be successfully diverted from crime without recourse to court proceedings, provided the response is clear, firm and constructive'.[4]

Secondly, where the opportunity offered is not taken, and the juvenile offends again, there must be swift and appropriate action. In this context, a warning by the police is often the most effective way of preventing further crime. Around 68% of offenders who are cautioned for the first time are not cautioned again or re-convicted within two years. However, cautions grow less effective as they are repeated. The Audit Commission in 1996 pointed to evidence suggesting that after three occasions, prosecution is more effective than cautioning in preventing re-offending.[5] *No More Excuses* characterised the existing system as too haphazard; too often the caution failed to result in follow-up action, so that the opportunity for early intervention to turn young offenders against crime was lost.[6] It stated that 'inconsistent, repeated and ineffective cautioning has allowed some children and young people to feel that they can offend with impunity'. Reforms in the cautioning system have not been successful in achieving greater consistency in practice between forces. It is with the intent of achieving a more consistent and effective scheme that the new Act introduces a new scheme of reprimands and final warnings.

---

1 The Royal Commission on Criminal Procedure, Cmnd 8092 (1981) had drawn attention to the wide variations in practice in the use of cautions throughout the country. See also Wilkinson and Evans *Police Cautioning of Juveniles – The Impact of Home Office Circular 14/1985* [1990] Crim LR 165; Westwood *The Effects of Home Office Guidelines on the Cautioning of Offenders* [1991] Crim LR 591; Evans *Police Cautioning and the Young Adult Offender* [1991] Crim LR 598.
2 Cm 2263 (1993), at ch 5, paras 57 et seq.
3 *Young People and Crime* (Home Office Research Study no 145, 1996).
4 *Tackling Youth Crime: A Consultation Paper* (Home Office, 1997), para 54.
5 Ibid; *No More Excuses – A New Approach to Tackling Youth Crime in England and Wales*, Cm 3809 (1997), para 5.9.
6 Op cit, para 5.10.

3.67   The scheme in essence is as follows:

- a first offence might be met by the response of a police reprimand, provided it is not serious;
- any further offence would have to result in a final warning or prosecution;
- in no circumstances should an offender receive two reprimands;
- if a first offence results in a final warning, any subsequent offence should normally lead to prosecution;
- only where two years have elapsed since a final warning and the subsequent offence is minor should prosecution not follow for an offence subsequent to a final warning;
- the police can always decide to prosecute for any offence.

Reprimands and final warnings will be recorded by the police, and may be taken into account subsequently by a sentencing court.

Application of the new scheme

3.68   After the commencement of s 65, no caution is to be given to any child or young person (s 65(8)). However, it should be noted that the provisions are being piloted, for a period running for 18 months from 30 September 1998 in the following areas: Hammersmith and Fulham, Kensington and Chelsea, and Westminster (jointly); Hampshire, Southampton, Portsmouth and the Isle of Wight (jointly); Sheffield; Wolverhampton; and Blackburn with Darwen.[1] Any caution given prior to commencement is to be regarded as a reprimand or warning. A first caution is to be treated as a reprimand, a second or subsequent caution as a warning (Sch 9, para 5). By s 65(1), the powers relating to reprimand and warning in s 65(2)–(5) apply where:

(a) a police officer has evidence that a child or young person ('the offender') has committed an offence;
(b) the police officer considers that the evidence is such that, if the offender were prosecuted for the offence, there would be a realistic prospect of his being convicted;
(c) the offender admits to the police officer that he committed the offence;
(d) the offender has not previously been convicted of an offence; and
(e) the police officer is satisfied that it would not be in the public interest for the offender to be prosecuted.

---

1 See Appendix II and *No More Excuses*, op cit, para 10.6.

The power to reprimand

3.69   The police officer may reprimand the offender if the offender has not previously been reprimanded or warned (s 65(2)). He must warn rather than reprimand if he considers the offence to be so serious as to require a warning (s 65(4)). It is intended that the Home Secretary will publish guidance as to the circumstances in which it is appropriate to give reprimands or warnings, including criteria as to levels of seriousness for the purposes of deciding whether a charge, or a warning, is appropriate, and the category of police officers by whom reprimands and warnings may be given, and their form (s 65(6)). Such guidance will be important in ensuring that the decisions taken by the police (whose responsibility it will be for deciding whether to reprimand, warn or charge a young offender) are consistent and fair.[1]

---

1 *Tackling Youth Crime: A Consultation Paper* (Home Office, 1997), para 59.

The power to warn

3.70   By s 65(3), the police officer may warn the offender if:

(a) the offender has not previously been warned; or
(b) where the offender has previously been warned, the offence was committed more than two years after the date of the previous warning and the police officer considers the offence to be not so serious as to require a charge to be brought.

No person may be warned under paragraph (b) above more than once.

The giving of the reprimand or warning

3.71   By s 65(5), the police officer must:

(a) give any reprimand or warning at a police station and, where the offender is under the age of 17,[1] in the presence of an appropriate adult;[2] and
(b) explain to the offender and, where he is under that age, the appropriate adult in ordinary language –
   (i)   in the case of a reprimand, the effect of s 66(5)(a) (that a reprimand may be cited in criminal proceedings in the same way as a conviction);
   (ii) in the case of a warning, the effect of s 66(1), (2), (4), (5)(b) and (c) (reference to youth offending team,[3] participation in rehabilitation programme, restriction on availability of conditional discharge power and citation in like circumstances as criminal conviction) and of any guidance about rehabilitation programmes issued by the Home Secretary under s 66(3).

---

1 See general annotations.
2 For the meaning of 'appropriate adult', see annotations to s 65.
3 See paras **2.1–2.21**.

3.72   A reprimand or warning may be cited in criminal proceedings in the same way as a conviction (s 66(5)). The provisions of the Rehabilitation of Offenders Act 1974 do not appear to apply to reprimands or warnings.

Where a warning is given the police officer must refer the person to a youth offending team (s 66(1)); the effect of that is that usually the offender will be placed on a programme of intervention prepared by the team, the purpose of which will be to help the offender (and his or her family) to change the attitudes and behaviour which led to the offending so as to prevent any further offending.[1] The team is under a duty to assess the person referred and, unless considered inappropriate to do so, it must arrange for him to participate in a rehabilitation programme (s 66(2)). A 'rehabilitation programme' is defined by s 66(6) as a programme the purpose of which is to rehabilitate participants and prevent them from re-offending. There appear to be no limits as to what can be included in a programme for this purpose, although s 66(3) requires the Home Secreary to issue guidance as to what should be included. The programme might include an assessment of the offender to establish the reasons for offending behaviour including any problems requiring attention, and may include work with parents to help them to become more effective in supervising their child, short-term counselling or group work with the young offender to bring about behavioural change, reparation to victims, supervised community or youth activities, or work to improve attendance and achievement at school.

---

1 This meets the recommendation of the Royal Commission on Criminal Justice: see para **3.66**.

3.73   Although there is a duty on the part of the police to refer the offender to the youth offending team, there is no obligation to delay the administration of the final warning until the youth offending team has determined whether an intervention programme is appropriate and, if so, what form it should take. Although such a requirement would have provided the police with more information on which to base their decision as to whether to issue a final warning, it would have introduced delay into the process and broken the direct link between offence and consequences of offending.

3.74   If a programme of intervention is proposed by the youth offending team, an offender cannot be prosecuted for failure to participate in that action plan, or to co-operate with it or to complete it fully or successfully. However, a report of failure by a person to participate in a rehabilitation programme arranged for him may be cited in criminal proceedings in the same circumstances as a conviction of his might be (s 66(5)). The meaning of this provision is far from clear. *Tackling Youth Crime*[1] states that 'any unreasonable non-compliance would be recorded on the individual's criminal record'.[1] Leaving on one side the fact that s 66(5) does not contain the qualifying word 'unreasonable', the term used by s 66(5) is 'failure by a person to participate', not 'non-compliance'. Although total failure to participate is clearly within s 66(5), anything which falls short of that, arguably, should not. After all, 'non-compliance' involves a qualitative assessment, with no opportunity for any disputes about that assessment to be determined or tested in court. It is submitted that 'failure to participate' should be construed narrowly. In cases where there is unsatisfactory levels of participation, the appropriate course of action is for the youth offending team to modify its programme of intervention.

---

1 *Tackling Youth Crime: A Consultation Paper* (Home Office, 1997), para 68.

3.75   The original intention of the Government was that a conditional discharge should not be available in respect of a person aged between 10 and 19 in respect of a further offence for which he is convicted within two years of a final warning. This lack of any discretion was intended to provide a further incentive for the offender to remain out of trouble.[1] The absolute nature of that prohibition met resistance during the consultation period, and s 66 now permits such an order to be made, but only in exceptional circumstances. If the person is convicted of an offence within two years of the warning, the sentencing court cannot make a conditional discharge order under s 1 of the Powers of Criminal Courts Act 1973 unless it is of the opinion that there are exceptional circumstances which justify its doing so (s 66(4)). If the court does make a conditional discharge, it must state in open court[2] that it is of the opinion that there are such exceptional circumstances and why it is of that opinion (s 66(4)). There is no prohibition or limitation on the granting of an absolute discharge, which would be appropriate in cases where the offence is a technical one and there are overwhelming mitigating circumstances,[3] but the normal expectation is that, in the majority of cases, a person who commits a further offence after receiving a final warning will know that he faces significant punishment.

---

1 *Tackling Youth Crime*, op cit, para 69.
2 See amendments to s 9.
3 *Tackling Youth Crime*, op cit.

Chapter 4

CHILDREN AND YOUNG PERSONS: SENTENCES

Reparation orders – Action plan orders – Amendments to supervision orders – Detention and training orders – Power of court to order parent or guardian to pay fine – Duty of magistrates' court to remit cases to youth court

4.1   The new Act introduces two orders, only applicable to young offenders: reparation orders and action plan orders. It makes modifications to the rules governing supervision orders. The new Act makes changes in respect of attendance centre orders: because these orders extend beyond children and young persons, to persons aged under 21, they are dealt with in Chapter 7. Schedules 7 and 8 also contain detailed amendments which affect other community orders. These changes are of more general application, and, again, are dealt with in Chapter 7.

The new Act also introduces a new community order: the drug treatment and testing order. This is an order which applies to persons aged 16 or over,[1] and, although therefore applicable to young offenders aged 16 and 17, is also applicable to adult offenders. It is dealt with at paras **7.29–7.49**.

---

1 See general annotations.

REPARATION ORDERS

4.2   Section 67 introduces the reparation order, a sentence requiring a young offender to make reparation to the victim of the offence or a person otherwise affected by it, or to the community at large. It will apply where a child or young person is convicted (after commencement) of an offence other than one for which the sentence is fixed by law (s 67(1)). It is intended to help show young offenders the harm which they have done to the community and to their victims, help to make the offender realise the distress and inconvenience that his or her criminal actions will have caused, and to accept responsibility for those acts. It will give the offender the opportunity to make amends whilst at the same time perhaps giving the victim a greater insight into the reasons for the offence, enabling that victim to put the offence behind him.[1] This particular form of restorative justice is regarded as particularly important by the Government: during debate on the Bill, Alun Michael, MP, Minister of State, observed that:

'the inclusion of reparation in [a reparation order], and in other kinds of sentence, such as supervision orders, should become an underlying principle of our criminal justice system and, more particularly, of our youth justice system.'[2]

In developing this principle, it builds on experimental and pilot schemes that have been introduced in the Thames Valley police force and other areas. However, this principle is not to be achieved through a single unified order which might combine reparation with other requirements or disposals, but rather through a range of different, but appropriate, orders. For example, if long-term work with the offender is appropriate, the right disposal might be to make a supervision order which includes as one of its requirements provision for the making of reparation. By contrast, reparation orders are particularly intended for cases where it is necessary to focus the attention of the offender over a short period of time.[3]

---

1 See Home Office draft Guidance, para 2.3.
2 Alun Michael, MP, Minister of State, Home Office, HC Committee, col 563.
3 Ibid, col 558.

4.3   The reparation order provisions are being piloted in four areas for an 18-month period which commenced on 30 September 1998.[1] The ability, where available, to make an order will be subject to the pre-condition that the conviction in respect of which the order is proposed to be made occurred on or after the date of commencement.[2]

---

1 See Appendix II; also see *No More Excuses: A New Approach to Tackling Youth Crime in England and Wales*, Cm 3809 (1997), para 10.6. The pilot areas for reparation orders are Hammersmith and Fulham, Kensington and Chelsea, Westminster (jointly); Hampshire, Southampton, Portsmouth, Isle of Wight (jointly); Wolverhampton; Sheffield.
2 For the pre-conditions to the making of the order see paras **4.6–4.8**.

When can an order be made?

4.4   Section 67 provides that, the court by or before which the child or young person[1] is convicted may make a 'reparation order', which requires the offender to make the reparation specified in the order:

(a) to a person or persons so specified; or
(b) to the community at large.

Any person so specified must be a person identified by the court as a victim of the offence or a person otherwise affected by it. The phrase 'make reparation' is defined by s 85 as meaning make reparation otherwise than by the payment of compensation. If, in any case, the court has power to make a reparation order but does not do so, it shall give reasons as to why it does not make an order (s 67(11)). It is intended that courts consider the making of an order in any case in which a compensation order is not imposed.[2]

The order is a court disposal, not a community sentence. For that reason the restrictions on the imposition of community sentences contained in ss 6 to 7 of the Criminal Justice Act 1991 do not apply.

1 See s 117.
2 *No More Excuses*, op cit, para 4.14.

Restrictions

4.5   Certain restrictions apply on the making of the order, and on its requirements.

4.6   The first is that a court must not make a reparation order unless it has been notified by the Home Secretary that arrangements for implementing such orders are available in the area proposed to be named in the order and the notice has not been withdrawn (s 67(3)). Obviously, local arrangements for the administration and management of reparation schemes must exist.

4.7   Secondly, a reparation order must not be combined with a custodial sentence (s 67(4)). It is the Government's view that to combine the two would be to combine two very different disposals, in an inappropriate way. This, however, was a view challenged strongly during the passage of the Act.

4.8   Thirdly, the court must not make a reparation order in respect of the offender if it proposes to make in respect of him a community service order, a combination order, a supervision order which includes requirements,[1] or an action plan order (s 67(4)).[2] The intention is to avoid a multiplicity of regimes and requirements. Community service and combination orders (through the community service element) already include elements of reparation. The National Standards for the Supervision of Offenders in the Community provide that the main purpose of the community service order is to prevent offending by re-integrating the offender into the community.[3] This is to be achieved by means of punishment ('by means of positive and demanding unpaid work, keeping to disciplined requirements') and by reparation to the community ('by undertaking socially useful work'). Where a court wishes to impose an action plan order[2] or a supervision order with requirements,[1] but wishes the offender to make reparation, that reparation should be specified as part of the requirements of either of those orders, again to avoid multiplicity of regimes. It cannot impose a separate reparation order. This is intended to avoid conflict between the demands of different orders and to ensure that the reparative element is an integral part of the action plan or supervision order. Indeed, the National Standards identify reparation as one important process participants in supervision orders should engage in.[4]

In contrast, a reparation order can be combined with a compensation order. It was the original intention of the Government that this combination should not be possible, because it 'smacks too much of punishing the offender twice for the same offence'.[5] The rationale for prohibiting this combination was not entirely convincing, and, during the later stages of the passage of the Act, the Government conceded the point that it might be appropriate for a young offender to make both financial and non-financial reparation. To have continued the prohibition on combining the two would also have meant that victims would have needed to be warned that by agreeing to reparation their right to seek financial compensation (other than through the ordinary civil process) would be lost. The young offender who daubs paint on the outside of a house, or vandalises a motor vehicle, might be expected both to pay compensation for the damage and to be brought to understand the effect of his or her actions on victims by making reparation, for example by writing a letter of apology or apologising to the victim in person, weeding a garden, cleaning graffiti, collecting litter or doing other work to help the community. This change of heart by the Government is now reflected by the new Act, which permits the combination of compensation and reparation order.

---

1 Imposed in pursuance of ss 12 to 12C of the 1969 Act. See, generally, paras **4.43–4.47**, and annotations to s 67.
2 See paras **4.24–4.33**.
3 *National Standards for the Supervision of Offenders in the Community* (Home Office, 1995), para 2, p 34.
4 Ibid, para 19, p 29.
5 Alun Michael, MP, Minister of State, Home Office, HC Committee, col 570.

4.9   Before making an order, a court must obtain and consider a written report by a probation officer, social worker or member of youth offending team[1] indicating the type of work that is suitable for the offender, and the attitude of the victim or victims to the requirements proposed to be included in the order (s 68(1)). There is no obligation to act on the views of the victim, although those views are important on the question of whether an order is appropriate, and what activities it might require. Nor does the victim have to give consent in writing.[2] Where possible the report should be prepared in advance of the young person's appearance for sentence.[3]

This report is not a pre-sentence report, within the technical sense set out in the Criminal Justice Act 1991. The report writer should seek to do as much preparatory work as possible in a case where there is a reasonable chance that a reparation order might be made, in order to minimise delay in supplying a report to the court.[4] Such preparatory work might include ascertaining the victim's views about reparation, ascertaining the antecedents of the young person and any other relevant information. The report itself should indicate the type of reparative activity which, in the report writers' opinion, could usefully be included in the order, an opinion informed by the offender's needs and capabilities, by the nature of the offence which has been committed and by the wishes of the victim. Every effort should be made to ensure that the reparation relates as closely as possible to the offence itself.[4] The report writer should also consider whether it is appropriate to recommend the making of a parenting order, made under s 8 of the new Act.

It has already been noted that the court has to state in open court the reason why it does not make a reparation order.[5] Those reasons might be that the victim is unwilling to agree to reparation. Care should be taken to ensure that the victim is not embarrassed in public by a statement as to this refusal, and it may be that guidance is issued to this effect.[6] The matter should be dealt with in the report from the probation officer, or whoever, which no doubt in such circumstances would address the alternative possibility of reparation to the community generally.

1 See para **2.20**.
2 see para **4.11**.
3 *Tackling Youth Crime: A Consultation Paper* (Home Office, 1997), para 28.
4 Home Office draft Guidance, para 3.2.
5 See para **4.4**.
6 Alun Michael, MP, Minister of State, Home Office, HC Committee, col 577.

4.10   The court must, before making an order, explain to the offender in ordinary language the effect of the order and proposed requirements, the consequences of failure to comply, and the court's power to review the order on the application either of the offender or the responsible officer (s 68(2)).

In this context the parents of the offender have an important role to play, and where possible, should be present.[1] Their attendance can be compelled by a court under s 34A of the Children and Young Persons Act 1933, which obliges a court to require such attendance, unless the court is satisfied that it would be unreasonable to do so.

1 Home Office draft Guidance, para 3.11.

The content of the order

4.11   A reparation order must not require the offender:

(a) to work for more than 24 hours in aggregate; or
(b) to make reparation to any person without the consent of that person (s 67(5)).

Reparation should not include financial reparation.[1]

The purpose of s 67(5)(a) is to limit the scope of the order. The 24-hour requirement is a maximum: no minimum level is set. Some pressure was exerted on the Government during the passage of the Act to extend the extent of the reparation programme, which might be considered to be low, especially in respect of older offenders.[2] However, the 24-hour period is the maximum that might be required by the order. The Minister of State highlighted instances of offenders voluntarily continuing reparative work even after the conclusion of a relevant court order,[3] but did not identify how often offenders voluntarily engage in, or extend a period of reparation. It was also emphasised that the 24-hour maximum period was the equivalent to Saturday afternoon for three months. The short-term nature of the order was stressed. The reparation period is intended to allow 'the youngster to see the end of the task ahead', an objective which might be defeated by a longer programme of reparation.

There appears to be no prohibition on the reparation period continuing beyond the 18th birthday of the offender, provided the overall maximum period of statutory reparation is not exceeded.

The consent of the victim is required before reparation is made to him or her. That consent does not have to be in writing, but must, nevertheless, be forthcoming. This element of consent is particularly important, in that to require a victim to accept reparation when it was not wanted would, from the point of view of the victim, be to add insult to injury. There is, of course, nothing to prevent the court ordering the offender to make reparation generally to the community if the victim is unwilling to consent to such reparation.

1 See para **4.13**.
2 See, eg James Clappison, MP, HC Committee, cols 574–576.
3 See Alun Michael, MP, Minister of State, Home Office, HC Committee, col 575.

4.12   Subject to s 67(5) (which contains the limitations on the number of hours of reparation), requirements specified in a reparation order shall be such as in the opinion of the court are commensurate with the seriousness of the offence, or the combination of the offence and one or more offences associated with it (s 67(6)). In this regard, therefore, the general approach relating the requirements of a sentence with the seriousness of the offence for which it was passed, and contained in the 1991 Act, are maintained.[1]

Requirements so specified must, as far as practicable, be such as to avoid:

(a) any conflict with the offender's religious beliefs or with the requirements of any community order to which he may already be subject; and
(b) any interference with the times, if any, at which the offender normally works or attends school or any other educational establishment (s 67(7)).

1 See annotations to s 63.

4.13   Any reparation required by a reparation order:

(a) must be made under the supervision of the responsible officer (defined by s 67(10) to include probation officer, social worker or member of youth offending team); and
(b) must be made within a period of three months[1] from the date of the making of the order (s 67(8)).

A reparation order will require a young offender to make specific reparation to an individual victim, to a collective victim such as a school or community centre, or, if it is what the victim would prefer, to the community at large.[2] The intention is that the reparation should be in kind rather than financial. If courts wish to impose financial compensation they can do so through the compensation order. Typical examples of the types of activity which might constitute reparation have already been given.[3] Clearly, a court will need to have regard to the age of the offender in determining what is suitable reparation.

The responsible officer will, most likely, be a member of the youth offending team. The draft Home Office guidance identifies what that officer will need to do. He will need to:

(a) give the young person instructions as to when to attend to carry out any reparative action;

(b) meet with him regularly to measure progress against the reparation order, and monitor compliance with the requirements of the order;

(c) bring any breach proceedings;

(d) liaise with the young person's parents or guardian;

(e) liaise with those running any reparative programmes;

(f) ensure that the offender understands what is required by the order and what the consequences of non-compliance will be;

(g) supervise and direct the making of reparation.

The officer should make initial contact within five working days of the making of the order, and prepare a plan to support the order within 10 working days of the making of that order, which should include details as to frequency of meetings between offender and supervisor (at least weekly during the first month of the order).

---

1 See general annotations.
2 *Tackling Youth Crime*, op cit, paras 20–21.
3 See para **4.8**.

Variation and discharge

4.14   Schedule 5 to the new Act contains detailed provisions in respect of the variation and discharge of reparation orders. The same Schedule applies equally to action plan orders, discussed later.[1] Schedule 5 came into force on 30 September 1998: see Appendix II.

---

1 See paras **4.24–4.33**.

Who has the power to discharge or vary an order?

4.15   The power to discharge or vary a youth court order is vested in the youth court named in the order (Sch 5, para 1). That will be the youth court for the petty sessions area[1] in which the offender resides, or will reside (ss 67(9) and 69(9)). The power to discharge or vary includes the power to discharge or vary a Crown Court order. The language of Sch 5, para 2 (which deals with discharge or variance) in no way limits the power of the youth court to youth court orders.

Breach proceedings may be taken without prior warning to the offender, but in any event, no more than two warnings of non-compliance with the order should be given before breach proceedings are commenced.[2]

---

1 See general annotations.
2 Home Office draft Guidance, para 9.5.

What powers to discharge or vary are granted?

4.16   If it appears to the appropriate youth court on an application made by the responsible officer or by the offender that it is appropriate to do so, the court may discharge the order, or vary it:

(a) by cancelling any provision included in it; or
(b) by inserting in it (either in addition to or in substitution for any of its provisions) any provision which could have been included in the order if the court had then had the power to make the order and were in fact exercising it (Sch 5, para 2(1)).

The court has no power to discharge or vary of its own motion: there must be an application, although clearly a court can, if it wishes to do so, invite an application. If an application for discharge is made and dismissed, no further application for discharge can be made except with the consent of the court (Sch 5, para 2(2)).

Failure to comply with youth court order

4.17   Where the appropriate youth court is satisfied, on an application made by the responsible officer, that the offender has failed to comply with any requirement included in the order, it may (in addition to any order by way of discharge or variation) order the offender to pay a fine not exceeding £1,000, or make an attendance centre order[1] or curfew order in respect of him (Sch 5, para 3(2)(a)). The fine imposed is to be deemed to be a sum adjudged to be paid by a conviction (Sch 5, para 3(7)).

Alternatively, the youth court may discharge the order and deal with the offender for the offence in respect of which the order was made, in any manner in which he could have been dealt with for that offence by the court which made the order if the order had not been made (Sch 5, para 3(2)(b)). Thus, if the youth court wishes to impose a custodial sentence, in the form of a detention and training order,[2] it can do so only if the seriousness of the offence is such as to satisfy the custody threshold in s 1 of the Criminal Justice Act 1991.[3]

---

1 For the definition of an attendance centre order, see para **7.59**.
2 See paras **4.49** et seq.
3 See annotations to s 63.

4.18   However, if the court is proposing to deal with the offender for breach of the order, it must take into account the extent to which the offender has complied with the requirements of the order (Sch 5, para 3(8)). If the offender has attained the age[1] of 18 after the date of application, but before the date of hearing, the offender is to be dealt with as if he were still aged under 18 (Sch 5, para 5(6)). If he had attained the age of 18 prior to the application, he should be dealt with in accordance with that age.

---

1 See general annotations.

Failure to comply with Crown Court order

4.19   If the order was a Crown Court order, the youth court, following an application by the responsible officer, may deal with the offender as set out in para **4.17** above. Alternatively, it may (although is under no duty to do so) commit the offender in custody or release him on bail until he can be brought or appear before the Crown Court (Sch 5, para 3(2)(c)). Where the youth court follows that course of action it is under a duty to supply to the Crown Court a certificate, signed by a justice of the peace, giving:

(a) particulars of the offender's failure to comply with the requirement in question; and

(b) such other particulars of the case as may be desirable (Sch 5, para 3(4)).

Such a certificate purporting to be so signed, is admissible as evidence of the failure of the breach before the Crown Court. That phraseology permits other evidence to be adduced in the Crown Court to prove breach, or no breach, if such evidence exists and is relevant. Schedule 5, para 3(4), does not state that the justices' certificate shall be 'conclusive evidence'. Clearly, in all but exceptional cases the certificate is likely to suffice.

4.20   Where failure to comply is proved to the satisfaction of the Crown Court, the order must be revoked, if it is still in force (Sch 5, para 3(6)). The Crown Court may deal with the offender for the offence in respect of which the order was made, in any manner in which it could have dealt with him for that offence if he had not made the order (Sch 5, para 3(5)). Thus, if it wishes to impose a custodial sentence, in the form of a detention and training order,[1] it can only do so if the seriousness of the offence is such as to satisfy the custody threshold in s 1 of the Criminal Justice Act 1991.[2] Again, the court must take into account the extent to which the offender has complied with the requirements of the order (Sch 5, para 3(8)). If the offender has attained the age[3] of 18 after the date of application, but before the date of hearing, the offender is to be dealt with as if he were still under 18 (Sch 5, para 5(6)). If he had attained the age of 18 prior to the application,[4] he should be dealt with in accordance with that age.

---

1 See paras **4.49** et seq.
2 See annotations to s 63.
3 See general annotations.
4 See para **4.18**.

Procedure

4.21   The Act does not specify whether the application by the responsible officer must be in writing. However, no order can be made without the offender being present in court (Sch 5, para 4(1)), unless the order is one of discharge, cancelling a requirement contained in the order, altering the name of any area specified in the order, or changing the responsible officer named in the order (Sch 5, para 4(9)).

The attendance of the offender may be secured by the issue or a summons or warrant (in which circumstances the provisions of the Magistrates' Courts Act 1980, s 55(3) and (4) apply, with some modifications[1]) (Sch 5, para 4(2) and (3)).

If the offender is arrested pursuant to a warrant, and cannot immediately be brought before the appropriate court, the person in whose custody he is held may make arrangements for his detention in place of safety for a period of up to 72 hours from the time of arrest, bringing him before a youth court during that period (Sch 5, para 4(4)). That court may not necessarily be the appropriate youth court: if it is not, the youth court before which the offender is brought may remand to local authority accommodation (provided the offender is aged under 18) or direct his release (Sch 5, para 4(5)). If the offender has attained the age of 18 after the date of application, but before the date of hearing, the offender is to be dealt with as if he were still aged under 18 (Sch 5, para 5(6)). If he had attained the age of 18 prior to the application, he should be dealt with in accordance with that age.

If the offender is aged 18 or over he should be remanded to a remand centre, if such a centre is available, or, otherwise, to prison. He may, of course, alternatively be released (Sch 5, para 4(6)).

Where an application for discharge or variation is made under Sch 5, para 2(1) (as to which, see para **4.16**) the offender may be remanded to local authority accommodation if either his attendance has been secured by warrant, or if the court considers that remand (or further remand) will enable information to be obtained which is likely to assist the court in deciding whether, and if so, how, to exercise its powers (Sch 5, para 4(7)). The relevant local authority must be specified in accordance with the terms of Sch 5, para 4(8).

---

1 As modified (the modifications being italicised) these provide as follows:

'(3) The court shall not begin to hear the complaint in the absence of the defendant or issue a warrant under this section unless either it is proved to the satisfaction of the court, on oath or in such other manner as may be prescribed, that the summons *cannot be served or* was served on him within what appears to the court to be a reasonable time before the hearing or adjourned hearing or the defendant has appeared on a previous occasion to answer to the complaint.

(4) Where the defendant fails to appear at an adjourned hearing, the court shall not issue a warrant under this section unless it is satisfied that he has had adequate notice of the time and place of the adjourned hearing.'

Appeals

4.22   An offender may appeal to the Crown Court in respect of any order of discharge (or refusal to discharge), variation or failure to comply made by a youth court, other than an order that did not require his presence[1] (Sch 5, para 5(7)). There appears to be no right of appeal against such decisions taken by the Crown Court.

---

1 See para **4.21**.

Attendance centre orders

4.23 The power of a youth court to impose an attendance centre order has already been noted.[1] For this purpose, Sch 5, para 5(1), applies (in a modified form) the provisions of s 17 of the Criminal Justice Act 1982. The provisions of ss 18 and 19 of the 1982 Act also apply (in a modified form) to the discharge, variation and breach of such orders. These are discussed in more detail at para **7.59**.

1 See para **4.17**.

ACTION PLAN ORDERS

4.24 Section 69 makes provision for an action plan order, a new community penalty requiring a young offender to comply with an action plan intended to address his offending behaviour. Although there are distinct similarities between the action plan order introduced by s 69, and a supervision order with requirements for intermediate treatment,[1] the intention is that the action plan order should be a new kind of community penalty – one which provides the opportunity for a short but intensive programme of work with the young offender, and his or her parents, to tackle the causes of offending at an early stage.[2] Supervision orders with an intermediate treatment requirement are intended to be less focused and to last longer. The new order will be available to both youth courts and Crown Courts.

The content of the order will vary according to the particular offender and his or her offending. It will impose a series of requirements, individually tailored to the young offender and designed to address the specific causes of the offending. It may, for example, require the young offender to comply with educational arrangements, to make reparation to the victim, to observe the terms of a daily or weekly schedule stipulating whereabouts and activities, or to stay away from particular activities.

1 See para **4.43**, and annotations to s 67.
2 See *No More Excuses*, op cit, para 5.18. See also Alun Michael, MP, Minister of State, Home Office, HC Committee, col 587.

Application of s 69

4.25 The provisions of s 69 apply where a offender aged 10[1] and above but not more than 17 is convicted of an offence other than one for which the sentence is fixed by law, after the commencement[2] of the section (s 69(1)). Section 69 is being piloted in four areas for an 18-month period which commenced on 30 September 1998.[3]

1 See general annotations.
2 See para **1.4**.
3 See Appendix II. Also see *No More Excuses*, op cit, para 10.6. The pilot areas for action plan

orders are Hammersmith and Fulham, Kensington and Chelsea, and Westminster (jointly); Hampshire, Southampton, Portsmouth, Isle of Wight (jointly); Wolverhampton; and Sheffield.

Power to make the order

4.26 The action plan order introduced by s 69 is a community order and therefore subject to the requirements for, and restriction on, the making of such orders under ss 6 and 7 of the Criminal Justice Act 1991 (s 69(11)).[1] For young people whose offending is serious enough to justify a community sentence, it should be regarded as a first option.[2]

By s 69(2), the court by or before which the offender is convicted may, if it is of the opinion that it is desirable to do so in the interests of securing his rehabilitation, or of preventing the commission by him of further offences, make an order (an 'action plan order') which:

(a) requires the offender, for a period of three months beginning with the date of the order, to comply with an action plan, that is to say, a series of requirements with respect to his actions and whereabouts during that period;

(b) places the offender under the supervision for that period of the responsible officer; and

(c) requires the offender to comply with any directions given by that officer with a view to the implementation of that plan.

The three-month length of the order is intended to provide a short but intensive programme of intervention commensurate with the seriousness of the offending and aimed at tackling the causes of his or her offending.

1 See annotations to s 61.
2 Home Office draft Guidance, para 2.3.

Restrictions on the making of an action plan order

4.27 Several restrictions are placed on the making of an order. First, a court must not make an action plan order unless it has been notified by the Home Secretary that arrangements for implementing such orders are available in the area proposed to be named in the order and the notice has not been withdrawn (s 69(3)). Secondly, the court may not make an action plan order in respect of the offender if:

(a) he is already the subject of such an order; or

(b) the court proposes to pass on him a custodial sentence or to make in respect of him a probation order, a community service order, a combination order, a supervision order or an attendance centre order (s 69(4)).

The restriction on combining an action plan order with custody is perhaps self-evident, given that by definition custodial sentences and community sentences should not be combined.[1] Quite apart from differences in principle, the threshold for a custodial sentence in s 1 of the Criminal Justice Act 1991 will not have been crossed. Community service and combination orders are targeted at offenders aged 16 and over, and include an element of reparation. Supervision orders and attendance centre orders contain their own regimes designed to work with young offenders, and the differences in degree between action plan orders and supervision orders have already been noted.[2] A reparation order may not be combined with an action plan order s 67(4)(b). There is, however, no obstacle to combining an action plan order with a curfew order, fine or compensation order.

---

1 See 1991 Act, ss 1 and 6.
2 See para **4.24**.

Procedure when making an order

4.28   By s 70, before making an action plan order, a court must obtain and consider:

(a) a written report by a probation officer, a social worker of a local authority social services department or a member of a youth offending team,[1] indicating:
  (i)   the requirements proposed by that person to be included in the order;
  (ii) the benefits to the offender that the proposed requirements are designed to achieve; and
  (iii) the attitude of a parent or guardian of the offender to the proposed requirements; and
(b) where the offender is under the age of 16,[2] information about the offender's family circumstances and the likely effect of the order on those circumstances (s 70(1)).

This report replaces the normal pre-sentence report.

This requirement to consider the family circumstances does not apply in respect of offenders aged 16 or 17 who are being considered for an action plan order. Such persons will often have left home and be living independently. However, the Government intends to issue guidance, which may include asking for sensitivity in cases where offenders aged over 16 have family circumstances or arrangements to which it is appropriate for a court to give greater attention.[3]

It should be borne in mind that, to achieve a report containing the matters set out in s 70, a significant level of contact will have had to have occurred between the reporting officer and the offender, and, where appropriate, his family. It will be important that report writers do as much preparatory work as possible prior to the court hearing, in order to minimise the potential for delay. This should include liaison with schools and education authorities, to inquire about the achievements and failings of the offender and to ascertain the view of teachers as to whether an educational requirement is considered necessary or desirable. The report writer should also consider the desirability of recommending a parenting order.

1 See paras **2.19–2.21**.
2 See general annotations.
3 Alun Michael, MP, Minister of State, Home Office, HC Committee, col 589. See, now, draft
   Guidance, para 3.2.

4.29   Before making an action plan order, a court must explain to the
offender in ordinary language:

(a) the effect of the order and of the requirements proposed to be included in
     it;
(b) the consequences which may follow (under Sch 5)[1] if he fails to comply
     with any of those requirements; and
(c) that the court has power (under Sch 5) to review the order on the
     application either of the offender or the responsible officer (s 70(2)).

1 See paras **4.14–4.23**.

Requirements in an action plan order

4.30   By s 69(5), requirements included in an action plan order, or
directions given by a responsible officer, may require the offender to do all or
any of the following things, namely:

(a) to participate in activities specified in the requirements or directions at a
     time or times so specified;
(b) to present himself to a person or persons specified in the requirements or
     directions at a place or places and at a time or times so specified;
(c) to attend at an attendance centre specified in the requirements of
     directions for a number of hours so specified (but only if the offence is, in
     the case of an adult, punishable with imprisonment (s 69(7));
(d) to stay away from a place or places specified in the requirements or
     directions;
(e) to comply with any arrangements for his education specified in the
     requirements or directions;
(f) to make reparation specified in the requirements or directions to a person
     or persons so specified or to the community at large (provided that that
     person is a victim of or affected by the offence and consents to reparation
     (s 69(8))); and
(g) to attend any hearing fixed by the court under s 70(3).

Such requirements and directions must, as far as practicable, be such as to avoid
any conflict with the offender's religious beliefs or with the requirements of any
other community order to which he may be subject, and any interference with
the times, if any, at which he normally works or attends school or any other
educational establishment (s 69(6)).

The responsible officer has the discretion to give to the young offender any
directions considered necessary to enable the offender to complete the action

plan order successfully, a proposition not explicitly stated in the new Act but nevertheless emphasised by draft Guidance.[1] In every case, however, the requirements of the order should be tailored to the individual personal circumstances of the offender. These requirements can include provisions relating to reparation of a non-financial kind. If financial reparation is sought, the appropriate order is a compensation order. Any reparation ordered should, so far as possible, be linked to the type of offence for which reparation is to be made. Such reparation might include the removal of graffiti, if graffiti was daubed on walls during the commission of the offence, a meeting with an elderly victim to apologise and explain why the offence was committed and to observe the effect of the offence on the victim, repairing damage to a playground caused by the offender, or (in the case of an offence involving an elderly victim) supervised gardening work at an old people's home.[2]

1 Home Office draft Guidance, para 5.5.
2 See the examples given by the draft Guidance, at para 6.9.

4.31 The plan should be drawn up by a member of the youth offending team, in consultation with the young person and his parents. The question of full parental involvement is not a statutory requirement. National Standards will be drawn up by the Home Office, in consultation with the Youth Justice Board.[1]

1 See para **2.22**.

Subsequent action by the court

4.32 Immediately after making an action plan order, a court may fix a further hearing for a date not more than 21 days after the making of the order; and direct the responsible officer to make, at that hearing, a report as to the effectiveness of the order and the extent to which it has been implemented (s 70(3)).

At that hearing the court must consider the responsible officer's report, and:

(a) may, on the application of the responsible officer or the offender, vary the order, by cancelling any provision included in it; or
(b) by inserting in it (either in addition to or in substitution for any of its provisions) any provision that the court could originally have included in it (s 70(4)).

A hearing shortly after the making of the order is intended to provide an opportunity for the court, in discussion with the responsible officer, the young offender and his or her parents, to make an early assessment of whether the requirements are effective in practice and an opportunity to amend the order if appropriate. Such a hearing is not, however, a mandatory statutory requirement.

Discharge, variation and breach

4.33   Schedule 5 to the Act deals with failure to comply with the requirements of action plan orders, for varying such orders and for discharging them with or without the substitution of other sentences (s 70(5)). The relevant provisions are the same as those which relate to reparation orders, and reference should be made to paras **4.14–4.23**.

SUPERVISION ORDERS

4.34   Section 12 of the Children and Young Persons Act 1969 permits the making of supervision orders[1] with or without requirements. The new Act contains detailed amendments to the provisions of the 1969 Act, and other legislation appertaining to supervision orders.[2]

---

1 See annotations to s 67.
2 Some, but not all, of these changes came into force on 30 September 1998; the provisions brought into force then are s 71(5), s 72, Sch 7 and Sch 8, paras 16 and 18: see Appendix II.

Reparation requirements

4.35   Section 71(1)–(3) of the new Act amend s 12A of the 1969 Act to enable a court to attach conditions on a supervision order requiring the making of reparation to a specified person or persons or to the community at large. The importance of reparation is evident from the introduction of the new reparation orders.[1] It is not possible, however, to combine such an order with a supervision order, because that would create two different supervision regimes. Further, reparation orders are intended to be short term, as opposed to the longer-term objectives of supervision orders. If an offender is suitable to be made the subject of a supervision order, a reparation element should form a requirement of such an order. Before doing so, the court should consider the views of the victim.

---

1 See paras **4.2–4.22**.

Residence requirements

4.36   Section 12AA of the 1969 Act[1] provides the power to impose a residence requirement in a supervision order, where there has been a breach of a supervision requirement. The new Act amends s 12AA.

A residence requirement may, under s 12AA, be imposed only where the pre-conditions in s 12AA(6) are satisfied. These require there to have been a supervision order either with a residence requirement made under s 12(2) or with a requirement for specified activities under s 12A(3). The offender must also be found guilty of an imprisonable offence, committed during the duration of the order and which the court considers serious. The court must be satisfied that the behaviour which constituted the offence was due to a significant extent to the circumstances in which he was living.

The changes made by s 71(4) of the new Act make a residency requirement available to a court to impose in respect of any young person who breaches a supervision order, or who commits an offence whilst subject to a supervision order, provided the court is satisfied that the young person's living arrangements contributed to the failure to comply or to the offending. The requirement in respect of an imprisonable offence is removed. There is a pre-condition for prior consultation with the relevant local authority. The Government considers that, although removing a person from home is not a step to be undertaken lightly, where there are factors associated with the location in which that person lives which are leading to or encouraging offending, it may be in the offender's best interests to move him or her away from this influence for a short period of time.[2]

---

1 See annotations to s 67.
2 Lord Williams of Mostyn, Parliamentary Under-Secretary, Home Office, HL Committee, col 670.

Breaches of Crown Court supervision order

4.37   Section 72 substitutes certain provisions in s 15(3)–(8) of the 1969 Act. These provisions deal with the powers available to a court where there has been a breach of a Crown Court supervision order. The effect of the changes is to require a youth court to commit an offender to the Crown Court if there is a breach of requirements in a supervision order made by the Crown Court. The Crown Court may deal with the offender in any manner in which it could have dealt with the offender for that offence if it had not made the supervision order, and, if it deals with the offender, it must discharge the order.

Section 72 came into force on 30 September 1998.[1]

---

1 See Appendix II.

Supervision arrangements

4.38   Schedule 8, paras 16, 17 and 19, make minor and consequential amendments to the 1969 Act in the light of the creation of youth offending teams. An offender may be placed under the supervision of such a team, with a member of the team to act as supervisor.

Schedule 7 also makes detailed textual amendments to the 1969 Act including to the definition of 'parent' for the purposes of the 1969 Act (see Sch 7, paras 3 and 10). Schedule 7 came into force on 30 September 1998.[1]

One final change is in respect of repeals. The 1969 Act repealed references to 'child' and 'children' in ss 56 and 59 of the Children and Young Persons Act

1933. That repeal was never brought into effect, and Sch 7, para 11 of the new Act repeals that repeal.

---

1 See Appendix II.

Penalties for breach of supervision order

4.39   Section 15 of the 1969 Act deals, inter alia, with the breach of supervision orders. Powers to deal with breach are vested in the youth court, even in respect of Crown Court supervision orders. Subsection (3) sets out the power that exists where the court finds that the offender has failed to comply with any requirement. Hitherto, these have comprised a fine not exceeding £1,000, or an attendance centre order, or (if it discharges the order) the imposition of any punishment, other than detention in a young offenders' institution, that it could then have imposed if the offender had just been convicted.

In the search to provide a wider range of options to sentencing courts, s 72 amends s 15(3) to permit the making of a curfew order,[1] and to permit the committal of an offender found to be in breach of a Crown Court supervision order to the Crown Court. He may be committed in custody or on bail (1969 Act, s 95(3)(a)). However, there is no obligation to commit to the Crown Court. If the youth court does decide to commit to the Crown Court, then the new s 15(4), (5) and (6) provide for the documentation to be sent to the Crown Court and set out the powers of that court. Note should also be taken of the fact that the effect of the change is to remove the requirement that had previously existed, namely that the court should, pursuant to s 12D of the 1969 Act, have made a statement that the supervision order was made with requirements in place of custody.

---

1 See Criminal Justice Act 1991, s 12.

4.40   By s 15(4) of the 1969 Act, (inserted by s 72(2) of the 1998 Act), the committing court must send to the Crown Court a certificate signed by a justice of the peace giving:

(a) particulars of the supervised person's failure to comply with the requirement; and

(b) such other particulars of the case as may be desirable.

Such a certificate is evidence (but not conclusive evidence) of the failure to comply. If it is satisfied that the offender has failed to comply, the Crown Court may deal with the offender, for the offence in respect of which the order was made, in any manner in which it could have dealt with him if it had not made the order. In other words, the powers of the Crown Court to re-sentence are those available as at the date of the making of the order, not the date of re-sentencing.

Appeals against sentence where offender subject of supervision order

4.41   Section 10 of the Criminal Appeal Act 1968 provides for an appeal against sentence where an offender is dealt with by the Crown Court (otherwise than on appeal from a magistrates' court) for an offence of which he was not convicted on indictment (1968 Act, s 10(1)).

Section 10(2) of the 1968 Act provides that the proceedings from which an appeal lies under s 10 are those where an offender convicted of an offence by a magistrates' court:

(a) is committed to the Crown Court for sentence; or
(b) having been made the subject of an order for conditional discharge or a community order within the meaning of Part I of the Criminal Justice Act 1991, or given a suspended sentence of imprisonment,

he is put in breach of it by a later conviction and comes before the Crown Court to be further dealt with for his offence.

4.42   In respect of (b) above, a 'community order' is defined by reference to s 6(4) of the Criminal Justice Act 1991.[1] This includes, inter alia, a supervision order. Hitherto, s 10(2) of the 1968 Act excluded an appeal against sentence under s 10(2)(b) where a person had been the subject of a supervision order. That exclusion has been repealed by Sch 10, following the amendments made by the new Act to the provisions relating to breaches of supervision orders.[2] It is the only amendment made by the new Act to the 1968 Act. It remains the case that the offender may only appeal against sentence if:

(a) he is sentenced to six months' or more imprisonment (or detention in a young offender institution) either for the offence of which he was summarily convicted alone, or for that offence and others for which sentence was passed in the same proceeding; or
(b) the sentence passed is one which the magistrates' court had no power to pass; or
(c) the court in dealing with him for the offence either:
   (i)   recommends that he be deported, or
   (ii) disqualifies him from driving, or
   (iii) makes an order under s 23 of the Power of Criminal Courts Act 1973 activating a suspended sentence, or
   (iv) makes a restriction order or declaration of relevance under the Football Spectators Act 1989 (1968 Act, s 10(3)).

---

1 See annotations to s 61.
2 See paras **4.37–4.40**. The repeal came into force on 30 September 1998: see Appendix II.

Requirements in supervision orders

4.43   Sections 12, 12A and 12B of the Children and Young Persons Act 1969 contain powers in respect of requirements that may be imposed as part of a supervision order. These are amended by Sch 7, paras 4 and 5.[1] They are also amended by s 71.

---

1 For these provisions as amended, see annotations to s 67.

4.44   The general requirement to impose requirements, contained in s 12 of the 1969 Act is amended, so that it contains a provision equivalent to that which applies in respect of other community orders in respect of the offender's religious beliefs, education or the requirements of any other community order (Sch 7, para 4). When a supervisor gives directions to the offender to present himself to a specified person at a specified time, to participate in specified activities (1969 Act, s 12(2)(b) and (c)), such directions shall, so far as practicable,[1] be such as to avoid:

(a) any conflict with the offender's religious beliefs or with the requirements of any other community order (within the meaning of Part I of the Criminal Justice Act 1991) to which he may be subject; and
(b) any interference with the times, if any, at which he normally works or attends school or any other educational establishment.

---

1 See general annotations.

4.45   The power to impose intermediate treatment requirements in a supervision order is contained in s 12A of the 1969 Act. When dealing with the scope of the new reparation order,[1] the Government was anxious to avoid a multiplicity of regimes. Reparation orders may not be combined with supervision orders which include certain requirements.[2] Section 71 of the new Act amends s 12A(3) to entitle the making of a direction requiring reparation to be made by the offender whether to the person specified or to the community at large.[3] The total number of days during which the offender can be subject to reparation or other requirements is 90 (1969 Act, s 12A(5), as amended by 1998 Act, s 71(2)). Section 71(3) also extends to requirements in supervision orders the procedural safeguards, noted earlier,[4] in respect to the consent of a victim to reparation.

---

1 See paras **4.2–4.23**.
2 See s 67(4)(b).
3 See para **4.11**.
4 See para **4.11**.

4.46   Schedule 7, para 5, amends s 12B of the 1969 Act,[1] which provides for the imposition of requirements as to mental treatment, whether as a residential or non-residential patient by or under the direction of a medical practitioner. The new Act makes changes in terms of the definition of 'medical practitioner', but, more importantly, extends the category of requirements to include treatment by or under the direction of a chartered psychologist (as defined by a new s 12B(1A)). Thus a supervision order can now address psychological as well as medical problems suffered by young offenders.

---

1 See annotations to s 67.

4.47   Schedule 7, para 5(3), makes changes to s 12B. That section requires, as a pre-condition for the imposition of a requirement for mental treatment, that the court be satisfied, on the evidence of a medical practitioner, that the mental condition of a supervised person is such as requires and may be susceptible to treatment. The effect of these changes is to incorporate the means of proof set out in s 54(2) and (3) of the Mental Health Act 1983. This now entitles proof not only by a report from a medical practitioner, but also by, or on behalf of, the manager of a hospital. If such a report is tendered to the court, a copy must be given to the solicitor or counsel representing the offender. Except where the report relates only to arrangements for admission to hospital, the attendance at court of the signatory of the report may be required (1983 Act, s 54(3)).

Repeals

4.48   In the light of the above changes, and as part also of the pre-consolidation process, a number of provisions are repealed, or modified by deletion of words. These are set out in Sch 10. No substantive changes, other than those set out above, are involved.

DETENTION AND TRAINING ORDERS

4.49   Section 73 introduces a new custodial sentence which will initially apply to those aged[1] 12 or over and under 18, but which potentially can be extended to 10- and 11-year-olds. The detention and training order requires the offender to be subject to a period of detention and training, followed by a period of supervision. The new order replaces the secure training centre order, introduced by ss 1 to 4 of the Criminal Justice and Public Order Act 1994. Those provisions are repealed.

---

1 See general annotations.

4.50   The power to make a detention and training order will arise where after commencement[1] the offender is convicted of an offence punishable with imprisonment in the case of a person aged 21 or over (s 73(1)). It is the date of conviction that determines the availability of the order, not the date of the offence, which may be prior to the commencement date. It is intended that s 73 will come into force in mid-1999.[2]

1 See para **1.4**.
2 *No More Excuses: A New Approach to Tackling Youth Crime in England and Wales*, Cm 3809 (1997), para 10.5.

Background

4.51   There were four pre-existing powers to impose a custodial sentence on children and young persons. First, detention during Her Majesty's pleasure, under s 53(1) of the Children and Young Persons Act 1933,[1] on conviction for murder. Secondly, detention for certain serious offences, under s 53(2) of the 1933 Act,[1] served either in local authority secure accommodation or in prison service accommodation. Thirdly, detention of young offenders aged 15, 16 or 17,[2] for periods between two months and two years in a Young Offender Institution, pursuant to s 8 of the Criminal Justice Act 1982. Fourthly, the secure training order, which permitted detention of 12- to 14-year-old persistent offenders for periods of between six months and two years, in a secure training centre.[3]

1 See annotations to s 73.
2 See general annotations
3 See annotations to s 75.

4.52   The secure training order provisions contained in ss 1 to 4 of the 1994 Act were amongst the most controversial provisions in that Act, because they moved away from the principle inherent in earlier legislation that custodial sentences served no useful purpose for children and young persons, and that rehabilitation and educatative work should be undertaken within the community. Some 36 different organisations, including The Law Society, criticised the extension of custodial powers for 12- to 14-year-olds.[1] The Law Society observed that it was not the lack of powers which caused the then perceived problem, but rather the lack of facilities and resources, particularly in respect of local authority secure accommodation. Despite this level of criticism the secure training centre order formed a central part of Part I of the 1994 Act, with other provisions dealing with establishment of secure training centres. The intention was that five regional secure training centres be created, each capable of taking about 40 children.[2] One, at Medway, Kent, is currently in operation, although it has attracted significant criticism and calls for its closure.[3]

1 Home Affairs Select Committee, 6th Report, Juvenile Offenders, HC 44–I, para 147.
2 David Maclean, MP, Minister of State, Home Office, 1993, HC Standing Committee B, cols 98–102.
3 (1998) *The Times*, August 26.

4.53   The secure training centre order was opposed by the then Labour opposition during the passage of the 1994 Act. When the Labour Government took office it indicated that it intended to review the implementation of ss 1 to 4 of the 1994 Act.[1]

The result of that review was a decision to introduce those provisions. However, the Government considered the position relating to custodial sentences for young offenders to be unsatisfactory, for four distinct reasons.[1] First, the available accommodation is fragmented, and with regimes varying both in quality and cost. Secondly, courts' powers to remand young persons to secure facilities were inadequate and inappropriate. Thirdly, the sentencing framework could lead to arbitrary outcomes, with the kind of institution in which the sentence being served is to a large extent determined by the powers under which the young person was being sentenced rather than the needs of the young person. Finally, the structure of sentences did not allow for sufficient emphasis to be placed on preventing offending or responding to progress.

The response to this analysis was to establish a review of the availability and type of secure accommodation, the conferment of new powers on the proposed Youth Justice Board,[2] changes in the powers and arrangements in respect of remands to secure accommodation,[3] and the new detention and training order. This is intended to replace the secure training centre order, and also the sentence of detention in a young offenders' institution with 'a more constructive and flexible custodial sentence providing a clear focus on preventing offending'. The aim is to ensure that custodial sentences, where they are necessary, are more effective in preventing further crime.[4] Such custodial sentences are needed to protect the public by removing the young offender temporarily from the opportunity to re-offend. The increased emphasis on supervision after release, on a clear sentence plan to tackle the causes of offending behaviour and on continuity of supervision before and after release are intended to complement the other provisions in the new Act for more effective community penalties.

---

1 *No More Excuses*, op cit, para 6.2.
2 See paras **2.22–2.23**.
3 *No More Excuses*, op cit, para 6.11. See also Alun Michael, MP, Minister of State, Home Office, HC Committee, col 599.
4 Ibid, para 6.11.

The power to make the order

4.54   Section 73 provides that, subject to s 53 of the 1933 Act, and s 8 of the Criminal Justice Act 1982, and to the restrictions contained in s 73(2), where:

(a)   a child or young person is convicted of an offence which is punishable with imprisonment in the case of a person aged 21 or over; and
(b)   the court is of the opinion that either or both of paras (a) or (b) of s 1(2) of the Criminal Justice Act 1991[1] apply or the case falls within s 1(3) of the 1991 Act,[1]

the sentence that the court is to pass is a detention and training order.

The references to s 1 of the 1991 Act have the effect of maintaining the principles inherent in the 1991 Act, namely, that custody should be imposed only where the offence (together with associated offences) is so serious that only custody can be justified, or, in the case of a violent or sexual offence, where only custody would be adequate to protect the public from harm. Custody can nonetheless be imposed where the offender fails to express his willingness to comply with any requirement in a probation or supervision order that requires such willingness, or willingness to comply with a requirement in a drug treatment and testing order.[2] The detention and training order is a custodial sentence (s 73(4)).

---

1 See annotations to s 76.
2 See paras **7.29–7.49**.

4.55   The effect of s 73(1) is, therefore, that if a custodial sentence is imposed on a child or young person, it must be by way of a detention or training order unless imposed under s 53(1) or (2) of the 1933 Act or s 8 of the 1982 Act. There are, however, further pre-conditions.

Section 73(2) states that a court must not make a detention and training order:

(a)   in the case of an offender under the age of 15[1] at the time of the conviction, unless it is of the opinion that he is a persistent offender;
(b)   in the case of an offender under the age of 12 at that time, unless:
   (i)   it is of the opinion that only a custodial sentence would be adequate to protect the public from further offending by him; and
   (ii)   the offence was committed on or after such date as the Home Secretary may by order appoint.

In respect of 15-, 16- and 17-year-olds, the only pre-condition is that the seriousness conditions in s 1(2) of the 1991 Act or the unwillingness to consent provisions in s 1(3) of the 1991 Act apply. In respect of those aged 13 and 14, the court also must form the opinion that the offender is a persistent offender.

---

1 See general annotations.

4.56   The term 'persistent offender' is not defined. It is a question of fact in each case, to be judged by his past course of conduct, not necessarily by the likelihood of, or level of seriousness of, future offending. Clearly, however, a detention and training order might well be inappropriate in a case where there was no such likelihood of future offences of a level justifying custody.

The offences do not have to be offences in respect of which the offender has been convicted; they might be conduct for which a reprimand or final warning has been given, or which are admitted. Of course, a court should not make a finding of persistence in respect of matters which are denied.

The nature of 'persistence' is the continuance in a course of action.[1] Clearly, for that purpose more than one offence is required, but even two offences could scarcely be described with conviction as a course of conduct. Obviously, the more offences there are the clearer is the behavioural pattern and thus the easier it is to ascribe the label 'persistent'. In *No More Excuses*, reference is made, in another context, to persistence as involving at least three offences.

A further question arises: persistence in what? A 14-year-old may have a pattern of offending involving 'joy-riding' in motor vehicles. Clearly, he is a persistent offender if there is an on-going pattern of such crimes. What, however, if his offending propensity is more varied, involving shop-lifting, wanton vandalism and football hooliganism? He is, nevertheless, a persistent criminal, albeit that he may not 'persist' in types of particular crime. This conclusion fits with the general intent of the new order, namely, that a period of detention, training and supervision are necessary to divert the offender from offending behaviour. It fits also with other constructions of 'persistent': the courts have held that whether a person is 'persistent' is a matter of fact and degree. In *Re Arctic Engineering Ltd (No 2)*[2] it was held that on the true construction of s 188 of the Companies Act 1948, 'persistently' required some degree of continuance or repetition.

If the court is of the opinion that the offender is a persistent offender, it must state so in open court (s 74(1)),[3] as well as complying with the requirements of s 1(4) of the 1991 Act.

---

1 The *Oxford English Dictionary* defines the word 'persist' as 'To continue firmly or obstinately in a state, opinion, purpose or course of action'.
2 [1986] 2 All ER 346 (Ch D).
3 See annotations to s 9.

4.57   Section 73(2)(b) applies to offenders aged 10 and 11. The detention and training order will not be available for this age group until an order has been made by the Home Secretary. Its potential availability met fierce criticism in Parliament on the basis that it is wrong in principle, and a significant extension of the law, to impose custodial sentences on 10- and 11-year-olds for anything other than the most grave of offences.[1] The Government agreed that the need for such an extension had not been incontrovertibly established.[2] The intention, at this stage, is to provide a convenient legislative power should the need to extend the order to 10- and 11-year-olds become clear.

If and when this provision comes into effect, a court which proposes to impose a detention and training order must first be of the opinion that only a custodial sentence would be adequate to protect the public from further offending by him. If it is of that opinion, it must say so in open court (s 74(1)),[3] as well as complying with the requirements of s 1(4) of the 1991 Act. It is not enough that custody be the best way, or the most convenient way, of adequately protecting the public from further offending: it must be the only way of so doing. The wording of s 73(2)(b) does not require that the further offending has to be in respect of offences of a level of seriousness which would themselves justify the imposition of a custodial sentence. Although it could be argued that, because the order is a custodial sentence, the further offending behaviour should be of the same level of seriousness, it is the persistence in offending that enables the custody threshold to be crossed. The level of seriousness of the offences which are persistently committed is, arguably, more relevant to the question of whether an order should be made, not whether the pre-conditions for its making are satisfied.

1 For criticism, see James Clappison, MP, HC Committee, cols 595–596. For the powers in
   respect of grave crimes, see the Children and Young Persons Act 1933, s 53(2), set out in
   annotations to s 73.
2 Alun Michael, MP, Minister of State, Home Office, HC Committee, col 599.
3 See annotations to s 9.

Length of the order

4.58   A detention and training order is an order that the offender in respect
of whom it is made shall be subject, for the term specified in the order, to a
period of detention and training followed by a period of supervision. Subject to
the limitation as to overall length contained in s 73(6), the term of a detention
and training order shall be 4, 6, 8, 10, 12, 18 or 24 months.[1] This provision is
thus an exception to the general limitation on youth court powers.

The total length of the order (comprising both the period of detention and
training and also the period of supervision) may not exceed the maximum
term of imprisonment that a Crown Court could impose on an adult offender
(s 73(6)). This conclusion is self-evident, given that the term 'detention and
training order' includes both the elements of detention and of supervision. In
respect of an offender being convicted of more than one offence, a court may
make more than one order, either concurrent or consecutive, provided that
the term does not exceed 24 months (s 74(2)(a), and (3)). For this purpose the
terms of wholly or partly concurrent orders are to be regarded as a single term
(s 74(8)).

If a court inadvertently makes an order the effect of which is that the aggregate
term of the total order exceeds 24 months, the excess shall be treated as
remitted (s 74(4)). This provision, which replicates similar provisions in other
statutes,[2] caused debate during the passage of the Act as to the effects of a court
not making its wishes clear. It might simply order a period of detention, in the
form of 'sentence to detention for [x]', without making it clear that it is
detention under s 53(2) of the Children and Young Persons Act 1933 that the
court had in mind.[3] Clearly, there is a need for sentencers to be precise and
clear, an objective not always easily achieved in the light of the current morass
of sentencing legislation.

1 See general annotations.
2 See Criminal Justice Act 1982, s 1(B)(5).
3 See Stephen Hawkins, MP, HC Committee col 605, citing the opinion of Dr David Thomas,
   QC.

The making of an order in respect of a person detained in a young offender institution

4.59   Where an order is made in respect of a person subject to a sentence of
detention in a young offender institution, the rules are somewhat complex. If
he has been released pursuant to Part II of the Criminal Justice Act 1991, then
the order takes effect immediately. If, by contrast, he is still in detention, then

the new sentence takes effect on the day he would (but for the new sentence) be released on licence (s 79(2)). In calculating dates of release, the rules governing concurrent orders, set out in para **4.58**, apply equally in this context.

The position in respect of the conviction of an offender already subject to an order

4.60   An offender who re-offends by committing an imprisonable offence before the end of the order, having been released from the detention and training element of the order, may be required to serve a term of detention in secure accommodation, in addition to any other disposal (s 78(2)). If an offender is still serving the detention and training element of the first order,[1] a subsequent detention or training order, wholly or partly concurrent to the first, is to be treated as part of a single term (s 74(8)). If, by contrast, an offender has been released and is under supervision, a subsequent order is not regarded as part of a single term with the first.

---

1 See para **4.58**.

Examples

4.61   The following examples illustrate the effect of the above provisions.

EXAMPLE 1

In a case where a s 73 order is being imposed for offences A and B, a court may make two orders, each of 24 months, to run concurrently. It may not impose two orders of 24 months consecutively. If it wishes to impose consecutive orders, the total length in aggregate must not exceed 24 months.

EXAMPLE 2

An offender was made subject to a 12-month order on 1 January. On 1 April, the offender (who is still detained in custody) is before the court for a further offence. It may impose an order of no greater than 12 months to run consecutively from the end of the first order, or an 18-month order (or less) to run concurrently from 1 April.

EXAMPLE 3

An offender is made subject to an 18-month order on 1 January. After 12 months he is released, and is then subject to a period of 12 months' supervision. After another six months (ie 1 June the following year) he is sentenced for another offence. The court may impose a concurrent term of 24 months.

4.62   A person who is subject to a detention and training order may subsequently be sentenced to detention in a young offenders' institution. This may be because of his age, or because of the effect of s 79(5) which provides that where a person who has attained the age of 18 is being dealt with in a manner in which a court on a previous occasion could have dealt with him, and is sentenced to a detention and training order, that person shall be treated as if he had been sentenced to detention in a young offenders' institution.

If a person is already subject to a detention and training order, and is then sentenced to detention in a young offenders' institution, that second sentence comes into effect at a time which depends on whether the offender has been released from the custodial element of the order. If he has, then the second sentence commences on the day on which it was passed (s 79(1)(a)). If, by contrast, the offender is still being detained, the order of detention will commence on the date when, by virtue of s 75(2), (3), (4), or (5) the offender would otherwise be released from the custodial element of the order (s 79(1)(b)). In any case where the offender is subject concurrently to a detention and training order and to a sentence of detention in a young offenders' institution, he is to be treated for the purposes of ss 75 to 78 of the new Act,[1] for the purposes of s 1C of the Criminal Justice Act 1982 and for the purposes of Part II of the Criminal Justice Act 1991 as if the offender were subject only to one of those terms, that term being the one imposed on the later occasion (s 79(3)). However, the effect of s 79(4) is that the offender shall not be released in respect of either the order or the sentence unless and until he is required to be released in respect of each of them.

---

1 See paras **4.66–4.67**.

Length of the order

4.63   It will have been noted that s 73(5) limits the permissible length of an order to certain specified, even-numbered months (4, 6, 8, 10, 12, 18 and 24). The even numbers can perhaps be explained on the basis that the normal split of time between detention and training on the one hand, and supervision on the other, is 50 : 50 (s 75(2)).[1] More seriously, the question arises as to why other options are not left to the court. The explanation[2] given for these discrete periods was, first, that they make the sentence simpler and easier for the young offender to understand. Secondly, it is desired that supervisors in the youth offending team[3] and those who deal with the young person in custody are able to produce a constructive sentence plan that is based on a fixed predetermined period. A fixed period aids such sentence planning. Thirdly, the fixed periods chosen are designed to ensure that those who receive a lengthy order, but who receive the benefit of early release,[4] do not serve less than those who are made the subject of shorter orders. These explanations may provide some justification for the approach taken (although whether a convincing justification is a different matter), but do not address all the concerns that arise. Section 48 of the Criminal Justice and Public Order Act 1994 entitles an accused who pleads guilty to receive a discount on the sentence that would otherwise be imposed. Clearly, the effect of the fixed point approach taken by s 73(5) is that discount, if it is to be given, must reflect that scale, thus distorting both the discount which a court may wish to grant and the whole sentencing levels for other offenders in a case of multiple defendants.

---

1 See para **4.67**.
2 See Alun Michael, MP, Minister of State, Home Office, HC Committee, col 607.
3 See para **2.19**.
4 See para **4.67**.

4.64 In determining the length of a detention and training order the court is under a duty to take account of any period for which the offender has been remanded in custody in connection with the offence, or any other offence the charge for which was founded on the same facts or evidence (s 74(5)). Because the custodial element of the order is only, usually,[1] one-half of the total length of the order, if the period of time spent in custody is to be reflected in accordance with s 74(5), the order must be reduced by a period equal to twice the period of time spent on remand. The wording of s 74(5) ('... determining the term of a detention and training order') makes it quite clear that the allowance for time spent on remand should be against the total length of the order, not against the period to be spent in custody. The court must then, having made the appropriate deduction from what is otherwise considered to be the appropriate length of order, make a further adjustment to take the order to the nearest, and lower, permitted order length, a conclusion highlighting the lack of flexibility in the order lengths and discussed later.[1] It is clear, however, that the practice followed in respect of adults who spend time on remand, where time spent on remand is automatically credited to the offender, cannot be followed in the case of young offenders. The effect of doing so would be an order which would either not fit the regime chosen, rightly or wrongly, by the Government in respect of order length or, alternatively, shorten the custodial element of the order in a way that might negate the training aspect of the period of detention.

---

1 See para **4.67**.

Sentencing of persons currently subject to detention and training orders

4.65 The potential for concurrent, partly concurrent and consecutive orders has already been noted.[1] In addition, s 79(5) should be borne in mind. The effect of this is that where an offender, aged 18 or over and subject to a detention and training order, is convicted of one or more further offences for which he is liable to a sentence of detention in a young offender institution, the court has the power to pass one or more sentences of detention, such as in a young offender institution to run consecutively to the detention and training order.

---

1 See para **4.60**.

The period of detention and training

4.66 Section 75(1) provides that an offender shall serve the period of detention and training under a detention and training order in such secure accommodation as may be determined by the Home Secretary or by such other person as may be authorised by him for that purpose. That could be a secure training centre, a young offender institution, local authority secure accommodation, or a youth treatment centre (s 75(7)). The accommodation in which the offender is detained will depend on the age of the offender and the availability of accommodation.[1] Attempts were made during the passage of the Act[2] to introduce changes the effect of which would have been to require separate provision for offenders aged under 15[3] from those aged 15 or above.

As the law currently stood, 12-, 13- and 14-year-olds served terms of custody in different accommodation from those aged 15 or above. This approach was resisted by the Government. *No More Excuses* had indicated that how the new arrangements would work would, in part, depend upon the review of the secure accommodation estate currently being undertaken by the Government. It is intended that the Youth Justice Board will review the regimes put in place. However, flexibility in available regimes is considered important.[4] The precise accommodation should depend on the maturity of the offender and his or her needs. The provisions are also intended to permit different regimes to permit, for example, mental treatment or treatment as a young sex offender, and to keep open possibilities for innovative regimes for the future. Younger offenders will normally be dealt with discretely and differently from older offenders, but not always.[5] Different children mature at different rates, and chronological age is not an indicator of either maturity or vulnerability.

---

1 See *No More Excuses: A New Approach to Tackling Youth Crime in England and Wales*, Cm 3809 (1997), at para 6.18.
2 See James Clappison, MP, HC Committee, col 619.
3 See general annotations.
4 Alun Michael, MP, Minister of State, Home Office, HC Committee, col 629.
5 Ibid, col 630.

4.67 The period of detention and training under a detention and training order shall be one-half of the term of the order (s 75(2)). The Home Secretary may at any time release the offender if he is satisfied that exceptional circumstances exist which justify the offender's release on compassionate grounds (s 75(3)).

In addition, the Act contains provisions permitting early release and also extended periods of detention. The purpose of these provisions in s 75 is to provide some flexibility to reward good behaviour and progress, or to provide some sanction for poor behaviour and lack of progress. No guidelines have yet been established to give guidance as to how these powers are to be exercised.

By s 75(4), the Home Secretary may release the offender:

(a) in the case of an order for a term of eight months[1] or more but less than 18 months, one month before the half-way point of the term of the order; and
(b) in the case of an order for a term of 18 months or more, one month or two months before that point.

The converse situation is where an offender has not behaved or progressed under the order. In that case, there is clearly no possibility of extending the period to be served by executive order. Section 75(5) provides that, if an application is made by the Home Secretary and the youth court orders, the period of detention may be extended. If such an application is granted, the Home Secretary must release the offender:

(a) in the case of an order for a term of eight months or more but less than 18 months, one month after the half-way point of the term of the order; and

(b) in the case of an order for a term of 18 months or more, one month or two months after that point.

The Act does not specify to which youth court such an application should be made. The Act is silent on this point. Although s 77 defines the relevant petty session areas, for the purposes of breach proceedings, as the area in which the youth court which made the order is situated or the area in which the offender resides for the time being, it is unclear that this is the position with regard to applications under s 75(5). The phrase used is '*the* youth court' [our emphasis]. Arguably, the relevant youth court is the court which made the order. No doubt detailed regulations will be made to deal with these procedural matters.

The effect of these provisions relating to the period of detention can be seen in the table below.

Length of order	Minimum period possible	Maximum period possible*
4 months	2 months	2 months
6 months	3 months	3 months
8 months	3 months	5 months
10 months	4 months	6 months
12 months	5 months	7 months
18 months	7 months	11 months
24 months	10 months	14 months

* Pre-supposes youth court order under s 75(5).

Whilst it is true that these figures presuppose good behaviour and progress, the fact that, potentially, the difference between a six- and 10-month-order is only one month actually in custody, and that between a six-month and 24-month order is only seven months actually in custody, is striking.

---

1 See general annotations.

The period of supervision

4.68 On release from the period of detention and training, the offender is subject to a period of supervision. By s 76(1), the period of supervision of an offender who is subject to a detention and training order:

(a) begins with the offender's release, at whatever point that occurs; and

(b) subject to s 76(2), ends when the term of the order ends.

Thus, for example, an offender sentenced to an order of ten months in length, who is released at the earliest possible moment (ie four months) will be subject to a supervision period of six months. However, s 76(2) empowers the Home Secretary to make an order providing that the period of supervision shall end at such point as may be specified in the order. That point must be during the term of such an order, and thus there is no question of the Home Secretary extending the period of supervision.

4.69   Supervision of the offender under the order may be by a probation officer,[1] local authority social worker[2] or a member of a youth offending team (s 76(3)–(5)). The category of person who is appointed to supervise which orders will be determined by the Home Secretary. No guidance or national standards have been issued or made as at the date of going to press. Before the commencement of the period of supervision or the alteration in details of category of supervisor or change of requirements, the offender must be given a statutory notice setting out the category of person responsible for supervision and any requirements with which the offender must for the time being comply (s 76(6) and (7)). The new Act does not expressly authorise the imposition of requirements by a court, or, indeed, by the Home Secretary, but the terms of s 76(6) assume the right of the Home Secretary to impose conditions. There appears to be no limit, other than that of reasonableness or proportionality, on the requirements that may be imposed by the Home Secretary. Obviously, the imposition of conditions could, in an appropriate case, be subject to judicial review on normal judicial review principles.

---

1 The probation officer must be a probation officer appointed for or assigned to the petty sessions area within which the offender resides for the time being (s 76(4)).
2 The local authority social worker or member of a youth offending team must be a social worker or member of a team established by the local authority within whose area the offender resides for the time being (s 76(5)). For youth offending teams, see paras **2.19–2.22**.

4.70   The implicit power to impose requirements has already been noted. By s 77(1), where a detention and training order is in force in respect of an offender, and it appears on information to a justice of the peace acting for a relevant petty sessions area[1] that the offender has failed to comply with requirements under s 76(6)(b) above, the justice may:

(a) issue a summons requiring the offender to appear at the place and time specified in the summons before a youth court acting for the area; or
(b) if the information is in writing[1] and on oath, issue a warrant for the offender's arrest requiring him to be brought before such a court.

The 'relevant petty sessions area' for this purpose is the area in respect of which the order was made by a youth court acting for it, or in which the offender resides for the time being (s 77(2)).

If it is proved to the satisfaction of the youth court before which an offender appears or is brought under s 77 that he has failed to comply with requirements, that court may deal with the offender in accordance with s 77(3). A youth court before whom an offender appears or is brought otherwise than under s 77 does not have power to deal with any breach of requirements, or to discharge or vary the supervision requirements.

Where an offender appears, or is brought, before a youth court pursuant to s 77(1), that court may:

(a) order the offender to be detained, in such secure accommodation as the Home Secretary may determine, for such period, not exceeding the shorter of three months or the remainder of the term of the detention and training order, as the court may specify (s 77(3)(a)); or

(b) impose on the offender a fine not exceeding level 3 on the standard scale (s 77(3)(b)).[1]

There is no minimum length of detention for breach of requirements. If the breach occurs at the end of the supervision period, the short nature of the potential detention for breach will be a factor a court will bear in mind in determining whether to make an order under s 77(3)(a). If detention is ordered under that subsection, the secure accommodation in which the fresh period of detention is to be served does not, inevitably, have to be of the same type as that in which the original period of detention was served.

---

1 See general annotations.

POWER OF COURT TO ORDER PARENT OR GUARDIAN TO PAY FINE, ETC

4.71   Section 55 of the Children and Young Persons Act 1933 imposes a duty on a court to order the payment of a fine, compensation or costs to be paid by the parent of the child or young person[1] instead of by the child or young person himself. This duty arises where:

(a) a child or young person is convicted or found guilty of any offence for the commission of which a fine or costs may be imposed, or a compensation order made under s 35 of the Powers of Criminal Courts Act 1973; and

(b) the court is of the opinion that the case would best be met by the imposition or making of such an order.

The duty to order payment by a parent or guardian does not arise if the parent or guardian cannot be found, or it would be unreasonable in all the circumstances to make such an order. Nor does the duty arise for persons aged 16, where it is a power, not a duty.

---

1 See s 117.

4.72   These provisions are further amended by the new Act. Schedule 7, para 1, amends s 55(1A)(b) to make it clear that the duty (subject to the exceptions described above) applies where a fine is imposed for breach of an attendance centre order or attendance centre rules,[1] or for breach of a requirement of a relevant community order under Sch 2 to the Criminal Justice Act 1991.[2] This is very much a tidying up change, ensuring that the duty extends generally to all community orders, and extending it to fines in respect of attendance centre orders or rules.

1 Criminal Justice Act 1982, s 19(3).
2 Criminal Justice Act 1991, Sch 2, paras 3(1)(a) and 4(1)(a). See annotations to s 64.

4.73   Section 55 is also amended by defining 'parent' by reference to the definition in s 1 of the Family Law Reform Act 1987.[1]

1 Schedule 7, para 1(3).

DUTY OF MAGISTRATES' COURT TO REMIT CASES TO YOUTH COURT

4.74   Section 7(8) of the Children and Young Persons Act 1969 imposes a duty on a magistrates' court to remit a young person to a youth court for sentencing unless the court is of the opinion that the case is one which can properly be dealt with by means of:

(a) an absolute or conditional discharge,
(b) an order requiring his parent or guardian to enter into a recognizance to take proper care of him and exercise proper control of him.

Schedule 7, para 3, amends and extends that provision to include a child as well as a young person. Schedule 7, para 3, also provides that the reference to 'parent' in s 7(8) of the 1969 Act is to be construed in accordance with s 1 of the Family Law Reform Act 1987 (ie 'biological parent').

Chapter 5

ANTI-SOCIAL AND SEX OFFENDER ORDERS

Anti-social behaviour orders – Sex offender orders

ANTI-SOCIAL BEHAVIOUR ORDERS

5.1   Section 1 of the new Act grants to a magistrates' court a new power to make an anti-social behaviour order. Such an order is civil in nature and is an order which, if the pre-conditions for its making are satisfied, entitles a court to prohibit the defendant from doing anything described in the order. That is not a finding of guilt as to the commission of a criminal offence. Section 1 does not limit what acts may be prohibited by the order. If a person subject to an anti-social behaviour order without reasonable excuse does anything which he is prohibited from doing by an anti-social behaviour order he is guilty of an either-way offence.

To assist in the use and application of the new order, the Government proposes to issue guidance. Although that guidance will not be legally binding, it will be a matter to which those using the powers must have regard; a failure to do so might form part of an application for judicial review.[1] In any event, the spirit of the guidance was set out during the Committee stages of the Bill, and thus forms part of the parliamentary intent for the purposes of any *Pepper v Hart*[2] reference. The draft guidance referred to is the version produced by the Home Office in August 1998.

The provisions in s 1 are likely to come into force on 1 April 1999.[3]

---

1 See para **5.11**.
2 *Pepper (Inspector of Taxes) v Hart* [1993] AC 593, [1993] 1 All ER 42 (HL).
3 Draft Guidance, para 1.5A.

Rationale and background

5.2   The purpose of the anti-social behaviour order is 'to allow people to live their lives free from fear and intimidation'.[1] It attempts to achieve this objective by providing a civil remedy to prevent the repetition of anti-social conduct. Many, although not all, anti-social acts amount to criminal offences, such as those under the Public Order Act 1986, the Criminal Damage Act 1971, the Environmental Protection Act 1990 or the Noise Act 1996. Common law powers relating to breaches of the peace may be applicable: in particular the power to apply to a magistrates' court for a binding-over order is relevant. The fact that the binding-over power is now subject to challenge under art 6 of the European Convention on Human Rights,[2] and that that challenge may in the future be made in an English court,[3] provides an important context in which the powers in s 1, which similarly try to regulate future behaviour of an individual, should be judged.

---

1 *Community Safety Orders: A Consultation Paper* (Home Office, 1997), para 1.
2 *Steel v United Kingdom* (1997).
3 See Human Rights Bill 1998, cl 7.

5.3   Provisions introduced by the Housing Act 1996 give local authorities some power to prevent certain types of conduct in, or in the locality of, certain local authority housing.[1] In fact, it was during the passage of that Act that the then Labour opposition proposed, unsuccessfully, a new 'community safety order', which was restricted to acts which breached existing civil or criminal laws. That order would have permitted an order to be made if the defendant had committed at least five unlawful acts; it may be compared with the broad scope of the new order now introduced by s 1.

Section 144 of the 1996 Act amended and strengthened the provisions of Sch 2 to the Housing Act 1985, making it easier for a local authority to obtain re-possession of tenanted property. The extended grounds include behaviour likely to cause a nuisance or annoyance, or conviction for an arrestable offence in the locality of the property.

Section 152 of the 1996 Act gives to the High Court or a county court, on an application by a local authority, the power to grant an injunction prohibiting a person from:

(a) engaging in or threatening to engage in conduct causing or likely to cause a nuisance or annoyance to a person residing in, visiting or otherwise engaging in a lawful activity in residential premises to which s 152 applies or in the locality of such premises;

(b) using or threatening to use residential premises to which s 152 applies for immoral or illegal purposes; or

(c) entering residential premises to which s 152 applies or being found in the locality of any such premises.

This provision was introduced to combat the menace and nuisance caused by young persons, often in gangs, on local authority estates. Although the scope of a s 152 application might appear to be wide, the court has to be satisfied that the respondent has used, or threatened to use, violence against a person mentioned in s 152(1)(a), and that there is a significant risk of harm to that person or a person of that description if the injunction is not granted (1996 Act, s 152(3)). It will be seen that conduct which might found a s 152 application will almost always amount to anti-social behaviour. However, the new anti-social order goes further in that it is not subject to the limitations and pre-conditions set out above. It also is not confined to conduct in, or in the locality of, local authority housing.

1 Housing Act 1996, s 152, applies to residential premises which are dwelling-houses held under secure or introductory tenancies from the local authority, or accommodation provided under Part VII of the 1996 Act, or Part III of the Housing Act 1985 (homelessness) (1996 Act, s 152(2)).

5.4　　The Protection from Harassment Act 1997 gives individuals the right to seek the protection of the courts from a course of conduct which causes harassment. Civil actions in tort, such as an application for an injunction to prevent the continuance of a nuisance, are also a possibility, although the basis of the jurisdiction to grant such a remedy without a property interest being infringed is uncertain.[1] These provisions have distinct limitations. The 1997 Act focuses upon the harassment of individuals, and its provisions are not intended to deal with situations where harassment is aimed at a community, and may be less effective in dealing with such action. Civil actions in tort require the victim both to be able to finance such an action, whether privately or through the legal aid scheme, and be in a position to take such action.

1 See para **5.22**, fn 5.

 5.5　　The Public Order Act 1986 contains several criminal offences which may make unlawful conduct which potentially falls within the scope of the new order. Section 4 of the 1986 Act creates an offence of using towards another person threatening, abusive or insulting words or behaviour, or distributing or displaying to another person any writing, sign or visible representation which is threatening, abusive or insulting with intent to cause fear of (or to provoke immediate unlawful violence), or whereby such a result is likely to occur. It is concerned with the use, or threatened use, of violence.[1]

Section 4A of the Public Order Act 1986 makes it an offence to use threatening, abusive or insulting words or behaviour, or disorderly behaviour or to display any threatening, abusive or insulting writing, etc, with intent to cause a person harassment, alarm or distress, thereby causing that person, or another, harassment, alarm or distress.

Section 5 of the 1986 Act makes unlawful the use of threatening, abusive or insulting words or behaviour or disorderly behaviour, or the display of any writing, sign or other visible representation which is threatening, abusive or insulting, within the hearing or sight of a person likely to be caused harassment, alarm or distress thereby.

The common element in each of these offences is the characteristics of the conduct which is prohibited (ie the use of threatening, abusive words or behaviour, or disorderly behaviour) are identified clearly. By contrast, it will later be noted[2] that s 1 does not identify the characteristics of the conduct to be prohibited otherwise than by its result.

1 For detailed discussion of the constituent elements of these offences, see paras **8.60–8.65**.
2 See para **5.13**.

The pre-conditions for making an order

5.6   The pre-conditions for the making of an order are:

'(a) that the person has acted, since the commencement date,[1] in an anti-social manner, that is to say, in a manner that caused or was likely to cause harassment, alarm or distress[2] to one or more persons not of the same household[3] as himself; and

(b) that such an order is necessary to protect persons in the local government area[3] in which the harassment, alarm or distress was caused or was likely to be caused from further anti-social acts by him.' (s 2(4))

1 See para **1.4**.
2 See paras **5.24–5.26**.
3 See annotations to s 1.

5.7   An application under s 1 is made by a complaint to the magistrates' court whose commission area[1] includes the place where it is alleged that the harassment, alarm or distress[2] was caused or was likely to be caused. Where there is more than one such area, there is no reason why an application cannot be made to the court for any one of such areas, nor does the new Act prohibit multiple applications being made by the appropriate authority to different magistrates' courts. No jurisdiction exists for an order to be sought from, or made by, a county court or the High Court. Magistrates' courts are courts with which the police (who will make many of the applications) are familiar, and the criminal offence which will result from breach will be dealt with in the magistrates' court. The application is to be made by complaint. At the moment, proceedings by way of complaint can proceed in the absence of the defendant, provided it can be proved that the defendant has been served with a summons.[3] The rules have not been changed, and so a s 1 order may be made in the absence of a defendant if service can be proved and the pre-conditions otherwise satisfied.

1 See general annotations.
2 See paras **5.24–5.26**.
3 See Magistrates' Courts Act 1980, s 11.

Who can apply for an order?

5.8   An application for an order may be made by a relevant authority if it appears to it that the pre-conditions set out in para **5.13** are fulfilled with respect to a person aged[1] 10 or over. There is no obligation, in the case of a young offender, to consult a youth offending team.[2] The child or young person may not be known to that team, or even be guilty of offending conduct, bearing in mind that anti-social behaviour will not always be criminal in nature. However, one suspects that young persons potentially the subject of a s 1 application may be known to such teams, and processes of consultation prior to decisions as to whether an order should be made may include members of the relevant youth offending team. The alleged anti-social conduct may also be relevant to the question of the adoption of crime and disorder strategies, either generally or in respect of youth offending.[3]

1 See general annotations. For issues in respect of children and young persons, see para **5.39**.
2 See paras **2.19–2.21**.
3 See paras **2.16–2.17**.

5.9   'Relevant authority' means the council for the relevant local government area (in England, usually the district council or London borough, and, in Wales, a county or county borough) (s 1(1) and (12)), or, alternatively, the chief officer of police[1] for the police area any part of which lies within the local government area in which the conduct giving rise to the application for the order was caused or likely to be caused (s 1(1)). The terms of s 1(1) are such that whether the relevant authority is a local authority or the relevant chief officer of police, is left in the alternative. It is quite possible for an application to be made by either. However, one relevant authority must not make an application without consulting the other (s 1(2)). Thus a local authority must consult the relevant chief officer of police, and a chief officer of police must consult the local authority and any other chief officer. Which agency takes the lead will be a matter to be discussed and agreed locally within the framework of the statutory partnership to prevent crime created by ss 5 to 7 of the new Act.[2] The Government expects a local strategy for dealing with s 1 orders to be part of the crime and disorder strategy to be worked out for each area, within a context of the detailed guidance to be issued by the Government.[3] Implicit in the above framework is the fact that a court which is being asked to make an order should expect to have the view of both agencies before deciding whether or not to make an order, and is entitled to know what the result of the consultation was. The making of an order is not automatic: a court is entitled to decline to make an order until it is told what the views of both agencies are.

1 See annotations to s 1.
2 *Community Safety Orders: A Consultation Paper*, op cit, para 1.
3 Lord Williams of Mostyn, Parliamentary Under-Secretary, HL Committee, col 551; Lord Falconer of Thoroton, Solicitor-General, HL Committee, cols 553–554 (3 February).

5.10   The expression used in s 1(2) is 'shall not make an application'. The position as to what happens if one of the two agencies entitled to make an application does not consult the other is unclear. Despite the view taken by the Government in its Consultation Paper[1] that a court would be able to grant an order on the application of one agency if satisfied that it would be right to do so, even if the observations of one of the agencies are not available or the support of one of the agencies is not forthcoming, it is submitted that the requirement to consult is mandatory. This conclusion is reached not only because the words 'shall not' are indicative of a mandatory requirement, but also on the more pragmatic ground that, otherwise, the person who is the subject of the proposed application would be at risk of different approaches by the two agencies. It also appears to be the intent of the Government.[2]

1 *Community Safety Orders: A Consultation Paper*, op cit, para 6.
2 See Alun Michael, MP, Minister of State, Home Office, HC Committee, col 58.

5.11   An individual complainant may not apply to a magistrates' court for an anti-social behaviour order; only a 'relevant authority' may do that. No other individual has the right to make an application for an order under s 1. If an individual considers that there is a need for an order he will make representations to the relevant authority (ie the local authority or police), which will then consult. If neither of those bodies decide to seek a s 1 order, an individual who is suffering from anti-social conduct is left to seek his own remedy, for example under the Protection from Harassment Act 1997, or, possibly, in some cases may seek to challenge the decision not to proceed by an application for judicial review. Whether an application is made is a matter of executive discretion, and not subject to appeal. It may be likened to the decision to commence the prosecution process. For that reason, the decision to seek an order may, potentially, be subject to an application for judicial review.[1]

1 In *Solicitor-General, ex parte Taylor and Taylor* [1996] 1 FCR 206 (DC) it was held that the decision whether to bring proceedings for contempt of court was not justiciable. Cf *Chief Constable of Kent, ex parte L* [1993] 1 All ER 756 (DC), where the court stated that, where a policy exists in respect of cautioning juveniles, the decision to commence or discontinue criminal proceedings was subject to judicial review, but only where it could be shown that the decision was made regardless of, or contrary to, that policy. This was applied in *Commissioner of Police for the Metropolis, ex parte P* (1996) 8 Admin LR 6 (DC) where the cautioning of a juvenile improperly, and in contravention of the Code for Crown Prosecutors, was judicially reviewable. See also *Inland Revenue Commissioners, ex parte Mead* [1993] 1 All ER 772 (DC).

5.12   Because these are civil proceedings, the application will not be made by the Crown Prosecution Service but by an advocate instructed on behalf of the relevant authority.[1] The CPS will, however, be involved if a prosecution is brought for breach of the order.[2] In respect of the representation of the defendant, the legal aid regulations will be amended to make assistance by way of representation (ABWOR) available for anti-social orders.[3]

1 Alun Michael, MP, Minister of State, Home Office, HC Committee, col 58, quoting draft guidance, para 3.4.
2 See para **5.52**.
3 And for sex offender orders. For such orders, see paras **5.57** et seq.

The power to make an anti-social order

5.13   The power to make an order under s 1 will arise in respect of any act of anti-social behaviour, as defined for the purposes of the Act, which occurs after the date of commencement of s 1.[1]

The applicant must show not only that the defendant has acted in an anti-social manner (as defined by the Act) (s 1(1)(a)) but also that such an order is necessary to protect persons in the local government area where the harassment, alarm or distress was caused, or likely to be caused, from further anti-social acts by him (s 1(1)(b)).

---

1 See para **1.4**.

5.14   This must be an act, or acts, after commencement which amount to anti-social behaviour, ie causes, or is likely to cause, harassment, alarm or distress to one or more persons not of the same household as the person engaging in the act or acts. If that is not the case, no order can be made. There is no question of using pre-commencement acts in aggregation with post-commencement acts to establish anti-social behaviour. By this means, retro-spectivity is avoided. However, in cases which amount to a continuing course of conduct, such as on-going noise nuisance, it may well be important to establish that the acts are but the latest example of a series of acts or amount to a course of conduct. Although a court cannot take the pre-commencement conduct into account in determining whether the threshold condition for the making of an order has been satisfied (ie whether the acts caused, or was likely to cause, harassment, alarm or distress), it can take that pre-commencement conduct into account in determining whether, on the merits of the case, an order should be made. It is clearly important for a court to know that conduct is not isolated, but is conduct that has continued for some months. As initially drafted, the Act would have prohibited this, it initially providing that no evidence of anti-social acts committed before commencement was to be adduced. That restriction has been removed from the Act. There is now nothing to prevent evidence of such acts being adduced, and a court has the discretion to take such acts into account,[1] although in the early days of the operation of s 1 courts will need to take care to ensure that specific findings about post-commencement conduct are made. It should also be noted in this context that, because the provisions are civil in nature, nothing in the Criminal Evidence Act 1898, s 1(f), which restricts questioning of an accused as to past discreditable acts, applies to an application under s 1.

---

1 Lord Williams of Mostyn, Parliamentary Under-Secretary, Home Office, HL Committee, col 509.

5.15   Section 1(1)(a) requires the person against whom the application for an order is made to have 'acted' in an anti-social manner. 'Acted' encompasses not only a course of conduct but also single acts.[1] There is nothing in s 1 which prevents a court from making an order on the basis of one act that meets the threshold condition. This may be because only one act can be proved, or, less likely, because only one act occurred. A court should be slow to make an order based on a single act, given the rationale of the provisions is to prevent on-going anti-social behaviour. Section 1(1)(b) makes it clear that such an order must be necessary to protect persons in the local government area from further anti-social acts by him. The draft guidance, and the parliamentary debates[2] make it clear that the making of an order on the basis of criminal or 'sub-criminal' behaviour[3] should be unusual. The main test is whether there is a pattern of 'behaviour'[4] over a period of time.

---

1 See Alun Michael, MP, Minister of State, Home Office, HC Committee, col 38.
2 Ibid, col 48.
3 See para **5.19**.
4 Draft Guidance, para 3.9.

5.16   A pre-condition for an order under s 1 is that there must be an act or acts, which cause, or which are likely to cause, harassment, alarm or distress. An intent to cause harassment, alarm or distress is not needed.[1]

A question of fundamental importance is: what is an 'act'? This term is defined by the *Concise Oxford English Dictionary* as including 'something done, a deed, the process of doing something', and in its normal sense suggests a positive act. Omissions are not 'acts', and to apply 'act' in the context of s 1 in this way may lead to its scope being somewhat more limited than might have been supposed. Although many examples of 'acts' in this sense can be given (the shouting of racist abuse, 'joy-riding' in cars on estate roads, the daubing of slogans, and so on), others may be less easily brought within the scope of s 1, and, indeed, may not be so, unless the term 'act' is construed more broadly to equate with 'conduct' or 'behaviour'. The word 'conduct' is not used by s 1. However, the word 'behaviour' is, although not in the context of the pre-conditions for the making of an order. Not only is 'behaviour' used in the side-heading, the name of the order ('anti-social *behaviour* order') is used in s 1(4) and subsequent subsections. 'Behaviour' is something wider than 'act', being defined by the *Concise Oxford English Dictionary* as including 'the way one conducts oneself; manners; the treatment of others ...'. To construe 'act' to equate with 'behaviour' would take s 1 beyond situations where a positive 'act' is done, to clearly put within its potential operation situations where a state of affairs is allowed to subsist.

The straightforward examples given above are clear-cut, and obvious. But other examples are far less so, despite the fact that the examples may each cause, or be likely to cause, harassment, alarm or distress. How a court resolves them will turn on how the courts wish to construe the term 'act'. Although most of the examples used in the parliamentary debates are actions positive in nature, it by no means inevitably follows that s 1 will, or should, be narrowly construed. Some examples of these difficult cases can be given. The keeper of a dog, or flock of geese, is creating a state of affairs: arguably, perhaps, there is an 'act' (ie the creation of that state of affairs, and its maintenance through feeding and upkeep), but there is certainly 'behaviour'. Whether that act can be linked to the causing, or likely causing, of harassment, harm or distress is a different matter, and might depend on the nature of what, to take the above example, is being kept. The suburban householder who keeps an incessantly barking dog, or a noisy flock of geese, is, perhaps, creating a state of affairs where, inevitably given the nature of the animals, harassment, alarm or distress is likely to be caused.

Often an act and refusal to act go hand in hand. The youth engaging in loutish behaviour who refuses to desist is both acting and refusing to act. There is certainly 'behaviour'. Similarly with the continued refusal by a dog owner to prevent the incessant, and loud, barking of his animal. There is, perhaps, an act (the keeping of the noisy animal) and a refusal (to take action to quieten the animal), but no doubt exists that it is his 'behaviour' that occasions the problem.

The householder whose burglar alarm continuously sounds is not in a narrow sense engaging in an 'act' but is certainly engaging in anti-social 'behaviour' by allowing it to continue.[2] What, however, of the householder who returns home to find his children playing loud music incessantly, and to the distress of fellow residents, but who fails to take any action to moderate the sound and remove the source of distress? There is no 'act', unless, unusually in English law, we were to consider a refusal to be an 'act'. The 'behaviour', however, is to permit an on-going problem to remain unresolved. It is the child, or children, who are undertaking an act, the playing of loud music. They could, of course, themselves be the subject of a s 1 order, if aged at least 10. The practical answer may be to ask whether it matters: after all, the relevant authority should use the s 1 power against those who engage in anti-social behaviour over a period of time,[1] not in respect of isolated incidents. This does not answer the question as to what is the legal entitlement of the relevant authority to seek an order in such circumstances, whether in respect of an isolated or on-going refusal. This lack of clarity in the terms of the s 1 power is disturbing, given its breadth and consequences.

---

1 See para **5.15**.
2 In this, and other noise examples, the more appropriate remedy may be the use by a local authority of the powers contained in the Noise Act 1996.

5.17 The difficulties do not end there. Questions of causation are likely to arise. The householder who holds a late-night party clearly engages in an act. It is, however, not his act (the holding of the party) that causes the harassment, alarm or distress, but rather the raucous nature of the partygoers who ignore his pleas for moderation. This might possibly be distinguished from the keeping of the noisy dog or flock of geese, discussed above. The keeping of geese or incessantly noisy dogs is inappropriate to a suburban area. The same inevitability of inappropriate noise does not exist in respect of the holding of parties: partying is, after all, not an unusual or inherently unacceptable activity to engage in an urban area (at any rate, in moderation). Noise nuisance may result, but does not inevitably do so. The householder may be asked to bring the party to a close. On the analysis set out above, there is not, at this stage, power in law to make a s 1 order against the householder. The subsequent holding of such parties is an act, but questions remain as to whether it is the act of the party-giver, as opposed to his guests, that causes that harassment, alarm or distress. With a series of parties, there is a course of conduct: arguably, it is the repeated holding of parties that cause such harassment, alarm or distress and which would satisfy the threshold condition for a s 1 order.

Anti-social manner

5.18　　As part of the pre-conditions for an order the person against whom it is sought must be proved to have acted in an anti-social manner, that is to say, acts which cause, or are likely to cause harassment, alarm or distress. The term 'anti-social manner' is characterised by breadth and vagueness, and is open to objection on the basis that it will catch conduct which is unorthodox or unusual, eccentric or bizarre, but which, nevertheless, is conduct which ought not to be the subject of the legal process. It is not intended that it should have that result.[1] 'Anti-social manner' is limited to conduct causing, or likely to cause, harassment, alarm or distress by the use of the words, 'that is to say'. Despite some doubts expressed during the passage of the Act, it is clear that these words in s 1(1)(a) are intended to limit the anti-social behaviour which can be the subject of an order to conduct which does, or is likely to cause, harassment, alarm or distress.[2]

The wording of s 1(1)(b) is also relevant to the question of the meaning, in s 1, of the phrase 'anti-social behaviour'. As noted earlier, s 1(1)(b) creates a second pre-condition for the making of an order, namely, that such an order is necessary to protect persons in the local government area in which *the* harassment, alarm or distress was caused or was likely to be caused from *further* anti-social acts by him. The use of the italicised words 'the' and 'further' links the future anti-social acts which are anticipated with the past anti-social conduct which has occurred and which forms the basis for the application for an anti-social order. 'Anti-social' does not, therefore, bear a wider meaning in s 1(1)(b) than in s 1(1)(a). It is not possible, sensibly, to construe s 1 in a way that permits the making of an anti-social order in circumstances where there has not been, or there is not likely to be, any harassment, alarm or distress. The use of the word 'further' is intended to link such matters to those which fall within s 1(1)(a).[3]

The effect of all this is that the use of the term 'anti-social' in s 1 has no real legal significance other than to mark, in judgmental terms through the label 'anti-social', the objectionable nature of such conduct, measured by the effects of the conduct rather than the conduct itself.

1　See Alun Michael, MP, Minister of State, Home Office, HC Committee, col 48.
2　See Lord Williams of Mostyn, Parliamentary Under-Secretary, HL Committee, cols 512–513.
3　Ibid, col 514.

5.19　　The conduct does not have to be unlawful. Lawful conduct may be part of a pattern of behaviour put before a court as evidence of the necessity for the making of an order.[1] However, there is no requirement in law for there to be one or more acts that contravene the criminal law. Alun Michael, MP, Minister of State, stated, during the passage of the Act, that it was intended that the orders be used in respect of criminal or 'sub-criminal' activity,[2] not for 'run of the mill civil disputes between neighbours', petty intolerance, minor one-off disorderly acts or the penalising of the eccentric.[3] Where the relevant behaviour is criminal, the anti-social behaviour order should be used if criminal procedures might not be appropriate or might not prevent anti-social behaviour. The term 'sub-criminal' activity was not defined by the Minister, and is a term with which lawyers may feel unhappy: either behaviour is criminal, or it is not. However, the examples given indicate the sort of lawful behaviour which, it is envisaged, might fall within the scope of a s 1 order: arguments with neighbours, peppered with threats, persistent loud noise at anti-social hours, the posting of excrement through the letter-box of a neighbour who dared to complain; the dumping of refuse all over the place, perhaps in neighbours' gardens; abusive language and intimidating behaviour; the intimidation and bullying of neighbour's children on the way to and from school.

---

1 Alun Michael, MP, Minister of State, Home Office, HC Committee, col 40.
2 Ibid, col 47.
3 Ibid, col 48.

5.20   During the passage of the Act, attempts were made to restrict the ambit of s 1 to instances where it is proved that harassment, alarm or distress to one or more persons not of the same household have actually occurred. Those attempts were successfully resisted.[1] The intention of s 1 is to allow a court to restrain any conduct which is likely in the future to have this effect. This is, seemingly, a narrower formulation than that contained in the Government's Consultation Paper, *Community Safety Orders,* where it was stated that the order[2] would include conduct which caused harassment to a community, conduct which amounted to anti-social criminal conduct or was otherwise anti-social, conduct which disrupted the peaceful and quiet enjoyment of a neighbourhood by others, or conduct which intimidated a community or a section of it.[3] However, the breadth of the concepts of harassment, alarm or distress does create the potential for the application of s 1 to the wide extent envisaged by the Consultation Paper.

---

1 See eg, Lord Williams of Mostyn, Parliamentary Under-Secretary, Home Office, HL Committee, col 513.
2 Which was, at that time, to be called a 'community safety order'.
3 *Community Safety Orders: A Consultation Paper* (Home Office, 1997), para 9.

5.21   The terms 'harassment, alarm or distress' are well known in the context of public order and other legislation, and bear the same meaning. They are also used in the offence of the new racially-aggravated public order offence created by s 31 of the new Act.[1] Whether words or behaviour cause, or are likely to cause, harassment, alarm or distress is a question of fact for a magistrates' court to decide. These words are to be given their ordinary and natural meaning.[2] In *Chambers v DPP*[3] C and E were road protesters who had disrupted progress on a highway construction site by getting in the way of the beam created by a surveyor's theodolite; they thus prevented him from using it properly and caused him inconvenience and annoyance. They were prosecuted for, and convicted of, an offence of disorderly conduct contrary to s 5 of the Public Order Act 1986,[4] the magistrates' court concluding that their conduct was not only disorderly but also caused harassment to the surveyor. There was no threat or fear of violence, but the surveyor was inconvenienced and annoyed by the appellants' behaviour. On appeal they argued that an element of apprehension about one's personal safety was necessary in order to establish harassment. This argument was rejected by the Divisional Court, which concluded that whether conduct was disorderly was a question of fact, and needed no further judicial definition. Disorderly behaviour was intended to cover behaviour which was not threatening, abusive or insulting. Section 5 refers separately to the constituents of the offence as disorderly behaviour and likelihood of harassment being caused. It was to be assumed that Parliament intended to mean something separate and different in each case.

---

1 See para **8.52**.
2 *Brutus v Cozens* [1973] AC 854, [1972] 2 All ER 1297 (HL).
3 [1995] Crim LR 896 (DC).
4 See para **5.5**.

5.22 Conduct which falls within the ambit of the public order offences, particularly, s 5 of the 1986 Act,[1] will often, although not always, be within the ambit of the new civil order which s 1 creates. The individual who shouts threats and abuse, vandalises cars, throws stones or daubs slogans on an individual's house may well be guilty of an offence under these provisions.

There are differences. Under the 1986 Act, there needs to be threatening, abusive or insulting behaviour, or disorderly conduct. There is no such requirement in s 1. Section 5 of the 1986 Act requires the conduct, or display, to be within the sight or hearing of a person likely to be caused harassment, alarm or distress. No such limitation exists in respect of s 1 of the new Act. Thus a case such as *Chappell v DPP*[2] where the dropping of material through a letter box of an intended recipient was not a s 5 offence, because it was not within the 'hearing or sight' of such a person, but would be conduct which potentially falls within s 1. Further, an offence under s 4 of the 1986 Act must involve the 'use towards another' of threatening, abusive words or behaviour, meaning that the person at whom the behaviour was aimed must have been present to perceive it.[3] It is also concerned with the use, or threatened use, of immediate unlawful violence.[4] No such presence is needed for the purpose of s 1.

The defendant may also be guilty of other offences, like criminal damage. There is no provision in s 1, or elsewhere, which prevents the making of an application in respect of a person, who has already been prosecuted for a criminal offence based on the conduct that is relied upon to satisfy the threshold condition. Such an application can be made and the rules against double jeopardy do not prevent this. The justification for this conclusion is that the purposes of the two processes are different. A criminal prosecution is designed to punish an individual for his conduct. By contrast, the purpose of the s 1 order is to take legal action to seek a civil order to prevent the repetition of conduct of a certain type, which has specified consequences. A civil court would have no difficulty, on an application for an injunction, in making such an order to restrain offending behaviour if the grounds in law existed.[5] There is no difference in principle, although the potential criminal consequences of failure to comply with the order are significant.

1 See para **5.5**.
2 (1988) 89 Cr App Rep 896 (DC).
3 See *Atkin v DPP* (1989) 89 Cr App Rep 199 (DC).
4 See *Valentine v DPP* (unreported) 24 March 1997.
5 Whether they do is in fact open to doubt. *Khorasandjian v Bush* [1993] 3 All ER 669, which decided that an injunction could issue at common law to restrain acts of harassment, appears to have been overruled by *Hunter v Canary Wharf Ltd* [1997] 2 All ER 426 (HL). *Burris v Azadani* [1995] 4 All ER 802 (CA) survives *Hunter*. It decided that common law power exists to grant injunctions to restrain conduct not of itself tortious, if such an order was reasonably regarded as necessary for the protection of a plaintiff's legitimate interest. In this case the legitimate interest flowed from the making of a non-molestation order. Quaere, whether an interest arises where an individual has suffered from anti-social behaviour, and an order is made against the perpetrator of the acts under s 1 in the absence of the making of such an order.

5.23   Anti-social behaviour is defined by reference to its consequences or likely consequences. The nature of the conduct itself is irrelevant: it is those consequences or likely consequences that matter. Unlike conduct which might fall within the ambit of s 5 of the Public Order Act 1986, the conduct does not have to be threatening, abusive, insulting or disorderly,[1] although it will often be so. It is also interesting to note that it was thought necessary in s 7(2) of the Protection from Harassment Act 1997 to state that 'harassment' includes alarming or causing the person distress. No similar provision is contained in the new Act, harassment, alarm and distress being regarded as separate concepts, albeit ones that are not mutually exclusive.

Perfectly lawful conduct may cause harassment, alarm or distress, and thus be the trigger for an application to a court under s 1, although, as noted above,[2] often the conduct will be such as also to constitute an offence, whether under ss 4, 4A or 5 of the Public Order Act 1986, under some other statutory provision or which gives rise to the preventative powers of the police in respect of actual or apprehended breaches of the peace.

1 See *Chambers v DPP* [1995] Crim LR 896 (DC) (see para **5.21**).
2 See para **5.5**.

Harassment
5.24   Section 1 does not define the term 'harassment'. The *Shorter Oxford English Dictionary* suggests terms such as 'trouble', 'vex by repeated attacks', 'worry' and 'distress'. Such definitions are, at least in one sense, unhelpful: the common statutory habit of grouping 'harassment' with 'alarm' and 'distress' suggests that harassment means something different from the causing of alarm, worry or distress. It will be recalled that in *Chambers v DPP* the fact of 'inconvenience and annoyance' was sufficient to constitute harassment.[1]

In *Burke*[2] the court adopted the approach taken to the meaning of 'harassment' by the Court of Appeal in *Yuthiwathana*,[3] where, in the context of an alleged offence under s 1 of the Protection from Eviction Act 1977, the test applied was whether there was an act 'calculated to interfere with the peace and comfort' of [the tenant] with the intent to cause him to give up occupation of his room. That amounted to harassment, which was a matter of fact and degree in each case.

1 See para **5.21**.
2 [1990] 2 All ER 315 (CA).
3 (1984) 80 Cr App Rep 55 (CA).

Alarm

5.25   Again, it is a matter of fact. A magistrates' court will have to decide whether the conduct caused, or was likely to cause, alarm. It is unnecessary to show that the person alarmed, or likely to be alarmed, should be concerned at physical danger to himself; it may be alarm about the safety of an unconnected third person.[1] It is also clear that the alarm of an individual can be proved by the testimony of a person who witnessed the alarm.[1] The alarm, or likelihood of alarm, has to be judged on the facts of each case on the standards which apply in the individual circumstances: if the person in fact was alarmed, or, because of his or her own disposition, likely to be alarmed, the fact that others may be of stouter disposition is immaterial. The defendant must take the 'victim' as he finds him, and cannot successfully argue that his conduct should be judged by its effect, or likely effect, on a reasonable person. There is no requirement that the defendant knew, or ought to have known, that his conduct was likely to cause alarm. A police officer is a person who can be alarmed, although whether he is, or is likely to be, alarmed is, again, a question of fact for the court to decide.

1 *Lodge v DPP* (1988) *The Times*, 26 October (DC).

Distress

5.26   Yet again, this is a matter of fact. The lack of need for an awareness of the causing, or likelihood, of the state of mind of the victim has already been discussed,[1] and applies equally to 'distress' as it does to 'alarm'. A police officer is a person who potentially may be caused distress.[2] Whether he is likely to be so is a different matter, and a matter of fact.

1 See para **5.25**.
2 *DPP v Orum* [1988] 3 All ER 449 (DC).

5.27   Unlike the conduct which falls within s 4 of the 1986 Act, the anti-social conduct does not have to be towards another person. Nor, unlike s 5 of that Act, does the conduct have to be in the presence of a person likely to be caused harassment, alarm or distress. For these reasons, the scope of s 1 is extremely broad. Clearly, it includes conduct such as the making of threats, the targeting of racial abuse at an individual, the shouting of lewd and suggestive remarks at young women, or the victimisation of an individual. It will potentially include conduct such as the incessant following of a person, the making of 'silent' telephone calls, or repeated telephone calls, or the sending persistently of unwanted goods or services, such as home delivery pizzas, flowers, chocolates, or subscriptions to dating agencies. It includes conduct which is not immediately perceived: one example might be the daubing of the outside of a house with taunts or racial abuse, only seen by the occupants at whom it was aimed when they return home from holiday. Another example would be the on-going observation of the home of a court witness, who feels frightened and intimidated as a result. A third example is the deposit through a letter box of written taunts or abuse, fireworks, dead rats or even excrement. Noise nuisances, exuberant partying, or (perhaps)[1] the keeping of constantly barking dogs, or a flock of chickens or geese (liable to cause significant noise nuisance to a housing estate) may, potentially, be within the scope of s 1.

Some conduct falling within s 1 is clear-cut: the peering by young men over a hedge or fence at the occupants of a garden, or the stalking of a young woman by a man. Others are less clear-cut: the farmer who consistently parks an ugly tractor to block the scenic views of adjoining householders, does an act which causes the residents distress. It is scarcely the intention of Parliament that s 1 should extend to such matters. The fact that such conduct, in all probability, will be held to be reasonable,[2] should not disguise the sheer breadth of the s 1 power. The car insurance or double-glazing salesman who persistently telephones an individual touting for business may also be committing anti-social behaviour.

The use of the s 1 power should not extend to the making of an order to prevent minor or trivial behaviour.[2] One example given was that 'it is not the loud stereo that belongs to someone of a different colour or culture that is meant to be caught . . .'. However, that result is only achieved by the use of the courts' discretion, the monitoring function of the relevant authority or the use of the 'defence' of reasonableness.[3] Many might consider it unsatisfactory that the *legal scope* of an order should be so ill-defined as to require discretionary safeguards.

---

1 See the difficulties discussed at para **5.16**.
2 See para **5.28**.
3 See para **5.31**.

The seriousness of the conduct

5.28   As a pre-condition to the making of an order, the harassment, alarm or distress need not be serious. Nevertheless, the seriousness of such harassment, alarm or distress will clearly be a relevant factor when the relevant authority decides whether or not to make an application, or when a magistrates' court decides whether or not an order should be made. During the passage of the Act attempts were made to ensure that 'seriousness' was part of the pre-conditions for jurisdiction contained in s 1.[1] Such attempts were successfully resisted by the Government, which pointed out that a defence exists that the conduct was reasonable. However, the burden of proving reasonableness lies on a defendant to proceedings under s 1,[2] and it will be open to a court to consider an application based on matters which may not be regarded as serious. The fact that the relevant authority and the court each have a filtering role in respect of undeserving cases is, arguably, an insufficient safeguard.

---

1 See, eg, Lord Goodhart, HL Committee, cols 533–542.
2 See para **5.31**.

5.29   The harassment, alarm or distress, or likelihood of it, can be to one person or more than one person not of the same household[1] as the person against whom the order is sought. As noted earlier,[2] that person or persons do not have to be present. As originally drafted, the Act would have required that harassment, alarm or distress (or likelihood of it) to be caused to two or more persons. That is no longer required. The harassment, etc, or likelihood of it, can equally be suffered by one person. An old lady living alone on a housing estate may be caused alarm and distress, and possibly suffer harassment, from a group of youths playing football outside her house, using her house wall as a target against which to shoot the football. Such elderly people may be the subject of abuse or bullying, or, if she lives in a downstairs flat be incesssantly bothered, and distressed, by loud and oppressive heavy metal music from above, continuing regularly into the night. A black person, who is the only non-white in the area, may suffer racial taunts and abuse, and will likewise fall within the scope of s 1. Of course, in some circumstances, the fact that there is only one person who suffers, or is likely to suffer, harassment, etc, may be relevant to the question of the reasonableness of the conduct of the defendant, but, as the above examples show, that is by no means inevitably so.

This change is clearly desirable. The effects of the change are, however, not wholly clear. One of the intentions of the Government is that s 1 should not focus on individual disputes, but rather on matters which affect the community.[3] It is not intended to deal with neighbour disputes, such as, for example, the excessive growth of leylandia cypress trees, although the terms of the Act, as originally drafted, were wide enough to include the growth of such trees which results in two persons' (ie husband and wife) distress. The Act is aimed at conduct which is both anti-social and anti-community, and the fact that an application cannot be made by an individual but has to be made by a local authority or chief constable provides some means of ensuring the fulfilment of this aim. However, there is nothing in the terms of s 1 which adds 'anti-community' to the pre-conditions for the making of an order, and, arguably, the wording of s 1(1)(b)[4] extends the operation of the new order to cases where the future harassment, etc, is to one person only. Further, some of the examples given above are no more than neighbour disputes. There is no reason to single out particular forms of neighbour disputes as worthy of attention, and others not. Section 1 does not confine its operation to anti-social acts committed in a public place: so to confine it would remove from its operation cases such as where a group of youths gather in the garden of one of their number to shout racial abuse and taunts at a black neighbour. By contrast, domestic violence victims are not likely to be covered by s 1.[5]

1 For the meaning of this term, see annotations to s 1 and see also para **5.36**.
2 See para **5.27**.
3 See Lord Williams of Mostyn, Parliamentary Under Secretary, HL Committee, col 548.
4 See para **5.37**.
5 See para **5.36**.

5.30   Nothing in s 1 requires an intent to cause harassment, alarm or distress to exist. Further, the harassment, alarm or distress is not required, by the terms of s 1, to be serious in objective terms, although this may be of relevance to the issue of whether the conduct is reasonable, as discussed below.

Reasonableness

5.31   Section 1(5) does state that, in determining whether the condition in s 1(1)(a) is fulfilled, the court shall disregard any act of the defendant which he shows was reasonable in the circumstances. This mirrors the provision in s 5(3)(a) of the Public Order Act 1986, but with different wording.[1]

1 Section 5(3) of the 1986 Act begins with the words 'it shall be a defence for the accused to prove ...'.

5.32   This 'reasonableness' provision is not without difficulty. It is plainly intended to allow a court to make a judgment as to the acceptability of the conduct of the respondent. However, s 1 is not a conduct-based provision, but one which focused on the result or likely result of the conduct. The conduct which entitles a court to make an order is definable only by its consequences, or likely consequences. What amounts to anti-social behaviour is defined by reference to whether it causes, or is likely to cause, harassment, alarm or distress. By definition, conduct which does not cause, or is not likely to cause, harassment, alarm or distress, is not anti-social behaviour, and thus s 1(5) has no relevance. Section 1(5) applies to conduct that does have, or is likely to have, that effect. Section 1(5) therefore envisages conduct can be reasonable notwithstanding this effect or likelihood, but gives no indication as to where the balance should be struck.

To regard s 1(5) as providing a 'defence' would, strictly speaking, be inaccurate. It requires a court to disregard certain conduct in determining whether one of the pre-conditions for the making of a s 1 order is satisfied. It is intended to deal with situations where some complainants are unduly tetchy, susceptible or sensitive.[1] The strong, but unusual, smells created by exciting, adventurous cooking might cause distress but might be regarded (at any rate in isolation and moderation) as reasonable conduct. Other examples can be given: the charity worker calling door to door, and an aircraft company having aircraft flying over a residential area during permitted hours.[2] Trivial acts which cause distress or minor harassment might be regarded as reasonable. Clearly, the intention of s 1(5) is to take outside the scope of s 1 conduct which because of its triviality or because it conforms to the normal standards of give-and-take of everyday life ought not to be within it.

1 See Lord Williams of Mostyn, Parliamentary Under-Secretary, HL Committee, col 541.
2 Lord Williams of Mostyn, op cit, col 564.

5.33   Once it is established that the defendant's act or acts caused, or were likely to cause, harassment, alarm or distress, it is the reasonableness of the defendant's act or acts that has to be judged, not the reasonableness of the reaction, or likely reaction, of persons in the locality. Thus, to return to the example of noise emanating from a party, if it is established that there is an 'act' or 'acts' within the meaning of s 1 which cause, or are likely to cause, harassment, alarm or distress, a defendant may nonetheless show that he held the party at a reasonable hour, limited the invitations and took all reasonable steps to control noise from amplifying apparatus, car doors, and so on. This could (although not necessarily will) provide a basis for a court concluding that his conduct was reasonable notwithstanding the fact that significant distress was caused to persons in the locality. It will be a matter of fact for the court to judge the reasonableness of what was being done. A court might well take the view that, following a series of previous rowdy events, the holding of any further event, for whatever purpose, is unreasonable. It should also be borne in mind that some acts may be reasonable and some not.

What the court is not bound, or, strictly, entitled to consider under s 1(5) is the reasonableness of the reaction of persons in the locality, save only to deal with the question of likelihood of distress, or to the extent that this shows the reasonableness or otherwise of the defendant himself. It does not in terms deal with the unduly sensitive, although that is, arguably, how it may well be used.

5.34   As noted above, it is doubtful whether s 1(5) provides a 'defence'. It requires the defendant to exclude a particular act or acts from being taken into account in deciding whether the pre-condition in s 1(1)(a) is satisfied. The general rule is, of course, that the party in a civil case must prove the matters relied on by that party. The words in s 1(5) are 'which he [the person the subject of the application] shows was reasonable in the circumstances'. This clearly places the burden of establishing reasonableness on the respondent. The standard of proof will be the balance of probabilities.[1]

1 See para **5.41**.

5.35   Reasonableness will be an important concept in keeping the use of s 1 within the boundaries of what Parliament intended. The scope of the wording of s 1 potentially goes far beyond the general intent of the legislation. A similar position has arisen in the context of the Protection from Harassment Act 1997, where harassment has extended to persistent, abusive telephoning, uninvited visits to the applicants' house, threats against the complainant, threats of suicide and threats to cause damage. In *Huntingdon Life Sciences Ltd v Curtin*[1] the 1997 Act was relied on by counsel for H by analogy as a justification for the issue of injunction to prevent acts of legitimate protest against H. In upholding the application of the applicant to discharge an interim injunction, the court held that Parliament had clearly not intended the Act to be used to prevent individuals from exercising their right to protest and demonstrate about issues of public interest, and the courts would resist any attempts to interpret it widely. Such arguments apply with even more force in the context of s 1 of the new Act, which could on its wording apply very clearly not only to the obvious anti-social types of behaviour commonly found on housing estates, but also against protestors, anti-hunt and road protest groups and the like. The facts of *Chambers v DPP*[2] themselves demonstrate how s 1 could operate in a protest context. The scope of s 1 is wide, and there are no limits imposed by the new Act, given the extremely wide definition, and the clear rejection by Parliament of an approach which required reasonableness to be considered as part of the question: is there anti-social conduct? For that reason, the application of the reasonableness test in s 1(5) will be crucial, as will the exercise of discretion at both the application stage (by the police or local authority) and by the court, if an application is in fact made. The scope of s 1 can be limited by the courts themselves. The granting of an order is discretionary, not mandatory, even if the threshold conditions are satisfied: the court 'may' make an order (s 1(4)). It is open to the courts to refuse to grant applications which fall within the terms of s 1 but which appear to be neighbour rather than community disputes,[3] or which do not appear deserving of intervention by way of a s 1 order. The experience of the operation of the Protection from Harassment Act 1997, however, creates no confidence that that is likely to be the attitude of the courts in the context of s 1 of the new Act. It should also be borne in mind that courts will find it extremely difficult to distinguish between neighbour disputes which have an 'anti-community' element and those which do not.[4]

This discretion provides some safeguards. It is a matter of regret, and against normal principle, for safeguards against the misuse of powers to be dependent on executive or judicial discretion and not on clear legal pre-conditions and safeguards. We return to this point later.[5]

---

1 (1997) *The Times*, 11 December.
2 See para **5.21**.
3 See Lord Williams of Mostyn, Parliamentary Under-Secretary, HL Committee, col 545.
4 Ibid, cols 545–546.
5 See para **5.56**.

The effect of anti-social behaviour

5.36   The scope of s 1 is limited to acts of anti-social behaviour which cause harassment, etc, or which are likely to do so, to one or more persons not of the same household. 'Household' is not defined by the Act, and will, generally, be a question of fact and degree,[1] although there may be some cases where the only conclusion, as a matter of law a court can reach, is that persons are part of the same household.[2] It is not intended that s 1 should operate in cases of domestic incidents, disputes or violence. Thus, if violence or threatened violence occurs between man and wife, or unmarried partners while they are living together, the appropriate remedies are those available under the Family Law Act 1996; this may be so even where the spouses or partners have temporarily separated. However, if there is a formal separation, whether by court order or otherwise, then the two individuals will not be part of the same household and the potential arises for the grant of an order under s 1. Of course, in that situation a court will have to have regard to the appropriateness of the order being sought, bearing in mind the potential for an application for a non-molestation order (ex parte or otherwise) under s 42 or s 45 of the 1996 Act. Further, unlike such orders, an anti-social order can be sought only by the relevant local authority or chief constable. This provides a filter which enables what are basically individual, not community, disputes to be weeded out. However, circumstances can be envisaged where the conduct of a separated or divorced spouse was such as to give rise to distress or alarm in the community.

---

1 See annotations to s 1, and the authorities therein cited.
2 See Woolf J in *England v Secretary of State for Social Services* (1982) FLR 222, cited in annotations to s 1.

Section 1(1)(b) – the necessity for the order

5.37   The second pre-condition to be satisfied is that in s 1(1)(b), namely that the court must be satisfied that an order is necessary to protect persons in the local government area in which the harassment, alarm or distress was caused or was likely to be caused from further anti-social acts by him.

Some of the potential difficulties relating to this provision have already been dealt with, in particular the meaning of 'persons' and of 'further anti-social acts'.[1] No doubt some difficulties may arise in respect to what is the 'relevant local government area' in which persons should be protected. The point does not directly arise under s 1(1)(a), but does under s 1(1)(b), and may do so in a variety of ways that are not entirely improbable.

Section 1(6)[2] states that the prohibitions which may be imposed by an anti-social behaviour order are those necessary for the purpose of protecting from further anti-social acts by the defendant:

(a) persons in the local government area; and
(b) persons in any adjoining local government area specified in the application for the order.

It will be noted that the word used in s 1(6)(b) is 'adjoining', which, given its ordinary meaning, means 'contiguous'. Thus if defendant A, who lives in one local government area, shouts racial abuse and taunts at family X who live across the street and the local authority boundary runs through the middle of the street, the court can make an order prohibiting future such conduct in either local government area, provided the applicant specifies the area in the application. It would seem odd for a court not to have such a power if the applicant does not specify the adjoining local government area, but no doubt such points could be dealt with by an amendment to the application.

However, in other circumstances, s 1(6) may not assist. For example, defendant B tours the streets by motor car, broadcasting abuse through a loud hailer, across more than one local authority area. The evidence shows that he intends to repeat the conduct not in the same local authority area, but in others, not immediately adjacent to the areas in which the original acts occurred. Therefore, no order can be made in respect of those areas. Further, if defendant C, who lives in the area of local authority X, sends hate mail to the residents of Downtown estate in local authority Y, can an order be made if the evidence shows that he intends, for the future, to target the Uptown estate in local authority area Z? It would appear not, unless Z is adjoining Y. It can probably be assumed from the wording of s 1(1)(b) that the word 'caused' is to be linked to the area in which the victims were when they suffered that harassment, etc, rather than the area in which the acts were committed. That latter interpretation follows from the use of the wording 'protect persons in the local government area in which the harassment, alarm or distress was caused', and the use of the word 'caused' in s 1(1)(a) appears to relate not to the deed (ie the place where the defendant was) but to the effect (the harassment, etc).

1 See para **5.18**.
2 See paras **5.44–5.47**.

'Further anti-social acts'

5.38   Also to be considered is the meaning of the phrase 'further anti-social acts'. As already noted, the use of the word 'further' puts beyond doubt the fact that anti-social acts are those as defined in s 1(1)(a). That leaves the question whether what has to be shown is conduct of a similar or the same kind. A court will be expected to have regard to the defendant's current behaviour in formulating prohibitions.[1] However, prohibitions can only be formulated once the pre-condition in s 1(1)(b) is satisfied. An example given during debate tends to show that a repetition of exactly the same conduct is not envisaged. A defendant may, for example, commit different sorts of anti-social behaviour in a shopping centre. A court should arguably construe s 1(1)(b) to the effect that it must be proved that an order is necessary to protect persons from further anti-social acts of a similar type. Once it is accepted that prohibitions in an order should relate to the defendant's current behaviour, the conclusion stated above is clearly right and inevitable.

1 Lord Williams of Mostyn, Parliamentary Under-Secretary, HL Committee, col 563.

Applications in respect of juveniles

5.39   An order can be made against a juvenile, the minimum age being 10. It will be dealt with by a magistrates' court, not a youth court.

Section 1 does not make it explicit, but appears, theoretically, to permit an application in respect of a defendant who is 10 at the date of application. This would, again theoretically, permit an application against a 10-year-old based on anti-social acts when he was only nine. That, seemingly unfair, conclusion is mitigated by the fact that the use of the powers against juveniles is intended to be exceptional. The usual use of power under s 1 in respect of a juvenile is where the juvenile is one of several members of a family involved in a pattern of behaviour.[1] Where a juvenile is involved, the court will no doubt have regard to the welfare of the child, even though the duty under s 44 of the Children and Young Persons Act 1933 probably does not apply, these being civil proceedings.[1] Although the new Act does not say so specifically, there is nothing to prevent a court considering making an order asking for reports on that child or young person, although the need to take prompt action to prevent recurrence of anti-social acts will also need to be borne in mind. It should also be noted that the power to make a parenting order[2] arises where a court makes an anti-social behaviour order against a child or young person.[3]

1 Alun Michael, MP, Minister of State, Home Office, HC Committee, col 53. See also draft
  Guidance, to similar effect.
2 See para **3.38**.
3 1998 Act, s 8(1)(b).

Procedure

5.40   An order can be made in the absence of a defendant,[1] a conclusion which is inevitable given that there may well be, amongst those who engage in anti-social acts, a wilfully disobedient attitude to the law and its processes. There is no power of arrest at the civil stage of the proceedings. The proceedings will usually be in public, and may be so even in cases involving children or young persons.[2] It is intended that a court should, generally, deal with the case on first hearing. Paragraph 5.4 of the draft Guidance recommends that it should be made clear in the summons, or an accompanying notice, that the case will go ahead on the first occasion listed, if necessary in the absence of the defendant. On the other hand, it is generally preferable for the defendant to be present.[3]

If a child or young person is the defendant, a court may require a parent or guardian to attend the court.[4]

1 There is no provision to that effect in the Act, but see draft Guidance 5.4, and Alun Michael,
  MP, Minister of State, Home Office, HC Committee, col 89.
2 Alun Michael, MP, ibid.
3 Ibid, col 90.
4 Children and Young Persons Act 1933, s 34A.

The burden of proof

5.41   The burden of proof is on the applicant for the order, save in respect of any matters as to the reasonableness of any act which arise under s 1(5).[1] The key question is whether the pre-conditions in s 1 are satisfied.[2] Only then can the court go on to consider whether there is a need to make an order and, if so, what it should contain. Because the proceedings are civil proceedings, they attract the civil standard of proof, namely the balance of probabilities. It should, however, be clearly noted that it is wrong to regard the law of evidence as providing distinct and separate standards. The standard of proof in a civil case varies according to the nature of what has to be proved. Case-law suggests that allegations of crime or other similar serious allegations have to be proved to the criminal standard of beyond reasonable doubt.[3] In *Khawaja v Secretary of State for the Home Department*[4] Lord Scarman said that, in the context of an application for habeas corpus (where the liberty of the individual is at stake) the difference was 'largely a matter of words'. Although dicta exist to suggest that a civil court never adopts the criminal standard even where allegations of a criminal nature are being made,[5] findings by coroners' courts of suicide, and of unlawful killing have each been held to require proof beyond reasonable doubt.[6] So too in civil cases where the allegation is one of murder[7] or child abuse. Of course, allegations of anti-social acts do not fall into the same league of seriousness. Nevertheless, the consequences of the making of an order are that if breach of a requirement is shown, the defendant has committed a criminal offence, without any opportunity to demonstrate that his conduct was reasonable. For this reason, it is arguable that the courts should apply a high standard of proof in respect of the threshold conditions. Such an approach commended itself to Ministers during the passage of the Act, it being stressed that 'the more serious the allegation the more important it is to have a high standard of proof ... it is axiomatic that it is not just 51% ... it is a flexible instrument ... if the court has particular concerns, one would expect it to apply a higher test'.[8] This approach is surely confirmed by the requirements of the European Convention on Human Rights.[9]

---

1 See para **5.31**.
2 Lord Williams of Mostyn, Parliamentary Under-Secretary, HL Committee, cols 559–560.
3 See *Hornal v Neuberger Products Ltd* [1957] 1 QB 247, [1956] 3 All ER 970.
4 [1984] AC 74, [1983] 1 All ER 765 at 783, per Lord Scarman.
5 *Bater v Bater* [1951] P 35 at 37, per Denning LJ (as he then was).
6 See *West London Coroner, ex parte Gray* [1988] QB 467, [1987] 2 All ER 129 (DC).
7 *Halford v Brooks* (1991) *The Times*, 3 October (QBD).
8 Lord Williams of Mostyn, Parliamentary Under-Secretary, op cit, col 560.
9 See para **5.56**.

How are the pre-conditions to be proved?

5.42   Clearly, the pre-conditions must be proved by admissible evidence, although that need not be evidence from the 'victim'. Even in respect of a prosecution under s 5 of the Public Order Act 1986, there is no need to prove the harassment, alarm or distress by adducing evidence from the victim.[1] Nor is the presence of the complainant required.

These being civil proceedings, the provisions of the Civil Evidence Act 1995 apply, and relate to the admissibility of statements of persons who do not testify. The court can hear testimony, whether orally or on paper, which satisfies the relevant conditions for admissibility and establishes the threshold conditions. In cases where there is likelihood of victimisation or reprisals, it may be that it is inappropriate for the identity of the complainant to be disclosed as part of the application. However, the power to withhold the identity of a complainant, where the application is based upon actual harassment, alarm or distress, is doubtful. In such circumstances, the applicant may wish to rely instead on the 'likely to cause' approach permitted by s 1.

1 *Swanston v DPP* (1997) 161 JP 203 (DC).

The making of the order

5.43   If the pre-conditions in s 1(1) are satisfied, a court may make an order. It is not obliged to do so. If it does, the order will have effect for a period of not less than two years. The order shall continue for the specified period or until further order. The minimum length of the order applies irrespective of the age or maturity of the defendant, or the levels of seriousness of the anti-social acts complained of. Some criticism can be made of the fact that there is no power, especially for a youngster, to make a shorter order. The position is alleviated somewhat by the fact that, as noted later,[1] an order may, with the consent of both parties, be discharged by the court which made the order, even within the two-year period (s 1(8), (9)). The capacity, under s 1(7), to leave an order to run until further order is made does not entitle a court to make a further order within the two-year period. The two-year minimum order period is both explicit and clear.

1 See para **5.50**.

5.44   If an order is made, it prohibits the defendant from doing anything described in the order. The prohibitions which may be imposed are those necessary for the purpose of protecting persons in the local authority area from further anti-social acts by the defendant.

It is clear that the order can only contain prohibitions. There is no power to impose requirements to perform positive obligations. Thus an order should contain prohibitions restraining the defendant from doing things which will amount to further anti-social acts. The wording of s 1(6) refers to 'further anti-social acts by the defendant'. These words are equivalent to those in s 1(1)(b) (the pre-condition for the making of the order) and it is submitted that the prohibitions which may be imposed under s 1(6) must be in respect of the further anti-social acts from which the court considers, under s 1(1)(b), that it is necessary to protect persons in the local government area. A court cannot impose prohibitions that might prevent anti-social acts, of which there is no evidence, which might be committed in the future.

5.45   There appears to be no limit to what may be included in the order, subject to compliance with the terms of s 1(6), which states that the prohibitions which may be imposed by an anti-social order are those necessary for the protection of persons in the local government area from further anti-social acts by the defendant. No guidance is given by the Act as to what the word 'necessary' actually means. On one interpretation, a prohibition is not 'necessary' if the conduct can be prevented by other means. Thus, for example, a child might be brought under control by a parenting order. In one sense, therefore, prohibitions in an anti-social order are not 'necessary' unless there is no alternative. It is submitted that this is too narrow an approach. The purpose of the word 'necessary' is to limit the scope of any prohibition to the context which justifies the making of the order, and to prevent the imposition of prohibitions which are not directly related to that anti-social conduct. If it is not so related, it is not 'necessary'. A provision is 'necessary' if it is needed. A prohibition is needed even though there are alternative ways of achieving the protection sought. Thus, a binding-over order may provide an appropriate sanction for repetition of anti-social conduct, but the potential to make such an order does not prevent a court making an anti-social behaviour order. The fact that a woman might be able to gain a non-molestation order under the Family Law Act 1996 or an injunction under the Protection from Harassment Act 1997 will not debar a court from making an anti-social behaviour order if the court considers that such an order is needed, and the pre-conditions for the making of the order are satisfied.

5.46 The issues discussed earlier as to the meaning of 'persons', 'local government area' and 'further anti-social behaviour' apply equally in this context.

5.47 Whatever the restrictions imposed, they must be reasonable. The unreasonable decisions of magistrates' courts are judicially reviewable on normal judicial review grounds.[1] Further, it is submitted that they will need also to be proportionate. Proportionality is important in the context of the European Court of Human Rights. The Human Rights Bill, when enacted and in force, will require a court to have regard to the Convention, and to the jurisprudence of the Court of Human Rights.[2] Thus, restrictions or prohibitions which interfere with otherwise lawful acts of an individual must be proportionate to the harm that is sought to be prevented. Extreme orders, such as requiring a defendant not to visit property at which he lives, or not to go to a particular housing estate or street, are draconian in effect and would need the highest level of justification. A court will need to consider the effect of the proposed prohibition, and balance the effect of that prohibition on the defendant against the seriousness of the anti-social behaviour and the capacity to prevent its occurrence by other means. Arguably, a court should consider, and take into account, the range of different powers and orders which might appropriately be used or sought to prevent the anti-social behaviour, and also the overall intention of Parliament that s 1 is primarily designed to prevent 'anti-community' behaviour and not a means to achieve a private law remedy through public law process.

---

1 See para **5.11**.
2 See Human Rights Bill 1998, cl 3.

Appeals

5.48   A right of appeal exists from the decision of a magistrates' court to grant an anti-social behaviour order (s 4(1)).[1] The appeal against the making of the order is to the Crown Court. There is no appeal against the refusal to make an order, but since there are no restrictions upon the relevant authority making repeat applications, there is no obstacle to a fresh application being made in such circumstances, providing it does not amount to an abuse of process. A relevant authority might also, if the grounds exist, seek judicial review of the decision of a magistrates' court not to grant an order, although it is submitted that a divisional court would be slow to interfere with the judgments made by the magistrates' court which made the order.

---

1 The same provisions apply in respect of the making of a sex offender order: see para **5.76**.

5.49   On appeal, the Crown Court may make such orders as may be necessary to give effect to its determination of the appeal, and may make such incidental or consequential orders as appear to it to be just (s 4(2)). It can therefore remit the case to the magistrates' court for re-hearing. Alternatively, it may make an anti-social order (or sex offender order) and impose such prohibitions as are necessary for the purpose of protecting persons in the local government area from further anti-social acts (or, in the case of a sex offender order, for the purpose of protecting the public from serious harm from the defendant). Such an order will be deemed to be made by the magistrates' court from which the appeal to the Crown Court came (s 4(3)).

Variation or discharge of an order

5.50   No explicit power is given by s 1 to a court to vary an order, but that is clearly implicit from the fact that s 1(8) states that the applicant or the defendant may apply by complaint to the court which made an anti-social order for it to be varied or discharged. Except with the consent of both parties, no such order can be discharged before the end of the period of two years beginning with the date of service of the order. An order can be varied without the agreement of both parties, and the consent of both parties is not needed for discharge after the expiration of the two-year period.

Breach of the order

5.51   Breach of the order is a criminal offence. By s 1(10), if, without reasonable excuse, a person does anything which he is prohibited from doing by anti-social behaviour order, he shall be liable:

(a) on summary conviction, to imprisonment for a term not exceeding six months or to a fine not exceeding the statutory maximum, or to both; or
(b) on conviction on indictment, to imprisonment for a term not exceeding five years or to a fine, or to both.

Clearly, if the offence is committed by a child or young person, the case will be dealt with by the youth court, unlike the application for the making of the order.

5.52   The burden of proof of establishing the offence is on the prosecution. It will be the 'relevant authority', usually the police, that will prosecute. The prosecution will need to establish, to the criminal standard of proof, that an order was made and its terms. This will be done by producing to the court a copy of the order. The prosecution will also need to prove that there has been a breach of the order, by the accused doing something prohibited by the order. In many cases, that may be by an admission through a plea of guilty, or a formal admission under s 9 of the Criminal Justice Act 1967. If there is not a formal admission or a plea of guilty, the breach will be proved in the normal way through admissible evidence. These being criminal proceedings, the relevant rules of evidence governing hearsay evidence[1] will apply. Thus, there may be a need for the complainant to attend court, to testify about repeated acts of a type prohibited by the order, and to be cross-examined. This may be something not all complainants will wish to do. The prosecution does not need to prove that the acts complained of amount to anti-social behaviour, or have any specified effects or likelihood. The offence is committed by a breach of the requirements of the order, subject to that breach not being with reasonable excuse.

Clearly, an evidential burden of establishing reasonable excuse is placed on the accused. But on whom is the legal burden? This is unclear. Unlike some statutory provisions,[2] no express burden of proof is placed on the accused. The question, therefore, is whether the terms of s 101 of the Magistrates' Courts Act 1980 have that same effect. Section 101 was discussed earlier.[3] It is unclear whether this is such a case falling within s 101. All that the prosecution can do is to establish a breach of the order. The prosecution cannot know the circumstances which may make a breach of the order a criminal offence under s 1(10): it is the accused who can best explain what he did, and why. However, the balance of authority suggests that this is no more than an evidential burden. Such a conclusion clearly shows that the burden of showing lack of reasonable excuse under s 1(10) differs from that of showing reasonableness under s 1(5). Against that, however, the wording of s 1(5) specifically allocates the burden of proof. The failure to do so in s 1(10) seems to confirm that the general rule applies.

If the burden is indeed on the prosecution, the absence of reasonable excuse will have to be proved beyond reasonable doubt. If, by contrast, the burden of showing that reasonable excuse existed is on the accused, it is to the standard of the balance of probabilities.[4]

---

1 See, in particular, Criminal Justice Act 1991, ss 23–26.
2 See, eg, Prevention of Crime Act 1953, s 1.
3 See para **3.54**.
4 *Islington LBC v Panico* [1973] 3 All ER 485 (DC).

5.53   What is a reasonable excuse will be a matter of fact for the court to determine. Reasonable excuse should not be found simply because no harassment, alarm or distress was created, or likely to be created by the breach of the order. The reasonable excuse must relate to the conduct in breach of the prohibition, not the effect of that breach.

5.54   If convicted, the accused may be fined or sentenced to a term of imprisonment. It is not open to a court to impose a conditional discharge (s 1(11)).

5.55   Appeal against conviction for breach of such an order will lie in the same way as is applicable generally in criminal cases (ie to the Crown Court by way of re-hearing or Divisional Court by way of case stated).

Evaluation

5.56   Few people would disagree with the objective of preventing the lives of a community, or part of it, being ruined by the anti-social behaviour of others. Whether the solution contained in s 1 is appropriate is more open to argument. Quite extensive criminal powers already exist, but the new powers might nevertheless be justified in terms of protection from future acts and the difficulties of enforcement of the criminal law given the burden of proof. Nevertheless, the vagueness and breadth of the new power has already been noted, and a person can be subject to potential criminal liability in respect of such conduct established only on the balance of probabilities.

These provisions, although establishing a civil process, have in reality many of the consequences of criminal regulation. In determining compliance with the European Convention on Human Rights, the Court of Human Rights looks not simply at the classification of the proceedings in domestic law, but also at the general nature of the proceedings, and the consequences. The European Commission of Human Rights has categorised proceedings before magistrates following non-payment of council tax and binding-over proceedings as criminal,[1] despite their classification in English law as civil proceedings, with the result that the standards expected in such proceedings in terms of certainty, burden of proof and legal representation apply.[2] The Government believes that changes made to s 1 during the passage of the Act serve to meet concerns that might arise as to compatibility of s 1 with the Convention, pointing to, in particular, the addition of criteria relating to reasonable conduct, and the extension of legal aid to such proceedings.

Nevertheless, an individual can be made subject to an order of unlimited length, with ill-defined and broad powers to prohibit conduct, and with no direct link in the terms of criminal liability (as opposed to sentence) between the anti-social conduct and the breach of the order. An individual may be subject to this wide-ranging restriction established on the balance of probabilities. It not entirely clear that challenge under the Convention will inevitably fail.

1 See *Benham v United Kingdom* (1996) 22 EHRR 239; *Steel v United Kingdom* (Report of the Commission, 9 April, 1997).
2 See art 6 of the European Convention on Human Rights.

SEX OFFENDER ORDERS

5.57   Section 2 of the new Act gives to a magistrates' court a power to make a sex offender order which, in essence, is similar to the anti-social behaviour order. It is civil in nature and is an order which, if the pre-conditions for its making are satisfied, entitles a court to prohibit the defendant from doing anything described in the order. That is not a finding of guilt as to the commission of a criminal offence. Section 2 does not limit which acts may be prohibited by a sex offender order, provided those prohibitions are necessary for the purpose of protecting the public from serious harm from the defendant. If a person subject to a sex offender order without reasonable excuse does anything which he is prohibited from doing by the order, he is guilty of an either-way offence, triable either on indictment or summarily.

The provisions relating to sex offenders come into force on 1 December 1998: see Appendix II.

Rationale and background

5.58   The recent past has seen growing concern about the risks which sex offenders pose to the community, especially young and vulnerable members of it. The scale of the problem, in recent years, has become increasingly clear. There are an estimated 110,000 convicted male paedophiles in England and Wales, and, according to a Home Office study, of all men born in 1953, one in 60 had a conviction for a sexual offence by the time he was 40.[1] Special provisions relating to sex offenders have existed since s 44 of the Criminal Justice Act 1991 created the potential for extended supervision arrangements for sex offenders who had served a term of imprisonment. Since then, a range of legislation has been introduced to protect the public and to create a regime where supervision and treatment is available in respect of sex offenders. Section 2 of the Crime (Sentences) Act 1997 introduced mandatory life sentences for the commission of a second violent or sexual offence. The Sex Offenders Act 1997[2] provides for a scheme of registration for those cautioned for, or convicted of, a sexual offence, and also contains provisions designed to curb 'sex tourism'.[3] Part VI of the Police Act 1997 introduced measures designed to facilitate enhanced criminal conviction and criminal intelligence checks, which will assist in the checking of the character of those seeking to work in sensitive areas. As already noted,[4] the Protection from Harassment Act 1997 provides for injunctions to restrain acts of harassment, which can be used directly to prevent conduct such as stalking, sexual harassment and the targeting of individuals. The Sexual Offences (Protected Material) Act 1997 regulates access to victim statements in sex offence cases. The Criminal

Evidence (Amendment) Act 1997 extends police powers to obtain DNA in respect of all convicted sex offenders still serving a sentence.

The new Act adds to this range of measures. It does so by the provisions for extended sentences for sexual or violent offenders,[5] and by the new sex offender order, which is designed to enable a court to make an order prohibiting conduct, so as to prevent offences from occurring. Further measures involving a unification of registers of suspected sex offenders, and restrictions on their employment, are anticipated in the not too distant future.[6]

---

1 (1998) *The Times*, 25 August.
2 See annotations to ss 2–3.
3 Although not directly a public protection measure, it has the effect of child protection
   through the successful prosecution of those who seek to engage in unacceptable conduct
   with children or young persons, irrespective of where that conduct occurs.
4 See para **5.4**.
5 See paras **7.14–7.27**.
6 (1998) *The Times*, 5 June.

The pre-conditions for making the order

5.59   As noted earlier, a sex offender order is an order in respect of a sex offender, which prohibits him from doing any act specified in the order. An application for an order may be made by the chief officer of police in respect of a sex offender of any age provided the pre-conditions are satisfied. The first is, obviously, that the offender must be a sex offender.[1] The second is that the defendant has acted, since the relevant date, in such a way as to give reasonable cause to believe[2] that an order under s 2 is necessary to protect the public from serious harm from him.

---

1 See s 3 and annotations thereto.
2 See general annotations.

Sex offender

5.60   This term is defined by s 3, and means a person who:

(a) has been convicted of a sexual offence to which Part I of the Sex Offenders
     Act 1997 applies;[1]
(b) has been found not guilty of such an offence by reason of insanity, or
     found to be under a disability and to have done the act charged against
     him in respect of such an offence;
(c) has been cautioned, reprimanded or warned[2] by a police officer in
     England and Wales or Northern Ireland, in respect of such an offence
     which, at the time when the caution was given, he had admitted;[3]
(d) has been punished under the law in force in a country or territory outside
     the UK for an act which:
     (i)   constituted an offence under that law; and

(ii) would have constituted a sexual offence to which Part I of the 1997 Act applies if it had been done in any part of the UK.

The new order will, therefore, be available only in respect of a sex offender who was convicted of a sexual offence on or after the date of commencement of the 1997 Act (1 September 1997),[4] or in respect of an offender who was serving a term of imprisonment for a sexual offence on that date, or subject to statutory supervision on licence for such an offence (1997 Act, s 1(1), (3)). The new power will not be available in respect of those known to create a risk of serious harm to the public if they have not been convicted for, or cautioned in respect of, a sexual offence. In such cases, recourse may have to be made to the s 1 power, although, as noted later, this may not always be available.

---

1 See annotations to s 3.
2 See para **3.66**.
3 A caution, reprimand or warning will not be administered unless the individual admits the offence.
4 Sex Offenders Act 1997 (Commencement) Order 1997, SI 1997/1920.

5.61   The definition of 'sex offender' in s 3(1) is wider, in one respect, than that which appertains in the context of the Sex Offenders Act 1997. The notification requirement in the 1997 Act does not extend to those who commit a sexual offence abroad, but who have not been tried and convicted in the UK. By contrast, the effect of s 3(1)(d) is to extend the potential to make a s 2 order to a person who had been convicted overseas. The justification for not including such a person in the registration requirement in the 1997 Act was that to apply the notification requirements to persons convicted abroad would inevitably be partial, and potentially contrary to the European Convention on Human Rights. In addition, it was considered that 'to place an obligation on the authorities in respect of those who had been convicted abroad would undoubtedly imply recognition of the judgment of a foreign court. It would also assume that the sentences were compatible with the sentences that would have been imposed here and that the standards of evidence and procedure in the foreign courts were compatible with ours'.[1] No such inhibitions have troubled the present Government. The inclusion of persons convicted abroad, on or after 1 September 1997, rightly permits a court under s 2 to make an order against a person, such as a 'sex tourist', who may pose a serious risk to the public.

---

1 David Maclean, MP, Minister of State, Home Office, HC Deb vol 289, col 30.

5.62   'Sexual offence' bears the same meaning as in the Sex Offenders Act 1997[1] (new Act, s 3(1)(a)). The 1997 Act defines sexual offences in terms of the list of offences contained in Sch 1 to that Act. It follows that we have to have recourse to different definitions of the term 'sexual offence' for the purposes of different parts of the new Act. In particular, the definition contained in s 31 of the Criminal Justice Act 1991, which differs somewhat from that in Sch 1 to the 1997 Act, is the definition which applies in the context of extended sentences for violent or sexual offenders.[2] It is the 1997 Act definition which applies in the context of the sex offender order. This is despite the terms of s 18(2) of the new Act which on its face applies to Part I of the new Act the same definitions as are contained in Part I of the 1991 Act, unless the contrary intention appears. Such a contrary intention does appear from the terms of s 3.

1 See annotations to s 3.
2 See para **7.18** and annotations to s 58.

5.63   The question arises as to how the overseas conviction which falls to be considered under s 3(1)(d) is to be proved. That question is dealt with by s 3(6). Subject to the provisions of s 3(7), that condition is to be taken to be satisfied by the application stating the fact of such conviction unless, no later than a day to be specified by rules of court,[1] the defendant serves on the applicant for an order a notice:

(a) stating that, on the facts as alleged with respect to the act in question, the condition is not in his opinion satisfied;
(b) showing his grounds for that opinion; and
(c) requiring the applicant to show that it is satisfied.

If such a notice is served, it will be for the applicant for the order to prove that s 3(1)(d) is satisfied, by proving the offence under foreign law. Because an application for an order under s 2 amounts to civil proceedings the standard of proof will be to the civil standard, the balance of probabilities.[2]

1 None had been made as at the date of going to press.
2 But see the comments at para **5.41**.

Reasonable cause to believe necessary to protect the public from serious harm

5.64   Section 2(1)(b) requires that the defendant has acted, since the relevant date, in such a way as to give reasonable cause to believe[1] that an order under s 2 is necessary to protect the public from serious harm from him. The 'relevant date' will be either:

(a) the date of commencement of s 2;[2] or
(b) the date of conviction,[3] caution or punishment;

whichever is later (s 3(2)).

There is no question of an order being made against a sex offender if the conduct which gives rise to the reasonable belief was prior to this date, no matter how great the risk is to the public. However, if such a person engages in conduct which causes, or is likely to cause, harassment, alarm or distress, a possibility highly likely given public concerns about, and perceptions of, sex offenders, then it may well be that a court would be entitled to make an anti-social behaviour order, to achieve the same ends.[4]

---

1 See general annotations.
2 For commencement, see para **1.4**.
3 See annotations to s 2.
4 See para **5.66**.

5.65   An application under s 2 is made by a complaint to the magistrates' court whose commission area[1] includes any place where it is alleged that the defendant acted in such a way as to give rise to the reasonable belief. Where there is more than one such area, there is no reason why an application cannot be made to the court for any one of such areas, nor does the new Act prohibit multiple applications being made by the appropriate authority to different magistrates' courts. No jurisdiction exists for an order to be sought from, or made by, a county court or the High Court. Magistrates' courts are courts with which the police (who will make the application) are familiar, and the criminal offence which will result from breach will be dealt with in the magistrates' court.

Only the chief officer of police[2] may make an application. If an individual, or local authority or child support agency, considers that there is a need for protection against a sex offender, because of his conduct, that individual can, of course, make representations to the police or seek some individual remedy (perhaps, in some circumstances, under the Protection from Harassment Act 1997). The decision not to seek an order may also be challengable by an application for judicial review. Whether an order is applied for is a matter of executive discretion, and not subject to appeal. It may be likened to the decision to commence the prosecution process. For that reason, the decision to seek an order may, potentially, be subject to an application for judicial review.[3]

---

1 See general annotations.
2 See s 2 and annotations thereto.
3 See para **5.11**.

5.66   The word 'acted' in s 2(1)(a) encompasses not only a course of conduct but also single acts. There is nothing in s 2 which prevents a court from making an order on the basis of one act which meets the pre-condition. This may be because only one act can be proved, or because only one act has been committed. However, there must be an act: the fact that X is a known paedophile, and is considered to present a significant risk of serious harm to young children, is not sufficient.

The act in question does not have to be illegal or itself create serious harm. It is what the act in question shows about the future behaviour of the defendant that is important. The conduct may be quite broad-based in nature. Thus, the act in question by X might be the offering of sweets to children, standing at school gates at playtime or at the end-of-school, or frequenting fairgrounds or amusement arcades or other places where children might congregate, or similar acts. Another example might be the sex offender who is allowed contact with his own children on a supervised basis, at designated times, say, on Wednesday evenings and Saturday afternoons. The turning-up for unsupervised contact on Thursdays and Sundays potentially gives rise to reasonable cause to believe that serious harm may occur to that child. Whether an order can in fact be made in such circumstances depends on the approach to the word 'public'.

The nature of the 'act' may be important in determining whether an anti-social behaviour order under s 1 is available, either as an alternative to a sex offender order, or because the power to make a s 2 order does not exist. The terms of s 1 are more narrow than those of s 2. An anti-social behaviour order under s 1 will be available only if the act or acts by the defendant caused, or were likely to cause, harassment, alarm or distress to one or more persons not of the same household as himself. If the acts in question are acts in relation to a person who is part of the family unit in which the defendant lives, it will need to be shown that such harassment, alarm or distress was (or was likely to be) suffered by others, perhaps family members, neighbours, or (possibly) child support agencies (who may well suffer 'alarm'). Where, however, the acts engaged in are of a type described above, a s 1 order becomes a viable alternative to a s 2 order.

5.67   Although no definition of 'serious harm' is contained in the new Act directly, s 18(2) provides that in Chapter I of the Act expressions used in Part I of the Criminal Justice Act 1991 bear the same meanings as in that Part, unless the contrary intention appears. There is no evidence of such a contrary intention here. Thus, s 31(3) of the 1991 Act applies. Section 31(3) states that 'any reference, in relation to an offender convicted of a violent or sexual offence, to protecting the public from serious harm from him shall be construed as a reference to protecting members of the public from death or serious injury, whether physical or psychological occasioned by further such offences by him'. Section 2 of the new Act is not, of course, confined in its operation to persons who have been convicted of a sexual offence. Nevertheless, the terms of s 31(3) are apposite. The meaning of 'serious harm' in the context of sexual offences was considered in *Bowler*.[1] The Court of Appeal said in that case that the power to impose a longer than normal sentence under s 2(2)(b) of the 1991 Act was not limited to exceptional cases where the danger of serious harm was obvious and had actually been caused in the past, for a judge reasonably to form the opinion that there was a danger that serious harm might occur in the future. An indecent assault on a young girl might well lead to serious psychological injury, and some adult women might be seriously disturbed by a relatively minor indecent assault. The purpose of the section included the protection of those women, less robust than average, who might be vulnerable to that kind of conduct.[2]

---

1   (1994) 15 Cr App Rep (S) 78 (CA).

2   *Apelt* (1994) 15 Cr App Rep (S) 532 (CA); *Williams* (1994) 15 Cr App Rep (S) 330 (CA); see
    also *Creasy* (1994) 15 Cr App Rep (S) 671 (CA) for a case involving a minor assault on a boy.

5.68 The purpose of the power is to protect the public from sex offenders who pose a continuing danger as sex offenders.[1] For that reason the term 'serious harm' must relate to his potential to cause serious harm as a *sex offender*. Thus, s 2 should not be used if the defendant poses a risk of serious harm to the public (say, by violent crime of a non-sexual nature) if that risk is unrelated to the risk he creates as a sex offender. If further evidence is needed to support that conclusion, it is surely to be found in the name of the order.

---

1 *Community Safety Orders: A Consultation Paper* (Home Office, 1997), para 2.

5.69 It will be noted that s 2 does not use the word 'risk',[1] despite the fact that it is against sex offenders who pose a continuing risk of serious harm that the new order is aimed.[2] The choice of terminology is, arguably, not particularly significant. A risk of serious harm might exist, but be a remote risk. The court, in reality, will have to decide levels of risk, despite the fact that the word is not used, and also the danger which the public face. A court in determining whether a s 2 order should be made will need to decide, first, whether there is a risk of serious harm to the public from the defendant, and, secondly, whether an order is necessary to protect the public from that risk. If that risk were remote a court might well, and should, conclude that a sex offender order is not necessary. Arguably, all sex offenders pose some risk to the public, or elements of it. The use of the term 'necessary' makes clear that simply being a sex offender does not, of itself, entitle the making of the order, for otherwise the further pre-condition in s 2(1)(b) would be redundant.

---

1 The concept of risk should not be confused with that of 'danger'. 'Risk' relates to the probability that a harmful event or behaviour will occur; 'danger' describes the actual or potential exposure to harm, or the propensity of certain individuals or circumstances to present harm: see Kemshall *Reviewing Risk* (Home Office, 1997), p 3, and the sources therein cited.
2 *Community Safety Orders*, op cit, para 2.

5.70 The risk of serious harm must be a risk of serious harm to the public. The 'public' is not defined. Unlike some statutory provisions, there is no statutory reference to 'section of the public' but, arguably, this does not matter. An offence against an individual, or even the targeting of an individual, potentially gives rise to a risk in respect of members of the public generally. Whether in fact it does so, and the level of that risk, will be for the court to decide, taking into account the conclusions of the agencies who know of the offender.

Clearly, the perpetrator of sexual offences against women poses a risk of serious harm to the public, ie to other potential victims. More difficulty arises in the case of 'marital rape'. The offender may be unlikely to offend sexually against other women. Although it might be argued that he posed a danger only to his wife, and thus there was no danger to the public, his conduct suggests a propensity to engage in inappropriate and unlawful sexual behaviour. The fact that the sexual offence was against his wife is relevant to the level of risk of future harm but a risk of harm to the community nevertheless exists. An offender who has targeted only one child has nonetheless caused concerns to arise not only for that child, but for other children, because the man has shown, by his conduct, that he has a sexual attraction to children.

The power to make the order

5.71   By s 2(3), if it is proved that the pre-conditions for the making of an order are fulfilled, a magistrates' court may make a sex offender order. The burden of proof is on the applicant for the order. As these are civil proceedings, the civil standard of proof applies, although, as noted earlier, the test of 'balance of probabilities' is not a fixed and absolute standard.[1] The applicant will have to prove the fact that the offender is a sex offender, and that it is necessary to make an order to protect the public from serious harm. In all these matters, because these are civil proceedings the rules of evidence applicable to such proceedings apply. Thus, for example, s 73 of the Police and Criminal Evidence Act 1984 (which relates to the proof of previous convictions in criminal cases) has no application.

---

1 See para **5.41**.

Proof

5.72   Whether a person is a sex offender can be proved by proof of the relevant conviction, caution, reprimand, warning or prohibited act.[1] In terms of a conviction, that can be proved by the production of a certificate of conviction. The caution, etc, can be proved by production of the relevant record, and the prohibited act in accordance with the provisions of s 3(5) to (7). The applicant will also need to prove by admissible evidence the conduct of the defendant which gives rise to the reasonable belief that an order is necessary to protect the public from serious harm. Because these are civil proceedings, the hearsay rule will not operate and it will not be necessary to call witnesses directly. Their statements may well suffice.

The second matter which must be proved is the risk of serious harm. The police, when considering whether to make an application, and the court in deciding whether to grant an order, will need to take into account the views of expert witnesses such as psychiatrists, probation officers, housing officers or social workers. In reality, the level of risk, and the nature of the danger posed by the sex offender, will often be assessed through inter-agency co-operation. In many areas, multi-agency protocols for the exchange of information and management of the risk posed by sex offenders have been, or are being, developed. The level of risk and nature of the danger can be assessed through a wide range of information.

Draft Home Office Guidance identifies the factors that should be taken into account in making an assessment of risk. These include:

(a) the probability or likelihood that a further offence will be committed;

(b) the potential harm resulting from such behaviour, and the potential victims of the harm;
(c) the nature and circumstances of previous convictions;
(d) the current circumstances of an offender and how these might foreseeably change, eg work placements or environments, housing, family or relation-ships, stress, drink or drugs, proximity to schools or playgrounds;
(e) the disclosure implications if the order is applied for, and how the court process might affect the ability to manage the offender in the community;
(f) an assessment of the accuracy and currency of the information about the individual (including an assessment of the status of those expressing concern and their reasons for doing so);
(g) the nature and pattern of the behaviour giving rise to the concern, and any predatory behaviour which might indicate a likelihood of re-offending;
(h) compliance, or otherwise, with previous sentences, court orders or supervision arrangements;
(i) compliance or otherwise with therapeutic help and its outcome.

As noted above, the previous convictions of the defendant will be relevant, first, if they establish that the defendant is a sex offender, and, secondly, if they provide evidence as to whether the public needs to be protected from serious harm. The previous conviction does not, of itself, justify the making of an order: by definition, every sex offender (other than those cautioned) has a previous conviction. However, previous convictions are relevant in providing the context in which the need to protect the public, in the light of the acts of the defendant, can be judged. Thus, hanging around school gates takes on particular significance if a previous conviction was for a sexual assault against a child near a school. However, danger does not have to be established by showing the commission of offences other than that which fulfils the pre-condition for a s 2 order. Thus, an offender could be considered to create a danger of serious harm to the community in the light of known conduct, for which he had not been prosecuted, but having been cautioned for a sexual offence.

The third matter which must be proved is that the order is necessary to prevent serious harm.[2]

---

1 See para **5.62**.
2 See para **5.75**.

The making of the order

5.73   If the pre-conditions in s 2(1) are satisfied, a court may make an order. It is not obliged to do so. If it does, the order shall have effect for a period of not less than five years. The order will continue for the specified period or until further order. The minimum length of the order applies irrespective of the age or maturity of the defendant, or the levels of seriousness of the sex offences of which the defendant was convicted and which provide some means of judging the level of protection needed by the public. An order may, with the consent of both parties, be discharged by the court which made the order, even within the five-year period (s 2(7)). After the expiration of that five-year period, an order may be discharged on application by either the applicant or defendant (s 2(6)).

The capacity, under s 2(5), to leave an order to run until further order is made does not entitle a court to make a further order terminating the order within the five-year period save with the agreement of the parties. The five-year minimum order period is both explicit and clear.

5.74   If an order is made, it prohibits the defendant from doing anything described in the order. The prohibitions which may be imposed are those necessary for the purpose of protecting the public from serious harm from the defendant.

It is clear that the order can contain only prohibitions. There is no power to impose requirements to perform positive obligations, such as to agree to supervision by a probation officer, to comply with a child protection plan (other than in a negative sense) or to attend a sex offenders project. The position with respect to curfews is more difficult. In one sense, a curfew is a prohibition against doing certain acts (ie by going out outside the terms of the curfew). In another sense, a curfew imposes positive obligations (to remain in a stated place at specific times). For this reason it is not possible to impose a curfew by means of a s 2 order, a conclusion in line with the view of the Government in its Consultation Paper.[1]

An order should contain prohibitions restraining the defendant from doing things which are necessary to protect the public from serious harm. There appears to be no limit to what may be included in the order, subject to compliance with the terms of s 2(4), which states that the prohibitions which may be imposed by a sex offender order are those necessary for the protection of the public from serious harm. It should be noted that the potential serious harm is not limited to serious harm to members of the public in the police area where the chief officer of which made the application or in which the magistrates' court which hears the application is.

---

1 *Community Safety Orders*, op cit, para 12.

5.75   No guidance is given by the Act as to what the word 'necessary' actually means. On one interpretation, a prohibition is not 'necessary' if the conduct can be prevented by other means. As noted earlier,[1] this is too narrow an approach. The purpose of the word 'necessary' is to limit the scope of any prohibition to the danger that the defendant poses to the public, and to prevent the imposition of prohibitions which are not directly related to that level of danger. A provision is 'necessary' if it is needed. A prohibition is needed even though there are alternative ways of achieving the protection sought, although the fact that there are other options open to the police may be relevant in determining whether an order should in fact be granted.

Whatever the restrictions imposed, they must be reasonable. The unreasonable decisions of magistrates' courts are judicially reviewable on normal judicial review grounds.[2] Again, they will need also to be proportionate. Proportionality is important in the context of the European Court of Human Rights. The Human Rights Bill 1998, when enacted and in force, will require a court to have regard to the Convention, and to the jurisprudence of the Court of Human Rights. Thus, restrictions or prohibitions which interfere with otherwise lawful acts of an individual must be proportionate to the harm that is sought to be prevented. Extreme orders, such as prohibiting a defendant from visiting property where he lives, or a particular housing estate or street, are draconian in effect and would need the highest level of justification. A court will need to consider the effect of the proposed prohibition, and balance the effect of that prohibition on the defendant against the danger of serious harm to the public. However, once the court has decided that prohibition is necessary to prevent serious harm, it is almost inconceivable that a reviewing court could conclude that it was disproportionate to take steps needed to prevent serious harm.

---

1 See para **5.45**.
2 See para **5.11**.

5.76   A right of appeal exists against the making of a sex offender order (s 4(1)). On appeal, the Crown Court may make such orders as may be necessary to give effect to its determination of the appeal, and may make such incidental or consequential orders as appear to it to be just (s 4(2)). It can therefore remit the case to the magistrates' court for re-hearing. Alternatively, it may make a sex offender order and impose such prohibitions as are necessary for the purpose of protecting persons in the local government area from further anti-social acts (or, in the case of a sex offender order, for the purpose of protecting the public from serious harm from the defendant). Such an order will be deemed to be made by the magistrates' court from which the appeal to the Crown Court came (s 4(3)).

Breach of the order

5.77   Breach of the order is a criminal offence. By s 2(8), if, without reasonable excuse,[1] a person does anything which he is prohibited from doing by an anti-social behaviour order, he shall be liable:

(a) on summary conviction, to imprisonment to a term not exceeding six months or to a fine not exceeding the statutory maximum,[1] or to both; or
(b) on conviction on indictment, to imprisonment for a term not exceeding five years or to a fine, or to both.

Clearly, if the offence is committed by a child or young person, the case will be dealt with by the youth court.

---

1 See general annotations.

5.78   The burden of proof of establishing the offence is on the prosecution. The Crown Prosecution Service will prosecute the alleged offence. The prosecution will need to establish, to the criminal standard of proof, that an order was made and its terms. This will be done by producing to the court a copy of the order. The prosecution will also need to prove that there has been a breach of the order, by the accused doing something prohibited by the order. In many cases that may be by an admission through a plea of guilty, or a formal admission under s 9 of the Criminal Justice Act 1967. If there is not a formal admission or a plea of guilty, the breach will be proved in the normal way through admissible evidence. These being criminal proceedings, the relevant rules of evidence governing hearsay evidence[1] will apply. The prosecution does not need to prove that the acts complained of create a danger of serious harm to anybody, or to the public at large. The offence is committed by a breach of the requirements of the order, subject to that breach not being with reasonable excuse.

The position in respect of reasonable excuse is unclear, and has already been discussed in the context of anti-social behaviour orders.[2] Probably, the burden of showing lack of reasonable excuse is on the prosecution.

---

1 See, in particular, Criminal Justice Act 1991, ss 23–26.
2 See para **5.52**.

5.79   If convicted, the accused may be fined or sentenced to a term of imprisonment. It is not open to a court to impose a conditional discharge (s 2(9)).

Appeals

5.80   Appeal against conviction for breach of such an order will lie in the same way as is applicable generally in criminal cases (ie to the Crown Court by way of re-hearing or divisional court by way of case stated).

Chapter 6

REDUCING DELAY IN THE CRIMINAL JUSTICE SYSTEM

Management of the prosecution process: new powers for lay CPS staff – Case management in magistrates' courts – Abolition of committal proceedings for indictable-only offences and replacement by sending for trial procedure – Reducing delay in the youth justice system – Time limits

6.1   Part III of the Act contains provisions designed to improve the speed and efficiency of the criminal justice system by improving the management of the prosecution process and the management of cases once a prosecution has been instituted, so as to bring cases promptly to court, and by requiring cases which must be tried in the Crown Court to be sent there immediately. These and a number of other provisions, including new time limits and special provisions relating to juveniles, are dealt with in this chapter.

Many of the provisions in Part III spring from the *Review of Delay in the Criminal Justice System* (the Narey Report),[1] an internal review by the Home Office published in February 1997. Others stem from the White Paper, *No More Excuses*,[2] and the consultation paper which preceded it, *Tackling Delay in the Youth Justice System*.[3]

The Act does not implement the proposal in the Narey Report that those accused of either-way offences should lose their right to insist on being tried in the Crown Court and that the final decision about where such an accused who intended to plead not guilty should be tried should rest with the magistrates.[4] However, in July 1998 the Home Secretary announced that legislation would be introduced in the 1998–1999 Parliamentary session to give effect to this proposal.[5]

---

1 Home Office.
2 *No More Excuses – A New Approach to Tackling Youth Crime in England and Wales*, Cm 3809 (1997).
3 *Tackling Delay in the Youth Justice System: A Consultation Paper* (Home Office, 1997).
4 Op cit, pp 31–35. A similar recommendation was made by the Royal Commission on Criminal Justice in its Report, Cm 2263 (1993), ch 6, paras 4–14.
5 (1998) *The Times*, 30 July.

MANAGEMENT OF THE PROSECUTION PROCESS: NEW POWERS FOR LAY CROWN PROSECUTION SERVICE STAFF

6.2   The review which led to the Narey Report[1] received a significant amount of evidence that delay in the criminal justice process was at least partly the fault of the Crown Prosecution Service ('CPS'). The main complaint levelled at the CPS was that it did not deal promptly with the prosecution of straightforward cases.[2]

The Narey Report concluded that work was being done by Crown Prosecutors which could be done by lay staff under proper direction and supervision by legally qualified staff. It made a number of recommendations, only two of which required legislation:

(1) the Director of Public Prosecutions should have power to confer on lay staff the power of a Crown Prosecutor to review files;
(2) lay staff employed by the CPS should be able to present uncontested cases in magistrates' courts.

The two recommendations are given statutory effect by s 53. The latter recommendation accorded with the recommendation of the Royal Commission on Criminal Justice in 1993 that steps should be taken to reorganise the allocation of CPS staff to cases to ensure that legally qualified staff were used only on those tasks requiring their skills by using lay staff to present uncontested cases in magistrates' courts.[3]

---

1 *Review of Delay in the Criminal Justice System: A Report* (Home Office, 1997).
2 Ibid, p 9.
3 Report, Cm 2263 (1993), ch 5, para 13.

6.3   To appreciate the effect of s 53 in practice, it is necessary to understand some other recommendations made by the Narey Report in respect of the CPS, which are to be adopted.[1] To speed up the criminal justice process, the Report recommended that there should be improved coordination between the CPS and the police and magistrates' courts so that guilty pleas can be identified at an early stage in moderately straightforward cases. The Report considered that:

> 'The culprit behind the not infrequent breakdown in police CPS co-operation is the division of the post-investigative process of preparing cases for prosecution into two distinct parts, police file preparation and CPS file review. At its most damaging this is illustrated in court by CPS prosecutors not infrequently citing police inadequacies as the reason for seeking an adjournment. Even in the best of cases, however, this two-part system seems inevitably to be combative and time-consuming. Until prosecution files can be sent electronically (still some time away) the simple process of transferring papers can take a number of days, is expensive, and seems to result in files sometimes being mislaid.'[2]

The Narey Report concluded that CPS staff, in whatever number needed to deal with straightforward guilty pleas at magistrates' courts, should have a permanent presence at police stations with administrative support units

(ASUs) in order to bring closer together the two parts of the prosecution process. The CPS staff would work with the police (who would remain responsible for the investigation of offences and for charging) on the preparation of the prosecution file and prosecute all cases where a guilty plea was anticipated. The CPS staff would continue to be managed by senior CPS staff but the effort to prepare cases for court would be a shared police–CPS undertaking.[3] Such a change will doubtless significantly reduce delay in processing straightforward cases. However, bringing about a closer relationship between the police and the CPS must raise concerns about the independence of the prosecutor and about the clear distinction between investigation and prosecution, which was a fundamental principle of the *Report of the Royal Commission on Criminal Procedure* in which the origins of the CPS are to be found.[4]

The Narey Report concluded that, if prosecutors were located within police ASUs, it should be possible for simple guilty pleas ('those triable in magistrates' courts and where evidential requirements are immediately met') to be dealt with at the first court hearing, which would usually take place the day after the accused had been charged by the police. According to the Narey scheme of things, the CPS prosecutor in the police station would review the police file and determine which of the three types of hearing would be necessary:

(1) for an accused who was expected to plead guilty, a plea hearing before a full court at which he would plead (or, in an either-way case, indicate his plea) and either be sentenced or committed to the Crown Court for sentence;

(2) for an accused who was expected to plead not guilty, an early administrative hearing conducted by the clerk to the justices, after which the next stage would be a mode of trial hearing (in an either-way case) or a pre-trial review (see paras **6.24** to **6.27**);

(3) for an accused in an indictable-only custody case, a remand hearing from which he would be remanded direct to the Crown Court (see paras **6.34** to **6.54**).

The prosecutor would notify the magistrates' court by telephone (or e-mail, if available) of the hearing needed the next day in each particular case. Courts would then be organised accordingly.[5]

Narey thought that these changes would lead to the more effective management and speedier completion of all cases. Simple guilty plea cases would be completed and, unless there were pre-sentence or other reporting requirements, sentence passed the day after charge (or, if a court was not sitting on that day, within a day or so after that). However, Narey concluded that expediting cases in this way would depend on there being a minimum amount of paperwork. The report stated that the simple guilty plea cases just referred to would normally only require the completion of a file of no more than five pieces of paper. The contents of this 'super-abbreviated file' would be:

(1) the key witness statement(s);

(2) the accused's details;

(3) a copy of the charge sheet;

(4) a short descriptive note of the police interview with the accused; and

(5) a note of previous convictions and cautions.[6]

One may question whether the 'super-abbreviated file' will contain enough for an accused's solicitor to be properly informed in advising whether the accused is guilty in law and whether there is sufficient evidence against him.

---

1 *Annual Report of the Crown Prosecution Service 1997–98* (Stationery Office, 1998).

2 *Review of Delay in the Criminal Justice System,* op cit, p 11.

3 The Glidewell Report on the CPS (*Review of the Crown Prosecution Service,* Cm 3960 (1998)), proposes the amalgamation of some of the functions of the CPS Branch and the police ASU into a single integrated unit, the Criminal Justice Unit (which it recommends should be a CPS unit with some police staff). The Criminal Justice Unit would have sole conduct of fast-track cases. The recommendation builds on but goes further than recommendations for fast-track justice in the Narey Report. The Government has broadly accepted the thrust of the Report and had initiated representations about the details of the recommendations when this book went to press. See *Annual Report of the Crown Prosecution Service 1997–98,* op cit.

4 Cmnd 8092 (1981). This distinction was endorsed as a central feature of the criminal process by the Royal Commission on Criminal Justice in its Report, Cm 2263 (1993), ch 5, para 2.

5 As to the new general duty of a custody officer who grants bail, subject to a duty to appear before a magistrates' court, to appoint a date not later than the next sitting of the court as the date for the appearance, see para **9.24**.

6 The recommendations described in this paragraph are contained in ch 3 of the Report, op cit.

6.4   Narey concluded that, without significant additional resources for the CPS, the ideas set out above would require flexibility in the use of CPS staff, and that it would be necessary and sensible to use lay staff to carry out some of the duties of a Crown Prosecutor.[1]

Under s 1(6) of the Prosecution of Offences Act 1985, every Crown Prosecutor has all the powers of the Director of Public Prosecutions as to the institution and conduct of proceedings. Crown Prosecutors are, of course, legally qualified.[2] However, without special statutory provision, the delegation by the Director of Public Prosecutions of the conduct of proceedings to staff who are not Crown Prosecutors is impermissible. This was established by the Divisional Court in 1988 when the DPP attempted to delegate the review of files to executive officers in the CPS.[3] The necessary statutory provision to achieve the Narey proposals, a new s 7A of the 1985 Act, is substituted by s 53 which came into force on 30 September 1998 (see Appendix II).

---

1 *Review of Delay in the Criminal Justice System,* op cit, p 14.

2 See annotations to s 53.

3 *DPP, ex parte Association of First Division Civil Servants* (1988) 138 NLJ 158 (DC). It was held that a scheme whereby lay CPS staff would have screened the papers relating to summary offences to see whether a prosecution was prima facie justified, and would have referred the case to a Crown Prosecutor only if they thought the proceedings might be discontinued, was ultra vires because it effectively delegated to persons other than Crown Prosecutors decisions on the conduct (including discontinuance) of proceedings.

Powers of non-legal staff in the CPS

6.5   Section s 7A(1) of the 1985 Act, which remains the same as in the original version, empowers the Director of Public Prosecutions to designate, for the purposes of the section, members of the staff of the CPS who are not Crown Prosecutors, and therefore would not normally be legally qualified.

As enacted, s 7A(2) of the 1985 Act provided that a member of the CPS staff designated under s 7A(1) had all the powers of a Crown Prosecutor in relation to any application for or relating to bail in criminal proceedings, even in the Crown Court in a bail appeal,[1] but had to exercise those powers subject to any instructions given by the Director (or a Crown Prosecutor).[1]

---

1 This is the effect of the Prosecution of Offences Act 1985, ss 1(6) and 15(3), referred to in the annotations to s 53.

6.6   Consequent on a recommendation in the Narey Report, the powers of those designated by the Director of Public Prosecutions for the purposes of s 7A of the 1985 Act have been extended substantially by the new s 7A.[1]

The new s 7A(2) provides that a person designated for the purposes of the section will have such of the following as may be specified in the designation:

(a) the powers and rights of audience of a Crown Prosecutor in relation to:
    (i)   applications for, or relating to, bail in criminal proceedings;[2]
    (ii) the conduct of criminal proceedings[2] in magistrates' courts other than trials;[3]
(b) the powers of such a Prosecutor in relation to the conduct of criminal proceedings, contested or otherwise, not falling within (a)(ii) (eg the review of cases, but not decisions as to the institution of criminal proceedings).[4]

There is one major limitation on the powers which can be specified under s 7A(2). This is that, even in the case of bail application (and this is a new legislative limit),[5] they do not extend to any proceedings for an offence triable only on indictment, such as murder, manslaughter, wounding with intent, robbery and rape, or an either-way offence, such as unlawful wounding, theft and indecent assault:

(a) for which the accused has elected to be tried by a jury;
(b) which a magistrates' court has decided is more suitable to be so tried; or
(c) in respect of which a notice of transfer has been given under s 4 of the Criminal Justice Act 1987 or s 53 of the Criminal Justice Act 1991 (s 53(5) and (6)).[2]

It can be seen that the extent of the powers of those designated may vary, depending on the terms of the designation. For example, one designated person may have all the above powers whereas another may be limited to the power in (a)(i), perhaps depending on experience. In addition, s 7A(2) contemplates that a particular designation of a power may provide for exceptions to be specified in the designation.

As previously, a person designated for the purposes of s 7A must exercise his powers under s 7A(2) subject to instructions given to him by the Director (1985 Act, new s 7A(3)). Any such instruction may be given so as to apply generally (1985 Act, new s 7A(4)). It was indicated by the then Solicitor-General in Parliament that the instructions would require certain decisions to be referred to a Crown Prosecutor, eg the decision whether to accept a plea of guilty to a lesser offence.[6]

1 See Appendix II.
2 See annotations to s 53.
3 For this purpose, a trial begins with the opening of the prosecution case after the entry of a plea of not guilty and ends with the conviction or acquittal of the accused (1985 Act, s 7A(5)).
4 The decision to institute proceedings is usually taken by the police, and the type of cases where it falls to the CPS to take that decision are of a serious variety.
5 In practice, lay staff have not dealt with bail application proceedings involving an indictable-only offence: Lord Falconer of Thoroton, Solicitor-General, HL Report, col 230.
6 HC 3rd Reading, col 234.

6.7 It is noteworthy that the extension of advocacy and criminal litigation rights were not achieved via the mechanism of the Courts and Legal Services Act 1990, under whose procedures rights of audience or litigation can be given or extended by an 'authorised body' (which the Crown Prosecution Service is not)[1] if its conduct, education and training rules are approved. Had the Government wanted to do so it could have amended the 1991 Act so as make that Act applicable. The reason why the Government chose not to use the Act's procedure was its perception that:

> 'It grinds extremely slowly and it would literally take years before any progress was made ... Resolving [the Government's] concerns should not have to await the extremely cumbersome process of the 1990 Act.'[2]

The potentiality to widen the powers of lay CPS staff is yet another resource-driven erosion of the quality of the administration of justice. Prosecutions involve a variety of matters which require a professional mind; there are obviously issues of independence of mind where any full-time prosecutor is involved but a professionally trained mind is liable to be more independent than one which is not.

1 It is understood that the CPS has applied to be an 'authorised body'.
2 Lord Falconer of Thoroton, Solicitor-General, HL Committee, col 584.

6.8 The use of 'lay presenters' in magistrates' courts by prosecuting authorities is not new. They are already used in a substantial number of cases by, for example, local authorities, Customs and Excise and the Health & Safety Executive, but the number of prosecutions conducted by these bodies falls into insignificance compared with those conducted by the CPS. 'Lay presenters' in the form of police officers were, of course, common in the days preceding the establishment of the CPS.

The limitation of CPS lay presenters to uncontested criminal proceedings does not necessarily mean that their work may be limited to formal proceedings. Uncontested criminal proceedings in the magistrates' court are not necessarily formal or straightforward. Decisions by prosecutors can require judgments about what is an acceptable plea or an acceptable basis for plea. They can involve difficult decisions with implications for the accused, for victims of crime, and for the running of the court. Unexpected points can crop up, as when the court clerk notices that someone has decided on a plea which is not appropriate. A *Newton* hearing on disputed facts relevant to sentence may have to take place; such a hearing can be complicated.[1]

It is the Government's intention that lay presenters should be used only in straightforward guilty plea cases[2] but how these are to be determined in advance has not yet been established, although an obvious and easily defined category would be a 'pleading guilty by post motoring case'.[2]

It was matters such as those referred to above that led to concerns in respect of the education and training of those CPS staff who are designated under s 7A of the 1985 Act, as to the rules of conduct which govern their work, and as to the supervision and monitoring of them. All that s 7A (and indeed the 1985 Act as a whole) says is that instructions may be given to them by the Director, which may be of general application (1985 Act, s 7A(3) and (4)). The reference in s 7A(3) to 'instructions given to him by the Director' covers, by virtue of s 1(7) of the 1985 Act, instructions given by a Crown Prosecutor.[3] Thus, CPS staff who are designated will also work under the direction of a Crown Prosecutor, as recommended by the Narey Report.

The Government gave assurances that guidance as to the deployment of lay reviewers and lay presenters (which is expressly authorised by s 7A(3) and (4)) will be given. The Government also gave assurances that designated lay staff would be suitably trained before being designated, although there would not be a requirement that they should have any formal qualification. The training programme will be a substantial one but, as the scheme is to be piloted in a few areas before general implementation, it should be manageable.[4]

In an attempt to allay fears about the operation of the new s 7A, s 7A(7),[5] inserted at the Committee stage in the House of Commons, requires details of the following for any year be set out in the Director's annual report to the Attorney-General which has to be laid before Parliament and published:

(a) the criteria applied by the Director in determining whether to designate persons under s 7A; and
(b) the training undergone by persons so designated; and
(c) any general instructions given by the Director under s 7A(4).

1 For further examples, see White *Crime, disorder – and suitable caseworkers* (1998) SJ 297.
2 Lord Falconer of Thoroton, Solicitor-General, HL 3rd Reading, col 229.
3 Ibid, HL Report, col 906, and HL 3rd Reading, col 230.
4 Ibid, HL 3rd Reading, col 231.
5 See annotations to s 53. The Director is already required to include the Code for Crown Prosecutors in the annual report (1985 Act, s 10(3)).

6.9   It is worth noting that the above changes were enacted within two months of the Glidewell Report on the CPS, a much wider-ranging review than the Narey Report, which concluded that the CPS 'has the potential to become a lively, successful and esteemed part of the criminal justice system but sadly, none of these adjectives applies to the service as a whole at present'.[1]

1 *The Review of the Crown Prosecution Service*, Cm 3960 (1998), para 26 of Summary.

CASE MANAGEMENT IN MAGISTRATES' COURTS

6.10   The importance of case management to ensure good progress by a case before trial has been recognised in the area of civil justice by the proposals in the Woolf Report, and in the Crown Court by the adoption of plea and direction hearings. The Narey Report[1] concluded that there was considerable scope for more rigorous management of a case in a magistrates' court before it went for trial, so as to reduce adjournments and lead to the earlier completion of contested cases.

The Narey Report recommended two mechanisms for case management in the magistrates' court be put on a statutory basis:

(1) pre-trial reviews so that cases are ready for trial when they come before the bench;
(2) early administrative hearings.

1 *Review of Delay in the Criminal Justice System: A Report* (Home Office, 1997), ch 5.

6.11   Pre-trial reviews ('PTRs') have become increasingly common on an informal basis in magistrates' courts. They have developed locally and there is no single model. The Narey Report concluded that:

> '[I]t is clear that, properly conducted, PTRs can make a significant contribution to case progress. They provide an opportunity for the [prosecution] to amend charges and for the defence to enter different pleas from those already indicated; they allow the issues in contention between the parties to be identified; and they clarify which witnesses need to attend. ...
>
> PTRs are also useful in estimating the amount of court time required to hear contested cases, allowing the time allocated to be used more productively, and making other practical arrangements for the trial.'[1]

The problem experienced in operating the various forms of PTR was that, because of their informal nature, some aspects of case management were beyond the powers of the clerks operating them and depended entirely on the co-operation of the parties. Consequently, the Narey Report recommended that the pre-trial review be put on a statutory basis by providing clerks with the necessary additional powers.

1 Op cit, p 26.

6.12 In some magistrates' courts early administrative hearings ('EAHs'), conducted by clerks, have been introduced so that the accused can hear what the court expects from him in terms of obtaining legal representation and supplying evidence to enable the court to consider a legal aid application. The clerk also explains to the defendant the nature of the forthcoming proceedings and the implications of the charge against him. In some cases this prompts a guilty plea; where the case is contested, experience has shown that overcoming the inertia of the accused in applying for legal aid helps to reduce the number of adjournments.[1]

The magistrates' court at Bexley is a pioneer in this field. It claims that the introduction of EAHs in 1993 has reduced from 55 per cent to less than 10 per cent the proportion of cases failing to make progress at first appearance because the defendant needs, but has not obtained, legal advice.[1] The Bexley hearings operate as follows:

> 'Defendants are bailed to appear, the first Tuesday or Thursday after arrest, at a hearing conducted by the Clerk to the Justices, the Deputy Clerk or a senior clerk with delegated powers. An independent volunteer helps the defendant to complete the legal aid application forms and to select a solicitor from a list of local firms. The clerk explains to the defendant the procedures of the court and the charges he is facing, and ascertains whether the defendant appears to be eligible for legal aid. If so, the volunteer makes a telephone appointment with the solicitor on the defendant's behalf, and the clerk sets as the date of the first hearing a day on which the solicitor is due to be in court (this link with the listing process is important).'[1]

Uncertainty over the extent of powers for the police to bail a defendant to appear at an EAH, or for the clerk to extend that bail to the first substantive appearance, has discouraged many courts from adopting EAHs. The Narey Report concluded that there was a strong case for legislating so as to put them on to a proper footing.

1 *Review of Delay in the Criminal Justice System,* op cit, p 28.

6.13 The Narey Report[1] also recommended that, as with the existing informal arrangements, both mechanisms should be operated by justices' clerks. Its reason was that a bench of three lay justices was not so well suited for a case management role; the need for agreement between members of the bench was not conducive to decisive action, and there was frequently no continuity, so that the next time the case came to court it would probably be before a differently constituted bench which might not be aware of the opinions and attitudes of the earlier bench. Narey admitted that the first of these difficulties could be overcome, and the second possibly reduced, by allowing hearings concerned with case management to be conducted by a single justice. However, it came down against this on the ground that lay justices did not generally have the detailed background knowledge of law procedure, or the confidence, which enabled stipendiary magistrates or professionally qualified clerks to take 'the type of robust decision necessary to drive the case forward'.[2]

Narey rejected the suggestion that the way forward lay in the total or very substantial replacement of the lay magistracy by stipendiaries, not for financial reasons but because of the widespread and firmly held belief that the lay magistracy is intrinsic to our legal system.

The Report concluded that justices' clerks (and other senior staff to whom they may delegate their powers) should be given the responsibility for managing cases in the magistrates' courts.

1 *Review of Delay in the Criminal Justice System*, op cit, pp 25–26.
2 Ibid, p 25.

6.14 Sections 49 and 50 make the necessary legislative changes to enable the introduction of the two new case management mechanisms proposed by the Narey Report. Although no doubt they will normally be operated by justices' clerks and their assistants, the sections also give case management powers to a single justice and then permit them to be extended with some derogations to justices' clerks. This is consistent with the situation under the Justices' Clerks Rules 1970,[1] which specify that certain functions exercisable by a single justice may be exercised by a justices' clerk or his assistant.

Section 49 is being piloted for a six-month period which commenced on 30 September 1998 in the following areas:

(a) the petty sessions areas of Bromley; Croydon; and Sutton.
(b) the petty sessional divisions of Aberconwy; Arfon; Blackburn, Darwen and Ribble Valley; Burnley and Pendle; Colwyn; Corby; Daventry; Dyffryn Clwyd; Eifionydd and Pwllheli; Gateshead; Kettering; Meirionnydd; New-castle-under-Lyme and Pirehill North; Newcastle-upon-Tyne; Northampton; Rhuddlan; Staffordshire Moorlands; Stoke-on-Trent; Towcester; Wellingborough; and Yns Mon/Angelsey.[2]

Section 50 came into force on 30 September 1998: see Appendix II.

1 SI 1970/ 231.
2 See Appendix II; also see HC Deb, vol 313, cols WA 219–220.

Pre-trial review

Pre-trial review: powers of magistrates' courts exercisable by single justice

6.15   Unless an enactment specifically provides to the contrary, a magistrates' court must normally consist of at least two justices.[1] This rule does not apply, of course, to stipendiary magistrates who may, and normally do, sit alone unless there is an express provision to the contrary.[2]

Committal proceedings, ie proceedings with a view to transferring the matter to the Crown Court for trial, may be conducted by a single lay justice, although normally two or three sit in such proceedings.[3]

---

1 Magistrates' Courts Act 1980, s 121.
2 Justices of the Peace Act 1997, s 15(1).
3 Magistrates' Courts Act 1980, s 4(1).

6.16   In order to enhance the ability of magistrates' courts to manage business, including pre-trial reviews, efficiently and expeditiously, s 49(1) provides that a number of powers of a magistrates' court may be exercised by any single (lay) justice of the peace for that area.[1]

The powers which are exercisable by a single justice under s 49 are:

(a) to extend bail or to impose or vary conditions of bail;

(b) to mark an information as withdrawn;

(c) to dismiss an information, or to discharge an accused in respect of an information, where no evidence is offered by the prosecution;

(d) to make an order for the payment of defence costs out of central funds;[2]

(e) to request a pre-sentence report following a plea of guilty and, for that purpose, to give an indication of the seriousness of the offence;[3]

(f) to request a medical report and, for that purpose, to remand the accused in custody or on bail;

(g) to remit an offender to another court (ie another magistrates' court) for sentence;

(h) where a person has been granted police bail to appear at a magistrates' court, to appoint an earlier time for his appearance;

(i) to extend, with the consent of the accused, a custody time limit or an overall time limit;

(j) where a case is to be tried on indictment, to grant representation under Part V of the Legal Aid Act 1988 for purposes of the proceedings in the Crown Court;

(k) where an accused has been convicted of an offence, to order him to produce his driving licence;

(l) to give a direction prohibiting the publication of matters disclosed or exempted from disclosure in court;

(m) to give, vary or revoke directions for the conduct of a trial, including directions as to the following matters, namely –

(i)   the timetable for the proceedings;

(ii) the attendance of the parties;

(iii) the service of documents (including summaries of any legal arguments relied on by the parties);

(iv) the manner in which evidence is to be given;[4] and

(n) to give, vary or revoke orders for the separate or joint trials in the case of two or more accused or two or more informations.

It will be noted that some of these functions, although derived from the Narey Report's recommendations, are not pre-trial functions. A notable absentee from the list of pre-trial functions is the assessment of the accused's bail or custody status. This remains reserved to a bench of justices.

---

1 See annotations to s 49.
2 This is a reference not to payment of costs after a trial (where the only tribunal able to deal with the matter is the bench that acquitted the accused, as reasons may have emerged during the trial that would make the award inappropriate), but to payment of costs at an interlocutory hearing: Mike O'Brien, MP, Parliamentary Under-Secretary, HC Committee, col 417.
3 The indication given to the Probation Service will not be binding.
4 This includes directions relating to the giving of evidence behind screens or by live television link or by video-recording.

Pre-trial review: powers of magistrates' courts exercisable by a justices' clerk

6.17   Section 45(1) of the Justices of the Peace Act 1997, a consolidating Act, provides that rules made in accordance with s 144 of the Magistrates' Courts Act 1980[1] may make provision enabling things authorised to be done by, to or before a single justice of the peace to be done instead by, to or before a justices' clerk, ie a clerk to the justices for a petty sessions area. Currently, only a barrister or solicitor of five years' standing, or a barrister or solicitor with five years' service as an assistant to a justices' clerk, is eligible to be appointed for the first time as a justices' clerk.[2]

Section 45(2) of the 1997 Act provides that such rules may also make provision enabling things authorised to be done by, to or before a justices' clerk (whether by virtue of s 45(1) or otherwise) to be done instead by, to or before a person appointed by a magistrates' courts committee to assist him; that person is not required to be legally qualified. Save to the extent that the rules may enable an assistant to exercise a power exercisable by a justices' clerk, any judicial power so exercisable may not be delegated to an assistant.[3]

---

1 See s 49 and annotations thereto.
2 Justices of the Peace Act 1997, s 43.
3 *Gateshead JJ, ex parte Tesco Stores Ltd* [1981] QB 470, [1981] 1 All ER 1027 (DC); *Manchester Stipendiary Magistrate, ex parte Hill* [1983] 1 AC 328, sub nom *Hill v Anderton* [1982] 2 All ER 963 (HL).

6.18   The Justices' Clerks Rules 1970,[1] made under the Justices of the Peace Act 1968, a precursor of the 1997 Act, provide that a number of functions of a single justice specified in Part I of the Rules may be exercised by a justices' clerk or a person appointed by a magistrates' courts committee to assist him.

---

1 SI 1970/231, rr 2 and 4.

6.19   Section 49(2) of the new Act gives further impetus to the power to make rules in respect of the exercise by a justices' clerk of a power exercisable by a single justice of the peace.

It provides that rules under s 144(1) of the 1980 Act may, subject to what is said below, provide that any of the things which, by virtue of s 49(1) of the new Act, are authorised to be done by a single justice for any area may, subject to any specified restrictions or conditions, be done by a justices' clerk for that petty sessions area (s 49(2)(a)). As indicated in para **6.14**, it is the Government's intention that, initially on a pilot basis, clerks should be authorised in some areas to exercise these powers.[1] For this reason, in particular, s 49(2)(b) provides that rules of the present type may make different provision for different areas. The 'piloted' rules will then be refined, if and as necessary, before being extended to magistrates in general.[2]

Unlike s 49(1), the original version of s 49(2) caused a fair amount of concern in the House of Lords on the ground that it was vital to preserve a clear and categorical distinction between the role of the justice as judicial decision maker and the role of the justices' clerk as the professional, legal adviser and, on occasion, administrator.[3]

---

1 Lord Williams of Mostyn, Parliamentary Under-Secretary, Home Office, HL 2nd Reading, col 535.
2 Lord Falconer of Thoroton, Solicitor-General, HL 2nd Reading, col 597. Section 49 came into force on 1 August 1998 for the purposes of making the rules mentioned in this paragraph.
3 Lord Bingham of Cornhill, HL 2nd Reading, col 561; Baroness Anelay of St Johns, HL Committee, col 372.

6.20   As a result of this concern, s 49(3) provides that there are some things falling within the purview of the powers listed in s 49(1) which the rules may not authorise a justices' clerk to do. They are all matters which involve significant discretionary decisions. The rules may not authorise a justices' clerk:

(a) without the consent of the prosecutor and the accused, to extend bail on conditions other than those (if any) previously imposed, or to impose or vary conditions of bail;
(b) to give an indication of the seriousness of an offence for the purposes of a pre-sentence report;
(c) to remand the accused in custody for the purposes of a medical report or, without the consent of the prosecutor and the accused, to remand the accused on bail for those purposes on conditions other than those (if any) previously imposed;
(d) to give a direction prohibiting the publication of matters disclosed or exempted from disclosure in court; or
(e) without the consent of the parties, to give, vary or revoke orders for separate or joint trials in the case of two or more accused or two or more informations.

6.21   There is no express provision for any powers exercisable under regulations relating to the matters covered by s 49 to be exercised by any assistant to the justices' clerk. However, it may be that, under the rules which are to be made, justices' clerks may delegate their powers to assistants or certain types of assistants as in the case of the functions currently specified in the Justices' Clerks Rules 1970.[1] The Act does not itself prescribe any minimum level of qualification or experience.

---

1 Lord Williams of Mostyn, Parliamentary Under-Secretary, Home Office, HL Report, cols 902–903.

6.22　　Rules made under s 144 of the Magistrates' Courts Act 1980 are made by the Lord Chancellor. They must be made by statutory instrument;[1] they are subject to annulment by a resolution of either House of Parliament.[2] By s 144(1) of the 1980 Act, the Lord Chancellor is empowered to make rules 'on the advice of or after consultation with' the Magistrates' Courts Rules Committee. On the other hand, there is not normally a requirement for consultation of justices and justices' clerks in respect of rules made under s 144. However, such consultation is required in respect of rules of the type mentioned in s 49(2) of the new Act. Section 49(4) requires the Lord Chancellor, before making any such rules in relation to any petty sessions area to consult justices of the peace and justices' clerks for that area. This provision, which will involve consultation before and after 'piloting regulations', is intended to ensure that the piloting and the lessons to be learnt from it are effective.[3] We dealt in para **3.7** with what consultation requires. A failure by the Lord Chancellor to consult (at all or properly) would be likely to lead a court to hold on an application of a person entitled to be committed that there had been a breach of a mandatory procedural requirement of s 49(4), rendering the rules invalid and of no effect.[4] On the other hand, if the Lord Chancellor failed to heed the views put forward during proper consultation, this would not in itself affect the validity of the rules. The Lord Chancellor's statutory duty is to consult and to be receptive to what consultatees say. It is not a duty to be dictated to by them. Serious views carefully advanced by consultees must not simply be ignored, but the weight to be given to them, balanced against all the other relevant factors, is for the Lord Chancellor to decide. However, if his conclusions are so unreasonable that no reasonable Lord Chancellor could ever have come to them, the courts could interfere under the *Wednesbury* principle[5] on an application for judicial review.

---

1 See annotations to s 114.

2 Magistrates' Courts Act 1980, s 144(4).

3 Mike O'Brien, MP, Parliamentary Under-Secretary, Home Office, HC Committee, col 415.

4 *Agricultural, Horticultural and Forestry Industry Training Board v Aylesbury Mushrooms Ltd* [1972] 1 All ER 200 (DC). Failure to consult in breach of a duty to do so will not necessarily lead a court to hold that the provision in question is invalid and of no effect. If the court concludes that there is a broad public interest in not upsetting the provision, in order, for example, to avoid consequential uncertainty, it may simply grant a declaration that the provision-maker has failed to comply with the duty to consult: see *Secretary of State for Social Services, ex parte Association of Metropolitan Authorities* [1986] 1 All ER 164 (DC).

5 *Associated Provincial Picture Houses Ltd v Wednesbury Corpn* [1948] 1 KB 223, [1947] 2 All ER 680 (CA).

Miscellaneous comments about pre-trial reviews

6.23   Pre-trial reviews will not be obligatory in magistrates' courts. It is anticipated that they will be used before trial in the majority of cases, but there may be cases where a pre-trial review would contribute nothing (as where it was possible to resolve preliminary issues on paper). It will be for the relevant person or persons at the court to decide whether a pre-trial review should take place in a particular case.

Save to the extent that one already exists, no right of appeal is given against a decision taken at a pre-trial review. Such a decision is, however, subject to judicial review.

Early administrative hearings (EAHs)

6.24   An accused charged with a straightforward summary or either-way offence[1] to which he is expected to plead guilty is intended, as a result of the changes relating to the CPS referred to in para **6.3**, to appear before magistrates the next day for sentencing or for committal for sentence. An accused thought likely to contest the charge will appear instead at an EAH, which have been put on a statutory footing by s 50, the day after charge or very soon afterwards. The purpose of the EAH is to enable arrangements to be made for the accused to obtain legal aid and to consult a legal adviser. At the EAH the accused will be remanded to a pre-trial review or to a mode of trial hearing, as appropriate. If an accused springs a surprise by indicating at the EAH that he intends to plead guilty, he can appear at a sentencing court that day or the next day.[2]

_____

1 See general annotations.
2 *Review of Delay in the Criminal Justice System*, op cit, p 28.

_____

6.25   Section 50 provides that, where a person charged with an offence at a police station appears or is brought before a magistrates' court for the first time in relation to the charge, that court may consist of a single justice of the peace (s 50(1)) or, as seems more likely, a justices' clerk (s 50(4)).

There is one exception. Section 50 does not apply where the accused falls to be dealt with under s 51, which provides new procedures where an offence triable only on indictment is involved. These procedures and their application are dealt with in paras **6.34** to **6.54**.

6.26   Section 50(2) provides that at a hearing conducted by a single justice under s 50:

(a) the accused must be asked whether he wishes to receive legal aid (ie representation under Part V of the Legal Aid Act 1988 (s 50(5))); and
(b) if he indicates that he does, his eligibility for it must be determined; and

(c) if it is determined that he is eligible for it, the necessary arrangements or grant must be made for him to obtain it.

If legal aid cannot be determined at the early administrative hearing because the accused may not have provided evidence of his income, it is anticipated that that evidence will be dealt with by the administrative procedure in the court, and that he should have seen a lawyer, before the next court appearance.[1]

The single justice may also exercise any other power which he possesses by virtue of s 49 or any other legislation (s 50(3)(a)). On adjourning the hearing, the single justice may remand the accused in custody or on bail for the first substantive appearance (s 50(3)(b)).

---

1 Mike O'Brien, MP, Parliamentary Under-Secretary, Home Office, HC Committee, col 418.

6.27   As already indicated, s 50 applies to a justices' clerk (ie the clerk to the justices for a petty sessions area)[1] as it applies in relation to a single justice (s 50(4)). The functions at a hearing would seem to be judicial, not administrative, despite the marginal note, and are therefore not delegable by a justices' clerk.[2] The Justices' Clerks Rules 1970 are to be amended[3] so as to permit a justices' clerk to delegate to one of the clerks the power to conduct an EAH,[4] as intended by the Narey Report. The relatively small number of justices' clerks means that such an amendment is necessary if members of the court staff are to carry out the bulk of EAH work. A hearing conducted under s 50 by a justices' clerk will involve the same procedure under s 50(2) as in the case of a single justice (s 50(4)). The clerk may exercise any power which he has by virtue of the Justices' Clerks Rules 1970 or under rules made under s 49 (s 50(3)(a) and (4)). However, although s 50(3)(b) (remanding the accused in custody or on bail on adjournment) applies to a justices' clerk (s 50(4)), nothing in it authorises a justices' clerk to remand the accused in custody or, without the consent of the prosecutor and the accused, to remand the accused on bail on conditions other than those (if any) previously imposed (ibid). The reason for this limitation is the same as other limitations on justices' clerks referred to in respect of s 49.

---

1 Section 49(5).
2 See para **6.17**.
3 This is implied in a somewhat obscure statement by Mike O'Brien, MP, Parliamentary Under-Secretary, Home Office, HC Committee, col 414.
4 The Justices of the Peace Act 1997, s 45(2), provides that rules made under the Magistrates' Courts Act 1980, s 144, may make provision enabling things to be done by, to or before a justices' clerk to be done instead by, to or before a person appointed by a magistrates' court committee to assist him. This has already been done, of course, in respect of the functions listed in Sch 1 to the Justices' Clerks Rules 1970, SI 1970/231.

6.28   Schedule 8, para 62, inserts a new section, s 47A, into the Police and Criminal Evidence Act 1984. This provides that, where a person has been charged with an offence at a police station, any requirement under Part IV of PACE for the person to appear or be brought before a magistrates' court is to be taken to be satisfied if the person appears or is brought before the clerk to the justices[1] for a petty sessional area in order for the clerk to conduct an early administrative hearing under s 50 of the new Act.

---

1 See note 4 to para **6.27**.

ABOLITION OF COMMITTAL PROCEEDINGS FOR INDICTABLE-ONLY OFFENCES

Background

6.29   In modern times, committal proceedings have been the subject of considerable scrutiny. Fundamental change was made by the Criminal Justice Act 1967, permitting committal without consideration of the evidence.[1] Subsequently, the effectiveness of committal proceedings as a filter to prevent weak cases being committed for trial has been doubted by two Royal Commissions in 1981 and in 1993, both of which recommended the abolition of such proceedings. In 1981 the Royal Commission on Criminal Procedure[2] recommended the replacement of committal proceedings by a new procedure to be known as an 'application for discharge'. Under this proposal the defence would have had the option of a hearing before magistrates at which to make a submission of no case to answer after the prosecution case had been disclosed in writing. No action was taken to implement that recommendation at that time, but in 1986 the Roskill Committee[3] recommended an interim procedural reform in respect of serious fraud cases, until such time as action might be taken by the Government to implement the Royal Commission's recommendations. The resulting changes were introduced by the Criminal Justice Act 1987.

---

1 Re-enacted by s 6(2) of the Magistrates' Courts Act 1980.
2 Cmnd 8092 (1981), paras 8.24–8.31.
3 *Report of the Fraud Trials Committee* (HMSO, 1986).

6.30   More recently, the Royal Commission on Criminal Justice[1] recommended that, in place of committal proceedings, an accused should have the opportunity to make a submission before trial of no case to answer to a stipendiary magistrate after a mode of trial decision in favour of trial in the Crown Court in the case of an either-way offence, or to the Crown Court in the case of an offence triable only on indictment. This submission would be considered on the papers, although the accused would be able to advance oral arguments in support and the prosecution would be able to reply. Witnesses would not be called.

---

1 Cm 2263 (1993), ch 6, paras 20–32.

6.31   Section 44 of the Criminal Justice and Public Order Act 1994 abolished committal proceedings. Section 44 of and Sch 4 to the 1994 Act replaced them with provisions for a system of transfer for trial, which had some similarity with the recommendations of the Royal Commission on Criminal Justice. Under this system, a person charged before a magistrates' court with an indictable offence, in relation to whom the prosecution had served a notice of the prosecution case on the magistrates' court, would have been transferred by the magistrates' court to the Crown Court for trial, unless he had made a successful application for dismissal. Unless the case was one of complexity or difficulty (where the court could grant an oral hearing), an application by a legally represented accused could only be made in writing.

It had been intended that the new provisions would come into effect in 1995, but their implementation date was postponed on three occasions and they were repealed by the Criminal Procedure and Investigations Act 1996, ss 44 and 49.[1]

---

1 1996 Act, ss 44(2) and 80 and Sch 5.

6.32   Instead of the transfer scheme described above, the 1996 Act sought to achieve the objectives of improved efficiency and protection of witnesses by modifying the form of committal proceedings.[1] In essence, committal proceedings involving the receipt of oral evidence, evidence from the defence and cross-examination of witnesses have been abolished. The evidence at a contested committal is limited to documentary evidence and exhibits tendered by the prosecution. However, the magistrates are able to consider any representations by the defence or the prosecution, in addition to the prosecution evidence, to help them reach their decision on whether to commit for trial or to discharge the accused.

---

1 Schedule 1 to the 1996 Act amended the provisions in the Magistrates' Courts Act 1980
   relating to committal proceedings.

6.33   The Narey Report[1] focused on committal proceedings as a cause of delay in the criminal justice system. It reported that indictable offences on average spent 87 days in a magistrates' court before committal for trial and recommended the adoption of the Royal Commission on Criminal Justice's recommendation in respect of offences triable only on indictment. This recommendation is implemented by the new Act, with some modifications, as we now explain.

---

1 *Review of Delay in the Criminal Justice System*, op cit, pp 35–37.

THE SENDING FOR TRIAL PROCEDURE UNDER SECTION 51

6.34   Sections 51 and 52 provide a new procedure – the sending for trial procedure – in place of committal proceedings where an offence triable (in the case of an adult) only on indictment, hereafter indictable-only offence, is involved. Schedule 3 to the Act makes further, detailed provisions which apply to the procedure (s 52(6)). The new provisions are to be piloted before being brought into general effect. It is understood that the pilot will commence on 4 January 1999 in the same areas as the piloting of s 49. Those areas are set out in para **6.14**.[2]

The new procedure generally applies only to an accused who is an adult (ie someone aged[2] 18 or over) (s 51(12)) or a corporation (s 51(12)). Hereafter 'adult' includes 'corporation'. The only time when the new procedure applies to a juvenile is where a juvenile is a co-accused of an adult, as explained below; otherwise, the committal for trial procedure will continue to apply to a juvenile charged with an indictable-only offence which in the case of a juvenile must be tried on indictment (offences of homicide) or which the magistrates decide should be so tried in view of its gravity.[3]

The new procedure will also operate to the exclusion of the provisions for a case to be transferred to the Crown Court by a notice of transfer under s 4 of the Criminal Justice Act 1987 (cases of serious or complex fraud) or s 53 of the Criminal Justice Act 1991 (violent or sexual offences against children).[4] Those provisions will now apply only where the only indictable offence(s) with which the adult accused is charged is (or are) an either-way one(s).

The Administration of Justice (Miscellaneous Provisions) Act 1933, s 2(2) which forbids the preferring of a bill of indictment except in specified cases is amended by Sch 8, para 5(1)(a) so as to add to these cases the case where the person charged has been sent for trial under s 51. The Indictments (Procedure) Rules 1971[5] will require amendment in consequence of the new procedure.

---

1 See Appendix II. The provisions will apply in any piloting area for the purposes of sending a person for trial under s 51 from that area. The power to make regulations and rules under Sch 3, paras 1 and 2(7) respectively, referred to in paras **6.47** and **6.48**, came into force on 30 September 1998.

2 See general annotations.

3 Magistrates' Courts Act 1980, s 24(1).

4 By Sch 8, paras 65 and 93, the respective notice of transfer provisions do not apply in any case to which s 51 applies.

5 SI 1971/2084.

6.35   As will be seen, the new provisions undoubtedly have the potential to speed up the criminal process without prejudicing justice to the accused. There is, however, the risk that the paperwork will not be sorted out before the case reaches the Crown Court. One role performed by a magistrates' court under the committal for trial system is to ensure that the paperwork served on the accused is sorted out as far as possible before the case reaches committal stage. This means that the Crown Court is able to get on with the case when it reaches it. The case paper management is transferred to the Crown Court in respect of indictable-only offences – this is the effect of s 51. The plea and directions hearing will take place much earlier in the life of the case involving an indictable-only offence. An earlier PDH will provide a clear point at which a plea of guilty might attract the maximum sentence discount.[1] Crown Court judges will have to become case managers, reviewing the progress of case papers and readiness for trial far more than is currently the case.[2] If, as is likely, the burden of this management falls on resident judges and senior nominated judges at the Crown Court centres, they will have less time (they are already heavily involved in plea and directions hearings) to preside over trials. Unless more judges are appointed there is a risk that delay in the criminal justice system will simply be passed down the process.

---

1 This point was made in the *Review of Delay in the Criminal Justice System*, op cit, p 36.
2 This point was made by Baroness Anelay of St Johns, HL 2nd Reading, cols 592–593.

Sending for trial

6.36   Under the new procedure, a person charged with an indictable-only offence must still appear or be brought before a magistrates' court.

6.37   Section 51(1) provides that, where an adult appears or is brought before a magistrates' court charged with an indictable-only offence, the court *must* send him forthwith to the Crown Court for trial:

(a) for that offence; and
(b) for any either-way[1] or summary offence[2] with which he is charged which fulfils the 'requisite conditions'.

The 'requisite conditions' are that:

(i)   the either-way or summary offence appears to the court to be related to the indictable-only offence; and
(ii) in the case of a summary offence, it is punishable with imprisonment or involves obligatory or discretionary disqualification from driving (s 51(11)).

An either-way offence is related to an indictable-only offence if the charge for the either-way offence could be joined in the same indictment as the charge for the indictable-only offence (s 51(12)(c)). By r 9 of the Indictment Rules 1971,[3] the test for joining charges in the same indictment is that they must be founded on the same facts, or form or be part of a series of offences of the same or a similar character.[4] On the other hand, a summary offence is related to an indictable-only offence if it arises out of circumstances which are the same as or connected with those giving rise to the indictable-only offence (s 51(12)(d)).

If a person is sent for trial for a summary offence, the trial of the information charging it is treated as having been adjourned sine die (s 51(9)).

---

1 'Either-way offence' means an offence which, if committed by an adult, is triable either on
  indictment or summarily (s 51(12)(b)).
2 See general annotations.
3 SI 1971/1253.
4 See, further, *Archbold: Criminal Pleading, Evidence and Practice* (1998 edn), paras 1-166–1-171.

6.38   Section 51(2) deals with the situation where an adult who has been
sent for trial under s 51(1) subsequently appears before or is brought before a
magistrates' court charged with an either-way offence or summary offence
which fulfils the 'requisite conditions' described above. Section 51(2) provides
that the magistrates' court *may* send the accused forthwith to the Crown Court
for trial for the either-way or summary offence.

In deciding whether to exercise this discretion the court will be able to take into
consideration the stage which the indictable-only case has reached. The
appearance on the related charge may follow soon after that for the
indictable-only one, in which instance it may well be appropriate for that case to
be sent forward too so that they can be dealt with together. If, on the other
hand, the indictable-only case had already progressed a long way, it is possible
that sending the related charge up to the Crown Court to join it would lead to
extra delay, in which case the discretion would be more likely to be exercised
against sending it up to the Crown Court.

Adult co-accused
6.39   Section 51(3) requires a magistrates' court in some cases, and permits
it in others, to send to the Crown Court for trial an adult who has only been
charged with an either-way offence but who is co-accused of that offence with
someone charged with an indictable-only offence.

Section 51(3) provides that, where:

(a) the court sends an adult for trial under s 51(1);
(b) another adult appears or is brought before the court on the same or a
     subsequent occasion charged *jointly* with him with an either-way offence;
     and
(c) that offence appears to the court to be related to[1] the indictable-only
     offence,

the court must where it is the same occasion, and may where it is a subsequent
occasion, send the other adult forthwith to the Crown Court for trial for the
either-way offence.

Section 51(3) does not permit a magistrates' court to send for trial an adult
co-accused who is charged only with a summary offence. On the other hand,
s 51(4) requires a magistrates' court which sends an adult for trial under
s 51(3) at the same time to send him to the Crown Court for trial for any
summary offence which fulfils the 'requisite conditions', viz:

(a) that that offence appears to the court to be related to[1] the indictable-only
     offence; and

(b) it is punishable with imprisonment or involves obligatory or discretionary disqualification from driving (s 51(11)).

In such a case, the trial of the information charging the summary offence is treated as having been adjourned sine die (s 51(9)).[2]

Likewise, s 51(4) requires a magistrates' court which sends an adult co-accused for trial under s 51(3) also to send him for trial for any either-way offence for which he is *not jointly charged* with the adult sent for trial under s 51(1) which appears to be related to[1] the indictable-only offence.

---

1 In respect of 'related to', see para **6.37**.
2 See annotations to s 51.

Juvenile co-accused

6.40   Although a magistrates' court cannot send a child[1] or young person[1] who is not jointly charged with an adult forthwith for trial under the above provisions, it can do so where the child or young person is jointly charged with an adult for an indictable offence (whether it is triable only on indictment or triable either way)[2] for which the adult is sent for trial.

Section 51(5) is the relevant provision. It provides that, where:

(a) the court sends an adult for trial under s 51(1) or (3) above; and
(b) a child or young person appears or is brought before the court on the same or a subsequent occasion charged jointly with the adult with an indictable offence for which the adult is sent for trial,

the court must, if it considers it necessary in the interests of justice to do so, send the child or young person forthwith to the Crown Court for trial for the indictable offence.

In relation to young people, this merely brings the section into line with the corresponding provisions relating to committal for trial in s 24(1) of the Magistrates' Courts Act 1980. In place of a simple discretion to send a young person to the Crown Court to be tried jointly with an adult on an indictable-only charge, the court is required to send him where it is necessary in the interests of justice. That is the same test as under the Magistrates' Courts Act 1980.

Where a court sends a child or young person for trial under s 51(5), it *may* at the same time send him to the Crown Court for trial for any either-way or summary offence with which he is charged which fulfils the 'requisite conditions' (s 51(6)), viz:

(a) that that offence appears to the court to be related to[3] the indictable-only offence; and
(b) in the case of a summary offence, it is punishable with imprisonment or involves obligatory or discretionary disqualification from driving (s 51(11)).

There is an obvious gap in all this. If juvenile X appears jointly charged with adult Y with robbery, an indictable-only offence, and charged on his own account only with a related wounding with intent, another indictable-only offence, and a related theft, an either-way offence, he can be sent for trial under the above provisions in respect of the robbery and the theft but not in respect of the wounding with intent because he is not charged jointly with Y for that offence and it is not an either-way or summary offence.

If a juvenile is sent for trial for a summary offence, the trial of the information charging it is treated as having been adjourned sine die (s 51(9)).

---

1 A 'child' means a person under 14; 'young person' means someone who has obtained the age of 14 and is under 18 (s 117(1)).
2 See general annotations.
3 In respect of 'related to', see para **6.37**.

What is a summary offence for the purpose of paras 6.36 to 6.40?

6.41   Normally, the answer is provided by applying the standard interpretation in s 5 of and Sch 1 to the Interpretation Act 1978, viz an offence which, if committed by an adult, is triable summarily only.

Special provision is, however, made by the Act to deal with those either-way offences listed in Sch 2 to the Magistrates' Courts Act 1980 which are triable only summarily where the value of the damage done or of the property destroyed is less than the 'relevant sum' (currently £5,000).

At present the list of offences in Sch 2 (hereafter the 'specified offences') is as follows:

(a) offences under the Criminal Damage Act 1971 (destroying or damaging property), excluding any damage committed by destroying or damaging property by fire;

(b) aiding, abetting, counselling or procuring the commission of any offence in (a); or attempting to commit, or inciting another to commit, any such offence; and

(c) offences under s 12A of the Theft Act 1968 (aggravated vehicle-taking) where only damage to the vehicle or other property is alleged as the aggravating feature.

Section 52(3) provides that, for the purposes of s 51, a magistrates' court is to treat a 'specified offence' as an indictable offence (ie triable on indictment, as opposed to triable only on indictment) *unless it is clear to the court, having regard to any representations made by the prosecutor or the accused,*[1] *that the value involved does not exceed the relevant sum.* In other words, for the purposes of s 51, it will be presumed by a magistrates' court that a 'specified offence' in respect of which a person appears or is brought before it is an either-way offence, unless it is 'clear' that the value involved does not exceed the relevant sum.

The point is important because the test of whether an either-way offence is 'related to' an indictable-only offence is different from the test of whether a summary offence is so related (see para **6.37**).

---

1 By analogy with similar provisions under the 1980 Act, s 22, the court is not obliged to hear representations: *Canterbury and St Augustine's JJ, ex parte Klisiak* [1982] QB 398, [1981] 2 All ER 129 at 137–138.

Legal aid

6.42   Schedule 8, para 67, amends ss 20 and 21 of the Legal Aid Act 1988 with respect to the grant and availability of representation under Part V of that Act. Under a 'new' s 20(4)(aa), a magistrates' court which sends a person for trial under s 51 of the new Act is competent to grant such representation as respects the proceedings before the Crown Court (Sch 8, para 67(1)), just as (for example) it is on committing a person for trial or sentence. In addition, under a 'new' s 20(5A), a magistrates' court which has a duty (or power) to send a person for trial under s 51 of the new Act is also competent to grant representation (the so-called 'through legal aid order'), before discharging that duty (or deciding to exercise that power), as respects any proceedings before the Crown Court on his trial (Sch 8, para 67(2)), just as a magistrates' court can when sitting as examining justices.

The provisions of s 21(3)(a) of the Legal Aid Act 1988 which provide that a person committed for trial on a charge of murder *must* be granted representation for his trial are extended to those sent for trial on such a charge under s 51 of the new Act (Sch 8, para 67(3)), as is the provision in s 21(4) of the 1988 Act that it is for the magistrates' courts committing a person for trial on a murder charge, and not for the Crown Court, to make the grant of representation (Sch 8, para 67(4)).

Sending to Crown Court in custody or on bail

6.43   By s 52(1), where a magistrates' court sends a person for trial under s 51, it may send him:

'(a) in custody, that is to say, by committing him to custody there to be safely kept until delivered in due course of law; or
(b) on bail in accordance with the Bail Act 1976, that is to say, by directing him to appear before the Crown Court for trial.'

This provision is subject to s 4 of the Bail Act 1976 (general right of bail to accused, except as provided by Sch 1 to that Act),[1] s 41 of the Magistrates' Courts Act 1980 (restriction on grant of bail in treason cases),[1] regulations relating to custody time limits under s 22 of the Prosecution of Offences Act 1985,[1] and s 25 of the Criminal Justice and Public Order Act 1994 (presumption against bail for accused charged with homicide or rape after previous conviction of such offences).[2]

Where an accused's release on bail is conditional on his providing one or more sureties, and the court is unable to release him because no surety or no suitable surety is then available, the court must commit the accused to custody in the meantime pending the recognizance(s) of the surety or sureties being entered into (s 52(2)).

---

1 See annotations to s 52.
2 See paras **9.20** to **9.23**.

Bail by the Crown Court

6.44   A person sent for trial in custody to the Crown Court for trial under s 51 will thereafter have to apply to the Crown Court, not the magistrates' court, for bail, just like a person who has been committed in custody for trial in the Crown Court or in relation to whom a notice of transfer has been given under s 4 of the Criminal Justice Act 1987 or s 53 of the Criminal Justice Act 1991. Schedule 8, para 48 amends s 81 of the Supreme Court Act 1981, the relevant provision about the powers of the Crown Court to grant bail, to this effect. As a result, an immediate application for bail can be made by a person who has been sent for trial under s 51.

Bail: variation of conditions where person sent for trial in respect of indictable-only offence

6.45   Where a magistrates' court has sent a person for trial on bail under s 51, that court or the Crown Court may on application:

(a) by or on behalf of the person to whom bail was granted; or
(b) by the prosecutor or a police officer,

vary the conditions of bail or impose conditions in respect of bail which has been granted unconditionally (Bail Act 1976, s 3(8), as applied by the Bail Act 1976, s 3(8B), inserted by Sch 8, para 37, to the new Act).

Adjournment

6.46   A magistrates' court may adjourn any proceedings under s 51, and if it does so must remand the accused (s 52(5)).

Statement of evidence against accused

6.47   At the time that the accused is sent for trial he may not know the evidence on which the charge or charges are based. Regulations are to be made requiring that, where an accused is sent for trial under s 51, copies of the documents containing evidence on which the charge or charges are based:

(a) are served on the accused; and

(b) are given to the Crown Court sitting at the place specified in the notice
     under s 51(7)[1] (Sch 3, para 1).

The copies must be served and given before 'the relevant date', which will be
prescribed in the regulations (Sch 3, para 1). Clearly, it is going to be important
that the 'relevant date' is set so as to ensure that a person sent for trial learns
swiftly the case against him.

The regulations will be made by the Attorney-General (Sch 3, para 1). They
must be made by statutory instrument and, unlike most regulations under the
Act, are subject to annulment in pursuance of a resolution of either House of
Parliament (s 114(1) and (2)).[2]

The requirement that a statement of evidence on which the charge or charges
are based is required to be served is of importance if the rules about
applications for dismissal described in paras **6.55** to **6.57** are to have any real
effect.

---

1 See para **6.53**.
2 See annotations to s 114.

Power of justices to take depositions etc

6.48   Schedule 3, para 4, empowers a justice of the peace to require and
take depositions and to require the production of documents or other exhibits
for the purposes of proceedings for an offence for which a person has been sent
for trial under s 51. This power will be used where a witness will not voluntarily
make a statement or produce a document or other exhibit.

More fully, Sch 3, para 4(1) provides that this power may be exercised:

'where a justice of the peace for any commission area[1] is satisfied that:

(a) any person in England and Wales ("the witness") is likely to be able to make on
     behalf of the prosecutor a written statement containing material evidence, or
     produce on behalf of the prosecutor a document or other exhibit likely to be
     material evidence, for the purposes of proceedings for an offence for which a
     person has been sent for trial under section 51 of this Act by a magistrates'
     court for that area; and
(b) the witness will not voluntarily make the statement or produce the document
     or other exhibit.'

Despite the reference to 'any person in England and Wales'[1] in sub-para (a),
the power to issue a summons may also be exercised if the justices are satisfied
that the witness is outside the British Islands[1] (Sch 3, para 4(4)). Thus, a
summons can be issued if the justice is satisfied that the witness is in France or
Australia, but not if the justice believes that the witness is in Scotland or Jersey
(or anywhere else in the British Islands other than England and Wales).

Where a justice is satisfied as to the specified things, he is required to issue a summons directed to the witness requiring that person to attend before a justice at the time and place appointed in the summons, and to have his evidence taken as a deposition or to produce the document or other exhibit (Sch 3, para 4(2)). Where a summons is issued with a view to taking a deposition, the time appointed must be such as to enable the evidence to be taken as a deposition before the 'relevant date' (which is to be prescribed by regulations)[2] (Sch 3, para 4(6)).

By virtue of the Justices' Clerks Rules 1970, the summons may be issued by the justices' clerk,[3] or by a member of his staff to whom he has delegated this power,[4] if the clerk, or delegate, is satisfied in respect of the requirements in Sch 3, para 4(1).

The accused person against whom the deposition is to be used is not entitled to the opportunity of attending at the taking of a deposition under the present provision and of cross-examining the witness.

---

1 See general annotations.
2 Schedule 3, paras 1(2) and 4(12). For the procedural requirements relating to such regulations, see s 114(1) and (2) and annotations thereto.
3 SI 1970/231, r 1 and Sch.
4 The delegation must be in accordance with r 4.

6.49   Some witnesses may be particularly unwilling to attend when they receive a summons. If a justice of the peace is satisfied by evidence on oath of the conditions set out in Sch 3, para 4(1), and also that it is probable that a summons under Sch 3, para 4(2), would not procure the result required by it, the justice may instead of issuing a summons issue a warrant to arrest the witness and to bring him before a justice at the time and place specified in the warrant (Sch 3, para 4(3)).[1] Unlike a summons under Sch 3, para 4(2), a warrant cannot be issued under Sch 3, para 4(3), unless the justice is satisfied by evidence on oath that the person is in England and Wales (Sch 3, para 4(4)).

Where a warrant is issued with a view to securing the taking of a deposition, the time specified in the warrant must be such as to enable the evidence to be taken as a deposition before the 'relevant date'.

---

1 The warrant may be executed by a police officer notwithstanding that it is not in his possession at the time, but it must (on the demand of the person arrested) be shown to him as soon as practicable (Magistrates' Courts Act 1980, s 125(4)(c)(iv), inserted by the new Act, Sch 8, para 44). The provisions of the Indictable Offences Act 1848 (which relate to the execution in the Isle of Man and Channel Islands of warrants for various offences) are extended to the present type of warrant for arrest (Magistrates' Courts Act 1980, s 126(e), inserted by the new Act, Sch 8, para 45). Schedule 8, paras 45 and 46 also amend the 1980 Act in the same way in respect of warrants of arrest under the 1980 Act, s 97A (depositions etc in committal proceedings).

6.50   If a summons under Sch 3, para 4, has been issued but the person summonsed fails to attend before a justice in answer to the summons, and:

(a) the justice is satisfied by evidence on oath that the witness is likely to be able to make a statement or produce a document or other exhibit as required;
(b) it is proved on oath, or in such other manner as may be prescribed, that he has been duly served with the summons and that a reasonable sum has been paid or tendered to him for costs and expenses; and
(c) it appears to the justice that there is no just excuse for the failure,

the justice may issue a warrant to arrest the witness and to bring him before a justice at the time and place specified in the warrant (Sch 3, para 4(5)).[1]

1 Note 1 to para **6.49** also applies to a warrant of arrest in these circumstances.

6.51   If any person attending or brought before a justice under Sch 3, para 4, refuses without just excuse to have his evidence taken as a deposition, or to produce the document or other exhibit, the justice may:

(a) commit him to custody until the expiration of such period not exceeding one month as may be specified in the summons or warrant or until he sooner has his evidence taken as a deposition or produces the document or other exhibit; or
(b) impose on him a fine not exceeding £2,500; or
(c) do both (Sch 3, para 4(7)).

What happens to a deposition taken or to an exhibit produced under Sch 3, para 4? The answer is that where a person:

(a) has his evidence taken as a deposition; or
(b) produces an exhibit which is a document,

the clerk to the justices must as soon as is reasonably practicable[1] send the deposition or a copy of the document (as the case may be) to the prosecutor and the Crown Court (Sch 3, para 4(9) and (10)).

Secondly, where a person produces an exhibit which is not a document, the clerk to the justices must as soon as is reasonably practicable[1] inform the prosecutor and the Crown Court of the fact and the nature of the exhibit (Sch 3, para 4(11)).

1 See general annotations.

6.52   With the exceptions listed below, a deposition taken under the above provisions may without further proof be read as evidence on the trial of the accused, whether for an offence for which he was sent for trial under s 51 or for any other offence arising out of the same transaction or set of circumstances (Sch 3, para 5).

The exceptions where this rule does not apply are if:

(a) it is proved that the deposition was not signed by the justice by whom it purports to have been signed;

(b) the court of trial at its discretion orders that the rule does not apply; or

(c) a party to the proceedings objects to the rule applying (Sch 3, para 5(3)).

In the last case (ie (c)), the court of trial may order that the objection shall have no effect if it considers it to be in the interests of justice so to order (Sch 3, para 5(4)).

Notice by magistrates' court

6.53 When a magistrates' court sends an accused for trial under any of the above provisions in s 51, it must specify in a notice the offence or offences for which the accused is sent for trial under the section and the place (ie the Crown Court location) at which he is to be tried (s 51(7)). A copy of the notice must be served on the accused and given to the Crown Court sitting at the place specified in it (s 51(7)).

There is an identical provision in respect of the magistrates' court's choice of the venue of the trial to that which applies under s 7 of the Magistrates' Courts Act 1980 in respect of committal for trial. It is provided by s 51(10), viz: in selecting the place of trial, the court must have regard to:

(a) the convenience of the defence, the prosecution and the witnesses;

(b) the desirability of expediting the trial; and

(c) any direction given by or on behalf of the Lord Chief Justice under s 75(1) of the Supreme Court Act 1981.[1]

In committal proceedings, magistrates' courts can be addressed by either party as to the place of trial. This, however, is not common and normally the magistrates' court will automatically commit to the Crown Court location which it has been told by the presiding judge of the relevant Crown Court circuit is the location to which it should commit, depending on the category of the offence.

Likewise, it would seem that a magistrates' court will normally send an accused for trial under s 51 to such a location. It is not clear, however, whether representations as to location can be made by either party in the magistrates' court. In any event, it would seem that if the location specified by the magistrates' court appears then or later to be unsuitable, a party can apply to the Crown Court for a change, just as he can in relation to committal proceedings. It would obviously be preferable that representations to the magistrates' court at the time of sending should be made if possible, rather than having to be delayed for consideration by the Crown Court.

---

1 See annotations to s 51.

6.54 Where there is more than one indictable-only offence and the court includes an either-way or a summary offence in the notice, the court must specify in that notice the indictable-only offence to which the either-way offence or, as the case may be, the summary offence appears to the court to be related (s 51(8)).

Cases sent for trial under s 51: proceedings in the Crown Court

Application for dismissal

6.55   There is no right of appeal as such against a sending for trial under s 51 by a magistrates' court, although an invalid 'sending' could be challenged by an application for judicial review. However, a person who is sent for trial under s 51 on any charge or charges may, at any time:

(a)   after he is served with copies of the documents containing the evidence on which the charge or charges are based; and

(b)   before he is arraigned (and whether or not an indictment has been preferred against him),

apply orally or in writing to the Crown Court for the charge, or any of the charges, in the case to be dismissed (Sch 3 para 2(1)) *on the ground that the evidence against him would not be sufficient for a jury properly to convict him.* This applies whether the charge in question relates to an indictable-only offence or an either-way one. On the other hand, the wording of these provisions indicates that they do not apply to a summary offence for which a person has been sent for trial under s 51. The application is to be made to the Crown Court sitting at the place specified in a notice under s 51(7) (Sch 3, para 2(1)).[1]

---

1 See para **6.53**.

6.56   The procedure in respect of an application for dismissal is modelled on that which applies to an application for dismissal after a complex or serious fraud or child abuse case has been transferred to the Crown Court under a notice of transfer under s 4 of the Criminal Justice Act 1987 or s 53 of the Criminal Justice Act 1991, respectively.

An oral application cannot be made unless the applicant has given to the Crown Court written notice of his intention to make the application (Sch 3, para 2(3)). Oral evidence may be given on such an application only with the leave of the judge or by his order. The judge can only give leave or make an order if it appears to him, having regard to any matters stated in the application for leave, that the interests of justice require him to do so (Sch 3, para 2(4)). The reference to the judge making an order indicates that there is a power for him to require a person to give evidence. Thus, although an accused who challenges the prosecution evidence cannot require a prosecution witness to attend the hearing of an application for dismissal, the judge can do so if he thinks that the interests of justice so require. If the judge gives leave permitting, or makes an order requiring, a person to give oral evidence, but that person does not do so, the judge may disregard any document indicating the evidence that he might have given (Sch 3, para 2(5)). The possibility of oral evidence being given on an application to dismiss where a case has been sent for trial under s 51, a process designed to reduce delay, is interesting in the light of the recent change to committal proceedings where oral evidence may now no longer be heard. It is open to the same objection as led to the change in respect of committal proceedings, viz the exposure of vulnerable witnesses to the ordeal of having to give evidence and being cross-examined twice, something which might be exploited by some accused in an attempt to deter witnesses from giving evidence at the trial. Of one thing one can be certain: applications for dismissal are going to take longer and be more costly than committal proceedings would be. Clearly, much is going to depend on how the judges interpret the 'interests of justice'.

Oral applications for dismissal may not, at the time this book went to press, be conducted by solicitors (unless they have obtained criminal higher court advocacy rights), although they are able to make the corresponding submission of 'no case to answer' in committal proceedings in magistrates' courts. The Law Society pressed unsuccessfully for an amendment to the Bill to permit solicitors to conduct such applications on the ground that it would, inter alia, save costs, speed up the criminal justice process and allow more flexible use of lawyers' skills.[1]

---

1 (1998) 148 NLJ 270.

6.57   If, after considering an oral or written application, it appears to the judge that the evidence against the applicant would not be sufficient for a jury properly to convict him of a charge which is the subject of the application, he must dismiss that charge (and accordingly quash any count relating to it in any indictment preferred against the applicant) (Sch 3, para 2(2)). It will not be uncommon for one charge against an applicant to be dismissed and another not.

If the charge, or any of the charges, against the applicant is dismissed:

(a) no further proceedings may be brought on the dismissed charge or charges except by means of the preferment of a voluntary bill of indictment;[1] and

(b) unless the applicant is in custody otherwise than on the dismissed charge or charges, he must be discharged (Sch 3, para 2(6)).

There is no right of appeal against the judge's decision on an application for dismissal, nor is it judicially reviewable because it is a 'decision relating to trial on indictment'.[2]

---

1 Administration of Justice (Miscellaneous Provisions) Act 1933, s 2.
2 Supreme Court Act 1981, s 29(3). See *Re Smalley* [1985] AC 622, [1985] 1 All ER 769 (HL); *Re Ashton* [1994] AC 9, [1993] 2 All ER 663 (HL); *Manchester Crown Court, ex parte DPP* [1993] 1 All ER 1524 (HL).

6.58   Further provisions in respect of applications for dismissal may be made by the Crown Court Rules (Sch 3, para 2(7)). It is anticipated that, in particular, they will make provision:

(a)   as to the time or stage in the proceedings at which anything required to be done is to be done (unless the court grants leave to do it at some other time or stage);
(b)   as to the contents and form of notices or other documents;
(c)   as to the manner in which evidence is to be submitted; and
(d)   as to persons to be served with notices or other material.

No doubt the rules made will be modelled on those which apply to an application for dismissal in transfer cases under the Criminal Justice Acts 1987 and 1991.[1]

---

1 Criminal Justice Act 1987 (Dismissal of Transferred Charges) Rules 1988, SI 1988/1695; Criminal Justice Act 1991 (Notice of Transfer) Regulations 1992, SI 1992/1670.

REPORTING RESTRICTIONS
6.59   Schedule 3, para 3, provides for reporting restrictions in respect of applications for dismissal, which are modelled on the restrictions which apply under s 8 of the Magistrates' Courts Act 1980 to reporting committal proceedings.

Subject to any exception set out below, it is unlawful:

(a)   to publish[1] in Great Britain[2] a written[2] report of an application for dismissal; or
(b)   to include in a relevant programme for reception in Great Britain[2] a report of such an application,

if (in either case) the report contains any matter other than that permitted by Sch 3, para 3[3] (Sch 3, para 3(1)). A 'relevant programme' means an item included in a 'programme service' within the meaning of the Broadcasting Act 1990.[2]

This restriction does not prevent the publication or inclusion in a relevant programme of a report of:

(a)   the identity of the court and the name of the judge;
(b)   the names, ages, home addresses and occupations of the accused and witnesses;
(c)   the offence or offences, or a summary of them, with which the accused is or are charged;
(d)   the names of counsel and solicitors engaged in the proceedings;
(e)   where the proceedings are adjourned, the date and place to which they are adjourned;
(f)   the arrangements as to bail;
(g)   whether legal aid was granted to the accused or any of the accused (Sch 3, para 3(8)).

---

1 'Publish', in relation to report, means publish the report, either by itself or as part of a newspaper or periodical, for distribution to the public (Sch 3, para 3(13)).
2 See general annotations.

3 This is in addition to, and not in derogation from, any provisions of any other enactment with respect to the publication of reports of court proceedings (Sch 3, para 3(12)). It follows that, even where reporting restrictions have been lifted as a result of an order under Sch 3, para 3(2), referred to in para **6.60**, the judge may order under the Contempt of Court Act 1981, s 4(2), that publication of reports of part or all of the proceedings be postponed (*Horsham Justices, ex parte Farquharson* [1982] QB 672, [1982] 2 All ER 269 (DC)).

6.60   By way of further exception, the judge dealing with the application for dismissal may order that the above restriction shall not apply to reports of that application (Sch 3, para 3(2)). Unlike the provision under s 8 of the 1980 Act, this power does not depend on an application by an accused. Indeed, the accused's consent is not expressly required but Sch 3, para 3(3) (below) implies that a 'lifting order' cannot be made if the accused (or all of a number of co-accused) objects.

What if there are two or more accused, and one objects to the making of a lifting order? Schedule 3, para 3(3) provides that in such a case the judge shall make the order if, and only if, he is satisfied, after hearing the representations of the accused, that it is in the interests of justice to do so. The case-law on the 'interests of justice' in the corresponding provision under s 8 of the 1980 Act would seem to be equally applicable here. In *Leeds Justices, ex parte Sykes*, Griffiths LJ said:

> 'without attempting any comprehensive definition, the interests of justice incorporate as a paramount consideration that the accused should have a fair trial. When the magistrates have to balance the request for the committal proceedings to be reported, they must bear in mind that the prima facie rule is that committal proceedings should not be reported, and only if a powerful case is made out for their reporting should they be prepared to make an order when one of the accused objects, particularly if the ground of objection is that very reason that led Parliament to provide that, as a general rule, proceedings should not be reported, namely that there is a risk that if the proceedings are widely reported, the reports may colour the views of the jury which ultimately has to try the case.'[1]

Griffiths LJ added, obiter, that an application for reporting restrictions to be lifted on the ground that publicity might induce potential witnesses for the accused making the application to come forward would 'merit really serious consideration' by the court in deciding whether or not it was in the interests of justice that the proceedings should be reported.[2]

The judge must give all the co-accused the chance to make representations. If he does not, there will be a breach of natural justice and the lifting order will be invalid.[3]

The validity of a decision to make (or not to make) a lifting order can be challenged by judicial review because it is neither an integral part of the process of a criminal trial nor does it affect the course or conduct of the trial and is therefore not 'a decision relating to trial on indictment'.[4] On request, the lifting order should be suspended in order for an application for judicial review to be made.

A 'lifting order' under Sch 3, para 3(2), will not apply to reports of proceedings under Sch 3, para 3(3), but any decision of the court to make or not to make such an order may be contained in reports published or included in a relevant programme before the time authorised by Sch 3, para 3(5) and (6), dealt with below (Sch 3, para 3(4)).

1 [1983] 1 All ER 460 at 462.
2 [1983] 1 All ER 460 at 464.
3 *Wirral District Magistrates' Court, ex parte Meikle* (1990) 154 JP 1035 (DC).
4 This was held to be so in respect of an order discharging a prohibition on press reports
   revealing the identity of a juvenile accused in the Crown Court in *Crown Court at Leicester, ex
   parte S (A Minor)* [1992] 2 All ER 659 (DC). What was said there is equally applicable in the
   present context.

6.61   It is not unlawful to publish or include in a relevant programme a report of an application for dismissal containing matter additional to what may normally be reported (under Sch 3, para 3(8)) where that application is successful (Sch 3, para 3(5)). However, where there are two or more jointly charged accused and more than one of them applies for dismissal, this provision only applies if all the applications are successful (Sch 3, para 3(6)).

It is not unlawful to publish or include in a relevant programme a report of an unsuccessful application at the conclusion of the trial of the person charged, or of the last of the persons charged to be tried (Sch 3, para 3(7)).

6.62   If a report is published or included in a relevant programme in contravention of the above provisions, the following are criminally liable:

(a) in the case of a publication of a written report as part of a newspaper or periodical, any proprietor, editor or publisher of the newspaper or periodical;

(b) in the case of a publication of a written report otherwise than as part of a newspaper or periodical, the person who publishes it;

(c) in the case of the inclusion of a report in a relevant programme, any body corporate which is engaged in providing the service in which the programme is included and any person having functions in relation to the programme corresponding to those of the editor of a newspaper (Sch 3, para 3(10)).

The above offence is summary only. It is not punishable with imprisonment. The maximum fine is one not exceeding level 5 on the standard scale[1] (s 52(6) and Sch 3, para 3(10)). A prosecution may only be instituted by or with the consent of the Attorney-General[2] (Sch 3, para 3(11)). It is likely that the offence will be interpreted as one of strict liability.

1 See general annotations.
2 Any function of the Attorney-General may be exercised by the Solicitor-General: Law Officers
   Act 1997, s 1(1).

Preparatory hearings and pre-trial hearings

6.63 The provisions of Parts III and IV of the Criminal Procedure and Investigations Act 1996 relating to preparatory hearings and pre-trial hearings apply where a case is sent for trial under s 51 (1996 Act, ss 28(1)(a) and 39(1), as amended by the new Act, Sch 8, paras 128 and 129).

Procedure where no indictable-only offence remains: adult accused

6.64 Schedule 3, paras 7 to 12, deals with the situation where, after a person has been sent for trial under s 51 but before he has been arraigned, the indictment on which he is charged has ceased to contain an indictable-only offence, whether as a result of an amendment of the indictment or as a result of a successful application for dismissal under Sch 3, para 2, or for any other reason (Sch 3, para 7(1)), but the indictment still contains an either-way offence or summary offence.

Schedule 3, paras 7 to 12, does not apply where the person sent for trial is a child or young person at the material time. The special provisions which apply in such a case are set out in para **6.71**.

As will be seen, the Crown Court has to decide whether to deal with the case or to remit it for trial at a magistrates' court. The procedure is modelled on that which applies to 'plea before venue proceedings' under ss 17A and 17B of the Magistrates' Courts Act 1980 in respect of either-way offences.

The first stage of the procedure under Sch 3, para 7, varies depending on whether or not the accused is present in court (as will normally be the case) or absent.

WHEN THE ACCUSED IS PRESENT IN COURT
6.65 Every part of the procedure set out below must take place with the accused present in court (Sch 3, para 7(2)).

The procedure is as follows by Sch 3, para 7(3) to (7):

(a) The Crown Court must cause to be read to the accused each count of the indictment that charges an either-way offence.

(b) The Crown Court must then explain to the accused in ordinary language that, in relation to each of those offences, he may indicate whether (if it were to proceed to trial) he would plead guilty or not guilty, and that if he indicates that he would plead guilty the court must proceed as mentioned in (d) below.

(c) The Crown Court must then ask the accused whether (if the offence in question were to proceed to trial) he would plead guilty or not guilty.

(d) If the accused indicates that he would plead guilty the Crown Court must proceed as if he had been arraigned on the count in question and had pleaded guilty.

(e) If the accused indicates that he would plead not guilty, or fails to indicate how he would plead, the Crown Court must consider whether the offence is more suitable for summary trial or for trial on indictment.

Subject to (d) above:

(a) asking the accused under Sch 3, para 7 whether (if the offence were to proceed to trial) he would plead guilty or not guilty;
(b) an indication by him under Sch 3, para 7, of how he would plead,

do not for any purpose constitute the taking of a plea (Sch 3, para 7(8)). Consequently, for example, an indication of an intention to plead not guilty does not constitute the taking of a plea of not guilty in a magistrates' court, if the case is subsequently transferred for trial to a magistrates' court, or in the Crown Court, if it is not.

The above provisions apply whether or not the accused is legally represented.

THE ABSENT ACCUSED

6.66 Just as in the case of plea before venue proceedings in a magistrates' court, special provision is made by Sch 3, para 8, for the Crown Court to proceed in the absence of the accused if he is disorderly, provided:

(a) the accused is represented by a legal representative;
(b) the court considers that by reason of the accused's disorderly conduct before the court it is not practicable[1] for proceedings under Sch 3, para 7, above to be conducted in his presence; and
(c) the court considers that it should proceed in the absence of the accused (Sch 3, para 8(1)).

It is noteworthy that in (a) 'legal representative' is used and not 'counsel or solicitor with advocacy rights in the superior criminal courts'. This wording is a neat way of describing these two types of advocate. It also recognises that, although currently only barristers in independent practice and 'solicitor-advocates' have a right of audience in the Crown Court, other bodies may currently be authorised under the Courts and Legal Services Act 1990 to grant such a right of audience.

---

1 See general annotations.

6.67 The following special procedure applies in the present type of case. First, the Crown Court must cause to be read to the legal representative each count of the indictment that charges an either-way offence. The Crown Court must ask the representative whether (if the offence were to proceed to trial) the accused would plead guilty or not guilty. If the representative indicates that the accused would plead guilty the Crown Court must proceed as if the accused had been arraigned on the count in question and had pleaded guilty (Sch 3, para 8(2)). However, subject to this, asking the representative how the accused would plead, and an indication by the representative of how the accused would plead, do not constitute the taking of a plea (Sch 3, para 8(3)).

If the representative indicates that the accused would plead not guilty or does not indicate how the accused would plead, the Crown Court must consider whether the offence is more suitable for summary trial or trial on indictment (Sch 3, para 8(2)).

The new procedure does not operate if a disorderly accused does not have a legal representative or if an accused is absent for some other reason. In these cases there will have to be an adjournment until the accused can be present, because (as explained below) mode of trial proceedings cannot take place unless, and until, an indication of intended plea of not guilty has been given.

WHERE THE ACCUSED INDICATES THAT HE WOULD PLEAD NOT GUILTY
6.68   In a case where the accused (or his legal representative) indicates that he would plead not guilty to an either-way offence, the Crown Court, before considering the question, must give first the prosecutor and then the accused an opportunity to make representations as to which mode of trial would be more suitable (Sch 3, para 9(2)).

In considering the question, the Crown Court must have regard to:

(a)   any representations made by the prosecutor or the accused;
(b)   the nature of the case;
(c)   whether the circumstances make the offence one of a serious character;
(d)   whether the punishment which a magistrates' court would have power to impose for it would be adequate; and
(e)   'any other circumstance which appear to the court to make it more suitable for the offence to be dealt tried [sic] in one way rather than the other' (Sch 3, para 9(3)).

If the Crown Court considers that an offence is more suitable for summary trial, it must explain to the accused in ordinary language:

(a)   'that it appears to the court more suitable for him to be tried summarily for the offence, and that he can either consent to be so tried or, of [sic] he wishes, be tried by a jury'; and
(b)   that if he is tried summarily and is convicted by the magistrates' court, he may be committed for sentence to the Crown Court under s 38 of the Magistrates' Courts Act 1980 if the convicting court is of such opinion as is mentioned in s 38(2) of that Act[1] (Sch 3, para 10(1) and (2)).

The Crown Court must then ask the accused whether he wishes to be tried summarily or by a jury, and:

(a)   if he indicates that he wishes to be tried summarily, must remit him for trial to a magistrates' court acting for the place where he was sent to the Crown Court for trial;
(b)   if he does not give such an indication, must retain its functions in relation to the offence and proceed accordingly (Sch 3, para 10(3)).

By Sch 3, para 11, if the Crown Court considers that an offence is more suitable for trial on indictment, it must:

(a) tell the accused that it has decided that it is more suitable for him to be tried by a jury; and

(b) retain its functions in relation to the offence and proceed accordingly.

---

1 By s 38(2) of the 1980 Act, if the magistrates' court is of the opinion:

   (a) that the offence or combination of the offence and other offences associated with it was so serious that greater punishment should be inflicted for the offence than the court has power to impose; or

   (b) in the case of a violent or sexual offence, that a custodial sentence for a term longer than the court has power to impose is necessary to protect the public from serious harm from him,

   the court may commit the offender in custody or on bail to the Crown Court for sentence.

6.69   The Crown Court may proceed in the absence of the accused in accordance with the above provisions (Sch 3, paras 9–11) subject to any variations set out below, if:

(a) the accused is represented by a legal representative who signifies to the court the accused's consent to the proceedings in question being conducted in his absence; and

(b) the court is satisfied that there is good reason for proceeding in the absence of the accused (Sch 3, para 15(1)).

However, if the accused's legal representative has indicated (or is deemed so to have indicated), under Sch 3, para 7 or 8, that the accused would plead not guilty and the court, having considered which is the more suitable mode of trial, has concluded that an offence is more suitable for summary trial, Sch 3, para 10, will not apply. Instead, if the legal representative indicates that the accused wishes to be tried summarily, the court must remit the accused for trial to a magistrates' court acting for the place where he was sent to the Crown Court for trial (Sch 3, para 15(3)(a)). On the other hand, if the legal representative does not indicate that the accused wishes to be tried summarily, the Crown Court will retain its functions and must proceed accordingly (Sch 3, para 15(3)(b)). In such a case, the requirement under Sch 3, para 11, for the Crown Court to tell the accused this does not apply (Sch 3, para 15(4)).

SPECIAL CASES

6.70   Where the prosecution is being carried on by the Attorney-General or the Solicitor-General and he applies for an offence which may be tried on indictment to be so tried, the procedural requirements, other than that relating to causing each count of the indictment to be read to the accused, set out above, do not apply and the Crown Court retains its function in relation to the offence and must proceed accordingly (Sch 3, para 12(1)). The same is true if the prosecution is being carried on by the Director of Public Prosecutions (as are all prosecutions carried on by the Crown Prosecution Service) and the Director applies for the offence to be tried on indictment (Sch 3, para 12(1)), but the Director may only so apply with the consent of the Attorney-General (Sch 3, para 12(2)). Thus, there is no general power for the

Crown Prosecution Service to cause the requirements set out in paras **6.64** to **6.69** to be side-stepped.

Procedure where no indictable-only offence remains: accused a child or young person

6.71   The above provisions are inappropriate in the case of those under 18, to whom the mode of trial procedure in a magistrates' court does not apply. So as to ensure that such an accused is not disadvantaged when he finds himself in the Crown Court for an either-way offence charged because it is associated with an indictable-only offence which is no longer being pursued, the Crown Court is required to deal with a juvenile in such a case on the same basis as would normally apply where magistrates are deciding whether to commit him for trial.

Schedule 3, para 13, sets out the procedure which applies if the indictment charging a child or young person sent for trial under s 51 who has not yet been arraigned no longer includes an indictable-only offence. It provides that, with two exceptions, the Crown Court must remit the child or young person for trial at a magistrates' court acting for the place where he was sent to the Crown Court for trial (Sch 3, para 13(2)).

The first exception is one where the child or young person is charged with an either-way offence covered in s 53(2) of the Children and Young Persons Act 1933, viz:

–   any offence punishable in the case of an adult with imprisonment for 14 years or more, not being an offence the sentence for which is fixed by law; or

–   an offence under s 14 (indecent assault on a woman) or s 15 (indecent assault on a man) of the Sexual Offences Act 1956,[1]

and the court considers that if he is found guilty of the offence it ought to be possible to sentence him under s 53(3) of the 1933 Act (Sch 3, para 13(2)(a)). Section 53(3) of the 1933 Act permits a court, if it is of the opinion that none of the other methods in which the case may legally be dealt with are suitable, to sentence the offender to be detained for such period not exceeding the maximum term of imprisonment with which the offence is punishable in the case of an adult as may be specified in the sentence.

The second exception is where the accused child or young person is charged jointly with a person aged 18 or over with an either-way offence and the Crown Court considers it necessary in the interests of justice that they both be tried for the offence in the Crown Court (Sch 3, para 13(2)(b)).

---

1 Section 53(2) also refers, in the case of a person of at least 14 and not more than 17, to an offence under s 1 of the Road Traffic Act 1988 (causing death by dangerous driving), or an offence under s 3A of the Road Traffic Act 1988 (causing death by careless driving while under the influence of drink or drugs), but as these are offences of homicide they are indictable-only (Magistrates' Courts Act 1980, s 24(1)).

6.72   The Crown Court may proceed in the absence of the juvenile accused in accordance with Sch 3, para 13 if:

(a) that accused is represented by a legal representative who signifies the accused's consent to the proceedings in question being conducted in his absence; and

(b) the court is satisfied that there is good reason for proceeding in that accused's absence (Sch 3, para 15(1)).

Power of Crown Court to deal with summary offence

6.73   Where a magistrates' court has sent a person for trial under s 51 for offences which include a summary offence, the summary offence will not be included in the indictment and the accused will not be asked to plead to the summary offence when arraigned (unless the summary offence has been included in the indictment under s 40 of the Criminal Justice Act 1988, which applies only to a few summary offences; see para **6.75**). Instead, the procedure is as follows. It is modelled on that which continues to apply where a person is committed for trial for an either-way offence and also to be dealt with for a related summary offence under s 41 of the Criminal Justice Act 1988.

If the accused pleads guilty or is found guilty on the indictment (whether for an indictable-only offence or a related either-way offence),[1] the Crown Court must consider whether the summary offence is related to the indictable-only offence or, as the case may be, any of the offences which are indictable-only (Sch 3, para 6(1) and (2)). In this context, an offence is related to another offence if it arises out of circumstances which are the same as or connected with those giving rise to the other offence (Sch 3, para 6(12)).

If the Crown Court considers that the summary offence is not so related to the indictable-only offence or any one or more of them, its functions cease in respect of the summary offence and that offence must be dealt with by the 'sending' magistrates' court. On the other hand, if the Crown Court considers that the summary offence is so related, the court must state to the accused person the substance of the offence and ask him whether he pleads guilty or not guilty (Sch 3, para 6(3)). If he pleads guilty, the Crown Court must convict him; it may deal with him in respect of the summary offence only in a manner in which a magistrates' court could have dealt with him (Sch 3, para 6(4)). This ensures that the sentencing function for offences arising from an incident are not divided between the Crown Court and the magistrates' court. On the other hand, if he pleads not guilty to the summary offence, the Crown Court's powers will cease in respect of it (Sch 3, para 6(5)) (and the case is returned to the magistrates' court to deal with), except that the court must dismiss the charge for that offence if the prosecution inform it that they would not desire to submit evidence in relation to it (Sch 3, para 6(6)).

If the accused is not convicted on the indictment, the powers of the Crown Court cease in respect of the summary offence,[2] and it must be dealt with by the 'sending' magistrates' court.

The Crown Court is required to inform the clerk of the 'sending' magistrates' court (ie the clerk to the justices for the petty sessions area for which that court is acting, or was acting at the time of the 'sending')[3] of the outcome of any proceedings in respect of a summary offence (Sch 3, para 6(7)). It will be remembered that summary proceedings in respect of the summary offence will have been adjourned sine die in the magistrates' court.[4]

---

1 By analogy with the Criminal Justice Act 1988, s 41, it would seem that this also includes the case where the conviction on the indictment is for a summary offence included in it under the Criminal Justice Act 1988, s 40 (see para **6.77**; *Bird* [1995] Crim LR 745 (CA)).
2 *Foote* (1992) 94 Cr App Rep 82 (CA).
3 Schedule 3, para 6(11), applying the Magistrates' Courts Act 1980, s 141.
4 See paras **6.37** and **6.39**.

DAMAGE OFFENCES: DETERMINING WHETHER SMALL VALUE

6.74   We explained in para **6.41** how a magistrates' court is to determine, for the purposes of s 51, whether one of the either-way offences listed in Sch 2 to the Magistrates' Courts Act 1980 which are triable only summarily where the value of the damage done or of the property destroyed is less than the 'relevant sum' (currently £5,000) is a summary offence for the purposes of the 'sending for trial' provisions in s 51.

6.75   Schedule 3, para 14, likewise lays down rules which apply where the Crown Court has to determine for the purposes of Sch 3, whether one of the 'specified offences' is a summary offence (Sch 3, para 14(1)). They correspond with the rules which apply under s 22 of the Magistrates' Courts Act 1980[1] where a magistrates' court has to determine the question in cases where the sending for trial procedure is not involved. It provides that the Crown Court must have regard to any representations made by the prosecutor or the accused[1] (Sch 3, para 14(2)). If it appears clear to the court that the value involved does not exceed the relevant sum, it must treat the offence as a summary one (Sch 3, para 14(3)), and the procedure set out in para **6.73** will apply, but if it appears clear to it that the sum involved exceeds that sum, it must treat the offence as an indictable one (Sch 3, para 14(4)).

If it appears to the Crown Court not clear whether the value involved does or does not exceed the relevant sum, the court must ask the accused whether he wishes the offence to be treated as a summary offence (Sch 3, para 14(5)). If the accused indicates that he wishes the offence to be treated as a summary offence, the court must so treat it (Sch 3, para 14(6)) (and the procedure set out in para **6.73** will apply). On the other hand, if he indicates the contrary, or gives no indication, the court must treat the offence as an indictable one (Sch 3, para 14(6)).

---

1 See annotations to s 52.

6.76   The Crown Court may proceed under the above provisions in the absence of the accused in accordance with Sch 3, para 14, if:

(a) the accused is represented by a legal representative who signifies to the court the accused's consent to the proceedings in question being conducted in his absence; and
(b) the court is satisfied that there is good reason for proceeding in the absence of the accused (Sch 3, para 15(1)).

If it does proceed, and it appears to the court not clear whether the value involved does or does not exceed the relevant sum, the provisions of Sch 3, paras 14(5) and (6), set out above will not apply. Instead:

(a) the court must ask the legal representative whether the accused wishes the offence to be treated as a summary offence;
(b) if the legal representative indicates that the accused wishes the offence to be treated as a summary offence, the court must so treat it;
(c) if the legal representative does not give such an indication, the court must treat the offence as an indictable offence (Sch 3, para 15(5)).

SUMMARY OFFENCES TO WHICH THE CRIMINAL JUSTICE ACT 1988, s 40, APPLIES
6.77   If the summary offence is one to which s 40 of the Criminal Justice Act 1988 applies, for example:

(a) common assault;
(b) taking a motor vehicle or other conveyance without authority etc (s 12(1) of the Theft Act 1968);
(c) driving a motor vehicle while disqualified (s 103(1)(b) of the Road Traffic Act 1988);
(d) an offence mentioned in the first column of Sch 2 to the Magistrates' Courts Act 1980 (criminal damage etc)[1] which would otherwise be triable only summarily by virtue of s 22(2) of that Act,

special provisions apply.

By s 40(1) of the 1988 Act, as amended (as italicised) by Sch 8, para 66 of the new Act, a count charging a person with one of these summary offences may be included in an indictment if the charge:

(a) is founded on the same facts or evidence as a count charging an indictable offence; or
(b) is part of a series of offences of the same or similar character as an indictable offence which is also charged,

but only if (in either case) the facts or evidence relating to the offence were disclosed to a magistrates' court inquiring into the offence as examining justices *or are disclosed by material which, in pursuance of the regulations referred to in para* **6.47** *has been served on the person charged.*

Where a count charging an offence to which s 40 of the 1988 Act applies is included in an indictment, the offence is tried in the same manner as if it were an indictable offence; but the Crown Court may only deal with the offender in respect of it in a manner in which a magistrates' court could have dealt with him (1988 Act, s 40(2)).

Schedule 3, para 6(8), provides that, where the summary offence for which the accused is sent for trial under s 51 is one to which s 40 applies, the Crown Court may (but not must) exercise in relation to it the power to try and to sentence conferred by s 40.[2] Where the accused is tried on indictment for such an offence, the functions of the Crown Court under Sch 3, para 6, in relation to the offence cease (Sch 3, para 6(8)).

---

1 See para **6.41** for the list of offences.
2 Whether or not it decides to do so will doubtless depend in particular on whether or not it proceeds to deal with the offence(s) sent for trial under s 51.

EFFECT OF SUCCESSFUL APPEAL IN RESPECT OF RELATED INDICTABLE OFFENCE
6.78   Where the Court of Appeal 'allows an appeal against conviction of an indictable-only offence which is related to a summary offence of which the appellant was convicted under [Sch 3, para 6]':

(a)   the Court of Appeal must set aside his conviction of the summary offence and give the clerk of the 'sending' magistrates' court notice that it has done so; and
(b)   it *may* direct that no further proceedings be taken in relation to the summary offence,

and the proceedings before the Crown Court in relation to the summary offence are thereafter to be disregarded for all purposes (Sch 3, para 6(9)). A notice under (a) must include particulars of any direction under (b) (Sch 3, para 6(10)).

The wording of this provision appears to make it apply where the accused was convicted of more than one indictable-only offence which is related to the summary offence in question, and an appeal against one of those convictions has been successful but not an appeal against the rest of such convictions. This is an odd result.

Substituted or additional charges in the bill of indictment
6.79   Section 2(2) of the Administration of Justice (Miscellaneous Provisions) Act 1933 is amended consequential on the provisions in s 51 so as to provide that, where an indictment is preferred in respect of a person sent for trial under s 51, the bill of indictment may include, either in substitution for or in addition to any count charging an offence specified in the notice under s 51(7),[1] any counts founded on material which in pursuance of the regulations referred to in para **6.47**, was served on the person charged, being counts which may be lawfully joined in the same indictment (Sch 8, para 5(2)).

---

1 See para **6.53**.

Disclosure

6.80   The rules about disclosure in Part I of the Criminal Procedure and Investigations Act 1996 are made applicable to cases where a person is sent for trial under s 51 by Sch 8, para 125(a), which adds this case to the list of cases in s 1(2) of the 1996 Act to which Part I of that Act applies. Generally speaking, the rules about disclosure which apply to a case sent for trial under s 51 are the same as in other cases. However, the requirements of s 5 of the 1996 Act relating to compulsory discharge by the accused do not apply unless copies of the documents containing the evidence have been served on the accused under the regulations referred to in para **6.47**, and a copy of the notice of the offence or offences for which the accused is sent for trial, referred to in para **6.53**, served on him (Criminal Procedure and Investigations Act 1996, s 5(3A), inserted by the new Act, Sch 8, para 126). This matches similar provisions in respect of transfers for trial under s 4 of the Criminal Justice Act 1987 and s 53 of the Criminal Justice Act 1991 (1996 Act, s 5(2) and (3)).

Until regulations are made as to the relevant time limit for primary disclosure by the prosecutor under s 3 of the 1996 Act, the prosecutor must act under s 3 as soon as is reasonably practicable[1] after the accused is sent for trial under s 51 (1996 Act, s 13(1)(cc), added by the new Act, Sch 8, para 127(a)).

---

1 See general annotations.

Discontinuance of proceedings

DISCONTINUANCE OF PROCEEDINGS IN MAGISTRATES' COURTS

6.81   Section 23(1) and (3) of the Prosecution of Offences Act 1985 provides that, where the Director of Public Prosecutions (ie the CPS) has the conduct of proceedings for an offence, he may at any stage during the preliminary stage of the proceedings give notice to the clerk of the court that he does not wish the proceedings to continue. If such a notice is given the proceedings are discontinued from the giving of that notice.[1]

The 'preliminary stage' of proceedings does not include, in the case of a summary offence, any stage after the court has begun to hear the prosecution's evidence at the trial, nor, in the case of an indictable offence, any stage after the accused has been committed for trial or the court has begun to hear the prosecution's evidence at a summary trial of the offence.[2] As a result of the terms of s 51, the definition of 'preliminary stage' has been amended so that, in addition, it does not include, in the case of any offence, any stage of the proceedings after the accused has been sent for trial under s 51 (Sch 8, para 63).

---

1 Prosecution of Offences Act 1985, s 23(3). The proceedings will, however, be revived if the accused wants them to continue and gives notice to this effect within the prescribed period: ibid, s 23(7).
2 Ibid, s 23(2).

DISCONTINUANCE OF PROCEEDINGS AFTER THE ACCUSED HAS BEEN SENT FOR TRIAL

6.82 This is dealt with by s 23A of the Prosecution of Offences Act 1985, which is inserted by Sch 8, para 64.

Section 23A deals with the situation where the accused has been sent for trial under s 51 of the 1998 Act for an offence, and the Director of Public Prosecutions or 'a public authority' has the conduct of the proceedings for that offence (1985 Act, s 23A(1)). It provides that where, at any time before the indictment is preferred, the Director or authority gives notice to the Crown Court to which an accused has been sent for trial under s 51 that he or it does not want the proceedings to continue, they are to be discontinued with effect from the giving of the notice (1985 Act, s 23A(2)).

For the above purpose, 'a public authority' means:

(a) a police force within the meaning of s 3 of the 1985 Act;

(b) the Crown Prosecution Service or any other government department;

(c) a local authority or other authority or body constituted for purposes of:
  (i) the public service or of local government; or
  (ii) carrying on under national ownership any industry or undertaking or part of an industry or undertaking; or

(d) any other authority or body whose members are appointed by Her Majesty or by any Minister of the Crown or government department or whose revenues consist wholly or mainly of money provided by Parliament (1985 Act, s 17(6), applied by 1985 Act, s 23A(1)).

In any notice given under s 23A(2) of the 1985 Act, the Director or public authority must give reasons for not wanting the proceedings to continue (1985 Act, s 23A(3)). As in the case of a discontinuance under s 23, the Director etc is not required to give a copy of the notice given to the Crown Court, or any indication of his reason for discontinuance to the accused, but he or it must inform the accused of the notice (1985 Act, s 27A(4)). However, unlike a discontinuance under s 23, the accused has no right to require the proceedings to continue.

As in the case of a discontinuance under s 23 (1985 Act, s 23(9)), the discontinuance of proceedings by virtue of s 23A of the 1985 Act does not prevent the institution of fresh proceedings in respect of the same offence (1985 Act, s 23A(5)).

Other consequential amendments

POWER TO REMIT JUVENILES TO YOUTH COURT FOR SENTENCE

6.83 By s 56(1) of the Children and Young Persons Act 1933, a Crown Court by or before which a child or young person is found guilty of an offence other than homicide must, unless satisfied that it would be undesirable to do so, remit the case to a youth court *acting for the place where the offender was committed for trial,* or if he was not committed for trial, to a youth court acting either for the same place as the remitting court or for the place where the offender habitually resides; where a case is so remitted, the youth court may deal with the offender in any way in which it might have dealt with him if it had tried and found him guilty. Schedule 8, para 3 to the new Act inserts into s 56 of the 1933 Act subs (1A), which provides that references to s 56(1) to an offender's being committed for trial are to include references to his being sent for trial under s 51 of the new Act.

ATTENDANCE OF WITNESSES

6.84   Section 2(4) of the Criminal Procedure (Attendance of Witnesses) Act 1965, as substituted by s 66 of the Criminal Procedure and Investigations Act 1996, provides that:

> 'where a person has been *committed for trial* for any offence to which the proceedings concerned relate, an application [for the issue of a witness summons under s 2 of the 1965 Act must be made] as soon as is reasonably practicable after the committal.'[1]

Schedule 8, para 8, amends this provision so as to make it apply also where a person has been sent for trial under s 51.

The substituted s 2(4), and indeed the whole of s 2 substituted by the 1996 Act, does not apply to any proceedings for the purpose of which no witness summons has been issued before the appointed day.[2] When this book went to press no day had been appointed for this purpose. There is no corresponding provision to be consequentially amended in the original s 2. Presumably, a day will have been appointed for the substituted s 2 by the time that the amendment in the new Act is brought into force.

---

1 Italics added.
2 1996 Act, s 66(7).

APPEAL AGAINST SENTENCE

6.85   By s 9(2) of the Criminal Appeal Act 1968,

> '[a] person who on conviction on indictment has also been convicted of a summary offence under s 41 of the Criminal Justice Act 1988 *(power of Crown Court to deal with summary offence where a person has been committed [for trial] for [an] either-way offence)* may appeal to the Court of Appeal against any sentence passed on him for the summary offence (whether on his conviction or in subsequent proceedings) under subsection (7) of [s 41].'

Schedule 8, para 12 extends this right of appeal to a person sent for trial under s 51 who has been sentenced for a related summary offence by the Crown Court, after pleading guilty to it under Sch 3, para 6. It does so by adding 'or paragraph 6 of Schedule 3 to the Crime and Disorder Act 1998 (power of Crown Court to deal with summary offences where person sent for trial for indictable-only offence)' after the words italicised above.

This amendment is odd for two reasons. First, the Crown Court's power to sentence someone sent for trial under s 51 for a summary offence to which he pleads guilty also applies to a co-accused who has been sent for trial only in respect of an either-way offence related to the indictable-only offence alleged against the other accused. Thus, the bracketed words quoted are strictly inaccurate. Secondly, as amended, the end of s 9(2) of the 1968 Act is odd because s 41(7) of the 1988 Act is only relevant to a sentence under s 41 of that Act. Although Sch 3, para 6, is to the same effect as s 41(7), it is not referred to in the amended provision.

---

1 The 1988 Act, s 41(7), provides that, where the accused pleads guilty, the Crown Court must convict him, but may deal with him only in a manner in which the magistrates' court could have dealt with him.

REDUCING DELAY IN THE YOUTH JUSTICE SYSTEM

6.86 In 1996, it took an average of 131 days (about four-and-a-half months) to deal with a young offender from offence to sentence. In the worst cases, young offenders were not dealt with until a year or more after the offence was committed.[1] Four out of five cases observed in a study published in 1996 were adjourned at least once and on average each young offender appeared in court four times during the progress of his case.[2]

In 1996, it took an average of 142 days between arrest and sentence to process a persistent young offender.[2] The Government intends to reduce this number to 71[3] and to ensure improvements in general.

In May 1997 the Lord Chancellor wrote to the chairmen of the youth courts to encourage them to take action to reduce delays during court proceedings and, in particular, to be more critical in granting adjournments in the youth courts.[4] In addition, a circular issued in October 1997 to courts, police, CPS and other relevant agencies set out good practice in reducing delays and asked local agencies to set up fast-track schemes for persistent young offenders.[5]

The new Act makes a number of changes to complement the improvements already being made under the existing legislative framework. These changes, set out in paras **6.87** to **6.93** below, are additional to those relating to time limits set out at the end of this chapter. The changes described in paras **6.87** to **6.94** came into force on 30 September 1998.[6]

---

1 *Tackling Delays in the Youth Justice System: A Consultation Paper* (Home Office, 1997), para 3; *No More Excuses – A New Approach to Tackling Youth Crime in England and Wales*, Cm 3809 (1997), para 7.1.
2 *Misspent Youth: Young People and Crime* (Audit Commission, 1996); *Misspent Youth '98* (Audit Commission, 1998).
3 *No More Excuses*, para 7.3.
4 *Tackling Delays in the Youth Justice System*, para 6.
5 Ibid, para 7; *No More Excuses*, para 7.4; *Misspent Youth '98*, p 68.
6 See Appendix II.

Juveniles in the Crown Court on grave charges: related offences

6.87 Section 47(6) implements a recommendation in the Narey Report.[1] It is concerned with cases where, under s 24(1) of the Magistrates' Courts Act

1980, *a juvenile is committed to the Crown Court for trial for homicide or one of the grave offences covered by s 53(2) of the Children and Young Persons Act 1933.* Hitherto, a magistrates' court has not had the power to commit a juvenile to the Crown Court for trial in respect of any other indictable offences, unless he was jointly charged with an adult and it was in the interests of justice to commit them both for trial (Magistrates' Courts Act 1980, s 24(1)(b)). Section 47(6) changes this in relation to related indictable offences. Section 47(6) effects this by inserting into s 24 of the Magistrates' Courts Act 1980 a new subsection (1A). Section 24(1A) provides that in the cases italicised above the court may also commit a juvenile for trial for any other indictable offence with which he is charged at the same time if the charges for both offences could be joined in the same indictment.[2]

---

1 *Review of Delay in the Criminal Justice System: A Report* (Home Office, 1997), p 45.
2 The 1980 Act, s 24(1)(a), is consequentially amended by Sch 8, para 40(2). Section 24 of the 1980 Act, as amended, is set out in the annotations to s 47. As to when charges may be joined in the same indictment, see the Indictment Rules 1971, SI 1971/1253, r 9; para **6.37**.

Effect on other proceedings of committal for trial of a juvenile

6.88 In *Khan*[1] the Court of Appeal held that, where a juvenile offender appeared before the youth court for a number of offences and the court committed him for trial in respect of one of them, they should (save in exceptional circumstances) postpone passing sentence for the other, ex hypothesi, lesser offences until after the Crown Court's proceedings.

This was regarded by the Government as leading to 'unwelcome delays in the youth court':

> 'What sometimes happens is that there is a committal on a charge that may be more serious. The outcome may be in doubt. The time scale may be longer and the whole situation becomes uncertain. Dealing with the lesser case more quickly can mean that some intervention and help to prevent reoffending can take place while the other case is waiting to be dealt with ... Freezing the situation because the more serious case is going forward can result in spree offending by youngsters[2] because no one is able to do anything. It is pernicious in its effect.'[3]

In *No More Excuses*, the Government indicated that the rule in *Khan* would be abolished so that, where a youth court commits a case to the Crown Court in respect of one offence, it need not await the outcome of the Crown Court trial before sentencing the same accused for another offence or offences.[4] This is implemented by s 47(5) which inserts into s 10 of the Magistrates' Courts Act 1980 a new subsection (3A)(a), which provides that 'a youth court shall not be required to adjourn any proceedings for an offence at any stage by reason only of the fact that the court commits the accused for trial for another offence'.

---

1 (1994) 158 JP 760 (CA).
2 'Spree offending' is a burst of offending. 'Spree offenders' may have no previous convictions, and often increase the frequency of their offending in anticipation of court appearances.

3 Alun Michael, MP, Minister of State, Home Office, HC Committee, col 404.
4 *No More Excuses – A New Approach to Tackling Youth Crime in England and Wales*, Cm 3809 (1997), para 7.8.

Effect on proceedings in juvenile court of other outstanding proceedings there

6.89   Although *Khan* was concerned specifically with situations where one or more charges are committed to the Crown Court for trial, in practice it has influenced the approach to multiple cases in the youth courts in cases where proceedings are not pending in the Crown Court.[1] In *No More Excuses*[2] the Government stated that the Act would clarify that 'where the youth court is dealing with offenders who face multiple charges (including so-called "spree" offenders), [the court does] not have to adjourn in order to tie up all outstanding charges'.

This is done by a new s 10(3A)(b) of the Magistrates' Courts Act 1980, inserted by s 47(5), which provides that 'a youth court shall not be required to adjourn any proceedings for an offence at any stage by reason only of the fact that the accused is charged with another offence'.[3]

1 *Tackling Delays in the Youth Justice System* (Home Office, 1997), para 26.
2 *No More Excuses – A New Approach to Tackling Youth Crime in England and Wales*, Cm 3809 (1997), para 7.9.
3 The 1980 Act, s 10, as amended is set out in the annotations to s 47.

Power of stipendiary magistrate to sit alone in youth court

6.90   One of the reforms to the youth court identified as necessary in *No More Excuses*[1] was speedier decisions on guilt or innocence, much closer to the offence and with less tolerance of adjournments. The Narey Report[2] also identified this as an issue.

Section 48 makes a contribution to achieving this reform. Justices sitting in the youth court (which must normally include a man and a woman and must never exceed three justices)[3] must be drawn from the youth court panel of justices specially qualified to deal with juvenile cases.[4] A stipendiary magistrate is ex officio a member of the panel.[5] Hitherto, a stipendiary magistrate has not normally sat alone in youth court proceedings. However, if at any sitting of a youth court, a stipendiary magistrate is the only member of the panel present and he thinks it inexpedient in the interests of justice for there to be an adjournment, he may sit alone.[6] This will remain the situation outside the London Metropolitan area. However, in that area, where the relevant rules were already slightly different, a significant change has been made by s 48. This amends the relevant legislation so as to provide that, as a general rule, a youth court in that area may consist *either* of a metropolitan stipendiary magistrate *or* (as now) a chairman and two other members (including one man and one woman). The relevant provisions, as amended, are set out in the annotations to s 48. Thus, a metropolitan stipendiary magistrate will be able to sit alone in the youth court without the need for any sort of special circumstances. Narey recommended that stipendiaries should specialise in the management of particularly complex cases.[7] This change provides the facility to avoid lengthy adjournments and should, therefore, for this and other reasons, speed up youth court proceedings. It remains to be seen to what extent the single metropolitan stipendiary magistrate supersedes lay justices in the youth court in the London Metropolitan area. Presumably, additional stipendiaries will have to be appointed for this to occur.

---

1 *No More Excuses – A New Approach to Tackling Youth Crime in England and Wales*, Cm 3809 (1997), para 9.3.
2 *Review of Delay in the Criminal Justice System*, op cit, p 45.
3 Youth Courts (Constitution) Rules 1954, SI 1954/1711, r 12(1). Three justices are normally required to sit (Children and Young Persons Act 1933, Sch 2, paras 15 and 17).
4 Youth Courts (Constitution) Rules 1954, r 11 (outside London Metropolitan area); Children and Young Persons Act 1933, Sch 2, para 15 (London Metropolitan area).
5 Youth Courts (Constitution) Rules 1954, r 2.
6 Ibid, r 12(3).
7 Loc cit.

Sittings of youth courts

6.91   Section 47(2) of the Children and Young Persons Act 1933 prohibited a youth court sitting in the same courtroom within an hour before or after a sitting of an 'adult' court. This ban was designed to protect juveniles from contact with older accused. The Narey Report regarded it as an inefficient arrangement which 'seems generally to be regarded as out of date and unnecessary' and recommended its abolition.[1] This is effected by s 47(7).[2]

---

1 *Review of Delay in the Criminal Justice System*, op cit, p 46.
2 The 1933 Act, s 47, as amended, is set out in the annotations to s 47.

Transferring from youth courts to adult courts juveniles who attain the age of 18

6.92   The Narey Report[1] recommended that 17-year-olds should cease to be dealt with by youth courts, on the ground that experience had shown that they are often disruptive and unco-operative and are therefore unsuitable for youth courts. This recommendation is not implemented by the Act.

On the other hand, the Act does implement another recommendation intended to address delay and increase effectiveness in the youth court,[2] viz that where a juvenile reaches the youth court age-limit after the commencement of his case in a youth court,[3] the youth court should have a discretion to remit the case to an adult magistrates' court. Section 47(1) is the relevant provision.

Section 47(1) provides that, where a person who appears or is brought before a youth court charged with an offence subsequently attains the age of 18,[4] the youth court may, at any time:

(a) before the start of the trial; or

(b) after conviction and before sentence,

remit the person for trial or, as the case may be, for sentence to a magistrates' court (other than a youth court) acting for the same petty sessions area[4] as the youth court.

For the above purpose, a trial starts when the court begins to hear prosecution evidence or, if the court accepts a guilty plea without so proceeding, when that plea is accepted.[5]

Whether the accused is suitable for the youth court in terms of maturity and attitude will be an important factor affecting the exercise of the court's discretion.

---

1 *Review of Delay in the Criminal Justice System: A Report* (Home Office, 1997), pp 43–44.
2 Ibid, p 45.
3 Proceedings are begun for this purpose when the young person first appears or is brought before the youth court (*Amersham Juvenile Court, ex parte Wilson* [1981] QB 974 (DC); *Uxbridge Youth Court, ex parte H* (1998) *The Times*, 7 April (DC). The youth court does not have an inherent power to transfer to an adult magistrates' court in the circumstances dealt with by s 47 (*Uxbridge Youth Court, ex parte H*).
4 See general annotations.
5 Section 47(1), applying the definition in the Prosecution of Offences Act 1985, s 22(11B); see annotations to s 43.

6.93   Where a person is remitted under s 47(1) the remitting youth court must adjourn proceedings in relation to the offence (s 47(2)(b)). The provisions of s 128 of the Magistrates' Courts Act 1980[1] and any other enactment relating to remand or the grant of bail in criminal proceedings apply in relation to the remitting youth court's power or duty to remand the person on the adjournment as if any reference to the court to or before which the person remanded is to be brought or appear after remand were a reference to the adult magistrates' court to which he is remitted (s 47(3)). The court to which the remission is made may deal with the case in any way in which it would have power to deal with it if all proceedings relating to the offence which took place before the remitting court had taken place before it (s 47(4)).

---

1 See annotations to s 47.

6.94   A person remitted under s 47(1) has no right of appeal against the order of remission (s 47(2)(a)).

TIME LIMITS IN RELATION TO CRIMINAL PROCEEDINGS

6.95   To reinforce the improved arrangements elsewhere in Part III of the Act to reduce delay, the provisions about time limits under s 22 of the Prosecution of Offences Act 1985 are strengthened, and the Government intends to promulgate further regulations under that section. In addition, the

Act introduces powers to make additional types of limit in the case of juveniles. With the exception of the changes to the power to make regulations mentioned in para **6.99**, the new provisions about time limits had not been brought into force when this book went to press. The new regime will be piloted.[1] The length of the time limits themselves will be set following consultation and the pilot trials.[2]

The new regime is summarised in the chart below.

TIME LIMITS

	CHARGE/	FIRST COURT	START OF		
ARREST →	INFORMATION →	APPEARANCE →	TRIAL →	CONVICTION →	SENTENCE

GENERAL SECTION 22 LIMITS

OVERALL TIME LIMIT ←————————→

CUSTODY TIME LIMITS ←——→

ADDITIONAL SECTION 22A LIMITS (JUVENILES ONLY)

INITIAL STAGE LIMIT ←————————→

CONVICTION– SENTENCE LIMIT ←——————→

---

1 Mike O'Brien, MP, HC Committee, col 816. See also HC Deb, vol 313, cols WA 219–220.
2 *No More Excuses* op cit, para 7.13. In addition to the statutory limits, there are national guidelines, produced by the Working Group on Pre-Trial Issues, setting maximum periods for the completion of the various stages in the progress of criminal cases within the sentencing limits. These guidelines mainly concern the preparation of the case by the police and the CPS. The Government intends to establish more demanding performance targets, which will be monitored by the Youth Justice Board: ibid, para 7.16.

General time limits in relation to the preliminary stages of criminal proceedings

6.96   By s 22(1) of the Prosecution of Offences Act 1985, the Home Secretary is empowered to make regulations to make provision, with respect to any specified 'preliminary stage' of proceedings for an offence, as to the maximum period:

(a) to be allowed to the prosecution to complete that stage (the 'overall time limit');[1]

(b) during which the accused may, while awaiting completion of that stage, be kept in custody (the 'custody time limit').[1]

---

1 Prosecution of Offences Act 1985, s 22(11).

Overall time limit

6.97   Although, as indicated by (a) at para **6.96**, the regulations may prescribe an overall time limit within which the prosecution must complete the preliminary stage of the proceedings in question, hitherto no such regulations have been made. However, the Government intends to make such regulations to reinforce the arrangements in the Act for improved case management etc.[1] They will define the period of the 'preliminary stage' to which they relate. By s 22(11) of the 1985 Act, 'preliminary stage' does not include any stage after the start of the trial, but the Act left open when that stage will start. To close this gap, subs (11ZA) has been added to s 22 whereby, for the purposes of s 22 proceedings for an offence are to be taken to begin when the accused is charged with the offence or, as the case may be, an information is laid charging him with the offence. Although the regulations may specify a period within these maxima, it would seem that they will provide the end and the beginning of the period just specified.

---

1 Lord Williams of Mostyn, Parliamentary Under-Secretary, Home Office, HL 2nd Reading, col 535.

Custody time limits

6.98   Regulations have, of course, been made in respect of (b) at para **6.96**, imposing maximum periods for which an accused may be remanded in custody while the preliminary stage in question is being completed. These are the Prosecution of Offences (Custody Time Limits) Regulations 1987[1] which relate only to indictable offences, other than treason. They define the 'preliminary stage' in a magistrates' court as the period between first appearance in that court and the start of summary trial or, as the case may be, a decision about whether or not to commit for trial, and in the Crown Court as the period between the committal for trial/preferment of a voluntary bill of indictment and the start of the trial. The Regulations need amendment in the light of the sending for trial provisions set out above.

---

1 SI 1987/299; see annotations to s 43. As to the application of the regulations to juveniles, see *Stratford Youth Court, ex parte S* (1998) 148 NLJ 870 (CA).

Changes to regulatory powers

6.99   As enacted, and as will still be the case, s 22(2) of the1985 Act provides that regulations may, inter alia, be made so as to apply only in relation to proceedings in specified areas and make different provision in respect to proceedings instituted in different areas.[1] However, as enacted, there is no express provision in s 22 whereby regulations may be made so as to apply in relation to proceedings of, or against persons of, specified classes or descriptions or whereby regulations may make different provision with respect to proceedings of, or against persons of, different classes or descriptions. Section

22(2) is amended by s 43(1) to enable regulations to be made to such an effect. One reason for this change is to enable stricter time limits to be introduced under s 22 in respect of juveniles, and particularly strong ones in respect of persistent juvenile offenders.[2] We consider the position of juveniles further in paras **6.103** to **6.113**. A persistent young offender will be defined as someone aged 10 to 17 who has been sentenced by any criminal court in the UK for one or more recordable offences[3] on three or more separate occasions and is arrested again (or has an information laid against him) for a further recordable offence within three years of last being sentenced.[4]

---

1 This enables time limits to be piloted.
2 *No More Excuses – A New Approach to Tackling Youth Crime in England and Wales*, Cm 3809
   (1997), para 7.11. Section 43(1) came into force on 30 September 1998: see Appendix II.
3 'Recordable offence' is defined by the National Police Records (Recordable Offences)
   Regulations 1985, SI 1985/1941, as amended. These regulations make certain offences, and
   others of which the accused is convicted on the same occasion, recordable on the police
   national computer. The offences which are recordable are: all offences punishable by
   imprisonment; and a number of offences which are not, such as offences under s 1 of the
   Street Offences Act 1959 (common prostitute loitering or soliciting for the purposes of
   prostitution); offences under s 12(5) of the Theft Act 1968 (taking or riding a pedal cycle
   without the owner's consent; offences under s 43 of the Telecommunications Act 1984
   (improper use of public telecommunications system); offences under s 5 of the Public Order
   Act 1986 (conduct likely to cause harassment, alarm or distress); offences under s 6(4) of the
   Road Traffic Act 1988 (failing to provide a 'screening' breath specimen); and offences under
   s 1 of the Malicious Communications Act 1988 (sending letters etc with intent to cause
   anxiety or distress).
4 *Tackling Delay in the Youth Justice System*, op cit, para 31; *No More Excuses*, op cit, para 7.17.

Effect of expiry of overall time limit

6.100   As enacted, s 22(4) of the 1985 Act provides that where, in relation to any proceedings for an offence, an overall time limit (whether as originally imposed or as extended or further extended) expires before the completion of the stage of the proceedings to which it relates, the accused is to be treated for all purposes as having been acquitted of that offence and proceedings cannot be re-instituted. The Government thought that this was too inflexible a 'punishment of the prosecution for overrunning a time limit'.[1] Consequently, s 22(4) is amended by s 43(3) to the effect that where an overall time limit expires in respect of an offence, the appropriate court must stay the proceedings. The 'appropriate court' is:

(a) where the accused has been committed for trial or indicted for the offence, the Crown Court; and
(b) in any other case, the magistrates' court specified in the summons or warrant in question or, where the accused has already appeared or been brought before a magistrates' court, a magistrates' court for the same area.[2]

This is a significant change because it enables fresh proceedings to be brought in respect of the offence. The effect of the original provision was to enable an accused successfully to plead the bar of autrefois acquit in respect of fresh proceedings for the offence in question. We deal further with the effect of a stay of proceedings in para **6.114**.

The pre-existing sanction for failing to meet a custody time limit, the accused's release on bail, continues in existence.

---

1 *No More Excuses*, op cit, para 7.14.
2 1985 Act, s 22(11).

Effect on overall time limit of escape by prisoner or failure to surrender to bail

6.101   As enacted, s 22(6) of the 1985 Act provided that:

'Where –

(a) a person escapes from the custody of a magistrates' court or the Crown Court; or

(b) a person who has been released on bail fails to surrender himself into the custody of the court at the appointed time;

the overall time limit which applies in his case in relation to the stage which the proceedings have reached at the time of the escape or, as the case may be, at the appointed time shall, so far as the offence in question is concerned, cease to have effect.'

The absence of any time limit as a result of the operation of this provision of the 1985 Act was hardly conducive to speed.

Section 22(6) of the 1985 Act has been extensively amended by s 43 of the new Act in respect of the two situations described in (a) and (b) above. Now the effect of a person becoming unlawfully at large is not that the overall time limit ceases to have effect; instead it results in a suspension (disregard) of the time limit. This is provided by s 22(6A) of the 1985 Act which is added by s 43(5).

Because the Government thought that a simple suspension of the period of absconding could be manipulated by an accused whose disappearance and re-appearance disrupted the prosecution, s 22(6A) permits the court to add a further period to the disregard. By s 22(6A), the following are to be disregarded where someone to whom a limit applies absconds:

(a) the period for which the person is unlawfully at large; and

(b) such additional period (if any) as the appropriate court may direct, having regard to the disruption of the prosecution occasioned by –

(i) the person's escape or failure to surrender; and

(ii) the length of the period mentioned in (a).

Where a magistrates' court decides to give a direction under s 22(6A), or refuses to do so, the accused, or the prosecution respectively, may appeal against that decision to the Crown Court (Prosecution of Offences Act 1985, s 22(7) and (8), as amended by s 43(6) and (7) of the new Act), just as is the case where a magistrates' court decides to extend, or further extend, an overall or custody time limit, or refuses to do so.

Extension of overall or custody time limit

6.102   As enacted, s 22(3) of the 1985 Act provided that 'the appropriate court' may at any time before the expiry of the time limit imposed by the regulations extend, or further extend, that limit, if it is satisfied:

(a) that there is good and sufficient cause for doing so; and
(b) that the prosecution has acted with due expedition.

Surprisingly, in the light of the court's strict interpretation of these criteria,[1] the Government's view was that this provision allowed the courts too wide a discretion in deciding whether to extend time limits: 'We know from the operation of existing custody time limits that extensions are not infrequently granted'.[2] It believed that the criteria for an extension needed to be made more prescriptive for the new time limit regime. Section 43(2) of the new Act substitutes for s 22(3) as set out above the following:

> '(3) the appropriate court may, at any time before the expiry of a time limit imposed by the regulations, extend, or further extend, that limit; but the court shall not do so unless it is satisfied –
>
> (a) that the need for the extension is due to –
>   (i) the illness or absence of the accused, a necessary witness, a judge or a magistrate;
>   (ii) a postponement which is occasioned by the ordering by the court of separate trials in the case of two or more accused or two or more offences; or
>   (iii) some other good and sufficient cause; and
> (b) that the prosecution has acted with all due diligence and expedition.'

In view of the retention of 'good and sufficient cause' as a ground for extension in (a)(iii), it cannot be accepted that the court's discretion has been limited. Indeed, the criteria for an extension have been widened by (a)(ii).

The discretionary power to order separate trials is exercisable, for example, where the court considers that the accused might be prejudiced in their defence as a result of a single trial. Without (a)(ii), where the court ordered separate trials there would be a risk that the time limit might expire before the later trial, with the result in the case of an overall time limit that the proceedings would have to be stayed and in the case of a custody time limit that the accused would have to be released on bail. The ordering of separate trials is a matter over which the prosecution has no control and it seemed to the Government that such a result should not follow if a trial were postponed for that reason.[2]

---

1 See the cases cited in *Archbold: Criminal Pleading, Evidence and Practice* (1998 edn), paras 1-273–1-274.
2 Lord Falconer of Thoroton, Solicitor-General, HL 3rd Reading, col 225.

Additional time limits for juveniles

6.103   As part of its strategy to reduce delay in the youth justice system, the Government intends to make more stringent time limits for persistent young offenders[1] than for other young offenders so as to ensure that they are 'fast-tracked' from the outset.

---

1 See para **6.99**.

6.104   The Home Secretary is given powers to make regulations specifying additional time limits in respect of those under aged 18[1] when the criminal process was instituted against them. These powers are given by a new s 22A of the Prosecution of Offences Act 1985, which is inserted by s 44 of the new Act.

The new time limits may be of two types:

(1) a maximum period between arrest and the ending of the date fixed for first appearance in court (the 'initial stage' limit); and
(2) a maximum period between the time of conviction and the time of sentence.

Once the regulations are in force under s 22A of the 1985 Act, time limits in respect of juveniles covered by them will, when those regulations are taken in conjunction with those existing and envisaged under s 22, cover most of the period from arrest to sentence. The only period not covered in the case of a juvenile who has been arrested will be the trial period itself. This omission is deliberate, as explained in *No More Excuses*:

> 'The period of the trial itself will not be covered by a time limit, as this would risk undermining the fairness of the court proceedings (and, in the vast majority of cases, the trial period does not contribute significantly to delay). In guilty plea cases, there would be no interval between start of trial and conviction.'[2]

---

1 See general annotations.
2 *No More Excuses – A New Approach to Tackling Youth Crime in England and Wales*, Cm 3809 (1997), para 7.12.

6.105   The time limits must be made by regulations (Prosecution of Offences Act 1985, s 22A(1)) made by statutory instrument subject to annulment in pursuance of a resolution of either House of Parliament (ibid, s 29).

General points about regulations under s 22A

6.106   Section 22A(2) of the 1985 Act applies, with amendments, s 22(2)[1] of that Act so as to provide that regulations under s 22A may, in particular:

(a) be made so as to apply only in relation to proceedings instituted in specified areas, or proceedings of, or against persons of, specified classes or descriptions;
(b) make different provision with respect to proceedings instituted in different areas, or different provision with respect to proceedings of, or against persons of, different classes or descriptions.[1]

As can be seen, these provisions not only permit piloting in particular areas but they also permit special provision to be made in respect of, for example, persistent young offenders.

---

1 See the annotations to s 43 for the full text of s 22(2).

Initial stage limit

6.107   Section 22A(1)(a) of the 1985 Act provides that the Home Secretary may by regulations make provision with respect to a person under the age of 18 at the time of his arrest in connection with an offence, as to the maximum period to be allowed for the completion of the stage beginning with his arrest and ending with the date fixed for his first appearance in court in connection with the offence. It will be noted that this time limit begins to run from arrest and not charge. An arrest will have been based on reasonable suspicion that the juvenile committed an offence. In some cases, there may be need for time to elapse in order to gather enough evidence for a charge to be brought: for example, a DNA test or other scientific evidence may be needed before the police can decide whether or not to charge the arrested juvenile. It may be difficult, therefore, for the police to comply with the limit in some cases, unless the period is extended.

A factor which might have made it difficult to comply with the initial stage limit is that hitherto there has been a practice, in some instances almost routine, of referring a case to a multi-agency panel before a decision as to whether a charge or a caution is appropriate. This has been the main cause of delay between arrest and charge. The Government has issued guidance that such referrals should be avoided and that decision-making should be based in most cases on the application of gravity-factors developed jointly by local agencies.[1] The new final warnings scheme under ss 65 and 66 should end the practice. That scheme allows the police simply to take decisions about whether or not to charge, without needing to consult others. Indeed, the Government specifically rejected calls for the final warning to be deferred until after the consultation with the youth offending team.[2]

---

1 *Misspent Youth '98* (Audit Commission, 1998), p 13.
2 See paras **2.19–2.21**.

Extension of initial stage time limit

6.108   At any time before the expiry of an initial stage time limit, a magistrates' court may extend or further extend that limit; but the court shall not do so unless it is satisfied:

(a) that the need for the extension is due to some good and sufficient cause; and

(b) that the investigation has been conducted, and (where applicable) the prosecution has acted, with all due diligence and expedition (1985 Act, s 22A(3)).

These criteria are, of course, similar to those specified in s 22 of the 1985 Act before it was amended by the new Act. They do not have the added degree of prescription which the Government thought so important in respect of s 22.

As is the case in respect of an overall time limit or a custody time limit, where a magistrates' court decides to extend, or further extend, an initial stage time limit (or refuses to extend it), the accused (or the prosecution as the case may be) may appeal against the decision to the Crown Court. An appeal by the prosecution may not be commenced after the expiry of the limit; but where such an appeal is commenced before the expiry of the limit, the limit is deemed not to have expired before the determination or abandonment of the appeal (1985 Act, s 22A(7), applying the 1985 Act, s 22(7)–(9)). Alternatively, the magistrates' court's decision could be challenged by an application for judicial review in appropriate cases.

The availability of a right of appeal against a decision to grant or refuse an extension to an initial stage time limit can be contrasted with the non-availability of a right of appeal in respect of an application for a warrant for further police detention under s 43 of the Police and Criminal Evidence Act 1984.

Expiry of initial stage time limit
6.109 Where the initial stage time limit (whether as originally imposed or as extended or further extended) expires before the person arrested is charged with the offence,[1] he must not be charged with it unless further evidence relating to it is obtained, and:

(a) if he is then under arrest, he must be released;
(b) if he is then on police bail, his bail (and any duty or conditions to which it is subject) must be discharged (1985 Act, s 22A(4)).

---

1 Being charged with an offence includes the laying of an information charging the offence (1985 Act, s 22A(9)).

6.110 A question unanswered by the new provisions is the situation where a juvenile is arrested and released on bail without charge, pending further inquiries, and is then re-arrested. In the absence of a provision to the contrary, it seems that the initial stage time limit is unaffected by release followed by a re-arrest, so that time continues to run from the first arrest.[1]

---

1 This was the view of Mike O'Brien, MP, Parliamentary Under-Secretary, Home Office, HC Committee, col 400.

6.111 Where the initial stage time limit (whether as originally imposed or as extended or further extended) expires after the person arrested is charged with the offence but before the date fixed for his first appearance in court in connection with it, the court must stay the proceedings (1985 Act, s 22A(5)). We deal with the effect of a stay of proceedings in para **6.114**.

Effect on initial stage time limit of escape by prisoner or failure to surrender to bail

6.112   Section 22A(6) of the 1985 Act deals with the effects on an initial stage time limit where:

(a) a person escapes from arrest; or
(b) a person who has been released on police bail fails to surrender himself at the appointed time,

and is accordingly unlawfully at large for any period.

It provides that, so far as the offence in question is concerned, *that* period (but not any other) must be disregarded for the purposes of the limit.

Conviction-sentence limit

6.113   Section 22A(1)(b) of the 1985 Act, inserted by s 44, provides that the Home Secretary may by regulation make provision:

> 'with respect to a person convicted of an offence who was under [18] at the time of his arrest for the offence or (where he was not arrested for it) the laying of the information charging him with it, as to the period within which the stage between his conviction and his being sentenced for the offence *should be* completed.'

The use of 'should be' indicates that, unlike the initial stage time limit, the conviction-sentence limit is an administrative time limit. Non-compliance with it would not lead to proceedings being stayed, but the limit would mean that court administrators would be obliged to set the date for sentencing within the time limit and that pre-sentence report writers or writers of other reports would be expected to meet that deadline. Because this time limit is not mandatory, a court could adjourn sentencing if, when the day fixed for sentencing arrived, there was insufficient information available on which to sentence.

Effect of staying a prosecution under s 22 or s 22A

6.114   Where a prosecution is stayed under s 22(4) or s 22A(5) of the 1985 Act, a prosecution will not necessarily be reactivated. There will be a discretion. How strictly it will be exercised remains to be seen. At the Second Reading in the House of Lords, Lord Williams of Mostyn, Parliamentary Under-Secretary, Home Office, said: 'Such prosecutions could be reactivated in exceptional circumstances'.[1] Section 22B(1) and (2) of the 1985 Act, added by s 45 of the new Act, certainly indicate that fresh proceedings should not be a matter of course by restricting the decision to bring them to senior prosecutors. It provides that, when proceedings have been stayed on the expiry of one of the above time limits, the institution of fresh proceedings requires a direction:

(a) where the original proceedings were conducted by the Director of Public Prosecutions (ie the Crown Prosecution Service), by the Director or a Chief Crown Prosecutor;[2]

(b) where the original proceedings were conducted by the Director of the Serious Fraud Office, the Commissioners of Inland Revenue or the Commissioners of Customs and Excise, by the Director or those Commissioners; or

(c) where the proceedings were not conducted by any of the above (as in the case of a private prosecution), by a person designated by the Home Secretary for the purpose of giving such a direction.

Although s 1(6) of the 1985 Act provides that 'every Crown Prosecutor shall have all the powers of the Director [of Public Prosecutions] as to the institution and conduct of proceedings but shall exercise those powers under the direction of the Director', it is submitted that this does not apply to s 22B(2)(a) in the light of the reference to a direction being given by the Director or a Chief Crown Prosecutor. If s 1(6) did apply, the reference to the latter would be otiose since a Chief Crown Prosecutor could institute proceedings under s 1(6). This interpretation is supported by statements in *No More Excuses*.[3]

---

1 HL 2nd reading, col 535.
2 See annotations to s 45.
3 *No More Excuses – A New Approach to Tackling Youth Crime*, Cm 3809 (1997), para 7.14.

Institution of fresh proceedings

6.115   Fresh proceedings are to be instituted:

(a) by preferring a bill of indictment, where the original proceedings were stayed by the Crown Court. The Administration of Justice (Miscellaneous Provisions) Act 1933, s 2(2) which forbids the preferring of a bill of indictment except in specified cases is amended by Sch 8, para 5(1)(b) so as to add to these the case where the bill is preferred in the present type of case. The Indictments (Procedure) Rules 1971[1] will require amendment in the light of the new provision. (For obvious reasons no committal proceedings are required in the case of an either-way offence);

(b) by laying an information, where the original proceedings were stayed by a magistrates' court (including a youth court) (1985 Act, s 22B(3)).

Fresh proceedings must be instituted within three months[2] (or such longer period as the court may allow) after the date on which the original proceedings were stayed by the court (1985 Act, s 22B(2)). An information laid under s 22B in respect of a summary offence more than six months[2] after the time when the offence was committed may be tried by a magistrates' court, notwithstanding the general prohibition on this in s 127(1) of the Magistrates' Courts Act 1980[3] (1985 Act, s 22B(4)). Other time limits, such as that in respect of the offence of unlawful intercourse with a girl under 16[4] and that in respect of the offences of gross indecency between men and of male homosexual buggery,[5] are not waived.

Where a decision is taken to re-institute proceedings, the court will have the discretion to remand the accused on bail or in custody. Presumably, any

applicable time limits of the types described in this part of this chapter will
begin to run de novo.

1 SI 1971/2084.
2 See general annotations.
3 See annotations to s 45.
4 Sexual Offences Act 1956, s 37(2) and Sch 2, para 10.
5 Sexual Offences Act 1967, s 7.

6.116   Where fresh proceedings are instituted under s 22(4) or s 22A(5) of
the 1985 Act, the court may direct that anything done in relation to the original
proceedings (other than disclosure under the Criminal Procedure and
Investigations Act 1996) shall be treated as done in relation to the fresh
proceedings (1985 Act, s 22B(5)). Presumably, such a direction will be the
norm and will apply to everything done in relation to the original proceedings.

6.117   The rules about disclosure in Part I of the Criminal Procedure and
Investigations Act 1996 apply to cases where fresh proceedings are brought
under s 22B(3) of the 1985 Act (1996 Act, s 1(1) and (2), as amended by the
new Act, Sch 8, para 125(b)). Until regulations are made as to the relevant time
limit for primary disclosure by the prosecutor under s 3 of the 1969 Act, the
prosecutor must act under s 3 as soon as is reasonably practicable[1] after the bill
of indictment is preferred or the accused pleads not guilty in a magistrates'
court (1996 Act, s 13(1), as amended by the new Act, Sch 8, para 127(b)).

Anything done in relation to the original proceedings by the prosecutor in
compliance or purported compliance with the prosecutor's duties of primary
disclosure under ss 3, 4, 7 and 9 of the Criminal Procedure and Investigations
Act 1996, or by the accused in compliance or purported compliance with his
duty of disclosure under s 5 of the 1996 Act or with s 6 of that Act (voluntary
disclosure by the accused), is automatically treated as done in relation to the
fresh proceedings, ie no direction by the court is required (1985 Act, s 22B(5)).
As a result, anything disclosed under the 1996 Act in respect of the original
proceedings need not be disclosed again in respect of the fresh proceedings.

Where disclosure has been made by someone in compliance with a duty
(whether statutory or common law) other than one under the 1996 Act, the
situation is governed by the rule set out in para **6.116**.

1 See general annotations.

6.118   Where a person is convicted of an offence in fresh proceedings
under s 22B of the 1985 Act, the institution of these proceedings cannot be
called into question in any appeal against that conviction (1995 Act, s 22B(6)).
This means that the exercise of the discretion under s 22B(2) to institute fresh
proceedings cannot be called into question in an appeal against conviction. A
refusal to extend a time limit in respect of the original proceedings which leads
to their staying and then to the institution of fresh proceedings cannot be
questioned in an appeal against conviction, but it may be subject to an appeal

under s 22(8) of the 1985 Act or to judicial review, depending on the circumstances. In contrast, there is no right of appeal against a prosecution decision to initiate or not to initiate fresh proceedings, although judicial review would be available in exceptional circumstances.[1]

---

1 *Chief Constable of Kent, ex parte L* [1993] 1 All ER 756 (DC); *Inland Revenue Commissioners, ex parte Mead* [1993] 1 All ER 772 (DC).

Chapter 7

DEALING WITH ADULT OFFENDERS

Sentencing guidelines and Sentencing Advisory Panel – Extended licence provisions for sexual or violent offenders – Drug treatment and testing orders – Other community sentences – Determinate sentences: length, early release and post-release supervision – Miscellaneous changes

7.1   In Chapter 4 the sentencing changes applicable to young offenders were discussed. In this chapter we deal with the changes relating to sentence made by the new Act. Part IV of the new Act contains a range of provisions in respect of how offenders may be dealt with. These include several new orders, including a drug treatment and testing order, and extended sentences for violent or sexual offenders. New institutional arrangements are put in place for providing guidelines for sentencers. In addition, detailed changes are made by Schs 7 and 8. Also dealt with in this chapter are the amended arrangements in respect of the release and supervision arrangements which apply in respect of those serving a determinate sentence.

The context of Schs 7 and 8 should be noted. The changes made by Sch 7 are of a minor or textual nature, or are made to remove anomalies which have been identified in existing legislation. These changes are a precursor to, arguably, long-overdue consolidation of sentencing legislation. They came into force on 30 September 1998: see Appendix II. Schedule 8 contains a wide range of detailed amendments, which are intended to make existing legislative provision, in content and terminology, reflect the substantive changes made by the new Act. This too, came into force on 30 September 1998: see Appendix II. Certain transitional provisions apply in the context of some of the changes made by Schs 7 and 8: see Appendix II.

SENTENCING GUIDELINES AND SENTENCING ADVISORY PANEL

7.2   Sections 80 and 81 create new machinery whereby the Court of Appeal (Criminal Division) can give guidance to sentencers in respect of sentences imposed in respect of indictable offences.[1] A duty is imposed on the court to consider whether to frame guidelines, or to revise existing guidelines, in respect of categories of indictable offences. The aim is to promote consistency in sentencing, promote the passing on an offender of the most effective sentence in order to prevent his re-offending and to promote public confidence in the criminal justice system.[2] This duty is supplemented by the creation of a new body, the Sentencing Advisory Panel, which, on its own initiative, may propose to the Court of Appeal that guidelines for particular categories of offence be adopted or revised (s 81(3)) and must do so if directed by the Home Secretary. In either situation, it will consult, consider and formulate views and furnish information to the court.

1 See general annotations.
2 Jack Straw, MP, Home Secretary, HC 2nd Reading, col 378. See the terms of s 80(3), dealing with the matters to which the court shall have regard, and set out at para **7.9**.

7.3   The duty imposed on the court by s 80 does not apply in any case where the Court of Appeal is seised of an appeal against sentence before that date of commencement (Sch 9, para 7).[1] The court is 'seised' of an appeal if leave to appeal against sentence has been granted either by the court or by a single judge, or, in a case where the sentencing judge granted a fitness for appeal,[2] if notice of appeal has been granted (s 80(7)). In such cases, no such duty arises. Clearly, however, there is nothing to prevent the court in any judgments setting out guidelines: that is how pre-existing sentencing guidelines have been developed, and there is nothing in the new Act to prevent this. The transitional provision is, arguably, of no great significance other than to define when the court is under a positive duty to consider the adoption of guidelines.

1 For commencement, see para **1.4**.
2 Under the Criminal Appeal Act 1968, s 9 or s 10.

Rationale for the new provisons

7.4   Except in cases of murder, where the mandatory life sentence applies, in cases which fall within s 2 or s 3 of the Crime (Sentences) Act 1997,[1] or where statute prescribes, in whole or in part, the order or penalty that may be imposed,[2] sentencing courts have a discretion as to the sentence that is imposed. However, it is of considerable importance that different courts sentence consistently for the same type of offence, and impose a penalty appropriate to the level of seriousness of the offence of which the offender is convicted. On the other hand, the existence of that judicial discretion free from executive interference is an equally important principle, and to some,[3] although not all,[4] a principle of constitutional principle. What is beyond doubt is that sentencers should be able, so far as possible, to sentence in accordance with the circumstances of the particular offence, but under the guidance of principles set out by the Court of Appeal. It was the concern of many to uphold this basic principle which led to the strong opposition to the introduction by the Crime (Sentences) Act 1997 of mandatory and minimum sentences.[5] In expressing his opposition to the changes then being proposed by the Bill that became the Crime (Sentences) Act 1997, Lord Bingham observed:

> 'It is a cardinal principle of just sentencing that the penalty should be fashioned to match the gravity of the offence and to take account of the circumstances in which it was committed. Any blanket or scatter-gun approach inevitably leads to injustice in individual cases.'[6]

1 Mandatory life sentence for second serious offence: s 2; minimum seven-year sentence for Class A drug trafficking offence: s 3.
2 See, eg, the mandatory disqualification provisions in respect of certain offences under the Road Traffic Act 1988.
3 See, eg, Ashworth *Sentencing and Penal Policy* (Weidenfeld and Nicholson, 1983) at p 54; Ashworth *Sentencing and Criminal Justice* (2nd edn) (Butterworths, 1995) at pp 40–51.
4 See, eg, Walker and Padfield *Sentencing Theory, Law and Practice* (Butterworths, 1996) at p 380, who see no constitutional principle which forbids or even discourages Parliament from limiting the discretion of sentencers if that has advantages.
5 See, eg, Lord Woolf, HL vol 577, col 997, where he complained of 'the legislature taking over what has been accepted to be the proper role of the judiciary'.
6 Crime (Sentences) Act 1997, HL vol 577, col 987.

7.5   The other side of the coin is, however, that there should be consistency of approach to sentencing by courts in individual cases, whilst ensuring an individually fashioned sentence. This consistency in sentencing can be achieved in various ways. One is through the statements as to general principle that are set out in decisions of the Court of Appeal, such as in respect of the credit to be given for a plea of guilty,[1] the application of principles of sentence totality (that the totality of the total sentence imposed should reflect the overall level, nature and seriousness of the offending)[2] or the principle of pro-portionality of longer than commensurate sentences passed under s 1(1)(b) of the Criminal Justice Act 1991.[3] A wide, but not comprehensive, range of guideline judgments also gives guidance as to mitigating and aggravating features of specific offences, and the appropriate sentence, and sentence length, in the case of custodial sentences.[4] These guideline judgments have added force in that the Attorney-General has the power to make a reference to the Court of Appeal in a case where the sentence imposed is considered to be unduly lenient.[5]

In respect of summary offences, the Magistrates' Association has issued Guidelines in respect of a wide range of offences, based on a timely plea of guilty.[6]

1 Although the Criminal Justice and Public Order Act 1994, s 48, makes statutory provision in respect of the principle, the detailed approach developed in the case-law is still relevant. See, eg, *Costen* (1989) 11 Cr App Rep (S) 182 (CA); *M (Sentence)* (1994) *The Times*, 1 March (CA); *Buffrey* (1993) 14 Cr App Rep (S) 511 (CA); *Stabler* (1984) 6 Cr App Rep (S) 129 (CA).
2 See, eg, *Hunter* (1979) 1 Cr App Rep (S) 7 (CA).
3 *Mansell* (1994) 15 Cr App Rep (S) 771 (CA).
4 See, eg, manslaughter (*Chambers* (1983) 5 Cr App Rep (S) 190 (CA); *Coleman* (1992) 13 Cr App Rep (S) 508 (CA)); rape (*Billham* (1986) 82 Cr App Rep 347 (CA)); burglary (*Mussell* (1990) 12 Cr App Rep (S) 607 (CA); *Brewster* (1997) *The Times*, 4 July (CA)). Many other examples exist.
5 Criminal Justice Act 1988, ss 35–36. For the principles as to how the court will act, see *A-G's Reference (No 4 of 1989)* (1989) 11 Cr App Rep 517 (CA).
6 See Wasik and Turner *Sentencing Guidelines for the Magistrates' Courts* [1993] Crim LR 345.

7.6   Despite this framework, there has continued to be a lack of clarity and consistency in sentencing and on-going public concern about what are perceived, rightly or wrongly, to be inadequate sentences for serious crime.

The Labour Party's manifesto for the 1997 General Election promised greater clarity and consistency. It is that promise which s 80 seeks to implement (and also s 81, which creates the Sentencing Advisory Panel) although not by the creation of the Sentencing Council which has been advocated for some years,[1] nor by the creation of a wider advisory council on criminal justice and the penal system, which would, if created, have played a role that went far beyond, sentencing matters. In the House of Lords, Lord Ackner led an impressive array of peers calling for the establishment of such a body, but the amendment successfully pressed by that group of peers was overturned by the House of Commons. In terms of consistency in sentencing the approach is to be through guideline judgments of the Court of Appeal, informed by guidance from a Sentencing Advisory Panel.

1 See Ashworth *Sentencing and Criminal Justice* op cit, pp 342–352.

Sentencing guidelines

7.7 Section 80(2) imposes a duty on the Court of Appeal (Criminal Division) to consider whether to frame guidelines as to the sentencing of offences which fall within the relevant category. The court must also consider whether it is appropriate to review existing sentencing guidelines (s 80(2)). The duty arises where the court:

(a) is seised of an appeal, or a reference under s 36 of the Criminal Justice Act 1988, against the sentence passed for an offence;[1] or

(b) receives a proposal under s 81 from the Sentencing Advisory Panel[2] in respect of the relevant category of offence (s 80(1)(b)).

'The relevant category' of offence is defined by s 80(1) as any category within which the offence falls or proposal relates. This gives the court the widest possible scope to focus in on groups of offence: for example, offences may be categorised by offence, offence type, level of financial loss, seriousness of personal harm suffered by the victim, method, age, gender or ethnicity of victim, or the locality of commission. Nothing in the new Act prescribes the type of categorisation that the court may adopt, and thus the potential for a wide range of guideline judgments exists.

1 For the definition of 'seised of an appeal' sees s 80(7).
2 See paras **7.11**–**7.13**.

7.8   The duty extends only to indictable offences (s 80(1), (9)), a phrase which includes both indictable-only and 'either way' offences.[1] Thus the potential for sentencing guidelines in respect of all types of cases tried at Crown Court exists. The duty does not extend to offences tried summarily. As noted above,[2] in respect of summary offences the Magistrates' Association has drawn up sentencing guidelines. Evidence exists that, despite these, considerable inconsistency in sentence for similar offences exists between different magistrates' courts.[3] Despite attempts to broaden the scope of ss 80 and 81, the Government concluded that it would be inappropriate to extend the role of the Court of Appeal to summary-only offences. In doing so it relied on the view of the Lord Chief Justice that to extend the sentencing guideline functions of the Court of Appeal to such offences would be inappropriate and disruptive of current arrangements, given that summary-only offences rarely came before the court.[4] Summary-only offences will thus continue to be governed by the Magistrates' Association guidelines, although magistrates' courts may well have regard informally to the guidance emanating from the Court of Appeal and the advice of the Sentencing Advisory Panel.

---

1 See general annotations.
2 See para **7.5**.
3 See Lord Henley, HL Committee, col 1149; Viscount Tenby, ibid.
4 See Lord Falconer of Thoroton, Solicitor-General, HL Committee, col 1150.

7.9   In framing or revising guidelines, the court is obliged to have regard to various matters (s 80(3)). These are:

(a) the need to promote consistency in sentencing;
(b) the sentences imposed by courts in England and Wales for offences of the relevant category;
(c) the cost of different sentences and their relative effectiveness in preventing re-offending;
(d) the need to promote public confidence in the criminal justice system; and
(e) the views communicated to the court by the Sentencing Advisory Panel.[1]

Guidelines framed or revised under s 80 must include criteria for determining the seriousness of offences, including (where appropriate) criteria for determining the weight to be given to any previous convictions of offenders or any failures of theirs to respond to previous sentences (s 80(4)).

---

1 See paras **7.11–7.13**.

7.10   Where guidance is framed by the Court of Appeal, it being seised of an appeal, the guidelines framed or revised under s 80 must, if possible, be included in the court's judgment in the appeal. However, there is the potential for significant delays to arise; it is clearly undesirable for individual appeals to be delayed whilst a consultation proceeds with the Sentencing Advisory Panel, and whilst the Panel conducts its own review. For that reason, s 80(6) states that guidelines framed or revised under s 80 must be included in a judgment of the court at the next appropriate opportunity (s 80(6)). This will be in the next case which falls within the same category of offence. Plainly, it would be wrong for individual cases to be subject to delay, and it is not the intention that the new provisions should work in a way that occasions such delay.[1]

---

1 See Alun Michael, MP, Minister of State, Home Office, HC Committee, col 654.

Sentencing Advisory Panel

7.11   Under powers conferred by s 81, the Lord Chancellor will establish a Sentencing Advisory Panel. This Panel will have the power to propose to the Court of Appeal (Criminal Division) that guidelines for sentencing in particular categories of indictable offence be framed or revised (s 81(1)). Although this power to propose guidelines is discretionary, it must do so if directed to do so by the Home Secretary (s 81(3)). Although the involvement of the Government, albeit indirectly, in the sentencing process might raise some concerns about the maintenance of judicial independence in the sentencing process, arguably it raises no fundamental issues of principle. The nature, types and levels of sentence passed for particular types of offences are a legitimate issue for the executive and Parliament: the new Act is itself an example. The Home Secretary would be likely to use the power to refer the question of guidelines to the Panel if there was a gap in a consideration of the main criminal offences, perhaps because no appeal had arisen in the relevant area, or if there were concerns about particular offences,[1] but the Home Secretary will not have the power to interfere with the contents of the Panel's advice: the line of reporting is from the Panel to the Court of Appeal, not from the Panel to the Home Secretary. In any event, the Court of Appeal is under no obligations to accept the advice or recommendations of the Panel.

1 Alun Michael, MP, Minister of State, Home Office, HC Committee, col 655.

7.12   The composition of the Panel is not prescribed by the new Act, and is at the discretion of the Lord Chancellor, on whom is conferred the power to remunerate members of the Panel (s 81(5)). The Panel is not, therefore, appointed directly by the Home Secretary, and thus no direct influence can be exerted through the nature of the appointments made to the Panel. The Lord Chancellor has held discussions with the Home Secretary and Lord Chief Justice concerning the potential composition of the Panel,[1] but no constraints exist on who should serve on the Panel. Its size, of around 12 persons, will 'be drawn from an appropriate range of experience', and may include sentencers (including a magistrate), persons with experience of the prison service and probation service, those with academic or research experience and persons wholly independent of the criminal justice system.[2] Members are likely to be appointed for a five-year period.[3]

1 Alun Michael, MP, Minister of State, Home Office, HC Committee, col 650.
2 Ibid, col 651.
3 Ibid, col 658.

7.13   The Panel will be under a duty to consult, to formulate its own views and communicate them to the Court of Appeal and to furnish information to the Court of Appeal about the sentences imposed by the courts in England and Wales for offences of the relevant category, the cost of different sentences and their relative effectiveness in preventing re-offending (s 81(4)).

EXTENDED LICENCE PROVISIONS FOR SEXUAL OR VIOLENT OFFENDERS

7.14   Sections 58 to 60 contain provisions which provide for extended licences for persons sentenced to a term of imprisonment for a sexual or violent offence,[1] by the passing of an extended sentence. The extended licence provisions for sexual offenders contained in the Criminal Justice Act 1991, s 44 are modified, s 59 substituting a new s 44 for that currently contained in the 1991 Act. The extended supervision provisions contained in ss 20 and 21 of the Crime (Sentences) Act 1997 were not brought into effect and are repealed by the new Act (Sch 10).

The new sentence is a custodial sentence, and therefore subject to the existing range of restrictions, in respect of the seriousness of the offence and in respect of children and young persons.

These provisions came into effect on 30 September 1998.[2]

---

1 The terms 'sexual offence' and 'violent offence' have the same meanings as in Part I of the Criminal Justice Act 1991 (s 58(8)). See annotations to s 58.
2 See Appendix II.

Background

7.15   These provisions mark the latest parliamentary attempt to create a regime whereby sex offenders and violent offenders, who may pose an on-going risk to the public at large, are subject to on-going supervision and licence after release from prison. Insofar as the new extended sentence provisions apply to sex offenders, they also form part of a package of measures intended to increase protection for the public.[1]

The pre-existing arrangements in respect of release of prisoners were those contained in the Criminal Justice Act 1991, enacted to implement the recommendations of the Carlisle Committee.[2] The scheme adopted by that Act was, broadly speaking, a system of early release, usually on licence, with the supervision of offenders on licence up until the three-quarters point of the total term of the sentence imposed. Thus an offender sentenced to four years' imprisonment for theft would be eligible for release after two years, and, if released, be subject to a period of licence for a further 12 months. That scheme applied to offenders sentenced to determinate terms of imprisonment for violent offences.

Special rules applied to those sentenced to determinate terms of imprisonment for a sexual offence, it being recognised that sex offenders may pose an on-going danger justifying extended supervision arrangements. The pre-existing s 44 of the 1991 Act provided that where a determinate sentence was imposed on an offender for a sexual offence, the court could (but was not required to) order that when the offender was released on licence in accordance with the rules governing early release, the period of licence should remain in force until the end of the sentence period, not simply until the expiration of three-quarters of that sentence. In considering whether to extend the period of licence in this way the court had to have regard to the need to protect the public from serious harm, and the desirability of preventing further offences by offenders and rehabilitating them. A sex offender could thus be supervised for a longer period than other offenders, but not for any period beyond the term of imprisonment imposed for the original offence, irrespective of the danger that offender might pose to the community or the benefits of on-going supervision on a statutory basis. In this context, the fact that no on-going supervisory regime could be achieved on a statutory (as opposed to voluntary) basis was a clear weakness, given the concerns about the continuing risks which certain sex offenders pose to the community.[3]

1 See para **5.58**.
2 *The Parole System in England and Wales* (HMSO, 1988), Cm 532. See also *Crime, Justice and Protecting the Public* (HMSO, 1990), Cm 965.
3 See the furore concerning Sydney Cook (a released paedophile): (1998) *The Times*, 27 April, (1998) *Guardian*, 4 April.

7.16   This regime was considered inadequate by the last Conservative Government. As part of the raft of legislative changes made by the Crime (Sentences) Act 1997 to try to achieve 'greater transparency' in the sentencing process,[1] and to try to ensure the concentration of supervision resources on those who posed the greatest danger to the community, new rules governing the supervision of sex offenders on their release were introduced, and similar (but not identical) arrangements extended to those sentenced to a term of imprisonment for a violent offence. Those rules are to be found in ss 20 and 21 of the 1997 Act, now repealed by Sch 10 to the new Act. In summary, these provided for the making of 'release supervision orders' as follows.

SEX OFFENDERS (1997 ACT, s 20)
The court had the power to direct that an extended supervision period should apply to a person sentenced to a term of imprisonment (of whatever length) for a sexual offence, and would have been obliged to so direct unless exceptional circumstances existed. The extended supervision period could be:

(a) one-half of the total sentence, or 12 months, whichever was longer; or
(b) such longer period, not exceeding 10 years, as the court considered necessary for the purpose of preventing the commission by the offender of further offences and securing his rehabilitation.

The supervision period could thus extend beyond the total length of the determinate sentence.

If no direction was made, the general rule introduced by the 1997 Act applied, namely, that offenders sentenced to a term of 12 months or more should be subject to a period of supervision of one-quarter of the term, or three months (whichever was greater) (1997 Act, s 16).

VIOLENT OFFENDERS (1997 ACT, s 21)
In respect of offenders sentenced to a determinate term of less than 12 months, generally there was no licence period. In respect of such offenders subject to a term of 12 months or more the normal rule was to be a period of one-quarter of the term, or three months, whichever was greater. The court had the power to order an extended supervision period of a specified length no greater than one-half of the total length of the term.

---

1 Michael Howard, MP, QC, Home Secretary, HC Deb, vol 284, no 9, col 912 (4 November 1996).

7.17 These provisions were never brought into effect by the Conservative Government, s 44 of the 1991 Act remaining the applicable power in respect of sex offenders. Despite the fact that no White Paper or Consultation Document was issued by the new Labour Government proposing changes to the arrangements put in place by the 1997 Act, it has taken the opportunity presented by a major piece of sentencing legislation to repeal the 1997 Act arrangements, set out above, and replace them with similar, but not identical, arrangements, in the form of a new extended sentence for sex or violent offenders. The Government considered that the provisions of the 1997 Act were not such as to provide an effective scheme for dealing with the periods to be served in respect of determinate sentences. It wished not to implement Part II of the 1997 Act, but, nevertheless, wished to make provision for extended supervision arrangements for sex and violent offenders. It thus sought to leave the basic scheme of the 1991 Act in place, but make new, and further, provision in respect of sex and violent offenders. It is, perhaps, a matter of opinion as to whether the detail of the new scheme is an improvement on that of the, never implemented, ss 20 and 21 of the 1997 Act. This emphasis on extended supervision for sex and violent offenders, and for recalled and returned prisoners, is a key part of the Government's proposals in the new Act. The result is likely to be additional supervisory costs of the probation service and for electronic monitoring in the region of £20 million per annum.[1]

---

1 Financial statement accompanying the Crime and Disorder Bill.

Application of the new power

7.18 The new extended sentence provisions will apply only where the sexual or violent offence[1] was committed on or after the date of commencement of s 58 (Sch 9, para 3). In respect of offences not governed by the new order, the pre-existing power in s 45 of the 1991 Act, set out at para **7.15**, will continue to apply.

For the purposes of the extended sentence, the terms 'sexual offence' and 'violent offence' bear the same meaning as ascribed to them by s 31 of the 1991 Act.[1] However, it has already been noted at para **5.62** that the definition of 'sexual offence' in s 31 differs from that applicable in respect of the Sex Offender Act 1997 and in respect of the new sex offender order. Care should be taken to ensure that, in this context, it is the s 31 definition that is applied.

---

1 See annotations to s 58.

7.19   The new power applies to any court which proposes to impose a custodial sentence for a sex or violent offence.[1] Because some of those offences are triable in a magistrates' court the power can be used by a magistrates' court, even though their powers in terms of the length of custodial sentence are in fact limited.[2] Although the effect of s 58(2)(a)[3] is to confine the length of the custodial term to pre-existing powers governing the imposition of custodial sentences, that does not restrict a magistrates' court in respect of the length of the extension period in respect of a sex offence[4] being tried summarily. Because an extended sentence is a custodial sentence, we therefore have the oddity that, now, in the sense described above, a magistrates' court may impose a custodial sentence in excess of six months.

---

1 See annotations to s 58.
2 Magistrates' Courts Act 1980, s 132.
3 See para **7.20**.
4 But not a violent offence, because of the effect of s 58(3), which would require a custodial
    term in excess of that in the 1980 Act, s 132, to be passed by a magistrates' court.

What is an extended sentence?

7.20   An 'extended sentence' is defined by s 58(2) as a custodial sentence the term of which is equal to the aggregate of:

(a)   the term of the custodial sentence which the court would have imposed if it had passed a custodial sentence otherwise than under s 58 ('the custodial term'); and

(b)   a further period ('the extension period') for which the offender is to be subject to a licence and which is of such length as the court considers necessary for the purpose mentioned in s 58(1), namely for the purposes of preventing the commission by him of further offences and securing the rehabilitation of the offender.

When may an extended sentence be imposed?

7.21   A court is not obliged to impose an extended sentence. If it does not do so, the normal rules governing release and supervision on licence, and applicable by virtue of s 44 of the 1991 Act will apply.[1] However, the power to pass an extended sentence under s 58(2) applies where a court which proposes to impose a custodial sentence for a sex or violent offence[2] considers that the period (if any) for which the offender would, if an extended sentence were not passed, be subject to a licence which would not be adequate for the purpose of preventing the commission by him of further offences and securing his rehabilitation (s 58(1)). A court will need to bear in mind that if it is a sentence of less than four years, and it decides not to impose an extended sentence, the home curfew arrangements (which will involve early release from prison) may potentially apply.[3]

Thus a court must determine, first, that a custodial sentence is appropriate, having regard to the offence seriousness criteria in s 1 of the 1991 Act,[4] and, secondly, determine that the extended period of supervision that the extended sentence permits[5] is necessary for the purposes set out in s 58(1). The court must also determine the total length of the sentence, a question dealt with below.

---

1 See para **7.15**.
2 See annotations to s 58.
3 See para **7.85**.
4 See Criminal Justice Act 1991, s 1.
5 See para **7.23**.

The length of the sentence

7.22   It has already been noted that an extended sentence comprises two elements: (1) a period of imprisonment (the 'custodial term'); and (2) the licence period ('the extension period'). A court will therefore need to address, individually, the question of the length of each of those two elements. The totality of the extended sentence for an offence must not, however, exceed the maximum term permitted for that offence (s 58(5)). The question of consecutive or concurrent extended sentences is dealt with later.[1]

THE CUSTODIAL TERM
Section 58(6) provides that s 2(2) of the Criminal Justice Act 1991 (length of custodial sentences) shall apply as if the term of an extended sentence did not include the extension period. The 'custodial term' must therefore reflect the seriousness of the offence or (if a longer than commensurate sentence) be proportionate.[2] It will be calculated in the normal way having regard to the matters to which regard is normally had (eg seriousness of the offence, aggravating or mitigating factors, any early indication of guilty plea, and the totality of the sentence).

If, in the case of a violent offence,[3] the appropriate custodial term is less than four years, a court may not pass an extended sentence (s 58(3)), and the normal licence provisions will apply.[4] No such minimum sentence length applies to sexual offences.[5]

THE EXTENSION PERIOD
This must not exceed:

(a) 10 years in the case of a sex offence; and
(b) five years in the case of a violent offence (s 58(4)).

The new Act confers a power on the Home Secretary to vary by order the
five-year period in respect of violent offences for a different period not
exceeding 10 years (s 58(7)).

---

1 See para **7.24**.
2 *Mansell* (1994) 15 Cr App Rep (S) 771 (CA).
3 See annotations to s 58.
4 See para **7.21**.
5 See annotations to s 58.

7.23   Although the extended sentence amounts in length to the aggregate
of the custodial term and extension period, there is no requirement that these
terms be equal in length. Thus an offender sentenced to a four-year or longer
custodial term could be made subject to an extension period of any length up
to five years, provided the two periods aggregated do not exceed the offence
maximum (s 58(3), (4) and (5)). An offender convicted of a sex offence can be
made the subject of an extension period of up to 10 years, irrespective of the
length of the custodial period, provided, again, that the two periods aggregated
do not exceed the offence maximum (s 58(4) and (5)).

Thus it is theoretically possible for a sex offender to be subject to an extended
sentence which comprises a six-month custodial term and a ten-year extension
period. This raises the question of whether the total length of the extended
sentence needs to be proportionate to the seriousness of the offence for which
the sentence is passed. In the context of 'longer than commensurate sentences'
under s 2 of the Criminal Justice Act 1991, the application of the doctrine of
proportionality has meant that such an extended term of custody should not be
disproportionate to the nature of the offending.[1] The extent to which this
principle will be applied equally in this context is unclear. Certainly, the effect
of s 58(6) is that the custodial element must be proportionate, and any 'longer
than commensurate' element in that custodial element must be proportionate
to the offending. However, the purpose of the extended period is to provide
on-going supervision within the community after release, to prevent the
commission of further offences and to secure his rehabilitation. Parliament has
specifically set the limits of that extended period (s 58(4)). Arguably, in many
cases a disproportionate extension period perhaps goes beyond what is
necessary for the purposes set out in s 58(1). In the example above, the fact that
only a six-month custodial term is imposed may cast doubt on whether the
danger posed by the offender is such to warrant a 10-year extension period.
However, it is difficult to imagine that an appeal court will readily accept an
argument that an extension period imposed on a violent or sex offender,
within the limits set by Parliament, is excessive provided the sentencing court

has approached carefully the task of identifying what extension period is needed to achieve the s 58(1) objectives. Arguably, the extension period must be commensurate with the risk of future offending or of harm to the public.

---

1 See para **7.5**.

Concurrent and consecutive sentences

7.24   An extended sentence is a custodial sentence imposed for an individual offence. There is nothing which prevents the imposition of concurrent or consecutive sentences in the normal way, in accordance with the relevant principles which govern the imposition and length of such sentences. Clearly, in the context of the custodial elements the totality of the sentences must reflect the nature and level of offending.[1] Whether it is appropriate to impose an extended sentence, and, if so, what is the appropriate length of the extension period will no doubt be judged in terms of when the offender will be released from custody. That is dealt with at paras **7.25–7.28**.

---

1 See para **7.23**.

The effect of the extended sentence

7.25   Section 59 substitutes a new s 44 for the pre-existing s 44 of the Criminal Justice Act 1991, and s 60 incorporates a new s 44A into the 1991 Act.

The new s 44 applies to a prisoner serving an extended sentence passed pursuant to s 58. The effect of s 44(2) is that the scheme dealing with the date of release and release on licence, contained in Part II of the 1991 Act,[1] applies to prisoners serving extended sentences.

The arrangements for early release depend on whether the prisoner is a 'long-term' or 'short-term' prisoner.[2] In this context, the provisions introduced by the new Act in respect of calculation of sentence length where there are two or more sentences should also be noted.[3] For all these purposes the length of the sentence is determined by the length of the custodial term sentence (1991 Act, s 44(2)).

Exceptions to this principle apply in respect of s 37(5),[4] and s 39(1) and (2)[5] of the 1991 Act, in which cases the question of whether the prisoner is a short-term or long-term prisoner is determined by the total length of the extended sentence (1991 Act, s 44(7)). Thus, subject to the limited exceptions mentioned above, if the custodial term is less than four years (which it may be in the case of a sex offence) the prisoner is a short-term prisoner, whilst if it is for four years or more (which it must be in the case of a violent offence and may be in respect of a sex offence) the prisoner is a long-term prisoner.

---

1 See para **7.73**.
2 See annotations to s 58.
3 See para **7.82**.

7.26   The date of release of a prisoner serving an extended sentence will be as follows:[1]

(a) Where the prisoner is a short-term prisoner, sentenced to a custodial term of less than four years, he must be released after serving one-half of his custodial term (1991 Act, s 33(1)(a) and (b), s 44(2)). This is unaffected by the new arrangements for short-term prisoners.[2]
(b) Where the prisoner is a long-term prisoner, with a custodial term of at least four years, he may be released after one-half of the custodial term, but must be released at the two-thirds point of the custodial term.

1 These statements assume no earlier release on compassionate grounds. For such release, see the 1991 Act, s 36, cited in annotations to s 59.
2 See para **7.25**.

7.27   The question then arises as to when the extension period described in para **7.20** begins. It begins as follows:

(a) where the prisoner is released on licence under Part II of the 1991 Act, the extension period begins on the date he would (but for his release) have served two-thirds of his custodial term (1991 Act, ss 44(5)(a), 37(1)). He will have been released on licence if:
   (i)   he is serving a custodial term of at least 12 months but less than four years, at the one-half of the custodial term point;
   (ii) he is serving a custodial term of four years or more, and released pursuant to a recommendation of the Parole Board after one-half, or automatically at the two-thirds of the custodial term point;
(b) where the prisoner would be released unconditionally under Part II of the 1991 Act (as he would be if serving a custodial term of less than 12 months) the extension period begins on the date when he would have been released (1991 Act, s 44(5)(b), s 33(1)(a)).

In short, the effect of the extension period is to extend the period of licence which would otherwise be served. 'Licence' bears the same meaning as in Part II of the 1991 Act, (new Act, s 58(8)) and nothing in the new Act alters the requirements which may be imposed as part of that licence or the arrangements for its management. A prisoner who is released on licence will remain on licence until the end of the extension period, unless the licence is revoked under s 39(1) or (2)[1] of the 1991 Act (1991 Act, s 44(3)). The picture can be best demonstrated by the following examples.

EXAMPLE 1
A is sentenced to an extended sentence of two years, the custodial term of which is nine months. He will be released after four-and-a-half months, and remain on licence for the remaining 19½ months.

EXAMPLE 2

B is sentenced to an extended sentence of four years, the custodial term of which is two years. He will be released after 12 months, on automatic conditional licence which lasts until the three-quarters sentence point (ie up to the 18 months point). He will then be subject to the extension period (ie a further two years' licence).

EXAMPLE 3

C is sentenced to an extended sentence of eight years, the custodial term of which is five years. He is released, on the recommendation of the Parole Board, at the one-half sentence point (ie after two years, six months). His parole licence continues until the three-quarters custodial term point (ie until three years, nine months after sentence). His extension period then commences (ie a further three years).

EXAMPLE 4

D is sentenced to an extended sentence of eight years, the custodial term of which is five years. The Parole Board declines to recommend discretionary conditional release. He is released on automatic conditional release at the two-thirds sentence point (ie after three years, four months). The licence continues until the three-quarters custodial term point (ie until three years, nine months after sentence). His extension period then commences (ie a further three years).

---

1 See annotations to s 59.

Re-release of prisoners serving extended sentences

7.28   Section 60 of the new Act inserts into the 1991 Act a new s 44A. This deals with the re-release of prisoners serving extended sentences, and who have been recalled to prison. Early release provisions are discussed at paras **7.81–7.85**, together with other provisions concerning release and re-release on licence.

DRUG TREATMENT AND TESTING ORDERS

7.29   Section 61 provides for a new community order (a 'drug treatment and testing order') for offenders aged 16 and over who are dependent on or have a propensity to misuse drugs. The age range should be noted: despite the fact that, for convenience of exposition, we deal with it in this chapter it is an order available in respect of persons aged 16 and over.

The order is not available in respect of offences for which the sentence is fixed by law or which is governed by the mandatory or minimum sentence provisions of ss 2 to 4 of the Crime (Sentences) Act 1997 (s 61(1)).[1]

The new order is not available in relation to an offence committed before the commencement of the section (Sch 9, para 4).[2] The new order came into force on 30 September 1998: see Appendix II.[3]

1 See annotations to s 61.
2 For commencement, see para **1.4**.
3 The order is being piloted under the management of the probation services in Merseyside (Liverpool), South-East London (Croydon) and Gloucestershire. See Home Office Circular 38/1998.

Background

7.30   The pre-existing provision to impose treatment for drug dependency as part of a sentence is contained in Sch 1A, para 6 to the Powers of Criminal Courts Act 1973, introduced by the Criminal Justice Act 1991, Sch 1A, para 6. That provision enables a court to impose a requirement as to treatment for drug or alcohol dependency as part of a probation order. Paragraph 6(2) of Sch 1A provides that a probation order may (where the pre-conditions in para 6(1) are satisfied) include a requirement that the offender shall submit, during the whole of the probation period or during such part of that period as may be specified in the order, to treatment by or under the direction of a person of experience with a view to the reduction or elimination of the offender's dependency on drugs or alcohol.

The pre-conditions contained in para 6(1) are that the court proposing to make a probation order is satisfied:

(a)   that the offender is dependent on drugs or alcohol;
(b)   that his dependency caused or contributed to the offence in respect of which the order is proposed to be made; and
(c)   that his dependency is such as requires and may be susceptible to treatment.

'Drug or alcohol dependency' is defined by para 6(9) as including a propensity towards the misuse of drugs or alcohol.

7.31   Schedule 1A, para 6(3) to the 1973 Act, specifies the treatment which may be required under such a requirement, which may be residential or non-residential.

If the person under whose direction an offender is being treated for dependency on drugs or alcohol pursuant to such a requirement is of the opinion that part of the treatment can be better or more conveniently given at or in an institution or place which is not specified in the order, or which is one at which the treatment given will be given under the direction by or under the direction of a person having the necessary qualifications or experience, that person who has formed that opinion may make arrangements for him to be treated accordingly, with the consent of the offender (1973 Act, Sch 1A, para 6(6)). The new Act in fact makes one detailed change in this regard. The pre-existing provision in Sch 1A, para 6(7) (which permitted such alternative arrangements to be in a place that could not have been specified for that purpose in the order) is repealed by Sch 10 to the new Act.

7.32   Paragraph 6 of Sch 1A to the 1973 Act remains in force after the new

Act comes into force. However, it is modified by Sch 8, para 34(2), to the new Act, which introduces a new para 6(1A) into Sch 1A to the 1973 Act. The effect of that is that if a court has been notified that arrangements for implementing drug treatment and testing orders are available in the area proposed to be specified in the probation order, para 6 of Sch 1A will no longer apply in respect of drug dependency, but only to alcohol dependency.

7.33   The Home Office has found that relatively little use has been made of the powers in Sch 1A, para 6, to the 1973 Act.[1] The reasons for this are believed to include:

–   the neutral policy position of both the Home Office and probation service, with no clear guidance on the use of the disposal being issued to sentencers;

–   a reluctance on the part of probation officers to make proposals for the use of such powers in pre-sentence reports, based on the view that coerced treatment is unlikely to be effective;

–   the lack of information for sentencers on what is available, what treatment involves and how it fits in with harm reduction strategies;

–   a perceived lack of enthusiasm on the part of treatment providers to operate mandatory programmes;

–   difficulties in getting the cost of treatment programmes met by local authorities under existing community care arrangements and the lack of any specific probation budget.

This apparent reluctance to utilise existing powers to the full is particularly significant given that 'drugs are at the root of much crime and disorder'.[2] It is also significant because many vulnerable young people with problems arising from drug or alcohol misusers have other behavioural or emotional problems.[3] The new order is therefore a classic combination of the Government's aim in respect of the new Act to be 'tough on crime, tough on the causes of crime'.[4]

---

1 See, generally, the Government's Consultation Paper *Breaking the Vicious Circle* (Home Office, 1997).
2 Jack Straw, MP, Home Secretary, HC 2nd Reading, col 377.
3 National Health Service Advisory Service Thematic review *Children and Young People Substance Misuse Services*, cited by Lord Henley, HL Committee, col 635.
4 See para **1.6**.

Who may be made the subject of an order?

7.34   Any person aged[1] at least 16. During the passage of the Act, concern was expressed that young drug users and misusers were to be subject to the same legislative regime as older offenders.[2] It was pointed out that the approach taken ought to take into account the age and relative understanding of the young person,[3] with a different range of services at different levels of intervention. Clearly, in respect of offenders aged under 18, youth offending teams will be able to make specific proposals in respect of the appropriate requirements to be imposed in a drug treatment and testing order, and these will be able to take into account the age and maturity of the offender. The court will, in the light of a pre-sentence report, be able to make an assessment as to whether a drug treatment and testing order is an appropriate order to make.[4] However, it should be borne in mind that the provision it replaces, namely a probation order with requirements,[5] has also been available in respect of offenders aged 16 and over.

---

1 See general annotations.
2 See Lord Henley, HL Committee, cols 634–636.
3 See *Substance Misuses and Young People* (Department of Health, 1997).
4 Lord Falconer of Thoroton, Solicitor-General, HL Committee, cols 637–638.
5 See para **7.31**.

The order

7.35   Section 61(2) provides that the court by or before which the offender is convicted may make an order (a 'drug treatment and testing order') which:

(a)   has effect for a period specified in the order of not less than six months nor more than three years ('the treatment and testing period'); and

(b)   includes the requirements and provisions mentioned in s 62.

A court must not make a drug treatment and testing order unless it has been notified by the Home Secretary that arrangements for implementing such orders are available in the area proposed to be specified in the order and the notice has not been withdrawn (s 61(3)). As already noted,[1] once such a notification has been given, and has not been withdrawn, the power to impose a requirement in respect of drug dependency in a probation order no longer arises. Instead the court will have to make a drug treatment and testing order.

---

1 See para **7.32**.

7.36   A drug treatment and testing order is a community order for the purposes of Part I of the Criminal Justice Act 1991 (s 61(4)), and thus the threshold for the making of a community order contained in s 6 of the Criminal Justice Act 1991 applies.[1] Like some, although not all, provisions relating to community orders, an order cannot be made unless the offender expresses his willingness to comply with its requirements (s 64(1)). However, if an offender fails to express his willingness to comply with its requirements, the effect of s 1(3) of the Criminal Justice Act 1991[2] is to entitle a court to impose a custodial sentence irrespective of the fact that the offence itself does not reach the custody threshold set out in s 1(2) of the 1991 Act. Alternatively, a community order not requiring consent could be made. These include a curfew order, and a probation order, although not one containing requirements for medical treatment, or for treatment in respect of alcohol.[3]

When a drug treatment and testing order is made, its effects and its requirements, the consequences of non-compliance, and availability of powers of review must be explained to the offender in ordinary language (s 64(1)).

1 See annotations to s 61.
2 See annotations to s 63.
3 See para **7.32**.

Combination of drug treatment and testing order with other orders and disposals

7.37   As already noted,[1] the order is a community order (s 61(4)). That not only means that the seriousness threshold for community order under s 6 of the Criminal Justice Act 1991 has to be crossed, but also that it is inappropriate to combine on the same occasion the order with a custodial sentence passed in respect of another offence.[2] It is not possible, for example, to combine a short custodial sentence with a drug treatment and testing order to address the addiction or drug misuse that motivated and underpinned the crime. However, there is nothing to prevent its combination with other community sentences. The Consultation Paper[3] clearly envisaged such combinations, particularly the combination of detention and treatment order and curfew and tagging. It noted that there was anecdotal evidence from chaotic drug misusers that electronic tagging has helped impose a degree of discipline on their lives as well as specific benefits of preventing them from going out to their dealers at particularly vulnerable moments.

1 See para **7.36**.
2 See *McElhorne* (1983) 5 Cr App Rep (S) 53.
3 *Breaking the Vicious Circle*, op cit.

Restriction on making a drug treatment and testing order

7.38   By s 61(5), a court must not make a drug treatment and testing order in respect of the offender unless it is satisfied:

(a) that he is dependent on or has a propensity to misuse drugs; and
(b) that his dependency or propensity is such as requires and may be susceptible to treatment.

These pre-conditions do not differ in material respects from the definition of drug dependency used in Sch 1A to the 1973 Act.[1] It will be for the court to determine whether a person is, or has a propensity to misuse drugs. For this purpose, alcohol is not a drug: if it were the amendments to Sch 1A, para 6 to the 1973 Act, discussed above,[1] would make little sense.

1 See para **7.30**.

Establishing misuse or propensity to misuse drugs
7.39   Section 61(6) provides that for the purpose of ascertaining for the purposes of s 61(5) whether the offender has any drug in his body, the court may by order require him to provide samples of such description as it may

specify; but the court must not make such an order unless the offender expresses his willingness to comply with its requirements.

Clearly, such an order can be made only against an 'offender'. There is thus no power whatsoever to make an order under s 61(5) in respect of a person who has yet to be convicted, and the Government rejected any suggestion of extending the law to permit testing of suspects pre-conviction.[1] Nor does it have to make such an order, and it is not envisaged that it will often be necessary to test before a drug treatment and testing order is made, on financial, logistical and practical grounds.[2] The pre-conditions for the making of a drug treatment and testing order do not of themselves require there to be evidence of the presence of a drug, or a particular level of drug, at any particular time, although, clearly, if a person is dependent or has a propensity to misuse then he may be unlikely to have no trace of drugs, or drug misuse, when tested. However, certain drugs have a quick metabolisation rate, whilst, of course, arrest and trial for the offence may occur a considerable period after the offence itself. It may be that it is the offence itself rather than the offender's current bodily state or behaviour which indicates a propensity to misuse drugs. However, the offence itself does not have to be a drugs offence. It might, for example, be a burglary committed with the motivation of obtaining cash to purchase drugs.

The crucial question is not whether there is evidence of the presence of a drug, but rather whether the court is satisfied that the conditions in s 61(5)(a) and (b) are met. This *could* be by the result of a sample, or by any other evidence before the court, including the details of the offence for which the offender is being sentenced. It could be by the opinion formed by the writer of a pre-sentence report.[3] There is no requirement in the legislation for a judicial finding to be made, nor any obligation to identify which drugs the offender has a dependency on or a propensity to misuse. The assessment of the offender by the probation service is therefore crucial. Any disputes about that assessment should be dealt with by a sentencing court in the normal way it would deal with challenges to the findings of, or statements in, a pre-sentence report. The Home Office has indicated that consideration should be given to the use of specialist probation assessors with effective contacts in police stations to assist in informal early assessment.[4] It is envisaged that the order will be aimed at drug misusers who are known to commit a high level of crime in order to fund their habit or who are violent and who show some willingness to co-operate with treatment.[5]

---

1 *Breaking the Vicious Circle*, op cit.
2 Ibid.
3 For the need for a pre-sentence report, see para **7.34**.
4 *Breaking the Vicious Circle*, op cit.
5 Ibid, para 6. See also Lord Falconer of Thoroton, Solicitor-General, HL Committee, col 637.

7.40   Where a court has requested the consent of the offender to the provision of samples prior to the making of the order, under s 61(6), his failure to consent does not of itself debar the court from making a drug treatment and testing order if there is other evidence of drug misuse or propensity to misuse. Of course, it is unlikely that if that other evidence existed the court would have sought to test at that stage in any event. In addition, such refusal makes it highly unlikely that the offender would be suitable for such an order, either because of an unwillingness to consent to the making of the order itself or because the refusal to provide samples may indicate to the court that there is no real willingness to co-operate. The courts should make an order only where the offender is assessed as suitable for it.[1]

---

1 Lord Falconer of Thoroton, Solicitor-General, HL Committee, col 637.

7.41   Section 61(3) imposes a further restriction on the making of an order. A court shall not make a drug treatment and testing order unless it is satisfied that arrangements have been or can be made for the treatment intended to be specified in the order (including arrangements for the reception of the offender where he is to be required to submit to treatment as a resident).

Requirements in drug treatment and testing orders

7.42   Section 62(1) provides that a drug treatment and testing order must include a requirement ('the treatment requirement') that the offender submit, during the whole of the treatment and testing period, to treatment by or under the direction of a specified person having the necessary qualifications or experience ('the treatment provider') with a view to the reduction or elimination of the offender's dependency on or propensity to misuse drugs.

The required treatment for any period must be:

(a)   treatment as a resident in such institution or place as may be specified in the order; or

(b)   treatment as a non-resident in or at such institution or place, and at such intervals, as may be so specified;

but the nature of the treatment must not be specified in the order except as specified by s 62(2)(a) and (b). The court will need to satisfy itself that arrangements can be, or have been, made for the specified treatment (including arrangements for the reception of the offender where he is to be required to submit for treatment as a resident) (s 62(3)).

7.43   These provisions are considered crucial to the practical success of the new order in dealing with drug-related crime. The order must be enforceable, and orders which have not been enforced properly, because of lack of clarity, have been one contributing factor to the lack of success of the pre-existing powers in the 1973 Act.[1] Clear definitions of the location, type, frequency and provider of treatment are intended to be key elements in the new order to provide a basis for effective enforcement.[2]

---

1 *Breaking the Vicious Circle*, op cit.
2 Ibid, para 14

7.44   The new Act imposes a duty on a court making an order for it to impose a testing requirement (s 62(4)). This is a requirement that, for the purpose of ascertaining whether he has any drug in his body during the treatment and testing period, the offender must provide during that period, at such times or in such circumstances as may be necessary (subject to the provisions of the order), samples of such description as may be so determined. The question of what samples, when given and in what circumstances, is a matter for the treatment provider, not the court, save only that the testing requirement must specify for each month the minimum number of occasions on which samples are to be provided (s 62(5)). The order will also specify the petty sessions area[1] in which it appears to the court making the order that the offender resides or will reside (s 62(6)).

Who undertakes the testing may vary. In *Breaking the Vicious Circle*[2] the Government suggested that offenders should be tested at least on a weekly basis, with a presumption that the person who carries out the tests should be the treatment provider. Confirmatory tests might, for evidential purposes, have to be analysed by a laboratory, but in some circumstances the Government suggests it makes sense for a probation officer, GP or independent clinic to carry out testing, given that testing in association with treatment, as opposed to isolation, is considered to be motivational.[3]

---

1 See general annotations.
2 Op cit, paras 11–12.
3 Ibid, para 12.

7.45   A drug treatment and testing order must:

(a) provide that, for the treatment and testing period, the offender be under the supervision of a 'responsible officer', that is to say, a probation officer appointed for or assigned to the petty sessions area specified in the order;
(b) require the offender to keep in touch with the responsible officer in accordance with such instructions as he may from time to time be given by that officer, and to notify him of any change of address; and
(c) provide that the results of the tests carried out on the samples provided by the offender in pursuance of the testing requirement be communicated to the responsible officer (s 62(7)).

The supervising probation officer does not, in the case of a 16- or 17-year-old, have to be a member of a youth offending team, although he or she might be.[1] The Government intends to issue guidance on the coordination that will need to occur if a drug treatment and testing order is made alongside another community order supervised by the youth offending team.

The levels of supervision are intended to be sufficient only for specified purposes. These are specified by s 62(7), and are to the extent necessary to enable him to report on the offender's progress, or on any failure, or to determine whether revocation or amendment of the order is appropriate (s 62(8)(a) to (c)). However, the potential coordinating role set out above needs also to be borne in mind.

Review of a drug treatment and testing order

7.46 A drug treatment and testing order must be kept under periodic review. By s 63(1), the order must:

(a) provide for the order to be reviewed periodically at intervals of not less than one month;

(b) provide for each review of the order to be made at a hearing held for the purpose by *the* court responsible for the order (a 'review hearing');

(c) require the offender to attend each review hearing;

(d) provide for the responsible officer to make to the court, before each review, a report in writing on the offender's progress under the order; and

(e) provide for each such report to include the test results communicated to the responsible officer under s 62(7)(c) and the views of the treatment provider as to the treatment and testing of the offender.

The words 'not less than one month' should not be misunderstood: it is intended that the minimum frequency, and the right frequency, is monthly,[1] although a longer frequency does not appear to be ruled out by the wording of s 63(1)(a).

Section s 62(7)(a) provides that the order must specify the responsible officer and state the petty sessions area.[2] Further, s 63(1)(b) provides for the review hearing being held by the court responsible for the order, which is presumably the court specified by virtue of s 62(7)(a), and that court has, by s 63(2), the power to amend any requirement or provision of the order. By these means the reviewing court may be changed from time to time, to accommodate, for example, changes in residence of the offender.

Although an offender must be present at a review hearing, there is one exception to that rule. By s 63(7), if at a review hearing the court, after considering the responsible officer's report, is of the opinion that the offender's progress under the order is satisfactory, it may amend the order to provide for each subsequent review to be made by a court without a hearing. A 'review without a hearing' is defined by s 63(10), in the case of the Crown Court, as a reference to a judge of the court, and, in the case of a magistrates' court, as a reference to a justice of the peace acting for the commission area[3] for which the court acts. Subsequent review hearings may therefore be held in the absence of the offender, but only if his progress is satisfactory. If at a review without a hearing the court, after considering the responsible officer's report, is of the opinion that the offender's progress under the order is no longer satisfactory, the court may require the offender to attend a hearing of the court at a specified time and place (s 63(8)). At that subsequent hearing the court, after considering that report, may exercise powers available at a review hearing, and may amend the order so as to provide for each subsequent review to be made at a review hearing (s 63(9)).

1 See Lord Williams of Mostyn, Parliamentary Under-Secretary, Home Office, HL Committee, col 642 in a somewhat obscure exchange with Viscount Colville of Culross.
2 See general annotations and s 117.
3 See general annotations.

Amendment of an order

7.47   At a review hearing the court, after considering the responsible officer's report, may amend any requirement or provision of the order (s 63(2)). The order may also be amended at other hearings without the offender being present, but only in accordance with s 63(9) (ie to provide for each subsequent review to be a review hearing). By s 63(3), the court:

(a) must not amend the treatment or testing requirement unless the offender expresses his willingness to comply with the requirement as amended;

(b) must not amend any provision of the order so as to reduce the treatment and testing period below the minimum specified in s 61(2), or to increase it above the maximum so specified; and

(c) except with the consent of the offender, must not amend any requirement or provision of the order while an appeal against the order is pending.

If the offender fails to express his willingness to comply with the treatment or testing requirement as proposed to be amended by the court, the court may:

(a) revoke the order; and

(b) may, unless the offender was aged 16 or 17 when the order was made, deal with him, for the offence in respect of which that order was made, in any manner in which it could deal with him if he had just been convicted by the court of the offence (s 63(4)).

In so dealing with him, the court must take into account the extent to which the offender has complied with the requirements of the order, and may impose a custodial sentence irrespective of the seriousness of the offence (s 63(5)). There will be no requirement for a pre-sentence report (although a court may require one), but obviously the responsible officer will have reported on the progress under the order. However, in the absence of a pre-sentence report there will not necessarily be a report on the offender's wider circumstances.

The powers in this respect of a court in respect of a person aged[1] under 18 at the date of the making of the order, and in respect of an offence triable only in indictment in the case of an adult, are limited to one of the following:

(a) a fine not exceeding £5,000; or

(b) to deal with the offender for that offence in any way in which it could deal with him if it had just convicted him of any offence punishable with imprisonment for a term not exceeding six months (s 63(6)).

1 See general annotations.

Breach

7.48   As a community order, Sch 2 to the Criminal Justice Act 1991[1] has effect in respect of the enforcement, etc, of drug treatment and testing orders. Schedule 2 has been amended in various respects by Sch 8 to the new Act. Those changes are dealt with at paras **7.62** to **7.70**.

1 See annotations to s 64.

7.49   Where it is alleged that an offender is in breach of an order he can be summonsed to appear before the relevant magistrates' court (1991 Act, Sch 2, para 2). If it is proved to the satisfaction of that court that the offender has without reasonable excuse failed to comply with the requirements of the order, the court may (Sch 2, para 3):[1]

(a)   impose on him a fine not exceeding £1,000;
(b)   make a community service order; or
(c)   make an attendance centre order;
(d)   deal with him for the offence in respect of which the drug treatment and testing order was made, in any manner it could have dealt with him if he had just been convicted by the court of the offence for which the order was made.

In respect of a Crown Court order it may (but is not required) to commit the offender in custody or release him on bail until he can be brought before the court (Sch 2, para 3(3)).[1]

A Crown Court has the powers contained in Sch 2, para 4 to the 1991 Act, which are similar to those exercisable by magistrates, save only that the power of imprisonment is not limited.

An offender who is required by a drug treatment and testing order to submit to treatment for his dependency on or propensity to misuse drugs must not be treated for the purposes as having failed to comply with that requirement on the ground only that he has refused to undergo any surgical, electrical or other treatment if, in the opinion of the court, his refusal was reasonable having regard to all the circumstances.

1 See annotations to s 64.

OTHER COMMUNITY SENTENCES

Probation orders

Discharge of probation and substitution of discharge
7.50   The power generally of a court to make a conditional discharge is contained in s 1A(1)(b) of the Powers of Criminal Courts Act 1973. The power to revoke a probation order is contained in Sch 2 to the Criminal Justice Act

1991.[1] It was, in one respect, increased by s 11 of the Powers of Criminal Courts Act 1973. This provided that where an application is made to a court having power to discharge a probation order, and the court considers the probation order to be no longer appropriate, the court could make an order of conditional discharge in substitution for that probation order.

The condition to which that discharge was subject is that the offender commits no offence during the period between the substitution and the date of expiration of the original probation order, had it continued.

---

1 See annotations to s 64.

7.51   Schedule 7, para 17, and Sch 10, repeal s 11 of the 1973 Act. This repeal took effect on 30 September 1998: see Appendix II. Section 11 is superseded by a new para 8A inserted into Sch 2 to the 1991 Act by Sch 7, para 46(11). It provides that a magistrates' court may, on the application of the offender or the responsible officer, make a conditional discharge and revoke the probation order, if it considers it in the interests of justice to do so. The application is made under para 8A, not under para 7 of Sch 2, which is the normal revocation power. The significant change made by para 8A is that, in respect of a Crown Court order, the magistrates may send the application to the Crown Court but have no power to dispose of the application themselves. Only the Crown Court henceforth will have the power to discharge a Crown Court probation order and substitute an order for conditional discharge. The new Sch 2, para 8A, permits an application to revoke and substitute a conditional discharge to be heard in the absence of the offender, if the application is made by the responsible officer, and that officer produces a statement to the court from the offender that he understands the effect of an order for conditional discharge and consents to the making of the application (Sch 2, para 8A(7)). If the substitution is in respect of a probation order made for an indictable-only offence, the offender being under 18 years of age at the time of the order, the conditional discharge is deemed to be made in those circumstances (Sch 2, para 11B). This affects how he may be dealt with if found subsequently to be in breach of the discharge.[1]

---

1 See para **7.71**.

7.52   Schedule 7, para 18, also amends s 12 of the 1973 Act, which makes supplementary provision relating to probation and discharge. It does so by making an amendment making it clear that if a power to revoke and impose a discharge is exercised on appeal, the order is deemed to be that of the court from which the appeal was made, not the Appeal Court. It also provides for the power to make an order for costs, disqualification or an order under various statutory provisions.

Requirements in probation orders

7.53   Schedule 1A, para 7 to the 1973 Act provided that instructions given by a probation officer under Sch 1A, para 2, of that Act must, so far as practicable, be such as to avoid any interference with the times, if any, at which the offender normally works or attends a school or other educational establishment. A similar provision is to be found in Sch 1A, para 3(4) (requirements to attend at probation centre). Both those provisions are replaced by new provisions (Sch 7, para 27). The purpose and effect of the change is to ensure that requirements or attendance be such as to avoid conflicts with the offender's religious beliefs or with the requirements of any other community order, as well as with the requirements of work or education.

7.54 Minor definitional changes are made by Sch 7, para 27(3) and (5) in respect of the terms 'registered medical practitioner' and 'chartered psychologist' found in Sch 1A, para 5 to the 1973 Act (requirements for treatment for medical condition). In that context, Sch 1A, para 5(7) is deleted by Sch 7, para 27(7): a requirement for treatment can no longer specify a place which could not have been specified in the probation order under para 5(3) of Sch 1A, ie as a residential or non-residential patient at a mental hospital or under the direction of a duly qualified medical practitioner.

7.55 Section 11 of the Criminal Justice Act 1991 deals with the combination of probation and community service. Schedule 7, para 40, of the new Act amends it to make it clear that the phrase 'punishable with imprisonment' contained therein means so punishable without regard to any prohibition or restriction imposed on the imprisonment of a young person.

Community service orders

7.56 The power to make a community service order is conferred by s 14 of the 1973 Act. Schedule 7, para 19, amends s 14 to make it clear that the power to impose a community service order does not apply to where the offence punishable by imprisonment is one where the sentence is fixed by law or one which is imposed by virtue of ss 2, 3 or 4 of the Crime (Sentences) Act 1997. This is not a change, but, rather, a clarification of the statutory provision.

7.57 The changes made, in respect of probation requirements, specifying the matters to which the responsible officer should have regard, were noted earlier.[1] An equivalent substitution is made in respect of community service (Sch 7, para 20), substituting a new s 15(3) for the pre-existing provision, and for the same reasons.

---

1 See para **7.53**.

Attendance centre orders

7.58 Schedule 7 makes a variety of amendments, of a detailed and drafting nature, to the Criminal Justice Act 1982. These are pre-consolidation amendments.[1]

7.59   In summary, the effect of these changes is as follows:

(a) The definition of an attendance order is textually amended (Sch 7, para 35), as is the definition of an attendance centre order (Sch 7, para 36). These changes are changes of definition rather than substance. The power to make an attendance centre order now arises in the circumstances set out in s 17 of the 1982 Act (as amended).

(b) The power to deal with breach of an attendance centre order by discharging it is amended. The existing s 18(4A) of the Criminal Justice Act 1982 provided that the power, which is exercisable by a court acting for the petty sessions area[1] in which the attendance centre is situated, or by the court which made the order, includes power to deal with the offender for the offence in respect of which the order was made, in any manner in which he could have been dealt with for that offence by the court which made the order if the order had not been made.

A new s 18(4A) is substituted by Sch 7, para 37. It provides that if a magistrates' court is discharging a magistrates' court order, or a Crown Court order, the power to re-sentence as before arises. It follows that, now, a magistrates' court cannot re-sentence in respect of a Crown Court order. A right of appeal from the magistrates' court to the Crown Court is created by a new s 18(4B). There is now power to re-sentence for the original offence if the offender has been ordered to attend at an attendance centre in default of the payment of a sum of money, or because of a failure to do (or abstain from doing) any matter (s 18(10), inserted by Sch 7, para 37(3)).

1 See general annotations.

7.60   Section 13 of the Criminal Justice Act 1982 deals with offenders who are the subject of attendance centre orders, and who attain the age of 21 (or, in limited circumstances, 18). When they attain that age they may be treated as if they had been sentenced to a term of imprisonment. However, they are not to be treated as if they were sentenced to a term of imprisonment for the purposes of supervision of young offenders (Sch 7, para 34). Section 13 is also amended to ensure that it applies not only to detention pursuant to s 8(2) of the 1982 Act, but also to detention pursuant to s 8(1) (detention in young offenders' institution for life, for murder).

Curfew orders

7.61   Amendments are made to s 12 of the 1991 Act, by Sch 7, para 41. These are minor amendments making it clear that the offender must be given a copy of the curfew order, as must the person responsible for monitoring the order, that references to the offender being under 16 are reference to his age on conviction, and also contain various textual changes.

Enforcement, etc of community orders

7.62   As noted earlier,[1] the provisions relating to the enforcement of community orders are to be found in Sch 2 to the 1991 Act. The new Act makes various changes to them, which are to be found in Sch 7, para 46, and Sch 8, para 96. The main changes are set out below.

---

1 See para **7.48**.

7.63   When a probation order, community service order or curfew order has been made on appeal, for the purposes of Sch 2, it will now be deemed to be made by the court from which the case under appeal came (eg magistrates' court, if it is a Crown Court appeal) (Sch 7, para 46(1)). A similar rule operates in respect of drug treatment and testing orders (Sch 8, para 96(1)).

7.64   The powers of magistrates' courts and Crown Courts for breach of a community order are contained, respectively, in paras 3 and 4 of Sch 2. Paragraphs 3(1)(c) and 4(1)(c) provided that the available powers were a fine not exceeding £1,000, a community service order (in the case of a probation order only) and revocation and re-sentencing. In the case of a probation order only and if the pre-condition contained in s 17 of the Criminal Justice Act 1982 was satisfied (ie the offender was aged under 21 and a place at an attendance centre was available) the court also has the power to make an attendance centre order.

The effect of the amendments in Sch 7, para 46(2) is to substitute new paras 3(1)(c) and 4(1)(c) to entitle a court to also make an attendance centre order where an offender aged under 16 had broken a curfew order.

7.65   Textual amendments are made to paras 3 and 4 of Sch 1 to put beyond doubt the fact that revocation of the community order when dealing with breach occurs only if the order is still in force. This addresses the situation where a breach hearing occurs after the expiration of the community order.

7.66   When dealing with a breach of a community order, a magistrates' court had to be satisfied that there was a failure to comply with the order without reasonable excuse. For reasons that are unclear, these words 'reasonable excuse' were not included in the equivalent Crown Court provision in para 4(1). That omission is rectified by Sch 7, para 46(3), which also makes a minor textual amendment.

7.67   Community service is not available in respect of a person aged under 16. The wording of Sch 2 did not make it clear that the power to make a community service order, explained above,[1] did not apply to a person under 16. Schedule 7, para 46(5), makes an appropriate amendment to para 6 of Sch 2, which is also amended to make it clear that an order continues notwithstanding the fact that an attendance centre order is made (Sch 7, para 46(4), amending Sch 2, para 6(1)(a)).

---

1 See para **7.56**.

7.68   Schedule 7, para 46(6), substitutes a new para 6(5) in Sch 2 to the 1991 Act. The pre-existing para 6(5) dealt with the powers which apply in respect of a failure to comply with a community service order made under paras 3 or 4 for breach of a community order (the 'original order'). In a complicated provision, the new para 6(5) makes it clear that a court can deal with a breach of the second order for failing to comply with it, and with similar powers in respect of revocation under paras 7 and 8 of Sch 2. It is the second order which is dealt with, the offender not being dealt with for the offence that gave rise to the original order.

7.69   Schedule 7, para 46 inserts a new para 6(6A) into Sch 2 to the 1991 Act. This increases the power of a magistrates' court in the case of an order made by such a court in the case of an offender aged under 18, in respect of offences triable only on indictment in the case of an adult. If the offender comes before the court for breach of the order after he reaches the age of 18, the court can:

(a)   impose a fine not exceeding £5,000; or
(b)   deal with him for that offence in any way in which a magistrates' court could deal with him if it had just convicted him of an offence punishable with imprisonment for a term not exceeding 12 months.

7.70   Paragraph 8(2) of Sch 2 to the 1991 Act deals with revocation of a magistrates' court order by a magistrates' court. It may either simply revoke or revoke and deal with the offender. Textual amendment is made by Sch 7, para 46(10), to make it clear that if it deals with the offender it may do so in the same way as if the court which imposed the order now had the offender before it for the offence for which the order was made.

Conditional discharge

7.71   The change in respect of conditional discharges and probation orders has already been noted.[1] In addition, changes are made in respect of the power to deal with the offender for a breach of a conditional discharge order imposed for an indictable-only offence. By s 1B(9) of the Powers of Criminal Courts Act 1973, if the offender later comes before the court for breach of the order having attained the age of 18, he can be dealt with as if the offence was an either-way offence and he had been tried summarily. The effect of a new Sch 2, para 11B is that if a probation order is being revoked and replaced by a conditional discharge, then if the original community order was made in the same circumstances as s 1B(9) sets out, then any provisions apply to the new conditional discharge.

---

1 See para **7.50**.

DETERMINATE SENTENCES – LENGTH, EARLY RELEASE AND POST-RELEASE SUPERVISION

7.72   The new Act contains a range of detailed changes concerning the length of time a prisoner must serve before being released on licence, the terms on which certain prisoners may be released on licence (including the power, in certain instances, to impose curfew conditions) and changes concerning recall to prison. Detailed changes are made to the licence provisions contained in Part II of the Criminal Justice Act 1991.

Some, but not all, of these changes came into effect on 30 September 1998: see Appendix II. The early release provisions contained in the Crime (Sentences) Act 1997 will not be implemented and are repealed by Sch 10.

The background and pre-existing law

7.73   As noted earlier,[1] the Criminal Justice Act 1991, Part II, sought to implement the recommendations of the Carlisle Report in respect of early release of prisoners. These provisions can be summarised as follows:

(a)   Section 33 of the 1991 Act distinguishes between a 'short-term' and a 'long-term' prisoner. The former is defined by s 33(5) of the 1991 Act as a person serving a sentence of imprisonment for a term of less than four years, the latter as a person serving a term of imprisonment of four years or more. The length of a sentence is to be calculated by aggregating consecutive terms of imprisonment, the overall total being regarded as a single term (1991 Act, s 51(2)).

(b)   A short-term prisoner is released unconditionally after having served one-half of his sentence, in the case of a term of imprisonment of less than 12 months (1991 Act, s 33(1)(a)).

(c)   A prisoner sentenced to a term of at least 12 months but less than four years is released automatically on licence (automatic conditional release) after one-half of his sentence, this licence extending in duration until the expiration of three-quarters of the sentence (1991 Act, ss 33(1)(b), 37(1)(a)). A prisoner sentenced to three years' imprisonment thus serves 18 months, is on licence for a further nine months, and at liberty unconditionally for a further three months. He remains subject to potential return to prison if convicted of a further imprisonable offence during the remaining period of the total sentence (1991 Act, s 40(1)), or for breach of the terms of the licence (1991 Act, s 38(1)).

(d)   A long-term prisoner sentenced to four years or more becomes eligible for conditional release after serving one-half of his sentence (discretionary conditional release) (1991 Act, s 35(1)). This discretionary conditional release is dependent on a recommendation for release by the Parole Board, and, if granted, extends until the expiration of three-quarters of the sentence (1991 Act, s 37(1)). If the prisoner is refused discretionary conditional release on licence, automatic conditional release occurs at the two-thirds point, the licence expiring at the three-quarters point. A prisoner sentenced to a term of six years thus must serve a minimum of three years before release. He may then be granted discretionary release, but in any event must be granted automatic conditional release after four years. Any release becomes unconditional after four years, six months. The prisoner may be returned to prison if convicted of a further imprisonable offence during the remaining period of the total sentence (1991 Act, s 40(1)), or if revocation of the licence is recommended by the Parole Board, or is expedient in the public interest (s 39(1), (2)).

(e) Special rules apply in respect of young offenders (1991 Act, s 43), sex offenders (1991 Act, s 44), fine defaulters and contemnors (1991 Act, s 45), persons liable to removal from the UK (1991 Act, s 46) and persons extradited to the UK (1991 Act, s 47).

(f) The calculation of sentence length can take into account remand time (1991 Act, s 41) and additional days for disciplinary offences (1991 Act, s 42).

---

1 See para **7.15**.

7.74   The last Conservative Government considered these provisions 'complicated'.[1] It took the view that 'the public, and sometimes even the courts, are frequently confused and increasingly cynical about what prison sentences actually mean'.[2] To achieve what it described as 'greater transparency' to the sentencing process[3] the Crime (Sentences) Act 1997 provided for a radically different scheme, where a prisoner would serve a period of time more closely approximating to that formally imposed by the court. That scheme, inter alia, provided for the repeal of Part II of the 1991 Act, only some six years after its introduction.

---

1 Michael Howard, MP, QC, Home Secretary, 4 November 1996.
2 *Protecting the Public*, Cm 3190 (1996), para 9.3.
3 Michael Howard, op cit.

7.75   In the view of the present Government, the provisions in the Crime (Sentences) Act 1997 relating to the length of sentence to be served by those subject to determinate sentences, and the early release of prisoners, were excessively complex and unsatisfactory. They are not to be implemented, and, with the exception of s 9 of the 1997 Act (which deals with credit for periods spent on remand, are repealed by s 107 and Sch 10). As already noted, the changes made by the new Act presuppose the continuance of the regime set out in the 1991 Act, albeit with considerable amendment.

Credit for periods of time in remand in custody

7.76   As noted in para **7.75**, s 9 of the 1997 Act is the one provision in that Act relating to the length of time to be served in respect of a determinate sentence to survive the new Act. The position, in recent years, regarding the credit to be given for periods spent in custody prior to sentence has been a confusing one, particularly in respect of the context of concurrent and consecutive sentences. The position was, until the 1997 Act, governed by s 67(1) of the Criminal Justice Act 1967, which stated that the length of any sentence of imprisonment imposed on an offender by a court must be reduced by any 'relevant period', defined by reference to periods spent in police detention or custody relating to those proceedings.

Section 9 replaced s 67(1), which was repealed by s 56(2) of and Sch 6 to the 1997 Act. The effect of s 9[1] is that, where it applies, a sentencing court must direct that the number of days for which the offender was remanded in custody in connection with an offence or a related offence[2] shall count as time served by him as part of the sentence (1997 Act, s 9(3)). Despite the fact that s 9(3) appears to contemplate that a court give a direction specifying the number of days actually spent on remand, the court may in fact give a direction in respect of a lesser number of days (or none at all), in accordance with rules made by the Home Secretary in respect of remand relating to concurrent or consecutive sentences (either wholly or partly) or if the test in s 9(4)(b) is satisfied (that 'in the opinion of the court just in all the circumstances not to give a direction …'). The court must state in open court the number of days for which the offender was remanded in custody and the number of days in relation to which the direction is given (1997 Act, s 9(5)).

---

1 See annotations to s 107.
2 See annotations to s 74.

7.77   The new Act makes various changes to s 9. Section 107 introduces a new s 9(7A), which clarifies the power to make rules conferred on the Home Secretary by s 9(4)(a) and (7) of the 1997 Act. Section 9(4)(a) grants power to release short-term prisoners on licence. The new s 9(7A) states that such rules may make such incidental, supplemental and consequential provisions as may appear to the Home Secretary to be necessary or expedient. Thus such rules as are made may deal with any matter relating to the credit to be given by a court to periods spent on remand, an issue which has caused considerable difficulty.[1] Section 107 came into force on 30 September 1998.

---

1 For the current position, see *Secretary of State for the Home Department, ex parte Naughton* [1997] 1 All ER 426 (CA); *Governor of Brockhill Prison, ex parte Evans* [1997] 1 All ER 439 (CA).

7.78   The second change made by s 107 is the incorporation into s 9 of a new subsection (11). This excludes from the operation of s 9 committals for defaults in paying any sum of money owed other than one adjudged to be paid by a conviction, for want of sufficient distress or for failure to do, or abstain from doing anything required to be done or left undone. This replicates the equivalent provision in s 27 of the 1997 Act (the interpretation section), which is, as indicated above, repealed by the new Act.

7.79   Thirdly, a new s 9(12) of the 1997 Act states that any reference in s 9 to a term of imprisonment to which a person has been sentenced, consecutive and concurrent (whether wholly or partly terms), are to be treated as a single term if:

(a) the sentences were passed on the same occasion; or
(b) where they were passed on different occasions, the person has not been released under Part II of the 1991 Act at any time during the period beginning with the first and ending with the last of these occasions.

This is similar to, but not identical with, the equivalent provision in s 27 of the 1997 Act, the textual differences making it clear that a term shall not be regarded as a single term if the period served has been interrupted by release on licence under the 1991 Act.

7.80   The final amendment to s 9 made by s 107 is a textual amendment which makes it clear that s 9 applies not only to sentences of imprisonment but also to a sentence of imprisonment in a young offenders' institution, detention for a determinate period under s 53 of the Children and Young Persons Act 1933 (1997 Act, s 9(9A), inserted by the new Act, s 107(5)). Section 9 does not apply to persons serving a detention and training order. In determining what are periods of remand in custody, such periods include remands to local authority secure accommodation or to hospital under ss 35, 36, 38 or 48 of the Mental Health Act 1983 (1997 Act, s 9(9A)(2)).

Early release: two or more sentences

7.81   The difficulties which have arisen in calculating sentence length have already been identified.[1] The new Act seeks to clarify the position and does so by substituting a new s 51(2) of the Criminal Justice Act 1991 for the pre-existing provision (s 101). Section 101 came into force on 30 September 1998: see Appendix II.

---

1 See para **7.76**.

7.82   Section 51(2) provides that any reference in Part II of the 1991 Act, however expressed, to a term of imprisonment for which a person has been sentenced or which, or part of which, he has served, consecutive or wholly or partly concurrent shall be treated as a single term if:

(a) the sentences were passed on the same occasion; or
(b) where they were passed on different occasions, the person has not been released under Part II of the 1991 Act at any time during the period beginning with the first and ending with the last of these occasions.

This provision is, in its material respects, identical with that inserted into s 9 of the Crime (Sentences) Act 1997, discussed earlier.[1] The new s 51(2) goes on to seek to clarify the operation of this principle in certain contexts:

(a) suspended sentences which are brought into effect are deemed to have been passed on the date when they are brought into effect (1991 Act, s 51(2A)). Thus a term of imprisonment and the term of a suspended sentence brought into effect on the same occasion are deemed to be part of a single term;

(b) where there are two or more terms of imprisonment which are wholly or partly concurrent and do not fall to be regarded as a single term, the following rules apply (1991 Act, s 51(2B)):

    (i) nothing in Part II of the 1991 Act requires the Home Secretary to release the prisoner in respect of any of the terms unless and until he is required to release him in respect of each of the others;

    (ii) nothing in Part II requires the Home Secretary or the Parole Board to consider the prisoner's release until each, or they, are required to consider his release in respect of each of the other sentences;

    (iii) on the prisoner's release under Part II, he will be on licence for so long, and subject to such conditions, as is required by Part II in respect of any of the sentences;

    (iv) the date mentioned in s 40 of the 1991 Act[2] will be that on which he would, but for his release have served each of his sentences in full;

(c) where a person has been sentenced to one or more determinate terms, and to one or more life sentences within the meaning of s 34 of the Crime (Sentences) Act 1997,[3] nothing in Part II of the 1991 Act requires the Home Secretary to release him until he is required to release him in respect of each of the life sentences, or requires consideration by him or the Parole Board of release until it is required in respect of each of the life sentences (1991 Act, s 51(2C)).

---

1 See paras **7.76–7.80**.
2 See annotations to s 59.
3 See annotations to s 101.

7.83   Section 51(2) is similar to, but not identical with, the equivalent provision in s 27 of the 1997 Act, the textual differences making it clear that a term shall not be regarded as a single term if the period served has been interrupted by release on licence under the 1991 Act.

Release of short-term prisoners on licence, subject to home curfew

7.84   The general rules relating to the release of short-term prisoners was noted earlier.[1] Section 99 provides for the release of some, although not all, short-term prisoners, on licence, and s 100 for a curfew condition to be imposed on that licence. Prisoners to whom the provisions apply will be eligible to apply for release on licence: if they are granted release on licence they will spend a period of time which they would otherwise spend in custody at home, under curfew. Eligibility for release on licence will occur after a 'requisite period' which can be as little as 30 days for a prisoner serving a term of three months but less than four months.

---

1 See para **7.73**.

Rationale for the change

7.85   Reducing the period of time served by prisoners is inevitably controversial. The Government's case was explained as follows:

> 'Typically, criminals lead disordered and irresponsible lives. They are often poor at making sensible decisions about their future and that of their families. They do not have to make decisions in prison or get to grips with their disorderly lives. The prison system makes decisions for them and imposes order on them. On release prisoners suddenly have to make decisions about what to do with every moment of the day. They must decide whether to drift back into crime and rejoin the company of criminal associates or whether to bring order into their lives. The criminal justice system must aim to punish criminals. It must also confront them with the reasons for their offending behaviour and make them change it. Prison imposes a straitjacket on criminals. Removal of the straitjacket often returns them to a disorderly lifestyle. Strict controls in their home environment forces criminals to change their behaviour, ensuring their compliance with a demanding set of rules. Those controls force order into life outside prison. Having learnt self-discipline, as opposed to acquiescence in prison discipline, offenders are more likely to carry that conduct into the period following the curfew, thus reducing their propensity to offend.'[1]

Whatever the cogency of that justification, and whether in fact it is as much a justification for reducing the number of short custodial sentences, the Government was clearly motivated by its judgment that the trials relating to electronic monitoring have proved a success, notwithstanding earlier doubts about its effectiveness at the time of the Criminal Justice Act 1991. The Government is examining the extension nation-wide of curfews and 'tagging' as a sentence,[2] but meanwhile sees the use of tagging as an effective means of bridging the transition from prison to home. There is also the tacit, although not overtly acknowledged,[3] benefit of reduction in the prison population at a time of over-stretched prison resources, the prison population having risen from 57,707 in March 1997 to 65,330 in May 1998. Latest projections suggest that the prison population will increase to 66,000 by September 1988, to 71,800 by September 1999 and 82,800 by 2002.[4] The benefits, in terms of prison resources, of reducing the time served in prison are clear.

---

1 Mike O'Brien, MP, Parliamentary Under-Secretary, Home Office, HC Committee, col 689.
2 Ibid, col 690.
3 The claim was made during debate on the Act that this was the real, and primary, justification for the new power, although not conceded as such by the Government: see the debate at HC Committee, cols 678–699.
4 Statistics cited by Mike O'Brien, op cit, col 691.

The new power

7.86   The new power is introduced through the insertion of new provisions into the Criminal Justice Act 1991. Section 99 of the new Act inserts a new s 34A into the 1991 Act. This has the effect of excluding a range of prisoners from the new early release provisions. Any short-term prisoner[1] aged[2] 18 or more, who is serving three months or more and who does not fall within this list of exclusions, will be eligible for early release on licence. The granting of a licence is not automatic (since s 34A(3) uses the term 'may').

---

1 See annotations to s 99.
2 See general annotations.

Who is not eligible?

7.87   By s 34A(2) of the 1991 Act, the following are not eligible:

(a) a prisoner serving an extended sentence within the meaning of s 58 of the Crime and Disorder Act 1998;[1]

(b) a prisoner serving a sentence for an offence under s 1 of the Prisoners (Return to Custody) Act 1995;[2]

(c) a prisoner serving a sentence imposed under paras 3(1)(d) or 4(1)(d) of Sch 2 to the 1991 Act[3] in a case where the prisoner had failed to comply with a requirement of a curfew order;

(d) the prisoner is subject to a hospital order, hospital direction or transfer direction under ss 37, 45A or 47 of the Mental Health Act 1983;

(e) the prisoner is liable to removal from the UK for the purposes of s 46 of the 1991 Act;

(f) the prisoner has been released on licence under s 34A of the 1991 Act at any time and has been recalled to prison under s 38A(1)(a);[4]

(g) the prisoner has been released on licence under ss 34A or 36 of the 1991 Act[5] during the currency of the sentence, and has been recalled to prison under s 39(1) or (2) of that Act;

(h) the prisoner has been returned to prison under s 40 of the 1991 Act at any time; or

  (i) the interval between the date on which the prisoner will have served the requisite period for the term of the sentence; and

  (ii) the date on which he will have served one-half of the sentence, is less than 14 days.

---

1 See paras **7.14** et seq.
2 See annotations to s 99.
3 See annotations to s 64.
4 See s 100.
5 See annotations to s 59.

7.88   After the 'requisite period', the Home Secretary may release the prisoner on licence. This phrase is defined by the new s 34A(4)) as follows:

(a) in respect of a prisoner serving a term of three months or more but less than four months, a period of 30 days;

(b) in respect of a prisoner serving a term of four months or more but less than eight months, a period equal to one-quarter of the term;

(c) in respect of a prisoner serving a term of eight months or more, a period
      that is 60 days less than one-half of the term.

There is thus no question of a prisoner receiving licence under s 34A. It should
be noted, however, that s 34A(5) confers an enabling power on the Home
Secretary, which permits him by order:

(a) to repeal the age requirement of '18 or over';
(b) to amend definition of the 'requisite period';
(c) to make such transitional provision as appears to him to be necessary or
      expedient in connection with the repeal or amendment.

The Home Secretary is under a duty to release the prisoner serving a term of 12
months or less at the expiration of one-half of the sentence (1991 Act, s 33(1)).
In respect of a prisoner serving more than 12 months but less than four years,
the duty to release on automatic conditional licence arises at the expiration of a
period of one-half sentence (1991 Act, s 33(1)(b)), the licence extending until
the three-quarter sentence point.

In calculating the period to be served, regard will need to be had to days to be
credited for time spent on remand (Crime (Sentences) Act 1997, s 9; see
para **7.76**). However, no such credit can have the effect of reducing the period
to be served actually in custody below the one-quarter sentence point (1991
Act, s 41(4), inserted by Sch 8, para 86(2))).

Effect of the short-term licence provision

7.89   It will be seen that the potential for early release arises after the
prescribed period, with the period between the date of that release and the
unconditional release point at the half-way stage[1] being a period under curfew.[2]
If no release occurs under s 34A, release will occur automatically at the half-way
point.

The effect of this is shown, in approximate terms, in the table below:

Length	Minimum period	Maximum period	Period of curfew
3 months	30 days	6 weeks	14 days
4 months	1 month	2 months	1 month
6 months	1.5 months	3 months	1.5 months
12 months	4 months	6 months	2 months
24 months	10 months	12 months	2 months

It will quickly become apparent that, if a magistrates' court is minded to
sentence an offender for a period short of three months, the offender may in
fact serve longer than might a prisoner serving three months. For example, a
prisoner sentenced to two months will actually serve one, whilst the person
serving 10 weeks will serve five weeks. Such conclusions point to some
inconsistencies which will inevitably arise. Whether these are to be regarded as
absurdities[3] may well depend upon whether the reasoning given in debate,

namely, the period served under curfew should be regarded as part of 'the whole process of the sentence'[4] is accepted.

---

1 See para **7.73**.
2 See para **7.90**.
3 See the debate at HC Committee, cols 678–699.
4 Mike O'Brien, MP, Parliamentary Under-Secretary, Home Office, HC Committee, col 693.

Power to include curfew condition in licence pursuant to s 34A(3)

7.90   As noted above, the power to release a short-term prisoner under s 34A(3) will be accompanied by a curfew order. Section 100(1) creates a new s 37A to the Criminal Justice Act 1991. It came into force on 30 September 1998: see Appendix II. Under this new provision, a person must not be released under s 34A(3) unless the licence includes a condition ('the curfew condition') which:

(a)   requires the released person to remain, for periods for the time being specified in the condition, at a place for the time being so specified (which may be an approved probation hostel); and

(b)   includes requirements for securing the electronic monitoring of his whereabouts during the periods for the time being so specified.

The curfew condition may specify different places or different periods for different days, but must not specify periods which amount to less than nine hours in any one day (excluding for this purpose the first and last days of the period for which the condition is in force) (s 37A(2)). The curfew condition must remain in force until the date when the released person would (but for his release) have served one-half of his sentence (s 37A(3)).

The curfew condition must include provision for making a person responsible for monitoring the released person's whereabouts during the periods for the time being specified in the condition; a person who is made so responsible must be of a description specified in an order made by the Home Secretary (s 37A(4)).

Enforcement of curfew conditions

7.91   This is governed by a new s 38A of the 1991 Act, introduced by s 100(2) of the new Act, but which is not yet in force. If it appears to the Home Secretary, as regards a person released on licence under s 34A(3):

(a)   that he has failed to comply with the curfew condition;

(b)   that his whereabouts can no longer be electronically monitored at the place for the time being specified in that condition; or

(c)   that it is necessary to do so in order to protect the public from serious harm from him,

the Home Secretary may revoke the licence and recall the person to prison.

A person whose licence under s 34A(3) is revoked under s 38A:

(a) may make representations in writing with respect to the revocation;
(b) on his return to prison, must be informed of the reasons for the revocation and of his right to make representations.

The Home Secretary may, after considering any representations made, or any other matters, cancel a revocation (s 38A(3)).

Effect of the early release provisions for short-term prisoners

7.92   It is estimated that between 45% and 60% of short-term prisoners will satisfy the test for early release under these provisions,[1] with some 7,200 prisoners being eligible.[2] Although it will not apply to those, such as sex offenders, who are serving extended sentences,[3] such sentences are not mandatory. A court will need to be alive to the early-release provisions in deciding whether or not to make an extended sentence order. In any event, draft documentation on risk assessment for home detention curfew, issued by the Home Office, states that sex offenders are to be released on home detention only in exceptional circumstances. Care will need to be taken on such matters to avoid accusations of different standards being applied for different types of prisoner, thus creating a potential for judicial review. Prisoners will be divided into two categories: those who receive a standard assessment and those who receive an enhanced assessment because they are considered to pose a greater risk. The risk assessment will take into account the nature of the offence, the level of risk posed by the offender and the proposed supervision arrangements. Eligibility of a sex offender, in practice (even if eligible in law because not the subject of an extended sentence), may depend on his attitude in prison, for example addressing his offending behaviour through a sex offender treatment programme. That, of course, assumes that such a programme is available in the prison to which he has been sent and, even if he is, whether he has been able to participate in it (which may not, in the case of short-term prisoners, always be the case).

---

1 Mike O'Brien, MP, Parliamentary Under-Secretary, HC Committee, col 701.
2 Ibid, col 701.
3 See para **7.14**.

Recall to prison of short-term prisoners

7.93   Section 103 provides that s 38 of the 1991 Act shall cease to have effect. That section created a criminal offence for the failure by a short-term prisoner to comply with licence provisions. No longer will the sanction for a failure to comply be a criminal prosecution. Instead, the extension of licence provisions in the way set out above justifies a change of approach, with the power in s 39 of the 1991 Act (hitherto applicable to long-term and life prisoners) to revoke the licence of a prisoner (on the recommendation of the Parole Board) extended to short-term prisoners (s 103(3)).

7.94   Further changes are made consequent upon this, dealing with the question of release on licence of a short-term prisoner who has been released on licence. Sections 104 and 105 modify the rules governing the release of prisoners who have been recalled to prison, or who have been returned to prison pursuant to s 40 of the 1991 Act, for the commission of a further offence during the currency of his original sentence. These provisions came into force on 30 September 1998: see Appendix II. The changes can be summarised as follows:

(a) The normal period of licence is up to the three-quarters sentence point. This is, for prisoners released on licence following recall to prison, extended to the whole of the sentence (1991 Act, s 37(1A), inserted therein by s 104(2)). Section 104(1) makes a textual amendment to s 33(1) of the 1991 Act to make it clear that all short-term prisoners are released on licence.

(b) Following return to prison, a court having passed a term of imprisonment of 12 months or less:
  (i) he shall be released on licence after one-half of the sentence;
  (ii) the licence shall remain in force for a period of three months;
  (iii) breach of the licence conditions renders him liable to summary conviction, punishable either by a fine or by imprisonment for 'the relevant period'. The 'relevant period' means a period equal in length to the period between the date on which the failure occurred or began and the date of the expiry of the licence. Any person so sentenced must be released having served one-half of the relevant period (Criminal Justice Act 1991, s 40A, inserted by s 105).

Conviction during currency of existing sentence

7.95 Section 40 of the Criminal Justice Act 1991 applies to a short-term or long-term prisoner released under Part II of the Act if:

(a) before the date on which he would (but for his release) have served his sentence in full, he commits an offence punishable with imprisonment; and

(b) whether before or after that date, he is convicted of that offence ('the new offence') (Criminal Justice Act 1991, s 40(1)).

The court by or before which a person to whom s 40 applies is convicted of the new offence may, whether or not it passes any other sentence on him, order him to be returned to prison for the whole or any part of the period which begins with the date of the order and is equal in length to the period between the date on which the new offence was committed and the date mentioned in (a) above (Criminal Justice Act 1991, s 40(2)). This is subject to a limitation in respect of a magistrates' court. It may not order a person to be returned to prison for a period exceeding six months (ibid, s 40(3)(a)). This is of obvious importance where the magistrates' court, having convicted someone of an either-way offence, has then committed him to the Crown Court for sentence and he has received a sentence in excess of the magistrates' powers.

There has hitherto been no appeal against an order for return to prison but provision is made for such an appeal where it is made by a Crown Court, although it has been possible to appeal to the Crown Court against such an order made by a magistrates' court (Magistrates' Courts Act 1980, s 108). The matter has been dealt with by Sch 8. Schedule 8, para 13 adds an order under s 40(2) to the list of orders in s 10(3) of the Criminal Appeal Act 1968 against which an offender may appeal to the Court of Appeal against sentence.

7.96   We referred above to a limitation on the power of a magistrates' court to order a person to be returned to prison for longer than six months to serve his original sentence. There is, however, an alternative; the magistrates' court may commit the person in custody or on bail to the Crown Court for sentence (Criminal Justice Act 1991, s 40(3)(b)). Hitherto, the Crown Court has had the same power to deal with the person committed in the same way as if he had been committed by or before it (ibid, s 40(3)(b)), but this has been changed by Sch 7, para 43, which inserts new subss (3A) and (3B) into the 1991 Act. Section 40(3A) provides that, where a person is committed to the Crown Court under s 40(3) of the 1991 Act, the Crown Court may, as previously, order him to be returned for the whole or any part of the period: (a) beginning with the date of the order; and (b) equal in length with the period between the date on which the new offence was committed and the date on which he would have served his sentence in full. Section 40(3B), however, adds that (b) does not confer on the magistrates power to commit to the Crown Court for sentence for the new offence.

MISCELLANEOUS CHANGES

7.97   The new Act makes various detailed changes of definition in a multiplicity of statutes, to which no specific mention need be made. These changes, mostly in Schs 7 and 8, came into force on 30 September 1998: see Appendix II.

7.98   It also makes changes in s 31 of the Powers of Criminal Courts Act 1973 relating to the power of the Crown Court in relation to fines and recognizances. Subsections (3B) and (3C) dealt with the maximum period of imprisonment in cases of part-payment. They now cease to have effect, the limits, based on part-payment as opposed to the sum owed, being removed (Sch 7, para 23). Other textual amendments are made to s 32 of that Act.

Of more substance is the change made in respect of remission of Crown Court fines or recognizances. Section 32 in some circumstances permitted a magistrates' court to remit Crown Court fines or recognizances. By virtue of a new s 32(4) (inserted by Sch 7, para 24), such an order, or one made by the Court of Appeal (Criminal Division) or House of Lords, cannot be remitted by a magistrates' court, save with the consent of that court.

7.99   Magistrates' courts have, hitherto, had the power to impose a community service order where it had the power to issue a warrant of commitment for default in paying a sum adjudged to be paid by a conviction of any court (Criminal Justice Act 1972, s 49). That power is removed by Sch 7, para 12.

7.100 Amendments are made by Sch 7, para 13 to s 1(6) of the Powers of Criminal Courts Act 1973, so as to make it clear that the power of a court to deal with an offender the passing of sentence upon whom has been deferred is the power to deal with him for the offence for which sentence was deferred.

7.101 A sentence of custody for life under s 8(2) of the Criminal Justice Act 1982[1] is a sentence in respect of which an offender aged between 18 and 21 may not be sentenced unless he is legally represented. Rather oddly, that requirement has not previously applied to a similar sentence passed under s 8(1). That omission is rectified (Sch 7, para 33).

---

1 See annotations to s 73.

7.102 Section 83 inserts a new subs (9A) into s 71 of the Criminal Justice Act 1988. That section confers a power on a magistrates' court and the Crown Court to make confiscation orders. The new subsection provides that when an offender is committed for sentence to the Crown Court then, for the purposes of the confiscation order provisions, the offender is to be treated as having been convicted by the Crown Court, not the magistrates' court. Section 83 came into effect on 30 September 1998: see Appendix II.

Chapter 8

RACIALLY-AGGRAVATED OFFENCES

Background – When is an offence racially-aggravated? – Racially-aggravated assaults – Racially-aggravated criminal damage – Racially-aggravated public order offences – Racially-aggravated harassment – Increase in sentences for racial aggravation – Final thoughts

BACKGROUND

8.1 Incidents of racial violence and harassment have increased substantially in recent years.[1] The impact of repeated acts of victimisation and violence on individuals is a matter of serious concern, as is the build-up of anger, fear and resentment among ethnic minority communities. Racial attacks and harassment do not just damage the victim, they also damage the fabric of our multiracial society. They are unreservedly condemned by all right-thinking people.

Racial incidents in England and Wales have been separately recorded by the police since 1988.[2] These have included incidents of verbal abuse and threatening behaviour, violence to the person and property damage. Figures have risen in almost every year since then. The number of racial incidents reported to the police (all forces in England and Wales) are:

1988	4,383
1989	5,044
1990	6,359
1991	7,882
1992	7,734
1993	9,218
April 1993–March 1994	9,762
April 1994–March 1995	11,878
April 1995–March 1996	12,222[3]

The police record as 'racial incidents' all incidents reported to them where any party suspects or alleges racial motivation, in accordance with the definition of a racial incident adopted in 1985 by the Association of Chief Police Officers, viz:

> 'Any incident in which it appears to the reporting or investigating officer that the complaint involves an element of racial motivation; or any incident which includes any allegation of racial motivation made by any person.'[2]

Data from the 1996 British Crime Survey[3] suggests that the above figures grossly understate the extent of the problem. The Survey estimated that the number of racially motivated offences against ethnic minorities in 1995 was 143,000 – 15%

of all offences against them, as opposed to 1% of all offences against white people in that year. In addition, a considerably higher percentage of members of ethnic minorities were found by the survey to have suffered racial harassment in 1995 than white people. Ethnic minorities also scored higher than white people on all the Survey's measures of fear of crime. In 1997, the New York-based group, Human Rights Watch, published a report showing that this country had one of the highest rates of racially motivated crime in Western Europe.[4]

---

1 See *Racially Motivated Crime: A British Survey* (Home Office Research and Planning Unit Paper 82, 1994).
2 *Racial Violence and Harassment: A Consultation Paper* (Home Office, 1997), para 2.2.
3 *Ethnicity and Victimisation: Findings from the 1996 British Crime Survey* (Home Office Statistical Bulletin Issue 6/98).
4 Lord Dholakia, HL 2nd Reading, col 577.

8.2   Racial violence or harassment is in a category of its own. First, the violence or harassment is directed against the victim not as an individual but as a member of a specific community or group. It injures and humiliates the victim because of the characteristics which come from the uncontrollable factor of birth. Secondly, there is a political dimension to a racially motivated attack or harassment. The violence signals a refusal to accept a specific community as members of the whole community, entitled to equal importance and respect. Thirdly, racial attacks arise from racism. Racism is the enemy of the values of a liberal democracy and of equal citizenship.

8.3   The criminal law is not lacking in offences which can successfully be charged in cases of racist violence or harassment or other conduct with a racial element. Part III of the Public Order Act 1986 contains a number of offences concerned with inciting racial hatred. These cover conduct such as the use of threatening, abusive or insulting words or behaviour, or the display, publication or distribution of threatening, abusive or insulting material, with intent to stir up racial hatred or whereby racial hatred is likely to be stirred up. In addition, the whole armoury of offences against the person, offences against public order, and so on, is available.

Racially-aggravated conduct can also often be dealt with by the new anti-social behaviour orders, described in Chapter 5. This chapter focuses on new provisions concerned with a direct criminal sanction.

8.4   In the 1993–94 session of Parliament, the Home Affairs Select Committee of the House of Commons called for specific offences to deal with racial violence and harassment, and so did the Commission for Racial Equality in 1992.[1]

Following Parliamentary debates on the Bill which became the Public Order Act 1986, and during Parliamentary debates for the ensuing Criminal Justice and Public Order Act 1994, the Conservative Government came under pressure to strengthen the law to deal with cases of racially motivated violence and racial harassment. For example, Opposition attempts to introduce an either-way offence of racially motivated violence, of which a person who committed manslaughter or one of a range of non-fatal offences, with racial motivation, would additionally be liable, failed.[2] Likewise, an attempt to insert a provision that, when racial motivation was proved in a criminal case, it should form an aggravating factor in sentencing also failed,[3] although such a rule was expressly laid down later that year by the Court of Appeal.[4] However, the Government did bow to pressure to the extent of introducing into the Public Order Act 1986 a new section, s 4A, which provides an offence of intentional harassment, alarm or distress.

The Labour manifesto in 1997 promised to create a new offence of racially motivated violence and a new offence of racial harassment. The new Act has achieved something different for two reasons. First, it provides a wider range of offences, not all requiring violence or harassment, which are simply aggravated versions of existing offences.[5] Secondly, it is not limited to 'racially motivated' conduct in the strict sense of that term – as will be seen later.

---

1 See *Racial Attacks and Harassment*, Home Affairs Select Committee, Third Report 1993–94, HC 71; *Second Review of the Race Relations Act 1976*, Commission for Racial Equality.
2 HL Deb, vol 555, cols 1910–1916.
3 Ibid, cols 1682–1699.
4 *Re A-G's Reference (Nos 29, 30 and 31 of 1994)* (1995) 16 Cr App Rep (S) 698; reported sub nom *Ribbans, Duggan and Ridley* (1994) *The Times*, 25 November (CA). See para **8.81**.
5 It proved very difficult to define a single offence covering racial violence against the person, because the maximum punishment would have had to be set at a level inappropriate for some behaviour covered: *Racial Violence: A Consultation Paper* (Home Office, 1997), para 5.4.

8.5   It may be questioned, as it was in both Houses of Parliament, why racial aggravation should be singled out for special treatment. Why should racial aggravation be treated differently from disability, sexual orientation and so on? This is a point which had previously been made in a leader in *The Times*, headed 'Blind Justice'.[1] It referred to the OJ Simpson case which, it said, showed how dangerous and distorting it can be when questions of racial motivation dominate a trial. It concluded:

> 'The figure of justice is blindfold for a reason. Using the criminal justice system to make symbolic genuflections to political causes, however noble, only undermines the effective operation of the rule of law and fetters proper judicial discretion. Punishment should not depend on creating a statutory hierarchy of wickedness which elevates racial prejudice over any of the ugly impulses towards criminality with which society must deal.'

The Government's justification for special provisions in respect of racially-aggravated offences was given as follows by Lord Hardie, the Lord Advocate, at the Report stage in the House of Lords:

> 'The particular evil of racial harassment is that offenders identify their victims because of their appearance and because of what they naturally and inescapably are. Other groups in society do become victims of crime, including racial groups, because of who they are, but none is so open to harassment, based purely on

prejudice, as the minority ethnic groups who form the majority of victims of racial crimes.

> All attacks on vulnerable groups are deplorable. [The provision] is intended to reinforce the protection given to those members of our society who are particularly vulnerable to the action of bigoted criminals, and builds on long-standing legislation which seeks to protect individuals from prejudice on grounds of race.'[2]

While this is a compelling answer in favour of special provisions in respect of racially-aggravated offences against members of ethnic minorities, it is less persuasive in respect of members of many groups other than ethnic minority groups caught by the definition of 'racial group' around which the new offences centre. We explain this definition in paras **8.8** to **8.13**.

---

1 (1997) *The Times*, 3 October; cited by Lord Monson, HL Committee, col 1291.
2 HL Report, col 706.

8.6   Part II of the Act introduces racially-aggravated offences parallel to the following 'basic' offences under the Offences against the Person Act 1861, Criminal Damage Act 1971, Public Order Act 1986 and the Protection from Harassment Act 1997. For each new offence, if the racial aggravation element is proved, significantly greater maximum penalties will be available than for their basic offence counterpart. The racially-aggravated offences are as follows:

(a) Racially-aggravated assaults (s 29):
  –   Offences against the Person Act 1861, s 20;
  –   Offences against the Person Act 1861, s 47;
  –   common assault.
(b) Racially-aggravated criminal damage (s 30).
(c) Racially-aggravated public order offences (s 31):
  –   Public Order Act 1986, s 4;
  –   Public Order Act 1986, s 4A;
  –   Public Order Act 1986, s 5.
(d) Racially-aggravated harassment (s 32):
  –   Protection from Harassment Act 1997, s 2;
  –   Protection from Harassment Act 1997, s 4.

The racially-aggravated offences are new offences in their own right;[1] ss 29–32 do not simply introduce new maximum sentences for the basic offences. They are intended to 'send a strong message to society at large that such crime is unacceptable and that it will be dealt with very seriously by the police and the courts'.[2]

In addition, s 82 gives statutory effect in other offences to the sentencing principle that racial aggravation is an aggravating factor meriting a stiffer sentence.

The above provisions came into force on 30 September 1998: see Appendix II. With a few modifications, they enact proposals set out in a Home Office consultation paper published in 1997.[3] They are not without precedent in other jurisdictions. Several American states have enacted statutes providing for

a greater penalty for racially motivated unlawful conduct. France has introduced legislation providing two years' imprisonment for crimes relating to
racial hatred and violence.[4] Nor are they wholly without precedent in other
contexts in English criminal law. Examples of other aggravated offences are
aggravated burglary[5] and aggravated vehicle-taking.[6]

---

1 This is clear from the wording of the relevant sections. Any possible doubts would be resolved
   by reference to the principle established by the House of Lords in *Courtie* [1984] AC 463,
   [1984] 1 All ER 740, viz where a greater maximum punishment can be imposed if a particular
   factual ingredient is established than if it is not, distinct offences exist.
2 *Racial Violence and Harassment: A Consultation Paper* (Home Office, 1997), para 2.4.
3 Ibid, para 3.
4 HL Deb, vol 555, col 1911.
5 Theft Act 1968, s 10.
6 Ibid, s 12A.

WHEN IS AN OFFENCE RACIALLY-AGGRAVATED?

8.7   The answer is provided by s 28(1) which states that an offence is
racially-aggravated for the purposes of the new offences if:

(a) at the time of committing the offence, or immediately before or after
     doing so, the offender demonstrates towards the victim of the offence
     hostility based on the victim's membership of, or presumed membership
     of, a racial group; or
(b) the offence is motivated (wholly or partly) by hostility towards members of
     a racial group based on their membership of that group.

Definition of racial group

8.8   Section 28(4) provides that racial group means a group of persons
defined by reference to race, colour, nationality (including citizenship) or
ethnic or national origins. There is a corresponding provision in s 17 of the
Public Order Act 1986 in respect of offences of inciting racial hatred and a
similar definition in s 3 of the Race Relations Act 1976. The result of the
wording of the definition is that there is a substantial overlap between parts of
it.

The definition of 'racial group' is clearly framed in somewhat flexible and
elusive language so as to prevent argument over the precise meaning of 'race'
and to leave no loopholes. Suppose, for example, that an immigrant from India
attacks a Pakistani because of his hatred of Pakistanis. He could hardly be said
to be motivated by, or to demonstrate, hostility towards that person on the basis
of his colour, and it could be argued that Pakistanis do not constitute a single
'race'. On the other hand, as will be seen below, it could hardly be argued that
Pakistanis do not all have the same national origin.[1]

Nevertheless, while there are understandable reasons behind the width and
flexibility of the definition of 'racial group', its definition means that the

provisions relating to racial aggravation go well beyond racist conduct as
normally understood. In the House of Lords, for example, Lord Howie of
Troon said this:

> 'What bothers me is that over the years a creeping lack of distinction has arisen
> between racism and nationalism. That is where I agree with the noble Lord, Lord
> Carlisle. I do not object to being called a Scotsman. I might object to being
> punched on the nose because I am a Scotsman but that is because I was punched on
> the nose rather than the reason. There is a real distinction between ...
> straightforward racism – which obviously I totally condemn and he will understand
> me in that regard – and nationalism.'[2]

Later, his Lordship said:

> 'Although I entirely support the Government's desire to oppose racialism and to
> deal with it, I believe that they are weakening their case by confusing racialism with
> nationalism. To be motivated against a coloured man or a coloured woman
> because of his or her skin or racial origin is quite different from being irritated by a
> Scotsman or even an Englishman – although I find that difficult to believe. These
> two things are different in degree.'[3]

---

1 See the opinion of Lord Cross of Chelsea in *London Borough of Ealing v Race Relations Board*
   [1972] 1 All ER 105 at 118.
2 HL Committee, col 1275.
3 HL Committee, col 1295.

8.9   It will be noted from s 28(4) that to be a member of a racial group the
person must be a member of a group of persons defined by reference to colour,
race, nationality or ethnic or national origins. Sikhs, for example, are not a
group defined by reference to colour, race or nationality, but (as we shall see)
they are a group defined by reference to their ethnic origins.

The courts do not appear to have enlarged on the meaning of 'colour' or 'race'
in the present context. 'Colour' clearly refers to skin colour, and not the colour
of hair or eyes, but one cannot be more specific and one can only speculate
about whether there are a limited number of colours in a spectrum or whether
light brown is a different colour from medium brown and so on. It is doubtful
whether the courts will ever need to consider the meaning of these terms, the
issues which would arise would almost inevitably be dealt with by another part
of the definition.

With respect to 'nationality (including citizenship)', the bracketed words
indicate that 'nationality' here is being used to indicate the fact of being a
citizen of a certain State, 'citizenship' being added to cover the case where
nationality is described by that term by the law of the State in question, as under
the British Nationality Act 1981. It is not easy to envisage situations where an
offence would be motivated by, or demonstrate, hostility based purely on
nationality in the above sense, as opposed to colour, race, national or ethnic
origins. An example, however, would be where a person who had a hatred for a
particular State and its citizens attacked a British-born person who was a

naturalised citizen of that State after he had seen him presenting that State's passport.

The other two terms in the definition, 'national origins' and 'ethnic origins', call for more explanation.

8.10   'National origins' means something different from mere nationality in the sense of citizenship of a certain state.[1] 'Origins' is a reference to a connection with a nation by birth or descent.[2] 'National' refers to:

> ' "nationality" as meaning membership of a certain nation in the sense of race. Thus, according to international law, Englishmen and Scotsmen are, despite their different nationality as regards race, all of British nationality as regards citizenship ... "[N]ational origins" means national in the sense of race and not citizenship. One result is that if a naturalised British citizen is attacked because he was born a German and the attacker has a grudge against Germans the attack will be motivated by his membership of a group defined by reference to national origins.'[3]

Further elucidation of 'national origins' can be derived from the speech of Lord Simon of Glaisdale in *London Borough of Ealing v Race Relations Board* which was concerned with that term in s 1 of the Race Relations Act 1968 (the forerunner of the Race Relations Act 1976) in the context of racial discrimination:

> ' "Nation" and "national", in their popular in contrast to their legal sense, are also vague terms. They do not necessarily imply statehood. For example, there were many submerged nations in the former Hapsburg empire. Scotland is not a nation in the eye of international law; but Scotsmen constitute a nation by reason of those most powerful elements in the creation of national spirit – tradition, folk memory, a sentiment of community. The Scots are a nation because of Bannockburn and Flodden, Culloden and the pipes at Lucknow, because of Jenny Geddes and Flora Macdonald, because of frugal living and respect for learning, because of Robert Burns and Walter Scott. So, too, the English are a nation – because Norman, Angevin and Tudor monarchs forged them together, because their land is mostly sea-girt, because of the common law and of gifts for poetry and parliamentary government, because (despite the Wars of the Roses and Old Trafford and Headingly) Yorkshiremen and Lancastrian feel more in common than in difference and are even prepared at a pinch to extend their sense of community to southern folk. By the Act of Union English and Scots lost their separate nationalities, but they retained their separate nationhoods; and their descendants have thereby retained their separate national origins. So, again, the Welsh are a nation – in the popular, though not in the legal, sense – by reason of Offa's Dyke, by recollection of battles long ago and pride in the present valour of their regiments, because of musical gifts and religious dissent, because of fortitude in the face of economic adversity, because of the satisfaction of all Wales that Lloyd George became an architect of the welfare state and prime minister of victory. To discriminate against Englishmen, Scots or Welsh, as such, would, in my opinion, be to discriminate against them on the ground of their "national origins".'[4]

---

1 *London Borough of Ealing v Race Relations Board* [1972] 1 All ER 105 at 112, per Viscount Dilhorne.
2 *London Borough of Ealing v Race Relations Board* [1972] 1 All ER 105 (HL).
3 Ibid, at 108, per Lord Donovan.
4 Ibid, at 116.

8.11   In respect of 'ethnic origins', 'origins' has the same meaning as in 'national origins', ie connection by birth or descent. The term 'ethnic' is construed relatively widely and, although a cultural or religious group is not per se defined by reference to its ethnic origins, 'ethnic' is used in a sense wider than the strictly racial or biological. This was held by the House of Lords in *Mandla v Dowell Lee*,[1] where Lord Fraser of Tullybelton, with whose speech the other Law Lords agreed, said:

> 'For a group to constitute an ethnic group in the sense of the Race Relations Act 1976, it must, in my opinion, regard itself, and be regarded by others, as a distinct community by virtue of certain characteristics. Some of these characteristics are essential; others are not essential but one or more of them will commonly be found and will help to distinguish the group from the surrounding community. The conditions which appear to me to be essential are these: (1) a long, shared history, of which the group is conscious as distinguishing it from other groups, and the memory of which it keeps alive; (2) a cultural tradition of its own, including family and social customs and manners, often but not necessarily associated with religious observance. In addition, to these two essential characteristics the following characteristics are, in my opinion, relevant: (3) either a common geographical origin, or descent from a small number of common ancestors; (4) a common language, not necessarily peculiar to the group; (5) a common literature peculiar to the group; (6) a common religion different from that of neighbouring groups or from the general community surrounding it; (7) being a minority or being an oppressed or a dominant group within a larger community, for example a conquered people ... and their conquerors might both be ethnic groups.'[2]

Pursuant to the above dictum, it is clear that Jews[3] are a group defined by reference to their ethnic origins, and so are Sikhs (as the House held in *Mandla*),[4] and so are Romany gypsies.[5] On the other hand, members of the 70-year-old Rastafarian movement are not,[6] and neither are tinkers nor travellers.[7]

---

1 [1983] 2 AC 548, [1983] 1 All ER 1062 (HL).
2 Ibid, at 562 and 1066–1067 respectively.
3 See also *Seide v Gillette Industries Ltd* [1980] IRLR 427 at 430 (EAT).
4 The Sikhs were originally a religious community, although this is no longer purely so, founded at about the end of the fifteenth century, which is now a distinctive and self-conscious community, with its own written language (which a small proportion of Sikhs can read): *Mandla v Dowell Lee* [1983] 1 All ER 1062 at 1069, per Lord Fraser.
5 *Commission for Racial Equality v Dutton* [1989] QB 783, [1989] 1 All ER 306 (CA).
6 *Dawkins v Crown Suppliers (PSB) Ltd* [1993] ICR 517 (CA). See Parpworth *Defining Ethnic Origins* (1993) 143 NLJ 610.
7 *Commission for Racial Equality v Dutton* [1989] QB 783, [1989] 1 All ER 306 (CA).

8.12   As can be seen, a group of persons defined by reference to religion is not a racial group and therefore falls outside the scope of Part II of the Act. The result is that, while the commission of an offence specified in ss 29 to 32 which demonstrates hostility based solely on the victim's membership of a religion, eg the Jewish, Muslim, Rastafarian or Roman Catholic religion, or is motivated solely by hostility towards members of his religion, is not covered, the commission of one of these offences which demonstrates hostility based on the fact that the victim is black-skinned, or Irish, or Pakistani, or a Jew, or a Sikh, is covered, because the 'attack' relates to his membership of a racial group. The essential difference between membership of a racial group and membership of a religious group is that the former is inherited whereas the latter involves personal choice. Of course, an attack on a member of a group identified by reference to a religion may be open to the interpretation that it is an attack on him as a member of a racial group identified with it, eg as Jews (or Sikhs) are associated with the Jewish (or Sikh) religion.[1] In addition, it is open to question how many attacks etc are triggered solely by hostility towards a person's religion. It is likely that the vast majority of attacks on members of ethnic minority groups associated with a particular religion, eg the Muslim religion, are triggered by racial hostility, and not solely by religious hostility.

The Government resisted pressure to extend the new provisions about racially-aggravated offences so as to include religious aggravation, on the ground that it was more difficult to define whether someone is a member of a religious group, which involves a subjective as well as objective element.[2] It did, however, announce that it was establishing research on the nature and scale of religious discrimination in order to establish the size of the problem, which would include research into religious attacks.[3] We return to the question of religious aggravation in para **8.19**.

---

1 *Brownlie's Law of Public Order and National Security* (2nd edn) p 17. Also see DGT Williams [1966] Crim LR 320 at 324; Hepple (1966) 29 MLR 306 at 308.
2 Jack Straw, MP, Home Secretary, HC Report, col 895.
3 Alun Michael, MP, Minister of State, Home Office, HC Committee, col 316.

8.13   The definition of 'racial group' does not include a group or person identified by reference to their language.[1] Suppose a Welsh language protester damages the holiday home in Wales of an English-speaking person. It would be difficult to prove that he has committed racially-aggravated criminal damage. The reason is that it would be difficult to prove that he was demonstrating hostility to the English-speaking person based on that person's membership of a racial group in terms of national or ethnic origins etc, or that he was motivated by hostility towards members of a racial group in such terms based on their membership of that group. His objection is to that person's language, and it would seem to be a matter of indifference what that person's national or ethnic origins are. Nevertheless, a jury might be invited to consider whether any hostility demonstrated by, or motivating, the protester was based on the victim's English national origins or the fact that he was English-speaking.

It may be noted, also, that 'racial group' does not include a group of persons defined by politics or culture; members of the National Front are not protected from vilification or abuse by the special protection of the new offences, nor are 'New Age Travellers'. Likewise, the new offences do not protect a person who is a victim because of his place of residence. The fact that a person is a 'Brummie' or a 'Geordie' does not make him a member of a racial group defined in terms of residents of Birmingham or Newcastle.

1 See *Gwynedd County Council v Jones* [1986] ICR 833 (EAT).

Racial aggravation

8.14   By s 28(1), any of the specified offences is racially-aggravated if:

'(a) at the time of committing the offence, or immediately before or after doing so, the offender demonstrates towards the victim of the offence hostility based on the victim's membership (or presumed membership) of a racial group, or

(b) the offence is motivated (wholly or partly) by hostility towards members of a racial group based on their membership of that group.'

The requirements of racial aggravation will not necessarily be satisfied simply because the victim is a member of a different racial group from the accused. Suppose that there is a dispute between neighbours over a boundary or the parking of vehicles, which ends up with one shouting abuse at the other or punching the other or threatening the other. Suppose that afterwards the shouter, puncher or threatener says to the police 'I am fed up with my Paki neighbour' or 'My Scottish neighbour deserved it'. That person might certainly be convicted of one of the basic offences which can give rise to a racially-aggravated offence if the requirements of racial aggravation are satisfied, but they are not on the facts: the victim's membership of a racial group was quite incidental to the commission of the basic offence on the facts given.

A matter which remains to be fully explained by the courts is the concept of membership of a racial group. There is clearly no problem where the group in question is defined by reference to colour, race or nationality: a person either is or is not a member of a group identified by reference to a particular colour, race or nationality. The difficulty relates to membership of a group identified by reference to its ethnic or national origins.

In *Mandla v Dowell Lee*[1] Lord Fraser of Tullybelton said, obiter, that an ethnic group would be capable of including converts, for example, persons who marry into the group, and of excluding apostates. He added: 'Provided a person who joins the group feels him or herself to be a member of it, and is accepted by other members, he is ... a member'. It would seem that a convert can be a member of a group identified by reference to its ethnic origins – the question is not his origins but that of the group – and that a person may cease to be a member of such a group by abandoning its traditions and his identity with it. Lord Fraser thought that the same would be true of other types of racial group. It is inconceivable that this could occur in practice in terms of colour or race, although it can in terms of nationality by the formal process of naturalisation. In addition, it seems possible that one can convert in and out of a group defined by reference to its national origins.[2]

1 [1983] 2 AC 548, [1983] 1 All ER 1062 at 1067.
2 Also see *Gwynedd County Council v Jones* [1986] ICR 833 at 836.

8.15   The importance of the precise meaning of 'membership' in s 28(1)
(a) is lessened by s 28(2), which provides that in s 28(1)(a) 'membership' in
relation to a racial group includes association with members of that group.
Thus, even if a convert does not become a 'member' in the strict sense of the
term, he is clearly in association with the group. So is a person who has not
converted but is the spouse of a member and thereby in association with that
member and members of his family etc who are members of the group. Thus, if
a white woman who is married to a Pakistani is attacked or abused because of
her association with Pakistanis, the offence will be racially-aggravated.

8.16   Sometimes hostility may be demonstrated towards someone in the
mistaken belief that he is a member of a racial group, as where a Bangladeshi is
the victim of hostility intended to be directed at a Pakistani. In such a case the
offence will be racially-aggravated because s 28(2) provides that the reference
to 'presumed membership' in s 28(1)(a) means presumed by the offender.
Likewise, if a white woman who has become a Muslim, and who is wearing a
chador – a religious face covering – is the subject of a racial attack or racial
abuse in the mistaken belief that she is a Pakistani, the offence will be
racially-aggravated.[1] Similarly, if a racist threatens a white woman whom he
mistakenly believes is associated with a Pakistani and his family, and the hostility
he demonstrates is based on that association, his offence is racially-aggravated
because of the definition of 'membership' and 'presumed membership'.

---

1 This example was given by Jack Straw, MP, Home Secretary, HC Report, col 893.

Demonstration of hostility based on victim's membership etc of a racial group
8.17   As can be seen, s 28(1)(a), the first of the two alternative types of racial
aggravation, means that the aggravated offences are not limited to racially
motivated offences. The reason for it is that it may be difficult to prove that the
reason why a person committed the offence (ie his motivation) was wholly or
partly hostility towards members of a racial group based on their membership
of that group. The first alternative is designed to prevent what are truly
racially-aggravated offences being incapable of proof by placing the emphasis
on the external manifestations of the conduct involved rather than the internal
motivation prompting it. The point was made as follows by the then
Solicitor-General. Referring to the first alternative, he said:

> 'So the effect is that if, as the noble Lord, Lord Carlisle, indicated, you say, "You are
> a Welsh something" or "a Paki something else", proved of itself that can establish
> the necessary racially-aggravating feature. That is the effect of the Bill. It was rightly
> identified by Members of the Committee. The reason it is put in is that everyone
> who is involved in race relations and the intervention of the courts in race relations
> discovers that it is notoriously difficult to prove racial motivation. It becomes an
> illusory matter of proof which lawyers are well able to demonstrate in court is
> difficult to prove. [Section 28](1)(a) is a practical and sensible attempt to try to

deal with the problem that if we had only [s 28] (1) (b), many cases which would fall within the racially-aggravated criminal offence definition would slip through. That is why we have done it.'[1]

It is over-optimistic to assume that 'the demonstration of racial hostility' will be easy to prove. The evidence will have to be confined to the time of the alleged incident, unless the accused conducts his case in such a way as to let the prosecution adduce evidence of, or ask questions about, his character or previous convictions or unless the facts are such that similar factual evidence is admissible (which will be rare).

Section 28(1)(a) requires that 'at the time of committing the offence, or immediately before or after doing so, the offender demonstrates towards the victim hostility based on the victim's membership or presumed membership of a racial group'.

'Racial group' has been dealt with already. So has 'membership' and 'presumed membership' of such a group. The reference to association with members of such a group clearly widens the ambit of this element of aggravation. The reference to 'hostility' seems to indicate that enmity or antagonism must be displayed on the stated ground. It might have been better if, as in a corresponding provision in Scots law (s 33)), reference had been made to the demonstration of malice and ill-will towards the victim. It is not obvious how hostility is going to be demonstrated other than by words, spoken or written.

In relation to the requirement that the hostility must be demonstrated at the time of committing the offence, or immediately before or after doing so, reference can be made to case-law on the offence of robbery. The definition of that offence refers to the use of threats of force 'immediately before or at the time of the stealing'. It has been held for the purposes of the offence that 'the time' of the stealing is not limited to the period (possibly a split second of time) during which the material act with mens rea of theft occurs, and that 'the time' of the stealing lasts as long as the theft can be said to be still in progress in common sense terms, ie so long as the accused is 'on the job'.[2] The addition by s 28(1)(a) of 'immediately after' is effective to extend that period.

---

1 Lord Falconer of Thoroton, Solicitor-General, HL Committee, col 1273.
2 *Hale* (1978) 68 Cr App Rep 415 (CA); *Atakpu* [1993] 4 All ER 215 at 224; *Lockley* [1995] Crim LR 656 (CA).

Motivation by hostility towards members of a racial group based on their membership of that group

8.18   In terms of the second alternative meaning of 'racially-aggravated' contained in s 28(1)(b), this has the effect in relation to the offences specified in ss 29 to 32 of making motive relevant to criminal liability, something which is exceptional[1] but which has a modern precursor in the offence of reprisals against witnesses, jurors and others, contrary to s 51(2) of the Criminal Justice and Public Order Act 1994. It is likely to be relied on only where hostility to a particular victim based on race is not demonstrated, as, for example, where racist graffiti is painted on the wall of a block of council flats.

It should be noted that the offence need not be motivated wholly by hostility towards members of a racial group based on their membership of that group, nor need it be principally so motivated. It may, for example, be motivated by religious, as well as racial, hostility. However, where it is partly so motivated – particularly where the racial motivation is subordinate to other motives – it will be particularly difficult to prove the necessary motivation.

1 Motive, good or bad, is normally irrelevant to criminal liability: *Sharpe* (1857) Dears & B 160; *Lewis v Cox* [1985] QB 509, [1984] 3 All ER 672 fn 1 (DC), although it may affect the punishment imposed (as is confirmed in the case of a racist motive by s 82).

8.19   The point just made is reinforced by s 28(3), which also makes a similar provision in respect of racial aggravation within s 28(1)(a). Section 28(3) provides that it is immaterial for the purposes of s 28(1)(a) or (b) whether or not the offender's hostility is also based, to any extent, on:

(a) the fact or presumption that any person or group of persons belongs to any religious group; or

(b) any other factor not mentioned in that paragraph.

This provision, inserted at the Committee stage in the House of Commons, is particularly intended to allay the concerns of the Muslim community that the Bill did not do enough to protect them. The effect of the provision is to make clear that, even if religious hostility is the principal or main trigger for what is done, racial aggravation will be established if an element of racial hostility is proved. In reality, the provision does not add anything to s 28; it does not catch 'the case where people are attacked, threatened or harassed solely because of their religion'. If D, an anti-Muslim fanatic, attacks a woman whom he knows is white, and whom he knows is not associated with members of an ethnic minority group, because she is wearing a chador or hajab as a badge of her religion the attack is not racially-aggravated. If, as has occurred, for example, in Slough, Hounslow and Southall, there is street-gang violence between Sikhs and Muslims,[1] triggered by each side's hostility for the other, the Sikhs' demonstration of, or motivation by, hostility towards the Muslim religion will not make their attack racially-aggravated. On the other hand, the Muslims' attack on the Sikhs will be racially-aggravated if, in part, it is triggered by hostility to Sikhs as an ethnic group, even if the principal trigger was hostility to the Sikh religion.

This problem is increased by the fact that religious hostility, unlike racial hostility,[2] has not yet been expressly identified as an aggravating factor when it comes to sentencing.

1 Fiona Mactaggart, MP, HC Report, col 898.

2 See paras **8.81** and **8.82**.

RACIALLY-AGGRAVATED ASSAULTS

8.20   The relevant provision is s 29, whose marginal note is 'Racially-aggravated assaults' (which, as explained later, is not strictly accurate).[1]

Section 29(1) provides that:

'A person is guilty of an offence under this section if he commits –

(a) an offence under section 20 of the Offences Against the Person Act 1861 (malicious wounding or grievous bodily harm);

(b) an offence under section 47 of that Act (actual bodily harm); or

(c) common assault,

which is racially aggravated[2] for the purposes of this section.'

Section 29(1) does not create one offence which can be committed in various ways but a number of separate ones.

1 See para **8.25**.
2 See paras **8.7–8.19**.

8.21   It seems likely that s 29 will be amended in the near future. The basic offences against the person referred to in it were reviewed by the Law Commission in its report on offences against the person and general defences. The Law Commission concluded that the offences referred to in s 29, and certain other non-fatal offences, were open to serious criticism, in that they do not deal adequately with modern situations and through their outdated language are liable to create scope for legal argument and costly appeals.[1] The appellate courts have agreed and called for reform.[2] The Law Commission promulgated a draft Criminal Law Bill.[1] In July 1997 the Government announced that it proposed to introduce legislation to reform the law of non-fatal offences, including the above ones.[3] A consultation paper, published in February 1998, *Violence: Reforming the Offences against the Person Act 1861*[4] was the first step in this process. It contained a draft Offences against the Person Bill which was in most respects in the same terms as the Law Commission's draft Bill in respect of offences against the person. The consultation paper recognised that the offences under s 29 will have to be re-formulated to follow the model of the proposed offences against the person if they are enacted.[5]

It is unfortunate that s 29 embodies 'archaic, confusing and unhelpful offences'[6] which are likely so soon to be abolished, possibly even before s 29 comes into force, with the consequent need to amend the section. Not only is there too much legislation in the area of criminal law, but it is also not unusual for it to be amended or repealed before it is ever brought into force.[7] This does not aid accurate knowledge or understanding of the law. Would it not have been better for the Government to have waited until an Offences against the Person Bill can be processed through Parliament?

1 Law Commission: *Legislating the Criminal Code: Offences against the Person and General Defences* (1993), Law Com No 218.
2 See, for example, *Lynsey* [1995] 3 All ER 654 at 654–655; *Mandair* [1995] 1 AC 208, [1994] 2 All ER 715 at 725, per Lord Mustill.
3 HC Deb, vol 299, col WA 578–579.
4 Home Office.
5 Op cit, para 3.7.
6 Op cit, para 2.2.
7 For a recent example, see the Criminal Justice and Public Order Act 1994, s 44 and Sch 4 (abolition of committal proceedings and their replacement by transfer proceedings) which was repealed by the Criminal Procedure and Investigations Act 1996, ss 44(2) and 80 before it came into force.

8.22   On a charge of an offence under s 29 the prosecution must prove that the accused has committed one of the relevant specified basic offences and that it (the basic offence) was racially-aggravated. The requirements of the specified basic offences are as follows.

An offence under s 20 of the Offences against the Person Act 1861

8.23   Section 20 of the 1861 Act provides that it is an offence unlawfully and maliciously to wound or inflict any grievous bodily harm upon any other person, either with or without a weapon or instrument. The last phrase adds nothing to the definition but was presumably added for the avoidance of doubt.

8.24   Section 20 creates two offences (with the result that there are two offences under s 29(1)(a)). The actus reus of one is an act resulting in the unlawful wounding of another, and of the other an act resulting in the unlawful infliction of grievous bodily harm on another. To constitute a wound, the inner and outer skin must actually be broken.[1] A bruise is not sufficient, but the wound need not be serious; a minor cut of both layers of skin will do. 'Grievous bodily harm', on the other hand, was defined by the House of Lords in *DPP v Smith*[2] as meaning really serious harm; it has since been held that 'really' adds nothing to 'serious harm' and that it is not a misdirection to direct a jury that 'grievous bodily harm' means serious harm.[3] 'Harm' refers to injury and 'bodily harm' is not limited to the skin, flesh and bones of the victim but also includes psychiatric injury. This was finally settled in 1997 by the House of Lords in the consolidated appeals *Ireland; Burstow*.[4] This is of obvious importance in the context of racially-aggravated offences.

1 *M'Loughlin* (1838) 8 C & P 635; *C (A Minor) v Eisenhower* [1984] QB 331, sub nom *JJC (A Minor) v Eisenhower* [1983] 3 All ER 230 (DC).
2 [1961] AC 290, [1960] 3 All ER 161 (HL).
3 *McMillan* (1984) unreported (CA); *Saunders* [1985] Crim LR 230 (CA).
4 [1997] 3 All ER 225 (HL). As in the case of an assault occasioning grievous bodily harm, where serious psychiatric injury is alleged but not admitted by the defence, the question whether or not the action caused such injury should not be left to the jury in the absence of expert evidence: ibid.

8.25   It was also established by the House of Lords' decision in *Ireland;*
Burstow that grievous bodily harm can be inflicted without the need for it to be
caused by an assault (fear of immediate application of unlawful force) or
battery (application of unlawful force), which offences are generically often
referred to as assaults. For this reason, the marginal note to s 29 is strictly
inaccurate in describing all offences covered by s 29 as racially-aggravated
assaults.

It is now clear from the decision in the House of Lords in *Ireland; Burstow* that
the application of force is not required for 'infliction'. As a result of this
decision, there can be no doubt that any act which causes serious bodily harm
in its extended sense constitutes inflicting such harm. Thus, someone who by
his racially-aggravated conduct causes another serious psychiatric injury or
causes him to run away in fear, in the course of which he trips and suffers
serious bodily harm, can be convicted of an offence under s 29(1)(a) – if he had
the necessary mens rea.

8.26   The grievous bodily harm must be inflicted or the wounding done
unlawfully, as must the necessary result in the other offences under s 29.
'Unlawfully' is simply a reference to the fact that a person cannot be convicted
of an offence under s 20 if his conduct is legally justified, for example by the fact
that he was using reasonable force in self-defence or to prevent crime or effect a
lawful arrest. It is inconceivable that grievous bodily harm or a wound could
ever be legally justified in the case of proven racial aggravation, and the same is
true in relation to the necessary result in the other offences under s 29.

8.27   The mens rea required for both offences is comprised by the word
'maliciously', which does not connote spite or ill-will.[1] To prove that the
accused acted maliciously, it is sufficient to prove that the accused intended his
act to result in *some* unlawful bodily harm (whether physical or psychiatric) to
some other person, albeit of a minor nature, or was subjectively reckless as to
the risk that his act might result in such harm.[2]

---

1 *Cunningham* [1957] 2 QB 396, [1957] 2 All ER 412 (CCA).
2 *Savage; DPP v Parmenter* [1992] 1 AC 699, [1991] 4 All ER 698 (HL).

An offence under s 47 of the Offences against the Person Act 1861

8.28   Section 47 provides two offences generically described as assaults
occasioning actual bodily harm (with the result that there are two offences
under s 29(1)(b)). The actus reus of one consists in the actus reus of an assault
(a term whose width is dealt with in para **8.33**) plus a requirement that it should
have caused actual bodily harm. The actus reus of the other consists in the actus
reus of a battery plus the same additional requirement.

The meaning of 'actual bodily harm' was explained by the Court of Appeal in
Chan-Fook.[1] The court held that 'harm' is a synonym for 'injury' (so that it would
not be enough that the victim's health or comfort had been interfered with, if

no injury had been caused), and that 'actual' indicates that the injury should not be so trivial as to be wholly insignificant (although there was no need for it to be permanent). The Court of Appeal also held that 'bodily harm' is capable of including an identifiable psychiatric injury, but not panic or an hysterical or nervous condition. *Chan-Fook* was approved by the House of Lords in *Ireland; Burstow.*[2]

---

1 [1994] 2 All ER 552 (CA). Also see *Miller* [1954] 2 QB 282, [1954] 2 All ER 529 at 534.
2 [1997] 4 All ER 225 (HL).

8.29 Although the accused's assault or battery must have been causally related to the actual bodily harm, the mens rea required to be proved is simply that for assault or battery, as the case may be; bodily harm to another does not have to have been intended or foreseen as a risk by the accused.[1]

---

1 *Savage; DPP v Parmenter* [1992] 1 AC 699, [1991] 4 All ER 698 (HL).

Common assault

8.30 'Common assault', the term used to describe a basic offence within s 29(1)(c), is a misleading term because it suggests that 'common assault' requires an 'assault' in its technical sense whereas it actually can be committed in the alternative by a battery, a separate offence. The two offences are now governed by s 39 of the Criminal Justice Act 1988. By s 39, assault and battery (described by the section as 'common assault and battery' but generally simply described as 'common assault')[1] are purely summary offences. It follows from the existence of two separate offences of 'common assault' that there are two offences under s 29(1)(c).

It would have been better if the Parliamentary draftsman had adopted the nomenclature used in the 1988 Act and had cited the statutory derivation for the offences, as is done in s 29(1)(a) and (b). This would have avoided any possible doubt on the meaning of common assault in s 29(1)(c).

---

1 They are so described for example in s 40 of the 1988 Act, as recognised by the Court of Appeal in *Lynsey* [1995] 3 All ER 654.

8.31 Because assault and battery are separate offences, a conviction of assault or battery will be quashed because a person cannot be convicted of alternative offences.[1] A person is guilty of an assault if he intentionally or subjectively recklessly causes another person to apprehend the application to his body of immediate, unlawful force. A person is guilty of battery if he intentionally or subjectively recklessly applies unlawful force to the body of another person.[2]

A battery generally includes an assault,[3] but this is not always so. Someone who hit another without having previously caused him to fear that unlawful force was about to be used against him, for example, because he had crept behind

him or because the victim was asleep, would commit battery even though no
assault had been committed.

---

1 *Jones v Sherwood* [1942] 1 KB 127, 111 LJKB 95 (DC); *Mansfield JJ, ex parte Sharkey* [1985] QB
  613, [1985] 1 All ER 193 (DC); *DPP v Little* [1992] 1 All ER 299 (DC).
2 *Fagan v Metropolitan Police Commissioner* [1969] 1 QB 439, [1968] 3 All ER 442 (DC); *Venna*
  [1976] QB 421, [1975] 3 All ER 788 (CA); *Kimber* [1983] 3 All ER 316 (CA); *Ireland; Burstow*
  [1997] 4 All ER 225 (HL).
3 *Rolfe* (1952) 36 Cr App Rep 4 (CCA); *DPP v Taylor; DPP v Little* [1992] 1 All ER 299 (DC).

8.32   Only one part of the above definition calls for further treatment in the
present context. This is the requirement for an assault that the victim must
apprehend the immediate application of unlawful force to his body.

The importance of this requirement is somewhat reduced by the fact that the
courts have taken a generous view of what is 'immediate'. For example, in *Smith
v Chief Superintendent, Woking Police Station*[1] a divisional court held that it had
been open to magistrates to infer that a woman, who had been frightened (as
he had intended) by seeing the accused looking at her through the window of
her bed-sitting room at 11pm, had apprehended the immediate application of
force.

In this case there was physical proximity between the accused and the victim
such that she could have feared that he would then and there apply force to her.
More extreme examples are provided by two recent cases involving 'stalking':
Ireland; Burstow[2] and *Constanza*[3]. There, between them, the House of Lords and
the Court of Appeal respectively held that an assault could be committed by
spoken words, a silent telephone call or a letter if it had the necessary effect.
What that effect consists of was apparently widened in these cases. In a curious
statement, the Court of Appeal in *Constanza*, albeit accepting the requirement
of the apprehension of immediate force, said that it was enough if the
prosecution proved fear of force 'at some time not excluding the immediate
future'. This cannot mean what it seems to mean, viz that a fear of force some
time in the distant future can suffice because this would deprive 'immediate' of
any meaning. One suggestion is that the Court of Appeal meant that there may
be an assault where the apprehension of force extends over a long period,
provided that it includes force in the immediate future.[4] This is ingenious but
not easy to square with the court's words. In *Ireland; Burstow*, Lord Steyn, with
whose speech the other Law Lords agreed, answered the question whether a
silent telephone caller may be guilty of an assault as follows:

> 'The answer to this question seems to me to be "Yes, depending on the facts". After
> all, there is no reason why a telephone caller who says to a woman in a menacing
> way "I will be at your door in a minute or two" may not be guilty of an assault if he
> causes his victim to apprehend immediate personal violence. Take now the case of
> the silent caller. He intends by his silence to cause fear and he is so understood.
> The victim is assailed by uncertainty about his intentions. Fear may dominate her
> emotions, and it may be the fear that the caller's arrival at her door may be
> imminent. She may fear the possibility of immediate personal violence. As a matter

of law the caller may be guilty of an assault: whether he is or not will depend on the circumstance and in particular on the impact of the caller's potentially menacing call or calls on the victim.'[5]

1 (1983) 76 Cr App Rep 234 (DC). Also see *Logdon v DPP* [1976] Crim LR 171 (DC).
2 [1997] 4 All ER 225 (HL).
3 [1997] Crim LR 576 (CA).
4 See comments by Professor Sir John Smith in [1997] Crim LR 576 at 577.
5 [1997] 4 All ER 225 at 236.

8.33   It is submitted that *Constanza* and *Ireland; Burstow* have gone too far in their liberal interpretation of the concept of apprehending immediate force. The dictionary definition of 'immediate' suggests that what must be apprehended is the application of force without delay,[1] as where the victim flinches at, or seeks to dodge, the force which he apprehends as the result of the accused's act. What was said on the point in the two decisions seems to equate 'immediate' with 'imminent', ie 'liable to happen soon',[1] a less stringent test. Indeed, in his speech in *Ireland; Burstow* Lord Steyn twice referred to the issue in terms of whether the accused had caused the victim to apprehend an imminent application of force. Moreover, on the second occasion, he thought that a fear of the possibility of imminent force would suffice. Despite this criticism, it must be admitted that there is support in another context for a liberal interpretation of 'immediate'; see para **8.56**.

1 *Collins English Dictionary.*

Why not other racially-aggravated offences against the person?

8.34   Arguments were made in Parliament in favour of providing racially-aggravated offences of murder, manslaughter and wounding or causing grievous bodily harm with intent to do grievous bodily harm, contrary to s 18 of the Offences against the Person Act 1861. Since murder carries a mandatory life sentence and the other two offences carry a maximum of life imprisonment, an aggravated offence is not required in order to give the courts an enhanced sentencing power – the requirement under s 82 to take racial aggravation into account in fixing the sentence is sufficient to achieve an increased sentence.[1] On the other hand, the other proclaimed purpose of the racially-aggravated offences – marking out the behaviour for particular opprobrium – would have been served by specific offences of racially-aggravated murder, manslaughter and wounding etc with intent. It would appear from this that the Government did not consider the latter rationale to be sufficient in itself for the creation of a racially-aggravated offence.

As discussed below, there are problems in terms of alternative verdicts with the fact that there is not an aggravated version of an offence under s 18 of the 1861 Act.

1 The reason given by Lord Williams of Mostyn, Parliamentary Under-Secretary, Home Office, for not introducing aggravated offences of these types: HL Committee, col 1280.

Trial and punishment

8.35   A non-aggravated offence under s 20 or s 47 of the Offences against the Person Act 1861 is triable either-way.[1] It is punishable with a maximum of five years' imprisonment or a fine, or both, on conviction on indictment,[2] and with a maximum of six months' imprisonment or a fine not exceeding the statutory maximum,[3] or both, on summary conviction.[4] The racially-aggravated offences of these two types are also triable either-way (s 29(2)(a) and (b)). They are subject to the same maximum punishment as their non-aggravated counterparts, except that the maximum term of imprisonment on conviction on indictment is seven years in respect of both offences (s 29(2)(b)).

Under the National Mode of Trial Guidelines[5] the guideline in respect of an alleged offence under s 20 or s 47, which is prefaced by the statement 'Cases should be tried summarily unless the [magistrates'] court considers that one or more of the following features is present *and* that its sentencing powers are insufficient', lists as one of these features the fact that 'the offence has clear racial motivation'. Presumably, the Guidelines will be amended in respect of the new offences.

1 Magistrates' Courts Act 1980, s 17(1) and Sch 1.
2 Offences against the Person Act 1861, ss 20 and 47.
3 See general annotations.
4 Magistrates' Courts Act 1980, ss 32 and 143; Criminal Justice Act 1991, s 17.
5 *Practice Note (Mode of Trial Guidelines)* [1990] 3 All ER 979 (CA). The Guidelines were revised and re-issued by the Criminal Justice Consultative Council, with the commendation of Lord Taylor CJ, in 1995. The revised version has not been reported but is to be found in *Archbold: Criminal Pleading, Evidence and Practice* and in *Blackstone's Criminal Practice*.

8.36   A simple offence of common assault or battery is triable summarily only and punishable with a maximum of six months' imprisonment or a fine not exceeding level 5 on the standard scale,[1] or both. However, by s 40 of the Criminal Justice Act 1988, a count charging a person with common assault or battery may be included in an indictment if the charge:

(a) is founded on the same facts or evidence as a count charging an indictable offence; or
(b) is part of a series of offences of the same or similar character as an indictable offence which is also charged,

but only if (in either case) the facts or evidence relating to the offence were disclosed in committal proceedings for the indictable offence or are disclosed in material served on a person sent for trial under s 51 of the new Act.

If a count for common assault or battery is included in an indictment under s 40 of the 1988 Act, the maximum punishment available on conviction is limited to the maximum for the offence available in a magistrates' court.

1 See general annotations.

8.37   The new offence of racially-aggravated 'common assault' is a significantly more serious one. It is triable either-way (s 29(3)) and punishable:

(a) on conviction on indictment, with a maximum of two years' imprisonment or a fine, or both;

(b) on summary conviction, with a maximum of six months' imprisonment or a fine not exceeding the statutory maximum,[1] or both.

The 300% increase in the maximum term of imprisonment for what will normally be a threat or push which has caused no harm (if it had a charge under s 47 is the appropriate one) is significant. Apparently two years was chosen on the ground that this is the normal lowest maximum specified for either-way offences. New offences triable on indictment are no longer created with a lower maximum and there are very few older ones with a maximum below that level.

Making the new offence an either-way one is in striking opposition to recent changes to the law designed to limit cases going to the Crown Court.

---

1 See general annotations.

Alternative verdicts

8.38   In relation to the basic forms of the offences referred to in s 29(1) the law is as follows. On an indictment under s 18 of the Offences against the Person Act 1861, the jury may convict the accused of an offence under s 20 or s 47, and on an indictment under s 20 of an offence under s 47 of that Act, although it has not been expressly included in the indictment, by virtue of s 6(3) of the Criminal Law Act 1967. The reason is that a charge under s 18 has been held to include a charge under s 20[1] which in turn has been held to include a charge under s 47.[2] In neither case is it now possible for an alternative verdict of an offence of common assault or common battery under s 39 of the Criminal Justice Act 1988 to be returned on an indictment under s 18 or s 20 or, for that matter, s 47 since an offence under s 39 is a summary one and is only within the Crown Court's jurisdiction if a specific count alleging it has been included in the indictment under s 40 of the 1988 Act.[3]

There is no equivalent provision to s 6(3) of the Criminal Law Act 1967 in respect of summary trials. It follows that a magistrates' court may not return an alternative verdict. They can reach a decision of guilty or not guilty only on the offence(s) charged only in the information(s) before them.[4] Potential problems which may result from the magistrates' incapacity in this respect can be avoided if the prosecution lays two or more informations, charging different offences, since the magistrates may try the informations together without the accused's consent, provided the facts are sufficiently closely connected to justify this course and there is no risk of injustice to the accused by its adoption.[5] A justification for the absence of provision for alternative verdicts appears to be that an accused in a magistrates' court on one charge may not be prepared to defend himself on another. However, given the availability of legal aid etc, is there any real distinction between the accused tried in the Crown Court and the accused tried in a magistrates' court?

1 *Mandair* [1995] 1 AC 208, [1994] 2 All ER 715 (HL).
2 *Wilson; Jenkins* [1984] AC 242, [1983] 3 All ER 448 (HL).
3 *Mearns* [1991] 1 QB 82, [1990] 3 All ER 989 (CA).
4 *Lawrence v Same* [1968] 2 QB 93, [1968] 1 All ER 1191 (DC).
5 *Chief Constable of Norfolk v Clayton* [1983] 2 AC 473, [1983] 1 All ER 984 (HL).

8.39   In terms of the new offences under s 29, the operation of s 6(3) of the Criminal Law Act 1967 is as follows in respect of trials on indictment. On a charge under s 18 of the Offences against the Person Act 1861, there cannot be an alternative conviction of any of the three 'racially-aggravated assaults', even though the prosecution opens its case on the basis that the offence was racially aggravated, because an alternative verdict is only possible under s 6(3) of the 1967 Act where the *allegations in the indictment* 'amount to or include (expressly or by implication) an allegation of another offence'.

'Amount to or include' are interpreted disjunctively, and, if the allegations in the indictment do not expressly amount to or include it, it is sufficient if they do so impliedly.[1] Provided one of these requirements is fulfilled, it is irrelevant that the other offence is not a necessary ingredient of the offence charged. Moreover, if the allegations in the indictment are *capable* of including (either expressly or impliedly) an allegation of another offence, the accused can be convicted of that other offence; the allegations need not necessarily involve the specific allegation of the other offence. Despite this liberal interpretation of the requirements of s 6(3) of the 1967 Act, it is indisputable that the allegations in an indictment for a s 18 offence do not satisfy them. Where the prosecution has evidence in a racially-aggravated case of wounding or serious harm that the accused intended to do grievous bodily harm, it will have to charge the racially-aggravated s 20 offence if it wants to have this offence in reserve in the event of an acquittal of the s 18 offence which it charges; otherwise the most the jury can do is to return an alternative verdict of an offence under s 20 unless an application to amend the indictment is successful. The success of such an application depends very much on the particular facts of the case.[2] If the prosecution does charge, or the indictment is amended to charge, a racially-aggravated s 20 offence, the jury will not need to consider whether racial aggravation is a factor in respect of the s 18 charge, but it will in respect to the charge of a racially-agravated s 20 offence. This is liable to make life difficult for the judges and to lead to confusion for jurors:

> 'A judge would first have to direct the jury on the offence of wounding with intent, which is count one on the indictment. He would have to tell the jury that it would have to decide whether the legal requirements of the offence had been made out and whether there had been a wounding. If so, the jury would have to decide whether the defendant caused the wound with intent to cause serious harm. Intent is the important difference between the two offences. It makes one more serious than the other.
>
> As the judge directs the jury on the first count of wounding with intent, he will make no mention of racial aggravation because it will not be a racially aggravated

offence ... However, if the judge is properly directing the jury and it is not satisfied on the first count, he will have to tell it to consider whether there has been an offence of wounding under s 20 [of the 1861 Act]. That is a less serious offence and does not involve intent. However, the judge will have to tell the jury to consider whether the wounding was racially aggravated, according to the meaning of racial aggravation in [s 28 of the new Act].

It is difficult to put ourselves in the place of the men and women who make up a jury and to speculate on what they might be thinking. If a jury is directed about wounding with intent and then wounding with aggravation, might it not ask itself, "Where has the concept of racial aggravation suddenly come from? Why has it come into the picture? Why do we have to consider racial aggravation on the less serious offence, but not on the more serious one?" Faced with those questions in the seclusion of the jury room, it is likely that most members of the jury will have some difficulty with them.'[3]

The Government stoutly resisted attempts to introduce a racially-aggravated offence under s 18 which would have permitted alternative verdicts of the other racially-aggravated offences at a trial involving a racially-aggravated wounding etc with intent. Its grounds were that it was neither necessary nor appropriate to create such an offence simply to offer the jury an alternative verdict, since it would require the prosecution to prove the additional element of racial aggravation without providing any additional maximum sentence.[4] Including a separate count in the indictment for the racially-aggravated offence was an adequate solution to the problem. It dismissed the suggestion that an indictment with a s 18 count and a racially-aggravated s 20 count would be one in respect of which there would be real difficulties about the summing up.[5]

---

1 *Wilson; Jenkins* [1984] AC 242, [1983] 3 All ER 448 (HL).
2 See *Archbold: Criminal Pleading, Evidence and Practice*, 1998 edn, para 1-147–1-153.
3 James Clappison, MP, HC Committee, col 323.
4 It is for the same reason that the Government explained the absence from the Act of offences of racially-aggravated murder or manslaughter: Alun Michael, MP, Minister of State, Home Office, HC Committee, col 325.
5 The fullest explanations of the Government's view are by Lord Falconer of Thoroton, Solicitor-General, HL Report, cols 701–702, and Alun Michael, MP, Minister of State, Home Office, HC Committee, cols 325–328.

8.40 On an indictment for a racially-aggravated s 20 offence, an alternative verdict will be available under s 6(3) of the 1967 Act for:

(a) a basic s 20 offence;
(b) a racially-aggravated s 47 offence;
(c) a basic s 47 offence; or
(d) a racially-aggravated 'common assault',

but not – for the reason given at the end of para **8.38** – for a basic 'common assault' offence.

Likewise on an indictment for a racially-aggravated s 47 offence, an alternative verdict will be available under s 6(3) for:

(a) a basic s 47 offence; or

(b) a racially-aggravated 'common assault',

but not for a basic 'common assault' offence.

On the other hand, no alternative verdict for an offence discussed in this part of the chapter will be available where the offence charged is a racially-aggravated 'common assault' because under s 6(3) of the 1967 Act the alternative must be an offence 'falling within the jurisdiction of the Crown Court' and the offence of common assault has been held not to be such an offence.[1] It is not obvious that an alternative verdict could be returned for any other offence. It would be prudent in the case of an indictment charging racially-aggravated 'common assault' to make use of s 40 of the Criminal Justice Act 1988 and include in the indictment a count charging 'common assault'.[2]

In view of the non-availability under s 6(3) of the 1967 Act of an alternative verdict of 'common assault', it is surprising that special provision is not made by the Act as it has been in similar contexts in ss 31 and 32.

---

1 *Mearns* [1991] 1 QB 82, [1990] 3 All ER 989 (CA).
2 See para **8.36**.

8.41   Of course, a jury will only return an alternative verdict on the invitation of the judge and after a direction by him. In addition, the House of Lords in *Wilson; Jenkins*[1] made it clear that a trial judge, before deciding to leave the possibility of conviction for another offence to the jury under s 6(3) of the 1967 Act, must always ensure that there was no risk of injustice to the accused and that he had had the opportunity of fully meeting that alternative in the course of his defence.[2]

---

1 [1984] AC 242, [1983] 3 All ER 448 (HL).
2 Further guidance is provided by *Fairbanks* (1968) 83 Cr App Rep 251 at 255–256, per Mustill
   LJ; *Maxwell* (1990) 88 Cr App Rep 173 at 176 (approved [1990] 1 All ER 806–807).

Arrest without warrant
8.42   The aggravated offences under ss 20 and 47 are, by virtue of their maximum punishment, arrestable offences under s 24(1) of the Police and Criminal Evidence Act 1984.[1] As an offence punishable with less than five years' imprisonment, the offences of aggravated 'common assault' are not arrestable offences under s 24(1) of the Police and Criminal Evidence Act 1984, nor are they in the list of arrestable offences in s 24(2) of that Act (although, strangely, an offence with the same maximum punishment on indictment under s 32 is). In the case of aggravated 'common assault', arrest may be possible either under the common law power to arrest for a breach of the peace or under s 25 of the Police and Criminal Evidence Act 1984[2] if one of the general arrest conditions is satisfied, depending on the circumstances.

---

1 The powers of police officers and private individuals in respect of arrestable offences are
   outlined in the annotations to s 32.
2 Under the Police and Criminal Evidence Act 1984, s 25, a police officer who reasonably

suspects that any offence which is not an arrestable offence has been, or is being, committed or attempted, may arrest without warrant any person whom he reasonably suspects of having committed or attempted, or of being in the course of committing or attempting, that offence. However, this power is only exercisable if it appears to the officer that service of a summons is impracticable or inappropriate because any of the 'general arrest conditions' is satisfied. These are:

(a) that the name of the suspect is unknown to the officer and cannot be ascertained by him; or
(b) that the officer has reasonable grounds for doubting whether the name furnished is the person's real name; or
(c) that the person has failed to furnish a satisfactory address, or that the officer has reasonable grounds for doubting whether the address furnished is a satisfactory address; or
(d) that the officer has reasonable grounds for believing that the arrest is necessary to prevent the suspect:
　　(i) causing physical harm to himself or another;
　　(ii) suffering physical injury;
　　(iii) causing loss of or damage to property;
　　(iv) committing an offence to public decency (provided members of the public going about their normal business cannot readily avoid the person to be arrested); or
(e) that there are reasonable grounds for believing that arrest is necessary to protect a child or other vulnerable person from the person to be arrested.

RACIALLY-AGGRAVATED CRIMINAL DAMAGE

8.43　　Hitherto, a court sentencing a person for simple criminal damage (other than by arson where the maximum punishment is life imprisonment)[1] involving racial motivation or hostility has had to sentence within the ordinary maximum. Given that the court must take into account racial motivation or hostility as an aggravating factor, this has not been a particular problem where the damage or aggregate damage exceeds £5,000 because the offence is triable either-way with a maximum on conviction on indictment of ten years' imprisonment and/or a fine.[2] However, it has been a problem where the value, or aggregate value, of the damage is less than £5,000 and the offence must be treated as if it was only triable summarily, the maximum sentence being three months' imprisonment and/or a fine not exceeding level 4 on the standard scale.[3] This low ceiling has allowed little scope for the aggravating element of racism to be taken into account in fixing the sentence.

---

1 Criminal Damage Act 1971, s 1(3).
2 Ibid, s 1(1).
3 Magistrates' Courts Act 1980, s 22(1) and (2) and s 33(1). This rule does not apply if the charge relates to two or more offences which form part of a series of two or more offences of the same or a similar character: ibid, s 22(11).

8.44　　Section 30(1) makes it an offence to commit an offence under s 1(1) of the Criminal Damage Act 1971 which is racially-aggravated. Because of the nature of the offence of simple criminal damage, the definition of racial aggravation in s 28(1)[1] has needed some modification, and this is achieved by s 30(3). As modified – the modification is in italics – s 28(1) provides that an offence is racially-aggravated for the purposes of s 30 if:

(a) at the time of committing the offence, or immediately before or after
     doing so, the offender demonstrates towards the *person to whom the property
     belongs or is treated as belonging for the purposes of the 1971 Act* hostility based
     on *that person's* actual or presumed membership of, or association with
     members of, a racial group; or
(b) the offence is motivated (wholly or partly) by hostility towards members of
     a racial group based on their membership of that group.

Section 10(2) of the 1971 Act explains what is meant by the words italicised. It is
noteworthy that, although they refer to *the* person to whom the property
belongs or is treated as belonging, s 10(2) recognises that property may belong
or be treated as belonging to more than one person. Where this is the case it
would seem that criminal damage is racially-aggravated if the offender
demonstrates towards one of the people to whom the property belongs or is
treated as belonging the necessary hostility.

Section 10(2) of the 1971 Act provides:

'Property shall be treated for the purposes of this Act as belonging to any person –

(a) having the custody or control of it; or
(b) having in it any proprietary right or interest (not being an equitable interest
     arising only from an agreement to grant or transfer an interest); or
(c) having a charge on it.'

'Custody or control' are not defined by the Act but it seems that 'custody' is
intended to mean 'physical custody' and 'control' to impart the notion of the
power to direct what shall be done with the thing in question.

It is most unlikely that the requirement of racial aggravation is going to be
satisfied solely in respect of those referred to in s 10(2)(c).[2]

---

1 See paras **8.7–8.19**.
2 The same is no doubt true in relation to people covered solely by s 10(3) which provides that
   where property is subject to a trust, the person to whom it belongs shall include any person
   having the right to enforce the trust.

8.45   In addition to the requirement of racial aggravation, the prosecution
must prove the elements of the offence of simple criminal damage contrary to
s 1(1) of the 1971 Act, viz that the accused has intentionally or recklessly, and
without lawful excuse, destroyed or damaged property belonging to another.
Because criminal damage by fire must be charged as arson, punishable with a
maximum of life imprisonment, contrary to s 1(1) and (3) of the 1971 Act, and
is therefore not merely an offence under s 1(1), the offence of racially-
aggravated criminal damage cannot be committed by fire.

8.46   'Damage' is, of course, a much wider term than 'destroy'. 'Destruction' requires that the property is reduced to nothing or to uselessness. Racists
who smash a window, snap off a sapling by its trunk or kill someone's pet,
destroy it. On the other hand, property is 'damaged' if it suffers permanent or
temporary physical harm or permanent or temporary impairment in its use or
value.[1] A wall is damaged, for example, if racist slogans are painted on it.

The test of physical harm or impairment of the property's use or value does not conclude the matter since, if the harm or impairment is minimal, there is no 'damage' for the purposes of the 1971 Act. Since it is not necessary that the effect of what has been done should be permanent, the fact that it is rectifiable does not prevent the property being damaged. However, where it is rectifiable the amount (and any cost) of rectification are relevant factors in determining the question of fact and degree;[2] if these are minimal it may be found that what has occurred is not 'damage'. In *Roe v Kingerlee*[3] a divisional court held that graffiti smeared in mud could be damage, even though it could be washed off. A case where it might be found as a matter of fact and degree that there was no damage might be spitting on someone's raincoat.[4] Such conduct would, however, amount to a battery since the slightest degree of force, eg a mere touching, will suffice, and it has been held that the touching of a person's clothes is the equivalent of touching him and that it is not necessary for a battery that the victim should feel anything.[5] If the battery was racially-aggravated, the offence of racially-aggravated common assault would be committed.

---

1 *Morphitis v Salmon* [1990] Crim LR 48 (DC); *Whiteley* (1991) 93 Cr App Rep 25 (CA).
2 See *Cox v Riley* (1986) 83 Cr App Rep 54 (DC) for an example of this.
3 [1986] Crim LR 735 (DC).
4 *A (A juvenile) v R* [1978] Crim LR 689 (Crown Ct). (Crown Court held on appeal, acquitting the accused, that such spitting was not damage on the facts before it.)
5 4 *Blackstone's Commentaries* (18th edn) 217, referring to 3 *Blackstone's Commentaries* (18th edn) 20; *Thomas* (1985) 81 Cr App Rep 331 at 334.

8.47 In order to commit an offence under s 1(1) of the 1971 Act, the accused must destroy or damage another's property 'without lawful excuse'. Section 5(2) provides that a person is to be treated as having a lawful excuse, whether or not he would be so treated apart from its provisions:

(a) if at the time of the act or acts alleged to constitute the offence he believed that the person or persons whom he believed to be entitled to consent to the destruction of or damage to the property had so consented, or would have so consented to it if he or they had known of the destruction or damage and its circumstances; or
(b) if he destroyed or damaged the property in question in order to protect property belonging to himself or another or a right or interest in property which was or which he believed to be vested in himself or another, and at the time of the act or acts alleged to constitute the offence he believed –
  (i) that the property, right or interest was in immediate need of protection; and
  (ii) that the means of protection adopted were reasonable in the circumstances.

For these purposes, it is immaterial whether the belief was justified or not, provided it was genuinely held.[1] In both situations the accused has the burden of adducing evidence to raise the issue.[2] It is difficult to imagine a case where those who damage or destroy another's property in circumstances amounting to racial aggravation are going to have a lawful excuse under s 5(2), particularly in the light of the case-law.

Blake v DPP[3] shows the limits of s 5(2)(a). D, a vicar, took part in a demonstration against the Gulf War. He wrote a Biblical quotation with a marker pen on a pillar outside the Houses of Parliament. He claimed that he was carrying out the instructions of God and, inter alia, that he had a lawful excuse under s 5(2)(a) because he believed that God was the person entitled to consent to the damage of the property. Dismissing D's appeal against conviction, the Divisional Court held that a belief that God had consented to the pillar being damaged and that God was entitled to consent could not amount to a lawful excuse under English law.

In relation to s 5(2)(b), the property intended to be protected, unlike that damaged, need not be tangible; it can consist of a right or interest in, for example, land. The test in s 5(2)(b) is partly subjective (in that it is applied on the basis of what was going on in the accused's mind, including whether he believed that the means of protection employed are reasonable) and partly objective (in that it is a question of law for the judge whether, on the facts as believed by the accused, the act done was one which protected property, or was capable of protecting property).[4] An example is provided by *Blake v DPP*, where D also claimed that he had a lawful excuse under s 5(2)(b) because he damaged the pillar to protect property in the Gulf States. Dismissing D's appeal against conviction for criminal damage, the Divisional Court held that, even if D had believed that he had a lawful excuse under s 5(2)(b), it was necessary for the court to adopt an objective view of whether, on the facts believed by D, what was done by him protected, or was capable of protecting, property. It held that his conduct could not be said to be done to protect property in the Gulf States as such protection was too remote from his conduct.

Section 5(5) provides that the provisions in s 5 are not to be construed as casting doubt on any defence recognised by law as a defence to a criminal charge, eg duress by threats or of circumstances.

It will be noted that s 5(5) refers to a defence recognised by law. Thus, a person who damages property in the belief that he has the consent of God to do so does not have a lawful excuse because such a belief does not constitute a defence recognised by English law. This was decided by the Divisional Court in *DPP v Blake*.

---

1 Criminal Damage Act 1971, s 5(3). Even a drunken belief will suffice: *Jaggard v Dickinson* [1981] QB 527, [1980] 3 All ER 716 (DC).
2 *Hill* (1989) 89 Cr App Rep 74 (CA).
3 [1993] Crim LR 586 (DC).
4 *Hunt* (1977) 66 Cr App Rep 105; *Hill* (1989) 89 Cr App Rep 74 (CA).

Trial and punishment
8.48   A person guilty of an offence under s 30 is liable:

(a) on summary conviction, to imprisonment for a term not exceeding six months or to a fine not exceeding the statutory maximum,[1] or to both;

(b) on conviction on indictment, to imprisonment for a term not exceeding 14 years or to a fine, or to both (s 30(2)).

This provision represents two differences between simple criminal damage and racially-aggravated criminal damage. On conviction on indictment, the latter is punishable with up to 14 years' imprisonment, as opposed to ten for the former. The specification of 14 years is important where the offender is under 18 because it permits a youth court to commit him for trial to the Crown Court and permits the Crown Court, if of the opinion that none of the other methods in which the case may legally be dealt with is suitable, to sentence the offender to be detained for such period not exceeding the maximum term of imprisonment with which the offence is punishable in the case of an adult as may be specified in the sentence (Children and Young Persons Act 1933, s 53(2) and (3)).

Perhaps even more important, the limitations on the trial and punishment of cases of damage or destruction not exceeding £5,000 in value in the case of simple criminal damage do not apply to racially-aggravated criminal damage. While these limitations are appropriate for the 'ordinary' case of criminal damage they are not for the more serious conduct inherent in racially-aggravated criminal damage.

Under the National Mode of Trial Guidelines,[2] the guideline in respect of an alleged offence under s 1 of the 1971 Act, which is prefaced by the statement 'Cases should be tried summarily unless the [magistrates'] court considers that one or more of the following features is present in the case and that its sentencing powers are insufficient', lists as one of these features the fact that 'the offence has clear racial motivation'. Presumably the Guidelines will be amended in respect of the new offence.

---

1 See general annotations.
2 *Practice Note (Mode of Trial Guidelines)* [1990] 3 All ER 979 (CA). See para **8.35**, note 5.

Alternative verdicts

8.49   Where the criminal damage exceeds £5,000, it will be possible at a trial on indictment for racially-aggravated criminal damage for the jury to return an alternative verdict of simple criminal damage under s 6(3) of the Criminal Law Act 1967. However, this will not be possible where the criminal damage does not exceed £5,000 because under s 6(3), as already explained in para **8.40**, the alternative must be an 'offence falling within the jurisdiction of the Crown Court' and it has been held that the offence of simple criminal damage which does not exceed £5,000 is not such an offence.[1]

---

1 *Burt* [1996] Crim LR 669 (CA).

8.50   In order to preserve a fall-back position, the prosecution should seek the inclusion of the criminal damage charge in the indictment under s 40 of the Criminal Justice Act 1988.[1] If a count is included in an indictment under the present provision the maximum punishment available on conviction is limited to the maximum for the offence available in a magistrates' court.

1 Section 40 provides that a count charging a person with criminal damage where the value is below £5,000 (or with being a party to such an offence or with attempting or inciting it) may be included in an indictment if the charge, inter alia, is founded on the same facts or evidence as a count charging an indictable offence, but only if in either case the facts or evidence relating to the offence were disclosed in committal proceedings relating to the indictable offence or are disclosed in material served on a person sent for trial under s 51 of the new Act.

Arrest without warrant

8.51   Like criminal damage itself, racially-aggravated criminal damage is an arrestable offence under s 24(1) of the Police and Criminal Evidence Act 1984.

RACIALLY-AGGRAVATED PUBLIC ORDER OFFENCES

8.52   Section 31(1) provides that:

'A person is guilty of an offence under this section if he commits –

(a) an offence under section 4 of the Public Order Act 1986 (fear or provocation of violence);

(b) an offence under section 4A of that Act (intentional harassment, alarm or distress); or

(c) an offence under section 5 of that Act (harassment, alarm or distress),

which is racially aggravated for the purposes of this section.'

As in the case of s 29(1), s 31(1) does not create one offence which can be committed in various ways; it creates three separate offences.[1]

1 Sections 4, 4A and 5 of the Public Order Act 1986 each create one offence: 1986 Act, s 7(2). See also *Winn v DPP* (1992) 156 JP 881 (DC).

8.53   On a charge of an offence under s 31, the prosecution must prove that the accused has committed the relevant specified basic offence and that it was racially-aggravated.[1]

1 See paras **8.7–8.19**.

An offence under s 4 of the Public Order Act 1986

8.54   Section 4(1) of the Public Order Act 1986 provides that a person is guilty of an offence if he:

(a) uses towards another person[1] ('an addressee') threatening, abusive or insulting words or behaviour; or

(b) distributes or displays to another person ('an addressee') any writing, sign or other visible representation which is threatening, abusive or insulting, with intent to cause that person (an addressee)[2] to believe that immediate unlawful violence[3] will be used against him or another by any person, or to provoke the immediate use of unlawful violence by that person (ie an addressee) or another, or whereby that person (an addressee) is likely to believe that such violence will be used or it is likely that such violence (by an addressee or another) will be provoked.

---

1 The requirement that the threatening, abusive or insulting words or behaviour must be 'used towards another' means that the words or behaviour in question must be used in the physical presence of and in the direction of another person directly: *Atkin v DPP* (1989) 89 Cr App Rep 199 (DC); if they are not one must fall back on the lesser offence under s 5 of the 1986 Act if it is applicable on the facts.
2 *Loade v DPP* [1990] 1 QB 1052, [1990] 1 All ER 36 (DC).
3 In the reference to an intention to cause, or the likelihood of causing, the apprehension of immediate unlawful violence or the provocation of it, 'violence' means any violent conduct: Public Order Act 1986, s 8. It includes fear or provocation of violent conduct towards property as well as violent conduct towards persons, and it is not restricted to conduct causing or intended to cause injury or damage but includes any other violent conduct (such as throwing at or towards a person a missile of a kind capable of causing injury which does not hit or falls short).

Distribution or display of any writing etc

8.55 The distribution or display of any writing, sign or other visible representation which is threatening, abusive or insulting covers handing out leaflets (distribution) or holding up a banner or placard. However, the requirement that it must be 'to another' would seem to require that the material be distributed or displayed directly to another, rather than simply being distributed (eg by leaving racist leaflets lying around in a shopping centre) or displayed (eg by sticking a racist poster on a wall in the middle of the night). If this is correct, writing racist graffiti on a wall or wearing a racist badge is unlikely, however threatening, abusive or insulting it may be, to constitute an offence under s 4 of the 1986 Act. Although someone ('an addressee') must be present to perceive the threatening etc words or behaviour, it is not necessary for him to give evidence that he had perceived what has taken place. The magistrates can rely solely on evidence given by other witnesses, such as police officers.[1]

---

1 *Swanston v DPP* (1997) 161 JP 203 (DC).

8.56 It will be noted that it is not necessarily an addressee who must be intended or likely to be provoked to immediate violence. It is sufficient that someone else present, towards whom the threatening etc behaviour etc was not directed, was intended or likely to be provoked. Thus if D shouts at a coloured person whom he knows cannot speak English, 'Yellow bastard, go home', intending that this should provoke immediate violence on the part of a group of skinheads who are in the near vicinity, the present offence is committed.

In relation to the alternative, fear of immediate violence intended or likely, the fear must be on the part of an addressee (although it need not be fear of violence against himself, nor of violence by the accused). The intended or likely fear instilled in an addressee must be of immediate unlawful violence. 'Immediate' does not mean 'instantaneous'; a relatively short period of time may elapse between the conduct which is threatening, abusive or insulting and the unlawful violence. 'Immediate' connotes proximity in time and in causation; that it is likely that violence will result within a relatively short period of time and without any other intervening occurrence.[1]

---

1 *Horseferry Road Stipendiary Magistrate, ex parte Siadatan* [1991] 1 QB 280, [1991] 1 All ER 324 (DC).

An offence under s 4A of the Public Order Act 1986

8.57   Section 4A, which was inserted by s 154 of the Criminal Justice and Public Order Act 1994, provides that a person is guilty of an offence if, with intent to cause a person harassment, alarm or distress, he:

(a) uses threatening, abusive or insulting words or behaviour, or disorderly behaviour; or

(b) displays any writing, sign or other visible representation which is threatening, abusive or insulting,

thereby causing that or another person harassment, alarm or distress.

In relation to any threatening, abusive or insulting writing, sign or other visible representation, the offence is limited to displaying it and cannot (unlike an offence under s 4) also be committed by distribution. One result is that handing out threatening, abusive or insulting leaflets is not caught by s 4A, unless the leaflets are so printed, and so held, that their contents can be said to be displayed in the sight of another. Another result is that a person who distributes threatening, abusive or insulting literature by simply delivering it through the letter boxes of intended recipients does not commit an offence under s 4A, since he does not display (and nor does he use) the threatening words.[1] An important application of s 4A will be the display of graffiti or slogans aimed at an individual which intentionally cause someone racial harassment.

---

1 *Chappell v DPP* (1988) 89 Cr App Rep 82 (DC).

8.58   Another distinction between this offence and that under s 4 is that the words or behaviour need not be used towards another person (nor need writing etc be displayed to another). It follows that words or behaviour need not be directed towards another, nor need written material be deliberately brought to the attention of another. Consequently, wearing a threatening, abusive or insulting badge is far more capable of being an offence under s 4A than under s 4, and the same is true if a T-shirt is worn bearing a racist slogan or picture which is threatening, abusive or insulting.

The fact that there has to be an identifiable victim means that some (possibly many) cases falling within s 4A will not be prosecuted under that section because victims of harassment may well be reluctant to go to the police for fear of reprisals. The offence is intended to protect the vulnerable, and the vulnerable are most likely to be influenced by the fear of reprisals. Does this augur well for the aggravated offence?

The offence is inadequate to deal with cases, such as generalised racist graffiti on walls or racist chanting, where there is no identifiable individual victim who is harassed, alarmed or distressed but, rather an offence to a section of the public at large. In the case of the graffiti the offence of racially-aggravated criminal damage would be more appropriate if the wall belonged to someone other than the writer of the graffiti.

The offence, like offences under ss 4 and 5 of the 1986 Act, and unlike those under the Protection from Harassment Act 1997, can be committed by an isolated piece of conduct; persistence is not required.

The accused must also intend his threatening etc words or behaviour or his display of a threatening etc visible representation to cause a person harassment, alarm or distress (s 4A(1)); it is irrelevant that the person actually caused the harassment etc was not the intended victim. The need for an intent to harass to be proved by the prosecution is a significant limiting factor on the offence, particularly because its proof may be difficult in practice.

An offence under s 5 of the Public Order Act 1986

8.59 Section 4A of the 1986 Act requires that harassment, alarm or distress has actually been caused and was intended to be caused by the accused. Section 5 deals with the case where one or other, or neither, of these two things can be proved.

Section 5(1) of the 1986 Act provides that a person is guilty of an offence if he:

(a) uses threatening, abusive or insulting words or behaviour or disorderly behaviour; or
(b) displays any writing, sign or other visible representation which is threatening, abusive or insulting,

within the hearing or sight of a person likely to be caused harassment, alarm or distress thereby.

For the purposes of the aggravated offence under s 31(1)(c), the definition of racial aggravation in s 28(1) has effect in the way specified by s 31(7), the effect of s 31(7) being italicised, as follows:

(a) at the time of committing the offence, or immediately before or after doing so, the offender demonstrates towards *the person (or persons)*[1] *likely to be caused harassment, alarm or distress* hostility based on that person's actual or presumed membership of, or association with members of, a racial group; or
(b) the offence is motivated (wholly or partly) by hostility towards members of a racial group based on their membership of that group.

While the accused's conduct need not be directed towards another (and written material need not be displayed by him to another), there must be a victim in the sense that what the accused does must be within the hearing or sight of a person likely to be caused harassment, alarm or distress thereby,[2] although no likelihood of violence being provoked or feared is required. Where threatening etc conduct is directed at a person or persons not likely to be caused harassment, alarm or distress, the offence is nevertheless committed if the conduct is in the hearing or sight of someone else who is likely to be caused harassment, alarm or distress thereby. In addition, it is not necessary, in a case where it is alleged that a person was likely to be caused alarm, that it was likely that that person would be caused alarm as to harm to himself. It is enough that he would be likely to be alarmed for the safety of an unconnected third party.[3]

---

1 As in the case of the offence under the 1986 Act, s 5, 'person' includes 'persons': Interpretation Act 1978, s 6.
2 Public Order Act 1986, s 5(1).
3 *Lodge v DPP* (1988) *The Times*, 26 October (DC).

General points about ss 4, 4A and 5 of the 1986 Act

Threatening, abusive, insulting or disorderly
8.60   The words 'threatening, abusive or insulting' do not bear an unusual legal meaning. Instead, it must be decided as a question of fact whether the accused's conduct was threatening, abusive or insulting in the ordinary meaning of those terms, and this is to be judged according to the impact which the conduct would have on a reasonable member of the public.[1] Behaviour is not threatening, abusive or insulting merely because it gives rise to a risk that immediate violence will be feared or provoked,[2] nor simply because it gives rise to anger, disgust or distress.[3]

If the conduct is threatening,[4] abusive or insulting, it does not matter whether or not anyone who witnessed it felt himself to be threatened, abused or insulted.[5]

A similar approach applies to 'disorderly', a term which does not require any element of violence, actual or threatened, or any threatening, abusive or insulting conduct.[6] On this basis, it is a question of fact whether the accused's conduct was disorderly in the ordinary meaning of the term.

---

1 *Brutus v Cozens* [1973] AC 854, [1972] 2 All ER 1297 (HL). See also *Simcock v Rhodes* (1977) 66 Cr App Rep 192 (CA).
2 *Brutus v Cozens* [1973] AC 854, [1972] 2 All ER 1297 (HL).
3 Ibid; *Parkin v Norman* [1983] QB 92 at 100.
4 This word is not limited to threats of violence, since an actual act of fighting can be 'threatening': *Oakwell* [1978] 1 All ER 1223 (CA).
5 *Parkin v Norman* [1983] QB 92, [1982] 2 All ER 583 (DC); *Marsh v Arscott* (1982) 75 Cr App Rep 211 (DC).

6 *Chambers v DPP* [1995] Crim LR 896 (DC).

Public or private place

8.61 With one exception, an offence under ss 4, 4A or 5 can be committed in private places,[1] such as factory premises, clubs or college premises, as well as in public places, such as football grounds, dance halls, public car parks and shopping precincts. The exception is that, in order to exclude domestic disputes, s 4(2) has the effect of providing that the use of words or behaviour inside a dwelling is only an offence under s 4 if 'the other person' (ie another person towards whom the words or behaviour are used or the writing etc is displayed) is not inside that dwelling or any other dwelling. Thus, to use threatening, abusive or insulting racist words towards someone else in the same house cannot be an offence under s 4, and the same is true if such words are shouted to someone in the house next door or displayed so as to be visible only to him. On the other hand, if threatening, abusive or insulting words are shouted by a racist in a house at a next-door neighbour from an ethnic minority who is in his back garden, an offence under s 4 will be committed, provided that the other elements of the offence are satisfied.

For the above purpose, 'dwelling' means any structure or part of a structure occupied as a person's home or as other living accommodation (whether the occupation is separate or shared with others) but does not include any part not so occupied,[2] such as a garage, a shop with accommodation over it or the communal parts of a block of flats (such as communal landings).[3] Thus, if threatening words are shouted from a flat to a shop below, an offence under s 4 may be committed, as is the case if the words are shouted from the shop to the flat upstairs. 'Structure' here includes a tent, caravan, vehicle, vessel or other temporary or movable structure.[2]

1 Public Order Act 1986, ss 4(2), 4A(2) and 5(2).
2 Ibid, s 8.
3 *Rukwira v DPP* [1993] Crim LR 882 (DC).

Harassment, alarm or distress

8.62 These terms appear in ss 4A and 5. They are wide terms, as explained in paras **5.21** to **5.26**.

Mens rea common to ss 4, 4A and 5

8.63 In ss 4 and 5 it is expressly required that the accused must either intend the words, behaviour or writing etc to be threatening, abusive or insulting (or disorderly in the case of s 5) or be aware that they or it may be.[1] No doubt the same requirement will be implied by the courts in relation to s 4A. This requirement will not be hard to prove if racial aggravation can be proved.

In relation to an offence under s 4 or s 5, a person whose awareness is impaired by intoxication must be taken to be aware of that of which he would be aware if not intoxicated, unless he proves either that his intoxication was not self-induced or that it was caused solely by the taking or administration of a substance in the course of medical treatment.[2]

---

1 Public Order Act 1986, s 6(3) and (4).
2 Ibid, s 6(5).

Defences

8.64   The 1986 Act provides two defences to a charge under s 4A or s 5, but not one under s 4. The accused has the onus of proving one of these defences on the balance of probabilities.[1]

Section 4A(3)(a) and s 5(3)(b) provide a defence for an accused who alleges that he was inside a dwelling at the material time. It states that it is a defence for him to prove that he was inside a dwelling and had no reason to believe that the words or behaviour used, or the writing, sign or other visible representation displayed, would be heard or seen by a person outside that or any other dwelling.

Section 4A(3)(b) and s 5(3)(c) provide that it is a defence for an accused to prove that his conduct was reasonable.[2] It is impossible to imagine a case where this defence could apply to conduct proved to be racially aggravated.

There is a further defence which applies only to a charge under s 5. An accused need not be proved to have intended or been aware that his conduct should be within the hearing or sight of a person likely to be caused harassment, alarm or distress thereby. On the other hand, s 5(3)(a) provides that it is a defence for the accused to prove[1] that he had no reason to believe that there was any person within hearing or sight who was likely to be caused harassment, alarm or distress.

---

1 The standard of proof is on the balance of probabilities: *Sodeman v R* [1936] 2 All ER 1138 (PC); *Carr-Briant* [1943] KB 607, [1943] 2 All ER 156 (CCA), as opposed to proof beyond reasonable doubt, which is the standard borne by the prosecution in relation to the prohibited conduct and the fault elements of the offence. The defence will satisfy this standard if the jury or magistrates are reasonably satisfied that 'the contrary' is the case or find it more probable than not that it is (*Miller v Minister of Pensions* [1947] 2 All ER 372 at 373–374).
2 Ie objectively reasonable: *DPP v Clarke* (1992) 94 Cr App Rep 359 (DC). In judging this, regard must be had to all the circumstances indicating the reason for the accused's conduct: *Morrow v DPP* [1994] Crim LR 58 (DC).

Trial and punishment

8.65   The basic offences under ss 4, 4A and 5 of the Public Order Act 1986 are all triable summarily only. Section 31(4) makes the racially-aggravated versions of the first two offences triable either way; the aggravated version of the offence under s 5 of the 1986 Act is triable only summarily.

The maximum punishment for a non-aggravated offence under ss 4 or 4A of the 1986 Act is six months' imprisonment or a fine not exceeding level 5 on the standard scale[1] or both.[2]

Section 31(4) provides the following maxima in respect of the racially-aggravated versions of these two offences:

(a) on summary conviction, imprisonment for a term not exceeding six months or a fine not exceeding the statutory maximum, or both;

(b) on conviction on indictment, imprisonment for a term not exceeding two years or a fine, or both.

The maximum punishment for a non-aggravated offence under s 5 of the 1986 Act is a fine not exceeding level 3 on the standard scale.[3] The racially-aggravated version of this offence is likewise not imprisonable, but s 31(5) raises the maximum fine to one not exceeding level 4 on the standard scale.[1]

---

1 See general annotations.
2 Public Order Act 1986, ss 4(4) and 4A(5).
3 Ibid, s 5(6). See general annotations.

Alternative verdicts

8.66 By section 31(6) of the new Act where a person is charged with an aggravated s 4 offence or an aggravated s 4A offence, and the jury find him not guilty of it, they may return a guilty verdict in respect of the corresponding non-aggravated offence, notwithstanding that both basic offences are triable summarily only.

An alternative verdict of the second aggravated public order offence at a trial on indictment for the first of the three aggravated offences (ie guilty of an aggravated s 4A offence on a charge of an aggravated s 4 offence) is not provided for by the new Act. This is not surprising because an allegation of the first offence does not expressly or impliedly amount to or include all the elements of the second. It is for this reason that the alternative verdict provisions of the Criminal Law Act 1967, s 6(3) are also inapplicable.

The comments made about alternative verdicts in paras **8.38** to **8.41** apply equally here. For the reasons given in para **8.38**, where any of the three aggravated public order offences is tried summarily there cannot be an alternative conviction for the corresponding non-aggravated offence or, indeed, any offence.

8.67 Although there can be an alternative conviction for the basic s 4 offence if the accused is acquitted in the Crown Court on a charge of violent disorder or affray,[1] there is no corresponding provision enabling an alternative verdict of the aggravated s 4 offence to be returned at a trial for violent disorder or affray. This is because offences of racially-aggravated violent disorder or affray have not been created, despite an attempt to do so in the House of Lords.[2] As in the case of the corresponding point in respect of s 18 of the Offences against the Person Act 1861, this is liable to lead to complications for the prosecution in a racially-aggravated case where the prosecution wishes to charge violent disorder or affray. The points were well put by Viscount Colville of Culross at the Committee stage in the House of Lords:

'I respectfully suggest that what will happen in these circumstances is this. If the prosecution wish to prosecute someone for a racially aggravated public order offence, they will have to decide whether they are going to go for ordinary violent disorder, ordinary affray – noble and learned Lords were right in saying that it will not be necessary for them in those circumstances to prove anything by way of racial aggravation – or they are going to go for racially aggravated threatening words and behaviour under what is now [s 31]. There is no alternative. The two things are not an alternative. They cannot be, because of the way the legislation is drafted. If they wish to proceed, for instance, on affray, it will not be necessary for them to prove any racial aggravation. They will just prove an affray in the ordinary fashion. There will be no alternative of racially aggravated threatening words and behaviour under section 4, because it cannot be an alternative. They will therefore have to put two counts. They will have to have ordinary affray, which by definition will not have to be racially aggravated, and they will have to have a second count of racially aggravated threatening words and behaviour. What the jury will make of that, I really do not know.

There is an added complication. Having been confronted with non-racially aggravated affray and the alternative of a racially-aggravated offence, the jury will also have a third alternative under [s 31(6)] whereby they can find a non-racially oriented offence under section 4. If the noble and learned Lord really wants judges in the Crown Court to sum up, and the prosecution to proceed, upon that basis, we will do it. There is no problem. What will happen, I shudder to think; but that is what we will do because we are bound, as a matter of law, to do it ...'[3]

---

1 Public Order Act 1986, s 7.
2 An amendment providing that a person could be charged with racially-aggravated offences under:

    (a) the Offences against the Person Act 1861, s 18; or
    (b) the Public Order Act 1986, s 2, and the Public Order Act 1986, s 3,

and providing that on such a charge a jury could return an alternative verdict of a racially-aggravated offence under the 1861 Act, s 20 or of a racially-aggravated offence under the 1986 Act, s 4 or s 4A, in the case of (a) and (b), respectively was withdrawn: HL Committee, cols 699–703.
3 HL Committee, cols 1301–1302.

Arrest

8.68   None of the racially-aggravated offences under s 31 is an arrestable offence. Section 31 does, however, provide police officers with the same powers of arrest without warrant as are available for the corresponding basic offences. These are more limited than those in respect of an arrestable offence.[1]

---

1 See annotations to s 32.

8.69   Section 31(2) provides that a police officer may arrest without warrant anyone whom he reasonably suspects[1] is committing an offence within s 31(1)(a) or (b). Where there are reasonable grounds for suspecting that one of these offences *has been* committed by a particular individual, a police officer may arrest him if it appears to him that service of a summons is impracticable or inappropriate because one of the general arrest conditions specified in s 25 of the Police and Criminal Evidence Act 1984 is satisfied.[2]

---

1 See annotations to s 31.
2 Police and Criminal Evidence Act 1984, s 25. See note 2 to para **8.42**. The power of arrest is, of course, also available in respect of an offence within s 31(1)(c).

8.70   Section 31(3) provides a police officer with a limited power of arrest without warrant in respect of an aggravated offence within s 31(1)(c). It provides that a police officer may arrest a person without warrant if:

(a) he engages in conduct which a police officer reasonably suspects[1] to constitute an offence falling within s 31(1)(c) (which means that the officer must reasonably suspect that the person ultimately arrested has used threatening etc words or behaviour or disorderly behaviour and has done so within the sight or hearing of a person likely to be caused harassment, alarm or distress, and that there is 'racial aggravation');
(b) he is warned[1] by that constable to stop; and
(c) he engages in further such conduct immediately or shortly after the warning.

The arresting officer is not required to be the officer who has given the warning referred to in (b).

The conduct mentioned in (a) and the further conduct need not be of the same nature (s 31(3)). If, on the first occasion, the person in question is warned for chanting racist slogans, and on the second he is brandishing a racist placard, the arrest power can operate, provided the conduct on the second occasion takes place 'immediately or shortly after' the first warning. A gap of a few minutes will no doubt satisfy this last requirement, whereas a gap of half-an-hour would not seem to, but it will be a question of fact in each case.

It should be noted that, just as on the first occasion the police officer must reasonably suspect that the conduct constitutes an offence within s 31(1)(c), so – on the second occasion – the officer must reasonably suspect that the conduct so constitutes an offence; the reference to 'further such conduct' is a reference to conduct of the type referred to in s 31(3)(a) in its entirety.

---

1 See annotations to s 31.

Why not other racially-aggravated public order offences?

8.71   It seems odd that the offences of riot, violent disorder and affray, contrary to ss 1 to 3 of the Public Order Act 1986 respectively, have not been given an aggravated version. We have already indicated that this is a potential source of difficulty in respect of alternative verdicts in the case of violent disorder and affray. These offences are the violent offences under the 1986 Act;

those under ss 4, 4A and 5 can be described as non-violent ones. It is surprising that, for example, a race riot is not regarded as an aggravated offence and that the court's sentencing powers, after allowing for the element of racial aggravation under s 82, are subject to the normal maximum for the offence. The Government gave two reasons. The first was that these offences 'are not directed against specific persons; they are mêlée or public order offences'.[1] This reason is not consistent with s 30, which provides the offence of racially-aggravated criminal damage. Criminal damage offences, including those involving racism, are frequently not directed against a specific individual or victim. As things now stand those who are guilty of taking part in a race riot are subject to a lower maximum penalty – 10 years' imprisonment[2] – than those guilty of racially-aggravated criminal damage. The Government's second reason is equally unconvincing. It was that the aggravated offences were intended to be aimed at the 'main' violence and harassment offences directed against the person, and that riot, violent disorder and affray fell outside the area of such offences.[3]

---

1 Lord Williams of Mostyn, Parliamentary Under-Secretary, Home Office, HL Committee, col 1281.
2 Public Order Act 1986, s 1.
3 Alun Michael, MP, Minister of State, Home Office, HC Committee, col 329.

RACIALLY-AGGRAVATED HARASSMENT

8.72   Section 32(1) provides that:

'A person is guilty of an offence under this section if he commits –

(a) an offence under section 2 of the Protection from Harassment Act 1997 (offence of harassment); or
(b) an offence under section 4 of that Act (putting people in fear of violence),

which is racially aggravated for the purposes of this section.'[1]

As in the case of ss 29(1) and 31(1), s 32(1) does not create one offence which can be committed in more than one way; it creates two separate offences.

On a charge of either of these aggravated offences the prosecution must prove that the accused has committed the relevant specified basic offence and that it was racially-aggravated. The requirements of the two basic offences are as follows (see paras **8.73** and **8.74**).

---

1 See paras **8.7–8.19**.

An offence under s 2 of the Protection from Harassment Act 1997

8.73   Section 2(1) of the 1997 Act makes it an offence to pursue a course of conduct in breach of the prohibition of harassment in s 1 of that Act.

The prohibition is framed as follows by s 1(1) of the Act:

'A person must not pursue a course of conduct –

(a) which amounts to harassment of another, and

(b) which he knows or ought to know amounts to harassment of the other.'

For there to be a 'course of conduct' there must be 'conduct' (a term which includes 'speech')[1] on at least two occasions.[2] This is true of 'course of conduct' whenever it appears in the following provisions. The reference to 'harassment of another' here, and elsewhere in the Act, includes alarming that person or causing that person distress.[3] What we said about these wide terms in paras **5.21–5.26** is equally applicable here.

Section 1(2) of the 1997 Act provides that the person whose course of conduct is in question ought to know that it amounts to harassment of another if a reasonable person in possession of the same information would think the course of conduct amounted to harassment of the other.

The prohibition of harassment in s 1(1) does not apply to a course of conduct if the person who pursued it proves:[4]

(a) that it was pursued for the purpose of preventing or detecting crime (eg by a police officer);

(b) that it was pursued under any enactment or rule of law or to comply with any condition or requirement imposed by any person under any enactment (eg by a court bailiff); or

(c) that in the particular circumstances the pursuit of the course of action was reasonable.[5]

It is inconceivable that any of these defences could be proved by an accused where the element of racial aggravation was proved by the prosecution.

---

1 Protection from Harassment Act 1997, s 7(4).
2 Ibid, s 7(3).
3 Ibid, s 7(2).
4 See note 1 to para **8.64**.
5 Protection from Harassment Act 1997, s 1(3).

An offence under s 4 of the Protection from Harassment Act 1997

8.74   Section 4(1) of the Act provides a more serious offence, which does not centre on a course of conduct in breach of the prohibition on harassment, but on a course of conduct putting people in fear of violence.

Section 4(1) provides that a person whose course of conduct causes another to fear, on at least two occasions, that violence will be used against him is guilty of an offence if he knows or ought to know that his course of conduct will cause the other so to fear on each of those occasions.

The provisions relating to the s 4 offence are markedly similar to the provisions relating to the prohibition of harassment, in that:

(a) there must be a 'course of conduct'; 'conduct' includes 'speech' and 'course of conduct' means conduct on at least two occasions;[1]
(b) the person whose course of conduct is in question ought to know that it will cause another to fear that violence will be used against him on any occasion if a reasonable person in possession of the same information would think the course of conduct would cause the other so to fear on that occasion;[2] and
(c) it is a defence for the accused to prove on the balance of probabilities[3] that:
   (i) his course of conduct was pursued for the purpose of preventing or detecting crime;
   (ii) his course of conduct was pursued under any enactment or rule of law or to comply with any condition or requirement imposed by any person under any enactment; or
   (iii) the pursuit of his course of conduct was reasonable for the protection of himself or another or for the protection of his or another's property.[4]

As with the corresponding defence under s 2, it is inconceivable that one of these defences could be established if the element of racial aggravation was proved.

---

1 Protection from Harassment Act 1997, s 7(3) and (4).
2 Ibid, s 4(2).
3 See note 1 to para **8.64**.
4 Protection from Harassment Act 1997, s 4(3).

Trial and punishment

8.75   The basic offence under s 2 of the 1997 Act is triable summarily only, and punishable with a maximum of six months' imprisonment or a fine not exceeding level 5 on the standard scale.[1] By s 32(3) of the new Act, an aggravated offence within s 32(1)(a) is triable either way and on conviction on indictment is punishable more severely than an offence under s 2. The increase in punishment corresponds with that in relation to racially-aggravated common assault.[2] The maximum punishment for an offence within s 32(1)(a) is:

(a) on summary conviction, imprisonment for a term not exceeding six months or a fine not exceeding the statutory maximum,[3] or both;
(b) on conviction on indictment, imprisonment for a term not exceeding two years or a fine, or both (s 32(3)).

A basic offence under s 4 of the 1997 Act is triable either way. On summary conviction, the maximum punishment is as for an offence under s 32(1)(a).[4] On a conviction on indictment, the maximum is five years' imprisonment or a fine, or both.[4] The maximum imprisonment on conviction on indictment for the aggravated offence within s 32(1)(b) is raised to seven years by s 32(4), which provides that the maximum sentence for such an offence is:

(a) on summary conviction, imprisonment for a term not exceeding six months or a fine not exceeding the statutory maximum,[3] or both;

(b) on conviction on indictment, imprisonment for a term not exceeding seven years or a fine, or both.

---

1 Protection from Harassment Act 1997, s 2(2).
2 See para **8.37**.
3 See general annotations.
4 Protection from Harassment Act 1997, s 4(4).

Alternative verdicts

Trials on indictment
8.76   Section 32(5) and (6) provide for alternative verdicts at a trial on indictment of a person charged with an offence within s 32(1)(a) or (b).

If the jury find an accused not guilty of an offence under s 32(1)(b), they may find him guilty of the basic offence under s 4 of the 1997 Act under the general alternative verdict provisions relating to trials on indictment contained in s 6(3) of the Criminal Law Act 1967. On the other hand, s 6(3) would not entitle a jury to return an alternative verdict for the relevant basic offence (that under s 2 of the 1997 Act) if they find an accused not guilty of an offence under s 32(1)(a), because that basic offence is a summary one. Section 32(5) provides that in such a case the jury may find the accused guilty of an offence under s 2 of the 1997 Act.

In addition, if at trial on indictment for an offence under s 32(1)(b), the jury find the accused not guilty, they are permitted by s 32(6) to find him guilty of an offence under s 32(1)(a). In such a case the alternative verdict could not otherwise have been possible because the terms of s 6(3) of the Criminal Law Act 1967 could not be satisfied.

Summary trials
8.77   The inability of a magistrates' court to convict of an alternative offence has already been noted.[1]

---

1 See para **8.38**.

Restraining orders

8.78   Section 5 of the 1997 Act provides a back-up to conviction and sentence in respect of an offence under s 2 or s 4, to restrain further conduct by the offender of the type in question. This is an important provision because some types of people who engage in harassment get fixated and tend not to be easily deterred.

Section 32(7) provides that s 5 of the 1997 Act has effect in relation to a person convicted of an aggravated offence under s 32. As amended, s 5 provides, in relation to such an offence, that a court sentencing or otherwise dealing with a person convicted of an offence under s 32 of the new Act may (as well as sentencing him or dealing with him in any other way) make a restraining order (1997 Act, s 5(1)).

The order may, for the purpose of protecting the victim of the offence, or any other person mentioned in the order, from further conduct which:

(a) amounts to harassment; or
(b) will cause a fear of violence,

prohibit the convicted person from doing anything described in the order (1997 Act, s 5(2)).

The order may have effect for a specified period or until further order (1997 Act, s 5(3)). It may be varied or discharged by the court which made it on application by the prosecutor, the convicted person or any other person mentioned in it (1997 Act, s 5(4)). Breach of a restraining order constitutes an offence under s 5(5) of the 1997 Act, which provides that, if without reasonable excuse the convicted person does anything which he is prohibited from doing by a restraining order, he is guilty of an offence. The offence is an either-way one, punishable in the same way as the basic offence under s 4[1] (1997 Act, s 5(6)).[2]

---

1 See para **8.74**.
2 The 1997 Act, s 5(1) is set out in the annotations to s 32.

Arrest without warrant

8.79   Offences under s 32(1)(b) and under ss 4 and 5 of the 1997 Act are arrestable offences under s 24(1) of the Police and Criminal Evidence Act 1984 by virtue of their maximum punishment.

Like an offence under s 2 of the 1997 Act, an offence under s 32(1)(a) is not an arrestable offence on that ground. On the other hand, like an offence under s 2 of the 1997 Act, an offence falling within s 32(1)(a) has been added to the list of arrestable offences in s 24(2) of the 1984 Act by s 32(2).[1]

---

1 See annotations to s 32.

INCREASE IN SENTENCES FOR RACIAL AGGRAVATION

8.80   Leaving aside offences where the sentence is fixed by law or whose circumstances attract a mandatory or minimum term of imprisonment under the Crime (Sentences) Act 1997, a court may not pass a custodial sentence unless:

(a) the offence, or combination of the offence and one or more associated offences, is so *serious* that only such a sentence can be justified; or

(b) where the offence is a violent or sexual offence, only such a sentence is adequate to protect the public from serious harm from the offender.[1]

Save when a custodial sentence is fixed or mandatory, it must be:

(a) such term (not exceeding the permitted maximum) as is commensurate with the *seriousness* of the offence, or the combination of the offence and one or more associated offences; or

(b) where the offence is a violent or sexual offence, for such longer term (not exceeding the permitted maximum) as is necessary to protect the public from serious harm from the offender.[2]

A court must not impose on an offender a community sentence[3] unless the offence, or the combination of the offence and one or more associated offences, is serious enough to warrant such a sentence.[4] Where a community sentence is passed it must be the most suitable for the offender and the restrictions on liberty imposed by it must be commensurate with the seriousness of the offence, or the combination of the offence and one or more associated offences.[5]

A court must take into account all information about the aggravating and mitigating circumstances of the offence before passing sentence.[6]

---

1 Criminal Justice Act 1991, s 1(1) and (2).
2 Ibid, s 2(1) and (2).
3 Ie a probation order, a community service order, a combination order, a curfew order, a supervision order, or an attendance centre order (ibid, s 6(4)).
4 Criminal Justice Act 1991, s 6(1).
5 Ibid, s 6(2).
6 Ibid, ss 3(3) and 7(1).

8.81   In 1995 in *Re A-G's Reference (Nos 29, 30 and 31 of 1994)*[1] the Court of Appeal stated that:

> 'It cannot be too strongly emphasised by this court that where there is a racial element in an offence of violence, that is a gravely aggravating feature ... [I]t is perfectly possible for the court to deal with any offence of violence which has a proven racial element in it, in a way which makes clear that that aspect invests the offence with added gravity and therefore must be regarded as an aggravating feature.'

Before the new Act the approach taken in *A-G's Reference (Nos 29, 30 and 31 of 1994)* was emphasised by the Magistrates' Association's sentencing guidelines[2] which expressly list racial aggravation as an aggravating factor in relation to offences of affray, inflicting grievous bodily harm, assault occasioning actual bodily harm, common assault, burglary, criminal damage, most offences under the Public Order Act 1986, and obstructing a constable in the execution of his duty. They also make it clear that in relation to any other offence the relevant list of aggravating factors is not exhaustive.

1 (1995) 16 Cr App Rep (S) 698; reported sub nom *Ribbans, Duggan and Ridley* (1994) *The Times*, 25 November (CA). See also *Re A-G's Reference (Nos 25, 26 and 27 of 1995)* [1996] 2 Cr App Rep (S) 390 (CA).
2 Revised 1997 guidelines.

8.82   Section 82 puts this element of racial aggravation, in respect of the *seriousness* of an offence, into statutory effect and extends it to offences in general. Section 82 states that it 'applies where a court is considering the seriousness of an offence other than one under ss 29 to 32' (s 82(1)). Because these offences are separate ones from their basic offences, their exclusion does not apply in respect of a basic offence which is therefore subject to the terms of s 82.

Section 82(2) provides that if the offence was racially aggravated, the court:

(a) must treat that fact as an aggravating factor (that is to say, a factor that increases the seriousness of the offence); and

(b) must state in open court[1] that the offence was so aggravated.

In the Crown Court, the question of racial aggravation will be determined by the judge, after a *Newton*[2] hearing if necessary, whereas where a racially-aggravated offence is charged it is for the jury.

Where a person is convicted of a racially-aggravated offence, it is submitted that the element of aggravation is built in within the tariff which exists under the increased penalty. To this extent, the sentencing principle in *A-G's Reference (Nos 29, 30 and 31 of 1994)* is superseded.

1 See annotations to s 9.
2 (1982) 77 Cr App Rep 13 (CA).

8.83   In the light of *A-G's Reference (Nos 29, 30 and 31 of 1994)* and of the Magistrates' Association guidelines, it is arguable that s 82 is unnecessary. On the other hand, placing sentencers under a statutory duty to treat racial aggravation as an aggravating factor does serve to reinforce good sentencing practice.

FINAL THOUGHTS

8.84   In the light of s 82, and indeed of its common law predecessor, one may question the need for the various racially-aggravated offences. The sentencing principle enshrined in s 82 ensures that the element of racial aggravation can be reflected in the sentence, and the requirement to state in open court that racial aggravation has aggravated the sentence would emphasise the special gravity of racial aggravation.

The need to prove the element of racial aggravation in order to obtain a conviction may be a disincentive to a prosecution being instituted or continued for a racially-aggravated offence, particularly in cases described above where an alternative verdict is not (or may not be) available. Prosecutors may decide in such cases not to opt for alternative charges for the sake of simplicity but simply to charge the basic offence and leave the element of racial aggravation to be taken into account under s 82.

8.85 There was a general assumption in Parliament that provisions such as those described above would have a strong deterrent effect; but will they, or are they just symbolic? It has been questioned whether singling out the racial aspects of violent crime does not magnify tensions and widen social divisions, increasing the difficulty of pursuing more constructive preventative policies.[1]

A recent Home Office research study concluded, inter alia, that:

'● The views held by all kinds of perpetrators towards ethnic minorities are shared by the wider communities to which they belong. Perpetrators see this as legitimising their actions. In turn, the wider community not only spawns such perpetrators, but fails to condemn them and actively reinforces their behaviour. The reciprocal relationship between the two suggests that the views of the 'perpetrator community' also need to be addressed in efforts to reduce racial harassment.

● For perpetrators, potential perpetrators and other individuals within the perpetrator community, expressions of racism often serve the function of distracting their own – and others' – attention away from real, underlying concerns which they feel impotent to deal with. These include a lack of identity, insecurity about the future and physical and/or mental health problems.

● Two main sets of factors appear to contribute to racial harassment and violence. These are factors which facilitate stress, delinquency or criminality; and factors which facilitate racial prejudice. Policies which aim to reduce either of these are likely to have an impact on racial harassment and violence.

● In their attempts to prevent racial harassment in the long term, the research suggests that agencies need to adopt a holistic approach consisting of three concentric strategies:

  – the identification of and effective action against *perpetrators*;
  – the identification of *potential perpetrators* and the development of strategies to divert them from actually becoming perpetrators;
  – the development of a range of strategies for consistently addressing the *perpetrator community's* general attitudes towards ethnic minorities.'[2]

As elsewhere in the Act, the provisions in this chapter are tough on crime, as opposed to the causes of crime.

---

1 Jacobs *Should Hate Be a Crime?* (1993) 113 *The Public Interest* 3, referred to in [1994] Crim LR 314.
2 *The Perpetrators of Racial Harassment and Racial Violence* (Home Office Research Study no 176, 1997).

Chapter 9

MISCELLANEOUS CHANGES

Criminal responsibility of children – Police powers – Bail – Forfeiture of recognizances – Remands and committals of children and young persons to secure accommodation – Evidence – Firearms – Restriction orders – Punishment of treason and piracy with violence – Right of appeal to the Crown Court

CRIMINAL RESPONSIBILITY OF CHILDREN

9.1   It is irrebuttably presumed that no child under the age[1] of ten years can be guilty of an offence.[2] Such a child is said to be doli incapax (not capable of crime). At common law the age of immunity from responsibility was seven. It was raised to eight by statute in 1933 and, again by statute, to ten in 1963. The age of ten can be contrasted with seven in Cyprus, Ireland and Switzerland, eight in Scotland and Northern Ireland, nine in Malta, 12 in Greece, the Netherlands and Turkey, 13 in France, 14 in Austria, Germany and Italy, 15 in the Scandinavian States, 16 in Portugal and Spain, and 18 in Belgium and Luxembourg.[3] The committee which monitors compliance with the UN Convention on the Rights of the Child has criticised the low age of criminal responsibility in the UK and proposed that consideration be given to raising it.[4]

---

1 See general annotations.
2 Children and Young Persons Act 1933, s 50, as amended by the Children and Young Persons Act 1963, s 16.
3 HL Deb, vol 564, col WA 82; (1995) 148 NLJ 1771 and 1880.
4 See *Family Policy Studies Centre Briefing Paper no 3* (1998).

Presumption of doli incapax

9.2   The common law laid down a special rule concerning children of 10 years or over but under the age of 14. They were presumed to be incapable of committing an offence, but this presumption might be rebutted by proof of a 'mischievous discretion', ie knowledge that what was done was seriously wrong.[1] Thus, a child aged between ten and 14 could be convicted only if the prosecution proved beyond reasonable doubt that he committed the actus reus with mens rea and knew he was doing something seriously wrong.[1] In relation to this last requirement, it was not enough merely to prove that the child realised that what he was doing was naughty or mischievous.[1] To rebut the presumption the prosecution had to adduce evidence separate from the facts of the alleged offence,[1] to show that the child knew the act in question was seriously wrong. Such evidence could include an admission in an interview with the police that the child knew what he was doing was seriously wrong, or the testimony of a teacher or other adult concerning the child's mental capacity and appreciation. This could lead to practical difficulties, delaying cases or even making it impossible for the prosecution to succeed. As the then Solicitor-General pointed out, at the Second Reading stage in the House of Lords, this process was:

> 'being used in a manipulative way in many courts by defendants, who say, "You have to bring a teacher, a social worker or some mature adult in order to prove this". It leads to difficulty with the calling of witnesses: it is hoped on the part of many defendants that this will make the Crown Prosecution Service bring its proceedings to a halt: it clogs up the youth court; and it is simply designed to make the proceedings more difficult.'[2]

These practical difficulties could prevent the conviction of a child, or even its prosecution. As Laws J said in the divisional court in *C v DPP*:

> '... [T]here will be cases in which in purely practical terms, evidence of the kind required simply cannot be obtained. The child defendant may have answered no questions at the police station, as is his right. He may decline to give evidence in court. That is his right also. He and his parents, or perhaps his schoolteachers, may well not co-operate with any prosecution attempt to obtain factual material about his background which may be adverse to him.'[3]

The prevention of a successful prosecution by such practical difficulties was not necessarily in the child's best interests, let alone those of justice or of the victim, because it could mean that appropriate action could not be taken to prevent re-offending.

---

1 *C v DPP* [1995] 2 All ER 43 (HL), [1994] 3 All ER 190 (DC).
2 HL 2nd Reading, col 595. See also *No More Excuses – A New Approach to Tackling Youth Crime in England and Wales*, Cm 3809 (1997), p 13.
3 [1994] 3 All ER 190 at 197.

9.3   The presumption of doli incapax was introduced in the reign of Edward III to mitigate the rigour of a penal system under which the sanction for those convicted of theft and other felonies was the death penalty. The criminal sanctions available for children are now very different, and for most young offenders the courts' emphasis is as much on preventing re-offending as on punishment. In this respect, the presumption was no longer necessary.

The special rule gave rise to the paradoxical result that, the more warped the child's moral standards, the safer he was from a finding of guilt and from the correctional treatment of the criminal law which can follow a finding of guilt.[1]

In *JBH and JH (Minors) v O'Connell* the presumption was criticised on another ground by Forbes J:

> 'That children between 10 and 14 are presumed to be exempt from criminal responsibility unless this presumption is rebutted by some evidence that they did the criminal act not only with mens rea but with a mischievous discretion is a common law rule that goes back certainly as far as Hale. No doubt it was a sensible

and merciful rule in Hale's days, but in these days of universal education from the age of five it seems ridiculous that evidence of some mischievous discretion should be required if a case of malicious damage is committed as it was in this case.'[2]

The presumption was also submitted to criticism by Bingham LJ (as he then was) in *C v DPP* as follows:

'I can understand very well the arguments against treating children of this age as criminals and for extending the scope of care proceedings but the statutory provisions to that end have not yet, as I understand, been implemented, so criminal charges may still be laid, but children have the benefit of the presumption which in this case and some others seem to me to lead to results inconsistent with common sense.'[3]

In 1994, a divisional court in *C v DPP*[4] held that the special rule was outdated and should be treated as no longer good law but the House of Lords reversed that decision and held that the special rule was still part of English law,[5] although it thought that, having regard to the anomalies and absurdities to which it gave rise, Parliament should review the rebuttable presumption.

---

1 See Williams *The Criminal Responsibility of Children* [1954] Crim LR 193 at 495–496.
2 (1981) unreported. The relevant parts of the transcripts are set out in *C v DPP* [1995] 2 All ER 43 at 54.
3 [1992] Crim LR 34 (DC). The relevant parts of the transcript are set out in *C v DPP* [1995] 2 All ER 43 at 57.
4 [1994] 3 All ER 190 (DC).
5 [1995] 2 All ER 43 (HL).

Abolition of presumption

9.4 In *Tackling Youth Crime*[1] the Government provisionally proposed the abolition of the presumption rather than simply its reversal (as some had suggested). Reversal would have meant that the 10- to 13-year-old accused would have been presumed to have had mischievous discretion unless the defence proved on the balance of probabilities that he did not. Of the 180 who responded on the point, 111 thought that the presumption should be abolished, 48 thought that it should be reversed and 21 favoured its retention as it was.[2]

In *No More Excuses*[3] the Government confirmed its proposal, emphasising that presuming that children aged between 10 and 14 do not know the difference between naughtiness and serious wrongdoing was contrary to common sense, and that abolition was necessary to remove the practical difficulties prosecutions and courts faced and which they would continue to face if the presumption were simply reversed.

---

1 *Tackling Youth Crime: A Consultation Paper* (Home Office, 1997), paras 3–18.
2 Lord Williams of Mostyn, Parliamentary Under-Secretary, Home Office, HL Committee, col 1329.
3 *No More Excuses – A New Approach to Tackling Youth Crime*, Cm 3809 (1997), paras 4.4 and 4.5.

9.5   The proposal in the White Paper is given statutory effect by s 34 which simply provides that: 'The rebuttable presumption of criminal law that a child aged 10 or over is incapable of committing an offence is hereby abolished'. Section 34 came into force on 30 September 1998.[1] Unlike s 2 of the Sexual Offences Act 1993 (which Act abolished the presumption of criminal law that a boy under 14 was incapable of sexual intercourse), s 34 does not apply to acts done before it comes into force (Sch 9). Consequently, it will be only in respect of offences committed on or after 30 September 1998 that children aged 10 to 13 will be criminally responsible in the same way as adults.

1 See Appendix II.

9.6   The abolition of the presumption of doli incapax has essentially been based on avoiding the practical difficulties which it generated rather than on a thorough-going analysis of when, and whether, it is proper to impose criminal responsibility on children aged 10 to 13. In view of the international criticism of the low age of criminal responsibility in the UK, it is surprising that, not only has that age not been raised, but that the softening effect of the intermediate stage (or 'twilight zone' as it has been called) between no criminal responsibility and full responsibility has been dispensed with. The abolition of the intermediate stage might have been reduced in its impact by revising the age of criminal responsibility, say to 12, particularly in the light of its relatively low level.

Alternatively, or in addition, concerns about the criminalisation of the very young could have been lessened by adopting the Youth Panel System which operates in Scotland under the Social Work (Scotland) Act 1968, and which has made an age of criminal responsibility of eight acceptable. If a child aged eight to 16 is brought before a Youth Panel, he is dealt with by the justices, the magistrates and the members of the Panel altogether. The child and his parents will be present while: the evidence is gone into; the mitigating circumstances are discussed; the reports are read; and the members of the Panel discuss among themselves and with the parents, in the child's presence, what is the best way to bring about redemption and rehabilitation.[1] Serious cases still end up in court but the system weeds out all the cases where court is not the most appropriate way to deal with children. The Youth Panel System enables many offending children to be effectively dealt with outside the criminal courts. It works well.[2]

It is noteworthy, in contrast, that s 4 of the Children and Young Persons Act 1969, which prohibited criminal proceedings for an offence (except homicide) by a child aged 10 to 13, and would have left such a child to be dealt with by care proceedings on the ground that he was guilty of an offence, was never brought into force and was repealed by the Criminal Justice Act 1991.[3]

1 This description was given by Lord Thomas of Gresford, HL Report, col 837.
2 This was stated by Lord Jauncey in *C v DPP* [1995] 2 All ER 43 at 45.
3 Section 72 and Sch 13.

POLICE POWERS

Power to order removal of face masks

9.7   Section 25 of the new Act extends the powers of a constable who is exercising the stop and search power contained in s 60 of the Criminal Justice and Public Order Act 1994. It does so by inserting a new subsection (4A) into s 60. This has the effect of permitting a constable who is authorised to exercise s 60 powers to require a person to remove any item which the constable reasonably believes that that person is wearing wholly or mainly for the purpose of concealing his identity. It confers consequential power to seize such items, and, in a new s 60A, provides for the retention and disposal of things seized under s 60. Section 25 will come into force, along with ancillary provisions in ss 26 and 27, on 1 December 1998: see Appendix II.

The background

9.8   Section 60 of the 1994 Act introduced a new, and potentially extremely wide, power of stop and search. It applies where a police officer, of at least superintendent rank,[1] or in cases of urgency an inspector or chief inspector, has granted an authorisation that the powers to stop and search persons and vehicles conferred by s 60 is exercisable at any place within a locality for a period not exceeding 24 hours. That authorisation may be granted where the officer reasonably believes[2] that:

(a) incidents involving serious violence may take place in any locality in his area; and

(b) it is expedient to do so to prevent their occurrence.

The period of authorisation may be extended by one further period of six hours (1994 Act, s 60(3)),[3] if it appears to the officer who gave the authorisation or to a superintendent that it is expedient to do so, having regard to offences which have, or are reasonably suspected to have, been committed in connection with any incident falling within the authorisation.

The term 'locality' is not defined by s 60. Its vagueness is intentional.[4] According to the *Shorter Oxford Dictionary*, a 'locality' has the quality of being local, begging the very question to be answered. A street, a housing estate, village, or district within a city can each be envisaged as being part of a 'locality'. What is the 'locality' for this purpose will be left essentially to the authorising officer, but the terms of Note 1G of Code A, issued under PACE, must be borne in mind. This stresses that the officer should not set a geographical area which is wider than he believes necessary for the purpose of preventing anticipated violence [or terrorism].[5] Nor is the position any clearer in respect of the meaning to be attributed to 'expedient', which is a subjective term which falls short of requiring 'necessity', not in respect of 'serious violence'.[6]

Under the pre-existing s 60, any police officer in uniform may:

(a) stop any pedestrian and search him or anything carried by him for offensive weapons or dangerous instruments;[7]

(b) stop any vehicle and search the vehicle, its driver and any passenger for offensive weapons or dangerous instruments.

The power to stop and search does not require the police officer to have any grounds for suspecting that the person or vehicle is carrying weapons or articles of that kind.

---

1 See 1994 Act, s 60(2).
2 See general annotations.
3 The wording of s 60 does not state this explicitly: see annotations to s 25. This conclusion can ·
   be justified on the wording of s 60: see Card and Ward: *The Criminal Justice and Public Order Act 1994* (Jordans, 1994) at paras 2.11–2.12.
4 See annotations to s 25.
5 The term 'locality' is used also in respect of the stop and search powers contained in s 81 of the 1994 Act. The words in square brackets refer to that power.
6 See para **9.10**.
7 See annotations to s 25. This power to stop and search a vehicle is not extended to stop and search for the purposes of the new provisions relating to masks, etc: see para **9.14**.

9.9   Increasingly, problems have arisen in respect of those who wear face coverings to avoid identification, in particular on occasions of public violence or demonstrations.[1] Serious disturbances have occurred on housing estates, including, for example, youths who, with balaclavas covering their faces, hi-jack cars and drive them at high speed around housing estates.[2] Other examples include the wearing of balaclavas or masks by some groups of anti-hunt saboteurs or some animal rights activists.[3] Existing powers are inadequate to deal with such situations. If a person wearing such an item is reasonably suspected of committing, or being about to commit, an arrestable offence, he can, of course, be arrested, under s 24 of PACE.[4] If the conduct, or even presence, of such a person, is such as to give a police officer reasonable cause to believe that a breach of the peace is imminent, or occurring, he can, in order to prevent it occurring or continuing, require the removal of that face-covering.[5] However, no power exists to require removal of such an item unless such circumstances occur, even if the removal of such an item would assist in the prevention of violence. It is that gap which the new Act is seeking to plug.

---

1 See Lord Williams of Mostyn, HL Consideration of Commons' Amendments, col 932.
2 Mike O'Brien, MP, Parliamentary Under-Secretary, Home Office, HC Committee, col 804. The example of car 'joyriders' is not altogether a happy one, because the new provisions will not necessarily apply in such circumstances: see para **9.10**.
3 See the debate at HC Committee, cols 788–806, focusing on an unsuccessful Conservative amendment.
4 See annotations to s 32.
5 *Humphries v O'Connor* (1864) 17 ICLR 1; *Moss v Maclachlan* [1985] IRLR 76 (DC).

The new power

9.10   Section 25 of the new Act inserts into s 60 of the 1994 Act a new s 60(4A), exercisable in the same situations as the power conferred by the pre-existing s 60(4). Thus, there must be:

–   *an authorisation by a senior officer*. The authorising officer will be of a superintendent rank or above, unless incidents involving serious violence are imminent and no superintendent is available. In that circumstance the authorisation may be given by an inspector or chief inspector (1994 Act, s 60(2));

–   *a reasonable belief*[1] that incidents involving serious violence may take place in any locality in his area.[2] As already noted, the term 'serious violence' is not defined. Although it is possible for violence to be against property as well as, or instead of, against a person, the whole context of s 60 of the 1994 Act suggests that it is serious violence against the person that must be anticipated. The examples given during the passage of the 1994 Act all related to incidents of personal violence. The motivation for a change in the law was the growth in violent crime against the person, and the articles that may be searched for under the pre-existing s 60(4), namely offensive weapons or dangerous instruments,[3] are all items which relate to violence against the individual.

The apprehension must be of violence, and of violence that is 'serious'. For this reason, the example of the car 'joyrider' driving maniacally round a housing estate[4] may not be a good one. Such behaviour by a youth, perhaps masked, may be frightening and annoying, and certainly dangerous, but will not of itself give rise to an apprehension of serious violence. Of course, it may form part of a course of conduct which does;

–   *the granting of the authorisation*. The granting of the authorisation must be expedient to prevent the occurrence of the apprehended incidents of serious violence (1994 Act, s 60(1)(b)). It does not have to be 'necessary' in order to prevent such violence.

Nothing in the new s 60(4A) authorises the use of the new power in circumstances where incidents of serious violence are not apprehended, or where no authorisation has in fact been issued. Such an authorisation must be in writing, or reduced to writing if it is impracticable for it to be issued in writing (1994 Act, s 60(9)). The requirement that there is the apprehension of serious violence is important, because this pre-condition amounts to the only real safeguard against the misuse of the s 60 stop and search power, although the approach of the new s 60(4A) is, in this respect, different from that of the pre-existing s 60(4).[5]

---

1 See general annotations.
2 See para **9.8**.
3 See annotations to s 25.
4 See para **9.8**.
5 See para **9.12**.

9.11   If an authorisation exists, or has been extended, not only may the police officer stop and search for offensive weapons or dangerous instruments, under s 60(4), but by the new s 60(4A), an officer in uniform may:

(a) require any person to remove any item which the officer reasonably believes that person is wearing wholly or mainly for the purposes of concealing his identity;

(b) seize any item which the officer reasonably believes any person intends to wear wholly or mainly for that purpose.

REASONABLE BELIEF

9.12   The requirement in s 60(4A) of reasonable belief[1] should be noted, because this mental state, or any other, is not required by s 60(4). If an authorisation has been issued, an officer may stop and search any person in the locality for offensive weapons or dangerous instruments. If, however, the officer wishes to require the removal of an item under s 60(4A), or to seize it, he must have reasonable belief that there is such an item. Most obviously that will arise because he can see it being worn, but there may be reasonable belief that it is being carried (eg the officer observing a face mask being stuffed inside an anorak or knapsack). There is no power to search for such items. This is deliberate and intended to provide a balance between the rights of the individual and the policing objectives of the new power. It is not clear how it does so. Although no power to search for such items is contained in s 60(4A), an officer may simply search under s 60(4), there being no reasonable suspicion or belief as a pre-requisite. The officer can then seize an item which falls under s 60(4)(a). Although, of course, police powers should be used properly, and for the purposes for which they are conferred, in many situations, given the apprehension of serious violence in the locality, an officer might well be justified in searching for offensive weapons or dangerous instruments, bearing in mind also the breadth of definition of these terms.[2]

---

1 See general annotations.
2 See annotations to s 25.

ITEMS WHICH FALL WITHIN s 60(4A)

9.13   The marginal note to s 25 of the new Act speaks of 'Powers to require removal of face-masks'. Certainly a face mask is, par excellence, a means of concealment of identity, and the new s 60(4A) will apply in any case where that is the intention, irrespective of what the motivation for that concealment is. It might be to prevent the glare of observation or the camera, or, on the other hand, to add realism to fancy-dress worn by a reveller on his or her way to a New-Year fancy dress party. We can, however, avoid the unreasonable use of s 60(4A) by concluding that, in the latter example, the purpose of it being worn is to provide amusement, ambience or to complete a costume rather than to conceal identity. It is the intention to conceal identity that matters, not the motivation for that concealment. The problem is probably academic: the party-goer will almost always be quite willing to remove the face mask voluntarily, if asked to do so. However, the breadth of s 60(4A) means that a refusal to do so might amount to the offence of wilful obstruction of a constable acting in the execution of his duty, under s 89 of the Police Act 1996, unless a court looks broadly at the purpose of wearing the mask and not the immediate objective.

Other obvious items which might fall within the power include balaclavas, helmets and scarves, if worn in a way that causes the officer to form the requisite belief. At the other end of the spectrum, no real difficulty surely exists with items worn for employment or similar purposes, such as the bee-keepers' headgear, or the protective headwear worn by workers with dangerous chemicals, bacteria or nuclear material (in the unlikely event that they are worn in public). Nor, surely, can it seriously be argued that the protective headgear of policemen in riot control gear falls within s 60(4A). In each of these cases there is no attempt to conceal identity, in whole or in part, but merely an intent to preserve the physical well-being of the wearer. A court would surely look with some incredulity on a statement by an officer that a reasonable belief as required by s 60(4A) existed, unless the context indicated otherwise very clearly.

Nor are there real difficulties with clothing worn for religious purposes, such as the yashmak, the double veil concealing the lower part of the face, worn by Muslim women in public. Although such an item might seem, potentially, to fall within the literal terms of s 60(4A), it would surely be both offensive and wrong to entitle an officer to require the removal of the yashmak, offending the legitimate religious beliefs and customs of the wearer, and, possibly, the European Convention on Human Rights. That is not the intention of Parliament.[1] A court should, again, look at the intention of the wearer: the intention of the wearer is to respect the requirements of her religion and culture, not to conceal identity.

There remains the question as to what is an 'item'. Masks, scarves, balaclavas, hoods and the like are all 'items' that can be 'worn'. But what of make-up, for example the person made-up as a clown, or the football supporters wearing woad or other garish make-up signifying national or other allegiance?[2] Arguably, make-up is not for this purpose an 'item' although in common parlance it is said to be 'worn'. In any event such make-up is not, in most cases, worn with the intention of concealing identity but to create an image or demonstrate allegiance. It would be an unusual case where a police officer could convince a court that he or she reasonably believed that there was an intent to conceal identity.

---

1 See Mike O'Brien, MP, Parliamentary Under-Secretary, Home Office, HC Committee, col 789.
2 See the discussion as to the position of Scottish World Cup supporters at HC Committee, cols 795–796.

9.14   The officer who makes the requirement, under s 60(4A)(a), or seizes the item under s 60(4A)(b), must be in uniform. Unlike the power conferred on him by s 60(4),[1] there is no power to require a vehicle to stop for this purpose, although, of course, a requirement for a vehicle to stop may be made by virtue of s 163 of the Road Traffic Act 1988. That section does not, however, authorise a police officer to require the driver of a vehicle to remain at rest. Nor does s 60(4A) (1998 Act, s 25(2) and (3)).

Articles seized under s 60(4A) may be retained by the police in accordance with regulations which are to be made by the Home Secretary pursuant to s 60A(2) of the 1994 Act (a new provision, inserted therein by the new Act, s 26). No such regulations have been made as at the date of going to press.

_____

1 See annotations to s 25.

_____

Criminal offence

9.15   A failure to comply with a requirement imposed by virtue of s 60(4A) of the 1994 Act has the same consequence as a failure to comply with any other requirement imposed by s 60 (1994 Act, s 60(8)(b), inserted by the new Act, s 25(3)). A person who so fails is liable on summary conviction to imprisonment for a term not exceeding one month or to a fine not exceeding level 3 on the standard scale,[1] or both.

_____

1 See general annotations.

_____

Power of arrest

9.16   An offence under s 60(8)(b) of the 1994 Act is added to the list of arrestable offences in s 24(2) of PACE by s 27(1) of the new Act.

Amendment of Part III of the Police Act 1997

9.17   Part III (ss 91 to 108) of the Police Act 1997 provides for the authorisation of covert entry upon and interference with property by the police, Customs and Excise, National Criminal Intelligence Service (NCIS) and the National Crime Squad (NCS). The main use of these powers is likely to be in connection with the installation of bugging devices, video surveillance or vehicle-tracking equipment. None of the operational sections of Part III, including those mentioned below, were in force when this book went to press.

Section 92 of the 1997 Act provides that no entry on or interference with property or with wireless telegraphy shall be unlawful if it is authorised by an authorisation under Part III of the Act. Authorisation is dependent on specified requirements being satisfied.

9.18   An authorisation must normally be given by an 'authorising officer', viz:

(a) a chief constable of a police force;
(b) the Commissioner, or an Assistant Commissioner, of the Metropolitan Police;
(c) the Commissioner of the City of London Police;

(d) the Director-General of the NCIS or of the NCS;

(e) the customs officer designated by the Commissioners of Customs and Excise (Police Act 1997, s 93(5)).

In respect of (e), it is proposed to designate the chief investigation officer of Customs and Excise, ie the head of the Customs National Investigation Service, as the authorising officer.[1]

By virtue of s 12(4) of the Police Act 1996, the assistant chief constable designated by the chief constable can exercise the chief constable's powers (and therefore exercise the chief constable's powers as an 'authorising officer') during the absence, incapacity or suspension of the chief constable, or a vacancy in the office of the chief constable. A similar provision exists in respect of the authorised deputy of the City of London Police Commissioner (City of London Police Act 1839, s 25). The Director-General of the NCIS or the NCS can designate a deputy to act in his absence (Police Act 1997, ss 8 and 54). These designated deputies can exercise the full powers under the 1997 Act of 'an authorising officer' (Police Act 1997, s 94(1) and (4)).

There was no provision in the 1997 Act for the exercise of an authorising officer's powers by someone appointed as the designated deputy of the person designated by the Commissioners of Customs and Excise. Such provision is now made by s 94(4)(d) of the Police Act 1997, inserted by s 113(3) of the new Act, which adds to the list of designated deputies in s 94(4) the customs officer designated by the Commissioners of Customs and Excise to act in the absence of the authorising officer for the purpose of exercising the powers of his 'authorising officer'. The deputy chief investigation officer of Customs and Excise is to be designated as the designated deputy.[1]

---

1 Lord McIntosh of Haringey, HL Report, col 937.

9.19   Section 94(1) and (2) of the Police Act 1997 provides that, where it is not reasonably practicable for an authorising officer to consider an application for an authorisation and:

(a) in the case of the Metropolitan Police, it is also not reasonably practicable for the application to be considered by any other authorising officer in that force; or

(b) in the case of a provincial police force, the City of London Police, the NCIS or the NCS and (as now amended) Customs and Excise, it is also not reasonably practicable for the authorising officer's designated deputy to consider it,

an authorisation can be considered, and an authorisation lasting 72 hours given in an urgent case, by:

(a) an assistant chief constable;

(b) a Commander (in the case of the Metropolitan or City of London forces);

(c) a person designated for the purposes of s 94 by the Director-General of the NCIS or (as the case may be) of the NCS;

(d) a customs officer designated by the Commissioners of Customs and Excise for the purposes of s 94 (s 94(2)).

As enacted, s 94(3) of the 1997 Act stated that a police member of the NCIS or NCS could not be designated under (c) 'unless he has held the rank of assistant chief constable in a police force maintained under [the Police Acts] or in the Royal Ulster Constabulary, or he has held the rank of Commander in the Metropolitan police force or the City of London police force'. This was a potential cause of problems where a police member moved to one of the two services on promotion to that rank in that Service or Squad.[1] As a result, s 113(2) changes the above rank requirement from 'has held ...' to 'holds the rank of assistant chief constable in that Service or Squad' so as to enable such officers to take decisions under s 94 of the 1997 Act.

---

1 Mike O'Brien, MP, Parliamentary Under-Secretary, Home Office, HC Committee, col 712.

BAIL

Bail: restriction in certain homicide and rape cases

9.20   As enacted, s 25 of the Criminal Justice and Public Order Act 1994 provided that, in the circumstances set out in s 25(3) below, a person who in any proceedings had been charged with or convicted of:

(a) murder;
(b) attempted murder;
(c) manslaughter;
(d) rape; or
(e) attempted rape;

must not be granted bail in those proceedings.[1]

By s 25(3) of the 1994 Act, s 25 applies only to a person previously convicted in any part of the UK of one of the above offences or of the Scottish offence of culpable homicide (which offence corresponds to manslaughter). Moreover, in the case of a previous conviction of manslaughter or culpable homicide, the prohibition applies only if the person charged or convicted was then sentenced to imprisonment or, if he was a child or young person, to long-term detention under s 53(2) of the Children and Young Persons Act 1933 (or the corresponding provisions in Scotland or Northern Ireland) (1994 Act, s 25(3)).

For the purposes of s 25 of the 1994 Act, 'conviction' is given a wide meaning. It includes a finding that a person is not guilty by reason of insanity, a finding in a case where a jury find the accused unfit to plead that he did the act or made the omission charged, and a conviction for an offence for which the offender is placed on probation or absolutely or conditionally discharged (1994 Act, s 25(5)).

---

1 1994 Act, s 25(1) and (2).

The objections to s 25 of the 1994 Act

9.21   As enacted, s 25 eroded the right to bail. It was open to criticism, especially in relation to those who are accused but not yet convicted. It was also open to question in that, when the 1994 Act was being debated in Parliament, the Government was unable to cite a case of the type covered by s 25 where a person released on bail in the circumstances covered by it had re-offended in a similar way.

There is no time-limit on the previous conviction and there is no requirement of any connection between the previous offence and the one in question. There is a world of difference between a person who was convicted of manslaughter 30 years ago on grounds of complicity in a suicide pact and who is now charged with attempted rape (of which he must be presumed innocent), and the person who was convicted of rape eight years ago and now faces another rape charge. The first person is not patently a risk to society and it is regrettable that bail had to be denied to him.

It may be that removing judicial discretion over the grant of bail contravened art 5 of the European Convention on Human Rights (no one to be deprived of his liberty except in specified circumstances and in accordance with procedures prescribed by law).[1] Currently two challenges to s 25, as enacted, have been declared admissible by the European Commission and are going to the European Court of Human Rights.[2]

---

1 The only specified circumstance relevant here refers to lawful arrest or detention in order to bring a person before the competent legal authority on reasonable suspicion of having committed an offence (art 5(1)(c)). Art 5(3) provides that everyone arrested or detained in accordance with art 5(1)(c) must be brought promptly before a judge or other officer authorised by law to exercise judicial power and is entitled to trial within a reasonable time, or to release pending trial. According to the interpretation of art 5(3) given by the European Court of Human Rights, a person charged with an offence must be released pending trial unless the State can show 'relevant and sufficient' reasons to justify his detention: *Wemhoff v Federal Republic of Germany* (1961) 1 EHRR 55. Four reasons have been found 'relevant and sufficient' by the Court:

(1) good reason to suppose that the accused, if released, would be likely to commit further offences (*Mitznetter v Austria* (1969) 1 EHRR 198; *Toth v Austria* (1991) 14 EHRR 551);

(2) good reason to believe that the accused, if released, would fail to appear at trial (*Stogmuller v Austria* (1969) 1 EHRR 155);

(3) good reason to suppose that the accused, if released, would interfere with the course of justice (*Wemhoff v Federal Republic of Germany*);

(4) crime grave and public reaction to the accused's release likely to give rise to public disorder (*Latellier v France* (1991) 14 EHRR 83); this can only justify a remand in custody temporarily (ibid).

2 Mike O'Brien, MP, Parliamentary Under-Secretary, Home Office, HC Committee, col 441.

The new rebuttable presumption against bail

9.22   The criticism of the absolute ban on bail in the circumstances outlined above is met by s 56 which amends s 25 of the 1994 Act. Section 56 came into force on 30 September 1998: see Appendix II. Section 56 removes the absolute ban, but it goes nowhere near reverting to the general presumption in favour of bail under the Bail Act 1976. Instead, it provides that in the situations with which s 25 is concerned bail is to be granted only if the court or custody officer is satisfied that there are exceptional circumstances which justify it. Section 56, in effect, introduces a strong rebuttable presumption against the grant of bail in such cases, in place of the absolute ban. This presumption can be rebutted by satisfying the court or, as the case may be, the custody officer considering the grant of bail that there are exceptional circumstances which justify the grant of bail. It would seem most unlikely that a custody officer would ever be so satisfied.

9.23   To what factors should the magistrates or custody officer have regard in determining wheher there are 'exceptional circumstances'?

In terms of the general presumption in favour of bail, a person:

(a)   who appears or is brought before a magistrates' court or the Crown Court in the course of or in connection with proceedings for the offence; or

(b)   who applies to a court for bail or for a variation of the conditions of bail in connection with the proceedings,

must be granted bail except as provided by Sch 1 whereby the accused need not be granted bail in specified circumstances, in particular if the court is satisfied that there are substantial grounds for believing that the accused, if bailed, would abscond, commit an offence or interfere with the course of justice. In reaching that decision, the court must have regard, inter alia, to the nature and seriousness of the offence and to the defendant's antecedents.

The circumstances and factors outlined in Sch 1 are strictly inapplicable to s 25 of the 1994 Act because they are specified as relevant to the general presumption in favour of bail. This would seem to leave at large what is meant by 'exceptional circumstances' justifying bail. The Government's view to the contrary that the court would have to consider the matters listed in Sch 1 to the 1976 Act simply does not fit with the wording of the relevant provisions, although no doubt the court will have regard to such matters in deciding whether there are exceptional circumstances under s 25.

Bail after arrest and charge: appointment of date for court appearances

9.24   Where, under Part IV of the Police and Criminal Evidence Act 1984 (PACE), a custody officer releases on bail an arrested person who has been charged, that release may be subject to a duty to appear before a magistrates' court at such time and such place as the custody officer may appoint. As enacted, s 47 of PACE did not provide any requirements or guidance as to the time to be appointed. In consequence, it has not been uncommon for accused to be bailed by a custody officer to appear in court weeks later. As part of the new Act's aim of speeding up the criminal process, and in accordance with a recommendation in the Narey Report,[1] s 47 of PACE is amended by s 46 so as to ensure that an early date is set for the first court appearance of a person bailed to appear before the court. Section 47(3A) of PACE, inserted by s 46(2), provides that where a custody officer grants bail to a person subject to a duty to appear before a magistrates' court, he must appoint for the appearance:

(a) a date which is not later than the first sitting of the court after the person is charged with the offence; or

(b) where he is informed by the clerk to the justices for the relevant petty sessions area that the appearance cannot be accommodated until a later date, that later date.

The idea is to enable 'simple guilty plea cases' (those triable in the magistrates' courts where evidential requirements are immediately met) to be dealt with as far as possible at the next court hearing. This change is being piloted from 30 September 1998 in the same areas as s 49, set out in para **6.14**; see Appendix II.

---

1 *Review of Delay in the Criminal Justice System: A Report* (Home Office, 1997), p 28.

Bail: increased power to require security

9.25   A person granted bail may be required to give security for his surrender to custody, ie to deposit with the court money or some other item of value which will be liable to forfeiture in the event of non-attendance in court to answer to bail (Bail Act 1976, s 3(5)). The security may be given by the person released on bail or on his behalf by somebody else (ibid). A security may be required either on bail from a police station or on bail from a court.

A security (like a surety, ie guarantee) may only be required if it is considered necessary to prevent absconding.[1] Hitherto, the giving of a security could not be required unless it appeared unlikely that the person bailed would remain in Great Britain until the time appointed for him to surrender to custody (Bail Act 1976, s 3(5)). There was no corresponding limitation in respect of the giving of a surety. The Government regarded the limitation as anomalous. The limitation in s 3(5) of the 1976 Act is deleted by s 54(1) which came into force on 30 September 1998 (see Appendix II). Lord Williams of Mostyn, Parliamentary Under-Secretary, Home Office, said: 'It is notorious that many cases are over-long delayed because bailed defendants simply do not bother to turn up on the due date. It is a constant feature and blemish, not least in magistrates' courts. We want to remove the limitation to give the court the opportunity to exercise its discretion'.[2]

---

1 This follows from a combination of the essence of a surety and the provisions of the Bail Act 1976, Sch 1, Part I, para 8, relating to when a condition may be imposed on bail.

2 HL Committee, col 589 (24 February).

Bail: power to impose a new condition

9.26   Section 3(6) of the Bail Act 1976 empowers a court granting bail to require a person to comply, before release on bail or later, with such requirements as appear to the court necessary to secure that:

(a) he surrenders to custody;

(b) he does not commit an offence while on bail;

(c) he does not interfere with witnesses or otherwise obstruct the course of justice whether in relation to himself or any other person;

(d) he makes himself available for the purpose of enabling inquiries or a report to be made to assist the court in dealing with him for the offence.

To this list is added, by s 54(2), paragraph (e) whose effect is to empower a court to insert such condition as appears to it necessary to secure that, before the time appointed for the person to surrender to custody, he attends an interview with an authorised advocate or authorised litigator.[1]

Although police bail may now[2] be made subject to conditions of the type referred to in paras (a), (b) and (c) above, the new type of condition may not be imposed in police bail. This is the effect of s 54(3),[3] which, together with s 54(2), came into force on 30 September 1998: see Appendix II.

1 As defined by the Courts and Legal Services Act 1990, s 19(1); see annotations to s 54.
2 Bail Act 1976, s 3A, inserted by the Criminal Justice and Public Order Act 1994.
3 Bail Act 1976, ss 3 and 3A, as amended, is set out in the annotations to s 54.

9.27   The reasoning behind the new provision was explained as follows by Lord Williams of Mostyn, Parliamentary Under-Secretary, Home Office, as follows:

> 'The purpose of the provision is plain. Again, it is notorious that some defendants simply do not take legal advice, have an adjournment on bail and come to the next hearing and say, "I haven't been to see my solicitor." That is a device that everyone who has been to a magistrates' court is familiar with. I recognise that it is less of a feature in the Crown Court for different and obvious reasons.
>
> What we are saying is that in some circumstances the charge against a defendant requires that he should be legally represented or at least legally advised, normally, of course, at public expense, and quite rightly too in appropriate cases. But a defendant often pays no attention to the fact that he also has obligations. If the state has an obligation to provide him with legal advice or legal representation, he has a corresponding obligation to take legal advice.
>
> This is a perfectly simple scheme saying to a defendant that the court may say, "a condition of your bail is that you take legal advice and have legal representation before the next hearing, which will be in 28 days". That will deal with an obvious, well-known blemish on the system which leads to endless, unjustified delays.'[1]

1 HL Committee, col 590 (24 February).

Bail: restriction of conditions of bail

9.28   Paragraph 8 of Sch 1 to the Bail Act 1976 provides that, where a person accused of an imprisonable offence is granted bail, no conditions which can be imposed under s 3(4) to (7) of that Act[1] (other than to secure that the accused makes himself available so as to enable inquiries or a report to be made to assist the court in dealing with him for the offence) may be imposed unless it appears to the court necessary to do so to prevent the accused failing to surrender to custody, or committing an offence while on bail, or interfering with witnesses or otherwise obstructing the course of justice. Another exception is added by Sch 8, para 38 to the new Act in respect of a condition under s 3(6)(e) of the 1976 Act, referred to in para **9.26**.

---

1 See annotations to s 54.

FORFEITURE OF RECOGNIZANCES

9.29   Section 55 makes technical changes to the provisions of s 120 of the Magistrates' Courts Act 1980 which governs the forfeiture of recognizances (agreed sums which it has been undertaken to pay in the event to which the undertaking relates) by a magistrates' court. Section 55 came into force on 30 September 1998: see Appendix II.

As enacted, s 120(1) of the 1980 Act provided:

> 'Where a recognizance to keep the peace or to be of good behaviour has been entered into before a magistrates' court or any recognizance is conditioned for the appearance of a person before a magistrates' court or for his doing any other thing connected with a proceeding before a magistrates' court, and the recognizance appears to the court to be forfeited, the court may, subject to subsection (2) below, declare the recognizance to be forfeited and adjudge the persons bound thereby, whether as principal or sureties, or any of them, to pay the sum in which they are respectively bound.'

This uniform treatment of the forfeiture of recognizances has been replaced by more complicated provisions (new subss (1), (1A) and (2) of s 120) which are substituted for the existing subss (1) and (2).

The principal aim of the new provisions is to make sureties to bail take their responsibilities more seriously. In the words of Lord Falconer of Thoroton, Solicitor-General:

> 'Stricter enforcement [of sureties' recognizances] is needed to ensure that defendants who are released on bail surrender to the custody of the court at the next hearing. Sureties are an important part of the bail process. The court may release a defendant on bail subject to providing a surety in cases where it considers that the defendant may not otherwise answer to bail ... The surety will ... be ... someone with influence over the defendant, who will promise to pay a sum to the court in the event that the defendant fails to appear at his next court hearing. This is a heavy responsibility and the surety should be certain that he or she would be able to ensure the defendant's appearance before making such an undertaking.'[1]

Under the new provisions, the rules relating to forfeiture of recognizances depend on which of the following three categories the case falls into:

(1) recognizance conditioned for the appearance of an accused before a magistrates' court (ie a recognizance by a surety to bail);

(2) recognizance to do any other thing connected with proceedings before a magistrates' court;

(3) recognizance to keep the peace or to be of good behaviour entered into before a magistrates' court.

---

1 HL 3rd Reading, cols 236–237.

Recognizance conditioned for the appearance of an accused before a magistrates' court

9.30   This situation is governed by the 'new' s 120(1A) of the 1980 Act. Hitherto, as indicated above, where an accused has failed to answer to bail, a surety's recognizance has not automatically been forfeited. Instead, the court has had first to consider the extent to which the surety was at fault before deciding whether the sum should be forfeited and, if so, whether in whole or in part. The Government thought that this approach might encourage someone to give a recognizance as a surety in respect of bail, perhaps in the belief that he will easily be able to persuade the court that he did all he could to ensure that the accused answered bail (and therefore was not at fault) and that therefore he will not be at risk of paying any of the sum in which he is bound. The new provision is intended to scotch such a belief and send a strong warning to prospective sureties about the seriousness of their undertaking and the potential consequences.[1]

---

1 Lord Falconer of Thoroton, Solicitor-General, HL 3rd Reading, col 237.

9.31   The 'new' s 120(1A) provides that, if the accused fails to appear in accordance with the condition, the court must:

(a) declare the recognizance to be forfeited;
(b) issue a summons directed to each person bound by the recognizance as surety, requiring him to appear before the court on a date specified in the summons to show cause why he should not be adjudged to pay the sum in which he is bound;

and on that date the court may proceed in the absence of any surety if it is satisfied that he has been served with the summons.

This provision contains two important changes. First, on non-appearance of the bailed accused the court must declare the forfeiture of the recognizance; it has no discretion as heretofore. Forfeiture is immediate and automatic. However, a surety will still have the chance to explain why the sum should not be paid. The difference is that the onus for establishing lack of culpability is shifted to the surety.

In the light of this change, it would seem that sureties to bail will be falling over themselves to appear before the court to show cause. Nevertheless, the procedure is strengthened by a second important change made by the new s 120(1A). Having ordered forfeiture of the recognizance, the court must issue a summons to the surety, requiring him to appear before the court on a specified date to show cause why he should not be adjudged to pay the sum in which he is bound; if he does not appear the court may proceed in his absence. Hitherto, there has been no statutory procedure in respect of the present type of recognizance for requiring a surety to appear. The practical importance of this second change is that it will enable the collection process to begin at an earlier stage than at present.

An oddity with the new provision is that if the surety or sureties does appear in court at the time that the absent accused should have appeared, as is not infrequently the case, it seems that the magistrates' court must first declare the recognizance forfeited and then issue a summons to each surety requiring him to appear. This would seem to be unnecessary. Why should a surety present throughout the occasion when the bailed accused fails to appear, and who admits his culpability, be put to the time, trouble and expense of having to await a summons and appear on the date specified in it?

9.32 The new provision applies only, of course, to proceedings in magistrates' courts. Forfeiture of a surety's recognizances in other courts is dealt with under subordinate legislation, eg the Crown Court Rules, and does not require primary legislation to amend them. The relevant rules are to be amended in line with the above provisions.

Recognizance to do any other thing connected with proceedings before a magistrates' court

9.33 This is governed by the 'new' s 120(2). This is along the same lines as the 'old' s 120(1), with one exception. It provides that, if the recognizance appears to the magistrates' court to be forfeited, it may:

> '(a) declare the recognizance to be forfeited; and
> (b) adjudge each person bound by it, whether as principal or surety, to pay the sum in which he is bound.'

As can be seen, forfeiture is not automatic even against the person who is bound by the recognizance as principal. An oddity with the drafting of this provision is that, whereas the 'old' s 120(1) provided that the court could 'adjudge the persons bound thereby, whether as principals or sureties, *or any of them* to pay the sum in which they are respectively bound', the 'new' provision seems to require a decision that either all or none should pay the sum in which each is bound.

In respect of the present type of recognizance, magistrates' courts have not been given a power to require a party to a recognizance to appear to show cause and can face a problem if such a person will not voluntarily appear. The editors of *Stone's Justices Manual*[1] have taken the view in respect of the 'old' s 120(1) that the court could not order forfeiture until the surety had been given notice that the court proposed to consider forfeiting his recognizance.

---

1 (1998 edn), para 1-2203.

Recognizance to keep the peace or to be of good behaviour entered into before a magistrates' court

9.34   With one exception, these are also dealt with by the 'new' s 120(2) in the same way as those just mentioned. The one exception is that, as in the case of the 'old' s 120,[1] s 120(2) provides that the court must not declare a recognizance of this type to be forfeited except by order made on complaint.

---

1 'Old' s 120(2).

REMANDS AND COMMITTALS OF CHILDREN AND YOUNG PERSONS TO SECURE ACCOMMODATION

9.35   By s 23(1) of the Children and Young Persons Act 1969, as amended by s 60 of the Criminal Justice Act 1991, where a court remands a child or young person aged under 17 charged with or convicted of one or more offences, or commits him for trial or sentence, and bail has been refused, the remand or committal is to be to local authority accommodation.

9.36   Section 60(1) of the Criminal Justice Act 1991 and s 20 of the Criminal Justice and Public Order Act 1994 also contained provisions to amend s 23 of the 1969 Act to allow courts in the above cases to remand or commit (hereafter simply 'remand') a 12- to 16-year-old directly to *secure* local authority accommodation if, but only if:

'(a)   he is charged with or has been convicted of a violent or sexual offence,[1] or an offence punishable in the case of an adult with imprisonment for a term of 14 years or more; or

(b)   he has a recent history of absconding while remanded to local authority accommodation, and is charged with or has been convicted of an imprisonable offence alleged or found to have been committed while he was so remanded,

and (in either case) the court is of opinion that only such a requirement would be adequate to protect the public from serious harm[2] from him.'

These conditions are described as the 'security requirement conditions' in the rest of this part of this book.

The amendments were not implemented because the necessary local authority secure accommodation had not been provided.

---

1 As defined by the Criminal Justice Act 1991, s 31 (1969 Act, s 23(12)).
2 The risk of 'serious harm' must be assessed by reference to the nature of the offences in respect of which the juvenile has been convicted or charged and the manner in which they had been carried out. It is not enough only to consider the risk that such offences might be repeated: *Croydon Youth Court, ex parte G* (1995) *The Times*, 3 May (DC).

9.37 Section 23 of the 1969 Act has hitherto been subject to temporary modification laid down by s 62 of the Criminal Justice Act 1991, which was intended to operate pending the general availability of local authority secure accommodation. Section 62 provided that where, in the case of a *male* young person aged 15 or 16, criteria almost identical to the 'security requirement conditions' were satisfied, he had to be remanded to a remand centre, if one was available, or, if not, to prison.

Although boys remanded to adult prisons are usually held in a wing on their own, the fact remains that even then they are within the culture and setting of an adult prison and that the prison officers who work with them will rotate between working with adult prisoners and working with them.[1] It is often a step towards turning them into adult criminals; sometimes it can result in suicide. There was universal agreement in Parliament that this was an undesirable state of affairs.

Complaint was also made in Parliament about remanding 15- and 16-year-olds to prison service establishments. Baroness Hilton of Eggardon, for example, said about remands to Feltham Young Offenders Institution and Remand Centre:

> 'In addition to the bullying, self-harm and even suicides of young boys, the regime is wholly inappropriate for 15 and 16-year-olds who should be attending school, who have truanted for many reasons and who are often illiterate. If they are lucky, they receive one hour a week of education in reading and writing. That is totally inappropriate to provide them with skills to cope with life thereafter. Those who are not bullied or commit suicide or who do not subject themselves to self-harm, are probably those who adapt to living in this regime with older boys of 18, 19 and 20. In many ways they are being hardened, adapted and taught to lead the lives of criminals. In my view it is wholly inappropriate to remand 15 and 16-year-olds to establishments such as Feltham, although the staff there do the best they can with something like a thousand young boys and young men who are locked up there.'[2]

---

1 James Clappison, MP, HC Committee, col 671.
2 HL Committee, col 1157 (3 March).

9.38 The previous Government began a building programme to provide 170 new local authority secure places. 160 of them had been completed by June 1998 and the remainder were due to be completed later in the summer. These new places, together with six additional places planned by the new Government since 1 May 1997, will bring to a total of 460 the number of local authority secure accommodation places.[1] The additional places will be insufficient to meet the full likely demand for secure remand places for 12- to 16-year-olds.[2] The reason is that, since the 170-place building plan was put into operation, the number of juveniles remanded in custody has increased significantly. For example, since January 1996 the number of boys aged 15 or 16 on remand in prison has not fallen below 200, and has been as high as 300. In January 1998, the number was 248 boys (75 15-year-olds and 173 16-year-olds) and at the beginning of June it was 228.[3]

The Government would not give any promises in Parliament as to when it would be possible to achieve the removal from prison of 15- and 16-year-olds by building more local authority secure accommodation. It implied that the provisions elsewhere in the Act to nip youth crime in the bud and to speed up the youth justice process and the encouragement by circular of non-custodial remands would reduce the number of places needed at some indeterminate point in the future.

---

1 HC Deb, vol 307, WA col 466.

2 *No More Excuses – A New Approach to Tackling Youth Crime in England and Wales*, Cm 3809 (1997), para 6.7. A child being looked after by a local authority may also be kept in local authority secure accommodation if the requirements of the Children Act 1989, s 25, are satisfied.

3 James Clappison, MP, HC Committee, col 670; Alun Michael, MP, Minister of State, Home Office, HC Committee, col 666, and HC Report, col 844.

9.39   The advent of the new local authority secure accommodation will enable the implementation of the power to order remands to such accommodation. However, the continuing insufficiency of local authority secure accommodation means that this must be done on an incremental basis rather than across the board in the way intended when s 60 of the Criminal Justice Act 1991 was enacted. As a result, s 23 of the 1969 Act, as amended by s 60 of the 1991 Act, has been further amended by ss 97 and 98 of the new Act. Section 62 of the 1991 Act and s 20 of the Criminal Justice and Public Order Act 1994 are repealed by Sch 10. It had been intended that these changes would come into operation in Autumn 1998, but the most recent information from the Home Office is that the implementation date is now undecided.[1]

There are two sets of provisions in respect of the amended s 23 of the 1969 Act. We set out below those provisions which are new.

–   The first introduces court-ordered remands direct to local authority secure accommodation for all 12- to 14-year-olds and for all 15- and 16-year-old girls (as soon as practicable) and (in due course) for all 15- and 16-year-old boys.

–   The second enables the most vulnerable 15- and 16-year-old boys to be remanded by the courts direct to local authority secure accommodation, rather than Prison Service accommodation, if a place has been identified. 'Vulnerable boys' are those whom a court considers should not be remanded to a remand centre or prison because of their physical or emotional immaturity or their propensity to harm themselves. The screening of vulnerability is not going to be foolproof, because prediction of how a youngster is going to react to custody in Prison Service accommodation will be difficult.

For the meantime, ie until more local authority secure accommodation places are available, other 15- and 16-year-old boys will continue to be remanded to

Prison Service accommodation. Regime standards are being developed by the Prison Service, which will include provisions to safeguard the welfare of young people, consistent with the need to protect the public and staff.

It will be noted that a remand to secure local authority accommodation is still prohibited in respect of a child under 12 (Children and Young Persons Act 1969, s 23(5)).

---

1 *No More Excuses – A New Approach to Tackling Youth Crime in England and Wales*, Cm 3809 (1997), para 10.5.

Child of 12 or 13, or a young person, of a prescribed description

9.40   Subsections (4) and (5) of the first of the new versions of s 23 provide that a court may remand a child of 12 or 13, or a young person, who (in either case) is of a specified description to secure local authority accommodation, provided the 'security requirement conditions' set out above are satisfied (s 23(5)).

The reference to 'prescribed description' means a description prescribed by reference to age or sex, or both, by an order of the Home Secretary (Children and Young Persons Act 1969, s 23(12)). It is intended as soon as practicable to prescribe girls under 17 and boys under 15.[1] This may have to be done by degrees, depending on the availability of secure accommodation. It is intended that as the amount of secure accommodation increases, the Home Secretary will incrementally extend the description to boys aged 15 or 16.

A court may only remand to local authority secure accommodation after consultation with the local authority (Children and Young Persons Act 1969, s 23(4)).

Where the juvenile is not legally represented in the court, the court must not remand or commit to local authority secure accommodation unless:

(a) the juvenile applied for legal aid and the application was refused on the ground that it did not appear his means were such that he required assistance; or

(b) having been informed of his right to apply for legal aid and had the opportunity to do so, he refused or failed to apply (Children and Young Persons Act 1969, s 23(5A)).

Apart from these changes, the provisions of s 23 of the 1969 Act in relation to the present type of juvenile remain in the form in which they were amended by s 60 of the 1991 Act. They are set out in the annotations to s 97.

---

1 *No More Excuses*, op cit, para 6.7.

Alternative provisions for 15- or 16-year-old boys not of a specified description

9.41   Section 98 of the new Act makes these alternative provisions for such boys who do not fall within the specified description referred to above. They take effect as alternative subsections to s 23 of the 1969 Act, which is most confusing!

These alternative provisions apply to a boy of 15 or 16 in respect of whom one of the 'security requirement conditions'[1] is satisfied (alternative s 23(5) of the 1969 Act, inserted by the new Act, s 98(3)).

A court must not declare a person who is not legally represented in the court to be a person who satisfied the 'security requirement conditions' unless:

(a) he applied for legal aid and the application was refused on the ground that it did not appear his means were such that he required assistance; or

(b) having been informed of his right to apply for legal aid and had the opportunity to do so, he refused or failed to apply (alternative s 23(4A) of the 1969 Act, inserted by s 98(3)).

Where a court, after consultation with a probation officer, a social worker of a local authority social services department or a member of a youth offending team,[2] declares a person to be one in respect of whom the 'security requirement conditions' are satisfied:

(a) it must remand him to local authority accommodation and require him to be placed and kept in secure accommodation, if:

    (i) it also, after such consultation, declares him to be a person to whom subsection (5A) below applies; and

    (ii) it has been notified that secure accommodation is available for him;

(b) it must remand him to a remand centre, if (a) above does not apply and it has been notified that such a centre is available for the reception from the court of persons in respect of whom the 'security requirement conditions' are satisfied; and

(c) it must remand him to a prison, if neither (a) nor (b) above applies (alternative s 23(4) of the 1969 Act, inserted by the new Act, s 98(3)).

Section 23(5A) referred to above applies to a person if the court is of opinion that, by reason of his physical or emotional immaturity or a propensity of his to harm himself, it would be undesirable for him to be remanded to a remand centre or a prison (inserted by the new Act, s 98(3)). It is a moot point whether 'physical or emotional immaturity' includes the likelihood of being bullied in a remand centre or prison, which is a major problem. Bullying is not necessarily associated with immaturity on the part of the victim; it can be associated with sexual orientation or timidity or some other characteristic or idiosyncracy.

The alternative provisions made by s 98 might have been more acceptable if, when a young person was remanded to a remand centre or prison, the relevant local authority was obliged to continue to look for suitable secure accommodation to which he would *automatically* be transferred if it was found. However, a proposed amendment to this effect was unsuccessful at the Report stage in the House of Commons.[3]

---

1 The precise wording of the 'security requirement conditions' is slightly different in its last part (although its effect is the same) from that described above which applies in the case of juveniles other than 15- and 16-year-old boys. See the 1969 Act, alternative s 23(5).

2 See paras **2.19–2.21**.
3 HC Report, cols 842–861.

9.42 The alternative provisions by made by s 98 may conflict with art 10 of the International Covenant on Civil and Political Rights to which the UK is a party. Article 10 requires accused juveniles to be separated from adults when detained.

The UK entered a reservation to art 10, but only in respect of the situation where there is a lack of suitable prison facilities or where the mixing of adults and juveniles is deemed to be mutually beneficial. It has been agreed that neither of these grounds seems to be applicable to the alternative provisions.[1]

---

1 Lord Goodhart, HL 2nd Reading, col 589.

EVIDENCE

Effect of child's silence at trial

9.43 Section 35 of the new Act amends s 35 of the Criminal Justice and Public Order Act 1994, to permit an inference to be drawn from the failure of a child to give evidence or, without good cause, to answer any question. Nothing in s 35 of the 1994 Act, or in the new amendment, requires a court to draw an inference or alters the purposes which an inference, if drawn, can serve. This section came into force on 30 September 1998: see Appendix II.

The background and rationale for change

9.44 The so-called 'right of silence' provisions in the Criminal Justice and Public Order Act 1994 were amongst the most contentious of all the provisions in that long and controversial Act. Sections 34, 36 and 37 of that Act empowered a court to draw such inference as it considered proper from a failure, at the investigation stage, to mention certain facts or give certain explanations or accounts. Those sections apply to all such failures by a suspect, irrespective of age.

By contrast, s 35 of the 1994 Act, which deals with silence at trial is age-limited. The pre-existing s 35 applies at the trial of any person who has attained the age[1] of 14 years.[2] The reason for this distinction has been explained[3] as the need to provide special protection for persons aged under 14 in the criminal justice system, although this does not really explain why that 'special protection' was thought unnecessary at the investigation stage, when, arguably, a child suspect would be even more vulnerable and deserving of protection. The 'right of silence' provisions of the 1994 Act were opposed by the then Labour opposition.

The new Act takes a different approach to alleged crime by children. As we have seen, it does so by abolishing the presumption of doli incapax relating to children aged 10 to 13,[4] and by making the new detention and training order[5] potentially available in respect of children as young as 10.[6] These changes tell 'young people [sic] that they must accept responsibility for what they have done. Any child knows that if he starts misbehaving he has to answer the basic questions "Did you do it?" and if so "why did you do it?" Any child will understand that before he reaches the age of 10. We are saying that once they have got to 10 it is logical, if there is a court case, for them to be given the opportunity and to be obliged to say whether they did it and if so, why they did it ...'.[7] Of course, it does not inevitably follow, logically, that because children aged 10 are criminally responsible in the same way as adults one inevitably removes all special procedures or rules. Nevertheless, in this context, age is now immaterial to the threshold condition for the drawing of an inference although not, one suspects, to the reality of whether a court will in fact draw an inference.

---

1 See general annotations.
2 See *Friend* [1997] Crim LR 817 (CA), where an argument that an accused aged 14 years, 5 months, and with a mental age of nine, should have the same immunity from adverse inferences as a person aged under 14 was rejected. Age is to be calculated in accordance with the Family Law Reform Act 1969, s 9.
3 James Clappison, MP, HC Committee, col 346.
4 See para **9.5**.
5 See paras **4.49–4.70**.
6 This power will not initially be implemented in respect of 10- and 11-year-olds: see para **4.49**.
7 Mike O'Brien, MP, Parliamentary Under Secretary, Home Office, HC Committee, col 350.

The effect of the change
9.45   The effect of s 35 of the new Act is that at the trial of a child (as well as a young person or an adult), and irrespective of whether that trial is at the youth court or Crown Court, then, unless the accused's guilt is not in issue (1994 Act, s 35(1)(a)), or it appears to the court that the physical or mental condition of the accused makes it undesirable for him to give evidence (1994 Act, s 35(1)(b)), s 35(2) of the 1994 Act will apply.

It may be noted that the age and maturity of the accused may be relevant to the question that may arise under s 35(1)(b) of the 1994 Act. Although the 11th Report of the Criminal Law Revision Committee[1] identified the main purpose of an exception in respect of mental condition as being to provide for cases of insanity or diminished responsibility, the exception in s 35(1)(b) is not confined to cases of diagnosed mental illness or disability, unless the word 'condition' is construed as referring to a medically diagnosable condition. Some support for this view comes from the decision in *Friend*[2] where the court held that no specific test exists to determine whether it is undesirable for the accused to give evidence: examples may include the risk of an epileptic fit, or a mental condition such as latent schizophrenia. Appeal courts will only interfere with the decision of the trial court if it is *Wednesbury* unreasonable.

On this basis, age will not be a factor in terms of the threshold condition, but rather as to whether an inference should in fact be drawn. In reality the two questions are blurred. In cases of illness, substance abuse, or, it is submitted, significant immaturity it matters not whether they are classified as matters which fall within s 35(1)(b) or whether they are matters which render the drawing of an inference undesirable. Whichever approach is correct the question is surely this: is it reasonable, given the accused's mental condition, to expect him to testify?

---

1 Cmnd 4991 (1972), para 115.
2 [1997] Crim LR 817 (CA).

9.46   If the conditions in s 35(1) are satisfied, and s 35(2) of the 1994 Act does apply, a court or jury may draw such inference as it considers proper from a failure to testify, or from a failure, without good cause, to answer any question, provided the procedural requirements of s 35(2) of the 1994 Act are satisfied. A court is under an obligation, at the conclusion of the prosecution case, to satisfy itself that the accused is aware of his right to give evidence and the potential for inferences to be drawn from a failure to do so, or from a failure, without good cause, to answer a question.

'Good cause' is dealt with by s 35(5). A refusal must be taken to be without good cause, unless:

(a) the accused is entitled to refuse to answer the question by virtue of any enactment, whenever passed or made, or on the ground of privilege; or

(b) the court in the exercise of its general discretion excuses him from answering it.

Of course, a question should not be asked, and need not be answered if it is not relevant to the matter before the court.

9.47   Whether an inference is in fact drawn will depend on the court of trial. The principles to be applied continue to be those stated by the Court of Appeal in *Cowan, Gayle and Riciardi*,[1] which require an evidential basis to be established to provide a basis for a finding of good cause. The evidential base required by that decision may well be supplied by evidence from a psychologist. In *Friend*[2] the Court of Appeal stated that a clinical psychologist's report could provide the evidential basis required by *Cowan*, but the court was entitled to take into account all the circumstances, including conduct prior to and after the commission of the offence.

It must be remembered, however, that nothing in s 35 requires a court to draw an inference, and a court may well decide in the case of a child not to do so. The practical significance of the change made by the new Act is far from clear, and in many cases an experienced advocate may be able to put a case to the court which will disincline a court in fact to draw an inference. It should also be remembered that an accused cannot be convicted solely on an inference: the prosecution must have established a prima facie case before an inference may be drawn (1994 Act, s 38(3)).

---

1 [1995] 4 All ER 939 (CA).
2 [1997] Crim LR 817 (CA).

Live television links at preliminary hearings

9.48   Section 57 of the new Act provides for the use of live television links at preliminary hearings before a court, where an accused is being held in custody in prison or other institution. The use of such a link (where it is possible) does not require the consent of the accused, or his legal adviser, but is a matter for the discretion of the court. Section 57 came into force on 30 September 1998: see Appendix II.

The rationale for the change

9.49   Unless a hearing is one which the law permits to be conducted in the absence of the accused, he must be physically present. At present, where a person is held in custody that may involve delays and costs associated with transporting defendants in custody back and forth between prison and court for hearings that often may be brief, and result in yet another remand.[1] In this respect the new power can be viewed as part of the strategy to reduce delay and cost, and intended, for example, to avoid situations where proceedings in court are delayed because vans carrying defendants fail to arrive at court on time, or go to the wrong court, or an accused is prevented from leaving prison to attend court for some logistic reason.[2] Whether the new power will in fact have this result is a different matter.

The new power is also intended to have the added advantage of contributing towards greater security of remand prisoners, and, indeed, was one of the main recommendations of the Learmont Report into security of prisoners, which followed the Parkhurst prison break-out.[3] During the passage of the Act through Parliament, it was indicated that there had been 11 escapes from escort or court by young offenders alone in the year to March 1988, nine of which were from the 'magistrates' court [sic]'.[4]

It will later be seen that the precise effectiveness of the technology to facilitate the working of the new power is by no means certain. It is for this reason that the Government intends to pilot the arrangements. The precise pilot arrangements are not yet known, but will be designed to ensure that defendants are not disadvantaged by the new procedure. The operation of the power will be expanded, as and when effective and adequate resources allow.[5] It may therefore be a long time, if ever, before such arrangements become universal.

---

1 Lord Falconer of Thoroton, Solicitor-General, HL Committee, col 591.
2 Examples given by Mike O'Brien, MP, Parliamentary Under-Secretary, Home Office, HC Committee, col 466.
3 See Lord Falconer of Thoroton, Solicitor-General, HL Committee, cols 591–592.
4 Mike O'Brien, MP, Parliamentary Under-Secretary, Home Office, HC Committee, col 467.
5 Ibid, col 465.

The power

9.50   By s 57(1), in any proceedings for an offence, a court, may, after hearing representations from the parties, direct that the accused shall be treated as being present in the court for any particular hearing before the start of the trial, if, during that hearing:

(a) he is held in custody in a prison or other institution; and

(b) whether by means of a live television link or otherwise, he is able to see and hear the court and to be seen and heard by it.

The term 'particular hearing' used in s 57(1) is in contradistinction to the term 'preliminary hearing' used in the marginal note to the section. This term 'preliminary hearing' is not used in the technical sense ascribed to a 'preparatory hearing' by s 29 of the Criminal Procedure and Investigations Act 1996, but refers to any hearing before either a magistrates' court or Crown Court before the start of the trial (s 57(1)). Nothing in s 57(1) otherwise limits the types of hearing to which it can potentially apply, which can include, for example, mode of trial hearings.

The phrase 'start of the trial' bears the same meaning as given by s 22(11A) or s 22(11B) of the Prosecution of Offences Act 1985,[1] which in cases being tried summarily will be the point when the court begins to hear evidence for the prosecution, or when a guilty plea is accepted. In a case being tried on indictment, the start of the trial is taken to occur when a jury is sworn to consider the issue of guilt or fitness to plead, or, if the court accepts a guilty plea before a jury is sworn, when that plea is accepted.

---

1 See annotations to s 43.

9.51 The power to use the s 57 procedure presupposes that it is available. As noted above, it is intended that the power be piloted. By s 57(2), a court cannot make a direction under s 57(1) unless:

(a) it has been notified by the Home Secretary that facilities are available for enabling persons held in custody in the institution in which the accused is or is to be held to see and hear the court and to be seen and heard by it; and

(b) the notice has not been withdrawn.

The facilities that must be available are those that enable, whether by a live television link or otherwise, the accused to see and hear the court and to be seen and heard by it (s 57(1)). Two points arise in this context. First, the words 'or otherwise' seem to be in s 57(1) to anticipate future technological developments, perhaps in the context of telephones or computer images. Secondly, the words in s 57(1) ('see and hear ...' etc) clearly in this context mean that the accused should have the same opportunities to see and hear as if he were in court. A literal interpretation which prevented the operation of the s 57(1) power in a case involving a visually or aurally impaired accused would surely be absurd and wrong, although such factors are clearly relevant to the question as to how the court should exercise its discretion.

9.52 The use of the power is a matter for the court's discretion. A court may only make an order under s 57(1) having heard representations from the parties. The term 'heard' clearly suggests that the representations should be at an oral hearing, and include all parties, or at any rate all parties who wish to make representations. Thus the court may balance the wishes of the accused to have his 'day in court' (however short) with the representations of the prosecution on matters of cost, convenience and security. The accused does not have to consent. No specific guidance is given by statute, or, indeed, by the parliamentary debates, as to how this discretion should be exercised but it surely is the case that the first consideration ought to be fairness to the accused, and whether his presence is necessary for the proceedings to be properly conducted. Where a magistrates' court with power to give a direction under s 57(1) does not do so, it must give its reasons (s 57(3)).

9.53   In this context, concerns arise about the ability of an advocate to take instructions from his client. Attempts were made during the passage of the Act to prevent the power from applying to proceedings where the mode of trial for an either-way offence is being considered.[1] These are proceedings where important decisions are made, and where existing legislation recognises the importance of the presence of the accused.[2] Access to his or her legal representative is fundamental, but particularly important in mode of trial proceedings.

Such arguments were met by the Government with assurances that adequate arrangements could be put in place to deal with matters of contact between advocate and accused. The legal representative will, it was argued, have to take the majority of his instructions beforehand. Pilot studies will allow for private and secret telephone links between legal representative and accused before the hearing, although the position in respect of instructions during the hearing was far less clearly articulated. The possibility of telephone link during a hearing was not ruled out, although one can well see that many of the claimed advantages of reducing delay may evaporate. One suggestion canvassed by the Government was that, during a hearing, 'a note could be passed by a clerk to an advocate through a telephone link [sic]'.[3] This startling suggestion of intrusion into the basic principle of absolute lawyer/client privilege serves only to confirm what was admitted by the Government in any event, namely, that pilot studies are intended to establish whether the use of the new power is practical, and, if so, in what circumstances.[4]

---

1 See amendments proposed by James Clappison, MP, HC Committee, cols 462–463.
2 See Magistrates' Courts Act 1980, s 18.
3 Mike O'Brien, MP, Parliamentary Under-Secretary, Home Office, HC Committee, col 466.
4 Ibid, cols 465–466.

9.54   It was noted earlier, at para **9.51**, that the proposed procedure can potentially be brought into operation in respect of any court, including the youth court. Particular care will need to be taken in respect of the use of the procedure with children. There will be a need to ensure that a child is aware of what is going on through appropriate advice, guidance and support.[1] However, the age of the accused is not intended to be a barrier to the use of the power.[2]

---

1 See James Clappison, MP, HC Committee, col 463.
2 Mike O'Brien, MP, Parliamentary Under-Secretary, Home Office, HC Committee, col 467.

FIREARMS

Possession of firearms by persons previously convicted of a crime

9.55   Section 21(1) and (2) of the Firearms Act 1968 provide the following prohibitions on the possession of firearms or ammunition by persons previously convicted of an offence. Contravention of one of the prohibitions is an either-way offence.[1] In the case of a person who has been sentenced to custody for life or to imprisonment for three years or more or detention in a young offender institution for such a term, the prohibition is an indefinite one.[2] In the case of a person who has been sentenced to imprisonment for three months or more but less than three years or to youth custody or detention in a young offender institution for such a term, or who has been sentenced to be detained for such a term in a detention centre or who has been subject to a secure training order, there is a five-year prohibition from the date of his release.[2] This latter provision is extended by Sch 8, para 14(1) to someone who has been made subject to a detention and training order whatever the period. In such a case the 'date of his release' for the purposes of the commencement of the five-year period is specified as follows by s 21(2A)(c) of the 1968 Act, added by Sch 8, para 14(2):

> 'in the case of a person who has been subject to a detention and training order –
>
> (i)   the date on which he is released from detention under the order;
> (ii) the date on which he is released from detention ordered under section 77 of the Crime and Disorder Act 1998;[3] or
> (iii) the date of the half-way point of the term of the order,
>
> whichever is the later.'

---

1 Firearms Act 1968, s 21(4). It is also an offence by the 1968 Act, s 21(5), for a person to sell or transfer a firearm or ammunition to, or to repair, test or prove a firearm or ammunition for, a person whom he knows or has reasonable grounds for believing to be prohibited by the 1968 Act, s 21, from having a firearm or ammunition in his possession. An offence under s 21(4) or (5) is punishable on conviction on indictment with a maximum of five years' imprisonment or a fine or both, and on summary conviction with a maximum of six months' imprisonment or a fine not exceeding the statutory maximum (see general annotations) or both: Firearms Act 1968, s 51 and Sch 6.
2 A person prohibited from possession can apply to the Crown Court for a removal of the prohibition: 1968 Act, s 21(6).
3 See para **4.70**.

Forfeiture and disposal of firearms

9.56   Section 52(1) of the Firearms Act 1968 empowers a court to order the forfeiture or disposal of a firearm or ammunition in certain cases listed in s 52(1) of that Act. At the time that the new Act received the Royal Assent, these included the case where a person is convicted of an offence under the 1968 Act (with minor exceptions) or is convicted of a crime for which he is sentenced to imprisonment, or detention in a young offender institution or is subject to a secure training order.

Consequent on the abolition of secure training orders and the introduction of detention and training orders,[1] s 52(1) above is amended so that an order under it can be made against someone who has been convicted and made subject to a detention and training order, and the reference to a secure training order is deleted (Sch 8, para 15).

---

1 See para **4.49**.

RESTRICTION ORDERS

9.57   Section 15(1) of the Football Spectators Act 1989 empowers a court by or before which a person is convicted of certain specified offences to make a restriction order against him. There is a second power under the 1989 Act to make a restriction order. By s 22 of the 1989 Act, there is a power by Order in Council to list offences under the law of a country other than England and Wales which correspond to offences specified in Sch 1 to the 1989 Act. Section 22 empowers a magistrates' court to make a restriction order against a person convicted of a specified listed offence.

The purpose of a restriction order is to prevent the person concerned attending designated football matches outside England and Wales. In terms of designated football matches in England or Wales, a person can be prohibited from attending by an exclusion order under Part IV (ss 30–37) of the Public Order Act 1986.

Unless exempted in respect of a particular occasion, a person who is subject to a restriction order is required to report 'on the occasion' of designated football matches outside England and Wales when required to do so at any police station in England and Wales at the time or between the times specified in the notice by which the requirement is made. A person who, without reasonable excuse, fails to comply with the duty to report imposed by a restriction order commits a summary offence (1989 Act, s 16(4)).

Public concern over the behaviour of so-called England supporters during the World Cup in France in June 1998 resulted in an addition being made to the Bill to strengthen the 1989 Act in two ways (see paras **9.58–9.59**). Both amendments came into force on 7 August 1998.[1]

---

1 Crime and Disorder Act 1998 (Commencement No 1) Order 1998, SI 1998/1883, art 3.

Arrest

9.58   As enacted, there was no power of arrest without warrant in respect of an offence under s 16(4) of the 1989 Act, other than the power of arrest given to a police officer by s 25 of the Police and Criminal Evidence Act 1984 (PACE). Under s 25, a police officer has a power of arrest if he reasonably suspects that a non-arrestable offence has been committed or attempted or is being committed or attempted, and it appears to him that service of a summons is impracticable or inappropriate because any of the general arrest conditions is satisfied, eg failure to give a name and address or giving a 'suspect' name and address.[1] The problem revealed by events surrounding the World Cup was that police officers were seeing individuals subject to restriction orders leaving the country, knowing full well that they would be failing to comply with their restriction orders but unable to do anything about it in terms of making an arrest.

Section 84(2) seeks to fill this gap by adding an offence under s 16(4) of the 1989 Act to the growing list of arrestable offences in s 24(2) of PACE.[2] It is doubtful, however, whether this will enable the police to arrest in a case such as that just mentioned. The reason is that the power to arrest without warrant in advance given to the police by s 24(7) of PACE requires the police officer to have reasonable grounds for suspecting that the arrestee is *about to commit* an arrestable offence. By the very nature of things, a person at a port or airport or at a Eurostar station en route to a football match abroad can hardly be said to be 'about to commit' an offence which cannot be committed until the time specified in the notice requiring him to report at a police station, which will almost cetainly be some time after embarkation.[3]

---

1 See note 1 to para **8.42**.
2 For a description of the powers of arrest in respect of an arrestable offence, see annotations to s 32.
3 Since the duty to report is 'on the occasion' of a designated match, it would be impermissible for the reporting time period to be significantly greater than the 'occasion' (ie the time of the match: *Collins English Dictionary*).

Punishment

9.59   The second strengthening of the law relating to restriction orders relates to increasing the punishment for the summary[1] offence of failing to comply with a restriction order, so as to increase its deterrent effect. Hitherto, the punishment for that offence has been imprisonment for up to one month or a fine not exceeding level 3 on the standard scale[1] or both. Section 84(1) increases this maximum to six months' imprisonment or a fine not exceeding level 5[1] or both. These increases do not apply where the offence was committed before 7 August 1998 (Sch 9, para 9).

One must question whether either of these two amendments to the 1989 Act is anything more than cosmetic, a knee-jerk reaction to public concern – like the Dangerous Dogs Act 1991. Not only is the new power of arrest of doubtful effect, but in addition few people are subject to restriction orders. In the five years preceding June 1998, there were 20,000 convictions for football-related offences, but only 71 people were subject to restriction orders in that month.[2]

---

1 See general annotations.

2 Sir Norman Fowler, MP, and Jack Straw, MP, Home Secretary, HC Report, col 725.

PUNISHMENT OF TREASON AND PIRACY WITH VIOLENCE

9.60   Section 36 abolishes the last vestiges of capital punishment, otherwise than in respect of certain offences under military law. This section and its associated repeals came into force on 30 September 1998: see Appendix II.

It does so by amending or repealing the various statutes which provided that the only punishment for treason was death (for repeals see also s 120(2) and Sch 10), and by amending s 2 of the Piracy Act 1837 which provided that the offence of piracy with violence under that section was punishable with a mandatory death sentence. In respect of each statutory provision, s 36 provides that a person convicted 'shall be liable to imprisonment for life'. The effect is to substitute a *maximum,* not a mandatory, sentence of life imprisonment, just as the corresponding words do in respect of other offences (such as robbery and aggravated burglary)[1] carrying a maximum of life imprisonment. The terminology used can be contrasted with the mandatory life sentence provision in respect of a person convicted of murder: 'shall ... be *sentenced* to imprisonment for life'.[2] The maximum punishment for treason is now the same as for treason felony contrary to s 3 of the Treason Felony Act 1848.

The change in the law is not one of great practical importance in contemporary society. The last person to be convicted of treason was James Joyce (Lord Haw-Haw) who was convicted in 1946 (and hung in 1947), and in respect of the offence of piracy with violence the death sentence was last carried out before the passing of the 1837 Act, in 1830.[3]

Certain IRA terrorist activities in modern times may have constituted treason, for example the rocket attack on 10 Downing Street and the Brighton hotel bombing, but they have not been prosecuted as such, in order to avoid the creation of martyrs. It could be that the change in the penalty for treason might affect decisions about prosecutions for treason, but it is thought unlikely.

1 Theft Act 1968 ss 8(2) and 19(2).
2 Murder (Abolition of Death Penalty) Act 1965, s 1(1), italics supplied.
3 Lord Archer of Sandwell, HL Report, col 842.

9.61   Prior to the Act there were two offences of treason, (high) treason under the Treason Act 1351 and treason under the Treason Act 1795, both of which were punishable with a mandatory sentence of death, and treason felony, punishable with a maximum of life imprisonment. The offence under the 1795 Act simply confirmed in statutory form the judicial construction of one of the forms of treason under the 1351 Act, 'compassing the death of the King, or his Queen or their eldest son and heir', whereby that term came to mean compassing the end of the Sovereign's political existence and also compassing the bodily harm or restraint of the Sovereign, his heirs and successors. The 1795 Act is repealed by s 36 and Sch 10.[1] This repeal has no effect on the extent of treason, since the Treason Act 1351 as judicially construed continues to apply to these situations.

Apart from the repeal of one of the two offences of treason, the Act does not amend the requirements of the offences of treason and piracy with violence. In 1977 the Law Commission published a working paper provisionally advocating the repeal of all the legislation dealing with treason and treason felony and its replacement by legislation more in tune with the twentieth century.[2] The Law Commission's work in this area seems to have progressed no further. This is not surprising in view of the desuetude of these offences.

---

1 Consequential on the repeal of the 1795 Act, the Treason Act 1817, which made the 1795 Act perpetual and made other provisions in respect of it, and the Sentence of Death (Expectant Mothers) Act 1931, which substituted life imprisonment for a mandatory death sentence for expectant mothers, are repealed, as are other related enactments (s 36(6) and Sch 10).
2 Law Commission Working Paper No 72: *Codification of the Criminal Law: Treason, Sedition and Allied Offences* (1977).

9.62   As indicated above, the Act does not completely abolish the death penalty in this country because the death penalty remains under ss 24 to 26 of the Army Act (and corresponding provisions in the legislation relating to the Royal Navy and Royal Air Force) for five grave military offences in time of war: mutiny, failure to suppress mutiny with intent to assist the enemy, assisting the enemy, misconduct in action, and obstructing operations.[1] The death penalty is not mandatory for these offences.[1]

One reason why these offences are not dealt with by the Act is that it deals with the civil law and an amendment to military law could not have been properly made by it. The Government is reviewing the future operation of armed forces legislation relating to the death penalty.[2]

---

1 Army Act 1955, ss 24, 25, 26, 31 and 32; Air Force Act 1955, ss 24, 25, 26, 31 and 32; Naval Discipline Act 1957, ss 2, 3, 4, 9 and 10.
2 Mike O'Brien, MP, Parliamentary Under-Secretary, Home Office, HC Committee, col 364.

9.63   The abolition of the death penalty otherwise than under military law in time of war will enable the Government to ratify the Sixth Protocol to the European Convention on Human Rights (which by February 1998 had been ratified by 28 States) and the Second Optional Protocol to the International Covenant on Civil and Political Rights (by February 1998 ratified by 31 States), both of which outlaw the death penalty in civil law although they permit a State to make provision in its law for use of a death penalty in time of war.[1]

---

1 Under the Second Optional Protocol the death penalty is only permissible in wartime if expressly reserved by a State when ratifying or acceding to the Protocol (art 2(1)).

AMENDMENT OF RIGHT OF APPEAL TO THE CROWN COURT

9.64   As enacted, s 108(2) of the Magistrates' Courts Act 1980 gave to a person sentenced by a magistrates' court for an offence in respect of which a probation order or an order of conditional discharge had previously been made, a right of appeal to the Crown Court against that sentence. Section 108(2) is amended by Sch 8, para 43,[1] which deletes the above right of appeal in respect of a probation order. Thus, where a person in breach of a probation order made by a magistrates' court is sentenced by a magistrates' court for the offence in respect of which a probation order was made, he can no longer appeal to the Crown Court against that sentence.

---

1 Came into force on 30 September 1998: see Appendix II.

APPENDIX I

Crime and Disorder Act 1998

(1998 c. 37)

ARRANGEMENT OF SECTIONS

PART I

PREVENTION OF CRIME AND DISORDER

CHAPTER I

ENGLAND AND WALES

Crime and disorder: general

PART IV

DEALING WITH OFFENDERS

CHAPTER I

ENGLAND AND WALES

Sexual or violent offenders

Offenders dependent etc. on drugs

Young offenders: reprimands and warnings

Young offenders: non-custodial orders

Young offenders: detention and training orders

Sentencing: general

Miscellaneous and supplemental

CHAPTER II

SCOTLAND

Sexual or violent offenders

Offenders dependent etc. on drugs

Racial aggravation

PART V

MISCELLANEOUS AND SUPPLEMENTAL

Remands and committals

Release and recall of prisoners

Miscellaneous

Supplemental

SCHEDULES

An Act to make provision for preventing crime and disorder; to create certain racially-aggravated offences; to abolish the rebuttable presumption that a child is doli incapax and to make provision as to the effect of a child's failure to give evidence at his trial; to abolish the death penalty for treason and piracy; to make changes to the criminal justice system; to make further provision for dealing with offenders; to make further provision with respect to remands and committals for trial and the release and recall of prisoners; to amend Chapter I of Part II of the Crime (Sentences) Act 1997 and to repeal Chapter I of Part III of the Crime and Punishment (Scotland) Act 1997; to make amendments designed to facilitate, or otherwise desirable in connection with, the consolidation of certain enactments; and, for connected purposes.   [31st July 1998]

GENERAL ANNOTATIONS

Certain recurring terms are annotated here, and cross-reference is made to these annotations at the appropriate places.

Commencement—See s 121(2) and paras **1.4** and **1.5** of the text.

Age—A person reaches a particular age at the commencement of the relevant anniversary of the birth (Family Law Reform Act 1969, s 9). By s 117(3) of the present Act, for the purposes of this Act, the age of a person is deemed to be that which it appears to the court to be after considering any available evidence.

British Islands—'British Islands' means the United Kingdom (qv), the Channel Islands and the Isle of Man (Interpretation Act 1978, s 5 and Sch 1).

Commission area—See 'petty sessions area', below.

Constable—A 'constable' is anyone holding the office of constable, whatever his rank in a particular police force.

The expression 'constable' includes special constables. Unlike other constables who are members of a police force as established by a police authority (who can exercise their powers throughout England and Wales and the adjacent United Kingdom waters), a special constable can only exercise his powers in the police area for which he is appointed, and any adjacent United Kingdom waters, and any police area contiguous to his own (Police Act 1996, s 30(1)–(3)).

'Constable' also includes those who hold office as police officers under police forces established for specific purposes. See, eg, British Transport police (British Transport Commission Act 1949, s 53; Railways Act 1993, s 132), Civil Aviation police (Civil Aviation Act 1982, s 57), Ministry of Defence Police (Ministry of Defence Police Act 1987, s 1).

Every prison officer while acting as such has all the powers, authority, protection and privileges of a constable (Prison Act 1952, s 8). On the other hand, the term 'constable' does not extend to persons who have, for limited purposes, powers of constables (see, eg, water bailiffs, pursuant to the Salmon and Freshwater Fisheries Act 1975, s 36).

Day(s)—'The term 'day' is used in more senses than one. A day is strictly the period of time which begins with one midnight and ends with the next. It may also denote the period of 24 hours, and again it may denote the period of time between sunrise and sunset' (45 *Halsburys Laws* (4th edn Revised, para 1113)). Clearly, it is the first of these three meanings which is appropriate to 'day' in the context of the Act's provisions in which it appears.

Either-way offence—See 'Indictable offence, etc', below.

England—'England' means, subject to any alteration of boundaries under Part IV of the Local Government Act 1972, the area consisting of the counties established by ss 1 and 20 of that Act, Greater London and the Isles of Scilly (Interpretation Act 1978, s 5 and Sch 1).

Fine not exceeding the statutory maximum—The 'statutory maximum' is the prescribed sum within the meaning of s 32 of the Magistrates' Courts Act (Criminal Justice Act 1982, s 74), which is the maximum fine which can be imposed on a summary conviction for an offence triable either way (see below). The Home Secretary has power to change this sum by order in the light of a change in the value of money (Magistrates' Courts Act 1980, s 143(1)). At the time of going to press, the statutory maximum was £5,000 (Criminal Justice Act 1991, s 17(2)(c)).

An order under s 143(1) must be made by statutory instrument subject to annulment in pursuance of a resolution of either House of Parliament, and may be revoked by a subsequent order thereunder; it does not affect the punishment for an offence committed before it comes into force (Magistrates' Courts Act 1980, s 143(6)).

Great Britain—See 'United Kingdom', below.

Indictable offence, summary offence and offence triable either way—'Indictable offence' means an offence which if committed by an adult, is triable on indictment, whether it is exclusively so triable or triable either way (Interpretation Act 1978, s 5 and Sch 1). Some offences are triable only on indictment; they are otherwise known as 'indictable-only offences'.

'Summary offence' means an offence which, if committed by an adult, is triable summarily only (Interpretation Act 1978, s 5 and Sch 1).

An 'offence triable either way' means an offence, other than an offence triable on indictment only by virtue of Part V of the Criminal Justice Act 1988 (which empowers the Crown Court to try a summary offence on indictment in certain cases if it is related to an indictable offence charged in the indictment), which, if committed by an adult, is triable either on indictment or summarily (Interpretation Act 1978, s 5 and Sch 1).

Month(s)—'Month(s)' are calendar months (Interpretation Act 1978, s 5 and Sch 1).

Petty sessions area—This term can only be understood by explaining that magistrates' courts are organised on the basis of commission areas, petty sessional divisions and petty sessions areas. These are defined as follows:

(a) *Commission areas* in England comprise the following geographical units—
    (i) every metropolitan county;
    (ii) every 'retained county' (ie the area of non-metropolitan county created by Part I of the Local Government Act 1972, as it stood immediately before 1 April 1995);
    (iii) every London Commission area (ie the inner London area and four outer London areas);
    (iv) the City of London area (Justices of the Peace Act 1997, s 1(1) and (3)).
    In Wales, commission areas comprise the following:
    (i) the Gwent and South Wales commission areas;
    (ii) every 'retained county' no part of which falls within the above two commission areas (ibid, s 1(2) and (3)).
(b) *Petty sessional divisions*. The Lord Chancellor has power to divide the area of any magistrates' courts committee, other than that for the City of London, into petty sessional divisions in accordance with the Justices of the Peace Act 1997, ss 33 and 34.
(c) *Petty sessions areas*. The following areas are petty sessions areas: any 'specified area' (ie a retained county, a metropolitan district, the inner London area or an outer London borough) which is not divided into petty sessional divisions; any petty sessional division of a specified area; and the City of London (Justices of the Peace Act 1997, s 4).

Practicable—See 'Reasonably practicable' below.

Programme service, within the meaning of the Broadcasting Act 1990—The Broadcasting Act 1990, s 202(1) provides that '"programme" includes an advertisement and, in relation to any service, includes any item included in that service'.

By the 1990 Act, s 201(1), a 'programme service', for the purposes of that Act is defined as meaning:

'any of the following services (whether or not it is, or it requires to be, licensed under this Act), namely—

(a)   any television broadcasting service or other television programme service (within the meaning of Part I of this Act);

(b)   any sound broadcasting service or licensable sound programme service (within the meaning of Part III of this Act);

(c)   any other service which consists in the sending, by means of a telecommunication system, of sounds or visual images or both either—

(i)   for reception at two or more places in the United Kingdom (whether they are so sent for simultaneous reception or at different times in response to requests made by different users of the service); or

(ii)   for reception at a place in the United Kingdom for the purpose of being presented there to members of the public or to any group of persons.

(2) Subsection (1)(c) does not apply to—

(a)   a local delivery service (within the meaning of Part II of this Act);

(b)   a service where the running of the telecommunication system does not require to be licensed under Part II of the Telecommunications Act 1984; or

(c)   a two-way service (as defined by section 46(2)(c) [of the 1990 Act].'

Reasonably believes/reasonable cause to believe—'Belief' is something more than suspicion, a term defined in the annotations to s 31: *Forsyth* [1997] Crim LR 589 (CA).

'Reasonably believes/reasonable cause to believe' means that the person concerned must have reasonable grounds to believe. However, it is not enough that he has reasonable grounds to believe that the specified facts exist, he must also actually believe that they do (see *Banks* [1916] 2 KB 621 (CCA); *Harrison* [1938] 3 All ER 134 (CCA), which were concerned with 'reasonable grounds for suspecting').

The existence of the reasonable grounds, and of the belief founded on them, is ultimately a matter to be decided in the light of the circumstances disclosed by the evidence. The grounds on which the person concerned formed the belief must be sufficient to induce in a reasonable person the required belief (*McArdle v Egan* (1933) 150 LT 412 (CA); *Nakkuda Ali v Jayaratne* [1951] AC 66 (PC); *IRC, ex parte Rossminster Ltd* [1980] AC 952, [1980] 1 All ER 80 at 84, 92, 103 and 104 (HL)).

Reasonably practicable—'Practicable' is defined by the *Oxford English Dictionary* as 'capable of being carried out in action' or 'feasible' (adopted by Goddard LCJ in *Lee v Nursery Furnishings Ltd* [1945] 1 All ER 387 at 389), and by *Webster's Dictionary* as 'possible to be accomplished with known means or resources' (adopted by Parker J in *Adsett v K & L Steelfounders and Engineers Ltd* [1953] 1 All ER 97 at 98).

'Reasonably practicable' imposes a less strict standard than 'practicable'. It has been held, in relation to a court order to do something so far 'as reasonably practicable', that that phrase was sufficiently general to embrace considerations going beyond what was physically feasible and was apt to include financial considerations (*Jordan v Norfolk County Council* [1994] 4 All ER 218 (DC)).

Standard scale—The 'standard scale' of fines applies only to offences which are only triable summarily. The meaning of the standard scale is that given by s 37 of the Criminal Justice Act 1982 and Sch 1 to the Interpretation Act 1978. When this book went to press the standard scale was as follows:

level 1   £200
level 2   £500
level 3   £1,000
level 4   £2,500
level 5   £5,000

(Criminal Justice Act 1991, s 17). The Home Secretary has powers by order to change the amounts specified in the standard scale in the light of a change in the value of money (Magistrates' Courts Act 1980, s 143(1) as amended by the Criminal Justice Act 1982, s 48). An order under s 143(1) must be made by statutory instrument subject to annulment in pursuance of a resolution of either House of Parliament, and may be revoked by a subsequent order thereunder; it does not affect the punishment for an offence committed before it comes into force (Magistrates' Courts Act 1980, s 143(6)).

Summary offence—See 'Indictable offence, etc', above.

United Kingdom—'United Kingdom', means Great Britain and Northern Ireland (Interpretation Act 1978, s 5 and Sch 1). 'Great Britain' means England (qv), Scotland and Wales (qv) (Union with Scotland Act 1706, preamble, art 1; Wales and Berwick Act 1746, s 3).

Wales—'Wales' means the combined area of the counties which were created by s 20 of the Local Government Act 1972, as originally enacted, but subject to any alteration made under s 73 of that Act (consequential alterations of boundary following alterations of watercourse) (Interpretation Act 1978, s 5 and Sch 1).

Writing—Includes printing, lithography, photography and other mode of representing or reproducing words in a visible form, and expressions referring to writing are to be construed accordingly (Interpretation Act 1978, s 5 and Sch 1).

PART I

PREVENTION OF CRIME AND DISORDER

CHAPTER I

ENGLAND AND WALES

Crime and disorder: general

1 Anti-social behaviour orders

(1) An application for an order under this section may be made by a relevant authority if it appears to the authority that the following conditions are fulfilled with respect to any person aged 10 or over, namely—

(a) that the person has acted, since the commencement date, in an anti-social manner, that is to say, in a manner that caused or was likely to cause harassment, alarm or distress to one or more persons not of the same household as himself; and

(b) that such an order is necessary to protect persons in the local government area in which the harassment, alarm or distress was caused or was likely to be caused from further anti-social acts by him;

and in this section 'relevant authority' means the council for the local government area or any chief officer of police any part of whose police area lies within that area.

(2) A relevant authority shall not make such an application without consulting each other relevant authority.

(3) Such an application shall be made by complaint to the magistrates' court whose commission area includes the place where it is alleged that the harassment, alarm or distress was caused or was likely to be caused.

(4) If, on such an application, it is proved that the conditions mentioned in subsection (1) above are fulfilled, the magistrates' court may make an order under this section (an 'anti-social behaviour order') which prohibits the defendant from doing anything described in the order.

(5) For the purpose of determining whether the condition mentioned in subsection (1)(a) above is fulfilled, the court shall disregard any act of the defendant which he shows was reasonable in the circumstances.

(6) The prohibitions that may be imposed by an anti-social behaviour order are those necessary for the purpose of protecting from further anti-social acts by the defendant—

(a) persons in the local government area; and

(b) persons in any adjoining local government area specified in the application for the order;

and a relevant authority shall not specify an adjoining local government area in the application without consulting the council for that area and each chief officer of police any part of whose police area lies within that area.

(7) An anti-social behaviour order shall have effect for a period (not less than two years) specified in the order or until further order.

(8) Subject to subsection (9) below, the applicant or the defendant may apply by complaint to the court which made an anti-social behaviour order for it to be varied or discharged by a further order.

(9) Except with the consent of both parties, no anti-social behaviour order shall be discharged before the end of the period of two years beginning with the date of service of the order.

(10) If without reasonable excuse a person does anything which he is prohibited from doing by an anti-social behaviour order, he shall be liable—

(a) on summary conviction, to imprisonment for a term not exceeding six months or to a fine not exceeding the statutory maximum, or to both; or

(b) on conviction on indictment, to imprisonment for a term not exceeding five years or to a fine, or to both.

(11) Where a person is convicted of an offence under subsection (10) above, it shall not be open to the court by or before which he is so convicted to make an order under subsection (1)(b) (conditional discharge) of section 1A of the Powers of Criminal Courts Act 1973 ('the 1973 Act') in respect of the offence.

(12) In this section—
'the commencement date' means the date of the commencement of this section;
'local government area' means—

(a) in relation to England, a district or London borough, the City of London, the Isle of Wight and the Isles of Scilly;

(b) in relation to Wales, a county or county borough.

Explanatory text—See paras **5.1–5.55**.

Age (subs (1))—See general annotations.

Harassment, alarm or distress (subss (1) and (3))—See discussion at paras **5.24–5.26**.

Household (subs (1))—See discussion at para **5.36**. The *Shorter Oxford English Dictionary* defines 'household' as including 'the maintaining of a house or family; the contents of a house collectively; the inmates of a house collectively'. A 'householder' is defined as 'The person who hold or occupies a house as his own dwelling and that of his household'. In *Simmons v Pizzey* [1979] AC 37, [1977] 2 All ER 432 (HL), the question whether the persons living in a house formed a 'single household', was a question of fact and degree, there being no certain indicia, the presence or absence of any of which was by itself conclusive. In *England v Secretary of State for Social Services* (1982) 3 FLR 222 the question arose as to what comprised a household for the purposes of the Family Income Supplement Act 1970. The correct approach was identified by Woolf J as follows:

'Although the speeches [in *Simmons v Pizzey*] to which I have made reference make it clear that in the majority of cases the question as to who is or is not a member of the household will not involve any question of law, there are a minority of cases which will still give rise to questions of law. Indeed in *Simmons v Pizzey* itself the House of Lords dismissed an appeal from the decision of the Divisional Court overruling the decision of the justices. The position as I see it is as follows: there are three categories of situation which can arise before the tribunal of fact. The first category are those where the only decision which the tribunal can, as a matter of law, come to is that the persons concerned are members of the household. The second category of cases are those where the only decision which the tribunal of fact can come to is that the persons concerned are not members of the household. The third category of cases, which in practice will be the largest, are those where it is proper to regard the persons concerned either as being members or not being members of the household, depending on the view which the fact-finding tribunal takes of all the circumstances as a matter of fact and degree.'

See also *London Borough of Hackney v Ezedinma* [1981] 3 All ER 438 (CA); *Birmingham Juvenile Court, ex parte N* [1984] 2 All ER 688 (DC).

Chief officer of police (subss (1) and (6))—This has the meaning given by s 18(1), by reference to the Police Act 1996, s 101(1), extracted in the annotations to s 18.

Police area (subss (1) and (6))—This has the meaning given by s 18(1), by reference to the Police Act 1996, s 1(2), extracted in the annotations to s 18.

Statutory maximum (subs (10))—See general annotations.

Section 1A of the Powers of Criminal Courts Act 1973 (subs (11))—As amended by Sch 8 to the new Act, this provides:

'1A.—(1) Where a court by or before which a person is convicted of an offence (not being an offence the sentence for which is fixed by law) is of opinion, having regard to the circumstances including the nature of the offence and the character of the offender, that it is inexpedient to inflict punishment, the court may make an order either—

    (a)   discharging him absolutely; or

    (b)   if the court thinks fit, discharging him subject to the condition that he commits no offence during such period, not exceeding three years from the date of the order, as may be specified in the order.

(1A) Subsection (1)(b) above has effect subject to section 62(4) of the Crime and Disorder Act 1998 (effect of reprimands and warnings).

(2) An order discharging a person subject to such a condition is in this Act referred to as "an order for conditional discharge", and the period specified in any such order as "the period of conditional discharge".

(3) Before making an order for conditional discharge the court shall explain to the offender in ordinary language that if he commits another offence during the period of conditional discharge he will be liable to be sentenced for the original offence.

(4) Where, under the following provisions of this Part of this Act, a person conditionally discharged under this section is sentenced for the offence in respect of which the order for conditional discharge was made, that order shall cease to have effect.

(5) The Secretary of State may by order direct that subsection (1) above shall be amended by substituting, for the maximum period specified in that subsection as originally enacted or as previously amended under this subsection, such period as may be specified in the order.'

2 Sex offender orders

(1) If it appears to a chief officer of police that the following conditions are fulfilled with respect to any person in his police area, namely—

    (a) that the person is a sex offender; and

    (b) that the person has acted, since the relevant date, in such a way as to give reasonable cause to believe that an order under this section is necessary to protect the public from serious harm from him,

the chief officer may apply for an order under this section to be made in respect of the person.

(2) Such an application shall be made by complaint to the magistrates' court whose commission area includes any place where it is alleged that the defendant acted in such a way as is mentioned in subsection (1)(b) above.

(3) If, on such an application, it is proved that the conditions mentioned in subsection (1) above are fulfilled, the magistrates' court may make an order under this section (a 'sex offender order') which prohibits the defendant from doing anything described in the order.

(4) The prohibitions that may be imposed by a sex offender order are those necessary for the purpose of protecting the public from serious harm from the defendant.

(5) A sex offender order shall have effect for a period (not less than five years) specified in the order or until further order; and while such an order has effect, Part I of the Sex Offenders Act 1997 shall have effect as if—

    (a) the defendant were subject to the notification requirements of that Part; and

    (b) in relation to the defendant, the relevant date (within the meaning of that Part) were the date of service of the order.

(6) Subject to subsection (7) below, the applicant or the defendant may apply by complaint to the court which made a sex offender order for it to be varied or discharged by a further order.

(7) Except with the consent of both parties, no sex offender order shall be discharged before the end of the period of five years beginning with the date of service of the order.

(8) If without reasonable excuse a person does anything which he is prohibited from doing by a sex offender order, he shall be liable—

    (a) on summary conviction, to imprisonment for a term not exceeding six months or to a fine not exceeding the statutory maximum, or to both; or

    (b) on conviction on indictment, to imprisonment for a term not exceeding five years or to a fine, or to both.

(9) Where a person is convicted of an offence under subsection (8) above, it shall not be open to the court by or before which he is so convicted to make an order under subsection (1)(b) (conditional discharge) of section 1A of the 1973 Act in respect of the offence.

Explanatory text—See paras **5.57–5.80**.

Chief officer of police (subs (1)); police area (subs (1))—See s 18 and annotations thereto.

Sex offender (subs (1))—See s 3(1).

Protect the public from serious harm (subss (1) and (4))—This phrase is to be found in that Criminal Justice Act 1991, s 1(2)(b) (criteria for imposition of a custodial sentence in respect of violent or sex offender) and s 2(2)(b) (longer than commensurate sentences in respect of violent or sex offenders). The conclusion that the public may be at risk from serious harm is one that should be based on evidence: see *Swain* (1994) 15 Cr App Rep (S) 768 (CA); *Bowler* (1994) 15 Cr App Rep (S) 78 (CA). In *Bowler* it was held that it was not necessary for serious harm to have occurred in the past for a court to conclude that the risk of such harm occurring in the future existed. The harm may be physical or psychological, and a relatively minor sexual offence may give rise to serious psychological injury: *Apelt* (1994) 15 Cr App Rep (S) 532 (CA); cf (in the context of violent offences) *Fishwick* [1996] 1 Cr App Rep (S) 359 (CA). The risk of serious harm does not have to be to the public at large: it can be in respect of an individual or small group of individuals: *Hashi* (1995) 16 Cr App Rep (S) 121 (CA).

Part I of the Sex Offenders Act 1997 (subs (5))—Part I of the Sex Offenders Act 1997 requires persons convicted or contained (after the commencement of Part I (1 September 1997)) of certain sex offences (as to which see annotations to s 3) to notify the police of their names and addresses, and subsequent changes. The same provisions apply to those, after commencement, serving a term of imprisonment or who are under statutory supervision for such an offence.

Length of notification period

Description of person	Applicable period
Offender sentenced to life or term of 30 months or more	Indefinite period
Offender admitted to hospital subject to restriction order*	Indefinite period
Offender sentenced to term of more than 6 months but less than 30 months	10 years, beginning with relevant date
Offender sentenced to term of 6 months or less	7 years, beginning with relevant date
Admitted to hospital without restriction order*	7 years, beginning with relevant date
Person of any other description	5 years, beginning with relevant date

* In the 1997 Act, a 'restriction order' means an order under the Mental Health Act 1983, s 41.

Relevant date (subs (5))—Defined by s 3(2). The 'relevant date' for the purposes of the Sex Offender Act 1997 determines the commencement of the applicable period during which the notification requirement applies. The definition in s 3(2), by reference to the date of one of the four events specified in s 3(1), is wider than that in the 1997 Act. By s 1(8) of that Act the 'relevant date' is the relevant date of conviction, finding of disability or of the caution and does not include the circumstance set out in s 3(1)(d) of the new Act. The notification requirements of the 1997 Act also apply whilst a sex offender order made under s 2 of the new Act is in force (1998 Act, s 2(5)).

Section 1A of the 1973 Act (subs (9))—'The 1973 Act' means the Powers of Criminal Courts Act 1973; see annotations to s 1.

---

3 Sex offender orders: supplemental

(1) In section 2 above and this section 'sex offender' means a person who—

  (a) has been convicted of a sexual offence to which Part I of the Sex Offenders Act 1997 applies;

  (b) has been found not guilty of such an offence by reason of insanity, or found to be under a disability and to have done the act charged against him in respect of such an offence;

  (c) has been cautioned by a constable, in England and Wales or Northern Ireland, in respect of such an offence which, at the time when the caution was given, he had admitted; or

  (d) has been punished under the law in force in a country or territory outside the United Kingdom for an act which—

(i) constituted an offence under that law; and

(ii) would have constituted a sexual offence to which that Part applies if it had been done in any part of the United Kingdom.

(2) In subsection (1) of section 2 above 'the relevant date', in relation to a sex offender, means—

(a) the date or, as the case may be, the latest date on which he has been convicted, found, cautioned or punished as mentioned in subsection (1) above; or

(b) if later, the date of the commencement of that section.

(3) Subsections (2) and (3) of section 6 of the Sex Offenders Act 1997 apply for the construction of references in subsections (1) and (2) above as they apply for the construction of references in Part I of that Act.

(4) In subsections (1) and (2) above, any reference to a person having been cautioned shall be construed as including a reference to his having been reprimanded or warned (under section 65 below) as a child or young person.

(5) An act punishable under the law in force in any country or territory outside the United Kingdom constitutes an offence under that law for the purposes of subsection (1) above, however it is described in that law.

(6) Subject to subsection (7) below, the condition in subsection (1)(d)(i) above shall be taken to be satisfied unless, not later than rules of court may provide, the defendant serves on the applicant a notice—

(a) stating that, on the facts as alleged with respect to the act in question, the condition is not in his opinion satisfied;

(b) showing his grounds for that opinion; and

(c) requiring the applicant to show that it is satisfied.

(7) The court, if it thinks fit, may permit the defendant to require the applicant to show that the condition is satisfied without the prior service of a notice under subsection (6) above.

Explanatory text—See paras **5.57–5.80**.

Sexual offence to which Part I of the Sex Offenders Act 1997 applies (subs (1))—Part I of the 1997 Act applies to offences under the law of England and Wales set out in Sch 1, para 1 to that Act. They include the following offences under the Sexual Offences Act 1956, references to age being to the age as at the date of commission of the offence (Sch 1, para 5).

(1) section 1 (rape);

(2) section 5 (intercourse with a girl under 13);

(3) section 6 (intercourse with a girl between 13 and 16) (Part I does not apply to offences committed by a person under 20);

(4) section 10 (incest by a man) (Part I does not apply where the other party is aged 18 or over);

(5) section 12 (buggery) (Part I does not apply to such offences committed by a person under 20, or where the other party is aged 18 or over);

(6) section 13 (indecency between men) (Part I does not apply to such offences committed by a person under 20, or where the other party is aged 18 or over);

(7) section 14 (indecent assault on a woman) (Part I does not apply where the other party is aged 18 or over, unless the offender is, or has been sentenced to imprisonment for a term of 30 months or more, or is admitted to a hospital subject to a restriction order);

(8) section 15 (indecent assault on a man) (Part I does not apply where the other party is aged 18 or over, unless the offender is, or has been sentenced to imprisonment for a term of 30 months or more, or is admitted to a hospital subject to a restriction order);

(9)   section 16 (assault with intent to commit buggery) (Part I does not apply where the other party is aged 18 or over);
(10)   subsection 28 (causing of, or encouraging prostitution of, intercourse with, or indecent assault on, girl under 16).

Schedule 1, para 1, to the 1997 Act also identifies certain other offences. These are as follows:

(1)   an offence under the Indecency with Children Act 1960, s 1 (indecent conduct towards young child);
(2)   an offence under the Criminal Law Act 1977, s 54 (inciting girl under 16 to have incestuous sexual intercourse) (for this purpose a person shall be taken to have been under the age of 16 at any time if it appears from the evidence as a whole that [she] was under that age at that time);
(3)   an offence under the Protection of Children Act 1978, s 1 (indecent photographs or pseudo-photographs of children);
(4)   an offence under Customs and Excise Management Act 1979, s 170 (penalty for fraudulent evasion of duty, etc) unless the prohibited goods did not include indecent photographs of persons under 16;
(5)   an offence under the Criminal Justice Act 1991, s 160 (possession of indecent photographs or pseudo-photographs of children).

Paragraph 2 of Sch 1 to the 1997 Act deals with the offences under Scottish law, in respect of which the conviction, or caution, of an individual, or caution in respect of which, will trigger the notification requirement. The relevant offences split into four categories.

(1)   The first set of offences are offences at common law, and include: rape, clandestine injury to women, abduction of a woman or girl with intent to rape, assault with intent to rape or ravish, indecent assault, lewd indecent or libidinous behaviour or practices, shameless indecency, and sodomy.
(2)   The second set comprises offences relating to indecent images of children, under the Civic Government (Scotland) Act 1982, s 52 and s 52A.
(3)   The third are offences under the Criminal Law (Consolidation) (Scotland) Act 1995, ss 1–3, 5–6, 8, 10 and 13(2). These are sexual offences which broadly, but not precisely, correspond with the offences which arise in England and Wales.
(4)   Finally, there is the offence under the Customs and Excise Management Act 1979, s 170.

In respect of offences for a person convicted in Northern Ireland, para 3 of Sch 1 to the 1997 Act specifies the following offences:

(1)   rape;
(2)   offences under the Offences against the Person Act 1861, s 52 (indecent assault upon a female person), s 61 (buggery) and s 62 (assault with intent to commit buggery or indecent assault upon a male person);
(3)   offences under the Criminal Law Amendment Act 1885, s 4 (unlawful carnal knowledge of a girl aged under 14) and s 5 (unlawful carnal knowledge of a girl aged under 17);
(4)   an offence under the 1885 Act, s 11 (committing, or being party to the commission of, or procuring or attempting to procure the commission of, any act of gross indecency with another male);
(5)   an offence under the Punishment of Incest Act 1908 (incest by males);
(6)   offences under the Children and Young Persons Act (Northern Ireland) 1968 (causing or encouraging seduction or prostitution of a girl aged under 17) and s 22 (indecent conduct towards a child);
(7)   an offence under the Prosecution of Children (Northern Ireland) Order 1978, art 3 (indecent photographs of children);
(8)   an offence under the Customs and Excise Management Act 1979, s 170 (fraudulent evasion of duty, etc) (unless the prohibited goods did not include indecent photographs of persons who were under the age of 16);
(9)   an offence under the Criminal Justice (Northern Ireland) Order 1980, art 9 (inciting a girl under the age of 16 to have incestuous sexual intercourse); and
(10)   an offence under the Criminal Justice (Evidence, etc) (Northern Ireland) Order, art 15 (possession of indecent photographs of children).

The offences in (2), (4) and (5) above do not apply where the victim, or, as the case may be, the other party to the offence was aged 18 or over. There is, however, one further exception to that exception. If an offence under s 52 (of indecent assault on a female) or under s 62 of the 1861 Act (indecent assault on a male) is committed, and the offender is sentenced to a term of 30 months or more or is, or has been, admitted to a hospital subject to a restriction order, then the offence is indeed a qualifying offence for the purpose of para 3 of Sch 1 to the 1997 Act.

England and Wales (subs (1))—See general annotations.

Cautioned (subss (1), (2), and (4))—See ss 3(4) and 65 and para **3.66**.

Constable (subs (1))—See general annotations.

United Kingdom (subss (1) and (5))—See general annotations.

Sex Offenders Act 1997, s 6(2), (3) (subs (3))—Sections 6(2) and (3) provide as follows:

'(2) In this Part any reference to a conviction includes—

    (a)   a reference to a finding in summary proceedings, where the court makes an order under section 37(3) of the Mental Health Act 1983, section 58(3) of the Criminal Procedure (Scotland) Act 1995 or Article 44(4) of the Mental Health (Northern Ireland) Order 1986, that the accused did the act charged; and

    (b)   a reference to a finding in summary proceedings in Scotland, where the court makes an order under section 246(3) of the Criminal Procedure (Scotland) Act 1995 discharging the accused absolutely, that the accused committed the offence;

and cognate references shall be construed accordingly.

(3) In this Part any reference to a person being or having been found to be under a disability and to have done the act charged against him in respect of a sexual offence to which this Part applies includes a reference to his being or having been found—

    (a)   unfit to be tried for such an offence;

    (b)   to be insane so that his trial for such an offence could not proceed; or

    (c)   unfit to be tried and to have done the act charged against him in respect of such an offence.'

Child or young person (subs (4))—A 'child' is a person under the age of 14; young person is aged 14–17: see s 117(1).

---

4 Appeals against orders

(1) An appeal shall lie to the Crown Court against the making by a magistrates' court of an anti-social behaviour order or sex offender order.

(2) On such an appeal the Crown Court—

    (a)   may make such orders as may be necessary to give effect to its determination of the appeal; and

    (b)   may also make such incidental or consequential orders as appear to it to be just.

(3) Any order of the Crown Court made on an appeal under this section (other than one directing that an application be re-heard by a magistrates' court) shall, for the purposes of section 1(8) or 2(6) above, be treated as if it were an order of the magistrates' court from which the appeal was brought and not an order of the Crown Court.

Explanatory text—See paras **5.48 and 5.76**.

Anti-social behaviour order (subs (1))—See ss 18(1) and 1(4).

Sex offender order (subs (1))—See ss 18(1) and 2(3).

Crime and disorder strategies

5 Authorities responsible for strategies

(1) Subject to the provisions of this section, the functions conferred by section 6 below shall be exercisable in relation to each local government area by the responsible authorities, that is to say—

   (a) the council for the area and, where the area is a district and the council is not a unitary authority, the council for the county which includes the district; and

   (b) every chief officer of police any part of whose police area lies within the area.

(2) In exercising those functions, the responsible authorities shall act in co-operation with the following persons and bodies, namely—

   (a) every police authority any part of whose police area lies within the area;

   (b) every probation committee or health authority any part of whose area lies within the area; and

   (c) every person or body of a description which is for the time being prescribed by order of the Secretary of State under this subsection;

and it shall be the duty of those persons and bodies to co-operate in the exercise by the responsible authorities of those functions.

(3) The responsible authorities shall also invite the participation in their exercise of those functions of at least one person or body of each description which is for the time being prescribed by order of the Secretary of State under this subsection.

(4) In this section and sections 6 and 7 below 'local government area' means—

   (a) in relation to England, each district or London borough, the City of London, the Isle of Wight and the Isles of Scilly;

   (b) in relation to Wales, each county or county borough.

Explanatory text—See paras **2.5** and **2.6**.

Police area (subss (1) and (2)); chief officer of police (subs (1))—See s 18 and annotations thereto.

Police authority (subs (2))—Section 3 of the Police Act 1996 states that there shall be a police authority for each police area. For 'police area' see s 18 and annotations thereto.

Probation committee (subs (2))—A Committee established pursuant to the Probation Services Act 1993.

City of London (subs (4))—See s 18(5).

---

6 Formulation and implementation of strategies

(1) The responsible authorities for a local government area shall, in accordance with the provisions of section 5 above and this section, formulate and implement, for each relevant period, a strategy for the reduction of crime and disorder in the area.

(2) Before formulating a strategy, the responsible authorities shall—

   (a) carry out a review of the levels and patterns of crime and disorder in the area (taking due account of the knowledge and experience of persons in the area);

(b) prepare an analysis of the results of that review;
(c) publish in the area a report of that analysis; and
(d) obtain the views on that report of persons or bodies in the area (including those of a description prescribed by order under section 5(3) above), whether by holding public meetings or otherwise.

(3) In formulating a strategy, the responsible authorities shall have regard to the analysis prepared under subsection (2)(b) above and the views obtained under subsection (2)(d) above.

(4) A strategy shall include—

(a) objectives to be pursued by the responsible authorities, by co-operating persons or bodies or, under agreements with the responsible authorities, by other persons or bodies; and
(b) long-term and short-term performance targets for measuring the extent to which such objectives are achieved.

(5) After formulating a strategy, the responsible authorities shall publish in the area a document which includes details of—

(a) co-operating persons and bodies;
(b) the review carried out under subsection (2)(a) above;
(c) the report published under subsection (2)(c) above; and
(d) the strategy, including in particular—
    (i) the objectives mentioned in subsection (4)(a) above and, in each case, the authorities, persons or bodies by whom they are to be pursued; and
    (ii) the performance targets mentioned in subsection (4)(b) above.

(6) While implementing a strategy, the responsible authorities shall keep it under review with a view to monitoring its effectiveness and making any changes to it that appear necessary or expedient.

(7) In this section—
    'co-operating persons or bodies' means persons or bodies co-operating in the exercise of the responsible authorities' functions under this section;
    'relevant period' means—

(a) the period of three years beginning with such day as the Secretary of State may by order appoint; and
(b) each subsequent period of three years.

Explanatory text—See paras **2.5–2.10**.

Local government area (subs (1))—See s 5(4).

Publish in the area (subs (5))—The Act gives no indication as to how such publication is to occur, and would appear to be within the discretion of the authority subject only to normal standards of reasonableness.

---

7 Supplemental

(1) The responsible authorities for a local government area shall, whenever so required by the Secretary of State, submit to the Secretary of State a report on such matters

connected with the exercise of their functions under section 6 above as may be specified in the requirement.

(2) A requirement under subsection (1) above may specify the form in which a report is to be given.

(3) The Secretary of State may arrange, or require the responsible authorities to arrange, for a report under subsection (1) above to be published in such manner as appears to him to be appropriate.

Explanatory text—See paras **2.5–2.10**.

Local government area (subs (1))—See s 5(4).

Youth crime and disorder

8 Parenting orders

(1) This section applies where, in any court proceedings—

   (a) a child safety order is made in respect of a child;

   (b) an anti-social behaviour order or sex offender order is made in respect of a child or young person;

   (c) a child or young person is convicted of an offence; or

   (d) a person is convicted of an offence under section 443 (failure to comply with school attendance order) or section 444 (failure to secure regular attendance at school of registered pupil) of the Education Act 1996.

(2) Subject to subsection (3) and section 9(1) below, if in the proceedings the court is satisfied that the relevant condition is fulfilled, it may make a parenting order in respect of a person who is a parent or guardian of the child or young person or, as the case may be, the person convicted of the offence under section 443 or 444 ('the parent').

(3) A court shall not make a parenting order unless it has been notified by the Secretary of State that arrangements for implementing such orders are available in the area in which it appears to the court that the parent resides or will reside and the notice has not been withdrawn.

(4) A parenting order is an order which requires the parent—

   (a) to comply, for a period not exceeding twelve months, with such requirements as are specified in the order; and

   (b) subject to subsection (5) below, to attend, for a concurrent period not exceeding three months and not more than once in any week, such counselling or guidance sessions as may be specified in directions given by the responsible officer;

and in this subsection 'week' means a period of seven days beginning with a Sunday.

(5) A parenting order may, but need not, include such a requirement as is mentioned in subsection (4)(b) above in any case where such an order has been made in respect of the parent on a previous occasion.

(6) The relevant condition is that the parenting order would be desirable in the interests of preventing—

   (a) in a case falling within paragraph (a) or (b) of subsection (1) above, any repetition of the kind of behaviour which led to the child safety order, anti-social behaviour order or sex offender order being made;

(b) in a case falling within paragraph (c) of that subsection, the commission of any further offence by the child or young person;

(c) in a case falling within paragraph (d) of that subsection, the commission of any further offence under section 443 or 444 of the Education Act 1996.

(7) The requirements that may be specified under subsection (4)(a) above are those which the court considers desirable in the interests of preventing any such repetition or, as the case may be, the commission of any such further offence.

(8) In this section and section 9 below 'responsible officer', in relation to a parenting order, means one of the following who is specified in the order, namely—

(a) a probation officer;

(b) a social worker of a local authority social services department; and

(c) a member of a youth offending team.

Explanatory text—See paras **3.31–3.40** and **3.55–3.57**.

Child safety order (subss (1) and (6))—See ss 11(1) and 18(1).

Anti-social behaviour order (subss (1) and (6))—See ss 1(4) and 18(1).

Sex offender order (subss (1) and (6))—See ss 2(3) and 18(1).

Child or young person (subs (1))—'Child' means a person under the age of 14; 'young person' means a person who has attained the age of 14 and is under the age of 18 (s 117(1)).

Section 443 … or section 444 of the Education Act 1996 (subss (1) and (6)—These provide as follows:

'443—(1) If a parent [or a person with responsibility or care for a child (s 576)] on whom a school attendance order is served fails to comply with the requirements of the order, he is guilty of an offence, unless he proves that he is causing the child to receive suitable education otherwise than at school.

(2) If, in proceedings for an offence under this section, the parent is acquitted, the court may direct that the school attendance order shall cease to be in force.

(3) A direction under subsection (2) does not affect the duty of the local education authority to take further action under section 437 if at any time the authority are of the opinion that, having regard to any change of circumstances, it is expedient to do so.

(4) A person guilty of an offence under this section is liable on summary conviction to a fine not exceeding level 3 on the standard scale.

444—(1) If a child of compulsory school age who is a registered pupil at a school fails to attend regularly at the school, his parent [or a person with responsibility or care for a child (s 576)] is guilty of an offence.

(2) Subsections (3) to (6) below apply in proceedings for an offence under this section in respect of a child who is not a boarder at the school at which he is a registered pupil.

(3) The child shall not be taken to have failed to attend regularly at the school by reason of his absence from the school—

(a) with leave,

(b) at any time when he was prevented from attending by reason of sickness or any unavoidable cause, or

(c) on any day exclusively set apart for religious observance by the religious body to which his parent belongs.

(4) The child shall not be taken to have failed to attend regularly at the school if the parent proves—

(a) that the school at which the child is a registered pupil is not within walking distance of the child's home, and

(b) that no suitable arrangements have been made by the local education authority or the funding authority for any of the following—

(i) his transport to and from the school,

(ii) boarding accommodation for him at or near the school, or

(iii) enabling him to become a registered pupil at a school nearer to his home.

(5) In subsection (4) 'walking distance'—

(a) in relation to a child who is under the age of eight, means 3.218688 kilometres (two miles), and

(b) in relation to a child who has attained the age of eight, means 4.828032 kilometres (three miles),

in each case measured by the nearest available route.

(6) If it is proved that the child has no fixed abode, subsection (4) shall not apply, but the parent shall be acquitted if he proves—

(a) that he is engaged in a trade or business of such a nature as to require him to travel from place to place,

(b) that the child has attended at a school as a registered pupil as regularly as the nature of that trade or business permits, and

(c) if the child has attained the age of six, that he has made at least 200 attendances during the period of 12 months ending with the date on which the proceedings were instituted.

(7) In proceedings for an offence under this section in respect of a child who is a boarder at the school at which he is a registered pupil, the child shall be taken to have failed to attend regularly at the school if he is absent from it without leave during any part of the school term at a time when he was not prevented from being present by reason of sickness or any unavoidable cause.

(8) A person guilty of an offence under this section is liable on summary conviction to a fine not exceeding level 3 on the standard scale.

(9) In this section 'leave', in relation to a school, means leave granted by any person authorised to do so by the governing body or proprietor of the school.'

Guardian (subs (2))—See s 117(1) and annotations thereto.

Three months (subs (4))—See general annotations.

Seven days (subs (4))—See general annotations.

Probation officer (subs (8))—See s 18(3) and annotations thereto.

Youth offending team (subs (8))—See s 39(4) (s 117(1)).

---

9 Parenting orders: supplemental

(1) Where a person under the age of 16 is convicted of an offence, the court by or before which he is so convicted—

(a) if it is satisfied that the relevant condition is fulfilled, shall make a parenting order; and

(b) if it is not so satisfied, shall state in open court that it is not and why it is not.

(2) Before making a parenting order—

(a) in a case falling within paragraph (a) of subsection (1) of section 8 above;

(b) in a case falling within paragraph (b) or (c) of that subsection, where the person concerned is under the age of 16; or

(c) in a case falling within paragraph (d) of that subsection, where the person to whom the offence related is under that age, a court shall obtain and consider information about the person's family circumstances and the likely effect of the order on those circumstances.

(3) Before making a parenting order, a court shall explain to the parent in ordinary language—

(a) the effect of the order and of the requirements proposed to be included in it;
(b) the consequences which may follow (under subsection (7) below) if he fails to comply with any of those requirements; and
(c) that the court has power (under subsection (5) below) to review the order on the application either of the parent or of the responsible officer.

(4) Requirements specified in, and directions given under, a parenting order shall, as far as practicable, be such as to avoid—

(a) any conflict with the parent's religious beliefs; and
(b) any interference with the times, if any, at which he normally works or attends an educational establishment.

(5) If while a parenting order is in force it appears to the court which made it, on the application of the responsible officer or the parent, that it is appropriate to make an order under this subsection, the court may make an order discharging the parenting order or varying it—

(a) by cancelling any provision included in it; or
(b) by inserting in it (either in addition to or in substitution for any of its provisions) any provision that could have been included in the order if the court had then had power to make it and were exercising the power.

(6) Where an application under subsection (5) above for the discharge of a parenting order is dismissed, no further application for its discharge shall be made under that subsection by any person except with the consent of the court which made the order.

(7) If while a parenting order is in force the parent without reasonable excuse fails to comply with any requirement included in the order, or specified in directions given by the responsible officer, he shall be liable on summary conviction to a fine not exceeding level 3 on the standard scale.

Explanatory text—See paras **3.41**, **3.42**, **3.48–3.55**.

Under the age of 16 (subs (1))—See general annotations.

Parenting order (subss (1), (2), (3), (4), (5), (6) and (7))—See ss 8(4) and 18(1).

Open court (sub (1))—In *Denbigh Justices, ex parte Williams* [1974] QB 759, [1974] 2 All ER 1052 (DC), Lord Widgery CJ stated as follows, in the context of a submission that a hearing had not been in open court:

'The trial should be "public" in the ordinary common-sense acceptation of that term. The doors of the courtroom are expected to be kept open, the public are entitled to be admitted, and the trial is to be public in all respects ... with due regard to the size of the courtroom, the conveniences of the court, the right to exclude objectionable characters and youth of tender years, and to do other things which may facilitate the proper conduct of the trial.'

A trial is conducted in open court even though reporting restrictions are in force under the Children and Young Persons Act 1933, s 39 or s 49, the Magistrates' Courts Act 1980, s 80, the Contempt of Court Act 1981, s 4, or any other statute.

Responsible officer (subs (5))—See ss 8(8) and 18(1).

Level 3 on the standard scale (subs (7))—See general annotations.

---

10 Appeals against parenting orders

(1) An appeal shall lie—

    (a) to the High Court against the making of a parenting order by virtue of paragraph (a) of subsection (1) of section 8 above; and

    (b) to the Crown Court against the making of a parenting order by virtue of paragraph (b) of that subsection.

(2) On an appeal under subsection (1) above the High Court or the Crown Court—

    (a) may make such orders as may be necessary to give effect to its determination of the appeal; and

    (b) may also make such incidental or consequential orders as appear to it to be just.

(3) Any order of the High Court or the Crown Court made on an appeal under subsection (1) above (other than one directing that an application be re-heard by a magistrates' court) shall, for the purposes of subsections (5) to (7) of section 9 above, be treated as if it were an order of the court from which the appeal was brought and not an order of the High Court or the Crown Court.

(4) A person in respect of whom a parenting order is made by virtue of section 8(1)(c) above shall have the same right of appeal against the making of the order as if—

    (a) the offence that led to the making of the order were an offence committed by him; and

    (b) the order were a sentence passed on him for the offence.

(5) A person in respect of whom a parenting order is made by virtue of section 8(1)(d) above shall have the same right of appeal against the making of the order as if the order were a sentence passed on him for the offence that led to the making of the order.

(6) The Lord Chancellor may by order make provision as to the circumstances in which appeals under subsection (1)(a) above may be made against decisions taken by courts on questions arising in connection with the transfer, or proposed transfer, of proceedings by virtue of any order under paragraph 2 of Schedule 11 (jurisdiction) to the Children Act 1989 ('the 1989 Act').

(7) Except to the extent provided for in any order made under subsection (6) above, no appeal may be made against any decision of a kind mentioned in that subsection.

Explanatory text—See paras **3.43–3.47**.

Any order under paragraph 2 of Schedule 11 to the Children Act 1989 (subs (6))—Paragraph 2 of Sch 11 provides:

'(1) The Lord Chancellor may by order provide that in specified circumstances the whole, or any specified part of, specified proceedings to which this paragraph applies shall be transferred to—

    (a) a specified level of court;

    (b) a court which falls within a specified class of court; or

    (c) a particular court determined in accordance with, or specified in, the order.

(2) Any order under this paragraph may provide for the transfer to be made at any stage, or specified stage, of the proceedings and whether or not the proceedings, or any part of them, have already been transferred.

(3) The proceedings to which this paragraph applies are—

    (a)   any proceedings under this Act;

    (b)   any proceedings under the Adoption Act 1976;

    (c)   any other proceedings which—

        (i)   are family proceedings for the purposes of this Act [proceedings under the new Act, ss 11 and 12 are such: Sch 8, para 68], other than proceedings under the inherent jurisdiction of the High Court; and

       (ii) may affect, or are otherwise connected with, the child concerned.

(4) Proceedings to which this paragraph applies by virtue of sub-paragraph (3)(c) may only be transferred in accordance with the provisions of an order made under this paragraph for the purpose of consolidating them with proceedings under—

    (a)   this Act;

    (b)   the Adoption Act 1976;

   (bb) s 20 (appeal) or s 27 (reference to court for declaration of parentage) of the Child Support Act 1991; or

    (c)   the High Court's inherent jurisdiction with respect to children.

(5) An order under this paragraph may make such provision as the Lord Chancellor thinks appropriate for excluding proceedings to which this paragraph applies from the operation of any enactment which would otherwise govern the transfer of those proceedings, or any part of them.'

The principal order made under this provision is the Children (Allocation of Proceedings) Order 1991, SI 1991/1677, as amended.

---

11 Child Safety orders

(1) Subject to subsection (2) below, if a magistrates' court, on the application of a local authority, is satisfied that one or more of the conditions specified in subsection (3) below are fulfilled with respect to a child under the age of 10, it may make an order (a 'child safety order') which—

    (a) places the child, for a period (not exceeding the permitted maximum) specified in the order, under the supervision of the responsible officer; and

    (b) requires the child to comply with such requirements as are so specified.

(2) A court shall not make a child safety order unless it has been notified by the Secretary of State that arrangements for implementing such orders are available in the area in which it appears that the child resides or will reside and the notice has not been withdrawn.

(3) The conditions are—

    (a) that the child has committed an act which, if he had been aged 10 or over, would have constituted an offence;

    (b) that a child safety order is necessary for the purpose of preventing the commission by the child of such an act as is mentioned in paragraph (a) above;

    (c) that the child has contravened a ban imposed by a curfew notice; and

    (d) that the child has acted in a manner that caused or was likely to cause harassment, alarm or distress to one or more persons not of the same household as himself.

(4) The maximum period permitted for the purposes of subsection (1)(a) above is three months or, where the court is satisfied that the circumstances of the case are exceptional, 12 months.

(5) The requirements that may be specified under subsection (1)(b) above are those which the court considers desirable in the interests of—

(a) securing that the child receives appropriate care, protection and support and is subject to proper control; or

(b) preventing any repetition of the kind of behaviour which led to the child safety order being made.

(6) Proceedings under this section or section 12 below shall be family proceedings for the purposes of the 1989 Act or section 65 of the Magistrates' Courts Act 1980 ('the 1980 Act'); and the standard of proof applicable to such proceedings shall be that applicable to civil proceedings.

(7) In this section 'local authority' has the same meaning as in the 1989 Act.

(8) In this section and section 12 below, 'responsible officer', in relation to a child safety order, means one of the following who is specified in the order, namely—

(a) a social worker of a local authority social services department; and

(b) a member of a youth offending team.

Explanatory text—See paras **3.16–3.25**.

Local authority (subss (1) and (8))—This has the same meaning as in the Children Act 1989 (subs (7)). The 1989 Act, s 105, provides that a 'local authority' means, in relation to England, the council of a county, a metropolitan district, a London borough or the Common Council of the City of London and, in relation to Wales, the council of a Welsh county or county borough.

Age (subss (1) and (3))—See general annotations.

Three months/12 months (subs (4))—See general annotations.

Family proceedings for the purposes of the 1989 Act or section 65 of the Magistrates' Courts Act 1980 (subs (6))—'The 1989 Act' is the Children Act 1989 (s 117(1)). Schedule 8, para 68, adds proceedings under ss 11 and 12 to the list of 'family proceedings' in the 1989 Act, s 8(4). Schedule 8, para 42, adds proceedings under ss 11 and 12 to the list of 'family proceedings' in the 1980 Act, s 65. The proceedings under ss 11 or 12 will be heard by a magistrates' court sitting as a 'family proceedings court'. For the composition of a family proceedings court, see the 1980 Act, ss 66 and 67, and for other provisions relating to them, see the 1980 Act, ss 65 and 68–74.

The standard of proof ... applicable to civil proceedings (subs (6))—This standard of proof is proof on the balance of probabilities. This standard will be satisfied if the magistrates are reasonably satisfied that it is more probable than not that the matter in question is proved (*Miller v Minister of Pensions* [1947] 2 All ER 372 at 373–374). See, further, para **5.41**.

Youth offending team (subs (8))—See s 39(4) (s 117(1)).

---

12 Child safety orders: supplemental

(1) Before making a child safety order, a magistrates' court shall obtain and consider information about the child's family circumstances and the likely effect of the order on those circumstances.

(2) Before making a child safety order, a magistrates' court shall explain to the parent or guardian of the child in ordinary language—

(a) the effect of the order and of the requirements proposed to be included in it;

   (b) the consequences which may follow (under subsection (6) below) if the child fails to comply with any of those requirements; and

   (c) that the court has power (under subsection (4) below) to review the order on the application either of the parent or guardian or of the responsible officer.

(3) Requirements included in a child safety order shall, as far as practicable, be such as to avoid—

   (a) any conflict with the parent's religious beliefs; and

   (b) any interference with the times, if any, at which the child normally attends school.

(4) If while a child safety order is in force in respect of a child it appears to the court which made it, on the application of the responsible officer or a parent or guardian of the child, that it is appropriate to make an order under this subsection, the court may make an order discharging the child safety order or varying it—

   (a) by cancelling any provision included in it; or

   (b) by inserting in it (either in addition to or in substitution for any of its provisions) any provision that could have been included in the order if the court had then had power to make it and were exercising the power.

(5) Where an application under subsection (4) above for the discharge of a child safety order is dismissed, no further application for its discharge shall be made under that subsection by any person except with the consent of the court which made the order.

(6) Where a child safety order is in force and it is proved to the satisfaction of the court which made it or another magistrates' court acting for the same petty sessions area, on the application of the responsible officer, that the child has failed to comply with any requirement included in the order, the court—

   (a) may discharge the order and make in respect of him a care order under subsection (1)(a) of section 31 of the 1989 Act; or

   (b) may make an order varying the order—

      (i) by cancelling any provision included in it; or

      (ii) by inserting in it (either in addition to or in substitution for any of its provisions) any provision that could have been included in the order if the court had then had power to make it and were exercising the power.

(7) Subsection (6)(a) above applies whether or not the court is satisfied that the conditions mentioned in section 31(2) of the 1989 Act are fulfilled.

Explanatory text—See paras **3.26, 3.28–3.30**.

Child safety orders (subss (1), (2), (3), (4), (5) and (6))—See ss 11(1) and 18(1).

Guardian (sub (2))—See s 117(1) and annotations thereto.

As far as practicable (sub (3))—See general annotations.

Responsible officer (subss (4) and (6))—This has the meaning given by s 11(8).

Proved to the satisfaction of the court (sub (6))—See annotations to s 11.

Petty sessions area (sub (6))—See general annotations.

A care order under subs (1)(a) of s 31 of the 1989 Act (sub (6))—The 1989 Act means the Children Act 1989 (s 117(1)). Such an order places the child under the care of a designated local authority (1989 Act, s 31(1)(a)).

The local authority designated in a care order must be—

(a)　the authority within whose area the child is ordinarily resident; or
(b)　where the child does not reside in the area of a local authority, the authority within whose area any circumstances arose in consequence of which the order is being made (1989 Act, s 31(8)).

The conditions mentioned in section 31(2) of the 1989 Act (subs (7))—The 1989 Act, s 31(2) provides:

'A court may only make a care order or supervision order if it is satisfied—

(a)　that the child concerned is suffering, or is likely to suffer, significant harm; and
(b)　that the harm, or likelihood of harm, is attributable to—
　(i)　the care given to the child, or likely to be given to him if the order were not made, not being what it would be reasonable to expect a parent to give to him; or
　(ii)　the child's being beyond parental control.'

13 Appeals against child safety orders

(1)　An appeal shall lie to the High Court against the making by a magistrates' court of a child safety order; and on such an appeal the High Court—

(a)　may make such orders as may be necessary to give effect to its determination of the appeal; and
(b)　may also make such incidental or consequential orders as appear to it to be just.

(2)　Any order of the High Court made on an appeal under this section (other than one directing that an application be re-heard by a magistrates' court) shall, for the purposes of subsections (4) to (6) of section 12 above, be treated as if it were an order of the magistrates' court from which the appeal was brought and not an order of the High Court.

(3)　Subsections (6) and (7) of section 10 above shall apply for the purposes of subsection (1) above as they apply for the purposes of subsection (1)(a) of that section.

Explanatory text—See para **3.27**.

Child safety order (subs (1))—See ss 11(1) and 18(1)).

14 Local child curfew schemes

(1)　A local authority may make a scheme (a 'local child curfew scheme') for enabling the authority—

(a)　subject to and in accordance with the provisions of the scheme; and
(b)　if, after such consultation as is required by the scheme, the authority considers it necessary to do so for the purpose of maintaining order,

to give a notice imposing, for a specified period (not exceeding 90 days), a ban to which subsection (2) below applies.

(2)　This subsection applies to a ban on children of specified ages (under 10) being in a public place within a specified area—

(a)　during specified hours (between 9 pm and 6 am); and
(b)　otherwise than under the effective control of a parent or a responsible person aged 18 or over.

(3)　Before making a local child curfew scheme, a local authority shall consult—

(a) every chief officer of police any part of whose police area lies within its area; and
(b) such other persons or bodies as it considers appropriate.

(4) A local child curfew scheme shall be made under the common seal of the local authority and shall not have effect until it is confirmed by the Secretary of State.

(5) The Secretary of State—

(a) may confirm, or refuse to confirm, a local child curfew scheme submitted under this section for confirmation; and
(b) may fix the date on which such a scheme is to come into operation;

and if no date is so fixed, the scheme shall come into operation at the end of the period of one month beginning with the date of its confirmation.

(6) A notice given under a local child curfew scheme (a 'curfew notice') may specify different hours in relation to children of different ages.

(7) A curfew notice shall be given—

(a) by posting the notice in some conspicuous place or places within the specified area; and
(b) in such other manner, if any, as appears to the local authority to be desirable for giving publicity to the notice.

(8) In this section—

'local authority' means—

(a) in relation to England, the council of a district or London borough, the Common Council of the City of London, the Council of the Isle of Wight and the Council of the Isles of Scilly;
(b) in relation to Wales, the council of a county or county borough;

'public place' has the same meaning as in Part II of the Public Order Act 1986.

Explanatory text—See paras **3.2–3.10** and **3.15**.

90 days (subs (1))—See general annotations.

Specified age; aged 18 or over (subs (2))—See general annotations.

Between 9pm and 6am (subs (2))—Subject to s 3 of the Summer Time Act 1972 (construction of references to points of time during the period of summer time), the times referred to refer to Greenwich mean time (Interpretation Act 1978, s 9).

Chief officer of police (subs (3))—See s 18(1) and annotations thereto.

Police area (subs (3))—See s 18(1) and annotations thereto.

City of London (subs (8))—For the purposes of this provision the Inner Temple and Middle Temple form part of the City of London (s 18(5)).

England; Wales (subs (8))—See general annotations.

'Public place' (subs (8))—This has the same meaning as in Part II of the Public Order Act 1986 (subs (8)) which is:

(a) any highway ..., and
(b) any place to which at the material time the public or any section of the public has access, on payment or otherwise, as of right or by virtue of express or implied permission (Public Order Act 1986, Part II, s 16).

'Any highway' in (a) refers to roads and streets (and the pavements alongside them), public footpaths or bridleways. It also includes a 'walkway', a species of highway, which consists of a way over, through or under buildings or structures. Under s 35 of the Highways Act 1980 these are created by an agreement between the local highway authority or district council and any person who owns or has an interest in the land, on which a building is, or is proposed to be, situated, for the provision of ways over, through or under such buildings, and for the dedication by that person of those ways as footpaths. The agreement may provide certain limitations and conditions, eg by making provision for the periodic closure of the walkway.

In addition, many cities and towns have local Acts making similar provisions to those in s 35. Pedestrian ways established under these local Acts are also 'highways' for present purposes.

In relation to (b), whether a place is a 'public place' is a question of degree and fact (*Waters* (1963) 47 Cr App Rep 149 (CCA)). If the public or any section of it have access to a place by express or implied permission, eg to enter a shopping precinct, it is irrelevant that the occupier of the place has the right to refuse entry or to restrict who may enter (*Lawrenson v Oxford* [1982] Crim LR 185 (DC)). It is nevertheless a 'public place' under the present definition.

Since the public must have access, by right or permission, at the material time, a place which is open at certain times but closed at others is a public place when it is open but not when it is closed (*Sandy v Martin* [1974] Crim LR 258 (DC)). A place to which people have, or are permitted to have, access is only a public place if the class of such persons is wide enough for them to be described as 'the public' or a 'section of the public'. In *Britton* [1967] 2 QB 51, [1967] 1 All ER 486 (CA)) Lord Parker CJ said, obiter, that 'section of the public' refers to some identifiable group, 'in other words members of a club or association'. It is submitted that the term is not limited to this but covers any identifiable group whose connection is not a private relationship (ie not a familial or domestic one), provided that that group is identifiable by some common interest or characteristic.

Communal areas in a block of flats have been held to be a 'public place' in circumstances where there is nothing to prevent access (*Knox v Anderton* (1983) 76 Cr App Rep 156 (DC)). In *Williams v DPP* (1992) 95 Cr App Rep 415 (DC), the landing of a communal block of flats, to which access could be gained only by way of a key, security code, tenants' intercom or the caretaker was held not to be a 'public place' because only those admitted by or with the implied consent of the occupiers of the flats had access. People with access were, therefore, not present as members of the public.

A place can be a 'public place' even though access is dependent on payment. Stadia, cinemas, and the like are public places on occasions when access is permitted to any member of the public or section of the public on payment for a ticket. It is not necessary, of course, that all who gain access should have paid for a ticket.

---

15 Contravention of curfew notices

(1) Subsections (2) and (3) below apply where a constable has reasonable cause to believe that a child is in contravention of a ban imposed by a curfew notice.

(2) The constable shall, as soon as practicable, inform the local authority for the area that the child has contravened the ban.

(3) The constable may remove the child to the child's place of residence unless he has reasonable cause to believe that the child would, if removed to that place, be likely to suffer significant harm.

(4) In subsection (1) of section 47 of the 1989 Act (local authority's duty to investigate)—

    (a) in paragraph (a), after sub-paragraph (ii) there shall be inserted the following sub-paragraph—
       '(iii) has contravened a ban imposed by a curfew notice within the meaning of Chapter I of Part I of the Crime and Disorder Act 1998; or'; and
    (b) at the end there shall be inserted the following paragraph—

'In the case of a child falling within paragraph (a)(iii) above, the enquiries shall be commenced as soon as practicable and, in any event, within 48 hours of the authority receiving the information.'

Explanatory text—See paras **3.11–3.14**.

Constable (subss (1), (2) and (3))—See general annotations.

Reasonable cause to believe (subss (1) and (3))—See general annotations.

Curfew notice (subs (1))—This term has the meaning given by s 14(6) (s 18(1)).

As soon as practicable (subss (2) and (4))—See general annotations.

Subsection (1) of s 47 of the 1989 Act—'The 1989 Act' means the Children Act 1989 (s 117). As amended, s 47(1) of the 1989 Act provides (the amendments are italicised):

'Where a local authority—

   (a)   are informed that a child who lives, or is found, in their area—
       (i)   is the subject of an emergency protection order; or
       (ii) is in police protection; or
       (iii) has contravened a ban imposed by a curfew notice within the meaning of Chapter I of Part I of the Crime and Disorder Act 1998; or
   (b)   have reasonable cause to suspect that a child who lives, or is found, in their area is suffering, or is likely to suffer, significant harm,

the authority shall make, or cause to be made, such enquiries as they consider necessary to enable them to decide whether they should take any action to safeguard or promote the child's welfare. *In the case of a child falling within paragraph (a)(iii) above, the enquiries shall be commenced as soon as practicable and, in any event, within 48 hours of the authority receiving the information.*'

---

16 Removal of truants to designated premises etc

(1) This section applies where a local authority—

   (a)   designates premises in a police area ('designated premises') as premises to which children and young persons of compulsory school age may be removed under this section; and
   (b)   notifies the chief officer of police for that area of the designation.

(2) A police officer of or above the rank of superintendent may direct that the powers conferred on a constable by subsection (3) below—

   (a)   shall be exercisable as respects any area falling within the police area and specified in the direction; and
   (b)   shall be so exercisable during a period so specified;

and references in that subsection to a specified area and a specified period shall be construed accordingly.

(3) If a constable has reasonable cause to believe that a child or young person found by him in a public place in a specified area during a specified period—

   (a)   is of compulsory school age; and
   (b)   is absent from a school without lawful authority,

the constable may remove the child or young person to designated premises, or to the school from which he is so absent.

(4) A child's or young person's absence from a school shall be taken to be without lawful authority unless it falls within subsection (3) (leave, sickness, unavoidable cause or day set apart for religious observance) of section 444 of the Education Act 1996.

(5) In this section—

'local authority' means—

(a) in relation to England, a county council, a district council whose district does not form part of an area that has a county council, a London borough council or the Common Council of the City of London;
(b) in relation to Wales, a county council or a county borough council;

'public place' has the same meaning as in section 14 above;
'school' has the same meaning as in the Education Act 1996.

Explanatory text—See paras **3.58–3.65**.

Police area (subs (1))—See s 18(1) and annotations thereto.

Children and young persons of compulsory school age (subss (1), (3) and (4))—As to children and young persons, see s 8.

'Compulsory school age' is defined by the Education Act 1996, s 8(2)–(4). Section 8(2) was amended with associated transitional provisions by the Education Act 1997, s 52, which applies until the amendments come into force (which they had not when this book went to press), as follows:

'52—(1) Section 8 of the Education Act 1996 (compulsory school age) shall be amended in accordance with subsections (2) and (3).

(2) For subsection (2) there shall be substituted—

"(2) A person begins to be of compulsory school age—

(a) when he attains the age of five, if he attains that age on a prescribed day, and
(b) otherwise at the beginning of the prescribed day next following his attaining that age."

(3) For subsection (4) there shall be substituted—

"(4) The Secretary of State may by order—

(a) provide that such days in the year as are specified in the order shall be, for each calendar year, prescribed days for the purposes of subsection (2);
(b) determine the day in any calendar year which is to be the school leaving date for that year."

(4) The Secretary of State may also make an order providing that such days in the year as are specified in the order shall be, for each calendar year during the whole or part of which section 8 of the Education Act 1996 is not wholly in force, prescribed days for the purposes of paragraph 1(2) of Schedule 40 to that Act (transitory provisions pending coming into force of section 8 of that Act) as it has effect in accordance with subsection (5) below.

(5) Where a person does not attain the age of five on any of those prescribed days, he shall be regarded for the purposes of paragraph 1(2) of that Schedule—

(a) as not attaining that age, and
(b) accordingly as not being of compulsory school age,
until the beginning of the prescribed day next following his fifth birthday.'

The 1996 Act, s 8(3) and (4), provides:

'(3) A person ceases to be of compulsory school age at the end of the day which is the school leaving date for any calendar year—

(a)   if he attains the age of 16 after that day but before the beginning of the school year next following,

(b)   if he attains that age on that day, or

(c)   (unless paragraph (a) applies) if that day is the school leaving date next following his attaining that age.

(4) The Secretary of State may by order determine the day in any calendar year which is to be the school leaving date for that year.'

Chief officer of police (subs (1))—See s 18(1) and annotations thereto.

Constable (subs (3))—See general annotations. It is clear from s 16(1) that only a constable who is a member of one of the 41 provincial police forces or of the Metropolitan or City of London police can act under subs (3).

Reasonable cause to believe (subs (3))—See general annotations.

Subsection (3) of section 444 of the Education Act 1996 (subs (4))—See annotations to s 8.

'School' has the same meaning as in the Education Act 1996 (subs (5))—The 1996 Act, s 4 provides:

'(1) In this Act 'school' means an educational institution which is outside the further education sector and the higher education sector and is an institution for providing—

(a)   primary education,

(b)   secondary education, or

(c)   both primary and secondary education,

whether or not the institution also provides part-time education suitable to the requirements of junior pupils or further education.

(2) Nothing in subs (1) shall be taken to preclude the making of arrangements under s 19(1) (exceptional educational provision) under which part-time education is to be provided at a school; and for the purposes of this Act an educational institution that would fall within subsection (1) but for the fact that it provides part-time rather than full-time education shall nevertheless be treated as a school if that part-time education is provided under arrangements made under section 19(1) [which deals with exceptional provision of education for the education of children who for reasons of illness, exclusion from school or otherwise would not receive suitable education unless such provision was made for them].'

Miscellaneous and supplemental

17 Duty to consider crime and disorder implications

(1) Without prejudice to any other obligation imposed on it, it shall be the duty of each authority to which this section applies to exercise its various functions with due regard to the likely effect of the exercise of those functions on, and the need to do all that it reasonably can to prevent, crime and disorder in its area.

(2) This section applies to a local authority, a joint authority, a police authority, a National Park authority and the Broads Authority.

(3) In this section—

'local authority' means a local authority within the meaning given by section 270(1) of the Local Government Act 1972 or the Common Council of the City of London;

'joint authority' has the same meaning as in the Local Government Act 1985;
'National Park authority' means an authority established under section 63 of the
Environment Act 1995.

Explanatory text—See para **2.11**.

'Joint authority' has the same meaning as in the Local Government Act 1985 (subs (3))—Ie any authority established by Part IV of the 1985 Act (1985 Act, s 105(1)). The term refers to joint authorities for fire and civil defence in Metropolitan counties, the London Fire and Civil Defence Authority and Metropolitan county passenger transport authorities.

Police authority (subs (2))—See s 18(1) and annotations thereto.

'National Park authority' means an authority established under s 63 of the Environment Act 1995 (subs (3))—Section 63(1) of the 1995 Act provides:

'The Secretary of State may—

(a)   in the case of any National Park for which there is an existing authority, or
(b)   in connection with the designation of any area as a new such Park, by order establish an authority (to be known as 'a National Park authority') to carry out in relation to that Park the functions conferred on such an authority by or under this Part.'

Broads Authority (subs (2))—This refers to the Broads Authority established under the Norfolk and Suffolk Broads Act 1988, s 1.

'Local authority' has the meaning given by s 270(1) of the Local Government Act 1972 (subs (3))—Ie in England, a county council, a district council, a London borough council or a parish council and, in relation to Wales, a county council, county borough council or community council.

---

18 Interpretation etc. of Chapter I

(1) In this Chapter—

'anti-social behaviour order' has the meaning given by section 1(4) above;
'chief officer of police' has the meaning given by section 101(1) of the Police Act 1996;
'child safety order' has the meaning given by section 11(1) above;
'curfew notice' has the meaning given by section 14(6) above;
'local child curfew scheme' has the meaning given by section 14(1) above;
'parenting order' has the meaning given by section 8(4) above;
'police area' has the meaning given by section 1(2) of the Police Act 1996;
'police authority' has the meaning given by section 101(1) of that Act;
'responsible officer'—

(a)   in relation to a parenting order, has the meaning given by section 8(8) above;
(b)   in relation to a child safety order, has the meaning given by section 11(8) above;

'sex offender order' has the meaning given by section 2(3) above.

(2) In this Chapter, unless the contrary intention appears, expressions which are also used in Part I of the Criminal Justice Act 1991 ('the 1991 Act') have the same meanings as in that Part.

(3) Where directions under a parenting order are to be given by a probation officer, the probation officer shall be an officer appointed for or assigned to the petty sessions area

within which it appears to the court that the child or, as the case may be, the parent resides or will reside.

(4) Where the supervision under a child safety order is to be provided, or directions under a parenting order are to be given, by—

(a) a social worker of a local authority social services department; or
(b) a member of a youth offending team,

the social worker or member shall be a social worker of, or a member of a youth offending team established by, the local authority within whose area it appears to the court that the child or, as the case may be, the parent resides or will reside.

(5) For the purposes of this Chapter the Inner Temple and the Middle Temple form part of the City of London.

'Chief officer of police' has the meaning given by section 101(1) of the Police Act 1996 (subs (1))—Ie:

(a) in relation to a police force maintained for each police area (see below) outside London by a police authority (see below), the Chief Constable;
(b) in relation to the metropolitan police force, the Commissioner of Police of the Metropolis, and
(c) in relation to the City of London police force, the Commissioner of Police for the City of London.

This definition has the effect of excluding the chief constables of entities such as the Transport Police, Civil Aviation Police or Ministry of Defence Police from the term 'chief officer of police' for the purposes of this Chapter of the Act.

Police area has the meaning given by section 1(2) of the Police Act 1996 (subs (1))—By s 1(2) of the 1996 Act, there are 43 police areas:

(a) the 41 listed in Sch 1 to the Police Act 1996;
(b) the metropolitan police district; and
(c) the City of London police area.

Police authority has the meaning given by section 101(1) of that Act [ie the Police Act 1996] (subs (1))—Ie 'police authority' means—

(a) in relation to one of the 41 police areas listed in Schedule 1 to the 1996 Act, the authority established under s 3 of the Act,
(b) in relation to the metropolitan police district, the Home Secretary, and
(c) in relation to the City of London police area, the Common Council.

Probation officer (subs (3))—See Probation Service Act 1993, s 1. The duties of probation officers are defined in the 1993 Act, s 14.

Youth offending team (subs (4))—See s 39(4).

CHAPTER II

SCOTLAND

19 to 24 [*Applies to Scotland only.*]

CHAPTER III

GREAT BRITAIN

25 Powers to require removal of masks etc.

(1) After subsection (4) of section 60 (powers to stop and search in anticipation of violence) of the Criminal Justice and Public Order Act 1994 ('the 1994 Act') there shall be inserted the following subsection—

'(4A) This section also confers on any constable in uniform power—

(a) to require any person to remove any item which the constable reasonably believes that person is wearing wholly or mainly for the purpose of concealing his identity;

(b) to seize any item which the constable reasonably believes any person intends to wear wholly or mainly for that purpose.'

(2) In subsection (5) of that section, for the words 'those powers' there shall be substituted the words 'the powers conferred by subsection (4) above'.

(3) In subsection (8) of that section, for the words 'to stop or (as the case may be) to stop the vehicle' there shall be substituted the following paragraphs—

'(a) to stop, or to stop a vehicle; or

(b) to remove an item worn by him,'.

Explanatory text—See paras **9.7–9.16**.

Section 60 ... of the Criminal Justice and Public Order Act 1994 (subs (1))—Section 60 of the 1994 Act provides as follows:

'(1) Where a police officer of or above the rank of superintendent reasonably believes that—

(a) incidents involving serious violence may take place in any locality in his area, and

(b) it is expedient to do so to prevent their occurrence,

he may give an authorisation that the powers to stop and search persons and vehicles conferred by this section shall be exercisable at any place within that locality for a period not exceeding twenty-four hours.

(2) The power conferred by subsection (1) above may be exercised by a chief inspector or an inspector if he reasonably believes that incidents involving serious violence are imminent and no superintendent is available.

(3) If it appears to the officer who gave the authorisation or to a superintendent that it is expedient to do so, having regard to offences which have, or are reasonably suspected to have, been committed in connection with any incident falling within the authorisation, he may direct that the authorisation shall continue in being for a further six hours.

(4) This section confers on any constable in uniform power—

(a) to stop any pedestrian and search him or anything carried by him for offensive weapons or dangerous instruments;

(b) to stop any vehicle and search the vehicle, its driver and any passenger for offensive weapons or dangerous instruments.

(4A) [See 1998 Act, s 25].

(5) A constable may, in the exercise of those powers, stop any person or vehicle and make any search he thinks fit whether or not he has any grounds for suspecting that the person or vehicle is carrying weapons or articles of that kind.

(6) If in the course of a search under this section a constable discovers a dangerous instrument or an article which he has reasonable grounds for suspecting to be an offensive weapon, he may seize it.

(7) This section applies (with the necessary modifications) to ships, aircraft and hovercraft as it applies to vehicles.

(8) A person who fails to stop or (as the case may be) to stop the vehicle when required to do so by a constable in the exercise of his powers under this section shall be liable on summary conviction to imprisonment for a term not exceeding one month or to a fine not exceeding level 3 on the standard scale or both.

(9) Any authorisation under this section shall be in writing signed by the officer giving it and shall specify the locality in which and the period during which the powers conferred by this section are exercisable and a direction under subsection (3) above shall also be given in writing or, where that is not practicable, recorded in writing as soon as it is practicable to do so.

(10) Where a vehicle is stopped by a constable under this section, the driver shall be entitled to obtain a written statement that the vehicle was stopped under the powers conferred by this section if he applies for such a statement not later than the end of the period of twelve months from the day on which the vehicle was stopped and similarly as respects a pedestrian who is stopped and searched under this section.

(11) In this section—

'dangerous instruments' means instruments which have a blade or are sharply pointed: Evidence Act 1984; and
'vehicle' includes a caravan as defined in section 29(1) of the Caravan Sites and Control of Development Act 1960.

(12) The powers conferred by this section are in addition to and not in derogation of, any power otherwise conferred.'

Reasonably believes (1994 Act (subs 4A)); constable (subs (4A))—See general annotations.

---

26 Retention and disposal of things seized

After section 60 of the 1994 Act there shall be inserted the following section—

'Retention and disposal of things seized under section 60

60A—(1) Any things seized by a constable under section 60 may be retained in accordance with regulations made by the Secretary of State under this section.

(2) The Secretary of State may make regulations regulating the retention and safe keeping, and the disposal and destruction in prescribed circumstances, of such things.

(3) Regulations under this section may make different provisions for different classes of things or for different circumstances.

(4) The power to make regulations under this section shall be exercisable by statutory instrument which shall be subject to annulment in pursuance of a resolution of either House of Parliament.'

Explanatory text—See para **9.14**.

1994 Act, s 60A(4)—See annotations to s 114.

---

27 Power of arrest for failure to comply with requirement

(1) In section 24(2) (arrestable offences) of the Police and Criminal Evidence Act 1984 ('the 1984 Act'), after paragraph (n) there shall be inserted—

'(o) an offence under section 60(8)(b) of the Criminal Justice and Public Order Act 1994 (failing to comply with requirement to remove mask etc.);'.

(2) [*Applies to Scotland only.*]

Explanatory text—See para **9.16**.

PART II

CRIMINAL LAW

Racially-aggravated offences: England and Wales

28 Meaning of 'racially aggravated'

(1) An offence is racially aggravated for the purposes of sections 29 to 32 below if—

   (a) at the time of committing the offence, or immediately before or after doing so, the offender demonstrates towards the victim of the offence hostility based on the victim's membership (or presumed membership) of a racial group; or

   (b) the offence is motivated (wholly or partly) by hostility towards members of a racial group based on their membership of that group.

(2) In subsection (1)(a) above—

'membership', in relation to a racial group, includes association with members of that group;
'presumed' means presumed by the offender.

(3) It is immaterial for the purposes of paragraph (a) or (b) of subsection (1) above whether or not the offender's hostility is also based, to any extent, on—

   (a) the fact or presumption that any person or group of persons belongs to any religious group; or

   (b) any other factor not mentioned in that paragraph.

(4) In this section 'racial group' means a group of persons defined by reference to race, colour, nationality (including citizenship) or ethnic or national origins.

Explanatory text—See paras **8.7–8.19**.

---

29 Racially-aggravated assaults

(1) A person is guilty of an offence under this section if he commits—

   (a) an offence under section 20 of the Offences Against the Person Act 1861 (malicious wounding or grievous bodily harm);

    (b)   an offence under section 47 of that Act (actual bodily harm); or

    (c)   common assault,

which is racially aggravated for the purposes of this section.

(2) A person guilty of an offence falling within subsection (1)(a) or (b) above shall be liable—

    (a)   on summary conviction, to imprisonment for a term not exceeding six months or to a fine not exceeding the statutory maximum, or to both;

    (b)   on conviction on indictment, to imprisonment for a term not exceeding seven years or to a fine, or to both.

(3) A person guilty of an offence falling within subsection (1)(c) above shall be liable—

    (a)   on summary conviction, to imprisonment for a term not exceeding six months or to a fine not exceeding the statutory maximum, or to both;

    (b)   on conviction on indictment, to imprisonment for a term not exceeding two years or to a fine, or to both.

Explanatory text—See paras **8.20–8.42**.

Racially aggravated (subs (1))—See s 28(1).

The statutory maximum (subss (2) and (3))—See general annotations.

---

30 Racially-aggravated criminal damage

(1) A person is guilty of an offence under this section if he commits an offence under section 1(1) of the Criminal Damage Act 1971 (destroying or damaging property belonging to another) which is racially aggravated for the purposes of this section.

(2) A person guilty of an offence under this section shall be liable—

    (a)   on summary conviction, to imprisonment for a term not exceeding six months or to a fine not exceeding the statutory maximum, or to both;

    (b)   on conviction on indictment, to imprisonment for a term not exceeding fourteen years or to a fine, or to both.

(3) For the purposes of this section, section 28(1)(a) above shall have effect as if the person to whom the property belongs or is treated as belonging for the purposes of that Act were the victim of the offence.

Explanatory text—See paras **8.43–8.51**.

Racially aggravated (subs (1))—See s 28(1) and subs (3).

The statutory maximum (subs (2))—See general annotations.

---

31 Racially-aggravated public order offences

(1) A person is guilty of an offence under this section if he commits—

    (a)   an offence under section 4 of the Public Order Act 1986 (fear or provocation of violence);

(b)   an offence under section 4A of that Act (intentional harassment, alarm or distress); or

(c)   an offence under section 5 of that Act (harassment, alarm or distress),

which is racially aggravated for the purposes of this section.

(2) A constable may arrest without warrant anyone whom he reasonably suspects to be committing an offence falling within subsection (1)(a) or (b) above.

(3) A constable may arrest a person without warrant if—

(a)   he engages in conduct which a constable reasonably suspects to constitute an offence falling within subsection (1)(c) above;

(b)   he is warned by that constable to stop; and

(c)   he engages in further such conduct immediately or shortly after the warning.

The conduct mentioned in paragraph (a) above and the further conduct need not be of the same nature.

(4) A person guilty of an offence falling within subsection (1)(a) or (b) above shall be liable—

(a)   on summary conviction, to imprisonment for a term not exceeding six months or to a fine not exceeding the statutory maximum, or to both;

(b)   on conviction on indictment, to imprisonment for a term not exceeding two years or to a fine, or to both.

(5) A person guilty of an offence falling within subsection (1)(c) above shall be liable on summary conviction to a fine not exceeding level 4 on the standard scale.

(6) If, on the trial on indictment of a person charged with an offence falling within subsection (1)(a) or (b) above, the jury find him not guilty of the offence charged, they may find him guilty of the basic offence mentioned in that provision.

(7) For the purposes of subsection (1)(c) above, section 28(1)(a) above shall have effect as if the person likely to be caused harassment, alarm or distress were the victim of the offence.

Explanatory text—See paras **8.52–8.70.**

Racially aggravated (subs (1))—See s 28(1).

Constable (subss (2) and (3))—See general annotations.

Reasonably suspects (subss (2) and (3))—It is not enough that the constable has reasonable grounds to suspect the stipulated thing; he must also actually suspect it (*Banks* [1916] 2 KB 621 (CCA); *Harrison* [1938] 3 All ER 134 (CCA)), and the use of 'reasonably suspects' makes the point even clearer. Also see *Chapman v DPP* (1988) 89 Cr App Rep 190 (DC).

'Suspicion' is something less than belief (*Johnson v Whitehouse* [1984] RTR 38 (DC)). 'Suspicion in its ordinary meaning is a state of conjecture or surmise when proof is lacking' (*Shaaben Bin Hussien v Chong Fook Kam* [1970] AC 942 at 948, [1969] 3 All ER 1626, per Lord Devlin).

The existence of the reasonable grounds and of the suspicion founded on them is ultimately a question of fact to be decided in the light of the circumstances disclosed by the evidence. The grounds on which the constable acted must be sufficient to induce in a reasonable person the required suspicion (*McArdle v Egan* (1933) 150 LT 412 (CA); *Nakkuda Ali v M F De S Jayaratne* [1951] AC 66 (PC); *IRC v Rossminster Ltd* [1980] 1 All ER 80 at 84, 92, 103 and 104).

A suspicion may be reasonable even though the material on which it is founded would not amount to a prima facie case for conviction of an offence (*Dumbell v Roberts* [1944] 1 All ER 326 (CA); *Shaabin Hussien v Chong Fook Kam* [1970] AC 942, [1969] 3 All ER 1626 (PC)), or where it would not be admissible evidence, eg because it is hearsay (*McArdle v Egan* above; *O'Hara v Chief Constable of the Royal Ulster Constabulary* [1997] 1 All ER 129 (HL)). Thus, the constable's suspicion need not be based on his own observations but could be based on what he has been told, or on information given to him anonymously. It is not necessary for him to prove what was known to his informant or that any of the facts on which he based his suspicion were in fact true. Whether such information provides reasonable grounds for the constable's suspicion depends on the source and context, viewed in the light of the surrounding circumstances (*O'Hara v Chief Constable of the Royal Ulster Constabulary*, above). However, the mere fact that an arresting constable has been instructed by a superior officer to effect the arrest is not capable of amounting to reasonable grounds for the necessary suspicion (ibid).

Warned (subs (3))—In relation to the requirement under ss 1 and 2 of the Road Traffic Offenders Act 1988 that certain motoring offences may not be prosecuted unless the person concerned has been 'warned' that the question of prosecuting him would be taken into consideration (or certain other procedural stages have been adopted), it has been held that, to be effective, a warning must be heard and understood by the person to whom it is addressed (*Gibson v Dalton* [1980] RTR 410 (DC)). No doubt, the same is true of a warning under s 31(3).

The statutory maximum (subs (4))—See general annotations.

Level 4 on the standard scale (subs (5))—See general annotations.

---

32 Racially-aggravated harassment etc

(1) A person is guilty of an offence under this section if he commits—

    (a) an offence under section 2 of the Protection from Harassment Act 1997 (offence of harassment); or

    (b) an offence under section 4 of that Act (putting people in fear of violence),

which is racially aggravated for the purposes of this section.

(2) In section 24(2) of the 1984 Act (arrestable offences), after paragraph (o) there shall be inserted—

    '(p) an offence falling within section 32(1)(a) of the Crime and Disorder Act 1998 (racially-aggravated harassment);'.

(3) A person guilty of an offence falling within subsection (1)(a) above shall be liable—

    (a) on summary conviction, to imprisonment for a term not exceeding six months or to a fine not exceeding the statutory maximum, or to both;

    (b) on conviction on indictment, to imprisonment for a term not exceeding two years or to a fine, or to both.

(4) A person guilty of an offence falling within subsection (1)(b) above shall be liable—

    (a) on summary conviction, to imprisonment for a term not exceeding six months or to a fine not exceeding the statutory maximum, or to both;

    (b) on conviction on indictment, to imprisonment for a term not exceeding seven years or to a fine, or to both.

(5) If, on the trial on indictment of a person charged with an offence falling within subsection (1)(a) above, the jury find him not guilty of the offence charged, they may find him guilty of the basic offence mentioned in that provision.

(6) If, on the trial on indictment of a person charged with an offence falling within subsection (1)(b) above, the jury find him not guilty of the offence charged, they may find him guilty of an offence falling within subsection (1)(a) above.

(7) Section 5 of the Protection from Harassment Act 1997 (restraining orders) shall have effect in relation to a person convicted of an offence under this section as if the reference in subsection (1) of that section to an offence under section 2 or 4 included a reference to an offence under this section.

Explanatory text—See paras **8.72–8.78**.

Racially aggravated (subs (1))—See s 28(1).

Subsection (2)—This adds an offence under s 32(1)(a) to the list of offences declared by s 24(2) of the 1984 Act to be 'arrestable offences' for the purposes of s 24 although they do not carry sentence fixed by law or a maximum sentence of five years' imprisonment or more.

Section 24 of the 1984 Act confers various powers of arrest in respect of an arrestable offence, which also apply to the offences of:

(a)   conspiracy to commit any arrestable offence;
(b)   attempting to commit any such offence other than an offence under the Theft Act 1968, s 12(1);
(c)   inciting, aiding, abetting, counselling or procuring any such offence (1984 Act, s 24(3)).

These offences are deemed to be arrestable offences for the purposes of the 1984 Act (ibid). The powers to arrest without warrant for an arrestable offence are as follows.

Section 24(4) and (5) of the 1984 Act provides that *any person* may arrest without a warrant:

(a)   anyone who is *in the act of committing* an arrestable offence; and
(b)   anyone whom he has reasonable grounds for suspecting *to be committing* such an offence;

and that where an arrestable offence *has been committed*, any person may arrest without a warrant:

(a)   anyone who is guilty of the offence; and
(b)   anyone whom he has reasonable grounds for suspecting to be guilty of it.

It is important to note that an arrest, purportedly on the basis that an arrestable offence has been committed, will not be covered by the latter provision – and will be unlawful – not only if it transpires that no actus reus of such an offence has ever been committed but also if it transpires that, while an actus reus was committed, the actor lacked the required mens rea for the offence. Section 24(6) and (7) provides further powers to *a constable* (see general annotations) to arrest without a warrant as follows:

(a)   where a constable has reasonable grounds for suspecting that an arrestable offence has been committed, he may arrest without a warrant anyone whom he has reasonable grounds for suspecting to be guilty of the offence;
(b)   a constable may arrest without a warrant anyone who is about to commit an arrestable offence; and
(c)   a constable may arrest without a warrant anyone whom he has reasonable grounds for suspecting to be about to commit an arrestable offence.

The statutory maximum (subss (3) and (4))—See general annotations.

Subs (7)—The 1997 Act, s 5(1) provides:

'A court sentencing or otherwise dealing with a person ("the defendant") convicted of an offence under section 2 or 4 may (as well as sentencing him or dealing with him in any other way) make a restraining order under this section.'

Racially-aggravated offences: Scotland

33 [*Applies to Scotland only.*]

Miscellaneous

34 Abolition of rebuttable presumption that a child is doli incapax

The rebuttable presumption of criminal law that a child aged 10 or over is incapable of committing an offence is hereby abolished.

Explanatory text—See paras **9.1–9.6**.

Aged 10 or over—See general annotations.

35 Effect of child's silence at trial

In section 35 of the 1994 Act (effect of accused's silence at trial), the following provisions shall cease to have effect, namely—

    (a) in subsection (1), the words 'who has attained the age of fourteen years'; and

    (b) subsection (6).

Explanatory text—See paras **9.43–9.47**.

Section 35 of the 1994 Act—The 1994 Act means the Criminal Justice and Public Order Act 1994 (s 117(1)). Section 35, as amended, provides as follows:

'(1) At the trial of any person, subsections (2) and (3) below apply unless—

    (a)   the accused's guilt is not in issue; or

    (b)   it appears to the court that the physical or mental condition of the accused makes it undesirable for him to give evidence;

but subsection (2) below does not apply if, at the conclusion of the evidence for the prosecution, his legal representative informs the court that the accused will give evidence or, where he is unrepresented, the court ascertains from him that he will give evidence.

(2) Where this subsection applies, the court shall, at the conclusion of the evidence for the prosecution, satisfy itself (in the case of proceedings on indictment, in the presence of the given for the defence and that he can, if he wishes, give evidence and that, if he chooses not to give evidence, or having been sworn, without good cause refuses to answer any question, it will be permissible for the court or jury to draw such inferences as appear proper from his failure to give evidence or his refusal, without good cause, to answer any question.

(3) Where this subsection applies, the court or jury, in determining whether the accused is guilty of the offence charged, may draw such inferences as appear proper from the failure of the accused to give evidence or his refusal, without good cause, to answer any question.

(4) This section does not render the accused compellable to give evidence on his own behalf, and he shall accordingly not be guilty of contempt of court by reason of a failure to do so.

(5) For the purposes of this section a person who, having been sworn, refuses to answer any question shall be taken to do so without good cause unless—

    (a)   he is entitled to refuse to answer the question by virtue of any enactment, whenever passed or made, or on the ground of privilege; or

(b)   the court in the exercise of its general discretion excuses him from answering it.

[subs (6) repealed]

(7) This section applies—

(a)   in relation to proceedings on indictment for an offence, only if the person charged with the offence is arraigned on or after the commencement of this section;

(b)   in relation to proceedings in a magistrates' court, only if the time when the court begins to receive evidence in the proceedings falls after the commencement of the section.'

No inference from a failure to give evidence may be drawn where the judge, or magistrates, have failed to observe the requirements of s 35(2) that the accused is aware of the potential for inferences to be drawn if he does not testify: *Price* [1996] Crim LR 736 (CA).

36 Abolition of death penalty for treason and piracy

(1) [*Applies to Northern Ireland only.*]

(2) In the following enactments, namely—

(a) [*applies to Northern Ireland only*]

(b) [*applies to Northern Ireland only*]

(c) section 3 of the Treason Act 1702 (endeavouring to hinder the succession to the Crown etc. punishable as high treason);

(d) [*applies to Northern Ireland only*]

for the words 'suffer pains of death' there shall be substituted the words 'be liable to imprisonment for life'.

(3) The following enactments shall cease to have effect, namely—

(a) the Treason Act 1790;

(b) the Treason Act 1795.

(4) In section 1 of the Treason Act 1814 (form of sentence in case of high treason), for the words 'such person shall be hanged by the neck until such person be dead', there shall be substituted the words 'such person shall be liable to imprisonment for life'.

(5) In section 2 of the Piracy Act 1837 (punishment of piracy when murder is attempted), for the words 'and being convicted thereof shall suffer death' there shall be substituted the words 'and being convicted thereof shall be liable to imprisonment for life'.

(6) The following enactments shall cease to have effect, namely—

(a) the Sentence of Death (Expectant Mothers) Act 1931; and

(b) [*applies to Northern Ireland only*].

Explanatory text—See paras **9.60–9.63**.

Treason Act 1790 (subs (3))—This prescribed the punishment for treason as death by hanging.

Treason Act 1795 (subs (3))—This confirmed that 'constructive treasons' acts held by judicial construction to satisfy the Treason Act 1351 were treason and punishable with death.

Sentence of Death (Expectant Mothers) Act 1931 (subs (6))—This prohibited the passing of the death penalty on expectant mothers, who had to be sentenced to life imprisonment instead.

PART III

CRIMINAL JUSTICE SYSTEM

Youth justice

37 Aim of the youth justice system

(1) It shall be the principal aim of the youth justice system to prevent offending by children and young persons.

(2) In addition to any other duty to which they are subject, it shall be the duty of all persons and bodies carrying out functions in relation to the youth justice system to have regard to that aim.

Explanatory text—See paras **2.14–2.15**.

---

38 Local provision of youth justice services

(1) It shall be the duty of each local authority, acting in co-operation with the persons and bodies mentioned in subsection (2) below, to secure that, to such extent as is appropriate for their area, all youth justice services are available there.

(2) It shall be the duty of—

   (a) every chief officer of police or police authority any part of whose police area lies within the local authority's area; and

   (b) every probation committee or health authority any part of whose area lies within that area,

to co-operate in the discharge by the local authority of their duty under subsection (1) above.

(3) The local authority and every person or body mentioned in subsection (2) above shall have power to make payments towards expenditure incurred in the provision of youth justice services—

   (a) by making the payments directly; or

   (b) by contributing to a fund, established and maintained by the local authority, out of which the payments may be made.

(4) In this section and sections 39 to 41 below 'youth justice services' means any of the following, namely—

   (a) the provision of persons to act as appropriate adults to safeguard the interests of children and young persons detained or questioned by police officers;

   (b) the assessment of children and young persons, and the provision for them of rehabilitation programmes, for the purposes of section 66(2) below;

   (c) the provision of support for children and young persons remanded or committed on bail while awaiting trial or sentence;

   (d) the placement in local authority accommodation of children and young persons remanded or committed to such accommodation under section 23 of the Children and Young Persons Act 1969 ('the 1969 Act');

   (e) the provision of reports or other information required by courts in criminal proceedings against children and young persons;

   (f) the provision of persons to act as responsible officers in relation to parenting orders, child safety orders, reparation orders and action plan orders;

(g) the supervision of young persons sentenced to a probation order, a community service order or a combination order;

(h) the supervision of children and young persons sentenced to a detention and training order or a supervision order;

(i) the post-release supervision of children and young persons under section 37(4A) or 65 of the 1991 Act or section 31 of the Crime (Sentences) Act 1997 ('the 1997 Act');

(j) the performance of functions under subsection (1) of section 75 below by such persons as may be authorised by the Secretary of State under that subsection.

(5) The Secretary of State may by order amend subsection (4) above so as to extend, restrict or otherwise alter the definition of 'youth justice services' for the time being specified in that subsection.

Explanatory text—See para **2.16**.

Local authority area (subs (1))—See s 42(1).

Chief officer of police; police authority (subs (1))—See s 42 and annotations to s 18.

Children and Young Persons Act 1969, s 23 (subs (4))—See annotations to s 97.

Section 37(4A) or 65 of the 1991 Act (subs (4))—'The 1991 Act' means the Criminal Justice Act 1991 (s 117(1)). For s 37, see annotations to s 59.

Section 31 of the Crime (Sentences) Act 1997 (subs (4))—This provides as follows:

'(1) Where a life prisoner is released on licence, the licence shall, unless previously revoked under section 32(1) or (2) below, remain in force until his death.

(2) A life prisoner subject to a licence shall comply with such conditions as may for the time being be specified in the licence; and the Secretary of State may make rules for regulating the supervision of any description of such persons.

(2A) The conditions so specified shall include on the prisoner's release conditions as to his supervision by:

    (a) a probation officer appointed for or assigned to the petty sessions area within which the prisoner resides for the time being;

    (b) where the prisoner is under the age of 22, a social worker of the social services department of the local authority within whose area the prisoner resides for the time being; or

    (c) where the prisoner is under the age of 18, a member of a youth offending team established by that local authority under section 39 of the Crime and Disorder Act 1998.

(3) The Secretary of State shall not include on release, or subsequently insert, a condition in the licence of a life prisoner, or vary or cancel any such condition, except—

    (a) in the case of the inclusion of a condition in the licence of a life prisoner to whom section 28 above applies, in accordance with recommendations of the Parole Board; and

    (b) in any other case, after consultation with the Board.

(4) For the purposes of subsection (3) above, the Secretary of State shall be treated as having consulted the Parole Board about a proposal to include, insert, vary or cancel a condition in any case if he has consulted the Board about the implementation of proposals of that description generally or in that class of case.

(5) The power to make rules under this section shall be exercisable by statutory instrument which shall be subject to annulment in pursuance of a resolution of either House of Parliament.

(6) In relation to a life prisoner who is liable to removal from the United Kingdom (within the meaning given by *section 46(3)* of the 1991 Act) subsection (2) above shall have effect as if *subsection (2A)* were omitted.'

---

39 Youth offending teams

(1) Subject to subsection (2) below, it shall be the duty of each local authority, acting in co-operation with the persons and bodies mentioned in subsection (3) below, to establish for their area one or more youth offending teams.

(2) Two (or more) local authorities acting together may establish one or more youth offending teams for both (or all) their areas; and where they do so—

(a) any reference in the following provisions of this section (except subsection (4)(b)) to, or to the area of, the local authority or a particular local authority shall be construed accordingly, and

(b) the reference in subsection (4)(b) to the local authority shall be construed as a reference to one of the authorities.

(3) It shall be the duty of—

(a) every chief officer of police any part of whose police area lies within the local authority's area; and

(b) every probation committee or health authority any part of whose area lies within that area,

to co-operate in the discharge by the local authority of their duty under subsection (1) above.

(4) The local authority and every person or body mentioned in subsection (3) above shall have power to make payments towards expenditure incurred by, or for purposes connected with, youth offending teams—

(a) by making the payments directly; or

(b) by contributing to a fund, established and maintained by the local authority, out of which the payments may be made.

(5) A youth offending team shall include at least one of each of the following, namely—

(a) a probation officer;

(b) a social worker of a local authority social services department;

(c) a police officer;

(d) a person nominated by a health authority any part of whose area lies within the local authority's area;

(e) a person nominated by the chief education officer appointed by the local authority under section 532 of the Education Act 1996.

(6) A youth offending team may also include such other persons as the local authority thinks appropriate after consulting the persons and bodies mentioned in subsection (3) above.

(7) It shall be the duty of the youth offending team or teams established by a particular local authority—

(a) to co-ordinate the provision of youth justice services for all those in the authority's area who need them; and

(b) to carry out such functions as are assigned to the team or teams in the youth justice plan formulated by the authority under section 40(1) below.

Explanatory text—See paras **2.19–2.21**.

Local authority area (subs (1))—See s 42(1).

Chief officer of police (subs (3))—See s 42 and annotations to s 18.

Probation Committee (subs (3))—See annotations to s 5.

---

40 Youth justice plans

(1) It shall be the duty of each local authority, after consultation with the relevant persons and bodies, to formulate and implement for each year a plan (a 'youth justice plan') setting out—

(a) how youth justice services in their area are to be provided and funded; and
(b) how the youth offending team or teams established by them (whether alone or jointly with one or more other local authorities) are to be composed and funded, how they are to operate, and what functions they are to carry out.

(2) In subsection (1) above 'the relevant persons and bodies' means the persons and bodies mentioned in section 38(2) above and, where the local authority is a county council, any district councils whose districts form part of its area.

(3) The functions assigned to a youth offending team under subsection (1)(b) above may include, in particular, functions under paragraph 7(b) of Schedule 2 to the 1989 Act (local authority's duty to take reasonable steps designed to encourage children and young persons not to commit offences).

(4) A local authority shall submit their youth justice plan to the Board established under section 41 below, and shall publish it in such manner and by such date as the Secretary of State may direct.

Explanatory text—See para **2.17**.

Local authority area (subs (1))—See s 42(1).

---

41 The Youth Justice Board

(1) There shall be a body corporate to be known as the Youth Justice Board for England and Wales ('the Board').

(2) The Board shall not be regarded as the servant or agent of the Crown or as enjoying any status, immunity or privilege of the Crown; and the Board's property shall not be regarded as property of, or held on behalf of, the Crown.

(3) The Board shall consist of 10, 11 or 12 members appointed by the Secretary of State.

(4) The members of the Board shall include persons who appear to the Secretary of State to have extensive recent experience of the youth justice system.

(5) The Board shall have the following functions, namely—

(a) to monitor the operation of the youth justice system and the provision of youth justice services;
(b) to advise the Secretary of State on the following matters, namely—
    (i) the operation of that system and the provision of such services;

    (ii) how the principal aim of that system might most effectively be pursued;

    (iii) the content of any national standards he may see fit to set with respect to the provision of such services, or the accommodation in which children and young persons are kept in custody; and

    (iv) the steps that might be taken to prevent offending by children and young persons;

(c) to monitor the extent to which that aim is being achieved and any such standards met;

(d) for the purposes of paragraphs (a), (b) and (c) above, to obtain information from relevant authorities;

(e) to publish information so obtained;

(f) to identify, to make known and to promote good practice in the following matters, namely—

    (i) the operation of the youth justice system and the provision of youth justice services;

    (ii) the prevention of offending by children and young persons; and

    (iii) working with children and young persons who are or are at risk of becoming offenders;

(g) to make grants, with the approval of the Secretary of State, to local authorities or other bodies for them to develop such practice, or to commission research in connection with such practice; and

(h) themselves to commission research in connection with such practice.

(6) The Secretary of State may by order—

(a) amend subsection (5) above so as to add to, subtract from or alter any of the functions of the Board for the time being specified in that subsection; or

(b) provide that any function of his which is exercisable in relation to the youth justice system shall be exercisable concurrently with the Board.

(7) In carrying out their functions, the Board shall comply with any directions given by the Secretary of State and act in accordance with any guidance given by him.

(8) A relevant authority—

(a) shall furnish to the Board any information required for the purposes of subsection (5)(a), (b) or (c) above; and

(b) whenever so required by the Board, shall submit to the Board a report on such matters connected with the discharge of their duties under the foregoing provisions of this Part as may be specified in the requirement.

A requirement under paragraph (b) above may specify the form in which a report is to be given.

(9) The Board may arrange, or require the relevant authority to arrange, for a report under subsection (8)(b) above to be published in such manner as appears to the Board to be appropriate.

(10) In this section 'relevant authority' means a local authority, a chief officer of police, a police authority, a probation committee and a health authority.

(11) Schedule 2 to this Act (which makes further provision with respect to the Board) shall have effect.

Explanatory text—See paras **2.22–2.23**.

Local authority (subs (10))—See s 42.

Chief officer of police; police authority (subs (10))—See s 42 and annotations to s 18.

---

42 Supplementary provisions

(1) In the foregoing provisions of this Part and this section—
'chief officer of police' has the meaning given by section 101(1) of the Police Act 1996;
'local authority' means—

(a) in relation to England, a county council, a district council whose district does not form part of an area that has a county council, a London borough council or the Common Council of the City of London;
(b) in relation to Wales, a county council or a county borough council;

'police authority' has the meaning given by section 101(1) of the Police Act 1996;
'youth justice system' means the system of criminal justice in so far as it relates to children and young persons.

(2) For the purposes of those provisions, the Isles of Scilly form part of the county of Cornwall and the Inner Temple and the Middle Temple form part of the City of London.

(3) In carrying out any of their duties under those provisions, a local authority, a police authority, a probation committee or a health authority shall act in accordance with any guidance given by the Secretary of State.

Explanatory text—See, generally, paras **2.22–2.23**.

Chief officer of police (subs (1))—See annotations to s 18.

'Police authority' (subss (1) and (3))—See annotations to s 18.

Time limits etc.

43 Time limits

(1) In subsection (2) of section 22 (time limits in relation to criminal proceedings) of the Prosecution of Offences Act 1985 ('the 1985 Act'), for paragraphs (a) and (b) there shall be substituted the following paragraphs—

'(a) be made so as to apply only in relation to proceedings instituted in specified areas, or proceedings of, or against persons of, specified classes or descriptions;
(b) make different provision with respect to proceedings instituted in different areas, or different provision with respect to proceedings of, or against persons of, different classes or descriptions;'.

(2) For subsection (3) of that section there shall be substituted the following subsection—

'(3) The appropriate court may, at any time before the expiry of a time limit imposed by the regulations, extend, or further extend, that limit; but the court shall not do so unless it is satisfied—

   (a)   that the need for the extension is due to—
         (i)   the illness or absence of the accused, a necessary witness, a judge or a
                magistrate;
         (ii)   a postponement which is occasioned by the ordering by the court of
                separate trials in the case of two or more accused or two or more
                offences; or
         (iii) some other good and sufficient cause; and
   (b)   that the prosecution has acted with all due diligence and expedition.'

(3) In subsection (4) of that section, for the words from 'the accused' to the end there
shall be substituted the words 'the appropriate court shall stay the proceedings'.

(4) In subsection (6) of that section—

   (a)   for the word 'Where' there shall be substituted the words 'Subsection (6A) below
         applies where'; and
   (b)   for the words from 'the overall time limit' to the end there shall be substituted the
         words 'and is accordingly unlawfully at large for any period.'

(5) After that subsection there shall be inserted the following subsection—

   '(6A) The following, namely—

   (a)   the period for which the person is unlawfully at large; and
   (b)   such additional period (if any) as the appropriate court may direct, having
         regard to the disruption of the prosecution occasioned by—
         (i)   the person's escape or failure to surrender; and
         (ii)   the length of the period mentioned in paragraph (a) above,

   shall be disregarded, so far as the offence in question is concerned, for the purposes
   of the overall time limit which applies in his case in relation to the stage which the
   proceedings have reached at the time of the escape or, as the case may be, at the
   appointed time.'

(6) In subsection (7) of that section, after the words 'time limit,' there shall be inserted
the words 'or to give a direction under subsection (6A) above,'.

(7) In subsection (8) of that section, after the words 'time limit' there shall be inserted
the words ', or to give a direction under subsection (6A) above,'.

(8) After subsection (11) of that section there shall be inserted the following
subsection—

   '(11ZA) For the purposes of this section, proceedings for an offence shall be taken
   to begin when the accused is charged with the offence or, as the case may be, an
   information is laid charging him with the offence.'

Explanatory text—See paras **6.95–6.102**.

Section 22 of the Prosecution of Offences Act 1985—As amended by the above subsections,
provides as follows (the amendments are italicised):

   '(1) The Secretary of State may by regulations make provision, with respect to any specified
   preliminary stage of proceedings for an offence, as to the maximum period:

   (a)   to be allowed to the prosecution to complete that stage;
   (b)   during which the accused may, while awaiting completion of that stage, be—

(i)   in the custody of a magistrates' court; or
(ii) in the custody of the Crown Court,

in relation to that offence.

(2) The regulations may, in particular—

(a)   *be made so as to apply only in relation to proceedings instituted in specified areas, or proceedings of, or against persons of, specified classes or descriptions;*

(b)   *make different provision with respect to proceedings instituted in different areas, or different provision with respect to proceedings of, or against persons of, different classes or descriptions;*

(c)   make such provision with respect to the procedure to be followed in criminal proceedings as the Secretary of State considers appropriate in consequence of any other provision of the regulations;

(d)   provide for the Magistrates' Courts Act 1980 and the Bail Act 1976 to apply in relation to cases to which custody or overall time limits apply subject to such modifications as may be specified (being modifications which the Secretary of State considers necessary in consequence of any provision made by the regulations); and

(e)   make such transitional provision in relation to proceedings instituted before the commencement of any provision of the regulations as the Secretary of State considers appropriate.

(3) The appropriate court may, at any time before the expiry of a time limit imposed by the regulations, extend, or further extend, that limit; but the court shall not do so unless it is satisfied—

(a)   *that the need for the extension is due to—*
  (i)   *the illness or absence of the accused, a necessary witness, a judge or a magistrate;*
  (ii) *a postponement which is occasioned by the ordering by the court of separate trials in the case of two or more accused or two or more offences; or*
  (iii) *some other good and sufficient cause; and*
(b)   *that the prosecution has acted with all due diligence and expedition.*

(4) Where, in relation to any proceedings for an offence, an overall time limit has expired before the completion of the stage of the proceedings to which the limit applies, the *appropriate court shall stay the proceedings.*

(5) Where—

(a)   a person escapes from the custody of a magistrates' court or the Crown Court before the expiry of a custody time limit which applies in his case; or

(b)   a person who has been released on bail in consequence of the expiry of a custody time limit—
  (i)   fails to surrender himself into the custody of the court at the appointed time; or
  (ii) is arrested by a constable on a ground mentioned in section 7(3)(b) of the Bail Act 1976 (breach, or likely breach, of conditions of bail);
  the regulations shall, so far as they provide for any custody time limit in relation to the preliminary stage in question, be disregarded.

(6) Subsection (6A) below applies where—

(a)   a person escapes from the custody of a magistrates' court or the Crown Court; or

(b)   a person who has been released on bail fails to surrender himself into the custody of the court at the appointed time;

and is accordingly unlawfully at large for any period.

(6A) The following, namely—

(a)   *the period for which the person is unlawfully at large; and*

(b)   *such additional period (if any) as the appropriate court may direct, having regard to the disruption of the prosecution occasioned by—*
  (i)   *the person's escape or failure to surrender; and*

(ii) the length of the period mentioned in paragraph (a) above,
shall be disregarded, so far as the offence in question is concerned, for the purposes of the overall time limit which applies in his case in relation to the stage which the proceedings have reached at the time of the escape or, as the case may be, at the appointed time.

(7) Where a magistrates' court decides to extend, or further extend, a custody or overall time limit, *or to give a direction under subsection (6A) above,* the accused may appeal against the decision to the Crown Court.

(8) Where a magistrates' court refuses to extend a custody or overall time limit, *or to give a direction under subsection (6A) above,* the prosecution may appeal against the refusal to the Crown Court.

(9) An appeal under subsection (8) above may not be commenced after the expiry of the limit in question; but where such an appeal is commenced before the expiry of the limit the limit shall be deemed not to have expired before the determination or abandonment of the appeal.

(10) Where a person is convicted of an offence in any proceedings, the exercise, in relation to any preliminary stage of those proceedings, of the power conferred by subsection (3) above shall not be called into question in any appeal against that conviction.

(11) In this section—

"appropriate court" means—

    (a)   where the accused has been committed for trial or indicted for the offence, the Crown Court; and

    (b)   in any other case, the magistrates' court specified in the summons or warrant in question or, where the accused has already appeared or been brought before a magistrates' court, a magistrates' court for the same area;

"custody" includes local authority accommodation to which a person is remanded or committed by virtue of section 23 of the Children and Young Persons Act 1969, and references to a person being committed to custody shall be construed accordingly;

"custody of the Crown Court" includes custody to which a person is committed in pursuance of—

    (a)   section 6 of the Magistrates' Courts Act 1980 (magistrates' court committing accused for trial); or

    (b)   section 43A of that Act (magistrates' court dealing with a person brought before it following his arrest in pursuance of a warrant issued by the Crown Court); or

    (c)   section 5(3)(a) of the Criminal Justice Act 1987 (custody after transfer order in fraud case); or

    (d)   paragraph 2(1)(a) of Schedule 6 to the Criminal Justice Act 1991 (custody after transfer order in certain cases involving children);

"custody of a magistrates' court" means custody to which a person is committed in pursuance of section 128 of the Magistrates' Courts Act 1980 (remand);

"custody time limit" means a time limit imposed by regulations made under subsection (1)(b) above or, where any such limit has been extended by a court under subsection (3) above, the limit as so extended;

"preliminary stage" in relation to any proceedings does not include any stage after the start of the trial (within the meaning given by subsections (11A) and (11B) below);

"overall time limit" means a time limit imposed by regulations made under subsection (1)(a) above or, where any such limit has been extended by a court under subsection (3) above, the limit as so extended; and

"specified" means specified in the regulations.

(11ZA) For the purposes of this section, proceedings for an offence shall be taken to begin when the accused is charged with the offence or, as the case may be, an information is laid charging him with the offence.

(11A) For the purposes of this section, the start of a trial on indictment shall be taken to occur when a jury is sworn to consider the issue of guilt or fitness to plead or, if the court accepts a plea of guilty before a jury is sworn, when that plea is accepted; but this is subject to section 8 of the Criminal Justice Act 1987 and section 30 of the Criminal Procedure and Investigations Act 1996 (preparatory hearings).

(11B) For the purposes of this section, the start of a summary trial shall be taken to occur—

    (a)   when the court begins to hear evidence for the prosecution at the trial or to consider whether to exercise its power under section 37(3) of the Mental Health Act 1983 (power to make hospital order without convicting the accused), or

    (b)   if the court accepts a plea of guilty without proceeding as mentioned above, when that plea is accepted.

(12) For the purposes of the application of any custody time limit in relation to a person who is in the custody of a magistrates' court or the Crown Court—

    (a)   all periods during which he is in the custody of a magistrates' court in respect of the same offence shall be aggregated and treated as a single continuous period; and

    (b)   all periods during which he is in the custody of the Crown Court in respect of the same offence shall be aggregated and treated similarly.

(13) For the purposes of section 29(3) of the Supreme Court Act 1981 (High Court to have power to make prerogative orders in relation to jurisdiction of Crown Court in matters which do not relate to trial on indictment) the jurisdiction conferred on the Crown Court by this section shall be taken to be part of its jurisdiction in matters other than those relating to trial on indictment.'

The current regulations made under the 1985 Act, s 22(1)(b), are the Prosecution of Offences (Custody Time limits) Regulations 1987, SI 1987/299. Their principal provisions are:

'2—(1) In these Regulations—

"the 1980 Act" means the Magistrates' Courts Act 1980;

"the 1985 Act" means the Prosecution of Offences Act 1985.

(2) In these Regulations, a reference to a person's first appearance in relation to proceedings in a magistrates' court for an offence is—

    (a)   in a case where that person has made an application under section 43B of the 1980 Act, a reference to the time when he appears before the court on the hearing of that application;

    (b)   in a case where that person appears or is brought before the court in pursuance of section 5B of the Bail Act 1976 and the decision which is to be, or has been, reconsidered under that section is the decision of a constable, a reference to the time when he so appears or is brought; and

    (c)   in any other case, a reference to the time when first he appears or is brought before the court on an information charging him with that offence.

(3) In these Regulations any reference to the start of the trial shall be construed in accordance with section 22(11A) and (11B) of the 1985 Act.

(4) Any maximum period set by these Regulations during which a person may be in the custody of a court does not include the day on which the custody commenced.

(5) A custody time limit which would, apart from this paragraph, expire on any of the days to which this paragraph applies shall be treated as expiring on the next preceding day which is not one of those days.

The days to which this paragraph applies are Saturday, Sunday, Christmas Day, Good Friday and any day which under the Banking and Financial Dealings Act 1971 is a bank holiday in England and Wales.

4 Custody time limits in magistrates' courts

(1) ... the maximum period during which a person accused of an indictable offence other than treason may be in the custody of a magistrates' court in relation to that offence while awaiting

completion of any preliminary stage of the proceedings specified in the following provisions of this Regulation shall be as stated in those provisions.

(2) Except as provided in paragraph (3) below, in the case of an offence triable either way the maximum period of custody between the accused's first appearance and the start of summary trial or, as the case may be, the time when the court decides whether or not to commit the accused to the Crown Court for trial shall be 70 days ...

(3) In the case of an offence triable either way if, before the expiry of 56 days following the day of the accused's first appearance, the court decides to proceed to summary trial in pursuance of sections 19 to 24 of the 1980 Act the maximum period of custody between the accused's first appearance and the start of the summary trial shall be 56 days.

(4) In the case of an offence triable on indictment exclusively the maximum period of custody between the accused's first appearance and the time when the court decides whether or not to commit the accused to the Crown Court for trial, shall be 70 days ...

(5) The foregoing provisions of this regulation shall have effect as if any reference therein to the time when the court decides whether or not to commit the accused to the Crown Court for trial were a reference—

    (a)   where a court proceeds to inquire into an information as examining justices in pursuance of section 6(1) of the 1980 Act, to the time when it begins to hear evidence for the prosecution at the inquiry;

    (b)   where a notice has been given under section 4(1)(c) of the Criminal Justice Act 1987 (in these Regulations referred to as a "notice of transfer"), to the date on which notice of transfer was given.

5 Custody time limits in the Crown Court

(1) [Revoked]

(2) Where—

    (a)   a person accused of an indictable offence other than treason is committed to the Crown Court for trial; or

    (b)   a bill of indictment is preferred against a person under section 2(2)(b) of the Administration of Justice (Miscellaneous Provisions) Act 1933,

the maximum period during which he may be in the custody of the Crown Court in relation to that offence, or any other offence included in the indictment preferred against him, while awaiting the preliminary stage of the proceedings specified in the following provisions of this Regulation shall be as stated in those provisions.

(3) The maximum period of custody—

    (a)   between the time when the accused is committed for trial and the start of the trial; or

    (b)   where a bill of indictment is preferred against him under the said section 2(2)(b), between the preferment of the bill and the start of the trial,

shall, subject to the following provisions of this Regulation, be 112 days.

(4) Where, following a committal for trial, the bill of indictment preferred against the accused (not being a bill preferred under the said section 2(2)(b)) contains a count charging an offence for which he was committed for trial at that committal together with a count charging an offence for which he was committed for trial on a different occasion, paragraph (3) above applies in relation to each offence separately.

   ...

(6A) The foregoing provisions of this regulation shall have effect, where notice of transfer is given in respect of a case, as if references to committal for trial and to offences for which a person was or was not committed for trial included references to the giving of notice of transfer and to charges contained or not contained in the notice of transfer.'

44 Additional time limits for persons under 18

After section 22 of the 1985 Act there shall be inserted the following section—

'22A Additional time limits for persons under 18

(1) The Secretary of State may by regulations make provision—

(a) with respect to a person under the age of 18 at the time of his arrest in connection with an offence, as to the maximum period to be allowed for the completion of the stage beginning with his arrest and ending with the date fixed for his first appearance in court in connection with the offence ("the initial stage");

(b) with respect to a person convicted of an offence who was under that age at the time of his arrest for the offence or (where he was not arrested for it) the laying of the information charging him with it, as to the period within which the stage between his conviction and his being sentenced for the offence should be completed.

(2) Subsection (2) of section 22 above applies for the purposes of regulations under subsection (1) above as if—

(a) the reference in paragraph (d) to custody or overall time limits were a reference to time limits imposed by the regulations; and

(b) the reference in paragraph (e) to proceedings instituted before the commencement of any provisions of the regulations were a reference to a stage begun before that commencement.

(3) A magistrates' court may, at any time before the expiry of the time limit imposed by the regulations under subsection (1)(a) above ("the initial stage time limit"), extend, or further extend, that limit; but the court shall not do so unless it is satisfied—

(a) that the need for the extension is due to some good and sufficient cause; and

(b) that the investigation has been conducted, and (where applicable) the prosecution has acted, with all due diligence and expedition.

(4) Where the initial stage time limit (whether as originally imposed or as extended or further extended under subsection (3) above) expires before the person arrested is charged with the offence, he shall not be charged with it unless further evidence relating to it is obtained, and—

(a) if he is then under arrest, he shall be released;

(b) if he is then on bail under Part IV of the Police and Criminal Evidence Act 1984, his bail (and any duty or conditions to which it is subject) shall be discharged.

(5) Where the initial stage time limit (whether as originally imposed or as extended or further extended under subsection (3) above) expires after the person arrested is charged with the offence but before the date fixed for his first appearance in court in connection with it, the court shall stay the proceedings.

(6) Where—

(a) a person escapes from arrest; or

(b) a person who has been released on bail under Part IV of the Police and Criminal Evidence Act 1984 fails to surrender himself at the appointed time,

and is accordingly unlawfully at large for any period, that period shall be disregarded, so far as the offence in question is concerned, for the purposes of the initial stage time limit.

(7) Subsections (7) to (9) of section 22 above apply for the purposes of this section, at any time after the person arrested has been charged with the offence in question, as if any reference (however expressed) to a custody or overall time limit were a reference to the initial stage time limit.

(8) Where a person is convicted of an offence in any proceedings, the exercise of the power conferred by subsection (3) above shall not be called into question in any appeal against that conviction.

(9) Any reference in this section (however expressed) to a person being charged with an offence includes a reference to the laying of an information charging him with it.'

Explanatory text—See paras **6.95, 6.103–6.113**.

1985 Act—Ie the Prosecution of Offences Act 1985.

Under the age of 18 (1985 Act, s 22A(1))—See general annotations.

1985 Act, s 22A(2)—Section 22(2) is set out in the annotations to s 43.

Bail under Part IV of the Police and Criminal Evidence Act 1984 (1985 Act, s 22A(4) and (6))—Ie release on police bail of a person who has been arrested.

---

45 Re-institution of stayed proceedings

After section 22A of the 1985 Act there shall be inserted the following section—

'22B Re-institution of proceedings stayed under section 22(4) or 22A(5)

(1) This section applies where proceedings for an offence ("the original proceedings") are stayed by a court under section 22(4) or 22A(5) of this Act.

(2) If—

(a) in the case of proceedings conducted by the Director, the Director or a Chief Crown Prosecutor so directs;

(b) in the case of proceedings conducted by the Director of the Serious Fraud Office, the Commissioners of Inland Revenue or the Commissioners of Customs and Excise, that Director or those Commissioners so direct; or

(c) in the case of proceedings not conducted as mentioned in paragraph (a) or (b) above, a person designated for the purpose by the Secretary of State so directs,

fresh proceedings for the offence may be instituted within a period of three months (or such longer period as the court may allow) after the date on which the original proceedings were stayed by the court.

(3) Fresh proceedings shall be instituted as follows—

(a) where the original proceedings were stayed by the Crown Court, by preferring a bill of indictment;

(b) where the original proceedings were stayed by a magistrates' court, by laying an information.

(4) Fresh proceedings may be instituted in accordance with subsections (2) and (3)(b) above notwithstanding anything in section 127(1) of the Magistrates' Courts Act 1980 (limitation of time).

(5) Where fresh proceedings are instituted, anything done in relation to the original proceedings shall be treated as done in relation to the fresh proceedings if the court so directs or it was done—

(a) by the prosecutor in compliance or purported compliance with section 3, 4, 7 or 9 of the Criminal Procedure and Investigations Act 1996; or

(b) by the accused in compliance or purported compliance with section 5 or 6 of that Act.

(6) Where a person is convicted of an offence in fresh proceedings under this section, the institution of those proceedings shall not be called into question in any appeal against that conviction.'

Explanatory text—See paras **6.114–6.118**.

The Director (Prosecution of Offences Act 1985, s 22B(2))—Ie the Director of Public Prosecutions, the head of the Crown Prosecution Service (1985 Act, s 1(1)(a)).

A Chief Crown Prosecutor (Prosecution of Offences Act 1985, s 22B(2))—Ie the Chief Crown Prosecutors, designated by the Director under the 1985 Act, s 1(4), for each area of England and Wales into which the Crown Prosecution Service has been divided by the Director under the 1985 Act, s 1(4).

Three months (Prosecution of Offences Act 1985, s 22B(2))—See general annotations.

Notwithstanding anything in section 127(1) of the Magistrates' Courts Act 1980 (Prosecution of Offences Act 1985, s 22B(4))—Section 127(1) and (2) provides:

'(1) Except as otherwise expressly provided by any enactment and subject to subsection (2) below, a magistrates' court shall not try an information or hear a complaint unless the information was laid, or the complaint made, within 6 months from the time when the offence was committed, or the matter of complaint arose.

(2) Nothing in—

(a) subsection (1) above; or

(b) subject to subsection (4) below, any other enactment (however framed or worded) which, as regards any offence to which it applies, would but for this section impose a time-limit on the power of a magistrates' court to try an information summarily or impose a limitation on the time for taking summary proceedings,

shall apply in relation to any indictable offence.'

---

46 Date of first court appearance in bail cases

(1) In subsection (3) of section 47 of the 1984 Act (bail after arrest), for the words 'subsection (4)' there shall be substituted the words 'subsections (3A) and (4)'.

(2) After that subsection there shall be inserted the following subsection—

'(3A) Where a custody officer grants bail to a person subject to a duty to appear before a magistrates' court, he shall appoint for the appearance—

(a) a date which is not later than the first sitting of the court after the person is charged with the offence; or

(b) where he is informed by the clerk to the justices for the relevant petty sessions area that the appearance cannot be accommodated until a later date, that later date.'

Explanatory text—See para **9.24**.

1984 Act (subs (1))—Ie the Police and Criminal Evidence Act 1984. Section 47 of that Act, as amended (in italics) by the present provision, provides:

'(1) Subject to subsection (2) below, a release on bail of a person under this Part of this Act shall be a release on bail granted in accordance with sections 3, 3A, 5 and 5A of the Bail Act 1976 as they apply to bail granted by a constable.

(1A) The normal powers to impose conditions of bail shall be available to him where a custody officer releases a person on bail under section 38(1) above (including that subsection as applied by section 40(10) above) but not in any other cases.

In this subsection, "the normal powers to impose conditions of bail" has the meaning given in section 3(6) of the Bail Act 1976.

(2) Nothing in the Bail Act 1976 shall prevent the re-arrest without warrant of a person released on bail subject to a duty to attend at a police station if new evidence justifying a further arrest has come to light since his release.

(3) Subject to subsection*s (3A) and* (4) below, in this Part of this Act references to "bail" are references to bail subject to a duty—

(a) to appear before a magistrates' court at such time and such place; or

(b) to attend at such police station at such time,

as the custody officer may appoint.

(3A) Where a custody officer grants bail to a person subject to a duty to appear before a magistrates' court, he shall appoint for the appearance—

(a) a date which is not later than the first sitting of the court after the person is charged with the offence; or

(b) where he is informed by the clerk to the justices for the relevant petty sessions area that the appearance cannot be accommodated until a later date, that later date.

(4) Where a custody officer has granted bail to a person subject to a duty to appear at a police station, the custody officer may give notice in writing to that person that his attendance at the police station is not required.

...

(6) Where a person who has been granted bail and either has attended at the police station in accordance with the grant of bail or has been arrested under section 46A above is detained at a police station, any time during which he was in police detention prior to being granted bail shall be included as part of any period which falls to be calculated under this Part of this Act.

(7) Where a person who was released on bail subject to a duty to attend at a police station is re-arrested, the provisions of this Part of this Act shall apply to him as they apply to a person arrested for the first time; but this subsection does not apply to a person who is arrested under section 46A above or has attended a police station in accordance with the grant of bail (and who accordingly is deemed by section 34(7) above to have been arrested for an offence).'

47 Powers of youth courts

(1) Where a person who appears or is brought before a youth court charged with an offence subsequently attains the age of 18, the youth court may, at any time—

   (a) before the start of the trial; or
   (b) after conviction and before sentence,

remit the person for trial or, as the case may be, for sentence to a magistrates' court (other than a youth court) acting for the same petty sessions area as the youth court.

In this subsection 'the start of the trial' shall be construed in accordance with section 22(11B) of the 1985 Act.

(2) Where a person is remitted under subsection (1) above—

   (a) he shall have no right of appeal against the order of remission;
   (b) the remitting court shall adjourn proceedings in relation to the offence; and
   (c) subsections (3) and (4) below shall apply.

(3) The following, namely—

   (a) section 128 of the 1980 Act; and
   (b) all other enactments (whenever passed) relating to remand or the granting of bail in criminal proceedings,

shall have effect in relation to the remitting court's power or duty to remand the person on the adjournment as if any reference to the court to or before which the person remanded is to be brought or appear after remand were a reference to the court to which he is being remitted ('the other court').

(4) The other court may deal with the case in any way in which it would have power to deal with it if all proceedings relating to the offence which took place before the remitting court had taken place before the other court.

(5) After subsection (3) of section 10 of the 1980 Act (adjournment of trial) there shall be inserted the following subsection—

   '(3A) A youth court shall not be required to adjourn any proceedings for an offence at any stage by reason only of the fact—

   (a) that the court commits the accused for trial for another offence; or
   (b) that the accused is charged with another offence.'

(6) After subsection (1) of section 24 of the 1980 Act (summary trial of information against child or young person for indictable offence) there shall be inserted the following subsection—

   '(1A) Where a magistrates' court—

   (a) commits a person under the age of 18 for trial for an offence of homicide; or
   (b) in a case falling within subsection (1) (a) above, commits such a person for trial for an offence,

the court may also commit him for trial for any other indictable offence with which
he is charged at the same time if the charges for both offences could be joined in
the same indictment.'

(7) In subsection (2) of section 47 (procedure in youth courts) of the Children and
Young Persons Act 1933 ('the 1933 Act'), the words from the beginning to 'court; and'
shall cease to have effect.

Explanatory text—See paras **6.87–6.89, 6.91–6.93**.

Age of 18 (subs (1))—See general annotations.

Youth court (subs (1))—By the Children and Young Persons Act 1933, s 45, these are courts of
summary jurisdiction, with the result that trial in them is merely a form of summary trial (ie trial is
not trial on indictment with a jury as it is in the Crown Court). Whereas an adult may never be tried
summarily for an offence triable only on indictment and, if he intends to plead not guilty, always has
the right to elect trial on indictment for an offence triable either way (according to the law as it was
when this book went to press), a person under 18, may be, and normally is, tried summarily for such
offences in the youth court, whatever his wishes as to the mode of trial.

Petty sessions area (subs (1))—See general annotations.

**'Start of the trial' shall be construed in accordance with section 22(11B) of the 1985 Act
(subs (1))**—Ie the Prosecution of Offences Act 1985 (s 117(1)). Section 22(11B) is set out in the
annotations to s 43.

Subs (3)—The 1980 Act means the Magistrates' Courts Act 1980 (s 117(1)). Section 128 of that Act
governs the periods for which a person may be remanded in custody prior to committal
proceedings or summary trial: see also the 1980 Act, s 128A. As to 'bail in criminal proceedings' see
the annotations to s 53.

Section 10 of the 1980 Act (subs (2))—Ie the Magistrates' Courts Act 1980 (s 117(1)). Section 10 of
that Act, as amended (in italics), provides:

'(1) A magistrates' court may at any time, whether before or after beginning to try an
information, adjourn the trial, and may do so, notwithstanding anything in this Act, when
composed of a single justice.

(2) The court may when adjourning either fix the time and place at which the trial is to be
resumed, or, unless it remands the accused, leave the time and place to be determined later by
the court; but the trial shall not be resumed at that time and place unless the court is satisfied that
the parties have had adequate notice thereof.

(3) A magistrates' court may, for the purpose of enabling inquiries to be made or of determining
the most suitable method of dealing with the case, exercise its power to adjourn after convicting
the accused and before sentencing him or otherwise dealing with him; but, if it does so, the
adjournment shall not be for more than 4 weeks at a time unless the court remands the accused
in custody and, where it so remands him, the adjournment shall not be for more than 3 weeks at a
time.

*(3A) A youth court shall not be required to adjourn any proceedings for an offence at any stage by reason only
of the fact—*

    (a)   that the court commits the accused for trial for another offence; or
    (b)   that the accused is charged with another offence.

(4) On adjourning the trial of an information the court may remand the accused and, where the
accused has attained the age of 18, shall do so if the offence is triable either way and—

    (a)   on the occasion on which the accused first appeared, or was brought before the court to
        answer to the information he was in custody or, having been released on bail,
        surrendered to the custody of the court; or

(b)   the accused has been remanded at any time in the course of proceedings on the information;

and, where the court remands the accused, the time fixed for the resumption of the trial shall be that at which he is required to appear or be brought before the court in pursuance of the remand or would be required to be brought before the court but for section 128(3A) below.'

Section 24 of the 1980 Act (subs (6))—Section 24, as amended (in italics) by subs (3) and by Sch 8, para 40, provides:

'(1) Where a person under the age of 18 appears or is brought before a magistrates' court on an information charging him with an indictable offence other than homicide, he shall be tried summarily unless—

(a)   the offence is such as is mentioned in subsection (2) of section 53 of the Children and Young Persons Act 1933 (under which young persons convicted on indictment of certain grave crimes may be sentenced to be detained for long periods) and the court considers that if he is found guilty of the offence it ought to be possible to sentence him in pursuance of *subsection (3) of that section*; or

(b)   he is charged jointly with a person who has attained the age of 18 and the court considers it necessary in the interests of justice to commit them both for trial;

and accordingly in a case falling within paragraph (a) or (b) of this subsection the court shall commit the accused for trial if either it is of opinion that there is sufficient evidence to put him on trial or it has power under section 6(2) above so to commit him without consideration of the evidence.

(1A) Where a magistrates' court—

(a)   *commits a person under the age of 18 for trial for an offence of homicide; or*

(b)   *in a case falling within subsection (1)(a) above, commits such a person for trial for an offence,*

the court may also commit him for trial for any other indictable offence with which he is charged at the same time if the charges for both offences could be joined in the same indictment.

(2) Where, in a case falling within subsection (1)(b) above, a magistrates' court commits a person under the age of 18 for trial for an offence with which he is charged jointly with a person who has attained that age, the court may also commit him for trial for any other indictable offence with which he is charged at the same time (whether jointly with the person who has attained that age or not) if *the charges for both offences could be joined in the same indictment.*

(3) If on trying a person summarily in pursuance of subsection (1) above the court finds him guilty, it may impose a fine of an amount not exceeding £1,000 or may exercise the same powers as it could have exercised if he had been found guilty of an offence for which, but for section 1 (1) of the Criminal Justice Act 1982, it could have sentenced him to imprisonment for a term not exceeding—

(a)   the maximum term of imprisonment for the offence on conviction on indictment; or

(b)   six months,

whichever is the less.

(4) In relation to a person under the age of 14 subsection (3) above shall have effect as if for the words "£1,000" there were substituted the words "£250".'

The Children and Young Persons Act 1933, s 53(2), is described in para **6.71**.

Section 47 of the Children and Young Persons Act 1933 (subs (7))—As amended this provides:

'(1) Youth courts shall sit as often as may be necessary for the purposes of exercising any jurisdiction conferred on them by or under this or any other Act.

(2) No person shall be present at any sitting of a youth court except—

(a)   members and officers of the court;

(b)   parties to the case before the court, their solicitors and counsel, and witnesses and other persons directly concerned in that case;

    (c)   bona fide representatives of newspapers or news agencies;

    (d)   such other persons as the court may specially authorise to be present.'

48 Youth courts: power of stipendiary magistrates to sit alone

(1) In paragraph 15 of Schedule 2 to the 1933 Act (constitution of youth courts)—

    (a)   in paragraph (a), after the word 'shall', in the first place where it occurs, there shall be inserted the words 'either consist of a metropolitan stipendiary magistrate sitting alone or' and the word 'shall', in the other place where it occurs, shall cease to have effect;

    (b)   in paragraph (b), after the words 'the chairman' there shall be inserted the words '(where applicable)'; and

    (c)   in paragraph (c), after the words 'the other members' there shall be inserted the words '(where applicable)'.

(2) In paragraph 17 of that Schedule, the words 'or, if a metropolitan stipendiary magistrate, may sit alone' shall cease to have effect.

Explanatory text—See para **6.90**.

Paragraphs 15 and 17 of Schedule 2 to the 1933 Act (subss (1) and (2))—'The 1933 Act' means the Children and Young Persons Act 1933 (s 117(1)). As amended (the amendments are italicised), para 15 of Sch 2 to the 1933 Act provides:

'Subject to the following provisions of this Schedule—

    (a)   each youth court shall *either consist of a metropolitan stipendiary magistrate sitting alone or* consist of a chairman and two other members and ... have both a man and a woman among its members;

    (b)   the chairman *(where applicable)* shall be a person nominated by the Lord Chancellor to act as chairman of youth courts for the metropolitan area and shall be either a metropolitan stipendiary magistrate or a lay justice for the inner London area selected, in such manner as may be provided by an order of the Lord Chancellor, from a panel of such justices from time to time nominated by him; and

    (c)   the other members *(where applicable)* shall be justices so selected from that panel.'

As amended, para 17 of Sch 2 provides:

'Where it appears to the chairman that a youth court cannot, without adjournment, be fully constituted, and that an adjournment would not be in the interests of justice, the chairman may sit with one other member (whether a man or a woman).'

49 Powers of magistrates' courts exercisable by single justice etc.

(1) The following powers of a magistrates' court for any area may be exercised by a single justice of the peace for that area, namely—

    (a)   to extend bail or to impose or vary conditions of bail;

    (b)   to mark an information as withdrawn;

    (c)   to dismiss an information, or to discharge an accused in respect of an information, where no evidence is offered by the prosecution;

    (d)   to make an order for the payment of defence costs out of central funds;

    (e)   to request a pre-sentence report following a plea of guilty and, for that purpose, to give an indication of the seriousness of the offence;

    (f)   to request a medical report and, for that purpose, to remand the accused in custody or on bail;

   (g) to remit an offender to another court for sentence;

   (h) where a person has been granted police bail to appear at a magistrates' court, to appoint an earlier time for his appearance;

   (i) to extend, with the consent of the accused, a custody time limit or an overall time limit;

   (j) where a case is to be tried on indictment, to grant representation under Part V of the Legal Aid Act 1988 for purposes of the proceedings in the Crown Court;

   (k) where an accused has been convicted of an offence, to order him to produce his driving licence;

   (l) to give a direction prohibiting the publication of matters disclosed or exempted from disclosure in court;

   (m) to give, vary or revoke directions for the conduct of a trial, including directions as to the following matters, namely—

       (i) the timetable for the proceedings;

      (ii) the attendance of the parties;

     (iii) the service of documents (including summaries of any legal arguments relied on by the parties);

     (iv) the manner in which evidence is to be given; and

   (n) to give, vary or revoke orders for separate or joint trials in the case of two or more accused or two or more informations.

(2) Without prejudice to the generality of subsection (1) of section 144 of the 1980 Act (rules of procedure)—

   (a) rules under that section may, subject to subsection (3) below, provide that any of the things which, by virtue of subsection (1) above, are authorised to be done by a single justice of the peace for any area may, subject to any specified restrictions or conditions, be done by a justices' clerk for that area; and

   (b) rules under that section which make such provision as is mentioned in paragraph (a) above may make different provision for different areas.

(3) Rules under that section which make such provision as is mentioned in subsection (2) above shall not authorise a justices' clerk—

   (a) without the consent of the prosecutor and the accused, to extend bail on conditions other than those (if any) previously imposed, or to impose or vary conditions of bail;

   (b) to give an indication of the seriousness of an offence for the purposes of a pre-sentence report;

   (c) to remand the accused in custody for the purposes of a medical report or, without the consent of the prosecutor and the accused, to remand the accused on bail for those purposes on conditions other than those (if any) previously imposed;

   (d) to give a direction prohibiting the publication of matters disclosed or exempted from disclosure in court; or

   (e) without the consent of the parties, to give, vary or revoke orders for separate or joint trials in the case of two or more accused or two or more informations.

(4) Before making any rules under that section which make such provision as is mentioned in subsection (2) above in relation to any area, the Lord Chancellor shall consult justices of the peace and justices' clerks for that area.

(5) In this section and section 50 below 'justices' clerk' has the same meaning as in section 144 of the 1980 Act.

Explanatory text—See paras **6.11**, **6.14–6.23**.

Justice of the peace for that area (subss (1), (2) and (4))—Ie a Justice of the Peace for the petty sessions area in question (see Justices of the Peace Act 1997, especially s 6). As to petty sessions areas, see general annotations.

Subsection (1) of section 144 of the 1980 Act (subs (2))—'The 1980 Act' means the Magistrates' Courts Act 1980 (s 117(1)). The 1980 Act, s 144(1) provides:

'The Lord Chancellor may appoint a rule committee for magistrates' courts, and may on the advice of or after consultation with the rule committee make rules for regulating and prescribing the procedure and practice to be followed in magistrates' courts and by justices' clerks.'

'Justices' clerk' has the same meaning as in section 144 of the1980 Act (subs (5))—Ie a clerk to the justices for a petty sessional area (1980 Act, s 144(5)). As to petty sessions area, see general annotations. By the Justices of the Peace Act 1997, s 43, no person may be appointed as justices' clerk unless either:

(a)   at the time of appointment:
   (i)   he has a 5-year magistrates' courts qualification (within the meaning of the Courts and Legal Services Act 1990, s 71); or
   (ii) he is a barrister or solicitor and has served for not less than five years as assistant to a justices' clerk; or
(b)   he then is or has previously been a justices' clerk.

The Justices of the Peace Act 1997, s 45, provides, inter alia:

'(1) Rules made in accordance with section 144 of the Magistrates' Courts Act 1980 may (except to the extent that any enactment passed after this Act otherwise directs) make provision enabling things authorised to be done by, to or before a single justice of the peace to be done instead by, to or before a justices' clerk.

(2) Such rules may also make provision enabling things authorised to be done by, to or before a justices' clerk (whether by virtue of subsection (1) above or otherwise) to be done instead by, to or before a person appointed by a magistrates' courts committee to assist him.

(3) Any enactment (including any enactment contained in this Act) or any rule of law which—

(a)   regulates the exercise of any jurisdiction or powers of justices of the peace; or
(b)   relates to things done in the exercise or purported exercise of any such jurisdiction or powers,

shall apply in relation to the exercise or purported exercise of any such jurisdiction or powers by the clerk to any justices by virtue of subsection (1) above as if he were one of those justices.'

The relevant rules, the Justices' Clerks Rules 1970, made under the predecessor to the 1997 Act, continue in force.

---

50 Early administrative hearings

(1) Where a person ('the accused') has been charged with an offence at a police station, the magistrates' court before whom he appears or is brought for the first time in relation to the charge may, unless the accused falls to be dealt with under section 51 below, consist of a single justice.

(2) At a hearing conducted by a single justice under this section—

(a)   the accused shall be asked whether he wishes to receive legal aid; and
(b)   if he indicates that he does, his eligibility for it shall be determined; and
(c)   if it is determined that he is eligible for it, the necessary arrangements or grant shall be made for him to obtain it.

(3) At such a hearing the single justice—

(a) may exercise, subject to subsection (2) above, such of his powers as a single justice as he thinks fit; and

(b) on adjourning the hearing, may remand the accused in custody or on bail.

(4) This section applies in relation to a justices' clerk as it applies in relation to a single justice; but nothing in subsection (3)(b) above authorises such a clerk to remand the accused in custody or, without the consent of the prosecutor and the accused, to remand the accused on bail on conditions other than those (if any) previously imposed.

(5) In this section 'legal aid' means representation under Part V of the Legal Aid Act 1988.

Explanatory text—See paras **6.12**, **6.14** and **6.24–6.28**.

Justices' clerk (subs (4))—See s 49(5) and annotations thereto.

---

51 No committal proceedings for indictable-only offences

(1) Where an adult appears or is brought before a magistrates' court ('the court') charged with an offence triable only on indictment ('the indictable-only offence'), the court shall send him forthwith to the Crown Court for trial—

(a) for that offence, and

(b) for any either-way or summary offence with which he is charged which fulfils the requisite conditions (as set out in subsection (11) below).

(2) Where an adult who has been sent for trial under subsection (1) above subsequently appears or is brought before a magistrates' court charged with an either-way or summary offence which fulfils the requisite conditions, the court may send him forthwith to the Crown Court for trial for the either-way or summary offence.

(3) Where—

(a) the court sends an adult for trial under subsection (1) above;

(b) another adult appears or is brought before the court on the same or a subsequent occasion charged jointly with him with an either-way offence; and

(c) that offence appears to the court to be related to the indictable-only offence,

the court shall where it is the same occasion, and may where it is a subsequent occasion, send the other adult forthwith to the Crown Court for trial for the either-way offence.

(4) Where a court sends an adult for trial under subsection (3) above, it shall at the same time send him to the Crown Court for trial for any either-way or summary offence with which he is charged which fulfils the requisite conditions.

(5) Where—

(a) the court sends an adult for trial under subsection (1) or (3) above; and

(b) a child or young person appears or is brought before the court on the same or a subsequent occasion charged jointly with the adult with an indictable offence for which the adult is sent for trial,

the court shall, if it considers it necessary in the interests of justice to do so, send the child or young person forthwith to the Crown Court for trial for the indictable offence.

(6) Where a court sends a child or young person for trial under subsection (5) above, it may at the same time send him to the Crown Court for trial for any either-way or summary offence with which he is charged which fulfils the requisite conditions.

(7) The court shall specify in a notice the offence or offences for which a person is sent for trial under this section and the place at which he is to be tried; and a copy of the notice shall be served on the accused and given to the Crown Court sitting at that place.

(8) In a case where there is more than one indictable-only offence and the court includes an either-way or a summary offence in the notice under subsection (7) above, the court shall specify in that notice the indictable-only offence to which the either-way offence or, as the case may be, the summary offence appears to the court to be related.

(9) The trial of the information charging any summary offence for which a person is sent for trial under this section shall be treated as if the court had adjourned it under section 10 of the 1980 Act and had not fixed the time and place for its resumption.

(10) In selecting the place of trial for the purpose of subsection (7) above, the court shall have regard to—

(a) the convenience of the defence, the prosecution and the witnesses;
(b) the desirability of expediting the trial; and
(c) any direction given by or on behalf of the Lord Chief Justice with the concurrence of the Lord Chancellor under section 75(1) of the Supreme Court Act 1981.

(11) An offence fulfils the requisite conditions if—

(a) it appears to the court to be related to the indictable-only offence; and
(b) in the case of a summary offence, it is punishable with imprisonment or involves obligatory or discretionary disqualification from driving.

(12) For the purposes of this section—

(a) 'adult' means a person aged 18 or over, and references to an adult include references to a corporation;
(b) 'either-way offence' means an offence which, if committed by an adult, is triable either on indictment or summarily;
(c) an either-way offence is related to an indictable-only offence if the charge for the either-way offence could be joined in the same indictment as the charge for the indictable-only offence;
(d) a summary offence is related to an indictable-only offence if it arises out of circumstances which are the same as or connected with those giving rise to the indictable-only offence.

Explanatory text—See paras **6.29–6.85**.

Child or young person (subs (6))—See s 117(1).

Section 10 of the 1980 Act (subs (9))—'The 1980 Act' means the Magistrates' Courts Act 1980. The 1980 Act, s 10, is set out in the annotations to s 47.

Section 75(1) of the Supreme Court Act 1981 (subs (10)(c))—This provides:

'The cases or classes of cases in the Crown Court suitable for allocation respectively to a judge of the High Court and to a Circuit Judge or Recorder, and all other matters relating to the distribution of Crown Court business, shall be determined in accordance with directions given by or on behalf of the Lord Chief Justice with the concurrence of the Lord Chancellor.'

The current direction is the *Practice Direction (Crown Court: Allocation of Business)* [1995] 2 All ER 900.

Aged 18 or over (subs (12))—See general annotations.

52 Provisions supplementing section 51

(1) Subject to section 4 of the Bail Act 1976, section 41 of the 1980 Act, regulations under section 22 of the 1985 Act and section 25 of the 1994 Act, the court may send a person for trial under section 51 above—

(a) in custody, that is to say, by committing him to custody there to be safely kept until delivered in due course of law; or

(b) on bail in accordance with the Bail Act 1976, that is to say, by directing him to appear before the Crown Court for trial.

(2) Where—

(a) the person's release on bail under subsection (1)(b) above is conditional on his providing one or more sureties; and

(b) in accordance with subsection (3) of section 8 of the Bail Act 1976, the court fixes the amount in which a surety is to be bound with a view to his entering into his recognisance subsequently in accordance with subsections (4) and (5) or (6) of that section,

the court shall in the meantime make an order such as is mentioned in subsection (1)(a) above.

(3) The court shall treat as an indictable offence for the purposes of section 51 above an offence which is mentioned in the first column of Schedule 2 to the 1980 Act (offences for which the value involved is relevant to the mode of trial) unless it is clear to the court, having regard to any representations made by the prosecutor or the accused, that the value involved does not exceed the relevant sum.

(4) In subsection (3) above 'the value involved' and 'the relevant sum' have the same meanings as in section 22 of the 1980 Act (certain offences triable either way to be tried summarily if value involved is small).

(5) A magistrates' court may adjourn any proceedings under section 51 above, and if it does so shall remand the accused.

(6) Schedule 3 to this Act (which makes further provision in relation to persons sent to the Crown Court for trial under section 51 above) shall have effect.

Section 4 of the Bail Act 1976 (subs (1))—This provides, inter alia:

'(1) A person to whom this section applies shall be granted bail except as provided in Schedule 1 to this Act.

(2) This section applies to a person who is accused of an offence when—

(a) he appears or is brought before a magistrates' court or the Crown Court in the course of or in connection with proceedings for the offence, or

(b) he applies to a court for bail or for a variation of the conditions of bail in connection with the proceedings.

This subsection does not apply as respects proceedings on or after a person's conviction of the offence or proceedings against a fugitive offender for the offence.

(5) Schedule 1 to this Act also has effect as respects conditions of bail for a person to whom this section applies.

(7) This section is subject to section 41 of the Magistrates' Courts Act 1980 (restriction of bail by magistrates' court in cases of treason).

(8) This section is subject to section 25 of the Criminal Justice and Public Order Act 1994 ([restrictions on] bail in cases of homicide and rape).

(8A) Where a custody time limit has expired this section shall have effect as if, in subsection (1), the words "except as provided in Schedule 1 to this Act" were omitted.'

In a case to which a custody time limit applies, section 4 has effect as if subsection (8A) were inserted at the end thereof: Prosecution of Offences (Custody Time Limits) Regulations 1987, SI 1987/299, reg 8.

Section 41 of the 1980 Act (subs (1))—Ie the Magistrates' Courts Act 1980 (s 117(1)). The 1980 Act, s 41, provides:

'A person charged with treason shall not be granted bail except by order of a judge of the High Court or the Secretary of State.'

Regulations under s 22 of the 1985 Act (subs (1))—The current regulations are the Prosecution of Offences (Custody Time Limits) Regulations 1987, SI 1987/299. The new procedure for sending for trial will require their consequential amendment.

Section 25 of the 1994 Act (subs (1))—'The 1994 Act' means the Criminal Justice and Public Order Act 1994 (s 117(1)). See annotations to s 56.

Subsections (3), (4), (5) and (6) of section 8 of the Bail Act 1976 (subs (2))—Section 8 provides:

'(1) This section applies where a person is granted bail in criminal proceedings on condition that he provides one or more surety or sureties for the purpose of securing that he surrenders to custody.

(2) In considering the suitability for that purpose of a proposed surety, regard may be had (amongst other things) to—

    (a)   the surety's financial resources;
    (b)   his character and any previous convictions of his; and
    (c)   his proximity (whether in point of kinship, place of residence or otherwise) to the person for whom he is to be surety.

(3) Where a court grants a person bail in criminal proceedings on such a condition but is unable to release him because no surety or no suitable surety is available, the court shall fix the amount in which the surety is to be bound and subsections (4) and (5) below, or in a case where the proposed surety resides in Scotland subsection (6) below, shall apply for the purpose of enabling the recognizance of the surety to be entered into subsequently.

(4) Where this subsection applies the recognizance of the surety may be entered into before such of the following persons or descriptions of persons as the court may by order specify or, if it makes no such order, before any of the following persons, that is to say—

    (a)   where the decision is taken by magistrates' court, before a justice of the peace, a justices' clerk or a police officer who either is of the rank of inspector or above or is in charge of a police station or, if magistrates' courts rules so provide, by a person of such other description as is specified in the rules;
    (b)   where the decision is taken by the Crown Court, before any of the persons specified in paragraph (a) above or, if Crown Court rules so provide, by a person of such other description as is specified in the rules;
    (c)   where the decision is taken by the High Court or the Court of Appeal, before any of the persons specified in paragraph (a) above or, if Supreme Court rules so provide, by a person of such other description as is specified in the rules;
    (d)   where the decision is taken by the Courts-Martial Appeal Court before any of the persons specified in paragraph (a) above or, if Courts-Martial Appeal rules so provide, by a person of such other description as is specified in the rules;

and Supreme Court rules, Crown Court rules, Courts-Martial Appeal rules or magistrates' court rules may also prescribe the manner in which a recognizance which is to be entered into before such a person is to be entered into and the persons by whom and the manner in which the recognizance may be enforced.

(5) Where a surety seeks to enter into his recognizance before any person in accordance with subsection (4) above but that person declines to take his recognizance because he is not satisfied of the surety's suitability, the surety may apply to—

(a) the court which fixed the amount of the recognizance in which the surety was to be bound, or

(b) a magistrates' court for the petty sessions area in which he resides,

for that court to take his recognizance and that court shall, if satisfied of his suitability, take his recognizance.

(6) Where this subsection applies, the court, if satisfied of the suitability of the proposed surety, may direct that arrangements be made for the recognizance of the surety to be entered into in Scotland before any constable, within the meaning of the Police (Scotland) Act 1967, having charge at any police office or station in like manner as the recognizance would be entered into in England or Wales.

(7) Where, in pursuance of subsection (4) or (6) above, a recognizance is entered into otherwise than before the court that fixed the amount of the recognizance, the same consequences shall follow as if it had been entered into before that court.'

Schedule 2 to the 1980 Act (subs (3))—Ie the Magistrates' Courts Act 1980. The first column of the 1980 Act, Sch 2, lists the following offences:

1. Offences under s 1 of the Criminal Damage Act 1971 (destroying or damaging property), excluding any offence committed by destroying or damaging property by fire.

2. The following offences, namely:

(a) aiding, abetting, counselling or procuring the commission of any offence mentioned in paragraph 1 above;

(b) attempting to commit any offence so mentioned; and

(c) inciting another to commit any offence so mentioned.

3. Offences under s 12A of the Theft Act 1968 (aggravated vehicle-taking) where no allegation is made under subs (1)(b) other than of damage, whether to the vehicle or other property or both.

Section 22 of the 1980 Act (subs (4))—Ie the Magistrates' Courts Act 1980 (s 117(1)). The material facts of s 22 of this Act are set out in the explanatory text (para **6.41**).

Miscellaneous

53 Crown Prosecution Service: powers of non-legal staff

For section 7A of the 1985 Act there shall be substituted the following section—

'7A Powers of non-legal staff

(1) The Director may designate, for the purposes of this section, members of the staff of the Crown Prosecution Service who are not Crown Prosecutors.

(2) Subject to such exceptions (if any) as may be specified in the designation, a person so designated shall have such of the following as may be so specified, namely—

(a) the powers and rights of audience of a Crown Prosecutor in relation to—

(i) applications for, or relating to, bail in criminal proceedings;

(ii) the conduct of criminal proceedings in magistrates' courts other than trials;

(b) the powers of such a Prosecutor in relation to the conduct of criminal proceedings not falling within paragraph (a)(ii) above.

(3) A person so designated shall exercise any such powers subject to instructions given to him by the Director.

(4) Any such instructions may be given so as to apply generally.

(5) For the purposes of this section—

(a) "bail in criminal proceedings" has the same meaning as it would have in the Bail Act 1976 by virtue of the definition in section 1 of that Act if in that section "offence" did not include an offence to which subsection (6) below applies;
(b) "criminal proceedings" does not include proceedings for an offence to which subsection (6) below applies; and
(c) a trial begins with the opening of the prosecution case after the entry of a plea of not guilty and ends with the conviction or acquittal of the accused.

(6) This subsection applies to an offence if it is triable only on indictment, or is an offence—

(a) for which the accused has elected to be tried by a jury;
(b) which a magistrates' court has decided is more suitable to be so tried; or
(c) in respect of which a notice of transfer has been given under section 4 of the Criminal Justice Act 1987 or section 53 of the Criminal Justice Act 1991.

(7) Details of the following for any year, namely—

(a) the criteria applied by the Director in determining whether to designate persons under this section;
(b) the training undergone by persons so designated; and
(c) any general instructions given by the Director under subsection (4) above,

shall be set out in the Director's report under section 9 of this Act for that year.'

Explanatory text—See paras **6.4–6.9**.

The 1985 Act—Ie the Prosecution of Offences Act 1985 (s 117(1)).

The Director (Prosecution of Offences Act 1985, s 7A(1) and (3))—Ie the Director of Public Prosecutions (1985 Act, s 15(11)).

The Crown Prosecution Service (1985 Act, s 7A(1))—By the 1985 Act, s 1(1):

'There shall be a prosecuting service for England and Wales (to be known as "the Crown Prosecution Service") consisting of—

(a) the Director of Public Prosecutions, who shall be head of the Service;
(b) the Chief Crown Prosecutors, designated under subsection (4) below, each of whom shall be the member of the Service responsible to the Director for supervising the operation of the Service in his area; and
(c) the other staff appointed by the Director under this section.'

Crown Prosecutors (1985 Act, s 7A(1) and (2))—By the 1985 Act, s 1(3):

'The Director may designate any member of the Service who has a general qualification (within the meaning of section 71 of the Courts and Legal Services Act 1990) for the purposes of this subsection, and any person so designated shall be known as a Crown Prosecutor.'

By the 1990 Act, s 71(3)(c):

'a person has a "general qualification" if he has a right of audience in relation to any class of proceedings in any part of the Supreme Court or all proceedings in county courts or magistrates' courts.'

Currently such a right is only possessed by a barrister, whether in independent practice or employed, or a solicitor.

Every Crown Prosecutor has the powers of the Director as to the 'conduct of any proceedings' but exercises them under the direction of the Director (1985 Act, s 1(6)). 'The conduct of proceedings' is defined as including the making of representations in respect of application for bail (1985 Act, s 15(3)).

Prosecution of Offences Act 1985, s 7A(5)(a)—The Bail Act 1976, s 1(1), defines 'bail in criminal proceedings' as follows:

'In this Act "bail in criminal proceedings" means—

(a)   bail grantable in or in connection with proceedings for an offence to a person who is accused or convicted of the offence, or

(b)   bail grantable in connection with an offence to a person who is under arrest for the offence or for whose arrest for the offence a warrant (endorsed for bail) is being issued.'

A notice of transfer under section 4 of the Criminal Justice Act 1987 or section 53 of the Criminal Justice Act 1991 (subs (6))—These sections make provision for the transfer of a case involving an either-way offence, without the need for committal proceedings, after a notice of transfer has been served by the Director of Public Prosecutions (or certain other designated authorities in the case of the 1987 Act) in cases of serious or complex fraud (1987 Act, s 4) or by the Director in certain cases involving physical or sexual abuse of children (1991 Act, s 53).

The Director's report under section 9 of this [ie 1985] Act for that year (subs (7))—The relevant part of s 9 provides:

'(1) As soon as practicable after 4th April in any year the Director shall make to the Attorney General a report on the discharge of his functions during the year ending with that date.

(2) The Attorney General shall lay before Parliament a copy of every report received by him under subsection (1) above and shall cause every such report to be published.'

---

54 Bail: increased powers to require security or impose conditions

(1) In subsection (5) of section 3 of the Bail Act 1976 (general provisions as to bail), the words 'If it appears that he is unlikely to remain in Great Britain until the time appointed for him to surrender to custody' shall cease to have effect.

(2) In subsection (6) of that section, after paragraph (d) there shall be inserted the following paragraph—

'(e)   before the time appointed for him to surrender to custody, he attends an interview with an authorised advocate or authorised litigator, as defined by section 119(1) of the Courts and Legal Services Act 1990;'.

(3) In subsection (2) of section 3A of that Act (conditions of bail in the case of police bail), for the words 'paragraph (d)' there shall be substituted the words 'paragraph (d) or (e)'.

Explanatory text—See paras **9.25–9.27**.

Bail Act 1976, ss 3 and 3A (subss (1), (2) and (3))—As amended by the present section and Sch 8, para 37, these provide as follows; the amendments are in italics:

'3.—(1) A person granted bail in criminal proceedings shall be under a duty to surrender to custody, and that duty is enforceable in accordance with section 6 of this Act.

(2) No recognizance for his surrender to custody shall be taken from him.

(3) Except as provided by this section—

    (a)   no security for his surrender to custody shall be taken from him,
    (b)   he shall not be required to provide a surety or sureties for his surrender to custody, and
    (c)   no other requirement shall be imposed on him as a condition of bail.

(4) He may be required, before release on bail, to provide a surety or sureties to secure his surrender to custody.

(5) He may be required, before release on bail, to give security for his surrender to custody. The security may be given by him or on his behalf.

(6) He may be required ... to comply, before release on bail or later, with such requirements as appear to the court to be necessary to secure that—

    (a)   he surrenders to custody,
    (b)   he does not commit an offence while on bail,
    (c)   he does not interfere with witnesses or otherwise obstruct the course of justice whether in relation to himself or any other person,
    (d)   he makes himself available for the purpose of enabling inquiries or a report to be made to assist the court in dealing with him for the offence,
    (e)   *before the time appointed for him to surrender to custody, he attends an interview with an authorised advocate or authorised litigator, as defined by section 119(1) of the Courts and Legal Services Act 1990;*

and, in any Act, "the normal powers to impose conditions of bail" means the powers to impose conditions under paragraph (a), (b) or (c) above.

(6ZA) Where he is required under subsection (6) above to reside in a bail hostel, he may also be required to comply with the rules of the hostel.

(6A) In the case of a person accused of murder the court granting bail shall, unless it considers that satisfactory reports on his mental condition have already been obtained impose as conditions of bail—

    (a)   a requirement that the accused shall undergo examination by two medical practitioners for the purpose of enabling such reports to be prepared; and
    (b)   a requirement that he shall for that purpose attend such an institution or place as the court directs and comply with any other directions which may be given to him for that purpose by either of those practitioners.

(6B) Of the medical practitioners referred to in subsection (6A) above at least one shall be a practitioner approved for the purposes of section 12 of the Mental Health Act 1983.

(7) If a parent or guardian of a child or young person consents to be surety for the child or young person for the purposes of this subsection, the parent or guardian may be required to secure that the child or young person complies with any requirement imposed on him by virtue of subsection (6) or (6A) above, but—

    (a)   no requirement shall be imposed on the parent or the guardian of a young person by virtue of this subsection where it appears that the young person will attain the age of seventeen before the time to be appointed for him to surrender to custody; and
    (b)   the parent or guardian shall not be required to secure compliance with any requirement to which his consent does not extend and shall not, in respect of those requirements to which his consent does extend, be bound in a sum greater than £50.

(8) Where a court has granted bail in criminal proceedings that court or, where the court has committed a person on bail to the Crown Court for trial or to be sentenced or otherwise dealt with, that court or the Crown Court may on application—

(a) by or on behalf of the person to whom bail was granted, or
(b) by the prosecutor or a constable,

vary the conditions of bail or impose conditions in respect of bail which has been granted unconditionally.

(8A) Where a notice of transfer is given under a relevant transfer provision, subsection (8) above shall have effect in relation to a person in relation to whose case the notice is given as if he had been committed on bail to the Crown Court for trial.

(8B) Subsection (8) above applies where a court has sent a person on bail to the Crown Court for trial under section 51 of the Crime and Disorder Act 1998 as it applies where a court has committed a person on bail to the Crown Court for trial.

(9) This section is subject to subsection (2) of section 30 of the Magistrates' Courts Act 1980 (conditions of bail on remand for medical examination).

(10) This section is subject, in its application to bail granted by a constable, to section 3A of this Act.

(10) [sic] In subsection (8A) above "relevant transfer provision" means—

(a) section 4 of the Criminal Justice Act 1987, or
(b) section 53 of the Criminal Justice Act 1991.

(10A) Where a custody time limit has expired this section shall have effect as if—

(a) subsections (4) and (5) (sureties and security for his surrender to custody) were omitted;
(b) in subsection (6) (conditions of bail) for the words "before release on bail or later" there were substituted the words "after release on bail".

3A.—(1) Section 3 of this Act applies, in relation to bail granted by a custody officer under Part IV of the Police and Criminal Evidence Act 1984 in cases where the normal powers to impose conditions of bail are available to him, subject to the following modifications.

(2) Subsection (6) does not authorise the imposition of a requirement to reside in a bail hostel or any requirement under paragraph (d) *or (e)*.

(3) Subsections (6ZA), (6A) and (6B) shall be omitted.

(4) For subsection (8), substitute the following—

"(8) Where a custody officer has granted bail in criminal proceedings he or another custody officer serving at the same police station may, at the request of the person to whom it was granted, vary the conditions of bail; and in doing so he may impose conditions or more onerous conditions.".

(5) Where a constable grants bail to a person no conditions shall be imposed under subsections (4), (5), (6) or (7) of section 3 of this Act unless it appears to the constable that it is necessary to do so for the purpose of preventing that person from—

(a) failing to surrender to custody, or
(b) committing an offence while on bail, or
(c) interfering with witnesses or otherwise obstructing the course of justice, whether in relation to himself or any other person.

(6) Subsection (5) above also applies on any request to a custody officer under subsection (8) of section 3 of this Act to vary the conditions of bail.'

Authorised advocate or authorised litigator (Bail Act 1976, s 3(6)(e))—These are defined by section 119(1) of the Courts and Legal Services Act 1990 as follows:

'authorised advocate' means any person (including a barrister or solicitor) who has a right of audience granted by an authorised body in accordance with the provisions of the 1990 Act;

'authorised litigator' means any person (including a solicitor) who has a right to conduct litigation granted by an authorised body in accordance with the provisions of the 1990 Act.

55 Forfeiture of recognizances

For subsections (1) and (2) of section 120 of the 1980 Act (forfeiture of recognizances) there shall be substituted the following subsections—

'(1) This section applies where—

(a) a recognizance to keep the peace or to be of good behaviour has been entered into before a magistrates' court; or

(b) any recognizance is conditioned for the appearance of a person before a magistrates' court, or for his doing any other thing connected with a proceeding before a magistrates' court.

(1A) If, in the case of a recognizance which is conditioned for the appearance of an accused before a magistrates' court, the accused fails to appear in accordance with the condition, the court shall—

(a) declare the recognizance to be forfeited;

(b) issue a summons directed to each person bound by the recognizance as surety, requiring him to appear before the court on a date specified in the summons to show cause why he should not be adjudged to pay the sum in which he is bound;

and on that date the court may proceed in the absence of any surety if it is satisfied that he has been served with the summons.

(2) If, in any other case falling within subsection (1) above, the recognizance appears to the magistrates' court to be forfeited, the court may—

(a) declare the recognizance to be forfeited; and

(b) adjudge each person bound by it, whether as principal or surety, to pay the sum in which he is bound;

but in a case falling within subsection (1)(a) above, the court shall not declare the recognizance to be forfeited except by order made on complaint.'

Explanatory text—See paras **9.29–9.34**.

The 1980 Act—Ie the Magistrates' Courts Act 1980 (s 117(1)).

56 Bail: restrictions in certain cases of homicide or rape

In subsection (1) of section 25 of the 1994 Act (no bail for defendants charged with or convicted of homicide or rape after previous conviction of such offences), for the words 'shall not be granted bail in those proceedings' there shall be substituted the words 'shall be granted bail in those proceedings only if the court or, as the case may be, the constable considering the grant of bail is satisfied that there are exceptional circumstances which justify it'.

Explanatory text—See paras **9.20–9.23**.

The 1994 Act—Ie the Criminal Justice and Public Order Act 1994 (s 117(1)). As amended, s 25 of the 1994 Act provides:

'(1) A person who in any proceedings has been charged with or convicted of an offence to which this section applies in circumstances to to which it applies *shall be granted bail in those proceedings only if the court or, as the case may be, the constable considering the grant of bail is satisfied that there are exceptional circumstances which justify it.*

(2) This section applies, subject to subsection (3) below, to the following offences, that is to say—

(a) murder;
(b) attempted murder;
(c) manslaughter;
(d) rape; or
(e) attempted rape.

(3) This section applies to a person charged with or convicted of any such offence only if he has been previously convicted by or before a court in any part of the United Kingdom of any such offence or of culpable homicide and, in the case of a previous conviction of manslaughter or of culpable homicide, if he was then sentenced to imprisonment or, if he was then a child or young person, to long-term detention under any of the relevant enactments.

(4) This section applies whether or not an appeal is pending against conviction or sentence.

(5) In this section—

"conviction" includes—

(a) a finding that a person is not guilty by reason of insanity;
(b) a finding under section 4A(3) of the Criminal Procedure (Insanity) Act 1964 (cases of unfitness to plead) that a person did the act or made the omission charged against him; and
(c) a conviction of an offence for which an order is made placing the offender on probation or discharging him absolutely or conditionally;

and "convicted" shall be construed accordingly; and

"the relevant enactments" means—

(a) as respects England and Wales, section 53(2) of the Children and Young Persons Act 1933;
(b) as respects Scotland, sections 205(1) to (3) and 208 of the Criminal Procedure (Scotland) Act 1995;
(c) as respects Northern Ireland, section 73(2) of the Children and Young Persons Act (Northern Ireland) 1968.

(6) This section does not apply in relation to proceedings instituted before its commencement.'

---

57 Use of live television links at preliminary hearings

(1) In any proceedings for an offence, a court may, after hearing representations from the parties, direct that the accused shall be treated as being present in the court for any particular hearing before the start of the trial if, during that hearing—

(a) he is held in custody in a prison or other institution; and
(b) whether by means of a live television link or otherwise, he is able to see and hear the court and to be seen and heard by it.

(2) A court shall not give a direction under subsection (1) above unless—

(a) it has been notified by the Secretary of State that facilities are available for enabling persons held in custody in the institution in which the accused is or is to be so held to see and hear the court and to be seen and heard by it; and

(b) the notice has not been withdrawn.

(3) If in a case where it has power to do so a magistrates' court decides not to give a direction under subsection (1) above, it shall give its reasons for not doing so.

(4) In this section 'the start of the trial' has the meaning given by subsection (11A) or (11B) of section 22 of the 1985 Act.

Explanatory text—See paras **9.48–9.54.**

'Start of the trial' (subs (4))—For 1985 Act, s 22(11A) or (11B) see annotations to s 43.

PART IV

DEALING WITH OFFENDERS

CHAPTER I

ENGLAND AND WALES

Sexual or violent offenders

58 Sentences extended for licence purposes

(1) This section applies where a court which proposes to impose a custodial sentence for a sexual or violent offence considers that the period (if any) for which the offender would, apart from this section, be subject to a licence would not be adequate for the purpose of preventing the commission by him of further offences and securing his rehabilitation.

(2) Subject to subsections (3) to (5) below, the court may pass on the offender an extended sentence, that is to say, a custodial sentence the term of which is equal to the aggregate of—

(a) the term of the custodial sentence that the court would have imposed if it had passed a custodial sentence otherwise than under this section ('the custodial term'); and

(b) a further period ('the extension period') for which the offender is to be subject to a licence and which is of such length as the court considers necessary for the purpose mentioned in subsection (1) above.

(3) Where the offence is a violent offence, the court shall not pass an extended sentence the custodial term of which is less than four years.

(4) The extension period shall not exceed—

(a) ten years in the case of a sexual offence; and
(b) five years in the case of a violent offence.

(5) The term of an extended sentence passed in respect of an offence shall not exceed the maximum term permitted for that offence.

(6) Subsection (2) of section 2 of the 1991 Act (length of custodial sentences) shall apply as if the term of an extended sentence did not include the extension period.

(7) The Secretary of State may by order amend paragraph (b) of subsection (4) above by substituting a different period, not exceeding ten years, for the period for the time being specified in that paragraph.

(8) In this section—

'licence' means a licence under Part II of the 1991 Act;

'sexual offence' and 'violent offence' have the same meanings as in Part I of that Act.

Explanatory text—See paras **7.14–7.28**.

Custodial sentence (subss (1) and (2))—A 'custodial sentence' is defined by the Criminal Justice Act 1991, s 31(1) (as amended by Sch 8, para 78), as, in respect of a person aged 21 or over, a sentence of imprisonment, and, in relation to a person under that age, a detention and training order or a secure training order under the Criminal Justice and Public Order Act 1994, s 1, a sentence of detention in a young offenders' institution or under s 53(3) of the Children and Young Persons Act 1933 or a sentence of custody for life under s 8(2) of the Criminal Justice Act 1982. This is wider than the definition adopted for the specific purposes of Part I of the Crime (Sentences) Act 1997, s 3(6).

By the Supreme Court Act 1981, s 47, a sentence imposed, or other order made, by the Crown Court when dealing with an offender takes effect from the beginning of the day on which it is imposed, unless the court otherwise directs.

Sexual offence (subss (1), (4) and (8))—Criminal Justice Act 1991, s 31(1), as amended, states that the term 'sexual offence' means an offence under the Sexual Offences Act 1956 (other than an offence under ss 30, 31 or 33 to 36 of that Act), an offence under the Mental Health Act 1959, s 128, the Indecency with Children Act 1960, the Sexual Offences Act 1967, an offence of burglary with intent to commit rape, contrary to the Theft Act 1968, s 9, the Criminal Law Act 1977, s 54, or under the Protection of Children Act 1978. In addition, conspiracies, attempts and incitements to commit any of these offences amount to a sexual offence (1991 Act, s 31(3)).

Violent offence (subss (1), (3), (4) and (8))—By virtue of s 58(8), this bears the meaning ascribed to it by the Criminal Justice Act 1991, s 31(1). This states that 'violent offence' means an offence which leads, or is intended or likely to lead, to a person's death or physical injury to a person, and includes an offence which is required to be charged as arson (whether or not it would otherwise fall within this definition).

Robbery, in which the victim is threatened with a knife is a violent offence: *Cochrane* (1994) 15 Cr App Rep (S) 708 (CA). So too is robbery with a firearm: *Touriq Khan* (1995) 16 Cr App Rep (S) 180. An offence of threatening to kill which does not involve the actual use of force will not normally be a violent offence: *Richart* (1995) 16 Cr App Rep (S) 977 (CA).

The period ... be subject to a licence (subs (1))—'Licence' means a licence under Part II of the Criminal Justice Act 1991. The arrangements for early release of persons serving determinate sentences are contained in Part II of the Criminal Justice Act 1991, which is amended by ss 99–105 of the new Act (as to which see paras **7.72–7.96**), and Sch 9, paras 10 to 12. The 1991 Act, s 33, distinguishes between a 'short-term' and a 'long-term' prisoner. The former is defined by s 33(5) of that Act as a person serving a sentence of imprisonment for a term of less than four years, the latter as a person serving a term of imprisonment of four years or more. The length of a sentence is to be calculated by aggregating consecutive terms of imprisonment, the overall total being regarded as a single term (1991 Act, s 51(2), substituted by the new Act, s 101). For the applicable rules, see paras **7.82–7.83**.

Criminal Justice Act 1991, s 2(2) (subs (6))—The 1991 Act, s 2 provides as follows:

'(1) This section applies where a court passes a custodial sentence other than one fixed by law on falling to be imposed under s 2(2) of the Crime (Sentences) Act 1997.

(2) [Subject to sections 3(2) and 4(2) of that Act,] the custodial sentence shall be—

(a)   for such term (not exceeding the permitted maximum) as in the opinion of the court is commensurate with the seriousness of the offence, or the combination of the offence and one or more offences associated with it; or

(b)   where the offence is a violent or sexual offence, for such longer term (not exceeding that maximum) as in the opinion of the court is necessary to protect the public from serious harm from the offender.

(3) Where the court passes a custodial sentence for a term longer than is commensurate with the seriousness of the offence, or the combination of the offence and one or more offences associated with it, the court shall—

(a)   state in open court that it is of the opinion that subsection (2)(b) above applies and why it is of that opinion; and

(b)   explain to the offender in open court and in ordinary language why the sentence is for such a term.

(4) A custodial sentence for an indeterminate period shall be regarded for the purposes of subsections (2) and (3) above as a custodial sentence for a term longer than any actual term.

[(5) Subsection (3) above shall not apply in any case where the court passes a custodial sentence falling to be imposed under subsection (2) of section 3 or 4 of the Crime (Sentences) Act 1997 which is for the minimum term specified in that subsection.']

(*Words in square brackets not yet in force.*)

---

59 Effect of extended sentences

For section 44 of the 1991 Act there shall be substituted the following section—

'44 Extended sentences for sexual or violent offenders

(1) This section applies to a prisoner serving an extended sentence within the meaning of section 58 of the Crime and Disorder Act 1998.

(2) Subject to the provisions of this section and section 51(2D) below, this Part, except sections 40 and 40A, shall have effect as if the term of the extended sentence did not include the extension period.

(3) Where the prisoner is released on licence under this Part, the licence shall, subject to any revocation under section 39(1) or (2) above, remain in force until the end of the extension period.

(4) Where, apart from this subsection, the prisoner would be released unconditionally—

(a) he shall be released on licence; and

(b) the licence shall, subject to any revocation under section 39(1) or (2) above, remain in force until the end of the extension period.

(5) The extension period shall be taken to begin as follows—

(a) for the purposes of subsection (3) above, on the date given by section 37(1) above;

(b) for the purposes of subsection (4) above, on the date on which, apart from that subsection, the prisoner would have been released unconditionally.

(6) Sections 33(3) and 33A(1) above and section 46 below shall not apply in relation to the prisoner.

(7) For the purposes of sections 37(5) and 39(1) and (2) above the question whether the prisoner is a long-term or short-term prisoner shall be determined by reference to the term of the extended sentence.

(8) In this section "extension period" has the same meaning as in section 58 of the Crime and Disorder Act 1998.'

Explanatory text—See para 7.25.

The 1991 Act—Ie the Criminal Justice Act 1991 (s 117(1)).

Sections 33 to 41 (1991 Act, s 44)—These provisions, as amended, are as follows:

'33—(1) As soon as a short-term prisoner has served one-half of his sentence, it shall be the duty of the Secretary of State—

  (a) to release him unconditionally if that sentence is for a term of less than twelve months; and
  (b) to release him on licence if that sentence is for a term of twelve months or more.

(2) As soon as a long-term prisoner has served two-thirds of his sentence, it shall be the duty of the Secretary of State to release him on licence.

(3) As soon as a short-term or long-term prisoner who—

  (a) has been released on licence under *this Part*; and
  (b) has been recalled to prison under section 39(1) or (2) below,

would (but for his release) have served three-quarters of his sentence, it shall be the duty of the Secretary of State to release him unconditionally.

(3A) In the case of a prisoner to whom section 44A below applies, it shall be the duty of the Secretary of State to release him on licence at the end of the extension period (within the meaning of section 58 of the Crime and Disorder Act 1998).

(4) [repealed]

(5) In this Part—

  (a) "long-term prisoner" means a person serving a sentence of imprisonment for a term of four years or more;
  (b) "short-term prisoner" means a person serving a term of imprisonment for a term of less than four years.

33A—(1) As soon as a prisoner—

  (a) whose sentence is for a term of less than twelve months; and
  (b) who has been released on licence under section 34A(3) or 36(1) below and recalled to prison under section 38A(1) or 39(1) or (2) below,

would (but for his release) have served one-half of his sentence, it shall be the duty of the Secretary of State to release him unconditionally.

(2) As soon as a prisoner—

  (a) whose sentence is for a term of twelve months or more; and
  (b) who has been released on licence under section 34A(3) below and recalled to prison under section 38A(1) below,

would (but for his release) have served one-half of his sentence it shall be the duty of the Secretary of State to release him on licence.

(3) In the case of a prisoner who—

(a)   *has been released on licence under this Part and recalled to prison under section 39(1) or (2) below; and*

(b)   *has been subsequently released on licence under section 33(3) or (3A) above and recalled to prison under section 39(1) or (2) below,*

section 33 above shall have effect as if for the words "three quarters" there were substituted the words "the whole" and the words "on licence" were omitted.

34—(1) A life prisoner is a discretionary life prisoner for the purposes of this Part if—

(a)   his sentence was imposed for a violent or sexual offence the sentence for which is not fixed by law; and

(b)   the court by which he was sentenced for that offence ordered that this section should apply to him as soon as he had served a part of his sentence specified in the order.

(2) A part of the sentence so specified shall be such part as the court considers appropriate taking into account—

(a)   the seriousness of the offence, or the combination of the offence and other offences associated with it; and

(b)   the provisions of this section as compared with those of section 33(2) above and section 35(1) below.

(3) As soon as, in the case of a discretionary life prisoner—

(a)   he has served the part of his sentence specified in the order ("the relevant part"); and

(b)   the Board has directed his release under this section,

it shall be the duty of the Secretary of State to release him on licence.

(4) The Board shall not give a direction under subsection (3) above with respect to a discretionary life prisoner unless—

(a)   the Secretary of State has referred the prisoner's case to the Board; and

(b)   the Board is satisfied that it is no longer necessary for the protection of the public that the prisoner should be confined.

(5) A discretionary life prisoner may require the Secretary of State to refer his case to the Board any time—

(a)   after he has served the relevant part of his sentence; and

(b)   where there has been a previous reference of his case to the Board, after the end of the period of two years beginning with the disposal of that reference; and

(c)   where he is also serving a sentence of imprisonment for a term, after he has served one-half of that sentence;

and in this subsection "previous reference" means a reference under subsection (4) above or section 39(4) below made after the prisoner had served the relevant part of his sentence.

(6) In determining for the purpose of subsection (3) or (5) above whether a discretionary life prisoner has served the relevant part of his sentence—

(a)   account shall be taken of any corresponding relevant period; but

(b)   no account shall be taken of any time during which the prisoner was unlawfully at large within the meaning of section 49 of the Prison Act 1952 ("the 1952 Act").

(6A) In subsection (6)(a) above, "corresponding relevant period" means the period corresponding to the period by which a determinate sentence of imprisonment imposed on the offender would fail to be reduced under section 67 of the Criminal Justice Act 1967 (reduction of sentences to take account of police detention or remands in custody).

(7) In this Part "life prisoner" means a person serving one or more sentences of life imprisonment; but—

(a)   a person serving two or more such sentences shall not be treated as a discretionary life prisoner for the purposes of this Part unless the requirements of subsection (1) above are satisfied as respects each of those sentences; and

(b) subsections (3) and (5) above shall not apply in relation to such a person until after he has served the relevant part of each of those sentences.

34A [see s 99].

35—(1) After a long-term prisoner has served one-half of his sentence, the Secretary of State may, if recommended to do so by the Board, release him on licence.

(2) If recommended to do so by the Board, the Secretary of State may, after consultation with the Lord Chief Justice together with the trial judge if available, release on licence a life prisoner who is not a discretionary prisoner.

(3) The Board shall not make a recommendation under subsection (2) above unless the Secretary of State has referred the particular case, or the class of case to which that case belongs, to the Board for its advice.

36—(1) The Secretary of State may at any time release a short-term or long-term prisoner on licence if he is satisfied that exceptional circumstances exist which justify the prisoner's release on compassionate grounds.

(2) Before releasing a long-term or life prisoner under subsection (1) above, the Secretary of State shall consult the Board, unless the circumstances are such as to render such consultation impracticable.

37—(1) Subject to subsections *(1A), (1B) or (2)* below, where a short-term or long-term prisoner is released on licence, the licence shall, subject to any revocation under section 39(1) or (2) below, remain in force until the date on which he would (but for his release) have served three-quarters of his sentence.

(1A) Where a prisoner is released on licence under section 33(3) or (3A) above, subsection (1) above shall have effect as if for the reference to three-quarters of his sentence there were substituted a reference to the whole of that sentence.

(1B) Where a prisoner whose sentence is for a term of 12 months or more is released on licence under section 33A(2) or section 34A(3) above, subsection (1) above shall have effect as if for the reference to three-quarters of his sentence there were substituted a reference between—

(a) the proportion of his sentence; and
(b) the duration of the curfew condition to which he is or was subject.

(2) Where a prisoner whose sentence is for a term of less than 12 months is released on licence under subsection *34A(3) or 36(1)* above, subsection (1) above shall have effect as if for the reference to three-quarters of his sentence there were substituted a reference to one-half of that sentence.

(3) Where a life prisoner is released on licence, the licence shall, unless previously revoked under section 39(1) or (2) below, remain in force until his death.

(4) A person subject to a licence under *this Part* shall comply with such conditions as may for the time being be specified in the licence; and the Secretary of State may make rules for regulating the supervision of any description of such persons.

(4A) The conditions so specified may in the case of a person released on licence under section 34A above whose sentence is for a term of less than twelve months, and shall in any other case, include on the person's release conditions as to his supervision by—

(a) a probation officer appointed for or assigned to the petty sessions area within which the person resides for the time being; or
(b) where the person is under the age of 18 years, a member of a youth offending team established by the local authority within whose area the person resides for the time being.

(5) The Secretary of State shall not include on release, or subsequently insert, a condition in the licence of a long-term prisoner, or vary or cancel any such condition, except after consultation with the Board.

(6) For the purposes of subsection (5) above, the Secretary of State shall be treated as having consulted the Board about a proposal to include, insert, vary or cancel a condition in any case if he has consulted the Board about the implementation of proposals of that description generally or in that class of case.

(7) The power to make rules under this section shall be exercisable by statutory instrument which shall be subject to annulment in pursuance of a resolution of either House of Parliament.

37A [see s 100].

38 [repealed].

38A [see s 100].

39—(1) If recommended to do so by the Board in the case of a short-term or long-term or life prisoner who has been released on licence under this Part, the Secretary of State may revoke his licence and recall him to prison.

(2) The Secretary of State may revoke the licence of any such person and recall him to prison without a recommendation by the Board, where it appears to him that it is expedient in the public interest to recall that person before such a recommendation is practicable.

(3) A person recalled to prison under subsection (1) or (2) above—

(a) may make representations in writing with respect to his recall; and
(b) on his return to prison, shall be informed of the reasons for his recall and of his right to make representations.

(4) The Secretary of State shall refer to the Board—

(a) the case of a person recalled under subsection (1) above who makes representations under subsection (3) above; and
(b) the case of a person recalled under subsection (2) above.

(5) Where on a reference under subsection (4) above the Board recommends in the case of any person his immediate release on licence under this section, the Secretary of State shall give effect to the recommendation.

(5A) *In the case of a prisoner to whom section 44A below applies, subsections (4)(b) and (5) of that section apply in place of subsection (5) above.*

(6) On the revocation of the licence of any person under this section, he shall be liable to be detained in pursuance of his sentence and, if at large, shall be deemed to be unlawfully at large.

40—(1) This section applies to a short-term or long-term prisoner who is released under this part if—

(a) before the date on which he would (but for his release) have served his sentence in full, he commits an offence punishable with imprisonment; and
(b) whether before or after that date, he is convicted of that offence ("the new offence").

(2) Subject to subsection (3) below, the court by or before which a person to whom this section applies is convicted of the new offence may, whether or not it passes any other sentence on him, order him to be returned to prison for the whole or any part of the period which—

(a) begins with the date of the order; and
(b) is equal in length to the period between the date on which the new offence was committed and the date mentioned in subsection (1) above.

(3) A magistrates' court—

(a) shall not have power to order a person to whom this section applies to be returned to prison for a period of more than six months; but

(b)   subject to section 25 of the Criminal Justice and Public Order Act 1994 may commit him in custody or on bail to the Crown Court for sentence and the Crown Court to which he has been so committed may make such an order with regard to him as is mentioned in subsection (2) above.

(4) The period for which a person to whom this section applies is ordered under subsection (2) above to be returned to prison—

(a)   shall be taken to be a sentence of imprisonment for the purposes of this Part;

(b)   shall, as the court may direct, either be served before and be followed by, or be served concurrently with, the sentence imposed for the new offence; and

(c)   in either case shall be disregarded in determining the appropriate length of that sentence.

(5) Where the new offence is found to have been committed over a period of two or more days, it shall be taken for the purposes of this section to have been committed on the last of those days.

(6) For the purposes of any enactment conferring rights of appeal in criminal cases, any such order as is mentioned in subsection (2) above made with regard to any person shall be treated as a sentence passed on him for the offence for which the sentence referred to in subsection (1) above was passed.

40A [See s 105 of the new Act].

41—(1) Where a person is sentenced to imprisonment for a term in respect of an offence, this section applies to him if the court directs under section 9 of the Crime (Sentences) Act 1997 that the number of days for which he was remanded in custody in connection with—

(a)   the offence; or

(b)   any other offence the charge for which was founded on the same facts or evidence,

shall count as time served by him as part of the sentence.

(2) For the purposes of determining for the purposes of this Part whether a person to whom this section applies—

(a)   has served, or would (but for his release) have served, a particular proportion of his sentence; or

(b)   has served a particular period,

the number of days specified in the direction shall, subject to subsections (3) and (4) below, be treated as having been served by him as part of that sentence or period.

(3) Nothing in subsection (2) above shall have the effect of reducing the period for which a licence granted under this Part to a short-term or long-term prisoner remains in force to a period which is less than—

(a)   one-quarter of his sentence in the case of a short-term prisoner; or

(b)   one-twelfth of his sentence in the case of a long-term prisoner.

(4) Where the period for which a licence granted under section 33A(2), 34A(3) or 36(1) above to a short-term prisoner remains in force cannot exceed one-quarter of his sentence, nothing in subsection (2) above shall have the effect of reducing that period.'

Released on licence (1991 Act, s 44(3), (4))—See annotations to s 58.

60 Re-release of prisoners serving extended sentences

After section 44 of the 1991 Act there shall be inserted the following section—

'44A Re-release of prisoners serving extended sentences

(1) This section applies to a prisoner serving an extended sentence within the meaning of section 58 of the Crime and Disorder Act 1998 who is recalled to prison under section 39(1) or (2) above.

(2) Subject to subsection (3) below, the prisoner may require the Secretary of State to refer his case to the Board at any time.

(3) Where there has been a previous reference of the prisoner's case to the Board (whether under this section or section 39(4) above), the Secretary of State shall not be required to refer the case until after the end of the period of one year beginning with the disposal of that reference.

(4) On a reference—

    (a) under this section; or
    (b) under section 39(4) above,

the Board shall direct the prisoner's release if satisfied that it is no longer necessary for the protection of the public that he should be confined (but not otherwise).

(5) If the Board gives a direction under subsection (4) above it shall be the duty of the Secretary of State to release the prisoner on licence.'

Explanatory text—See para **7.28**.

The 1991 Act—Ie the Criminal Justice Act 1991 (s 117(1)).

Subsection 39(1) or (2) of the 1991 Act (1991 Act, s 44A)—See annotations to s 59.

Offenders dependent etc. on drugs

61 Drug treatment and testing orders

(1) This section applies where a person aged 16 or over is convicted of an offence other than one for which the sentence—

    (a) is fixed by law; or
    (b) falls to be imposed under section 2(2), 3(2) or 4(2) of the 1997 Act.

(2) Subject to the provisions of this section, the court by or before which the offender is convicted may make an order (a 'drug treatment and testing order') which—

    (a) has effect for a period specified in the order of not less than six months nor more than three years ("the treatment and testing period"); and
    (b) includes the requirements and provisions mentioned in section 62 below.

(3) A court shall not make a drug treatment and testing order unless it has been notified by the Secretary of State that arrangements for implementing such orders are available in the area proposed to be specified in the order and the notice has not been withdrawn.

(4) A drug treatment and testing order shall be a community order for the purposes of Part I of the 1991 Act; and the provisions of that Part, which include provisions with

respect to restrictions on imposing, and procedural requirements for, community sentences (sections 6 and 7), shall apply accordingly.

(5) The court shall not make a drug treatment and testing order in respect of the offender unless it is satisfied—

    (a) that he is dependent on or has a propensity to misuse drugs; and

    (b) that his dependency or propensity is such as requires and may be susceptible to treatment.

(6) For the purpose of ascertaining for the purposes of subsection (5) above whether the offender has any drug in his body, the court may by order require him to provide samples of such description as it may specify; but the court shall not make such an order unless the offender expresses his willingness to comply with its requirements.

(7) The Secretary of State may by order amend subsection (2) above by substituting a different period for the minimum or maximum period for the time being specified in that subsection.

Explanatory text—See paras **7.29–7.49**.

Age (subs (1))—See general annotations.

Convicted/Convicted of an offence (subss (1) and (2))—The date of conviction is the date a guilty plea is entered or a finding of guilt is made: *T* [1979] Crim LR 588 (CA).

Sentence ... falls to be imposed under subsections 2(2), 3(2) or 4(2) of the 1997 Act (subs (1))—'The 1997 Act' means the Crime (Sentences) Act 1997 (s 117(1)). See s 85(6).

Community order for the purposes of Part I of the 1991 Act (subs (4))—'The 1991 Act' means the Criminal Justice Act 1991 (s 117(1)). The community orders for the purpose of Part I are probation orders, supervision orders, community service orders, combination orders and curfew orders as well as the new action plan orders created by the new Act.

Sections 6 and 7 of the Criminal Justice Act 1991 (subs (4))—These provide as follows:

'6—(1) A court shall not pass on an offender a community sentence, that is to say, a sentence which consists of or includes one or more community orders, unless it is of the opinion that the offence, or the combination of the offence and one or more offences associated with it, was serious enough to warrant such a sentence.

(2) Subject to subsection (3) below, where a court passes a community sentence—

    (a)   the particular order or orders comprising or forming part of the sentence shall be such as in the opinion of the court is, or taken together are, the most suitable for the offender; and

    (b)   the restrictions on liberty imposed by the order or orders shall be such as in the opinion of the court are commensurate with the seriousness of the offence, or the combination of the offence and one or more offences associated with it.

(3) In consequence of the provision made by section 11 below with respect to combination orders, a community sentence shall not consist of or include both a probation order and a community service order.

(4) In this Part "community order" means any of the following orders, namely—

    (a)   a probation order;

    (b)   a community service order;

    (c)   a combination order;

    (d)   a curfew order;

    (e)   a supervision order; and

    (f)   an attendance centre order.

7—(1) In forming any such opinion as is mentioned in subsection (1) or (2)(b) of section 6 above, a court shall take into account all such information about the circumstances of the offence and or (as the case may be) of the offence and the offence or offences associated with it (including any aggravating or mitigating factors) as is available to it.

(2) In forming any such opinion as is mentioned in subsection (2)(a) of that section, a court may take into account any information about the offender which is before it.

(3) Subject to subsection (3A) below, a court shall obtain and consider a pre-sentence report before forming an opinion as to the suitability for the offender of one or more of the following orders, namely—

   (a) a probation order which includes additional requirements authorised by Schedule 1A to
        the 1973 Act;
   (b) a community service order;
   (c) a combination order; and
   (d) a supervision order which includes requirements imposed under section 12, 12A, 12AA,
        12B or 12C of the Children and Young Persons Act 1969 ("the 1969 Act").

(3A) Subsection (3) above does not apply if, in the circumstances of the case, the court is of the opinion that it is unnecessary to obtain a pre-sentence report.

(3B) In the case of an offender under the age of eighteen years, save where the offence or any other offence associated with it is triable only on indictment, the court shall not form such an opinion as is mentioned in subsection (3A) above or subsection (5) below unless there exists a previous pre-sentence report obtained in respect of the offender and the court has had regard to the information contained in that report, or, if there is more than one such report, the most recent report.

(4) No community sentence which consists of or includes such an order as is mentioned in subsection (3) above shall be invalidated by the failure of a court to obtain and consider a pre-sentence report before forming an opinion referred to in that subsection, but any court on an appeal against such a sentence—

   (a) shall, subject to subsection (5) below, obtain a pre-sentence report if none was obtained
        by the court below; and
   (b) shall consider any such report obtained by it or by that court.

(5) Subsection (4)(a) above does not apply if the court is of the opinion—

   (a) that the court below was justified in forming an opinion that it was unnecessary to obtain
        a pre-sentence report, or
   (b) that, although the court below was not justified in forming that opinion, in the
        circumstances of the case at the time it is before the court, it is unnecessary to obtain a
        pre-sentence report.'

---

62 Requirements and provisions to be included in orders

(1) A drug treatment and testing order shall include a requirement ('the treatment requirement') that the offender shall submit, during the whole of the treatment and testing period, to treatment by or under the direction of a specified person having the necessary qualifications or experience ('the treatment provider') with a view to the reduction or elimination of the offender's dependency on or propensity to misuse drugs.

(2) The required treatment for any particular period shall be—

   (a) treatment as a resident in such institution or place as may be specified in the
        order; or
   (b) treatment as a non-resident in or at such institution or place, and at such
        intervals, as may be so specified;

but the nature of the treatment shall not be specified in the order except as mentioned in paragraph (a) or (b) above.

(3) A court shall not make a drug treatment and testing order unless it is satisfied that arrangements have been or can be made for the treatment intended to be specified in the order (including arrangements for the reception of the offender where he is to be required to submit to treatment as a resident).

(4) A drug treatment and testing order shall include a requirement ('the testing requirement') that, for the purpose of ascertaining whether he has any drug in his body during the treatment and testing period, the offender shall provide during that period, at such times or in such circumstances as may (subject to the provisions of the order) be determined by the treatment provider, samples of such description as may be so determined.

(5) The testing requirement shall specify for each month the minimum number of occasions on which samples are to be provided.

(6) A drug treatment and testing order shall include a provision specifying the petty sessions area in which it appears to the court making the order that the offender resides or will reside.

(7) A drug treatment and testing order shall—

    (a) provide that, for the treatment and testing period, the offender shall be under the supervision of a responsible officer, that is to say, a probation officer appointed for or assigned to the petty sessions area specified in the order;

    (b) require the offender to keep in touch with the responsible officer in accordance with such instructions as he may from time to time be given by that officer, and to notify him of any change of address; and

    (c) provide that the results of the tests carried out on the samples provided by the offender in pursuance of the testing requirement shall be communicated to the responsible officer.

(8) Supervision by the responsible officer shall be carried out to such extent only as may be necessary for the purpose of enabling him—

    (a) to report on the offender's progress to the court responsible for the order;

    (b) to report to that court any failure by the offender to comply with the requirements of the order; and

    (c) to determine whether the circumstances are such that he should apply to that court for the revocation or amendment of the order.

(9) In this section and sections 63 and 64 below, references to the court responsible for a drug treatment and testing order are references to—

    (a) the court by which the order is made; or

    (b) where another court is specified in the order in accordance with subsection (10) below, that court.

(10) Where the area specified in a drug treatment and testing order made by a magistrates' court is not the area for which the court acts, the court may, if it thinks fit, include in the order provision specifying for the purposes of subsection (9) above a magistrates' court which acts for that area.

Explanatory text—See paras **7.42–7.45**.

Drug treatment and testing order (subss (1), (3), (4), (6), (7), (9) and (10))—See ss 61 and 85(1).

Treatment and testing period (subss (1), and (2))—See ss 61(2) and 85(4).

Month (sub (5))—See general annotations.

Resides (sub (6))—Whether a person was resident in a particular place and whether that residence was permanent are questions of fact and degree to be determined by the tribunal of fact: *Hipperson v Electoral Registration Officer for the District of Newbury* [1995] 2 All ER 456. A person can reside in more than one place: a person may have both a weekday city residence and a weekend country retreat. In *Burdett v Joslin* [1985] 2 All ER 465 it was held that a residential connection arising out of the ownership of property which did not carry with it the right of occupation was not sufficient to show that an applicant for the grant of a firearm certificate under s 26 of the Firearms Act 1968 resided within the area in which he applied for the certificate.

Probation officer (subs 7))—See annotations to s 18.

Revocation or amendment of the order (subs (8))—Such procedures are in accordance with the Criminal Justice Act 1991, Sch 2, as amended (see new Act, s 64, and annotations thereto).

63 Periodic reviews

(1) A drug treatment and testing order shall—

   (a) provide for the order to be reviewed periodically at intervals of not less than one month;

   (b) provide for each review of the order to be made, subject to subsection (7) below, at a hearing held for the purpose by the court responsible for the order (a 'review hearing');

   (c) require the offender to attend each review hearing;

   (d) provide for the responsible officer to make to the court, before each review, a report in writing on the offender's progress under the order; and

   (e) provide for each such report to include the test results communicated to the responsible officer under section 62(7)(c) above and the views of the treatment provider as to the treatment and testing of the offender.

(2) At a review hearing the court, after considering the responsible officer's report, may amend any requirement or provision of the order.

(3) The court—

   (a) shall not amend the treatment or testing requirement unless the offender expresses his willingness to comply with the requirement as amended;

   (b) shall not amend any provision of the order so as to reduce the treatment and testing period below the minimum specified in section 61(2) above, or to increase it above the maximum so specified; and

   (c) except with the consent of the offender, shall not amend any requirement or provision of the order while an appeal against the order is pending.

(4) If the offender fails to express his willingness to comply with the treatment or testing requirement as proposed to be amended by the court, the court may—

   (a) revoke the order; and

   (b) deal with him, for the offence in respect of which the order was made, in any manner in which it could deal with him if he had just been convicted by the court of the offence.

(5) In dealing with the offender under subsection (4)(b) above, the court—

   (a) shall take into account the extent to which the offender has complied with the requirements of the order; and

(b) may impose a custodial sentence notwithstanding anything in section 1(2) of the 1991 Act.

(6) Where the order was made by a magistrates' court in the case of an offender under the age of 18 years in respect of an offence triable only on indictment in the case of an adult, the court's power under subsection (4)(b) above shall be a power to do either or both of the following, namely—

(a) to impose a fine not exceeding £5,000 for the offence in respect of which the order was made;

(b) to deal with the offender for that offence in any way in which it could deal with him if it had just convicted him of an offence punishable with imprisonment for a term not exceeding six months;

and the reference in paragraph (b) above to an offence punishable with imprisonment shall be construed without regard to any prohibition or restriction imposed by or under any enactment on the imprisonment of young offenders.

(7) If at a review hearing the court, after considering the responsible officer's report, is of the opinion that the offender's progress under the order is satisfactory, the court may so amend the order as to provide for each subsequent review to be made by the court without a hearing.

(8) If at a review without a hearing the court, after considering the responsible officer's report, is of the opinion that the offender's progress under the order is no longer satisfactory, the court may require the offender to attend a hearing of the court at a specified time and place.

(9) At that hearing the court, after considering that report, may—

(a) exercise the powers conferred by this section as if the hearing were a review hearing; and

(b) so amend the order as to provide for each subsequent review to be made at a review hearing.

(10) In this section any reference to the court, in relation to a review without a hearing, shall be construed—

(a) in the case of the Crown Court, as a reference to a judge of the court;

(b) in the case of a magistrates' court, as a reference to a justice of the peace acting for the commission area for which the court acts.

Explanatory text—See paras **7.46–7.47**.

Drug treatment and testing order (subs (1))—See ss 61(2) and 85(1).

Month (subs (1))—See general annotations.

Responsible officer (subss (1), (2), (6) and (7))—See ss 62(7) and 85(1).

Treatment and testing period (subs (3))—See ss 61(2) and 85(4).

Willingness to comply (subss (3) and (4))—The offender should have a full appreciation as to what the realistic alternatives before the court are, so that, having considered them, the offender can decide whether he wishes to consent: *Barnett* (1986) 8 Cr App Rep (S) 200 (CA); *Marquis* [1974] 2 All ER 1216 (CA).

Treatment or testing requirement (subs (4))—See ss 62(1) and (4) and 85(4).

Section 1(2) of the 1991 Act (subs (5))—Ie the Criminal Justice Act 1991 (s 117(1)). Section 1 of the 1991 Act, provides:

'(1) This section applies where a person is convicted of an offence punishable with a custodial sentence other than one fixed by law.

(2) Subject to subsection (3) below, the court shall not pass a custodial sentence on the offender unless it is of the opinion—

    (a)   that the offence, or the combination of the offence and one or more offences associated with it, was so serious that only such a sentence can be justified for the offence; or

    (b)   where the offence is a violent or sexual offence, that only such a sentence would be adequate to protect the public from serious harm from him.

(3) Nothing in subsection (2) above shall prevent the court from passing a custodial sentence on the offender if he fails to express his willingness to comply with—

    (a)   a requirement which is proposed by the court to be included in a probation order or supervision order and which requires an expression of such willingness; or

    (b)   a requirement which is proposed by the court to be included in a drug treatment and testing order or an order under section 57(6) of the Crime and Disorder Act 1998.

(4) Where a court passes a custodial sentence, it shall be its duty—

    (a)   in a case not falling within subsection (3) above, to state in open court that it is of the opinion that either or both of paragraphs (a) and (b) of subsection (2) above apply and why it is of that opinion; and

    (b)   in any case, to explain to the offender in open court and in ordinary language why it is passing a custodial sentence on him.

(5) A magistrates' court shall cause a reason stated by it under subsection (4) above to be specified in the warrant of commitment and to be entered in the register.'

---

64 Supplementary provisions as to orders

(1) Before making a drug treatment and testing order, a court shall explain to the offender in ordinary language—

    (a) the effect of the order and of the requirements proposed to be included in it;

    (b) the consequences which may follow (under Schedule 2 to the 1991 Act) if he fails to comply with any of those requirements;

    (c) that the order may be reviewed (under that Schedule) on the application either of the offender or of the responsible officer; and

    (d) that the order will be periodically reviewed at intervals as provided for in the order (by virtue of section 63 above);

and the court shall not make the order unless the offender expresses his willingness to comply with its requirements.

(2) Where, in the case of a drug treatment and testing order made by a magistrates' court, another magistrates' court is responsible for the order, the court making the order shall forthwith send copies of the order to the other court.

(3) Where a drug treatment and testing order is made or amended under section 63(2) above, the court responsible for the order shall forthwith or, in a case falling within subsection (2) above, as soon as reasonably practicable give copies of the order, or the order as amended, to a probation officer assigned to the court, and he shall give a copy—

    (a) to the offender;

    (b) to the treatment provider; and

    (c) to the responsible officer.

(4) Where a drug treatment and testing order has been made on an appeal brought from the Crown Court, or from the criminal division of the Court of Appeal, for the purposes of sections 62 and 63 above it shall be deemed to have been made by the Crown Court.

(5) Schedule 2 to the 1991 Act (enforcement etc. of community orders) shall have effect subject to the amendments specified in Schedule 4 to this Act, being amendments for applying that Schedule to drug treatment and testing orders.

Explanatory text—See para **7.36**.

Drug treatment and testing order (subss (1) and (2))—See ss 61(2) and 85(1).

Explain to offender in ordinary language (subs (1))—The explanation must be such as to enable the offender to make informed assessments of his own position: see annotations to 'willingness to comply' (s 63).

Schedule 2 to the 1991 Act (subss (1) and (3))—Ie the Criminal Justice Act 1991 (s 117(1)). Schedule 2 to the 1991 Act, as amended by Schedules 4 and 7 to the new Act, provides as follows:

'SCHEDULE 2

ENFORCEMENT ETC OF COMMUNITY ORDERS

PART I

Preliminary

1—(1) In this Schedule "relevant order" means any of the following orders namely, a probation order, a drug treatment and testing order, a community service order and a curfew order; and "the petty sessions area concerned" means—

    (a)   in relation to a probation, community service order or drug treatment and testing order, the petty sessions area for the time being specified in the order; and

    (b)   in relation to a curfew order, the petty sessions area in which the place for the time being specified in the order is situated.

(2) Subject to sub-paragraph (3) below, this Schedule shall apply in relation to combination orders—

    (a)   in so far as they impose such a requirement as is mentioned in paragraph (a) of subsection (1) of section 11 of this Act, as if they were probation orders, and

    (b)   in so far as they impose such a requirement as is mentioned in paragraph (b) of that subsection, as if they were community service orders.

(3) In its application to combination orders, paragraph (6)(3) below shall have effect as if the reference to section 14(1A) of the 1973 Act were a reference to section 11(1) of this Act.

(4) Where a probation order, community service order, combination order or curfew order has been made on appeal, for the purposes of this Schedule it shall be deemed—

    (a)   as if it was made on appeal brought from a magistrates' court, to have been made by a magistrates' court;

    (b)   if it was made on an appeal brought from the Crown Court or from the criminal division of the Court of Appeal, to have been made by the Crown Court.

PART II

BREACH OF REQUIREMENT OF ORDER

Issue of summons or warrant

2—(1) If at any time while a relevant order is in force in respect of an offender it appears on information to a justice of the peace acting for the petty sessions area concerned that the offender has failed to comply with any of the requirements of the order, the justice may—

    (a)   issue a summons requiring the offender to appear at the place and time specified in it; or

(b) if the information is in writing and on oath, issue a warrant for his arrest.

(2) Any summons or warrant issued under this paragraph shall direct the offender to appear or be brought—

(a) except where the relevant order is a drug treatment and testing order, before a magistrates' court acting for the petty sessions area concerned;
(b) in the excepted case, before the court by which the order was made.

Powers of magistrates' court

3—(1) If it is proved to the satisfaction of the magistrates' court before which an offender appears or is brought under paragraph 2 above that he has failed without reasonable excuse to comply with any of the requirements of the relevant order, the court may deal with him in respect of the failure in any one of the following ways, namely—

(a) it may impose on him a fine not exceeding £1,000;
(b) subject to paragraph 6(3) to (5) below, it may make a community service order in respect of him;
(c) where—
   (i) the relevant order is a probation order and the offender is under the age of twenty-one years, or
   (ii) the relevant order is a curfew order and the offender is under the age of sixteen years,
   and the court has been notified as required by subsection (1) of section 17 of the 1982 Act, it may (subject to paragraph 6(6) below) make in respect of him an order under that subsection (attendance centre orders); or
(d) where the relevant order was made by a magistrates' court, it may revoke the order and deal with him, for the offence in respect of which the order was made, in any manner in which it could deal with him if he had just been convicted by the court of the offence.

(2) In dealing with an offender under sub-paragraph (1)(d) above, a magistrates' court—

(a) shall take into account the extent to which the offender has complied with the requirements of the relevant order; and
(b) may assume, in the case of an offender who has wilfully and persistently failed to comply with those requirements, that he has refused to give his consent to a community sentence which has been proposed by the court and requires consent.

(3) Where a relevant order was made by the Crown Court and a magistrates' court has power to deal with the offender under sub-paragraph (1)(a), (b) or (c) above, it may instead commit him to custody or release him on bail until he can be brought or appear before the Crown Court.

(4) A magistrates' court which deals with an offender's case under sub-paragraph (3) above shall send to the Crown Court—

(a) a certificate signed by a justice of the peace certifying that the offender has failed to comply with the requirements of the relevant order in that respect specified in the certificate; and
(b) such other particulars of the case as may be desirable;

and a certificate purporting to be so signed shall be admissible as evidence of the failure before the Crown Court.

(5) A person sentenced under sub-paragraph (1)(d) above for an offence may appeal to the Crown Court against the sentence.

Powers of Crown Court

4—(1) Where under paragraph 2 or by virtue of paragraph 3(3) above an offender is brought or appears before the Crown Court and it is proved to the satisfaction of the court that he has failed without reasonable excuse to comply with any of the requirements of the relevant order, that court may deal with him in respect of the failure in any one of the following ways, namely—

(a)   it may impose on him a fine not exceeding £1,000;

(b)   subject to paragraph 6(3) to (5) below, it may make a community service order in respect of him;

(c)   where—

    (i)   the relevant order is a probation order and the offender is under the age of twenty-one years, or

    (ii)   the relevant order is a curfew order and the offender is under the age of sixteen years,

and the court has been notified as required by subsection (1) of section 17 of the 1982 Act, it may (subject to paragraph 6(6) below) make in respect of him an order under that subsection (attendance centre orders); or

(d)   it may revoke the order and deal with him, for the offence in respect of which the order was made, in any manner in which it could deal with him if he had not been convicted before the Crown Court of the offence.

(2) In dealing with an offender under sub-paragraph (1)(d) above, the Crown Court—

(a)   shall take into account the extent to which the offender has complied with the requirements of the relevant order; and

(b)   may assume, in the case of an offender who has wilfully and persistently failed to comply with those requirements, that he has refused to give his consent to a community sentence which has been proposed by the court and requires that consent.

(3) In proceedings before the Crown Court under this paragraph any question whether the offender has failed to comply with the requirements of the relevant order shall be determined by the court and not by the verdict of a jury.

Exclusions

5—(1) Without prejudice to paragraphs 7 and 8 below, an offender who is convicted of a further offence while a relevant order is in force in respect of him shall not on that account be liable to be dealt with under paragraph 3 or 4 above in respect of a failure to comply with any requirement of the order.

(2) An offender who—

(a)   is required by a probation order to submit to treatment for his mental condition, or his dependency on or propensity to misuse drugs or alcohol; or

(b)   is required by a drug treatment and testing order to submit to treatment for his dependency on or propensity to misuse drugs,

shall not be treated for the purposes of paragraph 3 or 4 above as having failed to comply with that requirement on the ground only that he has refused to undergo any surgical, electrical or other treatment if, in the opinion of the court, his refusal was reasonable having regard to all the circumstances.

Supplemental

6—(1) Any exercise by a court of its powers under paragraph 3(1)(a), (b) or (c), or 4(1)(a), (b) or (c) above shall be without prejudice to the continuance of the relevant order.

(2) A fine imposed under paragraph 3(1) or 4(1)(a) above shall be deemed, for the purposes of any enactment, to be a sum adjudged to be paid by a conviction.

(3) The number of hours which an offender may be required to work under a community service order made under paragraph 3(1) or 4(1)(b) above—

(a)   shall be specified in the order and shall not exceed 60 in the aggregate; and

(b)   where the relevant order is a community service order, shall not be such that the total number of hours under both orders exceeds the maximum specified in section 14(1A) of the 1973 Act.

(3A) A community service order shall not be made under paragraph 3(1)(b) or 4(1)(b) above in respect of a person who is under the age of sixteen years.

(4) Section 14(2) of the 1973 Act and, so far as applicable—

    (a)   the following provisions of that Act relating to community service orders; and

    (b)   the provisions of this Schedule so far as so relating,

shall have effect in relation to a community service order under paragraph 3(1)(b) or 4(1)(b) above as they have effect in relation to a community service order in respect of an offender.

(5) Where the provisions of this Schedule have effect as mentioned in sub-paragraph (4) above in relation to a community service order under paragraph 3(1)(b) or 4(1)(b) above—

    (a)   the power conferred on the court by each of paragraphs 3(1)(d) and 4(1)(d) above and paragraph 7(2)(a)(ii) below to deal with the offender for the offence in respect of which the order was made shall be construed as a power to deal with the offender, for his failure to comply with the original order, in any manner in which the court could deal with him if that failure to comply had just been proved to the satisfaction of the court;

    (b)   the reference in paragraph 7(1)(b) below to the offence in respect of which the order was made shall be construed as a reference to the failure to comply in respect of which the order was made; and

    (c)   the power conferred on the court by paragraph 8(2)(b) below to deal with the offender for the offence in respect of which the order was made shall be construed as a power to deal with the offender, for his failure to comply with the original order, in any manner in which the court which made the original order could deal with him if that failure had just been proved to the satisfaction of that court;

and in this sub-paragraph "the original order" means the relevant order the failure to comply with whose requirements led to the making of the community service order under paragraph 3(1)(b) or 4(1)(b).

(6) The provisions of sections 17 to 19 of the 1982 Act (making, discharge, variation and breach of attendance centre order) shall apply for the purposes of paragraphs 3(1)(c) and 4(1)(c) above but as if there were omitted—

    (a)   subsection (13) of section 17;

    (b)   from subsection (4A) of section 18 and subsections (3) and (5) of section 19, the words, "for the offence in respect of which the order was made", and "for that offence".

6A—(1) Where a relevant order was made by a magistrates' court in the case of an offender under 18 years of age in respect of an offence triable only on indictment in the case of an adult, any powers exercisable under paragraph 3(1)(d) above by that or any other court in respect of the offender after he has attained the age of 18 years shall be powers to do one of the following—

    (a)   to impose a fine not exceeding £5,000 for the offence in respect of which the order was made; or

    (b)   to deal with the offender for that offence in any way in which a magistrates' court could deal with him if it had just convicted him of an offence punishable with imprisonment for a term not exceeding six months.

(2) In sub-paragraph (1)(b) above any reference to an offence punishable with imprisonment shall be construed without regard to any prohibition or restriction imposed by or under any enactment on the imprisonment of young offenders.

PART III

REVOCATION OF ORDER

Revocation of order with or without re-sentencing

7—(1) This paragraph applies where a relevant order is in force in respect of any offender and, on the application of the offender or the responsible officer, it appears to a magistrates' court acting for the petty sessions area concerned or, where the relevant order is a drug treatment and testing order made by a magistrates' court, to that court, that, having regard to circumstances which have arisen since the order was made, it would be in the interests of justice—

   (a)   that the order should be revoked; or

   (b)   that the offender should be dealt with in some other manner for the offence in respect of which the order was made.

(2) The court may—

   (a)   if the order was made by a magistrates' court—

      (i) revoke the order; or

     (ii) revoke the order and deal with the offender, for the offence in respect of which the order was made, in any manner in which it could deal with him if he had just been convicted by the court of the offence; or

   (b)   if the order was made by the Crown Court, commit him to custody or release him on bail until he can be brought or appear before the Crown Court.

(3) The circumstances in which a probation order or drug treatment and testing order may be revoked under sub-paragraph (2)(a)(i) above shall include the offender's making good progress or his responding satisfactorily to supervision or, as the case may be, treatment.

(4) In dealing with an offender under sub-paragraph (2)(a)(ii) above, a magistrates' court shall take into account the extent to which the offender has complied with the requirements of the relevant order.

(5) An offender sentenced under sub-paragraph (2)(a)(ii) above for an offence may appeal to the Crown Court against the sentence.

(6) Where the court deals with an offender's case under sub-paragraph (2)(b) above, it shall send to the Crown Court such particulars of the case as may be desirable.

(7) Where a magistrates' court proposes to exercise its powers under this paragraph otherwise than on the application of the offender it shall summon him to appear before the court and, if he does not appear in answer to the summons, may issue a warrant for his arrest.

(8) No application may be made by the offender under sub-paragraph (1) above while an appeal against the relevant order is pending.

8—(1) This paragraph applies where an offender in respect of whom a relevant order is in force—

   (a)   is convicted of an offence before the Crown Court; or

   (b)   is committed by a magistrates' court to the Crown Court for sentence and is brought or appears before the Crown Court; or

   (c)   by virtue of paragraph 7(2)(b) above is brought or appears before the Crown Court.

(1A) This paragraph also applies where—

   (a)   a drug treatment and testing order made by the Crown Court is in force in respect of an offender; and

   (b)   the offender or the responsible officer applies to the Crown Court for the order to be revoked or for the offender to be dealt with in some other manner for the offence in respect of which the order was made.

(2) If it appears to the Crown Court to be in the interests of justice to do so, having regard to circumstances which have arisen since the order was made, the Crown Court may—

   (a)   revoke the order; or

   (b)   revoke the order and deal with the offender, for the offence in respect of which the order was made, in any manner in which it could deal with him if he had just been convicted by or before the court of the offence.

(3) The circumstances in which a probation order or drug treatment and testing order may be revoked under sub-paragraph (2)(a) above shall include the offender's making good progress or his responding satisfactorily to supervision or, as the case may be, treatment.

(4) In dealing with an offender under sub-paragraph (2)(b) above, the Crown Court shall take into account the extent to which the offender has complied with the requirements of the relevant order.

8A—(1) This paragraph applies where a probation order is in force in respect of any offender and on the application of the offender or the responsible officer it appears to a magistrates' court acting for the petty sessions area concerned that, having regard to circumstances which have arisen since the order was made, it would be in the interests of justice—

(a)   for the probation order to be revoked; and

(b)   for an order to be made under section 1A(1)(b) of the 1973 Act discharging the offender conditionally for the offence for which the probation order was made.

(2) No application may be made under paragraph 7 above for a probation order to be revoked and replaced with an order for conditional discharge under section 1A(1)(b) of the 1973 Act; but otherwise nothing in this paragraph shall affect the operation of paragraphs 7 and 8 above.

(3) Where this paragraph applies and the probation order was made by a magistrates' court—

(a)   the magistrates' court dealing with the application may revoke the probation order and make an order under section 1A(1)(b) of the 1973 Act discharging the offender in respect of the offence for which the probation order was made, subject to the condition that he commits no offence during the period specified in the order under section 1A(1)(b); and

(b)   the period specified in the order under section 1A(1)(b) shall be the period beginning with the making of that order and ending with the date when the probation period specified in the probation order would have ended.

(4) Where this paragraph applies and the probation order was made by the Crown Court, the magistrates' court may send the application to the Crown Court to be heard by that court, and if it does so shall also send to the Crown Court such particulars of the case as may be desirable.

(5) Where an application under this paragraph is heard by the Crown Court by virtue of sub-paragraph (4) above—

(a)   the Crown Court may revoke the probation order and make an order under section 1A(1)(b) of the 1973 Act discharging the offender in respect of the offence for which the probation order was made, subject to the condition that he commits no offence during the period specified in the order under section 1A(1)(b); and

(b)   the period specified in the order under subsection 1A(1)(b) shall be the period beginning with the making of that order and ending with the date when the probation period specified in the probation order would have ended.

(6) For the purposes of subparagraphs (3) and (5) above, subsection (1) of section 1A of the 1973 Act shall apply as if—

(a)   for the words from the beginning to "may make an order either" there were substituted the words "Where paragraph 8A of Schedule 2 to the Criminal Justice Act 1991 applies, the court under which sub-paragraph (3) or (5) of that paragraph has power to dispose of the application may (subject to the provisions of that sub-paragraph) make an order in respect of the offender", and

(b)   paragraph (a) of that subsection were omitted.

(7) An application under this paragraph may be heard in the offender's absence if—

(a)   the application is made by the responsible officer; and

(b)   that officer produces to the court a statement by the offender that the understands the effect of an order for conditional discharge and consents to the making of the application;

and where the application is so heard section 1A(3) of the 1973 Act shall not apply.

(8) No application may be made under this paragraph while an appeal against the probation order is pending.

(9) Without prejudice to paragraph 11 below, on the making of an order under section 1A(1)(b) of the 1973 Act by virtue of this paragraph the court shall forthwith give copies of the order to the responsible officer, and the responsible officer shall give a copy to the offender.

(10) Each of sections 1(11), 2(9) and 66(4) of the Crime and Disorder Act 1998 (which prevent a court from making an order for conditional discharge in certain cases) shall have effect as if the reference to the court by or before which a person is convicted of an offence there mentioned included a reference to a court dealing with an application under this paragraph in respect of the offence.

Revocation of order following custodial sentence

9—(1) This paragraph applies where—

    (a)   an offender in respect of whom a relevant order is in force is convicted of an offence—
        (i)   by a magistrates' court other than a magistrates' court acting for the petty sessions area concerned; or
        (ii)   where the relevant order is a drug treatment and testing order, by a magistrates' court which did not make the order, and
    (b)   the court imposes a custodial sentence on the offender.

(2) If it appears to the court, on the application of the offender or the responsible officer, that it would be in the interests of justice to do so having regard to circumstances which have arisen since the order was made, the court may—

    (a)   if the order was made by a magistrates' court, revoke it; and
    (b)   if the order was made by the Crown Court, commit the offender in custody or release him on bail until he can be brought or appear before the Crown Court.

(3) Where the court deals with an offender's case under sub-paragraph (2)(b) above, it shall send to the Crown Court such particulars of the case as may be desirable.

10—Where by virtue of paragraph 9(2)(b) above an offender is brought or appears before the Crown Court and it appears to the Crown Court to be in the interests of justice to do so, having regard to circumstances which have arisen since the relevant order was made, the Crown Court may revoke the order.

Supplemental

11—(1) On the making under this Part of this Schedule of an order revoking a relevant order, the clerk to the court shall forthwith give copies of the revoking order to the responsible officer.

(2) A responsible officer to whom in accordance with sub-paragraph (1) above copies of a revoking order are given shall give a copy to the offender and to the person in charge of any institution in which the offender was required by the order to reside.

11A—Paragraph 6A above shall apply for the purposes of paragraphs 7 and 8 above as it applies for the purposes of paragraph 3 above, but as if in paragraph 6A(1) for the words "powers exercisable under paragraph 3(1)(d) above" there were substituted the words "powers to deal with the offender which are exercisable under paragraph 7(2)(a)(ii) or 8(2)(b) below".

11B—Where under this Part of this Schedule a relevant order is revoked and replaced by an order for conditional discharge under section 1A(1)(b) of the 1973 Act and—

    (a)   the order for conditional discharge is not made in the circumstances mentioned in section 1B(9) of the 1973 Act (order made by magistrates' court in the case of an offender under 18 in respect of offence triable only on indictment in the case of an adult), but
    (b)   the relevant order was made in those circumstances, section 1B(9) of the 1973 Act shall apply as if the order for conditional discharge had been made in those circumstances.

PART IV

AMENDMENT OF ORDER

Amendment by reason of change of residence

12—(1) This paragraph applies where, at any time while a relevant order is in force in respect of an offender, a magistrates' court acting for the petty sessions area concerned is satisfied that the offender proposes to change, or has changed his residence from that petty sessions area to another petty sessions area.

(2) Subject to subparagraphs (3) and (4) below, the court may, and on the application of the responsible officer shall, amend the relevant order by substituting the other petty sessions area for the area specified in the order or, in the case of a curfew order, a place in that other area for the place so specified.

(3) The court shall not amend under this paragraph a probation or curfew order which contains requirements which, in the opinion of the court, cannot be complied with unless the offender continues to reside in the petty sessions area concerned unless, in accordance with paragraph 13 below, it either—

    (a)   cancels those requirements; or
    (b)   substitutes for those requirements other requirements which can be complied with if the offender ceases to reside in that area.

(4) The court shall not amend a community service order under this paragraph unless it appears to the court that provision can be made for the offender to perform work under the order under the arrangements which exist for persons who reside in the other petty sessions area to perform work under such orders.

(5) Where—

    (a)   the court amends a probation order or community service order under this paragraph;
    (b)   a local authority is specified in the order in accordance with section 2(2)(b) or 14(4)(c) of the 1973 Act; and
    (c)   the change, or promised change, of residence also is, or would be, a change of residence from the area of that authority to the area of another such authority,

the court shall further amend the order by substituting the other authority for the authority specified in the order.

(6) In subparagraph (5) above "local authority" has the meaning given by section 42 of the Crime and Disorder Act 1998 and references to the area of the local authority shall be construed in accordance with that section.

Amendment of requirements of probation or curfew order

13—(1) Without prejudice to the provisions of paragraph 12 above, but subject to subparagraph (2) below, a magistrates court for the petty sessions area concerned may, on the application of the offender or the responsible officer, by order amend a probation or curfew order—

    (a)   by cancelling any of the requirements of the order, or
    (b)   by inserting in the order (either in addition to or in substitution for any such requirement) any requirement which the court could include if it were then making the order.

(2) The power of a magistrates' court under subparagraph (1) above shall be subject to the following restrictions, namely—

    (a)   the court shall not amend a probation order—
        (i)   by reducing the probation period, or by extending that period beyond the end of three years from the date of the original order; or
        (ii) by inserting in it as requirement that the offender shall submit to treatment for his mental condition, or his dependency on drugs or alcohol, unless the amending order is made within three months after the date of the original order; and
    (b)   the court shall not amend a curfew order by extending the curfew periods beyond the end of six months from the date of the original order.

In this paragraph and paragraph 14 below, references to the offender's dependency on drugs or alcohol include references to his propensity towards the misuse of drugs or alcohol.

Amendment of certain requirements of probation order

14—(1) Where the medical practitioner or other person by whom or under whose direction an offender is being treated for his mental condition, or his dependency on drugs or alcohol, in pursuance of any requirement of a probation order—

    (a)   is of the opinion mentioned in subparagraph (2) below; or

    (b)   is for any reason unwilling to continue to treat or direct the treatment of the offender,

he shall make a report in writing to that effect to the responsible officer and that officer shall apply under paragraph 13 above to a magistrates' court for the petty sessions area concerned for the variation or cancellation of the requirement.

(2) The opinion referred to in subparagraph (1) above is—

    (a)   that the treatment of the offender should be continued beyond the period specified in that behalf in the order;

    (b)   that the offender needs different treatment, being treatment of a kind to which he could be required to submit in pursuance of a probation order;

    (c)   that the offender is not susceptible to treatment; or

    (d)   that the offender does not require further treatment.'

Young offenders: reprimands and warnings

65 Reprimands and warnings

(1) Subsections (2) to (5) below apply where—

    (a) a constable has evidence that a child or young person ('the offender') has committed an offence;

    (b) the constable considers that the evidence is such that, if the offender were prosecuted for the offence, there would be a realistic prospect of his being convicted;

    (c) the offender admits to the constable that he committed the offence;

    (d) the offender has not previously been convicted of an offence; and

    (e) the constable is satisfied that it would not be in the public interest for the offender to be prosecuted.

(2) Subject to subsection (4) below, the constable may reprimand the offender if the offender has not previously been reprimanded or warned.

(3) The constable may warn the offender if—

    (a) the offender has not previously been warned; or

    (b) where the offender has previously been warned, the offence was committed more than two years after the date of the previous warning and the constable considers the offence to be not so serious as to require a charge to be brought;

but no person may be warned under paragraph (b) above more than once.

(4) Where the offender has not been previously reprimanded, the constable shall warn rather than reprimand the offender if he considers the offence to be so serious as to require a warning.

(5) The constable shall—

    (a) give any reprimand or warning at a police station and, where the offender is under the age of 17, in the presence of an appropriate adult; and

(b) explain to the offender and, where he is under that age, the appropriate adult in ordinary language—

  (i)   in the case of a reprimand, the effect of subsection (5)(a) of section 66 below;

  (ii) in the case of a warning, the effect of subsections (1), (2), (4) and (5)(b) and (c) of that section, and any guidance issued under subsection (3) of that section.

(6) The Secretary of State shall publish, in such manner as he considers appropriate, guidance as to—

(a) the circumstances in which it is appropriate to give reprimands or warnings, including criteria for determining—

  (i)   for the purposes of subsection (3)(b) above, whether an offence is not so serious as to require a charge to be brought; and

  (ii) for the purposes of subsection (4) above, whether an offence is so serious as to require a warning;

(b) the category of constable by whom reprimands and warnings may be given; and

(c) the form which reprimands and warnings are to take and the manner in which they are to be given and recorded.

(7) In this section 'appropriate adult', in relation to a child or young person, means—

(a) his parent or guardian or, if he is in the care of a local authority or voluntary organisation, a person representing that authority or organisation;

(b) a social worker of a local authority social services department;

(c) if no person falling within paragraph (a) or (b) above is available, any responsible person aged 18 or over who is not a police officer or a person employed by the police.

(8) No caution shall be given to a child or young person after the commencement of this section.

(9) Any reference (however expressed) in any enactment passed before or in the same Session as this Act to a person being cautioned shall be construed, in relation to any time after that commencement, as including a reference to a child or young person being reprimanded or warned.

Explanatory text—See paras **3.66–3.71**.

Constable (subss (1), (2), (3), (4), (5) and (6))—See general annotations.

Child or young person (subss (1), (7) and (8))—See s 117(1).

Appropriate adult (subss (5) and (7))—Defined by Code C, made under the Police and Criminal Evidence Act 1984. The expression means:

(a) in the case of an arrested juvenile, his parent or guardian (or if he is on the case of a local authority, that authority) or a representative of the local authority social services department or another responsible adult who is not a police officer; and

(b) in the case of a person who is mentally ill or mentally handicapped, his nearest available relative or some other person who is responsible for his care or custody or another responsible adult who is not a police officer.

Age (subs (7))—See general annotations.

Commencement of this subsection (subs (8))—See para 1.4.

---

66 Effect of reprimands and warnings

(1) Where a constable warns a person under section 65 above, he shall as soon as practicable refer the person to a youth offending team.

(2) A youth offending team—

   (a) shall assess any person referred to them under subsection (1) above; and
   (b) unless they consider it inappropriate to do so, shall arrange for him to participate in a rehabilitation programme.

(3) The Secretary of State shall publish, in such manner as he considers appropriate, guidance as to—

   (a) what should be included in a rehabilitation programme arranged for a person under subsection (2) above;
   (b) the manner in which any failure by a person to participate in such a programme is to be recorded; and
   (c) the persons to whom any such failure is to be notified.

(4) Where a person who has been warned under section 65 above is convicted of an offence committed within two years of the warning, the court by or before which he is so convicted—

   (a) shall not make an order under subsection (1)(b) (conditional discharge) of section 1A of the 1973 Act in respect of the offence unless it is of the opinion that there are exceptional circumstances relating to the offence or the offender which justify its doing so; and
   (b) where it does so, shall state in open court that it is of that opinion and why it is.

(5) The following, namely—

   (a) any reprimand of a person under section 65 above;
   (b) any warning of a person under that section; and
   (c) any report on a failure by a person to participate in a rehabilitation programme arranged for him under subsection (2) above,

may be cited in criminal proceedings in the same circumstances as a conviction of the person may be cited.

(6) In this section 'rehabilitation programme' means a programme the purpose of which is to rehabilitate participants and to prevent them from re-offending.

Explanatory text—See paras **3.72–3.75**.

Youth offending team (subs (2))—See paras **2.19–2.21**.

Section 1A of the 1973 Act (subs (4))—'The 1973 Act' means the Powers of Criminal Courts Act 1973 (s 117(1)). The operative parts of s 1A are as follows:

   '(1) Where a court by or before which a person is convicted of an offence (not being an offence the sentence for which is fixed by law) is of opinion, having regard to the circumstances including the nature of the offence and the character of the offender, that it is inexpedient to inflict punishment, the court may make an order—

      (a) discharging him absolutely; or
      (b) if the court thinks fit, discharging him subject to the condition that he commits no offence during such period, not exceeding three years from the date of the order, as may be specified in the order.

   (1A) Subsection (1)(b) above has effect subject to section 66(4) of the Crime and Disorder Act 1998 (effect of reprimands and warnings).

(2) [omitted].

(3) Before making an order for conditional discharge the court shall explain to the offender in ordinary language that if he commits another offence during the period of conditional discharge he will be liable to be sentenced for the original offence.

(4) Where under the following provisions of this Part of the Act, a person conditionally discharged under this section is sentenced for the offence in respect of which the order was made, that order shall cease to have effect.

(5) [omitted].'

Young offenders: non-custodial orders

67 Reparation orders

(1) This section applies where a child or young person is convicted of an offence other than one for which the sentence is fixed by law.

(2) Subject to the provisions of this section and section 68 below, the court by or before which the offender is convicted may make an order (a 'reparation order') which requires the offender to make reparation specified in the order—

    (a) to a person or persons so specified; or
    (b) to the community at large;

and any person so specified must be a person identified by the court as a victim of the offence or a person otherwise affected by it.

(3) The court shall not make a reparation order unless it has been notified by the Secretary of State that arrangements for implementing such orders are available in the area proposed to be named in the order and the notice has not been withdrawn.

(4) The court shall not make a reparation order in respect of the offender if it proposes—

    (a) to pass on him a custodial sentence or a sentence under section 53(1) of the 1933 Act; or
    (b) to make in respect of him a community service order, a combination order, a supervision order which includes requirements imposed in pursuance of sections 12 to 12C of the 1969 Act or an action plan order.

(5) A reparation order shall not require the offender—

    (a) to work for more than 24 hours in aggregate; or
    (b) to make reparation to any person without the consent of that person.

(6) Subject to subsection (5) above, requirements specified in a reparation order shall be such as in the opinion of the court are commensurate with seriousness of the offence, or the combination of the offence and one or more offences associated with it.

(7) Requirements so specified shall, as far as practicable, be such as to avoid—

    (a) any conflict with the offender's religious beliefs or with the requirements of any community order to which he may be subject; and
    (b) any interference with the times, if any, at which the offender normally works or attends school or any other educational establishment.

(8) Any reparation required by a reparation order—

    (a) shall be made under the supervision of the responsible officer; and

  (b) shall be made within a period of three months from the date of the making of the
       order.

(9) A reparation order shall name the petty sessions area in which it appears to the
court making the order, or to the court varying any provision included in the order in
pursuance of this subsection, that the offender resides or will reside.

(10) In this section 'responsible officer', in relation to a reparation order, means one of
the following who is specified in the order, namely—

  (a) a probation officer;
  (b) a social worker of a local authority social services department; and
  (c) a member of a youth offending team.

(11) The court shall give reasons if it does not make a reparation order in a case where it
has power to do so.

Explanatory text—See paras **4.2–4.22**.

Supervision order which includes requirements in pursuance of sections 12 to 12C of the 1969 Act
(subs (4))—'The 1969 Act' is the Children and Young Persons Act 1969 (s 117(1)). These
provisions (as amended by the new Act) provide:

'12—(1) A supervision order may require the supervised person to reside with an individual
named in the order who agrees to the requirement, but a requirement imposed by a supervision
order in pursuance of this subsection shall be subject to any such requirement of the order as is
authorised by the following provisions of this section or by section 12A, 12B or 12C below.

(2) Subject to section 19(12) of this Act, a supervision order may require the supervised person to
comply with any directions given from time to time by the supervisor and requiring him to do all
or any of the following things—

  (a) to live at a place or places specified in the directions for a period or periods so specified;
  (b) to present himself to a person or persons specified in the directions at a place or places
       and on a day or days so specified;
  (c) to participate in activities specified in the directions on a day or days so specified;

but it shall be for the supervisor to decide whether and to what extent he exercises any power to
give directions conferred on him by virtue of this subsection and to decide the form of any
directions; and a requirement imposed by supervision order in pursuance of this subsection shall
be subject to any such requirement of the order as is authorised by section 12B(1) of this Act.

(3) The total number of days in respect of which a supervised person may be required to comply
with directions given by virtue of paragraph (a), (b), or (c) of subsection (2) above in pursuance
of a supervision order shall not exceed 90 or such lesser number, if any, as the order may specify
for the purposes of this subsection; and for the purpose of calculating the total number of days in
respect of which such directions may be given the supervisor shall be entitled to disregard any day
in respect of which directions were previously given in pursuance of the order and on which the
directions were not complied with.

12A—(1) This subsection applies to any supervision order made under section 7(7) of this Act
unless it requires the supervised person to comply with directions given by the supervisor under
section 12(2) of this Act.

(2) [Effectively repealed by the Children Act 1989, Sch 12].

(3) Subject to the following provisions of this section and to section 19(13) of this Act, a
supervision order to which subsection (1) of this section applies may require a supervised
person—

  (a) to do anything that by virtue of section 12(2) of this Act a supervisor has power, or would
       but for section 19(12) of this Act have power, to direct a supervised person to do;

    (aa) to make reparation specified in the order to a person or persons so specified or to the community at large;

    (b) to remain for specified periods between 6 p.m. and 6 a.m.—

        (i) at a place specified in the order; or

        (ii) at one of several places so specified;

    (c) to refrain from participating in activities specified in the order—

        (i) on a specified day or days during the period for which the supervision order is in force; or

        (ii) during the whole of that period or a specified portion of it.

(4) Any power to include a requirement in a supervision order which is exercisable in relation to a person by virtue of this section or the following provisions of this Act may be exercised in relation to him whether or not any other such power is exercised.

(5) The total number of days in respect of which a supervised person may be subject to requirements imposed by virtue of subsection (3) (a), (aa) or (b) above shall not exceed 90.

(6) The court may not include requirements under subsection (3) above in a supervision order unless—

    (a) it has first consulted the supervisor as to—

        (i) the offender's circumstances, and

        (ii) the feasibility of securing compliance with the requirements, and is satisfied, having regard to the supervisor's report, that it is feasible to secure compliance with them;

    (b) having regard to the circumstances of the case, it considers the requirements necessary for securing the good conduct of the supervised person or for preventing a repetition by him of the same offence or the commission of other offences; and

    (c) the supervised person or, if he is a child, his parent of guardian, consents to their inclusion.

(7) The court shall not include in such an order by virtue of subsection (3) above—

    (a) any requirement that would involve the co-operation of a person other than the supervisor and the supervised person unless that other person consents to its inclusion; or

    (aa) any requirement to make reparation to any person unless that person—

        (i) is identified by the court as a victim of the offence or a person otherwise affected by it; and

        (ii) consents to the inclusion of the requirement; or

    (b) any requirement requiring the supervised person to reside with a specified individual; or

    (c) any such requirement as is mentioned in section 12B(1) of this Act.

(8) The place, or one of the places, specified in a requirement under subsection (3)(b) above ('a night restriction') shall be the place where the supervised person lives.

(9) A night restriction shall not require the supervised person to remain at a place for longer than 10 hours on any one night.

(10) A night restriction shall not be imposed in respect of any day which falls outside the period of three months beginning with the date when the supervision order is made.

(11) A night restriction shall not be imposed in respect of more than 30 days in all.

(12) A supervised person who is required by a night restriction to remain at a place may leave it if he is accompanied—

    (a) by his parent or guardian;

    (b) by his supervisor; or

    (c) by some other person specified in the supervision order.

(13) A night restriction imposed in respect of a period of time beginning in the evening and ending in the morning shall be treated as imposed only in respect of the day upon which the period begins.

12AA—(1) Where the conditions mentioned in subsection (6) of this section are satisfied, a supervision order may impose a requirement ("a residence requirement") that a child or young person shall live for a specified period in local authority accommodation.

(2) A residence requirement shall designate the local authority who are to receive the child or young person and that authority shall be the authority in whose area the child or young person resides.

(3) The court shall not impose a residence requirement without first consulting the designated authority.

(4) A residence requirement may stipulate that the child or young person shall not live with a named person.

(5) The maximum period which may be specified in a residence requirement is six months.

(6) The conditions are that—

- (a) a supervision order has previously been made in respect of the child or young person;
- (b) that order imposed—
  - (i) a requirement under section 12, 12A or 12C of this Act; or
  - (ii) a residence requirement;
- (c) that he fails to comply with that requirement, or is found guilty of an offence committed while that order was in force; and
- (d) the court is satisfied that—
  - (i) the failure to comply with the requirement, or the behaviour which constituted the offence, was due to a significant extent to the circumstances in which he was living; and
  - (ii) the imposition of a residence requirement will assist in his rehabilitation.

Except that subparagraph (i) of paragraph (d) of this subsection does not apply where the condition in paragraph (b)(ii) is satisfied.

(7), (8) [Repealed by CJA 1991, Sch 13].

(9) A court shall not include a residence requirement in respect of a child or young person who is not legally represented at the relevant time in that court unless—

- (a) he has applied for legal aid for the purposes of the proceedings and the application was refused on the ground that it did not appear that his resources were such that he required assistance; or
- (b) he has been informed of his right to apply for legal aid for the purposes of the proceedings and has had the opportunity to do so, but nevertheless refused or failed to apply.

(10) In subsection (9) of this section—

- (a) "the relevant time" means the time when the court is considering whether or not to impose the requirement; and
- (b) "the proceedings" means—
  - (i) the whole proceedings; or
  - (ii) the part of the proceedings relating to the imposition of the requirement.

(11) A supervision order imposing a residence requirement may also impose any of the requirements mentioned in sections 12, 12A, 12B or 12C of this Act.

(12) [Repealed by CJA 1991, Sch 13].

Requirements as to mental treatment

12B—(1) Where a court which proposes to make a supervision order is satisfied, on the evidence of a medical practitioner approved for the purposes of section 12 of the Mental Health Act 1983, that the mental condition of a supervised person is such as requires and may be susceptible to treatment but is not such as to warrant his detention in pursuance of a hospital order under Part III of that Act, the court may include in the supervision order a requirement that the supervised person shall, for a period specified in the order submit to treatment of one of the following descriptions so specified, that is to say—

(a)   treatment by or under the direction of a fully registered medical practitioner specified in the order;
(b)   treatment as a non-resident patient at a place specified in the order; or
(c)   treatment as a resident patient in a hospital or mental nursing home within the meaning of the said Act of 1983, but not a special hospital within the meaning of that Act.

(2) A requirement shall not be included in a supervision order in pursuance of subsection (1) above—

(a)   in any case, unless the court is satisfied that arrangements have been or can be made for the treatment in question and, in the case of treatment as a resident patient, of the reception of the patient;
(b)   in the case of an order made or to be made in respect of a person who has attained the age of 14, unless he consents to its inclusion;

and a requirement so included shall not in any case continue in force after the supervised person becomes 18.

12C—(1) Subject to subsection (3) below, a supervision order to which section 12A(1) of this Act applies may require a supervised person, if he is of compulsory school age, to comply, for as long as he is of that age and the order remains in force, with such arrangements for his education as may from time to time be made by his parent, being arrangements for the time being approved by the local education authority.

(2) The court shall not include such a requirement in a supervision order unless it has consulted the local education authority with regard to its proposal to include the requirement and is satisfied that in the view of the local education authority arrangements exist for the child or young person to whom the supervision order will relate to receive efficient full-time education suitable to his age, ability and aptitude and to any special educational need he may have.

(3) Expressions used in subsection (1) above and in the Education Act 1944 have the same meaning there as in that Act.

(4) The court may not include a requirement under subsection (1) above unless it has first consulted the supervisor as to the offender's circumstances and, having regard to the circumstances of the case, it considers the requirement necessary for him of the same offence or the commission of other offences.

12D [repealed].

13—(1) A court shall not designate a local authority as the supervisor by a provision of a supervision order unless the authority agree or it appears to the court that the supervised person resides or will reside in the area of the authority.

(2) [repealed].

(3) Where a provision of a supervision order places a person under the supervision of a probation officer, the supervisor shall be a probation officer appointed for or assigned to the petty sessions area named in the order in pursuance of section 18(2)(a) of this Act and selected under arrangements made under section 4(1)(d) of the Probation Service Act 1993 (arrangements made by probation committee).'

Associated offence (subs (6))—By s 31(2) of the Criminal Justice Act 1991, an offence is associated with another if:

(a)   the offender is convicted of it in the proceedings in which he is convicted of the other offence, or (although convicted of it in earlier proceedings) is sentenced for it at the same time as he is sentenced for that offence; or

(b) the offender admits the commission of it in the proceedings in which he is sentenced for the other offence and requests the court to take it into consideration in sentencing him for that offence.

68 Reparation orders: supplemental

(1) Before making a reparation order, a court shall obtain and consider a written report by a probation officer, a social worker of a local authority social services department or a member of a youth offending team, indicating—

(a) the type of work that is suitable for the offender; and
(b) the attitude of the victim or victims to the requirements proposed to be included in the order.

(2) Before making a reparation order, a court shall explain to the offender in ordinary language—

(a) the effect of the order and of the requirements proposed to be included in it;
(b) the consequences which may follow (under Schedule 5 to this Act) if he fails to comply with any of those requirements; and
(c) that the court has power (under that Schedule) to review the order on the application either of the offender or of the responsible officer.

(3) Schedule 5 to this Act shall have effect for dealing with failure to comply with the requirements of reparation orders, for varying such orders and for discharging them with or without the substitution of other sentences.

Explanatory text—See paras **4.9–4.10**.

69 Action plan orders

(1) This section applies where a child or young person is convicted of an offence other than one for which the sentence is fixed by law.

(2) Subject to the provisions of this section and section 70 below, the court by or before which the offender is convicted may, if it is of the opinion that it is desirable to do so in the interests of securing his rehabilitation, or of preventing the commission by him of further offences, make an order (an 'action plan order') which—

(a) requires the offender, for a period of three months beginning with the date of the order, to comply with an action plan, that is to say, a series of requirements with respect to his actions and whereabouts during that period;
(b) places the offender under the supervision for that period of the responsible officer; and
(c) requires the offender to comply with any directions given by that officer with a view to the implementation of that plan.

(3) The court shall not make an action plan order unless it has been notified by the Secretary of State that arrangements for implementing such orders are available in the area proposed to be named in the order and the notice has not been withdrawn.

(4) The court shall not make an action plan order in respect of the offender if—

   (a) he is already the subject of such an order; or

   (b) the court proposes to pass on him a custodial sentence or a sentence under section 53(1) of the 1933 Act, or to make in respect of him a probation order, a community service order, a combination order, a supervision order or an attendance centre order.

(5) Requirements included in an action plan order, or directions given by a responsible officer, may require the offender to do all or any of the following things, namely—

   (a) to participate in activities specified in the requirements or directions at a time or times so specified;

   (b) to present himself to a person or persons specified in the requirements or directions at a place or places and at a time or times so specified;

   (c) to attend at an attendance centre specified in the requirements or directions for a number of hours so specified;

   (d) to stay away from a place or places specified in the requirements or directions;

   (e) to comply with any arrangements for his education specified in the requirements or directions;

   (f) to make reparation specified in the requirements or directions to a person or persons so specified or to the community at large; and

   (g) to attend any hearing fixed by the court under section 70(3) below.

(6) Such requirements and directions shall, as far as practicable, be such as to avoid—

   (a) any conflict with the offender's religious beliefs or with the requirements of any other community order to which he may be subject; and

   (b) any interference with the times, if any, at which he normally works or attends school or any other educational establishment.

(7) Subsection (5)(c) above does not apply unless the offence committed by the offender is punishable with imprisonment in the case of a person aged 21 or over.

(8) A person shall not be specified in requirements or directions under subsection (5)(f) above unless—

   (a) he is identified by the court or, as the case may be, the responsible officer as a victim of the offence or a person otherwise affected by it; and

   (b) he consents to the reparation being made.

(9) An action plan order shall name the petty sessions area in which it appears to the court making the order, or to the court varying any provision included in the order in pursuance of this subsection, that the offender resides or will reside.

(10) In this section 'responsible officer', in relation to an action plan order, means one of the following who is specified in the order, namely—

   (a) a probation officer;

   (b) a social worker of a local authority social services department; and

   (c) a member of a youth offending team.

(11) An action plan order shall be a community order for the purposes of Part I of the 1991 Act; and the provisions of that Part, which include provisions with respect to restrictions on imposing, and procedural requirements for, community sentences (sections 6 and 7), shall apply accordingly.

Explanatory text—See paras **4.24–4.33**.

Combination order (subs (4))—Section 11 of the Criminal Justice Act 1991, as amended by Sch 8, para 76, provides:

'(1) Where a court by or before which a person of or over the age of 16 years is convicted of an offence punishable with imprisonment (not being an offence for which the sentence is fixed by law or falls to be imposed under section 2(2)[, 3(2) or 4(2)] of the Crime (Sentences) Act 1997) is of the opinion mentioned in subsection (2) below, the court may make a combination order, that is to say, an order requiring him both—

(a) to be under the supervision of a probation officer for a period specified in the order, being not less than 12 months nor more than three years; and

(b) to perform unpaid work for a number of hours to be specified, being in the aggregate not less than 40 nor more than 100.

(2) The opinion referred to in subsection (1) above is that the making of a combination order is desirable in the interests of—

(a) securing the rehabilitation of the offender; or

(b) protecting the public from harm from him or preventing the commission by him of further offences.

(3) Subject to subsection (1) above, Part I of the 1973 Act shall apply in relation to combination orders—

(a) in so far as they impose such a requirement as is mentioned in paragraph (a) of that subsection, as if they were probation orders; and

(b) in so far as they impose such a requirement as is mentioned in paragraph (b) of that subsection, as if they were community service orders.'

(Words in square brackets not yet in force.)

Community service order (subs (4))—Section 14 of the Powers of Criminal Courts Act 1973 provides:

'(1) Where a person of or over 16 years of age is convicted of an offence punishable with imprisonment (not being an offence the sentence for which is fixed by law or falls to be imposed under section 2(2)[, 3(2) or 4(2)] of the Crime (Sentences) Act 1997), the court by or before which he is convicted may (but subject to subsection (2) below) make an order (in this Act referred to as a 'community service order') requiring him to perform unpaid work in accordance with the subsequent provisions of this Act.

The reference in this subsection to an offence punishable with imprisonment shall be construed without regard to any prohibition or restriction imposed by or under any enactment on the imprisonment of young offenders, and for the purposes of this subsection a sentence falls to be imposed under section 2(2)[, 3(2) or 4(2)] of the Crime (Sentences) Act 1997 if it is required by that provision and the court is not of the opinion there mentioned.

(1A) The number of hours which a person may be required to work under a community service order shall be specified in the order and shall be in the aggregate—

not less than 40 and not more than 240 …'.

(Words in square brackets not yet in force.)

[subsections (2)–(9) specify the procedural requirements].

Section 15(1) of the 1973 Act provides—

'An offender in respect of whom a community service order is in force shall—

keep in touch with the relevant officer in accordance with such instructions as he may from time to time be given by that officer and notify him of any change of address;

perform for the number of hours specified in the order such work at such times as he may be instructed by the relevant officer.'

Probation order (subs (4))—Section 2(1) of the Powers of Criminal Courts Act 1973, as amended by Sch 8, para 26(1), states:

'Where a court by or before which a person of or over the age of 16 years is convicted of an offence (not being an offence for which the sentence is fixed by law or falls to be imposed under section 2(2)[, 3(2) or 4(2)] of the Crime (Sentences) Act 1997) is of the opinion that the supervision of the offender by a probation officer is desirable in the interests of—

(a)   securing the rehabilitation of the offender; or

(b)   protecting the public from harm from him or preventing the commission by him of further offences,

the court may make a probation order, that is to say, an order requiring him to be under supervision for a period specified in the order of not less than six months nor more than three years …'.

(*Words in square brackets not yet in force.*)

Supervision order (subs (4))—A 'supervision order' is defined by s 11 of the Children and Young Persons Act 1969 as an order placing any person under the supervision of a local authority designated by the order or of a probation officer. For the powers of a court to deal with breaches of such orders, see 1969 Act, s 15.

Community order (subs (11))—See annotations to s 61.

---

70 Action plan orders: supplemental

(1) Before making an action plan order, a court shall obtain and consider—

(a)   a written report by a probation officer, a social worker of a local authority social services department or a member of a youth offending team, indicating—
  (i)   the requirements proposed by that person to be included in the order;
  (ii)   the benefits to the offender that the proposed requirements are designed to achieve; and
  (iii) the attitude of a parent or guardian of the offender to the proposed requirements; and

(b)   where the offender is under the age of 16, information about the offender's family circumstances and the likely effect of the order on those circumstances.

(2) Before making an action plan order, a court shall explain to the offender in ordinary language—

(a)   the effect of the order and of the requirements proposed to be included in it;

(b)   the consequences which may follow (under Schedule 5 to this Act) if he fails to comply with any of those requirements; and

(c)   that the court has power (under that Schedule) to review the order on the application either of the offender or of the responsible officer.

(3) Immediately after making an action plan order, a court may—

(a)   fix a further hearing for a date not more than 21 days after the making of the order; and

(b)   direct the responsible officer to make, at that hearing, a report as to the effectiveness of the order and the extent to which it has been implemented.

(4) At a hearing fixed under subsection (3) above, the court—

(a)   shall consider the responsible officer's report; and

(b)   may, on the application of the responsible officer or the offender, vary the order—
  (i)   by cancelling any provision included in it; or
  (ii)   by inserting in it (either in addition to or in substitution for any of its provisions) any provision that the court could originally have included in it.

(5) Schedule 5 to this Act shall have effect for dealing with failure to comply with the requirements of action plan orders, for varying such orders and for discharging them with or without the substitution of other sentences.

Explanatory text—See paras **4.28–4.29**.

Probation officer (subs (1))—See annotations to s 18.

Youth offending team (subs (1))—See paras **2.19–2.21**.

Age (subs (1))—See general annotations.

Responsible officer (subs (4))—See s 69(10).

71 Supervision orders

(1) In subsection (3) of section 12A of the 1969 Act (young offenders), after paragraph (a) there shall be inserted the following paragraph—

'(aa) to make reparation specified in the order to a person or persons so specified or to the community at large;'.

(2) In subsection (5) of that section, for the words 'subsection (3) (a) or (b)' there shall be substituted the words 'subsection (3) (a), (aa) or (b)'.

(3) In subsection (7) of that section, after paragraph (a) there shall be inserted the following paragraph—

'(aa) any requirement to make reparation to any person unless that person—
   (i) is identified by the court as a victim of the offence or a person otherwise affected by it; and
   (ii) consents to the inclusion of the requirement; or'.

(4) In subsection (6) of section 12AA of the 1969 Act (requirement for young offender to live in local authority accommodation), for paragraphs (b) to (d) there shall be substituted the following paragraphs—

'(b) that order imposed—
   (i) a requirement under section 12, 12A or 12C of this Act; or
   (ii) a residence requirement;
(c) he fails to comply with that requirement, or is found guilty of an offence committed while that order was in force; and
(d) the court is satisfied that—
   (i) the failure to comply with the requirement, or the behaviour which constituted the offence, was due to a significant extent to the circumstances in which he was living; and
   (ii) the imposition of a residence requirement will assist in his rehabilitation;';

and for the words 'the condition in paragraph (d)' there shall be substituted the words 'subparagraph (i) of paragraph (d)'.

(5) In section 13 of the 1969 Act (selection of supervisor), subsection (2) shall cease to have effect.

Explanatory texts—See paras **4.35–4.36**.

Section 12A of the 1969 Act (subss (1), (2), (3))—See annotations to s 67.

Section 12AA of the 1969 Act (subs (4))—See annotations to s 67.

Section 13 of the 1969 Act (subs (5))—See annotations to s 67.

72 Breach of requirements in supervision orders

(1) In subsection (3) of section 15 of the 1969 Act (variation and discharge of supervision orders), for paragraphs (a) and (b) there shall be substituted the following paragraphs—

> '(a) whether or not it also makes an order under subsection (1) above, may order him to pay a fine of an amount not exceeding £1,000, or make in respect of him—
>
> > (i)　subject to section 16A(1) of this Act, an order under section 17 of the Criminal Justice Act 1982 (attendance centre orders); or
> >
> > (ii)　subject to section 16B of this Act, an order under section 12 of the Criminal Justice Act 1991 (curfew orders);
>
> (b)　if the supervision order was made by a relevant court, may discharge the order and deal with him, for the offence in respect of which the order was made, in any manner in which he could have been dealt with for that offence by the court which made the order if the order had not been made; or
>
> (c)　if the order was made by the Crown Court, may commit him in custody or release him on bail until he can be brought or appear before the Crown Court.'

(2) For subsections (4) to (6) of that section there shall be substituted the following subsections—

> '(4) Where a court deals with a supervised person under subsection (3)(c) above, it shall send to the Crown Court a certificate signed by a justice of the peace giving—
>
> (a)　particulars of the supervised person's failure to comply with the requirement in question; and
>
> (b)　such other particulars of the case as may be desirable;
>
> and a certificate purporting to be so signed shall be admissible as evidence of the failure before the Crown Court.
>
> (5) Where—
>
> (a)　by virtue of subsection (3)(c) above the supervised person is brought or appears before the Crown Court; and
>
> (b)　it is proved to the satisfaction of the court that he has failed to comply with the requirement in question,
>
> that court may deal with him, for the offence in respect of which the order was made, in any manner in which it could have dealt with him for that offence if it had not made the order.
>
> (6) Where the Crown Court deals with a supervised person under subsection (5) above, it shall discharge the supervision order if it is still in force.'

(3) In subsections (7) and (8) of that section, for the words 'or (4)' there shall be substituted the words 'or (5)'.

Explanatory text—See para **4.37**.

Section 15 of the 1969 Act (subss (1), (2) and (3))—The 1969 Act means the Children and Young Persons Act 1969 (s 117(1)). These provisions provide for the variation and discharge of supervision orders:

> '(1) If while a supervision order is in force in respect of a supervised person it appears to a relevant court, on the application of the supervisor or the supervised person, that it is

appropriate to make an order under this section, the court may make an order discharging the supervision order or varying it—

(a) by cancelling any requirement included in it in pursuance of section 12, 12A, 12AA, 12B, 12C or 18(2)(b) of this Act; or

(b) by inserting in it (either in addition to or in substitution for any of its provisions) any provision which could have been included in the order if the court had then had power to make it and were exercising the power.

(2) The powers of variation conferred by subsection (1) above do not include power—

(a) to insert in the supervision order, after the expiration of three months beginning with the date when the order was originally made, a requirement in pursuance of section 12B(1) of this Act, unless it is in substitution for such a requirement already included in the order; or

(b) to insert in the supervision order a requirement in pursuance of section 12A(3)(b) of this Act in respect of any day which falls outside the period of three months beginning with the date when the order was originally made.

(3) If while a supervision order made under section 7(7) of this Act is in force in respect of a person it is proved to the satisfaction of a relevant court, on the application of the supervisor, that the supervised person has failed to comply with any requirement included in the supervision order in pursuance of section 12, 12A, 12AA, 12C or 18(2)(b) of this Act, the court—

(a) whether or not it also makes an order under subsection (1) above, may order him to pay a fine of an amount not exceeding £1,000 or, subject to section 16A(1) of this Act, may make in respect of him—

   (i) subject to section 16A(1) of this Act, an order under section 17 of the Criminal Justice Act 1982 (attendance centre orders); or

   (ii) subject to section 16B of this Act, an order under section 12 of the Criminal Justice Act 1991 (curfew orders); or

(b) if the supervision order was made by a relevant court, may discharge the order and deal with him, for the offence in respect of which the order was made, in any manner in which he could have been dealt with for that offence by the court which made the order if the order had not been made; or

(c) if the order was made by the Crown Court, may commit him in custody or release him on bail until he can be brought or appear before the Crown Court.

(4), (5) and (6) [see s 72(2) above].

(7) Section 18 of the Criminal Justice Act 1991 (fixing of certain fines by reference to units) shall apply—

(a) for the purposes of subsection (3)(a) above as if the failure to comply with the requirement were a summary offence punishable by a fine not exceeding level 3 on the standard scale; and

(b) for the purposes of subsections (3)(b) and (5) above as if the failure to comply with the requirement were a summary offence punishable by a fine not exceeding level 5 on that scale;

and a fine imposed under any of those provisions shall be deemed for the purposes of any enactment to be a sum adjudged to be paid by a conviction.

(8) In dealing with a supervised person under subsection (3) or (5) above, the court shall take into account the extent to which that person has complied with the requirements of the supervision order.

(9) If a medical practitioner by whom or under whose direction a supervised person is being treated for his mental condition in pursuance of a requirement included in a supervision order by virtue of section 12B(1) of this Act is unwilling to continue to treat or direct the treatment of the supervised person or is of opinion—

(a) that the treatment should be continued beyond the period specified in that behalf in the order; or

(b)   that the supervised person needs different treatment; or
(c)   that he is not susceptible to treatment; or
(d)   that he does not require further treatment,

the practitioner shall make a report in writing to that effect to the supervisor.

(10) On receiving a report under subsection (9) above, the supervisor shall refer it to a relevant court; and on such a reference, the court may make an order cancelling or varying the requirement.

(11) In this section "relevant court" means—

(a)   in the case of a supervised person who has not attained the age of 18, a youth court;
(b)   in the case of a supervised person who has attained that age, a magistrates' court other than a youth court.

(12) The provisions of this section shall have effect subject to the provisions of section 16 of this Act.'

Young offenders: detention and training orders

73 Detention and training orders

(1) Subject to section 53 of the 1933 Act, section 8 of the Criminal Justice Act 1982 ('the 1982 Act') and subsection (2) below, where—

(a)   a child or young person ('the offender') is convicted of an offence which is punishable with imprisonment in the case of a person aged 21 or over; and
(b)   the court is of the opinion that either or both of paragraphs (a) or (b) of subsection (2) of section 1 of the 1991 Act apply or the case falls within subsection (3) of that section,

the sentence that the court is to pass is a detention and training order.

(2) A court shall not make a detention and training order—

(a)   in the case of an offender under the age of 15 at the time of the conviction, unless it is of the opinion that he is a persistent offender;
(b)   in the case of an offender under the age of 12 at that time, unless—
(i)   it is of the opinion that only a custodial sentence would be adequate to protect the public from further offending by him; and
(ii)   the offence was committed on or after such date as the Secretary of State may by order appoint.

(3) A detention and training order is an order that the offender in respect of whom it is made shall be subject, for the term specified in the order, to a period of detention and training followed by a period of supervision.

(4) A detention and training order shall be a custodial sentence for the purposes of Part I of the 1991 Act; and the provisions of sections 1 to 4 of that Act shall apply accordingly.

(5) Subject to subsection (6) below, the term of a detention and training order shall be 4, 6, 8, 10, 12, 18 or 24 months.

(6) The term of a detention and training order may not exceed the maximum term of imprisonment that the Crown Court could (in the case of an offender aged 21 or over) impose for the offence.

(7) The following provisions, namely—

(a) section 1B of the 1982 Act (detention in young offender institutions: special provision for offenders under 18); and

(b) sections 1 to 4 of the 1994 Act (secure training orders),

which are superseded by this section and sections 74 to 78 below, shall cease to have effect.

Explanatory text—See paras **4.49–4.70**.

Section 53 of the 1933 Act (subs (1))—'The 1933 Act' means the Children and Young Persons Act 1933 (s 117(1)). Section 53(1)–(3) of the Children and Young Persons Act 1933 provides:

'(1) A person convicted of an offence who appears to the court to have been under the age of eighteen years at the time the offence was committed shall not, if he is convicted of murder, be sentenced to imprisonment for life … but in lieu thereof the court shall … sentence him to be detained during Her Majesty's pleasure, and if so sentenced shall be liable to be detained in such place and under such conditions … as the Secretary of State may direct [or arrange].

(2) Subsection (3) below applies—

(a) where a person of at least 10 but not more than 17 years is convicted on indictment of—
   (i) any offence punishable in the case of an adult with imprisonment for fourteen years or more, not being an offence the sentence for which is fixed by law, or
   (ii) an offence under section 14 (indecent assault on a woman) or section 15 (indecent assault on a man) of the Sexual Offences Act 1956;

(b) where a young person is convicted of—
   (i) an offence under section 1 of the Road Traffic Act 1988 (causing death by dangerous driving), or
   (ii) an offence under section 3A of the Road Traffic Act 1988 (causing death by careless driving while under influence of drink or drugs).

(3) Where this subsection applies, then, if the court is of opinion that none of the other methods in which the case may legally be dealt with is suitable, the court may sentence the offender to be detained for such period, not exceeding the maximum term of imprisonment with which the offence is punishable in the case of an adult, as may be specified in the sentence, and where such a sentence has been passed the child or young person shall, during that period, be liable to be detained in such place and on such conditions … as the Secretary of State may direct [or arrange].'

Section 8 of the Criminal Justice Act 1982 (subs (1))—Section 8(2) provides that where a person aged 18 or over but under the age of 21 years of age is convicted of any offence other than murder for which a person aged 21 years or over would be liable to imprisonment for life, the court shall, if it considers that a custodial sentence for life would be appropriate, sentence him to custody for life.

Provisions of sections 1 to 4 of the 1991 Act (subs (4))—Ie the Criminal Justice Act 1991 (s 117(1)). For sections 1–2, see annotations to ss 58 and 63.

Months (subs (5))—See general annotations.

---

74 Duties and powers of court

(1) On making a detention and training order in a case where subsection (2) of section 73 above applies, it shall be the duty of the court (in addition to the duty imposed by section 1(4) of the 1991 Act) to state in open court that it is of the opinion mentioned in paragraph (a) or, as the case may be, paragraphs (a) and (b)(i) of that subsection.

(2) Subject to subsection (3) below, where—

(a) an offender is convicted of more than one offence for which he is liable to a detention and training order; or

(b) an offender who is subject to a detention and training order is convicted of one or more further offences for which he is liable to such an order, the court shall have the same power to pass consecutive detention and training orders as if they were sentences of imprisonment.

(3) A court shall not make in respect of an offender a detention and training order the effect of which would be that he would be subject to detention and training orders for a term which exceeds 24 months.

(4) Where the term of the detention and training orders to which an offender would otherwise be subject exceeds 24 months, the excess shall be treated as remitted.

(5) In determining the term of a detention and training order for an offence, the court shall take account of any period for which the offender has been remanded in custody in connection with the offence, or any other offence the charge for which was founded on the same facts or evidence.

(6) The reference in subsection (5) above to an offender being remanded in custody is a reference to his being—

    (a) held in police detention;

    (b) remanded in or committed to custody by an order of a court;

    (c) remanded or committed to local authority accommodation under section 23 of the 1969 Act and placed and kept in secure accommodation; or

    (d) remanded, admitted or removed to hospital under section 35, 36, 38 or 48 of the Mental Health Act 1983.

(7) A person is in police detention for the purposes of subsection (6) above—

    (a) at any time when he is in police detention for the purposes of the 1984 Act; and

    (b) at any time when he is detained under section 14 of the Prevention of Terrorism (Temporary Provisions) Act 1989;

and in that subsection 'secure accommodation' has the same meaning as in section 23 of the 1969 Act.

(8) For the purpose of any reference in this section or sections 75 to 78 below to the term of a detention and training order, consecutive terms of such orders and terms of such orders which are wholly or partly concurrent shall be treated as a single term if—

    (a) the orders were made on the same occasion; or

    (b) where they were made on different occasions, the offender has not been released (by virtue of subsection (2), (3), (4) or (5) of section 75 below) at any time during the period beginning with the first and ending with the last of those occasions.

Explanatory text—See paras **4.57–4.58**.

Police detention (subs (6))—'Police detention' comes within the meaning of s 118(2) of the Police and Criminal Evidence Act 1984 ('PACE'). For this purpose, a person is in police detention if:

    (a) he has been taken to the police station after being arrested for an offence or after being arrested under s 14 of the Prevention of Terrorism (Temporary Provisions) Act 1989 or under para 6 of Sch 5 to that Act by an examining officer who is a constable; or

    (b) he is arrested at a police station after attending voluntarily at the police station or accompanying a constable to it,

and is detained there or is detained elsewhere in the charge of a constable, except that a person who is at a court after being charged is not in police detention for these purposes.

A person who is voluntarily at the police station is not in police detention for this purpose, although he is entitled to the protection of Code C relating to the treatment of suspects, made pursuant to s 66 of PACE.

Section 23 of the Children and Young Persons Act 1969 (subs (7))—See annotations to s 97 and (for different purposes) s 98.

Sections 35, 36, 38 or 48 of the Mental Health Act 1983 (subs (6))—By s 35(1), the Crown Court or a magistrates' court may remand an accused person to a hospital specified by the court for a report on his mental condition. The prerequisite for the exercise of this power is contained in s 35(3). It may be exercised if: (a) the court is satisfied, on the written or oral evidence of a registered medical practitioner, that there is reason to suspect that the accused person is suffering from mental illness, psychopathic disorder, severe mental impairment or mental impairment; and (b) the court is of the opinion that it would be impracticable for a report on his mental condition to be made if he were remanded on bail. The power is not exercisable in respect of a person convicted of an offence in respect of which the sentence is fixed by law. Section 35(4) provides that the court shall not remand an accused person to hospital under s 35 unless satisfied, on the written or oral evidence of the registered medical practitioner who would be responsible for making the report or for some other person representing the managers of the hospital, that arrangements have been made for his admission to the hospital and for his admission to it within the period of seven days beginning with the date of remand; and if the court is so satisfied it may, pending his admission, give directions for his conveyance to and detention in a place of safety.

Section 36(1) of the 1983 Act states that a Crown Court may, instead of remanding an accused person in custody remand him to a hospital specified by the court, if satisfied, on the written or oral evidence of two registered medical practitioners, that he is suffering from mental illness or severe mental impairment of a nature or degree which makes it appropriate for him to be detained in a hospital for medical treatment. The section contains similar procedural provisions as are contained in s 35.

Section 38(1) states that where a person is convicted before the Crown Court of an offence punishable with imprisonment (other than an offence the sentence for which is fixed by law) or is convicted by a magistrates' court of an offence punishable with imprisonment and the court before or by which he is convicted is satisfied, on the written or oral evidence of two registered medical practitioners: (a) that the offender is suffering from mental illness, psychopathic disorder, severe mental impairment or mental impairment; and (b) that there is reason to suppose that the mental disorder from which the offender is suffering is such that it may be appropriate for a hospital order to be made in his case, the court may, before making a hospital order or dealing with him in some other way, make an order (an 'interim hospital order') authorising his admission to such hospital as may be specified in the order and his detention there.

Section 14 of the Prevention of Terrorism (Temporary Provisions) Act 1989 (subs (7))—This provides as follows:

'Subject to subsection (2) below, a constable may arrest without warrant a person whom he has reasonable grounds for suspecting to be—

    (a)   a person guilty of an offence under section 2, 8, 9, 10 or 11 above,

    (b)   a person who is or has been concerned in commission, preparation or instigation of acts of terrorism to which this section applies, or

    (c)   a person subject to an exclusion order.

The acts of terrorism to which this section applies are—

    (a)   acts of terrorism connected with the affairs of Northern Ireland; and

    (b)   acts of terrorism of any other description except acts connected solely with the affairs of the United Kingdom or any part of the United Kingdom other than Northern Ireland.

Subject to subsection (5) below, a person arrested under this section shall not be detained in right of the arrest for more than 48 hours after his arrest.

The Secretary of State may, in any particular case, extend the period of 48 hours mentioned above by a period or periods specified by him, but any such period or further periods shall not exceed five days in all and if an application for such an extension is made the person detained shall as soon as practicable be given written notice of that fact and of the time when the application was made.'

75 The period of detention and training

(1) An offender shall serve the period of detention and training under a detention and training order in such secure accommodation as may be determined by the Secretary of State or by such other person as may be authorised by him for that purpose.

(2) Subject to subsections (3) to (5) below, the period of detention and training under a detention and training order shall be one-half of the term of the order.

(3) The Secretary of State may at any time release the offender if he is satisfied that exceptional circumstances exist which justify the offender's release on compassionate grounds.

(4) The Secretary of State may release the offender—

(a) in the case of an order for a term of 8 months or more but less than 18 months, one month before the half-way point of the term of the order; and

(b) in the case of an order for a term of 18 months or more, one month or two months before that point.

(5) If the youth court so orders on an application made by the Secretary of State for the purpose, the Secretary of State shall release the offender—

(a) in the case of an order for a term of 8 months or more but less than 18 months, one month after the half-way point of the term of the order; and

(b) in the case of an order for a term of 18 months or more, one month or two months after that point.

(6) An offender detained in pursuance of a detention and training order shall be deemed to be in legal custody.

(7) In this section and sections 77 and 78 below 'secure accommodation' means—

(a) a secure training centre;

(b) a young offender institution;

(c) accommodation provided by a local authority for the purpose of restricting the liberty of children and young persons;

(d) accommodation provided for that purpose under subsection (5) of section 82 of the 1989 Act (financial support by the Secretary of State); or

(e) such other accommodation provided for the purpose of restricting liberty as the Secretary of State may direct.

Explanatory text—See para **4.63**.

Detention and training order (subss (1), (2) and (6))—See ss 73(3) and 85(1).

Months (subss (4) and (5))—See general annotations.

Legal custody (sub (6))—The Prison Act 1952, s 43(1), is amended by the substitution of para (d) therein by a new para (d) (Sch 8, para 6). The effect of this change is to apply the provisions of the 1952 Act to a person detained in a secure training centre, subject to certain exceptions contained in the 1952 Act, s 5A (as inserted by the Criminal Justice and Public Order Act 1994, s 5(5)).

The offender is in lawful custody while confined in, or being taken to or from, any secure training centre; while he is working outside the centre; or while he is for any other reason outside the centre in the custody of, or under the control of, an officer of the centre (Prison Act 1952, s 13(2)). He is also in lawful custody if he is taken to a court for the purposes of any proceedings, or if he is taken to a hospital or other suitable place for medical examination or medical or surgical treatment (1952 Act, s 22).

It is a common law offence, punishable by fine and imprisonment, to escape from lawful custody. Such a person may be arrested without warrant and taken to the secure training centre in which he is required to be detained (1952 Act, s 49(2).

Secure training centre (subs (7))—The Criminal Justice and Public Order Act 1994, s 5, creates the power to make provision for children and young persons by way of secure training centres. Such a centre is defined by the Prison Act 1952, s 43(1)(d) (as substituted by the 1998 Act, Sch 8, para 6) as 'places in which offenders [under 18 years of age] in respect of whom detention and training orders have been made under section 73 of the Crime and Disorder Act 1998 may be detained and given training and education and prepared for their release'. Their management is governed by the Criminal Justice and Public Order Act 1994, ss 6–10. Secure training centre rules can be made (1952 Act, s 47(4A), as amended by the Criminal Justice and Public Order Act 1994, s 6(3)). The powers of custody officers at such centres are set out by the Criminal Justice and Public Order Act 1994, s 4. Any person who assaults, or who resists or wilfully obstructs a custody officer: (a) acting in the pursuance of escort arrangements; (b) performing custodial duties at a contracted-out secure training centre; or (c) performing contracted-out functions at a directly managed secure training centre is guilty of an offence, punishable on summary conviction to a fine not exceeding level 5 on the standard scale or to a term of imprisonment for a term not exceeding six months or both.

Young offender institution (subs (7))—Defined by the Prison Act 1952, s 43, as 'places for the detention of offenders sentenced to detention in a young offender institution or to custody for life'.

---

76 The period of supervision

(1) The period of supervision of an offender who is subject to a detention and training order—

- (a) shall begin with the offender's release, whether at the half-way point of the term of the order or otherwise; and
- (b) subject to subsection (2) below, shall end when the term of the order ends.

(2) The Secretary of State may by order provide that the period of supervision shall end at such point during the term of a detention and training order as may be specified in the order under this subsection.

(3) During the period of supervision, the offender shall be under the supervision of—

- (a) a probation officer;
- (b) a social worker of a local authority social services department; or
- (c) a member of a youth offending team;

and the category of person to supervise the offender shall be determined from time to time by the Secretary of State.

(4) Where the supervision is to be provided by a probation officer, the probation officer shall be an officer appointed for or assigned to the petty sessions area within which the offender resides for the time being.

(5) Where the supervision is to be provided by—

- (a) a social worker of a local authority social services department; or
- (b) a member of a youth offending team,

the social worker or member shall be a social worker of, or a member of a youth offending team established by, the local authority within whose area the offender resides for the time being.

(6) The offender shall be given a notice from the Secretary of State specifying—

(a) the category of person for the time being responsible for his supervision; and
(b) any requirements with which he must for the time being comply.

(7) A notice under subsection (6) above shall be given to the offender—

(a) before the commencement of the period of supervision; and
(b) before any alteration in the matters specified in subsection (6)(a) or (b) above comes into effect.

Explanatory text—See paras **4.68–4.69**.

Detention and training order (subss (1) and (2))—See ss 73(3) and 85(1).

Probation officer (subss (3) and (4))—See annotations to s 18.

Youth offending team (subss (3) and (5))—See paras **2.19–2.21**.

---

77 Breaches of supervision requirements

(1) Where a detention and training order is in force in respect of an offender and it appears on information to a justice of the peace acting for a relevant petty sessions area that the offender has failed to comply with requirements under section 76(6)(b) above, the justice—

(a) may issue a summons requiring the offender to appear at the place and time specified in the summons before a youth court acting for the area; or
(b) if the information is in writing and on oath, may issue a warrant for the offender's arrest requiring him to be brought before such a court.

(2) For the purposes of this section a petty sessions area is a relevant petty sessions area in relation to a detention and training order if—

(a) the order was made by a youth court acting for it; or
(b) the offender resides in it for the time being.

(3) If it is proved to the satisfaction of the youth court before which an offender appears or is brought under this section that he has failed to comply with requirements under section 76(6)(b) above, that court may—

(a) order the offender to be detained, in such secure accommodation as the Secretary of State may determine, for such period, not exceeding the shorter of three months or the remainder of the term of the detention and training order, as the court may specify; or
(b) impose on the offender a fine not exceeding level 3 on the standard scale.

(4) An offender detained in pursuance of an order under subsection (3) above shall be deemed to be in legal custody; and a fine imposed under that subsection shall be deemed, for the purposes of any enactment, to be a sum adjudged to be paid by a conviction.

78 Offences during currency of order

(1) This section applies to a person subject to a detention and training order if—

    (a) after his release and before the date on which the term of the order ends, he commits an offence punishable with imprisonment in the case of a person aged 21 or over; and

    (b) whether before or after that date, he is convicted of that offence ('the new offence').

(2) Subject to section 7(8) of the 1969 Act, the court by or before which a person to whom this section applies is convicted of the new offence may, whether or not it passes any other sentence on him, order him to be detained in such secure accommodation as the Secretary of State may determine for the whole or any part of the period which—

    (a) begins with the date of the court's order; and

    (b) is equal in length to the period between the date on which the new offence was committed and the date mentioned in subsection (1) above.

(3) The period for which a person to whom this section applies is ordered under subsection (2) above to be detained in secure accommodation—

    (a) shall, as the court may direct, either be served before and be followed by, or be served concurrently with, any sentence imposed for the new offence; and

    (b) in either case, shall be disregarded in determining the appropriate length of that sentence.

(4) Where the new offence is found to have been committed over a period of two or more days, or at some time during a period of two or more days, it shall be taken for the purposes of this section to have been committed on the last of those days.

(5) A person detained in pursuance of an order under subsection (2) above shall be deemed to be in legal custody.

79 Interaction with sentences of detention

(1) Where a court passes a sentence of detention in a young offender institution in the case of an offender who is subject to a detention and training order, the sentence shall take effect as follows—

(a) if the offender has been released by virtue of subsection (2), (3), (4) or (5) of section 75 above, at the beginning of the day on which it is passed;

(b) if not, either as mentioned in paragraph (a) above or, if the court so orders, at the time when the offender would otherwise be released by virtue of that subsection.

(2) Where a court makes a detention and training order in the case of an offender who is subject to a sentence of detention in a young offender institution, the order shall take effect as follows—

(a) if the offender has been released under Part II of the 1991 Act, at the beginning of the day on which it is made;

(b) if not, either as mentioned in paragraph (a) above or, if the court so orders, at the time when the offender would otherwise be released under that Part.

(3) Subject to subsection (4) below, where at any time an offender is subject concurrently—

(a) to a detention and training order; and

(b) to a sentence of detention in a young offender institution,

he shall be treated for the purposes of sections 75 to 78 above, section 1C of the 1982 Act and Part II of the 1991 Act as if he were subject only to the one of them that was imposed on the later occasion.

(4) Nothing in subsection (3) above shall require the offender to be released in respect of either the order or the sentence unless and until he is required to be released in respect of each of them.

(5) Where, by virtue of any enactment giving a court power to deal with a person in a manner in which a court on a previous occasion could have dealt with him, a detention and training order for any term is made in the case of a person who has attained the age of 18, the person shall be treated as if he had been sentenced to detention in a young offender institution for the same term.

Explanatory text—See para **4.62**.

Detention and training order (subss (1), (2), (3) and (5))—See ss 73(3) and 85(1).

Age (subs (5))—See general annotations.

Sentencing: general

80 Sentencing guidelines

(1) This section applies where the Court—

(a) is seised of an appeal against, or a reference under section 36 of the Criminal Justice Act 1988 with respect to, the sentence passed for an offence; or

(b) receives a proposal under section 81 below in respect of a particular category of offence;

and in this section 'the relevant category' means any category within which the offence falls or, as the case may be, the category to which the proposal relates.

(2) The Court shall consider—

(a) whether to frame guidelines as to the sentencing of offenders for offences of the relevant category; or

(a) where such guidelines already exist, whether it would be appropriate to review them.

(3) Where the Court decides to frame or revise such guidelines, the Court shall have regard to—

(a) the need to promote consistency in sentencing;
(b) the sentences imposed by courts in England and Wales for offences of the relevant category;
(c) the cost of different sentences and their relative effectiveness in preventing re-offending;
(d) the need to promote public confidence in the criminal justice system; and
(e) the views communicated to the Court, in accordance with section 81(4)(b) below, by the Sentencing Advisory Panel.

(4) Guidelines framed or revised under this section shall include criteria for determining the seriousness of offences, including (where appropriate) criteria for determining the weight to be given to any previous convictions of offenders or any failures of theirs to respond to previous sentences.

(5) In a case falling within subsection (1)(a) above, guidelines framed or revised under this section shall, if practicable, be included in the Court's judgment in the appeal.

(6) Subject to subsection (5) above, guidelines framed or revised under this section shall be included in a judgment of the Court at the next appropriate opportunity (having regard to the relevant category of offence).

(7) For the purposes of this section, the Court is seised of an appeal against a sentence if—

(a) the Court or a single judge has granted leave to appeal against the sentence under section 9 or 10 of the Criminal Appeal Act 1968; or
(b) in a case where the judge who passed the sentence granted a certificate of fitness for appeal under section 9 or 10 of that Act, notice of appeal has been given,

and (in either case) the appeal has not been abandoned or disposed of.

(8) For the purposes of this section, the Court is seised of a reference under section 36 of the Criminal Justice Act 1988 if it has given leave under subsection (1) of that section and the reference has not been disposed of.

(9) In this section and section 81 below—

'the Court' means the criminal division of the Court of Appeal;
'offence' means an indictable offence.

Explanatory text—See paras **7.7–7.10**.

England and Wales (subs (3))—See general annotations.

Section 9 or 10 of the Criminal Appeal Act 1968 (subs 7))—Section 9 provides for appeal against sentence following conviction on indictment; s 10 with appeal against sentence in other cases dealt with at the Crown Court.

---

81 The Sentencing Advisory Panel

(1) The Lord Chancellor, after consultation with the Secretary of State and the Lord Chief Justice, shall constitute a sentencing panel to be known as the Sentencing Advisory Panel ('the Panel') and appoint one of the members of the Panel to be its chairman.

(2) Where, in a case falling within subsection (1)(a) of section 80 above, the Court decides to frame or revise guidelines under that section for a particular category of offence, the Court shall notify the Panel.

(3) The Panel may at any time, and shall if directed to do so by the Secretary of State, propose to the Court that guidelines be framed or revised under section 80 above for a particular category of offence.

(4) Where the Panel receives a notification under subsection (2) above or makes a proposal under subsection (3) above, the Panel shall—

(a) obtain and consider the views on the matters in issue of such persons or bodies as may be determined, after consultation with the Secretary of State and the Lord Chief Justice, by the Lord Chancellor;

(b) formulate its own views on those matters and communicate them to the Court; and

(c) furnish information to the Court as to the matters mentioned in section 80(3)(b) and (c) above.

(5) The Lord Chancellor may pay to any member of the Panel such remuneration as he may determine.

Explanatory text—See paras **7.11–7.13**.

---

82 Increase in sentences for racial aggravation

(1) This section applies where a court is considering the seriousness of an offence other than one under sections 29 to 32 above.

(2) If the offence was racially aggravated, the court—

(a) shall treat that fact as an aggravating factor (that is to say, a factor that increases the seriousness of the offence); and

(b) shall state in open court that the offence was so aggravated.

(3) Section 28 above applies for the purposes of this section as it applies for the purposes of sections 29 to 32 above.

Explanatory text—See paras **8.80–8.83**.

Racially aggravated (subs (2))—See s 28.

Open court (subs (2))—See annotations to s 9.

Miscellaneous and supplemental

83 Power to make confiscation orders on committal for sentence

After subsection (9) of section 71 of the Criminal Justice Act 1988 (confiscation orders) there shall be inserted the following subsection—

'(9A) Where an offender is committed by a magistrates' court for sentence under section 38 or 38A of the Magistrates' Courts Act 1980 or section 56 of the Criminal Justice Act 1967, this section and sections 72 to 74C below shall have effect as if the offender had been convicted of the offence in the proceedings before the Crown Court and not in the proceedings before the magistrates' court.'

Explanatory text—See para **7.102**.

84 Football spectators: failure to comply with reporting duty

(1) In section 16(5) of the Football Spectators Act 1989 (penalties for failure to comply with reporting duty imposed by restriction order)—

    (a) for the words 'one month' there shall be substituted the words 'six months'; and

    (b) for the words 'level 3' there shall be substituted the words 'level 5'.

(2) In section 24(2) of the 1984 Act (arrestable offences), after paragraph (p) there shall be inserted—

    '(q) an offence under section 16(4) of the Football Spectators Act 1989 (failure to comply with reporting duty imposed by restriction order).'

Explanatory text—See paras **9.57–9.59**.

Level 5 on the standard scale (subs (1))—See general annotations.

Arrestable offences (subs (2))—See annotations to s 32.

85 Interpretation etc. of Chapter I

(1) In this Chapter—

    'action plan order' has the meaning given by section 69(2) above;
    'detention and training order' has the meaning given by section 73(3) above;
    'drug treatment and testing order' has the meaning given by section 61(2) above;
    'make reparation', in relation to an offender, means make reparation for the offence otherwise than by the payment of compensation;
    'reparation order' has the meaning given by section 67(2) above;
    'responsible officer'—

    (a) in relation to a drug treatment and testing order, has the meaning given by section 62(7) above;

    (b) in relation to a reparation order, has the meaning given by section 67(10) above;

    (c) in relation to an action plan order, has the meaning given by section 69(10) above.

(2) Where the supervision under a reparation order or action plan order is be provided by a probation officer, the probation officer shall be an officer appointed for or assigned to the petty sessions area named in the order.

(3) Where the supervision under a reparation order or action plan order is to be provided by—

    (a) a social worker of a local authority social services department; or

    (b) a member of a youth offending team,

the social worker or member shall be a social worker of, or a member of a youth offending team established by, the local authority within whose area it appears to the court that the child or young person resides or will reside.

(4) In this Chapter, in relation to a drug treatment and testing order—

'the treatment and testing period' has the meaning given by section 61(2) above;
'the treatment provider' and 'the treatment requirement' have the meanings given
   by subsection (1) of section 62 above;
'the testing requirement' has the meaning given by subsection (4) of that section.

(5) In this Chapter, unless the contrary intention appears, expressions which are also
used in Part I of the 1991 Act have the same meanings as in that Part.

(6) For the purposes of this Chapter, a sentence falls to be imposed under section 2(2),
3(2) or 4(2) of the 1997 Act if it is required by that provision and the court is not of the
opinion there mentioned.

Petty sessions area (subs (2))—See general annotations.

Youth offending team (subs (3))—See s 39 (s 117(1)).

CHAPTER II
SCOTLAND

Sexual or violent offenders

86 to 88 [*Applies to Scotland only.*]

Offenders dependent etc. on drugs

89–95 [*Applies to Scotland only.*]

Racial aggravation

96 [*Applies to Scotland only.*]

PART V
MISCELLANEOUS AND SUPPLEMENTAL

Remands and committals

97 Remands and committals of children and young persons

(1) In subsection (4) of section 23 of the 1969 Act (remands and committals to local
authority accommodation), for the words 'Subject to subsection (5) below,' there shall
be substituted the words 'Subject to subsections (5) and (5A) below,'.

(2) In subsection (5) of that section, for the words 'a young person who has attained the
age of fifteen' there shall be substituted the words 'a child who has attained the age of
twelve, or a young person, who (in either case) is of a prescribed description'.

(3) After that subsection there shall be inserted the following subsection—

'(5A) A court shall not impose a security requirement in respect of a child or young person who is not legally represented in the court unless—

(a) he applied for legal aid and the application was refused on the ground that it did not appear his means were such that he required assistance; or
(b) having been informed of his right to apply for legal aid and had the opportunity to do so, he refused or failed to apply.'

(4) In subsection (12) of that section, after the definition of 'imprisonable offence' there shall be inserted the following definition—

'"prescribed description" means a description prescribed by reference to age or sex or both by an order of the Secretary of State;'.

(5) Section 20 of the 1994 Act (which has not been brought into force and is superseded by this section) is hereby repealed.

Explanatory text—See paras **9.35–9.40**.

The 1969 Act (subs (1))—Ie the Children and Young Persons Act 1969 (s 117(1)). As amended by the present section (the amendments are italicised), s 23 of the 1969 Act provides as follows, except in relation to male persons of the type dealt with by s 98 of the new Act:

'(1) Where—

(a) a court remands a child or young person charged with or convicted of one or more offences, or commits him for trial or sentence; and
(b) he is not released on bail,

the remand or committal shall be to local authority accommodation; and in the following provisions of this section, any reference (however expressed) to a remand shall be construed as including a reference to a committal.

(2) A court remanding a person to local authority accommodation shall designate the local authority who are to receive him; and that authority shall be—

(a) in the case of a person who is being looked after by a local authority, that authority; and
(b) in any other case, the local authority in whose area it appears to the court that he resides or the offence or one of the offences was committed.

(3) Where a person is remanded to local authority accommodation, it shall be lawful for any person acting on behalf of the designated authority to detain him.

(4) Subject to subsections (5) and *(5A)* below, a court remanding a person to local authority accommodation may, after consultation with the designated authority, require that authority to comply with a security requirement, that is to say, a requirement that the person in question be placed and kept in secure accommodation.

(5) A court shall not impose a security requirement except in respect of a *child who has attained the age of twelve, or a young person, who (in either case) is of a prescribed description*, and then only if—

(a) he is charged with or has been convicted of a violent or sexual offence, or an offence punishable in the case of an adult with imprisonment for a term of fourteen years or more; or
(b) he has a recent history of absconding while remanded to local authority accommodation, and is charged with or has been convicted of an imprisonable offence alleged or found to have been committed while he was so remanded,

and (in either case) the court is of opinion that only such a requirement would be adequate to protect the public from serious harm from him.

(5A) A court shall not impose a security requirement in respect of a child or young person who is not legally represented in the court unless—

(a)   *he applied for legal aid and the application was refused on the ground that it did not appear his means were such that he required assistance; or*

(b)   *having been informed of his right to apply for legal aid and had the opportunity to do so, he refused or failed to apply.*

(6) Where a court imposes a security requirement in respect of a person it shall be its duty—

(a)   to state in open court that it is of such opinion as is mentioned in subsection (5) above; and

(b)   to explain to him in open court and in ordinary language why it is of that opinion;

and a magistrates' court shall cause a reason stated by it under paragraph (b) above to be specified in the warrant of commitment and to be entered in the register.

(7) A court remanding a person to local authority accommodation without imposing a security requirement may, after consultation with the designated authority, require that person to comply with any such conditions as could be imposed under section 3(6) of the Bail Act 1976 if he were then being granted bail.

(8) Where a court imposes on a person any such conditions as are mentioned in subsection (7) above, it shall be its duty to explain to him in open court and in ordinary language why it is imposing those conditions; and a magistrates' court shall cause a reason stated by it under this subsection to be specified in the warrant of commitment and to be entered in the register.

(9) A court remanding a person to local authority accommodation without imposing a security requirement may, after consultation with the designated authority, impose on that authority requirements—

(a)   for securing compliance with any conditions imposed on that person under subsection (7) above; or

(b)   stipulating that he shall not be placed with a named person.

(10) Where a person is remanded to local authority accommodation, a relevant court—

(a)   may, on the application of the designated authority, impose on that person any such conditions as could be imposed under subsection (7) above if the court were then remanding him to such accommodation; and

(b)   where it does so, may impose on that authority any requirements for securing compliance with the conditions so imposed.

(11) Where a person is remanded to local authority accommodation, a relevant court may, on the application of the designated authority or that person, vary or revoke any conditions or requirements imposed under subsection (7), (9) or (10) above.

(12) In this section—

"court" and "magistrates' court" include a justice;

"imprisonable offence" means an offence punishable in the case of an adult with imprisonment;

"prescribed description" means a description prescribed by reference to age or sex or both by an order of the Secretary of State;

"relevant court", in relation to a person remanded to local authority accommodation, means the court by which he was so remanded, or any magistrates' court having jurisdiction in the place where he is for the time being;

"secure accommodation" means accommodation which is provided in a community home, a voluntary home or a registered children's home for the purpose of restricting liberty, and is approved for that purpose by the Secretary of State;

"sexual offence" and "violent offence" have the same meanings as in Part I of the Criminal Justice Act 1991;

"young person" means a person who has attained the age of fourteen years and is under the age of seventeen years,

but, for the purposes of the definition of "secure accommodation", "local authority accommodation" includes any accommodation falling within section 61(2) of the Criminal Justice Act 1991.

(13) In this section—

    (a)   any reference to a person who is being looked after by a local authority shall be construed in accordance with section 22 of the Children Act 1989;

    (b)   any reference to consultation shall be construed as a reference to such consultation (if any) as is reasonably practicable in all the circumstances of the case;

    (c)   any reference, in relation to a person charged with or convicted of a violent or sexual offence, to protecting the public from serious harm from him shall be construed as a reference to protecting members of the public from death or serious personal injury, whether physical or psychological, occasioned by further such offences committed by him.

(14) This section has effect subject to—

    (a)   [repealed by Sch 10]

    (b)   section 128(7) of the Magistrates' Courts Act 1980 (remands to the custody of a constable for periods of not more than three days),

but section 128(7) shall have effect in relation to a child or young person as if for the reference to three clear days there were substituted a reference to 24 hours.'

Subs (5)—'The 1994 Act' means the Criminal Justice and Public Order Act 1994. Section 20 thereof provided for the substitution of lower age limits down to 12 in s 23(5) of the 1969 Act from the minimum age limit of 15 specified there.

---

98 Remands and committals: alternative provision for 15 or 16 year old boys

(1) Section 23 of the 1969 Act shall have effect with the modifications specified in subsections (2) to (6) below in relation to any male person who—

    (a) is of the age of 15 or 16; and

    (b) is not of a description prescribed for the purposes of subsection (5) of that section.

(2) In subsection (1), immediately before the words 'the remand' there shall be inserted the words 'then, unless he is remanded to a remand centre or a prison in pursuance of subsection (4)(b) or (c) below,'.

(3) For subsections (4) to (5A) there shall be substituted the following subsections—

    '(4) Where a court, after consultation with a probation officer, a social worker of a local authority social services department or a member of a youth offending team, declares a person to be one to whom subsection (5) below applies—

        (a) it shall remand him to local authority accommodation and require him to be placed and kept in secure accommodation, if—

            (i) it also, after such consultation, declares him to be a person to whom subsection (5A) below applies; and

            (ii) it has been notified that secure accommodation is available for him;

        (b) it shall remand him to a remand centre, if paragraph (a) above does not apply and it has been notified that such a centre is available for the reception from the court of persons to whom subsection (5) below applies; and

(c) it shall remand him to a prison, if neither paragraph (a) nor paragraph (b) above applies.

(4A) A court shall not declare a person who is not legally represented in the court to be a person to whom subsection (5) below applies unless—

(a) he applied for legal aid and the application was refused on the ground that it did not appear his means were such that he required assistance; or
(b) having been informed of his right to apply for legal aid and had the opportunity to do so, he refused or failed to apply.

(5) This subsection applies to a person who—

(a) is charged with or has been convicted of a violent or sexual offence, or an offence punishable in the case of an adult with imprisonment for a term of fourteen years or more; or
(b) has a recent history of absconding while remanded to local authority accommodation, and is charged with or has been convicted of an imprisonable offence alleged or found to have been committed while he was so remanded,

if (in either case) the court is of opinion that only remanding him to a remand centre or prison, or to local authority accommodation with a requirement that he be placed and kept in secure accommodation, would be adequate to protect the public from serious harm from him.

(5A) This subsection applies to a person if the court is of opinion that, by reason of his physical or emotional immaturity or a propensity of his to harm himself, it would be undesirable for him to be remanded to a remand centre or a prison.'

(4) In subsection (6)—

(a) for the words 'imposes a security requirement in respect of a young person' there shall be substituted the words 'declares a person to be one to whom subsection (5) above applies'; and
(b) for the words 'subsection (5) above' there shall be substituted the words 'that subsection'.

(5) In subsection (7), after the words 'a security requirement' there shall be inserted the words '(that is to say, a requirement imposed under subsection (4)(a) above that the person be placed and kept in secure accommodation)'.

(6) After subsection (9) there shall be inserted the following subsection—

'(9A) Where a person is remanded to local authority accommodation without the imposition of a security requirement, a relevant court may, on the application of the designated authority, declare him to be a person to whom subsection (5) above applies; and on its doing so, subsection (4) above shall apply.'

(7) Section 62 of the 1991 Act (which is superseded by this section) shall cease to have effect.

Explanatory text—See paras **9.35–9.39** and **9.41–9.42**.

The 1969 Act (subs (1))—Ie the Children and Young Persons Act 1969 (s 117(1)). As amended by the present section (the amendments are italicised) in respect of male persons to whom it applies, s 23 of the 1969 Act provides:

'(1) Where—

(a)   a court remands a child or young person charged with or convicted of one or more offences, or commits him for trial or sentence; and

(b)   he is not released on bail,

then, unless he is remanded to a remand centre or a prison in pursuance of subsection (4)(b) or (c) below, the remand or committal shall be to local authority accommodation; and in the following provisions of this section, any reference (however expressed) to a remand shall be construed as including a reference to a committal.

(2) A court remanding a person to local authority accommodation shall designate the local authority who are to receive him; and that authority shall be—

(a)   in the case of a person who is being looked after by a local authority, that authority; and

(b)   in any other case, the local authority in whose area it appears to the court that he resides or the offence or one of the offences was committed.

(3) Where a person is remanded to local authority accommodation, it shall be lawful for any person acting on behalf of the designated authority to detain him.

(4) Where a court, after consultation with a probation officer, a social worker of a local authority social services department or a member of a youth offending team, declares a person to be one to whom subsection (5) below applies—

(a)   *it shall remand him to local authority accommodation and require him to be placed and kept in secure accommodation, if—*

   (i)   *it also, after such consultation, declares him to be a person to whom subsection (5A) below applies; and*

   (ii)   *it has been notified that secure accommodation is available for him;*

(b)   *it shall remand him to a remand centre, if paragraph (a) above does not apply and it has been notified that such a centre is available for the reception from the court of persons to whom subsection (5) below applies, and*

(c)   *it shall remand him to a prison, if neither paragraph (a) nor paragraph (b) above applies.*

(4A) A court shall not declare a person who is not legally represented in the court to be a person to whom subsection (5) below applies unless—

(a)   *he applied for legal aid and the application was refused on the ground that it did not appear his means were such that he required assistance, or*

(b)   *having been informed of his right to apply for legal aid and had the opportunity to do so, he refused or failed to apply.*

(5) This subsection applies to a person who—

(a)   *is charged with or has been convicted of a violent or sexual offence, or an offence punishable in the case of an adult with imprisonment for a term of fourteen years or more; or*

(b)   *has a recent history of absconding while remanded to local authority accommodation, and is charged with or has been convicted of an imprisonable offence alleged or found to have been committed while he was so remanded,*

if (in either case) the court is of opinion that only remanding him to a remand centre or prison, or to local authority accommodation with a requirement that he be placed and kept in secure accommodation, would be adequate to protect the public from serious harm from him.

(5A) This subsection applies to a person if the court is of opinion that, by reason of his physical or emotional immaturity or a propensity of his to harm himself, it would be undesirable for him to be remanded to a remand centre or a prison.

(6) Where a court *declares a person to be one to whom subsection (5) above applies,* it shall be its duty—

(a)   to state in open court that it is of such opinion as is mentioned in *that subsection;* and

(b)   to explain to him in open court and in ordinary language why it is of that opinion;

and a magistrates' court shall cause a reason stated by it under paragraph (b) above to be specified in the warrant of commitment and to be entered in the register.

(7) A court remanding a person to local authority accommodation without imposing a security requirement *(that is to say, a requirement imposed under subsection (4)(a) above that the person be placed and kept in secure accommodation)* may, after consultation with the designated authority, require that person to comply with any such conditions as could be imposed under section 3(6) of the Bail Act 1976 if he were then being granted bail.

(8) Where a court imposes on a person any such conditions as are mentioned in subsection (7) above, it shall be its duty to explain to him in open court and in ordinary language why it is imposing those conditions; and a magistrates' court shall cause a reason stated by it under this subsection to be specified in the warrant of commitment and to be entered in the register.

(9) A court remanding a person to local authority accommodation without imposing a security requirement may, after consultation with the designated authority, impose on that authority requirements—

    (a)   for securing compliance with any conditions imposed on that person under subsection (7) above; or

    (b)   stipulating that he shall not be placed with a named person.

(9A) Where a person is remanded to local authority accommodation, without the imposition of a security requirement, a relevant court may, on the application of the designated authority, declare him to be a person to whom subsection (5) above applies, and on its doing so, subsection (4) above shall apply.

(10) Where a person is remanded to local authority accommodation, a relevant court—

    (a)   may, on the application of the designated authority impose on that person any such conditions as could be imposed under subsection (7) above if the court were then remanding him to such accommodation; and

    (b)   where it does so, may impose on that authority any requirements for securing compliance with the conditions so imposed.

(11) Where a person is remanded to local authority accommodation, a relevant court may, on the application of the designated authority or that person, vary or revoke any conditions or requirements imposed under subsection (7), (9) or (10) above.

(12) In this section—

"court" and "magistrates' court" include a justice;

"imprisonable offence" means an offence punishable in the case of an adult with imprisonment;

"relevant court", in relation to a person remanded to local authority accommodation, means the court by which he was so remanded, or any magistrates' court having jurisdiction in the place where he is for the time being;

"secure accommodation" means accommodation which is provided in a community home, a voluntary home or a registered children's home for the purpose of restricting liberty, and is approved for that purpose by the Secretary of State;

"sexual offence" and "violent offence" have the same meanings as in Part I of the Criminal Justice Act 1991;

"young person" means a person who has attained the age of fourteen years and is under the age of seventeen years,

but, for the purposes of the definition of "secure accommodation", "local authority accommodation" includes any accommodation falling within section 61(2) of the Criminal Justice Act 1991.

(13) In this section—

    (a)   any reference to a person who is being looked after by a local authority shall be construed in accordance with section 22 of the Children Act 1989;

    (b)   any reference to consultation shall be construed as a reference to such consultation (if any) as is reasonably practicable in all the circumstances of the case; and

(c)   any reference, in relation to a person charged with or convicted of a violent or sexual offence, to protecting the public from serious harm from him shall be construed as a reference to protecting members of the public from death or serious personal injury, whether physical or psychological, occasioned by further such offences committed by him.

(14) This section has effect subject to—

(a)   [repealed by Sch 10]; and

(b)   section 128(7) of the Magistrates' Courts Act 1980 (remands to the custody of a constable for periods of not more than three days),

but section 128(7) shall have effect in relation to a child or young person as if for the reference to three clear days there were substituted a reference to 24 hours.'

Age of 15 or 16 (subs (1))—See general annotations.

Youth offending team (subs (3))—See s 39 (s 117(1)).

Remand centre (subs (3))—See Prison Act 1952, s 43.

1991 Act (subs (7))—Ie the Criminal Justice Act 1991. Section 62 of that Act laid down transitory provisions pending provision of secure accommodation.

Release and recall of prisoners

99 Power to release short-term prisoners on licence

Immediately before section 35 of the 1991 Act there shall be inserted the following section—

'34A Power to release short-term prisoners on licence

(1) Subject to subsection (2) below, subsection (3) below applies where a short-term prisoner aged 18 or over is serving a sentence of imprisonment for a term of three months or more.

(2) Subsection (3) below does not apply where—

(a)   the sentence is an extended sentence within the meaning of section 58 of the Crime and Disorder Act 1998;

(b)   the sentence is for an offence under section 1 of the Prisoners (Return to Custody) Act 1995;

(c)   the sentence was imposed under paragraph 3(1)(d) or 4(1)(d) of Schedule 2 to this Act in a case where the prisoner had failed to comply with a requirement of a curfew order;

(d)   the prisoner is subject to a hospital order, hospital direction or transfer direction under section 37, 45A or 47 of the Mental Health Act 1983;

(e)   the prisoner is liable to removal from the United Kingdom for the purposes of section 46 below;

(f)   the prisoner has been released on licence under this section at any time and has been recalled to prison under section 38A(1)(a) below;

(g)   the prisoner has been released on licence under this section or section 36 below during the currency of the sentence, and has been recalled to prison under section 39(1) or (2) below;

(h)   the prisoner has been returned to prison under section 40 below at any time; or

    (j) the interval between—
        (i)   the date on which the prisoner will have served the requisite period for the term of the sentence; and
        (ii) the date on which he will have served one-half of the sentence,
    is less than 14 days.

(3) After the prisoner has served the requisite period for the term of his sentence, the Secretary of State may, subject to section 37A below, release him on licence.

(4) In this section "the requisite period" means—

    (a) for a term of three months or more but less than four months, a period of 30 days;
    (b) for a term of four months or more but less than eight months, a period equal to one-quarter of the term;
    (c) for a term of eight months or more, a period that is 60 days less than one-half of the term.

(5) The Secretary of State may by order made by statutory instrument—

    (a) repeal the words "aged 18 or over" in subsection (1) above;
    (b) amend the definition of "the requisite period" in subsection (4) above; and
    (c) make such transitional provision as appears to him necessary or expedient in connection with the repeal or amendment.

(6) No order shall be made under subsection (5) above unless a draft of the order has been laid before and approved by a resolution of each House of Parliament.'

Explanatory text—See paras **7.86–7.88**.

Short-term prisoner (Criminal Justice Act 1991, s 34A(1))—See annotations to s 59.

Prisoners (Return to Custody) Act 1995 (Criminal Justice Act 1991, s 34A(2))—The relevant parts of s 1 of the 1995 Act are as follows:

'1(1) Subject to subsection (2) below, a person who has been temporarily released in pursuance of rules made under section 47(5) of the Prison Act 1952 (rules for temporary release) is guilty of an offence if—

    (a)   without reasonable excuse, he remains unlawfully at large at any time after becoming so at large by virtue of the expiry of the period for which he was temporarily released; or
    (b)   knowing or believing an order recalling him to have been made and while unlawfully at large by virtue of such an order, he fails, without reasonable excuse, to take all necessary steps for complying as soon as reasonably practicable with that order.

(2) Subsection (1) above shall not apply in the case of a person temporarily released from a secure training centre.'

Liable to removal from the United Kingdom (1991 Act, s 34A(2))—Ie pursuant to powers in the Immigration Act 1971 and rules made thereunder.

Released on licence ... and recalled to prison (1991 Act, s 34A(2))—See annotations to s 59.

---

100 Curfew condition to be included in licence

(1) After section 37 of the 1991 Act there shall be inserted the following section—

'37A Curfew condition to be included in licence under section 34A

(1) A person shall not be released under section 34A(3) above unless the licence includes a condition ("the curfew condition") which—

- (a) requires the released person to remain, for periods for the time being specified in the condition, at a place for the time being so specified (which may be an approved probation hostel); and
- (b) includes requirements for securing the electronic monitoring of his whereabouts during the periods for the time being so specified.

(2) The curfew condition may specify different places or different periods for different days, but shall not specify periods which amount to less than 9 hours in any one day (excluding for this purpose the first and last days of the period for which the condition is in force).

(3) The curfew condition shall remain in force until the date when the released person would (but for his release) have served one-half of his sentence.

(4) The curfew condition shall include provision for making a person responsible for monitoring the released person's whereabouts during the periods for the time being specified in the condition; and a person who is made so responsible shall be of a description specified in an order made by the Secretary of State.

(5) The power conferred by subsection (4) above—

- (a) shall be exercisable by statutory instrument; and
- (b) shall include power to make different provision for different cases or classes of case or for different areas.

(6) Nothing in this section shall be taken to require the Secretary of State to ensure that arrangements are made for the electronic monitoring of released persons' whereabouts in any particular part of England and Wales.

(7) In this section "approved probation hostel" has the same meaning as in the Probation Service Act 1993.'

(2) Immediately before section 39 of the 1991 Act there shall be inserted the following section—

'38A Breach of curfew condition

(1) If it appears to the Secretary of State, as regards a person released on licence under section 34A(3) above—

- (a) that he has failed to comply with the curfew condition;
- (b) that his whereabouts can no longer be electronically monitored at the place for the time being specified in that condition; or
- (c) that it is necessary to do so in order to protect the public from serious harm from him,

the Secretary of State may, if the curfew condition is still in force, revoke the licence and recall the person to prison.

(2) A person whose licence under section 34A(3) above is revoked under this section—

    (a) may make representations in writing with respect to the revocation;

    (b) on his return to prison, shall be informed of the reasons for the revocation and of his right to make representations.

(3) The Secretary of State, after considering any representations made under subsection (2)(b) above or any other matters, may cancel a revocation under this section.

(4) Where the revocation of a person's licence is cancelled under subsection (3) above, the person shall be treated for the purposes of sections 34A(2)(f) and 37(1B) above as if he had not been recalled to prison under this section.

(5) On the revocation under this section of a person's licence under section 34A(3) above, he shall be liable to be detained in pursuance of his sentence and, if at large, shall be deemed to be unlawfully at large.

(6) In this section "the curfew condition" has the same meaning as in section 37A above.'

Explanatory text—See paras **7.90–7.91**.

---

101 Early release: two or more sentences

(1) For subsection (2) of section 51 of the 1991 Act (interpretation of Part II) there shall be substituted the following subsections—

'(2) For the purposes of any reference in this Part, however expressed, to the term of imprisonment to which a person has been sentenced or which, or part of which, he has served, consecutive terms and terms which are wholly or partly concurrent shall be treated as a single term if—

    (a) the sentences were passed on the same occasion; or

    (b) where they were passed on different occasions, the person has not been released under this Part at any time during the period beginning with the first and ending with the last of those occasions.

(2A) Where a suspended sentence of imprisonment is ordered to take effect, with or without any variation of the original term, the occasion on which that order is made shall be treated for the purposes of subsection (2) above as the occasion on which the sentence is passed.

(2B) Where a person has been sentenced to two or more terms of imprisonment which are wholly or partly concurrent and do not fall to be treated as a single term—

    (a) nothing in this Part shall require the Secretary of State to release him in respect of any of the terms unless and until the Secretary of State is required to release him in respect of each of the others;

    (b) nothing in this Part shall require the Secretary of State or the Board to consider his release in respect of any of the terms unless and until the Secretary of State or the Board is required to consider his release, or the Secretary of State is required to release him, in respect of each of the others;

    (c) on and after his release under this Part he shall be on licence for so long, and subject to such conditions, as is required by this Part in respect of any of the sentences; and

    (d) the date mentioned in section 40(1) above shall be taken to be that on which he would (but for his release) have served each of the sentences in full.

(2C) Where a person has been sentenced to one or more terms of imprisonment and to one or more life sentences (within the meaning of section 34 of the Crime (Sentences) Act 1997), nothing in this Part shall—

(a) require the Secretary of State to release the person in respect of any of the terms unless and until the Secretary of State is required to release him in respect of each of the life sentences; or

(b) require the Secretary of State or the Board to consider the person's release in respect of any of the terms unless and until the Secretary of State or the Board is required to consider his release in respect of each of the life sentences.

(2D) Subsections (2B) and (2C) above shall have effect as if the term of an extended sentence (within the meaning of section 58 of the Crime and Disorder Act 1998) included the extension period (within the meaning of that section).'

(2) After subsection (3) of section 34 of the 1997 Act (interpretation of Chapter II) there shall be inserted the following subsection—

'(4) Where a person has been sentenced to one or more life sentences and to one or more terms of imprisonment, nothing in this Chapter shall require the Secretary of State to release the person in respect of any of the life sentences unless and until the Secretary of State is required to release him in respect of each of the terms.'

Explanatory text—See paras **7.81–7.83**.

Life sentences within the meaning of section 34 of the Crime (Sentences) Act 1997 (1991 Act, s 51(2C))—Section 34(2) defines a life sentence as meaning:

'any of the following imposed for an offence, whether committed before or after the commencement of this Chapter, namely—

(a) sentence of imprisonment for life;

(b) a sentence of detention during Her Majesty's Pleasure or for life under section 53 of the 1933 Act; and

(c) a sentence of custody for life under section 8 of the 1982 Act.'

---

102 Restriction on consecutive sentences for released prisoners

(1) A court sentencing a person to a term of imprisonment shall not order or direct that the term shall commence on the expiration of any other sentence of imprisonment from which he has been released under Part II of the 1991 Act.

(2) Expressions used in this section shall be construed as if they were contained in that Part.

Explanatory text—see para **7.84**.

---

103 Recall to prison of short-term prisoners

(1) This section has effect for the purpose of securing that, subject to section 100(2) above, the circumstances in which prisoners released on licence under Part II of the 1991 Act may be recalled to prison are the same for short-term prisoners as for long-term prisoners.

Crime and Disorder Act 1998

(2) Section 38 of the 1991 Act (breach of licence conditions by short-term prisoners) shall cease to have effect.

(3) In subsection (1) of section 39 of the 1991 Act (recall of long-term prisoners while on licence), after the words 'in the case of a' there shall be inserted the words 'short-term or'.

Explanatory text—see para **7.93**.

Section 39 of the 1991 Act (subs (3))—See annotations to s 59.

---

104 Release on licence following recall to prison

(1) In subsection (3) of section 33 of the 1991 Act (duty to release short-term and long-term prisoners), for the word 'unconditionally' there shall be substituted the words 'on licence'.

(2) After subsection (1) of section 37 of that Act (duration and conditions of licences) there shall be inserted the following subsection—

'(1A) Where a prisoner is released on licence under section 33(3) or (3A) above, subsection (1) above shall have effect as if for the reference to three-quarters of his sentence there were substituted a reference to the whole of that sentence.'

Explanatory text—see para **7.94**.

Sections 33 and 37 of the 1991 Act (subss (1) and (2))—See annotations to s 59.

---

105 Release on licence following return to prison

After section 40 of the 1991 Act there shall be inserted the following section—

'40A Release on licence following return to prison

(1) This section applies (in place of sections 33, 33A, 37(1) and 39 above) where a court passes on a person a sentence of imprisonment which—

(a) includes, or consists of, an order under section 40 above; and
(b) is for a term of twelve months or less.

(2) As soon as the person has served one-half of the sentence, it shall be the duty of the Secretary of State to release him on licence.

(3) Where the person is so released, the licence shall remain in force for a period of three months.

(4) If the person fails to comply with such conditions as may for the time being be specified in the licence, he shall be liable on summary conviction—

(a) to a fine not exceeding level 3 on the standard scale; or
(b) to a sentence of imprisonment for a term not exceeding the relevant period,

but not liable to be dealt with in any other way.

(5) In subsection (4) above "the relevant period" means a period which is equal in length to the period between the date on which the failure occurred or began and the date of the expiry of the licence.

(6) As soon as a person has served one-half of a sentence passed under subsection (4) above, it shall be the duty of the Secretary of State to release him, subject to the licence if it is still subsisting.'

Explanatory text—See para **7.94**.

Miscellaneous

106 Pre-consolidation amendments

The enactments mentioned in Schedule 7 to this Act shall have effect subject to the amendments there specified, being amendments designed to facilitate, or otherwise desirable in connection with, the consolidation of certain enactments relating to the powers of courts to deal with offenders or defaulters.

Explanatory text—See paras **1.16** and **7.1**.

107 Amendments to Chapter I of Part II of 1997 Act

(1) Chapter I of Part II of the 1997 Act (which relates to the effect of determinate custodial sentences) shall be amended as follows.

(2) Sections 8 and 10 to 27 are hereby repealed.

(3) After subsection (7) of section 9 (crediting of periods of remand in custody) there shall be inserted the following subsection—

'(7A) Such rules may make such incidental, supplemental and consequential provisions as may appear to the Secretary of State to be necessary or expedient.'

(4) After subsection (10) of that section there shall be inserted the following subsections—

'(11) In this section "sentence of imprisonment" does not include a committal—

(a) in default of payment of any sum of money other than one adjudged to be paid by a conviction;
(b) for want of sufficient distress to satisfy any sum of money; or
(c) for failure to do or abstain from doing anything required to be done or left undone;

and cognate expressions shall be construed accordingly.

(12) For the purposes of any reference in this section, however expressed, to the term of imprisonment to which a person has been sentenced, consecutive terms and terms which are wholly or partly concurrent shall be treated as a single term if—

(a) the sentences were passed on the same occasion; or
(b) where they were passed on different occasions, the person has not been released under Part II of the 1991 Act at any time during the period beginning with the first and ending with the last of those occasions.'

(5) After that section there shall be inserted the following section—

'9A Provision supplementary to section 9

(1) Section 9 above applies to—

    (a) a sentence of detention in a young offender institution; and

    (b) a determinate sentence of detention under section 53 of the Children and Young Persons Act 1933 ("the 1933 Act"),

as it applies to an equivalent sentence of imprisonment.

(2) Section 9 above applies to—

    (a) persons remanded or committed to local authority accommodation under section 23 of the Children and Young Persons Act 1969 ("the 1969 Act") and placed and kept in secure accommodation; and

    (b) persons remanded, admitted or removed to hospital under section 35, 36, 38 or 48 of the Mental Health Act 1983 ("the 1983 Act"),

as it applies to persons remanded in or committed to custody by an order of a court.

(3) In this section "secure accommodation" has the same meaning as in section 23 of the 1969 Act.'

Explanatory text—See paras **7.77–7.80**.

Section 9 of the Crime (Sentences) Act 1997 (subs (2))—This provides:

'(1) This section applies where—

    (a) a court sentences an offender to imprisonment for a term in respect of an offence committed after the commencement of this section; and

    (b) the offender has been remanded in custody in connection with the offence or a related offence, that is to say, any other offence the charge for which was founded on the same facts or evidence.

(2) It is immaterial for that purpose whether the offender—

    (a) has also been remanded in custody in connection with other offences; or

    (b) has also been detained in connection with other matters.

(3) Subject to subsection (4) below, the court shall direct that the number of days for which the offender was remanded in custody in connection with the offence or a related offence shall count as time served by him as part of the sentence.

(4) Subsection (3) above shall not apply if and to the extent that—

    (a) rules made by the Secretary of State so provide in the case of—

        (i) a remand in custody which is wholly or partly concurrent with a sentence of imprisonment; or

        (ii) sentences of imprisonment for consecutive terms or for terms which are wholly or partly concurrent; or

    (b) it is in the opinion of the court just in all the circumstances not to give a direction under that subsection.

(5) Where the court gives a direction under subsection (3) above, it shall state in open court—

    (a) the number of days for which the offender was remanded in custody; and

    (b) the number of days in relation to which the direction was given.

(6) Where the court does not give a direction under subsection (3) above, or gives such a direction in relation to a number of days less than that for which the offender was remanded in custody, it shall state in open court—

(a)   that its decision is in accordance with rules made under paragraph (a) of subsection (4) above; or

(b)   that it is of the opinion mentioned in paragraph (b) of that subsection and what the circumstances are.

(7) The power to make rules under subsection (4)(a) above shall be exercisable by statutory instrument; but no such rules shall be made unless a draft of the rules has been laid before and approved by a resolution of each House of Parliament.

(7A) [see s 107(3)].

(8) For the purposes of this section a suspended sentence shall be treated as a sentence of imprisonment when it takes effect under section 23 of the Powers of Criminal Courts Act 1973 ("the 1973 Act") and as being imposed by the order under which it takes effect.

(9) References in this section to an offender being remanded in custody are references to his being—

(a)   held in police detention; or

(b)   remanded in or committed to custody by an order of the court.

(10) A person is in police detention for the purposes of this section—

(a)   at any time when he is in police detention for the purposes of the Police and Criminal Evidence Act 1984; and

(b)   at any time when he is detained under section 14 of the Prevention of Terrorism (Temporary Provisions) Act 1989.

(11) and (12) [See s 107(4)].'

Explanatory text—See paras **7.76–7.80**.

Section 53 of the Children and Young Persons Act 1933 (subs (5))—See annotations to s 73.

Section 23 of the Children and Young Persons Act 1969 (subs (5))—See annotations to s 97.

Sections 35, 36, 38 or 48 of the Mental Health Act 1983 (subs (5))—For sections 35–36 and 38, see annotations to s 74.

---

108 to 112 [*Applies to Scotland only.*]

113 Deputy authorising officer under Part III of Police Act 1997

(1) In subsection (1) of section 94 of the Police Act 1997 (authorisations given in absence of authorising officer), for the words '(f) or (g)' there shall be substituted the words '(f), (g) or (h)'.

(2) In subsection (3) of that section, for paragraphs (a) and (b) there shall be substituted the words 'he holds the rank of assistant chief constable in that Service or Squad'.

(3) In subsection (4) of that section, the word 'and' immediately preceding paragraph (c) shall cease to have effect and after that paragraph there shall be inserted the words 'and

(d)   in the case of an authorising officer within paragraph (h) of section 93(5), means the customs officer designated by the Commissioners of Customs and Excise to act in his absence for the purposes of this paragraph.'

Explanatory text—See paras **9.17–9.19**.

Section 94 of the Police Act 1997—As amended by the present section and in the light of the repeal of one word by Sch 10, the section provides (amendments are italicised):

'(1) Subsection (2) applies where it is not reasonably practicable for an authorising officer to consider an application for an authorisation under section 93 and—

    (a)   if the authorising officer is within paragraph (b) or (e) of section 93(5), it is also not reasonably practicable for the application to be considered by any of the other persons within the paragraph concerned; or

    (b)   if the authorising officer is within paragraph (a), (c), (d), (f), (g) or *(h)* of section 93(5), it is also not reasonably practicable for the application to be considered by his designated deputy.

(2) Where this subsection applies, the powers conferred on the authorising officer by section 93 may, in an urgent case, be exercised—

    (a)   where the authorising officer is within paragraph (a) or (d) of subsection (5) of that section, by a person holding the rank of assistant chief constable in his force;

    (b)   where the authorising officer is within paragraph (b) of that subsection, by a person holding the rank of commander in the metropolitan police force;

    (c)   where the authorising officer is within paragraph (c) of that subsection, by a person holding the rank of commander in the City of London police force;

    (d)   where the authorising officer is within paragraph (e) of that subsection, by a person holding the rank of assistant chief constable in the Royal Ulster Constabulary;

    (e)   where the authorising officer is within paragraph (f) or (g) of that subsection by a person designated for the purposes of this section by the Director General of the National Criminal Intelligence Service or, as the case may be, of the National Crime Squad;

    (f)   where the authorising officer is within paragraph (h) of that subsection, by a customs officer designated by Commissioners of Customs and Excise for the purposes of this section.

(3) A police member of the National Criminal Intelligence Service or the National Crime Squad appointed under section 9(1)(b) or 55(1)(b) may not be designated under subsection (2)(e) unless he *holds* the rank of assistant chief constable in *that Service or Squad.*

(4) In subsection (1), 'designated deputy'—

    (a)   in the case of an authorising officer within paragraph (a) or (d) of section 93(5), means the person holding the rank of assistant chief constable designated to act in his absence under section 12(4) of the Police Act 1996 or, as the case may be, section 5(4) of the Police (Scotland) Act 1967;

    (b)   in the case of an authorising officer within paragraph (c) of section 93(5), means the person authorised to act in his absence under section 25 of the City of London Police Act 1839;

    (c)   in the case of an authorising officer within paragraph (f) or (g) of section 93(5), means the person designated to act in his absence under section 8 or 54; *and*

    (d)   *in the case of an authorising officer within paragraph (h) of section 93(5), means the customs officer designated by the Commissioners of Customs and Excise to act in his absence for the purposes of this paragraph.'*

Supplemental

114   Orders and regulations

(1) Any power of a Minister of the Crown to make an order or regulations under this Act—

    (a)   is exercisable by statutory instrument; and

    (b)   includes power to make such transitional provision as appears to him necessary or expedient in connection with any provision made by the order or regulations.

(2) A statutory instrument containing an order under section 5(2) or (3) or 10(6) above, or regulations under paragraph 1 of Schedule 3 to this Act, shall be subject to annulment in pursuance of a resolution of either House of Parliament.

(3) No order under section 38(5), 41(6), 58(7), 61(7), 73(2)(b)(ii) or 76(2) above shall be made unless a draft of the order has been laid before and approved by a resolution of each House of Parliament.

General—This is a fairly standard provision as regards the grant to a Minister of powers to make orders or regulations.

The particularly rigorous 'affirmative resolution' procedure is reserved for orders of particular importance:

    (a)   orders amending the definition of 'youth justice services' in s 38(4) (s 38(5));

    (b)   orders amending the definition of the functions of the Youth Justice Board in s 41(5) or providing that the exercise of any of the Home Secretary's functions in relation to the youth justice system be exercisable concurrently with the Board (s 41(6));

    (c)   orders amending the extension period under s 58(4)(b) for the purposes of release on licence in the case of a violent offence (s 58(7));

    (d)   orders amending the duration of a drug testing order set out in s 61(2) (s 61(7));

    (e)   an order appointing the date on or after which the offence must have been committed if a detention and training order is to be available in respect of an offender under 12 at the time of conviction (s 73(2)(b)(ii)); and

    (f)   orders amending the end of a period of supervision of an offender subject to a detention and training order, set out in s 76(1) (s 76(2)).

The rather less rigorous 'negative resolution' procedure is reserved for:

    (a)   orders prescribing persons or bodies with whom there must be co-operation, or whose participation must be invited, in respect of the formulation of local crime and disorder strategies under s 6 (s 5(2) and (3));

    (b)   orders providing for the circumstances in which appeals to the High Court against the making of a parenting order by virtue of s 8(1)(a) against the making of a child safety order may be made against decisions taken by courts on questions arising in connection with the transfer, or proposed transfer, of proceedings by virtue of any order under the Children Act 1989, Sch 11, para 2 (s 10(6) and s 13(3)); and

    (c)   regulations providing that, where a person is sent for trial under s 51, copies of the documents containing the evidence on which the charge or charges are based, are served on that person and given to the Crown Court before the 'relevant date' (Sch 3, para 1).

Other orders or regulations under the Act, eg commencement orders under s 121, are not subject to either of the above procedures and are not even required to be laid before Parliament in order to be operative.

Statutory instrument (subss (1) and (2))—With regard to statutory instruments generally, see the Statutory Instruments Act 1946.

Subject to annulment in pursuance of a resolution of either House of Parliament (subs (2))—A statutory instrument containing an order of a type referred to in subs (2) must be laid before each House of Parliament before it comes into operation, unless it is essential that it should come into operation at an earlier date (in which case a special procedure must be followed), but it may be annulled by Order in Council pursuant to a resolution of either House of Parliament, that resolution being within the period of 40 days beginning with the day on which the instrument was laid: Statutory Instruments Act 1946, ss 4 and 5. Annulment does not prejudice the validity of anything previously done under the instrument: ibid, s 5(1). In reckoning the period of 40 days, account is to be taken of the day on which it was laid: *Hare v Gocher* [1962] 2 QB 641, [1962] 2 All ER 763; *Trow v Ind Coope (West Midlands) Ltd* [1967] 2 QB 899, [1967] 2 All ER 900 (CA). On the other hand, no account is to be taken of any time during which Parliament is dissolved or prorogued or during which both Houses are adjourned for more than four days: Statutory Instruments Act 1946, s 7(1).

Unless ... approved by a resolution of each House of Parliament (subs (3))—A statutory instrument containing an order or regulations of a type referred to in s 114(3) will not come into effect unless a draft of it has been laid before each House of Parliament and been approved by a resolution of each House. No amendment by either House is possible.

115 Disclosure of information

(1) Any person who, apart from this subsection, would not have power to disclose information—

(a) to a relevant authority; or

(b) to a person acting on behalf of such an authority,

shall have power to do so in any case where the disclosure is necessary or expedient for the purposes of any provision of this Act.

(2) In subsection (1) above 'relevant authority' means—

(a) the chief officer of police for a police area in England and Wales;

(b) the chief constable of a police force maintained under the Police (Scotland) Act 1967;

(c) a police authority within the meaning given by section 101(1) of the Police Act 1996;

(d) a local authority, that is to say—

(i) in relation to England, a county council, a district council, a London borough council or the Common Council of the City of London;

(ii) in relation to Wales, a county council or a county borough council;

(iii) in relation to Scotland, a council constituted under section 2 of the Local Government etc. (Scotland) Act 1994;

(e) a probation committee in England and Wales;

(f) a health authority.

Explanatory text—See para **1.17**.

116 Transitory provisions

(1) The Secretary of State may by order provide that, in relation to any time before the commencement of section 73 above, a court shall not make an order under—

(a) section 1 of the 1994 Act (secure training orders); or

(b) subsection (3)(a) of section 4 of that Act (breaches of supervision requirements),

unless it has been notified by the Secretary of State that accommodation at a secure training centre, or accommodation provided by a local authority for the purpose of restricting the liberty of children and young persons, is immediately available for the offender, and the notice has not been withdrawn.

(2) An order under this section may provide that sections 2 and 4 of the 1994 Act shall have effect, in relation to any such time, as if—

(a) for subsections (2) and (3) of section 2 there were substituted the following subsection—

'(2) Where accommodation for the offender at a secure training centre is not immediately available—

    (a) the court shall commit the offender to accommodation provided by a local authority for the purpose of restricting the liberty of children and young persons until such time as accommodation for him at such a centre is available; and

    (b) the period of detention in the centre under the order shall be reduced by the period spent by the offender in the accommodation so provided.';

  (b) in subsection (5) of that section, for the words 'subsections (2)(a)(ii) and (4)(b) apply' there were substituted the words 'subsection (4)(b) applies';

  (c) for subsection (8) of that section there were substituted the following subsection—

'(8) In this section "local authority" has the same meaning as in the Children Act 1989.'; and

  (d) in subsection (4) of section 4, for the words 'paragraphs (a), (b) and (c) of subsection (2) and subsections (5), (7) and (8) of section 2' there were substituted the words 'paragraphs (a) and (b) of subsection (2) and subsections (7) and (8) of section 2'.

(3) In relation to any time before the commencement of section 73 above, section 4 of the 1994 Act shall have effect as if after subsection (4) there were inserted the following subsection—

'(4A) A fine imposed under subsection (3)(b) above shall be deemed, for the purposes of any enactment, to be a sum adjudged to be paid by a conviction.'

(4) In relation to any time before the commencement of section 73 above, section 1B of the 1982 Act (special provision for offenders under 18) shall have effect as if—

  (a) in subsection (4), immediately before the words 'a total term' there were inserted the words 'a term or (in the case of an offender to whom subsection (6) below applies)';

  (b) in subsection (5)—

    (i) immediately before the words 'total term' there were inserted the words 'term or (as the case may be)'; and

    (ii) for the words 'the term' there were substituted the word 'it'; and

  (c) for subsection (6) there were substituted the following subsection—

'(6) This subsection applies to an offender sentenced to two or more terms of detention in a young offender institution which are consecutive or wholly or partly concurrent if—

    (a) the sentences were passed on the same occasion; or

    (b) where they were passed on different occasions, the offender has not been released under Part II of the Criminal Justice Act 1991 at any time during the period beginning with the first and ending with the last of those occasions;

and in subsections (4) and (5) above "the total term", in relation to such an offender, means the aggregate of those terms.'

(5) In this section 'local authority' has the same meaning as in the 1989 Act.

The 1994 Act (subs (1), (2) and (3)); the 1982 Act (subs (4)); the 1989 Act (subs (5))—See s 117(1).

117 General interpretation

(1) In this Act—

'the 1933 Act' means the Children and Young Persons Act 1933;
'the 1969 Act' means the Children and Young Persons Act 1969;
'the 1973 Act' means the Powers of Criminal Courts Act 1973;
'the 1980 Act' means the Magistrates' Courts Act 1980;
'the 1982 Act' means the Criminal Justice Act 1982;
'the 1984 Act' means the Police and Criminal Evidence Act 1984;
'the 1985 Act' means the Prosecution of Offences Act 1985;
'the 1989 Act' means the Children Act 1989;
'the 1991 Act' means the Criminal Justice Act 1991;
'the 1994 Act' means the Criminal Justice and Public Order Act 1994;
'the 1997 Act' means the Crime (Sentences) Act 1997;
'caution' has the same meaning as in Part V of the Police Act 1997;
'child' means a person under the age of 14;
'commission area' has the same meaning as in the Justices of the Peace Act 1997;
'custodial sentence' has the same meaning as in Part I of the 1991 Act;
'guardian' has the same meaning as in the 1933 Act;
'prescribed' means prescribed by an order made by the Secretary of State;
'young person' means a person who has attained the age of 14 and is under the age of 18;
'youth offending team' means a team established under section 39 above.

(2) [*Applies to Scotland only.*]

(3) For the purposes of this Act, the age of a person shall be deemed to be that which it appears to the court to be after considering any available evidence.

Under the age of 14/18 (subs (1))—See general annotations.

Commission area (subs (1))—See general annotations.

Custodial sentence has the same meaning as in Part I of the 1991 Act (subs (1))—Ie:

'(a) in relation to an offender of or over the age of twenty-one years, a sentence of imprisonment; and

(b) in relation to an offender under that age, a sentence of detention in a young offender institution or under section 53 of the Children and Young Persons Act 1933 ("the 1933 Act"), or a sentence of custody for life under section 8(2) of the 1982 Act.'

Guardian has the same meaning as in the 1933 Act (subs (1))—Ie Any person who, in the opinion of the court, has for the time being 'the care of the child or young person' (Children and Young Persons Act 1933, s 107).

---

118 [*Applies to Northern Ireland only.*]

119 Minor and consequential amendments

The enactments mentioned in Schedule 8 to this Act shall have effect subject to the amendments there specified, being minor amendments and amendments consequential on the provisions of this Act.

120 Transitional provisions, savings and repeals

(1) The transitional provisions and savings contained in Schedule 9 to this Act shall have effect; but nothing in this subsection shall be taken as prejudicing the operation of sections 16 and 17 of the Interpretation Act 1978 (which relate to the effect of repeals).

(2) The enactments specified in Schedule 10 to this Act, which include some that are spent, are hereby repealed to the extent specified in the third column of that Schedule.

121 Short title, commencement and extent

(1) This Act may be cited as the Crime and Disorder Act 1998.

(2) This Act, except this section, sections 109 and 111(8) above and paragraphs 55, 99 and 117 of Schedule 8 to this Act, shall come into force on such day as the Secretary of State may by order appoint; and different days may be appointed for different purposes or different areas.

(3) Without prejudice to the provisions of Schedule 9 to this Act, an order under subsection (2) above may make such transitional provisions and savings as appear to the Secretary of State necessary or expedient in connection with any provision brought into force by the order.

(4) Subject to subsections (5) to (12) below, this Act extends to England and Wales only.

(5) The following provisions extend to Scotland only, namely—

    (a) Chapter II of Part I;
    (b) section 33;
    (c) Chapter II of Part IV;
    (d) sections 108 to 112 and 117(2); and
    (e) paragraphs 55, 70, 71, 98 to 108, 115 to 124 and 140 to 143 of Schedule 8 and section 119 above so far as relating to those paragraphs.

(6) The following provisions also extend to Scotland, namely—

    (a) Chapter III of Part I;
    (b) section 36(3) to (5);
    (c) section 65(9);
    (d) section 115;
    (e) paragraph 3 of Schedule 3 to this Act and section 52(6) above so far as relating to that paragraph;
    (f) paragraph 15 of Schedule 7 to this Act and section 106 above so far as relating to that paragraph;
    (g) paragraphs 1, 7(1) and (3), 14(1) and (2), 35, 36, 45, 135, 136 and 138 of Schedule 8 to this Act and section 119 above so far as relating to those paragraphs; and
    (h) this section.

(7) Sections 36(1), (2)(a), (b) and (d) and (6)(b) and section 118 above extend to Northern Ireland only.

(8) Section 36(3)(b), (4) and (5) above, paragraphs 7(1) and (3), 45, 135 and 138 of Schedule 8 to this Act, section 119 above so far as relating to those paragraphs and this section also extend to Northern Ireland.

(9) Section 36(5) above, paragraphs 7(1) and (3), 45 and 134 of Schedule 8 to this Act, section 119 above so far as relating to those paragraphs and this section also extend to the Isle of Man.

(10) Section 36(5) above, paragraphs 7(1) and (3), 45 and 135 of Schedule 8 to this Act, section 119 above so far as relating to those paragraphs and this section also extend to the Channel Islands.

(11) The repeals in Schedule 10 to this Act, and section 120(2) above so far as relating to those repeals, have the same extent as the enactments on which the repeals operate.

(12) Section 9(4) of the Repatriation of Prisoners Act 1984 (power to extend Act to Channel Islands and Isle of Man) applies to the amendments of that Act made by paragraphs 56 to 60 of Schedule 8 to this Act; and in Schedule 1 to the 1997 Act—

  (a) paragraph 14 (restricted transfers between the United Kingdom and the Channel Islands) as applied in relation to the Isle of Man; and
  (b) paragraph 19 (application of Schedule in relation to the Isle of Man),

apply to the amendments of that Schedule made by paragraph 135 of Schedule 8 to this Act.

Commencement—This section (ie s 121) and the other provisions specified (which extend only to Scotland) came into force on Royal Assent (31 July 1998) (subs (2)).

Subsection (2)—A commencement order must be made by statutory instrument; see s 114 and annotations thereto. Also see para **1.4**.

England and Wales (subs (4))—See general annotations.

SCHEDULES

SCHEDULE 1
[Applies to Scotland only.]

Section 41(11)   SCHEDULE 2

THE YOUTH JUSTICE BOARD: FURTHER PROVISIONS

Membership

1 The Secretary of State shall appoint one of the members of the Board to be their chairman.

2—(1) Subject to the following provisions of this paragraph, a person shall hold and vacate office as a member of the Board, or as chairman of the Board, in accordance with the terms of his appointment.

(2) An appointment as a member of the Board may be full-time or part-time.

(3) The appointment of a person as a member of the Board, or as chairman of the Board, shall be for a fixed period of not longer than five years.

(4) Subject to sub-paragraph (5) below, a person whose term of appointment as a member of the Board, or as chairman of the Board, expires shall be eligible for re-appointment.

(5) No person may hold office as a member of the Board for a continuous period which is longer than ten years.

(6) A person may at any time resign his office as a member of the Board, or as chairman of the Board, by notice in writing addressed to the Secretary of State.

(7) The terms of appointment of a member of the Board, or the chairman of the Board, may provide for his removal from office (without cause being assigned) on notice from the Secretary of State of such length as may be specified in those terms, subject (if those terms so provide) to compensation from the Secretary of State; and in any such case the Secretary of State may remove that member from office in accordance with those terms.

(8) Where—

  (a) the terms of appointment of a member of the Board, or the chairman of the Board, provide for compensation on his removal from office in pursuance of sub-paragraph (7) above; and
  (b) the member or chairman is removed from office in pursuance of that sub-paragraph,

the Board shall pay to him compensation of such amount, and on such terms, as the Secretary of State may with the approval of the Treasury determine.

(9) The Secretary of State may also at any time remove a person from office as a member of the Board if satisfied—

  (a) that he has without reasonable excuse failed to discharge his functions as a member for a continuous period of three months beginning not earlier than six months before that time;

(b) that he has been convicted of a criminal offence;

(c) that a bankruptcy order has been made against him, or his estate has been sequestrated, or he has made a composition or arrangement with, or granted a trust deed for, his creditors; or

(d) that he is unable or unfit to discharge his functions as a member.

(10) The Secretary of State shall remove a member of the Board, or the chairman of the Board, from office in pursuance of this paragraph by declaring his office as a member of the Board to be vacant and notifying that fact in such manner as the Secretary of State thinks fit; and the office shall then become vacant.

(11) If the chairman of the Board ceases to be a member of the Board he shall also cease to be chairman.

Members and employees

3—(1) The Board shall—

(a) pay to members of the Board such remuneration;

(b) pay to or in respect of members of the Board any such allowances, fees, expenses and gratuities; and

(c) pay towards the provision of pensions to or in respect of members of the Board any such sums,

as the Board are required to pay by or in accordance with directions given by the Secretary of State.

(2) Where a member of the Board was, immediately before becoming a member, a participant in a scheme under section 1 of the Superannuation Act 1972, the Minister for the Civil Service may determine that his term of office as a member shall be treated for the purposes of the scheme as if it were service in the employment or office by reference to which he was a participant in the scheme; and his rights under the scheme shall not be affected by sub-paragraph (1)(c) above.

(3) Where—

(a) a person ceases to hold office as a member of the Board otherwise than on the expiry of his term of appointment; and

(b) it appears to the Secretary of State that there are special circumstances which make it right for him to receive compensation,

the Secretary of State may direct the Board to make to the person a payment of such amount as the Secretary of State may determine.

4—(1) The Board may appoint a chief executive and such other employees as the Board think fit, subject to the consent of the Secretary of State as to their number and terms and conditions of service.

(2) The Board shall—

(a) pay to employees of the Board such remuneration; and

(b) pay to or in respect of employees of the Board any such allowances, fees, expenses and gratuities,

as the Board may, with the consent of the Secretary of State, determine.

(3) Employment by the Board shall be included among the kinds of employment to which a scheme under section 1 of the Superannuation Act 1972 may apply.

5 The Board shall pay to the Minister for the Civil Service, at such times as he may direct, such sums as he may determine in respect of any increase attributable to paragraph 3(2) or 4(3) above in the sums payable out of money provided by Parliament under the Superannuation Act 1972.

House of Commons disqualification

6 In Part II of Schedule 1 to the House of Commons Disqualification Act 1975 (bodies of which all members are disqualified), there shall be inserted at the appropriate place the following entry—

'The Youth Justice Board for England and Wales'.

Procedure

7—(1) The arrangements for the procedure of the Board (including the quorum for meetings) shall be such as the Board may determine.

(2) The validity of any proceedings of the Board (or of any committee of the Board) shall not be affected by—

(a) any vacancy among the members of the Board or in the office of chairman of the Board; or

(b) any defect in the appointment of any person as a member of the Board or as chairman of the Board.

Annual reports and accounts

8—(1) As soon as possible after the end of each financial year of the Board, the Board shall send to the Secretary of State a report on the discharge of their functions during that year.

(2) The Secretary of State shall lay before each House of Parliament, and cause to be published, a copy of every report sent to him under this paragraph.

9—(1) The Board shall—

(a) keep proper accounts and proper records in relation to the accounts; and

(b) prepare a statement of accounts in respect of each financial year of the Board.

(2) The statement of accounts shall contain such information and shall be in such form as the Secretary of State may, with the consent of the Treasury, direct.

(3) The Board shall send a copy of the statement of accounts to the Secretary of State and to the Comptroller and Auditor General within such period after the end of the financial year to which the statement relates as the Secretary of State may direct.

(4) The Comptroller and Auditor General shall—

(a) examine, certify and report on the statement of accounts; and

(b) lay a copy of the statement of accounts and of his report before each House of Parliament.

10 For the purposes of this Schedule the Board's financial year shall be the period of twelve months ending with 31st March; but the first financial year of the Board shall be the period beginning with the date of establishment of the Board and ending with the first 31st March which falls at least six months after that date.

Expenses

11 The Secretary of State shall out of money provided by Parliament pay to the Board such sums towards their expenses as he may determine.

Section 52(6)   SCHEDULE 3

PROCEDURE WHERE PERSONS ARE SENT FOR TRIAL UNDER SECTION 51

Regulations

1 The Attorney General shall by regulations provide that, where a person is sent for trial under section 51 of this Act on any charge or charges, copies of the documents containing the evidence on which the charge or charges are based shall, on or before the relevant date—

  (a) be served on that person; and
  (b) be given to the Crown Court sitting at the place specified in the notice under subsection (7) of that section.

(2) In sub-paragraph (1) above 'the relevant date' means the date prescribed by the regulations.

Applications for dismissal

2—(1) A person who is sent for trial under section 51 of this Act on any charge or charges may, at any time—

  (a) after he is served with copies of the documents containing the evidence on which the charge or charges are based; and
  (b) before he is arraigned (and whether or not an indictment has been preferred against him),

apply orally or in writing to the Crown Court sitting at the place specified in the notice under subsection (7) of that section for the charge, or any of the charges, in the case to be dismissed.

(2) The judge shall dismiss a charge (and accordingly quash any count relating to it in any indictment preferred against the applicant) which is the subject of any such application if it appears to him that the evidence against the applicant would not be sufficient for a jury properly to convict him.

(3) No oral application may be made under sub-paragraph (1) above unless the applicant has given to the Crown Court sitting at the place in question written notice of his intention to make the application.

(4) Oral evidence may be given on such an application only with the leave of the judge or by his order; and the judge shall give leave or make an order only if it appears to him, having regard to any matters stated in the application for leave, that the interests of justice require him to do so.

(5) If the judge gives leave permitting, or makes an order requiring, a person to give oral evidence, but that person does not do so, the judge may disregard any document indicating the evidence that he might have given.

(6) If the charge, or any of the charges, against the applicant is dismissed—

  (a) no further proceedings may be brought on the dismissed charge or charges except by means of the preferment of a voluntary bill of indictment; and

  (b) unless the applicant is in custody otherwise than on the dismissed charge or charges, he shall be discharged.

(7) Crown Court Rules may make provision for the purposes of this paragraph and, without prejudice to the generality of this sub-paragraph, may make provision—

  (a) as to the time or stage in the proceedings at which anything required to be done is to be done (unless the court grants leave to do it at some other time or stage);

  (b) as to the contents and form of notices or other documents;

  (c) as to the manner in which evidence is to be submitted; and

  (d) as to persons to be served with notices or other material.

Reporting restrictions

3—(1) Except as provided by this paragraph, it shall not be lawful—

  (a) to publish in Great Britain a written report of an application under paragraph 2(1) above; or

  (b) to include in a relevant programme for reception in Great Britain a report of such an application,

if (in either case) the report contains any matter other than that permitted by this paragraph.

(2) An order that sub-paragraph (1) above shall not apply to reports of an application under paragraph 2(1) above may be made by the judge dealing with the application.

(3) Where in the case of two or more accused one of them objects to the making of an order under sub-paragraph (2) above, the judge shall make the order if, and only if, he is satisfied, after hearing the representations of the accused, that it is in the interests of justice to do so.

(4) An order under sub-paragraph (2) above shall not apply to reports of proceedings under sub-paragraph (3) above, but any decision of the court to make or not to make such an order may be contained in reports published or included in a relevant programme before the time authorised by sub-paragraph (5) below.

(5) It shall not be unlawful under this paragraph to publish or include in a relevant programme a report of an application under paragraph 2(1) above containing any matter other than that permitted by sub-paragraph (8) below where the application is successful.

(6) Where—

  (a) two or more persons were jointly charged; and

  (b) applications under paragraph 2(1) above are made by more than one of them,

sub-paragraph (5) above shall have effect as if for the words 'the application is' there were substituted the words 'all the applications are'.

(7) It shall not be unlawful under this paragraph to publish or include in a relevant programme a report of an unsuccessful application at the conclusion of the trial of the person charged, or of the last of the persons charged to be tried.

(8) The following matters may be contained in a report published or included in a relevant programme without an order under sub-paragraph (2) above before the time authorised by sub-paragraphs (5) and (6) above, that is to say—

  (a) the identity of the court and the name of the judge;
  (b) the names, ages, home addresses and occupations of the accused and witnesses;
  (c) the offence or offences, or a summary of them, with which the accused is or are charged;
  (d) the names of counsel and solicitors engaged in the proceedings;
  (e) where the proceedings are adjourned, the date and place to which they are adjourned;
  (f) the arrangements as to bail;
  (g) whether legal aid was granted to the accused or any of the accused.

(9) The addresses that may be published or included in a relevant programme under sub-paragraph (8) above are addresses—

  (a) at any relevant time; and
  (b) at the time of their publication or inclusion in a relevant programme.

(10) If a report is published or included in a relevant programme in contravention of this paragraph, the following persons, that is to say—

  (a) in the case of a publication of a written report as part of a newspaper or periodical, any proprietor, editor or publisher of the newspaper or periodical;
  (b) in the case of a publication of a written report otherwise than as part of a newspaper or periodical, the person who publishes it;
  (c) in the case of the inclusion of a report in a relevant programme, any body corporate which is engaged in providing the service in which the programme is included and any person having functions in relation to the programme corresponding to those of the editor of a newspaper;

shall be liable on summary conviction to a fine not exceeding level 5 on the standard scale.

(11) Proceedings for an offence under this paragraph shall not, in England and Wales, be instituted otherwise than by or with the consent of the Attorney General.

(12) Sub-paragraph (1) above shall be in addition to, and not in derogation from, the provisions of any other enactment with respect to the publication of reports of court proceedings.

(13) In this paragraph—

  'publish', in relation to a report, means publish the report, either by itself or as part of a newspaper or periodical, for distribution to the public;
  'relevant programme' means a programme included in a programme service (within the meaning of the Broadcasting Act 1990);
  'relevant time' means a time when events giving rise to the charges to which the proceedings relate occurred.

Power of justice to take depositions etc.

4—(1) Sub-paragraph (2) below applies where a justice of the peace for any commission area is satisfied that—

(a) any person in England and Wales ('the witness') is likely to be able to make on behalf of the prosecutor a written statement containing material evidence or produce on behalf of the prosecutor a document or other exhibit likely to be material evidence, for the purposes of proceedings for an offence for which a person has been sent for trial under section 51 of this Act by a magistrates' court for that area; and

(b) the witness will not voluntarily make the statement or produce the document or other exhibit.

(2) In such a case the justice shall issue a summons directed to the witness requiring him to attend before a justice at the time and place appointed in the summons, and to have his evidence taken as a deposition or to produce the document or other exhibit.

(3) If a justice of the peace is satisfied by evidence on oath of the matters mentioned in sub-paragraph (1) above, and also that it is probable that a summons under sub-paragraph (2) above would not procure the result required by it, the justice may instead of issuing a summons issue a warrant to arrest the witness and to bring him before a justice at the time and place specified in the warrant.

(4) A summons may also be issued under sub-paragraph (2) above if the justice is satisfied that the witness is outside the British Islands, but no warrant may be issued under sub-paragraph (3) above unless the justice is satisfied by evidence on oath that the witness is in England and Wales.

(5) If—

(a) the witness fails to attend before a justice in answer to a summons under this paragraph;

(b) the justice is satisfied by evidence on oath that the witness is likely to be able to make a statement or produce a document or other exhibit as mentioned in sub-paragraph (1)(a) above;

(c) it is proved on oath, or in such other manner as may be prescribed, that he has been duly served with the summons and that a reasonable sum has been paid or tendered to him for costs and expenses; and

(d) it appears to the justice that there is no just excuse for the failure,

the justice may issue a warrant to arrest the witness and to bring him before a justice at the time and place specified in the warrant.

(6) Where—

(a) a summons is issued under sub-paragraph (2) above or a warrant is issued under sub-paragraph (3) or (5) above; and

(b) the summons or warrant is issued with a view to securing that the witness has his evidence taken as a deposition,

the time appointed in the summons or specified in the warrant shall be such as to enable the evidence to be taken as a deposition before the relevant date.

(7) If any person attending or brought before a justice in pursuance of this paragraph refuses without just excuse to have his evidence taken as a deposition, or to produce the document or other exhibit, the justice may do one or both of the following—

(a) commit him to custody until the expiration of such period not exceeding one month as may be specified in the summons or warrant or until he sooner has his evidence taken as a deposition or produces the document or other exhibit;

(b) impose on him a fine not exceeding £2,500.

(8) A fine imposed under sub-paragraph (7) above shall be deemed for the purposes of any enactment, to be a sum adjudged to be paid by a conviction.

(9) If in pursuance of this paragraph a person has his evidence taken as a deposition, the clerk of the justice concerned shall as soon as is reasonably practicable send a copy of the deposition to the prosecutor and the Crown Court.

(10) If in pursuance of this paragraph a person produces an exhibit which is a document, the clerk of the justice concerned shall as soon as is reasonably practicable send a copy of the document to the prosecutor and the Crown Court.

(11) If in pursuance of this paragraph a person produces an exhibit which is not a document, the clerk of the justice concerned shall as soon as is reasonably practicable inform the prosecutor and the Crown Court of that fact and of the nature of the exhibit.

(12) In this paragraph—

'prescribed' means prescribed by rules made under section 144 of the 1980 Act;
'the relevant date' has the meaning given by paragraph 1(2) above.

Use of depositions as evidence

5—(1) Subject to sub-paragraph (3) below, sub-paragraph (2) below applies where in pursuance of paragraph 4 above a person has his evidence taken as a deposition.

(2) Where this sub-paragraph applies the deposition may without further proof be read as evidence on the trial of the accused, whether for an offence for which he was sent for trial under section 51 of this Act or for any other offence arising out of the same transaction or set of circumstances.

(3) Sub-paragraph (2) above does not apply if—

(a) it is proved that the deposition was not signed by the justice by whom it purports to have been signed;
(b) the court of trial at its discretion orders that sub-paragraph (2) above shall not apply; or
(c) a party to the proceedings objects to sub-paragraph (2) above applying.

(4) If a party to the proceedings objects to sub-paragraph (2) applying the court of trial may order that the objection shall have no effect if the court considers it to be in the interests of justice so to order.

Power of Crown Court to deal with summary offence

6—(1) This paragraph applies where a magistrates' court has sent a person for trial under section 51 of this Act for offences which include a summary offence.

(2) If the person is convicted on the indictment, the Crown Court shall consider whether the summary offence is related to the offence that is triable only on indictment or, as the case may be, any of the offences that are so triable.

(3) If it considers that the summary offence is so related, the court shall state to the person the substance of the offence and ask him whether he pleads guilty or not guilty.

(4) If the person pleads guilty, the Crown Court shall convict him, but may deal with him in respect of the summary offence only in a manner in which a magistrates' court could have dealt with him.

(5) If he does not plead guilty, the powers of the Crown Court shall cease in respect of the summary offence except as provided by sub-paragraph (6) below.

(6) If the prosecution inform the court that they would not desire to submit evidence on the charge relating to the summary offence, the court shall dismiss it.

(7) The Crown Court shall inform the clerk of the magistrates' court of the outcome of any proceedings under this paragraph.

(8) If the summary offence is one to which section 40 of the Criminal Justice Act 1988 applies, the Crown Court may exercise in relation to the offence the power conferred by that section; but where the person is tried on indictment for such an offence, the functions of the Crown Court under this paragraph in relation to the offence shall cease.

(9) Where the Court of Appeal allows an appeal against conviction of an indictable-only offence which is related to a summary offence of which the appellant was convicted under this paragraph—

- (a) it shall set aside his conviction of the summary offence and give the clerk of the magistrates' court notice that it has done so; and
- (b) it may direct that no further proceedings in relation to the offence are to be undertaken;

and the proceedings before the Crown Court in relation to the offence shall thereafter be disregarded for all purposes.

(10) A notice under sub-paragraph (9) above shall include particulars of any direction given under paragraph (b) of that sub-paragraph in relation to the offence.

(11) The references to the clerk of the magistrates' court in this paragraph shall be construed in accordance with section 141 of the 1980 Act.

(12) An offence is related to another offence for the purposes of this paragraph if it arises out of circumstances which are the same as or connected with those giving rise to the other offence.

Procedure where no indictable-only offence remains

7—(1) Subject to paragraph 13 below, this paragraph applies where—

- (a) a person has been sent for trial under section 51 of this Act but has not been arraigned; and
- (b) the person is charged on an indictment which (following amendment of the indictment, or as a result of an application under paragraph 2 above, or for any other reason) includes no offence that is triable only on indictment.

(2) Everything that the Crown Court is required to do under the following provisions of this paragraph must be done with the accused present in court.

(3) The court shall cause to be read to the accused each count of the indictment that charges an offence triable either way.

(4) The court shall then explain to the accused in ordinary language that, in relation to each of those offences, he may indicate whether (if it were to proceed to trial) he would plead guilty or not guilty, and that if he indicates that he would plead guilty the court must proceed as mentioned in sub-paragraph (6) below.

(5) The court shall then ask the accused whether (if the offence in question were to proceed to trial) he would plead guilty or not guilty.

(6) If the accused indicates that he would plead guilty the court shall proceed as if he had been arraigned on the count in question and had pleaded guilty.

(7) If the accused indicates that he would plead not guilty, or fails to indicate how he would plead, the court shall consider whether the offence is more suitable for summary trial or for trial on indictment.

(8) Subject to sub-paragraph (6) above, the following shall not for any purpose be taken to constitute the taking of a plea—

    (a) asking the accused under this paragraph whether (if the offence were to proceed to trial) he would plead guilty or not guilty;

    (b) an indication by the accused under this paragraph of how he would plead.

8—(1) Subject to paragraph 13 below, this paragraph applies in a case where—

    (a) a person has been sent for trial under section 51 of this Act but has not been arraigned;

    (b) he is charged on an indictment which (following amendment of the indictment, or as a result of an application under paragraph 2 above, or for any other reason) includes no offence that is triable only on indictment;

    (c) he is represented by a legal representative;

    (d) the Crown Court considers that by reason of his disorderly conduct before the court it is not practicable for proceedings under paragraph 7 above to be conducted in his presence; and

    (e) the court considers that it should proceed in his absence.

(2) In such a case—

    (a) the court shall cause to be read to the representative each count of the indictment that charges an offence triable either way;

    (b) the court shall ask the representative whether (if the offence in question were to proceed to trial) the accused would plead guilty or not guilty;

    (c) if the representative indicates that the accused would plead guilty the court shall proceed as if the accused had been arraigned on the count in question and had pleaded guilty;

    (d) if the representative indicates that the accused would plead not guilty, or fails to indicate how the accused would plead, the court shall consider whether the offence is more suitable for summary trial or for trial on indictment.

(3) Subject to sub-paragraph (2)(c) above, the following shall not for any purpose be taken to constitute the taking of a plea—

    (a) asking the representative under this section whether (if the offence were to proceed to trial) the accused would plead guilty or not guilty;

    (b) an indication by the representative under this paragraph of how the accused would plead.

9—(1) This paragraph applies where the Crown Court is required by paragraph 7(7) or 8(2)(d) above to consider the question whether an offence is more suitable for summary trial or for trial on indictment.

(2) Before considering the question, the court shall afford first the prosecutor and then the accused an opportunity to make representations as to which mode of trial would be more suitable.

(3) In considering the question, the court shall have regard to—

(a) any representations made by the prosecutor or the accused;

(b) the nature of the case;

(c) whether the circumstances make the offence one of a serious character;

(d) whether the punishment which a magistrates' court would have power to impose for it would be adequate; and

(e) any other circumstances which appear to the court to make it more suitable for the offence to be dealt tried in one way rather than the other.

10—(1) This paragraph applies (unless excluded by paragraph 15 below) where the Crown Court considers that an offence is more suitable for summary trial.

(2) The court shall explain to the accused in ordinary language—

(a) that it appears to the court more suitable for him to be tried summarily for the offence, and that he can either consent to be so tried or, if he wishes, be tried by a jury; and

(b) that if he is tried summarily and is convicted by the magistrates' court, he may be committed for sentence to the Crown Court under section 38 of the 1980 Act if the convicting court is of such opinion as is mentioned in subsection (2) of that section.

(3) After explaining to the accused as provided by sub-paragraph (2) above the court shall ask him whether he wishes to be tried summarily or by a jury, and—

(a) if he indicates that he wishes to be tried summarily, shall remit him for trial to a magistrates' court acting for the place where he was sent to the Crown Court for trial;

(b) if he does not give such an indication, shall retain its functions in relation to the offence and proceed accordingly.

11 If the Crown Court considers that an offence is more suitable for trial on indictment, the court—

(a) shall tell the accused that it has decided that it is more suitable for him to be tried for the offence by a jury; and

(b) shall retain its functions in relation to the offence and proceed accordingly.

12—(1) Where the prosecution is being carried on by the Attorney General, the Solicitor General or the Director of Public Prosecutions and he applies for an offence which may be tried on indictment to be so tried—

(a) sub-paragraphs (4) to (8) of paragraph 7, sub-paragraphs (2)(b) to (d) and (3) of paragraph 8 and paragraphs 9 to 11 above shall not apply; and

(b) the Crown Court shall retain its functions in relation to the offence and proceed accordingly.

(2) The power of the Director of Public Prosecutions under this paragraph to apply for an offence to be tried on indictment shall not be exercised except with the consent of the Attorney General.

13—(1) This paragraph applies, in place of paragraphs 7 to 12 above, in the case of a child or young person who—

(a) has been sent for trial under section 51 of this Act but has not been arraigned; and

(b) is charged on an indictment which (following amendment of the indictment, or as a result of an application under paragraph 2 above, or for any other reason) includes no offence that is triable only on indictment.

(2) The Crown Court shall remit the child or young person for trial to a magistrates' court acting for the place where he was sent to the Crown Court for trial unless—

(a) he is charged with such an offence as is mentioned in subsection (2) of section 53 of the 1933 Act (punishment of certain grave crimes) and the Crown Court considers that if he is found guilty of the offence it ought to be possible to sentence him in pursuance of subsection (3) of that section; or

(b) he is charged jointly with an adult with an offence triable either way and the Crown Court considers it necessary in the interests of justice that they both be tried for the offence in the Crown Court.

(3) In sub-paragraph (2) above 'adult' has the same meaning as in section 51 of this Act.

Procedure for determining whether offences of criminal damage etc. are summary offences

14—(1) This paragraph applies where the Crown Court has to determine, for the purposes of this Schedule, whether an offence which is listed in the first column of Schedule 2 to the 1980 Act (offences for which the value involved is relevant to the mode of trial) is a summary offence.

(2) The court shall have regard to any representations made by the prosecutor or the accused.

(3) If it appears clear to the court that the value involved does not exceed the relevant sum, it shall treat the offence as a summary offence.

(4) If it appears clear to the court that the value involved exceeds the relevant sum, it shall treat the offence as an indictable offence.

(5) If it appears to the court for any reason not clear whether the value involved does or does not exceed the relevant sum, the court shall ask the accused whether he wishes the offence to be treated as a summary offence.

(6) Where sub-paragraph (5) above applies—

(a) if the accused indicates that he wishes the offence to be treated as a summary offence, the court shall so treat it;

(b) if the accused does not give such an indication, the court shall treat the offence as an indictable offence.

(7) In this paragraph 'the value involved' and 'the relevant sum' have the same meanings as in section 22 of the 1980 Act (certain offences triable either way to be tried summarily if value involved is small).

Power of Crown Court, with consent of legally-represented accused, to proceed in his absence

15—(1) The Crown Court may proceed in the absence of the accused in accordance with such of the provisions of paragraphs 9 to 14 above as are applicable in the circumstances if—

(a) the accused is represented by a legal representative who signifies to the court the accused's consent to the proceedings in question being conducted in his absence; and

(b) the court is satisfied that there is good reason for proceeding in the absence of the accused.

(2) Sub-paragraph (1) above is subject to the following provisions of this paragraph which apply where the court exercises the power conferred by that sub-paragraph.

(3) If, where the court has considered as required by paragraph 7(7) or 8(2)(d) above, it appears to the court that an offence is more suitable for summary trial, paragraph 10 above shall not apply and—

    (a) if the legal representative indicates that the accused wishes to be tried summarily, the court shall remit the accused for trial to a magistrates' court acting for the place where he was sent to the Crown Court for trial;

    (b) if the legal representative does not give such an indication, the court shall retain its functions and proceed accordingly.

(4) If, where the court has considered as required by paragraph 7(7) or 8(2)(d) above, it appears to the court that an offence is more suitable for trial on indictment, paragraph 11 above shall apply with the omission of paragraph (a).

(5) Where paragraph 14 above applies and it appears to the court for any reason not clear whether the value involved does or does not exceed the relevant sum, sub-paragraphs (5) and (6) of that paragraph shall not apply and—

    (a) the court shall ask the legal representative whether the accused wishes the offence to be treated as a summary offence;

    (b) if the legal representative indicates that the accused wishes the offence to be treated as a summary offence, the court shall so treat it;

    (c) if the legal representative does not give such an indication, the court shall treat the offence as an indictable offence.

Section 64(5)   SCHEDULE 4

ENFORCEMENT ETC. OF DRUG TREATMENT AND TESTING ORDERS

Preliminary

1 Schedule 2 to the 1991 Act (enforcement etc. of community orders) shall be amended as follows.

Meaning of 'relevant order' etc.

2—(1) In sub-paragraph (1) of paragraph 1 (preliminary)—

    (a) after the words 'a probation order,' there shall be inserted the words 'a drug treatment and testing order,'; and

    (b) in paragraph (a), for the words 'probation or community service order' there shall be substituted the words 'probation, community service or drug treatment and testing order'.

(2) After sub-paragraph (3) of that paragraph there shall be inserted the following sub-paragraph—

    '(4) In this Schedule, references to the court responsible for a drug treatment and testing order shall be construed in accordance with section 62(9) of the Crime and Disorder Act 1998.'

Breach of requirements of order

3 In sub-paragraph (2) of paragraph 2 (issue of summons or warrant), for the words 'before a magistrates' court acting for the petty sessions area concerned' there shall be substituted the following paragraphs—

'(a) except where the relevant order is a drug treatment and testing order, before a magistrates' court acting for the petty sessions area concerned;

(b) in the excepted case, before the court responsible for the order.'

4 In sub-paragraph (1) of paragraph 4 (powers of Crown Court), after the word 'Where' there shall be inserted the words 'under paragraph 2 or'.

5 In sub-paragraph (2) of paragraph 5 (exclusions), for the words 'is required by a probation order to submit to treatment for his mental condition, or his dependency on drugs or alcohol,' there shall be substituted the following paragraphs—

'(a) is required by a probation order to submit to treatment for his mental condition, or his dependency on or propensity to misuse drugs or alcohol; or

(b) is required by a drug treatment and testing order to submit to treatment for his dependency on or propensity to misuse drugs,'.

Revocation of order

6—(1) In sub-paragraph (1) of paragraph 7 (revocation of order by magistrates' court), after the words 'the petty sessions area concerned' there shall be inserted the words 'or, where the relevant order is a drug treatment and testing order for which a magistrates' court is responsible, to that court'.

(2) In sub-paragraph (3) of that paragraph—

(a) after the words 'a probation order' there shall be inserted the words 'or drug treatment and testing order'; and

(b) after the word 'supervision' there shall be inserted the words 'or, as the case may be, treatment'.

7—(1) After sub-paragraph (1) of paragraph 8 (revocation of order by Crown Court) there shall be inserted the following sub-paragraph—

'(1A) This paragraph also applies where—

(a) a drug treatment and testing order made by the Crown Court is in force in respect of an offender; and

(b) the offender or the responsible officer applies to the Crown Court for the order to be revoked or for the offender to be dealt with in some other manner for the offence in respect of which the order was made.'

(2) In sub-paragraph (3) of that paragraph—

(a) after the words 'a probation order' there shall be inserted the words 'or drug treatment and testing order'; and

(b) after the word 'supervision' there shall be inserted the words 'or, as the case may be, treatment'.

8 In sub-paragraph (1) of paragraph 9 (revocation of order following custodial sentence), for paragraph (a) there shall be substituted the following paragraph—

'(a) an offender in respect of whom a relevant order is in force is convicted of an offence—

(i) by a magistrates' court other than a magistrates' court acting for the petty sessions area concerned; or

(ii) where the relevant order is a drug treatment and testing order, by a magistrates' court which is not responsible for the order; and'.

Amendment of order

9 In sub-paragraph (1) of paragraph 12 (amendment by reason of change of residence), after the words 'a relevant order' there shall be inserted the words '(other than a drug treatment and testing order)'.

10 After paragraph 14 there shall be inserted the following paragraph—

'Amendment of drug treatment and testing order

14A—(1) Without prejudice to the provisions of section 63(2), (7) and (9) of the Crime and Disorder Act 1998, the court responsible for a drug treatment and testing order may by order—

    (a) vary or cancel any of the requirements or provisions of the order on an application by the responsible officer under sub-paragraph (2) or (3)(a) or (b) below; or

    (b) amend the order on an application by that officer under sub-paragraph (3)(c) below.

(2) Where the treatment provider is of the opinion that the treatment or testing requirement of the order should be varied or cancelled—

    (a) he shall make a report in writing to that effect to the responsible officer; and

    (b) that officer shall apply to the court for the variation or cancellation of the requirement.

(3) Where the responsible officer is of the opinion—

    (a) that the treatment or testing requirement of the order should be so varied as to specify a different treatment provider;

    (b) that any other requirement of the order, or a provision of the order, should be varied or cancelled; or

    (c) that the order should be so amended as to provide for each subsequent review under section 63 of the Crime and Disorder Act 1998 to be made without a hearing instead of at a review hearing, or vice versa,

he shall apply to the court for the variation or cancellation of the requirement or provision or the amendment of the order.

(4) The court—

    (a) shall not amend the treatment or testing requirement unless the offender expresses his willingness to comply with the requirement as amended; and

    (b) shall not amend any provision of the order so as to reduce the treatment and testing period below the minimum specified in section 61(2) of the Crime and Disorder Act 1998 or to increase it above the maximum so specified.

(5) If the offender fails to express his willingness to comply with the treatment or testing requirement as proposed to be amended by the court, the court may—

    (a) revoke the order; and

    (b) deal with him, for the offence in respect of which the order was made, in any manner in which it could deal with him if he had just been convicted by the court of the offence.

(6) In dealing with the offender under sub-paragraph (5)(b) above, the court—

    (a) shall take into account the extent to which the offender has complied with the requirements of the order; and

    (b) may impose a custodial sentence notwithstanding anything in section 1(2) of this Act.

(7) Paragraph 6A above shall apply for the purposes of this paragraph as it applies for the purposes of paragraph 3 above, but as if for the words 'paragraph 3(1)(d) above' there were substituted the words 'paragraph 14A(5)(b) below'.

(8) In this paragraph—

"review hearing" has the same meaning as in section 63 of the Crime and Disorder Act 1998;

"the treatment requirement" and "the testing requirement" have the same meanings as in Chapter I of Part IV of that Act.'

11 In paragraph 16 (order not to be amended pending appeal), after the words 'paragraph 13 or 15 above' there shall be inserted the words 'or, except with the consent of the offender, under paragraph 14A above'.

12—(1) In sub-paragraph (1) of paragraph 18 (notification of amended order), after the words 'a relevant order' there shall be inserted the words '(other than a drug treatment and testing order)'.

(2) After that sub-paragraph there shall be inserted the following sub-paragraph—

    '(1A) On the making under this Part of this Schedule of an order amending a drug treatment and testing order, the clerk to the court shall forthwith give copies of the amending order to the responsible officer.'

(3) In sub-paragraph (2) of that paragraph, after the words 'sub-paragraph (1)' there shall be inserted the words 'or (1A)'.

Sections 68(3) and 70(5)   SCHEDULE 5

ENFORCEMENT ETC. OF REPARATION AND ACTION PLAN ORDERS

Preliminary

1 In this Schedule—

    'the appropriate court', in relation to a reparation order or action plan order, means the youth court acting for the petty sessions area for the time being named in the order in pursuance of section 67(9) or, as the case may be, section 69(9) of this Act;

    'local authority accommodation' means accommodation provided by or on behalf of a local authority (within the meaning of the 1989 Act).

General power to discharge or vary order

2—(1) If while a reparation order or action plan order is in force in respect of an offender it appears to the appropriate court, on the application of the responsible officer or the offender, that it is appropriate to make an order under this sub-paragraph, the court may make an order discharging the reparation order or action plan order or varying it—

    (a) by cancelling any provision included in it; or

(b) by inserting in it (either in addition to or in substitution for any of its provisions) any provision that could have been included in the order if the court had then had power to make it and were exercising the power.

(2) Where an application under this paragraph for the discharge of a reparation order or action plan order is dismissed, no further application for its discharge shall be made under this paragraph by any person except with the consent of the appropriate court.

Failure to comply with order

3—(1) This paragraph applies where a reparation order or action plan order is in force and it is proved to the satisfaction of the appropriate court, on the application of the responsible officer, that the offender has failed to comply with any requirement included in the order.

(2) The court—

(a) whether or not it also makes an order under paragraph 2 above, may order the offender to pay a fine of an amount not exceeding £1,000, or make an attendance centre order or curfew order in respect of him; or

(b) if the reparation order or action plan order was made by a youth court, may discharge the order and deal with him, for the offence in respect of which the order was made, in any manner in which he could have been dealt with for that offence by the court which made the order if the order had not been made; or

(c) if the reparation order or action plan order was made by the Crown Court, may commit him in custody or release him on bail until he can be brought or appear before the Crown Court.

(3) For the purposes of sub-paragraph (2)(b) and (c) above, a reparation order or action plan order made on appeal from a decision of a magistrates' court or the Crown Court shall be treated as if it had been made by a magistrates' court or the Crown Court, as the case may be.

(4) Where a court deals with an offender under sub-paragraph (2)(c) above, it shall send to the Crown Court a certificate signed by a justice of the peace giving—

(a) particulars of the offender's failure to comply with the requirement in question; and

(b) such other particulars of the case as may be desirable;

and a certificate purporting to be so signed shall be admissible as evidence of the failure before the Crown Court.

(5) Where—

(a) by virtue of sub-paragraph (2)(c) above the offender is brought or appears before the Crown Court; and

(b) it is proved to the satisfaction of the court that he has failed to comply with the requirement in question,

that court may deal with him, for the offence in respect of which the order was made, in any manner in which it could have dealt with him for that offence if it had not made the order.

(6) Where the Crown Court deals with an offender under sub-paragraph (5) above, it shall revoke the reparation order or action plan order if it is still in force.

(7) A fine imposed under this paragraph shall be deemed, for the purposes of any enactment, to be a sum adjudged to be paid by a conviction.

(8) In dealing with an offender under this paragraph, a court shall take into account the extent to which he has complied with the requirements of the reparation order or action plan order.

Presence of offender in court, remands etc.

4—(1) Where the responsible officer makes an application under paragraph 2 or 3 above to the appropriate court, he may bring the offender before the court and, subject to sub-paragraph (9) below, the court shall not make an order under that paragraph unless the offender is present before it.

(2) Without prejudice to any power to issue a summons or warrant apart from this sub-paragraph, the court to which an application under paragraph 2 or 3 above is made may issue a summons or warrant for the purpose of securing the attendance of the offender before it.

(3) Subsections (3) and (4) of section 55 of the 1980 Act (which among other things restrict the circumstances in which a warrant may be issued) shall apply with the necessary modifications to a warrant under sub-paragraph (2) above as they apply to a warrant under that section and as if in subsection (3) after the word 'summons' there were inserted the words 'cannot be served or'.

(4) Where the offender is arrested in pursuance of a warrant under sub-paragraph (2) above and cannot be brought immediately before the appropriate court, the person in whose custody he is—

    (a) may make arrangements for his detention in a place of safety for a period of not more than 72 hours from the time of the arrest (and it shall be lawful for him to be detained in pursuance of the arrangements); and

    (b) shall within that period bring him before a youth court.

(5) Where an offender is, under sub-paragraph (4) above, brought before a youth court other than the appropriate court, that court may—

    (a) direct that he be released forthwith; or

    (b) subject to sub-paragraph (6) below, remand him to local authority accommodation.

(6) Where the offender is aged 18 or over at the time when he is brought before the court, he shall not be remanded to local authority accommodation but may instead be remanded—

    (a) to a remand centre, if the court has been notified that such a centre is available for the reception of persons under this sub-paragraph; or

    (b) to a prison, if it has not been so notified.

(7) Where an application is made to a court under paragraph 2(1) above, the court may remand (or further remand) the offender to local authority accommodation if—

    (a) a warrant has been issued under sub-paragraph (2) of this paragraph for the purpose of securing the attendance of the offender before the court; or

    (b) the court considers that remanding (or further remanding) him will enable information to be obtained which is likely to assist the court in deciding whether and, if so, how to exercise its powers under paragraph 2(1) above.

(8) A court remanding an offender to local authority accommodation under this paragraph shall designate, as the authority who are to receive him, the local authority for the area in which the offender resides or, where it appears to the court that he does not reside in the area of a local authority, the local authority—

    (a) specified by the court; and

    (b) in whose area the offence or an offence associated with it was committed.

(9) A court may make an order under paragraph 2 above in the absence of the offender if the effect of the order is one or more of the following, that is to say—

    (a) discharging the reparation order or action plan order;

    (b) cancelling a requirement included in the reparation order or action plan order;

    (c) altering in the reparation order or action plan order the name of any area;

    (d) changing the responsible officer.

Supplemental

5—(1) The provisions of section 17 of the 1982 Act (attendance centre orders) shall apply for the purposes of paragraph 3(2)(a) above but as if—

    (a) in subsection (1), for the words from 'has power' to 'probation order' there were substituted the words 'considers it appropriate to make an attendance centre order in respect of any person in pursuance of paragraph 3(2) of Schedule 5 to the Crime and Disorder Act 1998'; and

    (b) subsection (13) were omitted.

(2) Sections 18 and 19 of the 1982 Act (discharge and variation of attendance centre order and breach of attendance centre orders or attendance centre rules) shall also apply for the purposes of that paragraph but as if there were omitted—

    (a) from subsection (4A) of section 18 and subsections (3) and (5) of section 19, the words ', for the offence in respect of which the order was made,' and 'for that offence'; and

    (b) from subsection (4B) of section 18 and subsection (6) of section 19, the words 'for an offence'.

(3) The provisions of section 12 of the 1991 Act (curfew orders) shall apply for the purposes of paragraph 3(2)(a) above but as if—

    (a) in subsection (1), for the words from the beginning to 'before which he is convicted' there were substituted the words 'Where a court considers it appropriate to make a curfew order in respect of any person in pursuance of paragraph 3(2)(a) of Schedule 5 to the Crime and Disorder Act 1998, the court'; and

    (b) in subsection (8), for the words 'on conviction' there were substituted the words 'on the date on which his failure to comply with a requirement included in the reparation order or action plan order was proved to the court'.

(4) Schedule 2 to the 1991 Act (enforcement etc. of community orders), so far as relating to curfew orders, shall also apply for the purposes of that paragraph but as if—

    (a) the power conferred on the magistrates' court by each of paragraphs 3(1)(d) and 7(2)(a)(ii) to deal with the offender for the offence in respect of which the order was made were a power to deal with the offender, for his failure to comply with a requirement included in the reparation order or action plan order, in any manner in which the appropriate court could deal with him for that failure to comply if it had just been proved to the satisfaction of that court;

   (b)   the power conferred on the Crown Court by paragraph 4(1)(d) to deal with the offender for the offence in respect of which the order was made were a power to deal with the offender, for his failure to comply with such a requirement, in any manner in which that court could deal with him for that failure to comply if it had just been proved to its satisfaction;

   (c)   the reference in paragraph 7(1)(b) to the offence in respect of which the order was made were a reference to the failure to comply in respect of which the curfew order was made; and

   (d)   the power conferred on the Crown Court by paragraph 8(2)(b) to deal with the offender for the offence in respect of which the order was made were a power to deal with the offender, for his failure to comply with a requirement included in the reparation order or action plan order, in any manner in which the appropriate court (if that order was made by a magistrates' court) or the Crown Court (if that order was made by the Crown Court) could deal with him for that failure to comply if it had just been proved to the satisfaction of that court.

(5) For the purposes of the provisions mentioned in sub-paragraph (4)(a) and (d) above, as applied by that sub-paragraph, if the reparation order or action plan order is no longer in force the appropriate court's powers shall be determined on the assumption that it is still in force.

(6) If while an application to the appropriate court in pursuance of paragraph 2 or 3 above is pending the offender attains the age of 18 years, the court shall, subject to paragraph 4(6) above, deal with the application as if he had not attained that age.

(7) The offender may appeal to the Crown Court against—

   (a)   any order made under paragraphs 2 or 3 above, except an order made or which could have been made in his absence (by virtue of paragraph 4(9) above);

   (b)   the dismissal of an application under paragraph 2 above to discharge a reparation order or action plan order.

Section 94(2)   SCHEDULE 6

[*Applies to Scotland only.*]

Section 106   SCHEDULE 7

PRE-CONSOLIDATION AMENDMENTS: POWERS OF CRIMINAL COURTS

Children and Young Persons Act 1933 (c.12)

1—(1) In subsection (1A) of section 55 of the 1933 Act (power to order parent or guardian to pay fine etc.), in paragraph (a), for the words 'section 15(2A)' there shall be substituted the words 'section 15(3)(a)'.

(2) For paragraph (b) of that subsection there shall be substituted the following paragraphs—

   '(b) a court would impose a fine on a child or young person under section 19(3) of the Criminal Justice Act 1982 (breach of attendance centre order or attendance centre rules); or (bb)a court would impose a fine on a child or young person under paragraph 3(1)(a) or 4(1)(a) of Schedule 2 to the Criminal Justice Act 1991 (breach of requirement of a relevant order (within the meaning given by that Schedule) or of a combination order);'.

(3) After subsection (5) of that section there shall be added the following subsection—

'(6) In relation to any other child or young person, references in this section to his parent shall be construed in accordance with section 1 of the Family Law Reform Act 1987.'

Criminal Justice Act 1967 (c.80)

2—(1) In subsection (1)(b)(i) of section 56 of the Criminal Justice Act 1967 (committal for sentence for offences tried summarily), for the words from 'section 93' to '34 to 36' there shall be substituted the words 'section 34, 35 or 36'.

(2) In subsection (2) of that section, for the words from 'section 8(6)' to the end there shall be substituted the words 'section 1B(5) of the Powers of Criminal Courts Act 1973 (conditionally discharged person convicted of further offence) and section 24(2) of that Act (offender convicted during operational period of suspended sentence).'

(3) Subsection (3) of that section shall cease to have effect.

(4) For subsection (5) of that section there shall be substituted the following subsections—

'(5) Where under subsection (1) above a magistrates' court commits a person to be dealt with by the Crown Court in respect of an offence, the Crown Court may after inquiring into the circumstances of the case deal with him in any way in which the magistrates' court could deal with him if it had just convicted him of the offence.

(5A) Subsection (5) above does not apply where under subsection (1) above a magistrates' court commits a person to be dealt with by the Crown Court in respect of a suspended sentence, but in such a case the powers under section 23 of the Powers of Criminal Courts Act 1973 (power of court to deal with suspended sentence) shall be exercisable by the Crown Court.

(5B) Without prejudice to subsections (5) and (5A) above, where under subsection (1) above or any enactment to which this section applies a magistrates' court commits a person to be dealt with by the Crown Court, any duty or power which, apart from this subsection, would fall to be discharged or exercised by the magistrates' court shall not be discharged or exercised by that court but shall instead be discharged or may instead be exercised by the Crown Court.

(5C) Where under subsection (1) above a magistrates' court commits a person to be dealt with by the Crown Court in respect of an offence triable only on indictment in the case of an adult (being an offence which was tried summarily because of the offender's being under 18 years of age), the Crown Court's powers under subsection (5) above in respect of the offender after he attains the age of 18 years shall be powers to do either or both of the following—

(a) to impose a fine not exceeding £5,000;
(b) to deal with the offender in respect of the offence in any way in which the magistrates' court could deal with him if it had just convicted him of an offence punishable with imprisonment for a term not exceeding six months.

(5D) For the purposes of this section the age of an offender shall be deemed to be that which it appears to the court to be after considering any available evidence.'

(5) Subsection (13) of that section shall cease to have effect.

Children and Young Persons Act 1969 (c.54)

3 After subsection (8) of section 7 of the 1969 Act (alterations in treatment of young offenders etc.) there shall be added the following subsection—

'(9) The reference in subsection (8) above to a person's parent shall be construed in accordance with section 1 of the Family Law Reform Act 1987 (and not in accordance with section 70(1A) of this Act).'

4 In section 12 of the 1969 Act (power to include requirements in supervision orders), after subsection (3) there shall be added the following subsection—

'(4) Directions given by the supervisor by virtue of subsection (2)(b) or (c) above shall, as far as practicable, be such as to avoid—

(a) any conflict with the offender's religious beliefs or with the requirements of any other community order (within the meaning of Part I of the Criminal Justice Act 1991) to which he may be subject; and

(b) any interference with the times, if any, at which he normally works or attends school or any other educational establishment.'

5—(1) In subsection (1) of section 12B of the 1969 Act (power to include in supervision order requirements as to mental treatment)—

(a) for the words 'medical practitioner', in the first place where they occur, there shall be substituted the words 'registered medical practitioner';

(b) for the words 'his detention in pursuance of a hospital order under Part III' there shall be substituted the words 'the making of a hospital order or guardianship order within the meaning';

(c) in paragraph (a), for the words 'fully registered medical practitioner' there shall be substituted the words 'registered medical practitioner';

(d) after that paragraph there shall be inserted the following paragraph—
'(aa) treatment by or under the direction of a chartered psychologist specified in the order;';

(e) in paragraph (b), for the words 'a place' there shall be substituted the words 'an institution or place'; and

(f) in paragraph (c), for the words 'the said Act of 1983' there shall be substituted the words 'the Mental Health Act 1983'.

(2) After that subsection there shall be inserted the following subsection—

'(1A) In subsection (1) of this section 'registered medical practitioner' means a fully registered person within the meaning of the Medical Act 1983 and 'chartered psychologist' means a person for the time being listed in the British Psychological Society's Register of Chartered Psychologists.'

(3) After subsection (2) of that section there shall be added the following subsection—

'(3) Subsections (2) and (3) of section 54 of the Mental Health Act 1983 shall have effect with respect to proof for the purposes of subsection (1) above of a supervised person's mental condition as they have effect with respect to proof of an offender's mental condition for the purposes of section 37(2)(a) of that Act.'

6 In section 16(11) of the 1969 Act (provisions supplementary to section 15), the words 'seventeen or' shall cease to have effect.

7—(1) In subsection (1)(a) of section 16A of the 1969 Act (application of sections 17 to 19 of Criminal Justice Act 1982), for the words 'section 15(2A) or (4)' there shall be substituted the words 'section 15(3)(a)'.

(2) In subsection (2)(b) of that section—

  (a) in sub-paragraph (i), after the word 'from' there shall be inserted the words 'subsection (4A) of section 18 and'; and
  (b) in sub-paragraph (ii), for the words 'subsection (6)' there shall be substituted the words 'subsection (4B) of section 18 and subsection (6) of section 19'.

8 In section 34(1)(c) of the 1969 Act (power of Secretary of State to amend references to young person), the words '7(7), 7(8),' shall cease to have effect.

9 Section 69(5) of the 1969 Act (power to include in commencement order certain consequential provisions) shall cease to have effect.

10 In section 70 of the 1969 Act (interpretation), for subsections (1A) and (1B) there shall be substituted the following subsections—

'(1A) In the case of a child or young person—

  (a) whose father and mother were not married to each other at the time of his birth, and
  (b) with respect to whom a residence order is in force in favour of the father,

any reference in this Act to the parent of the child or young person includes (unless the contrary intention appears) a reference to the father.

(1B) In subsection (1A) of this section, the reference to a child or young person whose father and mother were not married to each other at the time of his birth shall be construed in accordance with section 1 of the Family Law Reform Act 1987 and "residence order" has the meaning given by section 8(1) of the Children Act 1989.'

11 In Schedule 6 to the 1969 Act (repeals), the entries relating to sections 55, 56(1) and 59(1) of the 1933 Act (which entries have never come into force or are spent) are hereby repealed.

Criminal Justice Act 1972 (c.71)

12 Section 49 of the Criminal Justice Act 1972 (community service order in lieu of warrant of commitment for failure to pay fine etc.) shall cease to have effect.

Powers of Criminal Courts Act 1973 (c.62)

13—(1) In subsection (6) of section 1 of the 1973 Act (deferment of sentence), for the words '13(1), (2) and (5)' there shall be substituted the words '13(1) to (3) and (5)'.

(2) In subsection (8) of that section, for paragraph (a) there shall be substituted the following paragraph—

'(a) is power to deal with him, in respect of the offence for which passing of sentence has been deferred, in any way in which the court which deferred passing sentence could have dealt with him; and'.

14—(1) In subsection (9) of section 1B of the 1973 Act (commission of further offence by person conditionally discharged), for the words from 'those which' to the end there shall be substituted the words 'powers to do either or both of the following—

(a) to impose a fine not exceeding £5,000 for the offence in respect of which the order was made;
(b) to deal with the offender for that offence in any way in which a magistrates' court could deal with him if it had just convicted him of an offence punishable with imprisonment for a term not exceeding six months.'

(2) Subsection (10) of that section (which is superseded by provision inserted by this Schedule in section 57 of the 1973 Act) shall cease to have effect.

15 In section 1C(1) of the 1973 Act (effect of absolute or conditional discharge)—

(a) in paragraph (a), for the words 'the following provisions' there shall be substituted the words 'section 1B'; and
(b) paragraph (b) and the word 'and' immediately preceding it shall cease to have effect.

16 In section 2(1) of the 1973 Act (probation orders), the words from 'For the purposes' to 'available evidence' (which are superseded by provision inserted by this Schedule in section 57 of the 1973 Act) shall cease to have effect.

17 Section 11 of the 1973 Act (which is superseded by the paragraph 8A inserted by this Schedule in Schedule 2 to the 1991 Act) shall cease to have effect.

18—(1) For subsection (2) of section 12 of the 1973 Act (supplementary provision as to probation and discharge) there shall be substituted the following subsection—

'(2) Where an order for conditional discharge has been made on appeal, for the purposes of this Act it shall be deemed—

(a) if it was made on an appeal brought from a magistrates' court, to have been made by that magistrates' court;
(b) if it was made on an appeal brought from the Crown Court or from the criminal division of the Court of Appeal, to have been made by the Crown Court.'

(2) In subsection (3) of that section, for the words from 'any question whether a probationer' to 'period of conditional discharge,' there shall be substituted the words 'any question whether any person in whose case an order for conditional discharge has been made has been convicted of an offence committed during the period of conditional discharge'.

(3) For subsection (4) of that section there shall be substituted the following subsection—

'(4) Nothing in section 1A of this Act shall be construed as preventing a court, on discharging an offender absolutely or conditionally in respect of any offence, from making an order for costs against the offender or imposing any disqualification on him or from making in respect of the offence an order under section 35 or 43 of this Act or section 28 of the Theft Act 1968.'

19—(1) In subsection (1) of section 14 of the 1973 Act (community service orders in respect of convicted persons), after the word 'imprisonment', in the first place where it occurs, there shall be inserted the words '(not being an offence the sentence for which is fixed by law or falls to be imposed under section 2(2), 3(2) or 4(2) of the Crime (Sentences) Act 1997)'.

(2) In that subsection, after the words 'young offenders' there shall be inserted the words '; and for the purposes of this subsection a sentence falls to be imposed under section 2(2), 3(2) or 4(2) of the Crime (Sentences) Act 1997 if it is required by that provision and the court is not of the opinion there mentioned'.

(3) In subsection (7) of that section, for the words 'paragraph (b)(i) or (ii)' there shall be substituted the words 'paragraph (b)'.

(4) Subsection (8) of that section shall cease to have effect.

20 For subsection (3) of section 15 of the 1973 Act (obligations of person subject to community service order) there shall be substituted the following subsection—

'(3) The instructions given by the relevant officer under this section shall, as far as practicable, be such as to avoid—

   (a) any conflict with the offender's religious beliefs or with the requirements of any other community order (within the meaning of Part I of the Criminal Justice Act 1991) to which he may be subject; and
   (b) any interference with the times, if any, at which he normally works or attends school or any other educational establishment.'

21 In section 21(3)(b) of the 1973 Act (meaning of 'sentence of imprisonment' for purposes of restriction on imposing sentences of imprisonment on persons not legally represented), after the words 'contempt of court' there shall be inserted the words 'or any kindred offence'.

22 In subsection (3) of section 22 of the 1973 Act (suspended sentences of imprisonment)—

   (a) for the words 'make a probation order in his case in respect of another offence' there shall be substituted the words 'impose a community sentence in his case in respect of that offence or any other offence'; and
   (b) at the end there shall be inserted the words '; and in this subsection "community sentence" has the same meaning as in Part I of the Criminal Justice Act 1991.'

23—(1) In section 31 of the 1973 Act (powers etc. of Crown Court in relation to fines and forfeited recognizances), the following provisions shall cease to have effect—

   (a) in subsection (3A), the words 'Subject to subsections (3B) and (3C) below,';
   (b) subsections (3B) and (3C); and
   (c) in subsection (4), the words '4 or'.

(2) In subsection (6) of that section—

   (a) the words 'about committal by a magistrates' court to the Crown Court' shall cease to have effect; and
   (b) after the words 'dealt with him' there shall be inserted the words 'or could deal with him'.

(3) In subsection (8) of that section, for the words '(2) to (3C)' there shall be substituted the words '(2) to (3A)'.

24—(1) In subsection (2) of section 32 of the 1973 Act (enforcement etc. of fines imposed and recognizances forfeited by Crown Court), for the words 'section 85(1)' there shall be substituted the words 'section 85(2)'.

(2) In subsection (3) of that section, after the words 'to the Crown Court' there shall be inserted the words '(except the reference in subsection (1)(b) above)'.

(3) For subsection (4) of that section there shall be substituted the following subsection—

'(4) A magistrates' court shall not, under section 85(1) or 120 of the Magistrates' Courts Act 1980 as applied by subsection (1) above, remit the whole or any part of a fine imposed by, or sum due under a recognizance forfeited by—

(a) the Crown Court,
(b) the criminal division of the Court of Appeal, or
(c) the House of Lords on appeal from that division,

without the consent of the Crown Court.'

(4) Subsection (5) of that section shall cease to have effect.

25 In section 46 of the 1973 Act (reports of probation officers), after subsection (2) there shall be added the following subsection—

'(3) For the purposes of this section—

(a) references to an offender's parent shall be construed in accordance with section 1 of the Family Law Reform Act 1987; and
(b) "guardian" has the same meaning as in the Children and Young Persons Act 1933.'

26—(1) For subsection (5) of section 57 of the 1973 Act (interpretation) there shall be substituted the following subsection—

'(5) Where a compensation order or supervision order has been made on appeal, for the purposes of this Act (except section 26(5)) it shall be deemed—

(a) if it was made on an appeal brought from a magistrates' court, to have been made by that magistrates' court;
(b) if it was made on an appeal brought from the Crown Court or from the criminal division of the Court of Appeal, to have been made by the Crown Court.'

(2) After subsection (6) of that section there shall be added the following subsection—

'(7) For the purposes of any provision of this Act which requires the determination of the age of a person by the court, his age shall be deemed to be that which it appears to the court to be after considering any available evidence.'

27—(1) In paragraph 2 of Schedule 1A to the 1973 Act (additional requirements in probation orders), for sub-paragraph (7) there shall be substituted the following sub-paragraph—

'(7) Instructions given by a probation officer under sub-paragraph (4) or (6) above shall, as far as practicable, be such as to avoid—

(a) any conflict with the offender's religious beliefs or with the requirements of any other community order (within the meaning of Part I of the Criminal Justice Act 1991) to which he may be subject; and

(b) any interference with the times, if any, at which he normally works or attends school or any other educational establishment.'

(2) In paragraph 3 of that Schedule, for sub-paragraph (4) there shall be substituted the following sub-paragraph—

'(4) Instructions given by a probation officer under sub-paragraph (3) above shall, as far as practicable, be such as to avoid—

(a) any conflict with the offender's religious beliefs or with the requirements of any other community order (within the meaning of Part I of the Criminal Justice Act 1991) to which he may be subject; and
(b) any interference with the times, if any, at which he normally works or attends school or any other educational establishment.'

(3) In paragraph 5 of that Schedule, for the words 'duly qualified medical practitioner', wherever they occur, there shall be substituted the words 'registered medical practitioner'.

(4) In that paragraph (both as amended by subsection (3) of section 38 of the 1997 Act and so far as that paragraph has effect without that amendment), in sub-paragraph (4), after the words 'have been' there shall be inserted the words 'or can be'.

(5) In sub-paragraph (10) of that paragraph, before the definition of 'chartered psychologist' there shall be inserted the following definition—

'"registered medical practitioner" means a fully registered person within the meaning of the Medical Act 1983;'.

(6) In paragraph 6 of that Schedule (both as amended by subsection (4) of section 38 of the 1997 Act and so far as that paragraph has effect without that amendment), in sub-paragraph (4), after the words 'have been' there shall be inserted the words 'or can be'.

(7) Sub-paragraph (7) of that paragraph shall cease to have effect.

Magistrates' Courts Act 1980 (c.43)

28 In section 30(2)(a) of the 1980 Act (remand for medical examination), for the words 'duly qualified medical practitioner' there shall be substituted the words 'registered medical practitioner'.

29—(1) In subsection (2) of section 38 of the 1980 Act (committal for sentence on summary trial of offence triable either way), the words ', in accordance with section 56 of the Criminal Justice Act 1967,' shall cease to have effect.

(2) After that subsection there shall be inserted the following subsection—

'(2A) Where the court commits a person under subsection (2) above, section 56 of the Criminal Justice Act 1967 (which enables a magistrates' court, where it commits a person under this section in respect of an offence, also to commit him to the Crown Court to be dealt with in respect of certain other offences) shall apply accordingly.'

30—(1) In subsection (2) of section 38A of the 1980 Act (committal for sentence on indication of guilty plea to offence triable either way), the words ', in accordance with section 56 of the Criminal Justice Act 1967,' shall cease to have effect.

(2) In subsection (5) of that section, for the words 'the court might have dealt with him' there shall be substituted the words 'the magistrates' court could deal with him if it had just convicted him of the offence'.

(3) After that subsection there shall be inserted the following subsection—

'(5A) Where the court commits a person under subsection (2) above, section 56 of the Criminal Justice Act 1967 (which enables a magistrates' court, where it commits a person under this section in respect of an offence, also to commit him to the Crown Court to be dealt with in respect of certain other offences) shall apply accordingly.'

31 In section 39(6)(b) of the 1980 Act (cases where magistrates' court may remit offender to another such court for sentence), for the words 'section 34 or 36' there shall be substituted the words 'section 34, 35 or 36'.

32 In section 85(1)(a) of the 1980 Act (power to remit fine), for the words 'section 74' there shall be substituted the words 'section 77'.

Criminal Justice Act 1982 (c.48)

33 In section 3(1) of the 1982 Act (restriction on imposing custodial sentences on persons under 21 not legally represented)—

    (a) in paragraph (a), the words 'under section 1A above' shall cease to have effect;
    (b) in paragraph (c), for the words 'section 8(2)' there shall be substituted the words 'section 8(1) or (2)'; and
    (c) in paragraph (d), for the words 'section 53(2)' there shall be substituted the words 'section 53(1) or (3)'.

34—(1) In subsection (3) of section 13 of the 1982 Act (conversion of sentence of detention in a young offender institution to sentence of imprisonment), for the words 'section 15 below' there shall be substituted the words 'section 65 of the Criminal Justice Act 1991 (supervision of young offenders after release)'.

(2) In subsection (6) of that section, for the words 'section 8(2)' there shall be substituted the words 'section 8(1) or (2)'.

35 In subsection (2) of section 16 of the 1982 Act (meaning of 'attendance centre'), for the words from 'of orders made' to the end there shall be substituted the words 'of orders made under section 17 below.'

36—(1) In subsection (1) of section 17 of the 1982 Act (attendance centre orders), for the words 'Subject to subsections (3) and (4) below,' there shall be substituted the words 'Where a person under 21 years of age is convicted by or before a court of an offence punishable with imprisonment (not being an offence the sentence for which is fixed by law or falls to be imposed under section 2(2), 3(2) or 4(2) of the Crime (Sentences) Act 1997), or'.

(2) In that subsection, for paragraph (a) there shall be substituted the following paragraph—

'(a) would have power, but for section 1 above, to commit a person under 21 years of age to prison in default of payment of any sum of money or for failing to do or abstain from doing anything required to be done or left undone, or'.

(3) In that subsection, in paragraph (b), for the words 'any such person' there shall be substituted the words 'a person under 21 years of age' and after that paragraph there shall be inserted the following paragraph—

'(bb)   has power to deal with a person under 16 years of age under that Part of that Schedule for failure to comply with any of the requirements of a curfew order, or'.

(4) After that subsection there shall be inserted the following subsection—

'(1A) For the purposes of subsection (1) above—

(a)   the reference to an offence punishable with imprisonment shall be construed without regard to any prohibition or restriction imposed by or under any enactment on the imprisonment of young offenders; and

(b)   a sentence falls to be imposed under section 2(2), 3(2) or 4(2) of the Crime (Sentences) Act 1997 if it is required by that provision and the court is not of the opinion there mentioned.'

(5) For subsection (8) of that section there shall be substituted the following subsection—

'(8) The times at which an offender is required to attend at an attendance centre shall, as far as practicable, be such as to avoid—

(a)   any conflict with the offender's religious beliefs or with the requirements of any other community order (within the meaning of Part I of the Criminal Justice Act 1991) to which he may be subject; and

(b)   any interference with the times, if any, at which he normally works or attends school or any other educational establishment.'

37—(1) In section 18 of the 1982 Act (discharge and variation of attendance centre orders), for subsection (4A) there shall be substituted the following subsections—

'(4A) Any power conferred by this section—

(a)   on a magistrates' court to discharge an attendance centre order made by such a court, or

(b)   on the Crown Court to discharge an attendance centre order made by the Crown Court,

includes power to deal with the offender, for the offence in respect of which the order was made, in any manner in which he could have been dealt with for that offence by the court which made the order if the order had not been made.

(4B) A person sentenced by a magistrates' court under subsection (4A) above for an offence may appeal to the Crown Court against the sentence.'

(2) Subsection (7) of that section shall cease to have effect.

(3) In that section, after subsection (9) there shall be added the following subsections—

'(10) Where an offender has been ordered to attend at an attendance centre in default of the payment of a sum of money or for such a failure or abstention as is mentioned in section 17(1)(a) above, subsection (4A) above shall have effect in relation to the order as if the words ', for the offence in respect of which the order was made,' and 'for that offence' were omitted.

(11) Where an attendance centre order has been made on appeal, for the purposes of this section it shall be deemed—

(a) if it was made on an appeal brought from a magistrates' court, to have been made by that magistrates' court;

(b) if it was made on an appeal brought from the Crown Court or from the criminal division of the Court of Appeal, to have been made by the Crown Court;

and subsection (4A) above shall have effect in relation to an attendance centre order made on appeal as if the words "if the order had not been made" were omitted.'

38—(1) In subsection (1) of section 19 of the 1982 Act (breaches of attendance centre orders or attendance centre rules), for the words 'has been made' there shall be substituted the words 'is in force'.

(2) In subsection (5) of that section, after the word 'failed' there shall be inserted the words 'without reasonable excuse'.

(3) After subsection (7) of that section there shall be added the following subsections—

'(8) Where an offender has been ordered to attend at an attendance centre in default of the payment of a sum of money or for such a failure or abstention as is mentioned in section 17(1)(a) above, subsections (3) and (5) above shall have effect in relation to the order as if the words ', for the offence in respect of which the order was made,' and 'for that offence' were omitted.

(9) Where an attendance centre order has been made on appeal, for the purposes of this section it shall be deemed—

(a) if it was made on an appeal brought from a magistrates' court, to have been made by that magistrates' court;

(b) if it was made on an appeal brought from the Crown Court or from the criminal division of the Court of Appeal, to have been made by the Crown Court;

and, in relation to an attendance centre order made on appeal, subsection (3)(a) above shall have effect as if the words "if the order had not been made" were omitted and subsection (5) above shall have effect as if the words "if it had not made the order" were omitted.'

Criminal Justice Act 1988 (c.33)

39 Paragraph 40 of Schedule 15 to the Criminal Justice Act 1988 (minor and consequential amendments) shall cease to have effect.

Criminal Justice Act 1991 (c.53)

40 In section 11 of the 1991 Act (orders combining probation and community service), after subsection (1) there shall be inserted the following subsection—

'(1A) The reference in subsection (1) above to an offence punishable with imprisonment shall be construed without regard to any prohibition or restriction imposed by or under any enactment on the imprisonment of young offenders.'

41—(1) In subsection (5)(c) of section 12 of the 1991 Act (curfew orders), for the words 'supervising officer' there shall be substituted the words 'responsible officer'.

(2) After subsection (6A) of that section there shall be inserted the following subsection—

'(6B) The court by which a curfew order is made shall give a copy of the order to the offender and to the person responsible for monitoring the offender's whereabouts during the curfew periods specified in the order.'

(3) After subsection (7) of that section there shall be added the following subsection—

'(8) References in this section to the offender's being under the age of sixteen years are references to his being under that age on conviction.'

42 In section 31(1) of the 1991 Act (interpretation of Part I), in paragraph (b) of the definition of 'custodial sentence', for the words 'section 53' there shall be substituted the words 'section 53(3)'.

43—(1) In subsection (3) of section 40 of the 1991 Act (convictions during currency of original sentences), for the words from 'for sentence' to the end there shall be substituted the words 'to be dealt with under subsection (3A) below'.

(2) After that subsection there shall be inserted the following subsections—

'(3A) Where a person is committed to the Crown Court under subsection (3) above, the Crown Court may order him to be returned to prison for the whole or any part of the period which—

    (a) begins with the date of the order; and
    (b) is equal in length to the period between the date on which the new offence was committed and the date mentioned in subsection (1) above.

(3B) Subsection (3)(b) above shall not be taken to confer on the magistrates' court a power to commit the person to the Crown Court for sentence for the new offence, but this is without prejudice to any such power conferred on the magistrates' court by any other enactment.'

(3) In subsection (4) of that section, for the words 'subsection (2)' there shall be substituted the words 'subsection (2) or (3A)'.

44 In each of subsections (3)(b) and (4)(a) of section 57 of the 1991 Act (responsibility of parent or guardian for financial penalties), for the words 'section 35(4)(a)' there shall be substituted the words 'section 35(4)'.

45 In section 58 of the 1991 Act (binding over of parent or guardian), after subsection (8) there shall be added the following subsection—

'(9) For the purposes of this section—

    (a) "guardian" has the same meaning as in the 1933 Act; and
    (b) taking "care" of a person includes giving him protection and guidance and "control" includes discipline.'

46—(1) In paragraph 1 of Schedule 2 to the 1991 Act (enforcement etc. of community orders), after sub-paragraph (4) there shall be added the following sub-paragraph—

'(5) Where a probation order, community service order, combination order or curfew order has been made on appeal, for the purposes of this Schedule it shall be deemed—

(a) if it was made on an appeal brought from a magistrates' court, to have been made by a magistrates' court;

(b) if it was made on an appeal brought from the Crown Court or from the criminal division of the Court of Appeal, to have been made by the Crown Court.'

(2) In each of paragraphs 3(1) and 4(1) of that Schedule, for paragraph (c) there shall be substituted the following paragraph—

'(c) where—

    (i) the relevant order is a probation order and the offender is under the age of twenty-one years, or

    (ii) the relevant order is a curfew order and the offender is under the age of sixteen years,

and the court has been notified as required by subsection (1) of section 17 of the 1982 Act, it may (subject to paragraph 6(6) below) make in respect of him an order under that section (attendance centre orders); or'.

(3) In paragraph 4(1) of that Schedule—

(a) after the word 'failed' there shall be inserted the words 'without reasonable excuse'; and

(b) in paragraph (d), for the words 'by or before the court' there shall be substituted the words 'before the Crown Court'.

(4) In paragraph 6 of that Schedule, in sub-paragraph (1), for the words 'or (b)' there shall be substituted the words ', (b) or (c)'.

(5) After sub-paragraph (3) of that paragraph there shall be inserted the following sub-paragraph—

'(3A) A community service order shall not be made under paragraph 3(1)(b) or 4(1)(b) above in respect of a person who is under the age of sixteen years.'

(6) For sub-paragraph (5) of that paragraph there shall be substituted the following sub-paragraph—

'(5) Where the provisions of this Schedule have effect as mentioned in sub-paragraph (4) above in relation to a community service order under paragraph 3(1)(b) or 4(1)(b) above—

(a) the power conferred on the court by each of paragraphs 3(1)(d) and 4(1)(d) above and paragraph 7(2)(a)(ii) below to deal with the offender for the offence in respect of which the order was made shall be construed as a power to deal with the offender, for his failure to comply with the original order, in any manner in which the court could deal with him if that failure to comply had just been proved to the satisfaction of the court;

(b) the reference in paragraph 7(1)(b) below to the offence in respect of which the order was made shall be construed as a reference to the failure to comply in respect of which the order was made; and

(c) the power conferred on the court by paragraph 8(2)(b) below to deal with the offender for the offence in respect of which the order was made shall be construed as a power to deal with the offender, for his failure to comply with the original order, in any manner in which the court which made the original order could deal with him if that failure had just been proved to the satisfaction of that court;

and in this sub-paragraph "the original order" means the relevant order the failure to comply with whose requirements led to the making of the community service order under paragraph 3(1)(b) or 4(1)(b).'

(7) After sub-paragraph (5) of that paragraph there shall be added the following sub-paragraph—

'(6) The provisions of sections 17 to 19 of the 1982 Act (making, discharge, variation and breach of attendance centre order) shall apply for the purposes of paragraphs 3(1)(c) and 4(1)(c) above but as if there were omitted—

(a) subsection (13) of section 17;

(b) from subsection (4A) of section 18 and subsections (3) and (5) of section 19, the words ", for the offence in respect of which the order was made," and "for that offence".'

(8) After paragraph 6 of that Schedule there shall be inserted the following paragraph—

'6A—(1) Where a relevant order was made by a magistrates' court in the case of an offender under 18 years of age in respect of an offence triable only on indictment in the case of an adult, any powers exercisable under paragraph 3(1)(d) above by that or any other court in respect of the offender after he has attained the age of 18 years shall be powers to do either or both of the following—

(a) to impose a fine not exceeding £5,000 for the offence in respect of which the order was made;

(b) to deal with the offender for that offence in any way in which a magistrates' court could deal with him if it had just convicted him of an offence punishable with imprisonment for a term not exceeding six months.

(2) In sub-paragraph (1)(b) above any reference to an offence punishable with imprisonment shall be construed without regard to any prohibition or restriction imposed by or under any enactment on the imprisonment of young offenders.'

(9) In paragraph 7(5) of that Schedule, after the word 'above' there shall be inserted the words 'for an offence'.

(10) In paragraph 8(2) of that Schedule, for paragraph (b) there shall be substituted the following paragraph—

'(b) revoke the order and deal with the offender, for the offence in respect of which the order was made, in any manner in which the court which made the order could deal with him if he had just been convicted of that offence by or before the court which made the order.'

(11) After paragraph 8 of that Schedule there shall be inserted the following paragraph—

'8A—(1) This paragraph applies where a probation order is in force in respect of any offender and on the application of the offender or the responsible officer it appears to a magistrates' court acting for the petty sessions area concerned that, having regard to circumstances which have arisen since the order was made, it would be in the interests of justice—

(a) for the probation order to be revoked; and

(b) for an order to be made under section 1A(1)(b) of the 1973 Act discharging the offender conditionally for the offence for which the probation order was made.

(2) No application may be made under paragraph 7 above for a probation order to be revoked and replaced with an order for conditional discharge under section 1A(1)(b) of the 1973 Act; but otherwise nothing in this paragraph shall affect the operation of paragraphs 7 and 8 above.

(3) Where this paragraph applies and the probation order was made by a magistrates' court—

(a) the magistrates' court dealing with the application may revoke the probation order and make an order under section 1A(1)(b) of the 1973 Act discharging the offender in respect of the offence for which the probation order was made, subject to the condition that he commits no offence during the period specified in the order under section 1A(1)(b); and

(b) the period specified in the order under section 1A(1)(b) shall be the period beginning with the making of that order and ending with the date when the probation period specified in the probation order would have ended.

(4) Where this paragraph applies and the probation order was made by the Crown Court, the magistrates' court may send the application to the Crown Court to be heard by that court, and if it does so shall also send to the Crown Court such particulars of the case as may be desirable.

(5) Where an application under this paragraph is heard by the Crown Court by virtue of sub-paragraph (4) above—

(a) the Crown Court may revoke the probation order and make an order under section 1A(1)(b) of the 1973 Act discharging the offender in respect of the offence for which the probation order was made, subject to the condition that he commits no offence during the period specified in the order under section 1A(1)(b); and

(b) the period specified in the order under section 1A(1)(b) shall be the period beginning with the making of that order and ending with the date when the probation period specified in the probation order would have ended.

(6) For the purposes of sub-paragraphs (3) and (5) above, subsection (1) of section 1A of the 1973 Act shall apply as if—

(a) for the words from the beginning to 'may make an order either' there were substituted the words "Where paragraph 8A of Schedule 2 to the Criminal Justice Act 1991 applies, the court which under sub-paragraph (3) or (5) of that paragraph has power to dispose of the application may (subject to the provisions of that sub-paragraph) make an order in respect of the offender"; and

(b) paragraph (a) of that subsection were omitted.

(7) An application under this paragraph may be heard in the offender's absence if—

(a) the application is made by the responsible officer; and

(b) that officer produces to the court a statement by the offender that he understands the effect of an order for conditional discharge and consents to the making of the application;

and where the application is so heard section 1A(3) of the 1973 Act shall not apply.

(8) No application may be made under this paragraph while an appeal against the probation order is pending.

(9) Without prejudice to paragraph 11 below, on the making of an order under section 1A(1)(b) of the 1973 Act by virtue of this paragraph the court shall forthwith give copies of the order to the responsible officer, and the responsible officer shall give a copy to the offender.

(10) Each of sections 1(11), 2(9) and 66(4) of the Crime and Disorder Act 1998 (which prevent a court from making an order for conditional discharge in certain cases) shall have effect as if the reference to the court by or before which a person is convicted of an offence there mentioned included a reference to a court dealing with an application under this paragraph in respect of the offence.'

(12) After paragraph 11 of that Schedule there shall be inserted the following paragraphs—

'**11A** Paragraph 6A above shall apply for the purposes of paragraphs 7 and 8 above as it applies for the purposes of paragraph 3 above, but as if in paragraph 6A(1) for the words "powers exercisable under paragraph 3(1)(d) above" there were substituted the words "powers to deal with the offender which are exercisable under paragraph 7(2)(a)(ii) or 8(2)(b) below".

11B Where under this Part of this Schedule a relevant order is revoked and replaced by an order for conditional discharge under section 1A(1)(b) of the 1973 Act and—

  (a) the order for conditional discharge is not made in the circumstances mentioned in section 1B(9) of the 1973 Act (order made by magistrates' court in the case of an offender under eighteen in respect of offence triable only on indictment in the case of an adult), but
  (b) the relevant order was made in those circumstances,

section 1B(9) of the 1973 Act shall apply as if the order for conditional discharge had been made in those circumstances.'

Crime (Sentences) Act 1997 (c.43)

47 Section 1 of the 1997 Act (conditions relating to mandatory and minimum custodial sentences) shall cease to have effect.

48—(1) In subsection (2) of section 3 of the 1997 Act (minimum of seven years for third class A drug trafficking offence)—

  (a) for the words 'specific circumstances' there shall be substituted the words 'particular circumstances'; and
  (b) for the words 'the prescribed custodial sentence unjust' there shall be substituted the words 'it unjust to do so'.

(2) In subsection (3) of that section, for the words 'specific circumstances' there shall be substituted the words 'particular circumstances'.

49—(1) In subsection (2) of section 4 of the 1997 Act (minimum of three years for third domestic burglary)—

  (a) for the words 'specific circumstances' there shall be substituted the words 'particular circumstances'; and

(b) for the words 'the prescribed custodial sentence unjust' there shall be substituted the words 'it unjust to do so'.

(2) In subsection (3) of that section, for the words 'specific circumstances' there shall be substituted the words 'particular circumstances'.

50—(1) In subsection (2)(a) of section 35 of the 1997 Act (community sentences for fine defaulters), for the words 'and (11)' there shall be substituted the words ', (10) and (11)'.

(2) In subsection (5) of that section, paragraph (c) shall cease to have effect.

(3) In that subsection, the word 'and' at the end of paragraph (d) shall cease to have effect and after paragraph (e) there shall be added the following paragraphs—

'(f) the reference in paragraph 7(1)(b) of that Schedule to the offence in respect of which the order was made shall be construed as a reference to the default in respect of which the order was made;

(g) the power conferred by paragraph 7(2)(a)(ii) of that Schedule to deal with an offender for the offence in respect of which the order was made shall be construed as a power to deal with the person in respect of whom the order was made for his default in paying the sum in question; and

(h) paragraph 8(2)(b) of that Schedule shall not apply.'

(4) In subsection (7) of that section, for the words 'section 12(5)' there shall be substituted the words 'section 12(6)'.

(5) In subsection (8) of that section, the word 'and' at the end of paragraph (a) shall cease to have effect and after paragraph (b) there shall be added the following paragraphs—

'(c) the reference in paragraph 7(1)(b) of that Schedule to the offence in respect of which the order was made shall be construed as a reference to the default in respect of which the order was made;

(d) the power conferred by paragraph 7(2)(a)(ii) of that Schedule to deal with an offender for the offence in respect of which the order was made shall be construed as a power to deal with the person in respect of whom the order was made for his default in paying the sum in question; and

(e) paragraph 8(2)(b) of that Schedule shall not apply.'

(6) In subsection (10) of that section, for the words 'subsection (2)(b)' there shall be substituted the words 'subsection (2)(a) or (b)'.

51—(1) In subsection (3) of section 37 of the 1997 Act (community sentences for persistent petty offenders)—

(a) in paragraph (a), for the words '(4) and (6)' there shall be substituted the words '(4), (5A) and (6)'; and

(b) in paragraph (b), for the words '(5) and (6)' there shall be substituted the words '(5), (5A) and (6)'.

(2) For subsections (4) and (5) of that section there shall be substituted the following subsections—

'(4) In this section "community service order" has the same meaning as in the 1973 Act and—

(a) section 14(2) of that Act; and

(b) so far as applicable, the other provisions of that Act relating to community service orders and the provisions of Part I of the 1991 Act so relating,

shall have effect in relation to an order under subsection (3)(a) above as they have effect in relation to a community service order made under the 1973 Act in respect of an offender.

(5) In this section "curfew order" has the same meaning as in Part I of the 1991 Act and—

(a) section 12(6) of that Act; and

(b) so far as applicable, the other provisions of that Part relating to curfew orders,

shall have effect in relation to an order under subsection (3)(b) above as they have effect in relation to a curfew order made under that Act in respect of an offender.

(5A) A court shall not make an order under subsection (3)(a) or (b) above in respect of a person who on conviction is under 16.'

52 In section 50 of the 1997 Act (disclosure of pre-sentence reports), after subsection (6) there shall be added the following subsection—

'(7) In this section "guardian" has the same meaning as in the 1933 Act.'

53 In section 54 of the 1997 Act (general interpretation), after subsection (3) there shall be added the following subsection—

'(4) For the purposes of any provision of this Act which requires the determination of the age of a person by the court, his age shall be deemed to be that which it appears to the court to be after considering any available evidence.'

54 In section 55(2) of the 1997 Act (interpretation of minor and consequential amendments), for the words 'in any case where' (in both places where they occur) there shall be substituted the word 'and'.

Section 119   SCHEDULE 8

MINOR AND CONSEQUENTIAL AMENDMENTS

Children and Young Persons Act 1933 (c.12)

1 In subsection (4A) of section 49 of the 1933 Act (restrictions on reports of proceedings), for paragraph (e) there shall be substituted the following paragraph—

'(e) where a detention and training order is made, the enforcement of any requirements imposed under section 76(6)(b) of the Crime and Disorder Act 1998.'

2 In subsection (1A) of section 55 of the 1933 Act (power of court to order parent or guardian to pay fine imposed on child or young person), after paragraph (c) there shall be inserted the words 'or

(d) a court would impose a fine on a child or young person under section 77(3) of the Crime and Disorder Act 1998 (breach of requirements of supervision under detention and training order) or paragraph 3 of Schedule 5 to that Act (breach of requirements of reparation order or action plan order),'.

3 After subsection (1) of section 56 of the 1933 Act (powers of other courts to remit young offenders to youth courts) there shall be inserted the following subsection—

'(1A) References in subsection (1) above to an offender's being committed for trial include references to his being sent for trial under section 51 of the Crime and Disorder Act 1998.'

4 In section 58 of that Act (power of Secretary of State to send certain young offenders to approved schools), for the words 'subsection (2)', in both places where they occur, there shall be substituted the words 'subsection (3)'.

Administration of Justice (Miscellaneous Provisions) Act 1933 (c.36)

5—(1) In subsection (2) of section 2 of the Administration of Justice (Miscellaneous Provisions) Act 1933 (procedure for indictment of offenders)—

(a) after paragraph (ab) there shall be inserted the following paragraph—

'(ac)   the person charged has been sent for trial for the offence under section 51 (no committal proceedings for indictable-only offences) of the Crime and Disorder Act 1998 ("the 1998 Act"); or'; and

(b) after paragraph (b) there shall be inserted the words 'or

(c)   the bill is preferred under section 22B(3)(a) of the Prosecution of Offences Act 1985.'

(2) After paragraph (iA) of the proviso to that subsection there shall be inserted the following paragraph—

'(iB)   in a case to which paragraph (ac) above applies, the bill of indictment may include, either in substitution for or in addition to any count charging an offence specified in the notice under section 51(7) of the 1998 Act, any counts founded on material which, in pursuance of regulations made under paragraph 1 of Schedule 3 to that Act, was served on the person charged, being counts which may be lawfully joined in the same indictment;'.

Prison Act 1952 (c.52)

6 In subsection (1) of section 43 of the Prison Act 1952 (which enables certain institutions for young offenders to be provided and applies provisions of the Act to them), for paragraph (d) there shall be substituted the following paragraph—

'(d) secure training centres, that is to say places in which offenders in respect of whom detention and training orders have been made under section 73 of the Crime and Disorder Act 1998 may be detained and given training and education and prepared for their release.'

7—(1) In subsection (1) of section 49 of that Act (persons unlawfully at large), for the words from 'imprisonment' to 'secure training centre' there shall be substituted the words 'imprisonment or custody for life or ordered to be detained in secure accommodation or in a young offenders institution'.

(2) In subsection (2) of that section—

(a) for the words from 'imprisonment' to 'secure training centre' there shall be substituted the words 'imprisonment, or ordered to be detained in secure accommodation or in a young offenders institution'; and

(b) for the words from 'in a prison' to 'secure training centre' there shall be substituted the words 'in a prison or remand centre, in secure accommodation or in a young offenders institution'.

(3) After subsection (4) of that section there shall be inserted the following subsection—

'(5) In this section "secure accommodation" means—

(a) a young offender institution;
(b) a secure training centre; or
(c) any other accommodation that is secure accommodation within the meaning given by section 75(7) of the Crime and Disorder Act 1998 (detention and training orders).'

Criminal Procedure (Attendance of Witnesses) Act 1965 (c.69)

8 In subsection (4) of section 2 of the Criminal Procedure (Attendance of Witnesses) Act 1965 (issue of witness summons on application to Crown Court), after the words 'committed for trial' there shall be inserted the words ', or sent for trial under section 51 of the Crime and Disorder Act 1998,'.

Criminal Justice Act 1967 (c.80)

9—(1) In subsection (2) of section 56 of the Criminal Justice Act 1967 (committal for sentence for offences tried summarily—

(a) for the words 'sections 37, 38 and 38A' there shall be substituted the words 'sections 38 and 38A'; and
(b) for the words 'section 17(3) of the Crime (Sentences) Act 1997 (committal for breach of conditions of release supervision order)' there shall be substituted the words 'section 40(3)(b) of the Criminal Justice Act 1991 (committal for sentence for offence committed during currency of original sentence)'.

(2) Subsection (6) of that section shall cease to have effect.

10 In subsection (5) of section 67 of that Act (computation of sentences of imprisonment or detention passed in England and Wales)—

(a) in paragraph (b), for the words 'section 53(2)' there shall be substituted the words 'section 53(3)'; and
(b) paragraph (c) shall cease to have effect.

11 At the end of subsection (2) of section 104 of that Act (general provisions as to interpretation) there shall be inserted the words 'if—

(a) the sentences were passed on the same occasion; or
(b) where they were passed on different occasions, the person has not been released under Part II of the Criminal Justice Act 1991 at any time during the period beginning with the first and ending with the last of those occasions.'

Criminal Appeal Act 1968 (c.19)

12 In subsection (2) of section 9 of the Criminal Appeal Act 1968 (appeal against sentence following conviction on indictment), after the words 'for either way offence)' there shall be inserted the words 'or paragraph 6 of Schedule 3 to the Crime and Disorder Act 1998 (power of Crown Court to deal with summary offence where person sent for trial for indictable-only offence)'.

13—(1) In subsection (2) of section 10 of that Act (appeal against sentence in other cases dealt with at Crown Court), the words '(other than a supervision order within the meaning of that Part)' shall cease to have effect.

(2) In subsection (3) of that section, after paragraph (c) there shall be inserted the following paragraph—

'(cc)   where the court makes such an order with regard to him as is mentioned in section 40(3A) of the Criminal Justice Act 1991.'

Firearms Act 1968 (c.27)

14—(1) In subsection (2) of section 21 of the Firearms Act 1968 (possession of firearms by persons previously convicted of crime), after the words 'a secure training order' there shall be inserted the words 'or a detention and training order'.

(2) In subsection (2A) of that section, after paragraph (b) there shall be inserted the following paragraph—

'(c)   in the case of a person who has been subject to a detention and training order—
(i)   the date on which he is released from detention under the order;
(ii)   the date on which he is released from detention ordered under section 77 of the Crime and Disorder Act 1998; or
(iii) the date of the half-way point of the term of the order,

whichever is the later.'

15 In subsection (1) of section 52 of that Act (forfeiture and disposal of firearms), for the words 'secure training order' there shall be substituted the words 'detention and training order'.

Children and Young Persons Act 1969 (c.54)

16 In subsection (8) of section 7 of the 1969 Act (alterations in treatment of young offenders etc.), for the words from 'person guilty' to 'were begun' there shall be substituted the words 'child or young person guilty of an offence'.

17 In section 11 of the 1969 Act (supervision orders), for the words 'a local authority designated by the order or of a probation officer' there shall be substituted the following paragraphs—

'(a)   a local authority designated by the order;
(b)   a probation officer; or
(c)   a member of a youth offending team,'.

18 Section 12D of the 1969 Act (duty of court to state in certain cases that requirement in place of custodial sentence) shall cease to have effect.

19 After subsection (3) of section 13 of the 1969 Act (selection of supervisor) there shall be inserted the following subsection—

'(4) Where a provision of a supervision order places a person under the supervision of a member of a youth offending team, the supervisor shall be a member of a team established by the local authority within whose area it appears to the court that the supervised person resides or will reside.'

20—(1) In subsection (8) of section 16 of the 1969 Act (provisions supplementary to section 15), after the words 'under the preceding section' there shall be inserted the words 'by a relevant court (within the meaning of that section)'.

(2) Subsection (10) of that section shall cease to have effect.

21 After section 16A of the 1969 Act there shall be inserted the following section—

'16B Application of section 12 of Criminal Justice Act 1991 etc.

(1) The provisions of section 12 of the Criminal Justice Act 1991 (curfew orders) shall apply for the purposes of section 15(3)(a) of this Act but as if—

(a) in subsection (1), for the words from the beginning to 'before which he is convicted' there were substituted the words 'Where a court considers it appropriate to make a curfew order in respect of any person in pursuance of section 15(3)(a) of the Children and Young Persons Act 1969, the court'; and

(b) in subsection (8), for the words 'on conviction' there were substituted the words 'on the date on which his failure to comply with a requirement included in the supervision order was proved to the court'.

(2) Schedule 2 to the Criminal Justice Act 1991 (enforcement etc. of community orders), so far as relating to curfew orders, shall also apply for the purposes of that section but as if—

(a) the power conferred on the magistrates' court by each of paragraphs 3(1)(d) and 7(2)(a)(ii) to deal with the offender for the offence in respect of which the order was made were a power to deal with the offender, for his failure to comply with a requirement included in the supervision order, in any manner in which the relevant court could deal with him for that failure to comply if it had just been proved to the satisfaction of that court;

(b) the power conferred on the Crown Court by paragraph 4(1)(d) to deal with the offender for the offence in respect of which the order was made were a power to deal with the offender, for his failure to comply with such a requirement, in any manner in which that court could deal with him for that failure to comply if it had just been proved to its satisfaction;

(c) the reference in paragraph 7(1)(b) to the offence in respect of which the order was made were a reference to the failure to comply in respect of which the curfew order was made; and

(d) the power conferred on the Crown Court by paragraph 8(2)(b) to deal with the offender for the offence in respect of which the order was made were a power to deal with the offender, for his failure to comply with a requirement included in the supervision order, in any manner in which the relevant court (if that order was made by a magistrates' court) or the Crown Court (if that order was made by the Crown Court) could deal with him for that failure to comply if it had just been proved to the satisfaction of that court.

(3) For the purposes of the provisions mentioned in subsection (2)(a) and (d) above, as applied by that subsection, if the supervision order is no longer in force the relevant court's powers shall be determined on the assumption that it is still in force.

(4) In this section "relevant court" has the same meaning as in section 15 above.'

22 In subsection (14) of section 23 of the 1969 Act (remands and committals to local authority accommodation), paragraph (a) shall cease to have effect.

23 In subsection (1) of section 70 of the 1969 Act (interpretation), after the definition of 'young person' there shall be inserted the following definition—

> "youth offending team" means a team established under section 39 of the Crime and Disorder Act 1998.'

Superannuation Act 1972 (c.11)

24 In Schedule 1 to the Superannuation Act 1972 (kinds of employment to which a scheme under section 1 of that Act may apply), at the end of the list of 'Other Bodies' there shall be inserted the following entry—

> 'Youth Justice Board for England and Wales.'

Powers of Criminal Courts Act 1973 (c.62)

25 After subsection (1) of section 1A of the 1973 Act (absolute and conditional discharge) there shall be inserted the following subsection—

> '(1A) Subsection (1)(b) above has effect subject to section 66(4) of the Crime and Disorder Act 1998 (effect of reprimands and warnings).'

26—(1) In subsection (1) of section 2 of the 1973 Act (probation orders), the words 'by a probation officer' shall cease to have effect and for the words 'the supervision of a probation officer' there shall be substituted the word 'supervision'.

(2) In subsection (2) of that section, for the words 'a probation officer appointed for or assigned to that area' there shall be substituted the following paragraphs—

> '(a) a probation officer appointed for or assigned to that area; or
> (b) where the offender is under the age of 18 years when the order is made, a member of a youth offending team established by a local authority specified in the order.'

(3) After that subsection there shall be inserted the following subsection—

> '(2A) The local authority specified as mentioned in subsection (2)(b) above shall be the local authority within whose area it appears to the court that the offender resides or will reside.'

(4) In subsection (4) of that section, for the words 'the probation officer' there shall be substituted the words 'the person'.

(5) After that subsection there shall be inserted the following subsection—

> '(4A) In the case of an offender under the age of 18 years, the reference in subsection (4) above to a probation officer includes a reference to a member of a youth offending team.'

(6) In subsection (6) of that section—

> (a) for the words 'the probation officer' there shall be substituted the words 'the person'; and

(b) for the words 'that officer' there shall be substituted the words 'that person'.

27—(1) In subsection (4) of section 14 of the 1973 Act (community service orders), for the words from 'a probation officer' to the end there shall be substituted the following paragraphs—

'(a) a probation officer appointed for or assigned to the area for the time being specified in the order (whether under this subsection or by virtue of Part IV of Schedule 2 to the Criminal Justice Act 1991);
(b) a person appointed for the purposes of those provisions by the probation committee for that area; or
(c) in the case of an offender under the age of 18 years when the order is made, a member of a youth offending team established by a local authority for the time being specified in the order (whether under this subsection or by virtue of that Part).'

(2) After that subsection there shall be inserted the following subsection—

'(4A) The local authority specified as mentioned in subsection (4)(c) above shall be the local authority within whose area it appears to the court that the offender resides or will reside.'

(3) After subsection (8) of that section there shall be inserted the following subsection—

'(9) In the case of an offender under the age of 18 years, references in subsections (2), (5)(c) or (6) above to a probation officer include references to a member of a youth offending team.'

28 In subsection (2) of section 21 of the 1973 Act (restriction on imposing sentences of imprisonment etc. on persons not legally represented)—

(a) after the words 'sentence or trial,' there shall be inserted the words 'or sent to that Court for trial under section 51 of the Crime and Disorder Act 1998,'; and
(b) for the words 'which committed him' there shall be substituted the words 'which committed or sent him'.

29 In subsection (1)(b) of section 32 of the 1973 Act (enforcement etc. of fines imposed and recognizances forfeited by Crown Court), after the words 'or dealt with' there shall be inserted the words ', or by which he was sent to that Court for trial under section 51 of the Crime and Disorder Act 1998'.

30 After subsection (2) of section 23 of the 1973 Act (power of court on conviction of further offence to deal with suspended sentence) there shall be inserted the following subsection—

'(2A) The power to make an order under subsection (2) above has effect subject to section 102 of the Crime and Disorder Act 1998.'

31 In section 42 of the 1973 Act (power of Crown Court on committal for sentence), subsection (2) shall cease to have effect.

32 In subsection (1) of section 46 of the 1973 Act (reports of probation officers), after the words 'probation officer' there shall be inserted the words 'or a member of a youth offending team'.

33 In subsection (1) of section 57 of the 1973 Act (interpretation), after the definition of 'suspended sentence' there shall be inserted the following definition—

' "youth offending team" means a team established under section 39 of the Crime
    and Disorder Act 1998.'

34—(1) At the beginning of sub-paragraph (1) of paragraph 6 (requirements as to
drug or alcohol dependency) of Schedule 1A to the 1973 Act there shall be inserted the
words 'Subject to sub-paragraph (1A) below,'.

(2) After that sub-paragraph there shall be inserted the following sub-paragraph—

'(1A) If the court has been notified by the Secretary of State that arrangements for
    implementing orders under section 61 of the Crime and Disorder Act 1998 (drug
    treatment and testing orders) are available in the area proposed to be specified in
    the probation order, and the notice has not been withdrawn, this paragraph shall
    have effect as if the words 'drugs or', in each place where they occur, were omitted.'

(3) After that paragraph there shall be inserted the following paragraph—

'Interpretation

7 In the case of an offender under the age of 18 years, references in this Schedule
to a probation officer include references to a member of a youth offending team.'

Rehabilitation of Offenders Act 1974 (c.53)

35 After subsection (6) of section 5 of the Rehabilitation of Offenders Act 1974
(rehabilitation periods for particular sentences) there shall be inserted the following
subsection—

'(6A) Where in respect of a conviction a detention and training order was made
    under section 73 of the Crime and Disorder Act 1998, the rehabilitation period
    applicable to the sentence shall be—

    (a) in the case of a person aged fifteen years or over at the date of his conviction,
    five years if the order was, and three and a half years if the order was not, for a
    term exceeding six months;

    (b) in the case of a person aged under fifteen years at the date of his conviction,
    a period beginning with that date and ending one year after the date on
    which the order ceases to have effect.'

36 In subsection (2) of section 7 of that Act (limitations on rehabilitation under Act
etc.), after paragraph (b) there shall be inserted the following paragraph—

'(bb) in any proceedings on an application for a sex offender order under
    section 2 or, as the case may be, 20 of the Crime and Disorder Act 1998 or
    in any appeal against the making of such an order;'.

Bail Act 1976 (c.63)

37 After subsection (8A) of section 3 of the Bail Act 1976 (general provisions) there
shall be inserted the following subsection—

'(8B) Subsection (8) above applies where a court has sent a person on bail to the
    Crown Court for trial under section 51 of the Crime and Disorder Act 1998 as it
    applies where a court has committed a person on bail to the Crown Court for trial.'

38. In paragraph 8(1) of Schedule 1 to that Act (persons entitled to bail: supplementary provisions), after the words 'subsection (6)(d)' there shall be inserted the words 'or (e)'.

Magistrates' Courts Act 1980 (c.43)

39 In subsection (3) of section 11 of the 1980 Act (certain sentences and orders not to be made in absence of accused), for the words 'secure training order' there shall be substituted the words 'detention and training order'.

40—(1) In subsection (1)(a) of section 24 of the 1980 Act (summary trial of information against child or young person for indictable offence), for the words 'that subsection' there shall be substituted the words 'subsection (3) of that section'.

(2) In subsection (2) of that section, for the words from 'that other offence' to the end there shall be substituted the words 'the charges for both offences could be joined in the same indictment'.

41 Section 37 of the 1980 Act (committal to Crown Court with a view to greater term of detention in a young offender institution) shall cease to have effect.

42 In subsection (1) of section 65 of the 1980 Act (meaning of 'family proceedings'), after paragraph (p) there shall be inserted the following paragraph—

'(q) sections 11 and 12 of the Crime and Disorder Act 1998;'.

43 In subsection (2) of section 108 of the 1980 Act (right of appeal to the Crown Court), the words 'a probation order or' shall cease to have effect.

44 In subsection (4)(c) of section 125 of the 1980 Act (warrants)—

(a) the word 'and' at the end of sub-paragraph (ii) shall cease to have effect;
(b) in sub-paragraph (iii), for the words 'or 97 above' there shall be substituted the words ', 97 or 97A above; and'; and
(c) after that sub-paragraph there shall be inserted the following sub-paragraph—

'(iv) paragraph 4 of Schedule 3 to the Crime and Disorder Act 1998.'

45 In section 126 of the 1980 Act (execution of certain warrants outside England and Wales)—

(a) the word 'and' at the end of paragraph (c) shall cease to have effect;
(b) after that paragraph there shall be inserted the following paragraph—
'(cc)   warrants of arrest issued under section 97A above;'; and
(c) after paragraph (d) there shall be inserted the words '; and
(e) warrants of arrest issued under paragraph 4 of Schedule 3 to the Crime and Disorder Act 1998.'

46 At the beginning of subsection (1) of section 133 of the 1980 Act (consecutive terms of imprisonment) there shall be inserted the words 'Subject to section 102 of the Crime and Disorder Act 1998,'.

Supreme Court Act 1981 (c.54)

47 After subsection (1) of section 47 of the Supreme Court Act 1981 (sentences and other orders of Crown Court when dealing with offenders) there shall be inserted the following subsection—

'(1A) The power to give a direction under subsection (1) above has effect subject to section 102 of the Crime and Disorder Act 1998.'

48 In subsection (1)(a) of section 81 of the Supreme Court Act 1981 (bail), after the words 'Criminal Justice Act 1987' there shall be inserted the words 'or who has been sent in custody to the Crown Court for trial under section 51 of the Crime and Disorder Act 1998'.

Criminal Justice Act 1982 (c.48)

49 In subsection (2) of section 1 of the 1982 Act (general restriction on custodial sentences), for the words from 'remanded in custody' to the end there shall be substituted the following paragraphs—

'(a) remanded in custody;
(b) committed in custody for trial or sentence; or
(c) sent in custody for trial under section 51 of the Crime and Disorder Act 1998.'

50—(1) In subsection (1) of section 1A of the 1982 Act (detention in a young offender institution), for the words 'not less than 15 years of age' there shall be substituted the words 'not less than 18 years of age'.

(2) In subsection (3) of that section, for the words 'the minimum period applicable to the offender under subsection (4A) below' there shall be substituted the words '21 days'.

(3) In subsection (4) of that section, for the words 'the minimum period applicable' there shall be substituted the words '21 days'.

(4) Subsection (4A) of that section shall cease to have effect.

(5) At the beginning of subsection (6) of that section there shall be inserted the words 'Subject to section 102 of the Crime and Disorder Act 1998,'.

51 In subsection (2) of section 1C of the 1982 Act (accommodation of offenders sentenced to detention in a young offender institution), the words 'but if he is under 18 at the time of the direction, only for a temporary purpose' shall cease to have effect.

52—(1) In subsection (1) of section 3 of the 1982 Act (restriction on certain sentences where offender not legally represented), for paragraph (e) there shall be substituted the following paragraph—

'(e) make a detention and training order,'.

(2) In subsection (2) of that section—

(a) after the words 'sentence or trial,' there shall be inserted the words 'or sent to that Court for trial under section 51 of the Crime and Disorder Act 1998,'; and
(b) for the words 'which committed him' there shall be substituted the words 'which committed or sent him'.

53—(1) In subsection (3)(a) of section 19 of the 1982 Act (breaches of attendance centre orders or attendance centre rules), the words 'revoke it and' shall cease to have effect.

(2) In subsection (5) of that section, the words 'revoke the attendance centre order and' shall cease to have effect.

(3) In subsection (5A) of that section, for paragraph (b) there shall be substituted the following paragraph—

'(b) in the case of an offender who has wilfully and persistently failed to comply with those requirements, may impose a custodial sentence notwithstanding anything in section 1(2) of the Criminal Justice Act 1991.'

(4) After that subsection there shall be inserted the following subsection—

'(5B) Where a court deals with an offender under subsection (3)(a) or (5) above, it shall revoke the attendance centre order if it is still in force.'

Mental Health Act 1983 (c.20)

54 In subsection (8) of section 37 of the Mental Health Act 1983 (powers of courts to order hospital admission or guardianship), for the words from 'pass sentence of imprisonment' to 'in respect of the offender' there shall be inserted the following paragraphs—

'(a) pass a sentence of imprisonment, impose a fine or make a community order (within the meaning of Part I of the Criminal Justice Act 1991) in respect of the offence; or

(b) make an order under section 58 of that Act (binding over of parent or guardian) in respect of the offender,'.

Mental Health (Scotland) Act 1984 (c.36)

55—[*Applies to Scotland only.*]

Repatriation of Prisoners Act 1984 (c.47)

56 In subsection (4)(b) of section 2 (transfer of prisoners out of United Kingdom) of the Repatriation of Prisoners Act 1984, for sub-paragraph (i) there shall be substituted the following sub-paragraph—

'(i) released on licence under section 33(1)(b), (2) or (3), 33A(2), 34A(3) or 35(1) of the Criminal Justice Act 1991 or section 28(5) or 29(1) of the Crime (Sentences) Act 1997;'.

57 In subsection (9) of section 3 of that Act (transfer of prisoners into United Kingdom)—

(a) for the words 'section 48 of the Criminal Justice Act 1991 (discretionary life prisoners transferred to England and Wales)' there shall be substituted the words 'section 33 of the Crime (Sentences) Act 1997 (life prisoner transferred to England and Wales)'; and

(b) for the words 'section 34 of that Act (duty of Secretary of State to release discretionary life prisoners)' there shall be substituted the words 'section 28 of that Act (duty to release certain life prisoners)'.

58—(1) Paragraph 2 of the Schedule to that Act as it has effect, and is deemed always to have had effect, by virtue of paragraph 2 of Schedule 2 to the 1997 Act shall be amended as follows.

(2) In sub-paragraph (4), for the definition of 'the enactments relating to release on licence' there shall be substituted the following definition—

"'the enactments relating to release on licence" means sections 33(1)(b), (2) and (3), 33A(2), 34A(3), 35(1) and 37(1) and (2) of the Criminal Justice Act 1991 and section 28(5) and (7) of the Crime (Sentences) Act 1997;'.

59—(1) Paragraph 2 of the Schedule to that Act (operation of certain enactments in relation to the prisoner) as it has effect by virtue of paragraph 3 of Schedule 2 to the 1997 Act—

(a) shall have effect in relation to all prisoners repatriated to England and Wales after the commencement of Schedule 2; and
(b) as it so has effect, shall be amended as follows.

(2) In sub-paragraph (2), for the words '34(3) and (5) and 35(1) of the Criminal Justice Act 1991' there shall be substituted the words '35(1) of the Criminal Justice Act 1991 and section 28(5) and (7) of the Crime (Sentences) Act 1997'.

(3) In sub-paragraph (4), for the definition of 'the enactments relating to release on licence' there shall be substituted the following definition—

"'the enactments relating to release on licence" means sections 33(1)(b), (2) and (3), 33A(2), 34A(3), 35(1) and 37(1) and (2) of the Criminal Justice Act 1991 and section 28(5) and (7) of the Crime (Sentences) Act 1997;'.

60 For paragraph 3 of the Schedule to that Act there shall be substituted the following paragraph—

'Life imprisonment

3 Where the relevant provisions include provision equivalent to a sentence in relation to which subsection (1) of section 29 of the Crime (Sentences) Act 1997 (power to release certain life prisoners etc.) applies, that subsection shall have effect as if the reference to consultation with the trial judge if available were omitted.'

Police and Criminal Evidence Act 1984 (c.60)

61 After subsection (4) of section 27 of the 1984 Act (fingerprinting of certain offenders and recording of offences) there shall be inserted the following subsection—

'(4A) In subsection (4) above "conviction" includes—

(a) a caution within the meaning of Part V of the Police Act 1997; and
(b) a reprimand or warning given under section 65 of the Crime and Disorder Act 1998.'

62 After section 47 of the 1984 Act there shall be inserted the following section—

'47A Early administrative hearings conducted by justices' clerks

Where a person has been charged with an offence at a police station, any requirement imposed under this Part for the person to appear or be brought before a magistrates' court shall be taken to be satisfied if the person appears or is brought before the clerk to the justices for a petty sessions area in order for the clerk to conduct a hearing under section 50 of the Crime and Disorder Act 1998 (early administrative hearings).'

Prosecution of Offences Act 1985 (c.23)

63 In subsection (2) of section 23 of the 1985 Act (discontinuance of proceedings), after paragraph (b) there shall be inserted the following paragraph—

'(c) in the case of any offence, any stage of the proceedings after the accused has been sent for trial under section 51 of the Crime and Disorder Act 1998 (no committal proceedings for indictable-only and related offences).'

64 After that section there shall be inserted the following section—

'23A Discontinuance of proceedings after accused has been sent for trial

(1) This section applies where—

(a) the Director of Public Prosecutions, or a public authority (within the meaning of section 17 of this Act), has the conduct of proceedings for an offence; and

(b) the accused has been sent for trial under section 51 of the Crime and Disorder Act 1998 for the offence.

(2) Where, at any time before the indictment is preferred, the Director or authority gives notice under this section to the Crown Court sitting at the place specified in the notice under section 51 (7) of the Crime and Disorder Act 1998 that he or it does not want the proceedings to continue, they shall be discontinued with effect from the giving of that notice.

(3) The Director or authority shall, in any notice given under subsection (2) above, give reasons for not wanting the proceedings to continue.

(4) On giving any notice under subsection (2) above the Director or authority shall inform the accused of the notice; but the Director or authority shall not be obliged to give the accused any indication of his reasons for not wanting the proceedings to continue.

(5) The discontinuance of any proceedings by virtue of this section shall not prevent the institution of fresh proceedings in respect of the same offence.'

Criminal Justice Act 1987 (c.38)

65 After subsection (3) of section 4 of the Criminal Justice Act 1987 (notices of transfer in serious fraud cases) there shall be inserted the following subsection—

'(4) This section and sections 5 and 6 below shall not apply in any case in which section 51 of the Crime and Disorder Act 1998 (no committal proceedings for indictable-only offences) applies.'

66 In subsection (1) of section 40 of the Criminal Justice Act 1988 (power to join in indictment count for common assault etc.), at the end there shall be inserted the words 'or are disclosed by material which, in pursuance of regulations made under paragraph 1 of Schedule 3 to the Crime and Disorder Act 1998 (procedure where person sent for trial under section 51), has been served on the person charged'.

Legal Aid Act 1988 (c.34)

67—(1) In subsection (4) of section 20 of the Legal Aid Act 1988 (competent authorities to grant representation under Part V), after paragraph (a) there shall be inserted the following paragraph—

'(aa)   which sends a person for trial under section 51 of the Crime and Disorder Act 1998 (no committal proceedings for indictable-only offences),'.

(2) After subsection (5) of that section there shall be inserted the following subsection—

'(5A) A magistrates' court which has a duty or a power to send a person for trial under section 51 of the Crime and Disorder Act 1998 is also competent, before discharging that duty or (as the case may be) deciding whether to exercise that power, as respects any proceedings before the Crown Court on the person's trial.'

(3) In subsection (3)(a) of section 21 of that Act (availability of representation under Part V), after the word 'committed' there shall be inserted the words 'or sent'.

(4) In subsection (4) of that section, after the word 'commits' there shall be inserted the words 'or sends'.

Children Act 1989 (c.41)

68 In subsection (4) of section 8 of the 1989 Act (which defines 'family proceedings'), after paragraph (h) there shall be inserted the following paragraph—

'(i) sections 11 and 12 of the Crime and Disorder Act 1998.'

69 In subsection (3) of section 47 of the 1989 Act (local authority's duty to investigate), after the words 'this Act' there shall be inserted the words 'or section 11 of the Crime and Disorder Act 1998 (child safety orders)'.

Prisons (Scotland) Act 1989 (c.45)

70 to 71 [*Applies to Scotland only.*]

Criminal Justice Act 1991 (c.53)

72 For subsection (3) of section 1 of the 1991 Act (restrictions on imposing custodial sentences) there shall be substituted the following subsection—

'(3) Nothing in subsection (2) above shall prevent the court from passing a custodial sentence on the offender if he fails to express his willingness to comply with—

(a) a requirement which is proposed by the court to be included in a probation order or supervision order and which requires an expression of such willingness; or

(b) a requirement which is proposed by the court to be included in a drug treatment and testing order or an order under section 61(6) of the Crime and Disorder Act 1998.'

73 In subsection (5)(a) of section 3 of the 1991 Act (procedural requirements for custodial sentences), for the words 'a probation officer or by a social worker of a local authority social services department' there shall be substituted the following sub-paragraphs—

'(i)   a probation officer;

(ii)   a social worker of a local authority social services department; or

(iii) where the offender is under the age of 18 years, a member of a youth offending team;'.

74 In subsection (4) of section 6 of the 1991 Act (restrictions on imposing community sentences)—

(a) after paragraph (a) there shall be inserted the following paragraph—

'(aa)   a drug treatment and testing order;';

(b) the word 'and' immediately following paragraph (e) shall cease to have effect; and

(c) after paragraph (f) there shall be inserted the following paragraph—

'(g) an action plan order.'

75 In subsection (3) of section 7 of the 1991 Act (procedural requirements for community sentences), after paragraph (a) there shall be inserted the following paragraph—

'(aa)   a drug treatment and testing order;'.

76 In subsection (1) of section 11 of the 1991 Act (combination orders), for the words 'the supervision of a probation officer' there shall be substituted the word 'supervision'.

77 In subsection (3) of section 15 of the 1991 Act (regulation of community orders)—

(a) in paragraph (a), after the words 'probation officer' there shall be inserted the words 'or member of a youth offending team'; and

(b) after that paragraph there shall be inserted the following paragraph—

'(aa)   in relation to an offender who is subject to a drug treatment and testing order, the probation officer responsible for his supervision;'.

78 In subsection (1) of section 31 of the 1991 Act (interpretation of Part I)—

(a) immediately before the definition of 'attendance centre order' there shall be inserted the following definition—

'"action plan order" means an order under section 69 of the Crime and Disorder Act 1998;';

(b) in the definition of 'custodial sentence', in paragraph (b), after the word 'age,' there shall be inserted the words 'a detention and training order,' and the words 'or a secure training order under section 1 of the Criminal Justice and Public Order Act 1994' shall cease to have effect; and

(c) after that definition there shall be inserted the following definitions—

'"detention and training order" has the meaning given by section 73(3) of the Crime and Disorder Act 1998;

"drug treatment and testing order" means an order under section 61 of that Act;'.

79—(1) In subsection (1)(b) of section 32 of the 1991 Act (Parole Board), for the words 'the functions conferred by Part II of the Crime (Sentences) Act 1997 ("Part II")' there shall be substituted the words 'the functions conferred by this Part in respect of long-term and short-term prisoners and by Chapter II of Part II of the Crime (Sentences) Act 1997 ("Chapter II") in respect of life prisoners within the meaning of that Chapter'.

(2) In subsections (3), (4) and (6) of that section, for the words 'Part II' there shall be substituted the words 'this Part or Chapter II'.

80—(1) In subsection (3) of section 33 of the 1991 Act (duty to release short-term and long-term prisoners)—

(a) in paragraph (a), for the words 'subsection (1)(b) or (2) above or section 35 or 36(1) below' there shall be substituted the words 'this Part'; and
(b) in paragraph (b), for the words '38(2) or 39(1)' there shall be substituted the words '39(1) or (2)'.

(2) After that subsection there shall be inserted the following subsection—

'(3A) In the case of a prisoner to whom section 44A below applies, it shall be the duty of the Secretary of State to release him on licence at the end of the extension period (within the meaning of section 58 of the Crime and Disorder Act 1998).'

(3) Subsection (4) of that section shall cease to have effect.

81 After that section there shall be inserted the following section—

'33A Duty to release prisoners: special cases

(1) As soon as a prisoner—

(a) whose sentence is for a term of less than twelve months; and
(b) who has been released on licence under section 34A(3) or 36(1) below and recalled to prison under section 38A(1) or 39(1) or (2) below,

would (but for his release) have served one-half of his sentence, it shall be the duty of the Secretary of State to release him unconditionally.

(2) As soon as a prisoner—

(a) whose sentence is for a term of twelve months or more; and
(b) who has been released on licence under section 34A(3) below and recalled to prison under section 38A(1) below,

would (but for his release) have served one-half of his sentence, it shall be the duty of the Secretary of State to release him on licence.

(3) In the case of a prisoner who—

(a) has been released on licence under this Part and recalled to prison under section 39(1) or (2) below; and
(b) has been subsequently released on licence under section 33(3) or (3A) above and recalled to prison under section 39(1) or (2) below,

section 33(3) above shall have effect as if for the words 'three-quarters' there were substituted the words "the whole" and the words "on licence" were omitted.'

82 In subsection (1) of section 36 of the 1991 Act (power to release prisoners on compassionate grounds), for word 'prisoner' there shall be substituted the words 'short-term or long-term prisoner'.

83—(1) In subsection (1) of section 37 of the 1991 Act (duration and conditions of licences—

- (a) for the words 'subsection (2)' there shall be substituted the words 'subsections (1A), (1B) and (2)'; and
- (b) the words 'any suspension under section 38(2) below or, as the case may be,' shall cease to have effect.

(2) After subsection (1A) of that section there shall be inserted the following subsection—

'(1B) Where a prisoner whose sentence is for a term of twelve months or more is released on licence under section 33A(2) or 34A(3) above, subsection (1) above shall have effect as if for the reference to three-quarters of his sentence there were substituted a reference to the difference between—

- (a) that proportion of his sentence; and
- (b) the duration of the curfew condition to which he is or was subject.'

(3) In subsection (2) of that section, for the words 'section 36(1) above' there shall be substituted the words 'section 34A(3) or 36(1) above'.

(4) In subsection (4) of that section—

- (a) after the words 'a licence' there shall be inserted the words 'under this Part'; and
- (b) the words '(which shall include on his release conditions as to his supervision by a probation officer)' shall cease to have effect.

(5) After that subsection there shall be inserted the following subsection—

'(4A) The conditions so specified may in the case of a person released on licence under section 34A above whose sentence is for a term of less than twelve months, and shall in any other case, include on the person's release conditions as to his supervision by—

- (a) a probation officer appointed for or assigned to the petty sessions area within which the person resides for the time being; or
- (b) where the person is under the age of 18 years, a member of a youth offending team established by the local authority within whose area the person resides for the time being.'

(6) For subsection (5) of that section there shall be substituted the following subsection—

'(5) The Secretary of State shall not include on release, or subsequently insert, a condition in the licence of a long-term prisoner, or vary or cancel any such condition, except after consultation with the Board.'

84 After subsection (5) of section 39 of the 1991 Act (recall of prisoners while on licence) there shall be inserted the following subsection—

'(5A) In the case of a prisoner to whom section 44A below applies subsections (4)(b) and (5) of that section apply in place of subsection (5) above.'

85 After subsection (4) of section 40 of the 1991 Act (convictions during currency of original sentences) there shall be inserted the following subsections—

'(5) Where the new offence is found to have been committed over a period of two or more days, or at some time during a period of two or more days, it shall be taken for the purposes of this section to have been committed on the last of those days.

(6) For the purposes of any enactment conferring rights of appeal in criminal cases, any such order as is mentioned in subsection (2) or (3A) above made with regard to any person shall be treated as a sentence passed on him for the offence for which the sentence referred to in subsection (1) above was passed.'

86—(1) For subsections (1) and (2) of section 41 of the 1991 Act (remand time to count towards time served) there shall be substituted the following subsections—

'(1) Where a person is sentenced to imprisonment for a term in respect of an offence, this section applies to him if the court directs under section 9 of the Crime (Sentences) Act 1997 that the number of days for which he was remanded in custody in connection with—

(a) the offence; or
(b) any other offence the charge for which was founded on the same facts or evidence,

shall count as time served by him as part of the sentence.

(2) For the purpose of determining for the purposes of this Part whether a person to whom this section applies—

(a) has served, or would (but for his release) have served, a particular proportion of his sentence; or
(b) has served a particular period,

the number of days specified in the direction shall, subject to subsections (3) and (4) below, be treated as having been served by him as part of that sentence or period.'

(2) After subsection (3) of that section there shall be inserted the following subsection—

'(4) Where the period for which a licence granted under section 33A(2), 34A(3) or 36(1) above to a short-term prisoner remains in force cannot exceed one-quarter of his sentence, nothing in subsection (2) above shall have the effect of reducing that period.'

87—(1) In subsection (3) of section 43 of the 1991 Act (young offenders), for the words 'subsections (1)' there shall be substituted the words 'subsection (1)'.

(2) In subsection (5) of that section, for the words 'section 37(4)' there shall be substituted the words 'section 37(4A)'.

88—(1) In subsection (1) of section 45 of the 1991 Act (fine defaulters and contemnors), for the words 'except sections 35 and 40' there shall be substituted the words 'except sections 33A, 34A, 35 and 40'.

(2) In subsection (3) of that section—

(a) for the words 'subsections (1) to (4)' there shall be substituted the words 'subsections (1) to (3)'; and
(b) for the words 'section 38(2) or 39(1)' there shall be substituted the words 'section 39(1) or (2)'.

(3) In subsection (4) of that section—

(a) the words 'any suspension under section 38(2) below; or' shall cease to have effect; and

(b) for the words 'section 39(1)' there shall be substituted the words 'section 39(1) or (2)'.

89 In subsection (2) of section 46 of the 1991 Act (persons liable to removal from the United Kingdom), for the words from 'section 37(4)' to the end there shall be substituted the words 'section 37 above shall have effect as if subsection (4A) were omitted'.

90 For subsection (2) of section 47 of the 1991 Act (persons extradited to the United Kingdom) there shall be substituted the following subsection—

'(2) In the case of an extradited prisoner, section 9 of the Crime (Sentences) Act 1997 (crediting of periods of remand in custody) shall have effect as if the days for which he was kept in custody while awaiting extradition were days for which he was remanded in custody in connection with the offence, or any other offence the charge for which was founded on the same facts or evidence.'

91 In section 50 of the 1991 Act (transfer by order of certain functions to Board), for subsection (3) (including that subsection as applied by any order under subsection (1) of that section) there shall be substituted the following subsection—

'(3) In section 37 above, in subsection (5) for the words "after consultation with the Board" there shall be substituted the words "in accordance with recommendations of the Board", and subsection (6) shall be omitted.'

92 In subsection (4) of section 51 of the 1991 Act (interpretation of Part II)—

(a) for the words 'Subsections (2) and (3)' there shall be substituted the words 'Subsection (3)'; and

(b) for the words 'as they apply' there shall be substituted the words 'as it applies'.

93 After subsection (7) of section 53 of the 1991 Act (notices of transfer in certain cases involving children) there shall be inserted the following subsection—

'(8) This section shall not apply in any case in which section 51 of the Crime and Disorder Act 1998 (no committal proceedings for indictable-only offences) applies.'

94—(1) In subsection (1) of section 65 of the 1991 Act (supervision of young offenders after release), for the words from 'a probation officer' to the end there shall be substituted the following paragraphs—

'(a) a probation officer;

(b) a social worker of a local authority social services department; or

(c) in the case of a person under the age of 18 years on his release, a member of a youth offending team.'

(2) After that subsection there shall be inserted the following subsections—

'(1A) Where the supervision is to be provided by a probation officer, the probation officer shall be an officer appointed for or assigned to the petty sessions area within which the offender resides for the time being.

(1B) Where the supervision is to be provided by—

(a) a social worker of a local authority social services department; or

(b) a member of a youth offending team,

the social worker or member shall be a social worker of, or a member of a youth offending team established by, the local authority within whose area the offender resides for the time being.'

95 In subsection (1) of section 99 of the 1991 Act (general interpretation), after the definition of 'young person' there shall be inserted the following definition—

'"youth offending team" means a team established under section 39 of the Crime and Disorder Act 1998.'

96—(1) After sub-paragraph (5) of paragraph 1 of Schedule 2 to the 1991 Act (enforcement etc. of community orders) there shall be inserted the following sub-paragraph—

'(6) Where a drug treatment and testing order has been made on an appeal brought from the Crown Court, or from the criminal division of the Court of Appeal, for the purposes of this Schedule it shall be deemed to have been made by the Crown Court.'

(2) In sub-paragraph (1)(d) of paragraph 3 of that Schedule, the words 'revoke the order and' shall cease to have effect.

(3) After sub-paragraph (2) of that paragraph there shall be inserted the following sub-paragraph—

'(2A) Where a magistrates' court deals with an offender under sub-paragraph (1)(d) above, it shall revoke the relevant order if it is still in force.'

(4) In sub-paragraph (1)(d) of paragraph 4 of that Schedule, the words 'revoke the order and' shall cease to have effect.

(5) After sub-paragraph (2) of that paragraph there shall be inserted the following sub-paragraph—

'(2A) Where the Crown Court deals with an offender under sub-paragraph (1)(d) above, it shall revoke the relevant order if it is still in force.'

(6) After paragraph 12(4) of that Schedule there shall be inserted the following sub-paragraphs—

'(5) Where—

(a) the court amends a probation order or community service order under this paragraph;
(b) a local authority is specified in the order in accordance with section 2(2)(b) or 14(4)(c) of the 1973 Act; and
(c) the change, or proposed change, of residence also is or would be a change of residence from the area of that authority to the area of another such authority,

the court shall further amend the order by substituting the other authority for the authority specified in the order.

(6) In sub-paragraph (5) above "local authority" has the meaning given by section 42 of the Crime and Disorder Act 1998, and references to the area of a local authority shall be construed in accordance with that section.'

(7) In paragraph 17(1) of that Schedule, the words from 'and the court shall not' to the end shall cease to have effect.

97 In paragraph 1(2) of Schedule 5 to the 1991 Act (Parole Board: supplementary provisions), for the words 'its functions under Part II of this Act' there shall be substituted the following paragraphs—

'(a) its functions under this Part in respect of long-term and short-term prisoners; and

(b) its functions under Chapter II of Part II of the Crime (Sentences) Act 1997 in respect of life prisoners within the meaning of that Chapter'.

Prisoners and Criminal Proceedings (Scotland) Act 1993 (c.9)

98 to 108 [*Applies to Scotland only.*]

Probation Service Act 1993 (c.47)

109 In subsection (1)(dd) of section 4 of the Probation Service Act 1993 (functions of probation committee), for the words 'a secure training order (within the meaning of section 1 of the Criminal Justice and Public Order Act 1994)' there shall be substituted the words 'a detention and training order (within the meaning of section 73 of the Crime and Disorder Act 1998)'.

110—(1) In subsection (1) of section 17 of that Act (probation committee expenditure), for the words '(5) and (5A)' there shall be substituted the words 'and (5)'.

(2) Subsection (5A) of that section shall cease to have effect.

Criminal Justice and Public Order Act 1994 (c.33)

111 In subsection (3) of section 12 of the 1994 Act (escort arrangements and officers), after the words 'secure training orders' there shall be inserted the words 'or detention and training orders'.

112 In paragraph 4 of Schedule 1 to the 1994 Act (escort arrangements: England and Wales), in the definition of 'the offender', after the words 'section 1 of this Act' there shall be inserted the words 'or detention and training under section 73 of the Crime and Disorder Act 1998'.

113—(1) In sub-paragraph (1) of paragraph 3 of Schedule 2 to the 1994 Act (certification of custody officers: England and Wales)—

(a) in paragraph (b), for the words 'person in charge' there shall be substituted the word 'monitor'; and

(b) in paragraph (c), for the words 'person in charge' there shall be substituted the word 'governor'.

(2) In sub-paragraph (2) of that paragraph, for the words 'or person in charge' there shall be substituted the words ', monitor or governor'.

Drug Trafficking Act 1994 (c.37)

114 In subsection (7) of section 2 of the Drug Trafficking Act 1994 (confiscation orders), paragraph (a) shall cease to have effect.

Proceeds of Crime (Scotland) Act 1995 (c.43)

115 to 116 [*Applies to Scotland only.*]

Criminal Procedure (Scotland) Act 1995 (c.46)

117 to **124** [*Applies to Scotland only.*]

Criminal Procedure and Investigations Act 1996 (c.25)

125 In subsection (2) of section 1 of the Criminal Procedure and Investigations Act 1996 (application of Part I of that Act)—

(a) after paragraph (c) there shall be inserted the following paragraph—

'(cc) a person is charged with an offence for which he is sent for trial under section 51 (no committal proceedings for indictable-only offences) of the Crime and Disorder Act 1998,'; and

(b) at the end there shall be inserted the words 'or

(f) a bill of indictment charging a person with an indictable offence is preferred under section 22B(3)(a) of the Prosecution of Offences Act 1985.'

126 In section 5 of that Act (compulsory disclosure by accused), after subsection (3) there shall be inserted the following subsection—

'(3A) Where this Part applies by virtue of section 1(2)(cc), this section does not apply unless—

(a) copies of the documents containing the evidence have been served on the accused under regulations made under paragraph 1 of Schedule 3 to the Crime and Disorder Act 1998; and

(b) a copy of the notice under subsection (7) of section 51 of that Act has been served on him under that subsection.'

127 In subsection (1) of section 13 of that Act (time limits: transitional)—

(a) after the words 'section 1(2)(b) or (c),' there shall be inserted the words—

'(cc) the accused is sent for trial under section 51 of the Crime and Disorder Act 1998 (where this Part applies by virtue of section 1(2)(cc)),'; and

(b) after the words 'section 1(2)(e)' there shall be inserted the words 'or (f)'.

128 In subsection (1)(a) of section 28 of that Act (introduction to Part III), after the words 'committed for trial' there shall be inserted the words ', or sent for trial under section 51 of the Crime and Disorder Act 1998,'.

129 In subsection (1) of section 39 of that Act (meaning of pre-trial hearing), after the words 'committed for trial for the offence concerned' there shall be inserted the words ', after the accused has been sent for trial for the offence under section 51 of the Crime and Disorder Act 1998,'.

Crime (Sentences) Act 1997 (c.43)

130—(1) In subsection (3) of section 28 of the 1997 Act (duty to release certain life prisoners), after paragraph (b) there shall be inserted the words 'and

(c) the provisions of this section as compared with those of sections 33(2) and 35(1) of the Criminal Justice Act 1991 ("the 1991 Act")'.

(2) In subsection (7) of that section, in paragraph (c), for the words from 'the time when' to the end there shall be substituted the words 'he has served one-half of that sentence'.

131—(1) In subsection (2) of section 31 of the 1997 Act (duration and conditions of licences), the words '(which shall include on his release conditions as to his supervision by a probation officer)' shall cease to have effect.

(2) After that subsection there shall be inserted the following subsection—

'(2A) The conditions so specified shall include on the prisoner's release conditions as to his supervision by—

(a) a probation officer appointed for or assigned to the petty sessions area within which the prisoner resides for the time being;
(b) where the prisoner is under the age of 22, a social worker of the social services department of the local authority within whose area the prisoner resides for the time being; or
(c) where the prisoner is under the age of 18, a member of a youth offending team established by that local authority under section 39 of the Crime and Disorder Act 1998.'

(3) In subsection (6) of that section, for the words 'section 24(2) above' there shall be substituted the words 'section 46(3) of the 1991 Act', and for the words 'the words in parentheses' there shall be substituted the words 'subsection (2A) above'.

132—(1) In subsection (1) of section 35 of the 1997 Act (fine defaulters: general), for the words 'the 1980 Act' there shall be substituted the words 'the Magistrates' Courts Act 1980 ("the 1980 Act")'.

(2) In subsection (5)(e) of that section, for the words 'paragraph 3(2)(a)' there shall be substituted the words 'sub-paragraphs (2)(a) and (2A) of paragraph 3'.

(3) In subsection (8) of that section—

(a) in paragraph (a), the words 'to revoke the order and deal with an offender for the offence in respect of which the order was made' shall cease to have effect; and
(b) in paragraph (b), for the words 'paragraph 3(2)(a)' there shall be substituted the words 'sub-paragraphs (2)(a) and (2A) of paragraph 3'.

133 In section 54 of the 1997 Act (general interpretation), subsection (2) shall cease to have effect.

134 Subsection (5)(b) of section 57 of the 1997 Act (short title, commencement and extent) shall have effect as if the reference to the Channel Islands included a reference to the Isle of Man.

135—(1) Schedule 1 to the 1997 Act (transfer of prisoners within the British Islands) shall be amended as follows.

(2) In sub-paragraph (3) of paragraph 6—

(a) after paragraph (a) there shall be inserted the following paragraph—

'(aa) in relation to a person who is supervised in pursuance of a detention and training order, being ordered to be detained for any failure to comply with requirements under section 76(6)(b) of the Crime and Disorder Act 1998;'; and

(b) in paragraph (b), for the words 'recalled to prison under the licence' there shall be substituted the words 'recalled or returned to prison'.

(3) In paragraph 8—

(a) in sub-paragraph (2), for the words from 'sections 10' to '27 of this Act' there shall be substituted the words 'sections 33 to 39, 41 to 46 and 65 of the 1991 Act, paragraphs 8, 10 to 13 and 19 of Schedule 12 to that Act and sections 75 to 77 of the Crime and Disorder Act 1998';

(b) in sub-paragraph (4), for the words from 'sections 16' to '27 of this Act' there shall be substituted the words 'sections 37 to 39, 43 to 46 and 65 of the 1991 Act, paragraphs 8, 10 to 13 and 19 of Schedule 12 to that Act and sections 76 and 77 of the Crime and Disorder Act 1998';

(c) in sub-paragraph (5), after the words 'Any provision of' there shall be inserted the words 'Part II of the 1991 Act or'; and

(d) after sub-paragraph (5) there shall be inserted the following sub-paragraphs—

'(6) Section 41 of the 1991 Act, as applied by sub-paragraph (2) or (4) above, shall have effect as if section 67 of the Criminal Justice Act 1967 (computation of sentences of imprisonment passed in England and Wales) or, as the case may require, section 9 of this Act extended to Scotland.

(7) Section 65(7)(b) of the 1991 Act, as applied by sub-paragraph (2) or (4) above, shall have effect as if the reference to a young offender institution were a reference to a young offenders institution.'

(4) In paragraph 9—

(a) in sub-paragraph (1), paragraph (a) and, in paragraph (b), the words 'to that and' shall cease to have effect;

(b) in sub-paragraph (2), for the words from 'sections 10' to '27 of this Act' there shall be substituted the words 'sections 33 to 46 and 65 of the 1991 Act, paragraphs 8, 10 to 13 and 19 of Schedule 12 to that Act and sections 75 to 77 of the Crime and Disorder Act 1998';

(c) in sub-paragraph (4), for the words from 'section 16' to '27 of this Act' there shall be substituted the words 'sections 37 to 40A, 43 to 46 and 65 of the 1991 Act, paragraphs 8, 10 to 13 and 19 of Schedule 12 to that Act and sections 76 and 77 of the Crime and Disorder Act 1998';

(d) sub-paragraph (5) shall cease to have effect;

(e) in sub-paragraph (6), after the words 'Any provision of' there shall be inserted the words 'Part II of the 1991 Act or'; and

(f) after sub-paragraph (6) there shall be inserted the following sub-paragraphs—

'(7) Section 41 of the 1991 Act, as applied by sub-paragraph (2) or (4) above, shall have effect as if section 67 of the Criminal Justice Act 1967 or, as the case may require, section 9 of this Act extended to Northern Ireland.

(8) Section 65(7)(b) of the 1991 Act, as applied by sub-paragraph (1), (2) or (4) above, shall have effect as if the reference to a young offender institution were a reference to a young offenders centre.'

(5) In paragraph 10—

(a) in sub-paragraph (2)(a)—

    (i)   for the words from "sections" to "1997 Act")' there shall be substituted the words 'sections 1, 1A, 3, 3A, 5, 6(1)(a), 7, 9, 11 to 13, 15 to 21, 26A and 27 of, and Schedules 2 and 6 to, the Prisoners and Criminal Proceedings (Scotland) Act 1993 ("the 1993 Act")'; and

    (ii) after the word '3,' there shall be inserted words '6(1)(b)(i) and (iii)';

  (b) in sub-paragraph (2)(b), for the words 'sub-paragraphs (3) and (4)' there shall be substituted the words 'sub-paragraph (3)';

  (c) sub-paragraph (4) shall cease to have effect;

  (d) in sub-paragraph (5)(a), for the words from 'sections 15' to '37 of the 1997 Act' there shall be substituted the words 'sections 1A, 2(4), 3A, 11 to 13, 15 to 21, 26A and 27 of, and Schedules 2 and 6 to, the 1993 Act';

  (e) for sub-paragraph (6)(b) there shall be substituted the following sub-paragraph—

    '(b) in the said sub-paragraph (2) the reference to section 6(1)(b)(i) of the 1993 Act is a reference to that provision so far as it relates to a person sentenced under section 205(3) of the Criminal Procedure (Scotland) Act 1995.'; and

  (f) for sub-paragraph (7) there shall be substituted the following sub-paragraph—

    '(7) Any provision of Part I of the 1993 Act which is applied by sub-paragraph (2) or (5) above shall have effect (as so applied) as if any reference to a chief social work officer were a reference to a chief social worker of a local authority social services department.'

(6) In paragraph 11—

  (a) in sub-paragraph (2)(a)—

    (i)   for the words from "sections" to "1997 Act")' there shall be substituted the words 'sections 1, 1A, 3, 3A, 5, 6(1)(a), 7, 9, 11 to 13, 15 to 21, 26A and 27 of, and Schedules 2 and 6 to, the 1993 Act'; and

    (ii) after the word '3,' there shall be inserted the words '6(1)(b)(i) and (iii),';

  (b) in sub-paragraph (4)(a), for the words from 'sections 15' to '37 of the 1997 Act' there shall be substituted the words 'sections 1A, 3A, 11 to 13, 15 to 21, 26A and 27 of, and Schedules 2 and 6 to, the 1993 Act';

  (c) in sub-paragraph (5), for the words 'Sub-paragraph (5)' there shall be substituted the words 'Sub-paragraph (6)'; and

  (d) in sub-paragraph (6), the words 'or Part III of the 1997 Act' shall cease to have effect and, in the Table, for the entry relating to the expression 'young offenders institution' there shall be substituted the following entry—

'Probation officer appointed for or assigned to such petty sessions area	Probation Officer appointed by the Probation Board for Northern Ireland'.

(7) In sub-paragraph (5) of paragraph 12, in the Table, the entry relating to the expression 'Prison rules' shall cease to have effect.

(8) In sub-paragraph (5) of paragraph 13, in the Table, the entry relating to the expression 'Prison rules' shall cease to have effect.

(9) In sub-paragraph (1)(a) of paragraph 17 (prisoners unlawfully at large), after the words 'section 49(1)' there shall be inserted the words 'and (5)'.

(10) In sub-paragraph (1) of paragraph 20, in the definition of 'supervision', after the word 'purpose' there shall be inserted the words 'or a detention and training order'.

136 In Schedule 2 to the 1997 Act (repatriation of prisoners to the British Islands), paragraphs 4 and 8 are hereby repealed.

137 In Schedule 4 to the 1997 Act (minor and consequential amendments), the following provisions are hereby repealed, namely—

 (a) in paragraph 6, sub-paragraph (1)(b);
 (b) paragraphs 9 and 11; and
 (c) in paragraph 12, sub-paragraph (4).

138—(1) In Schedule 5 to the 1997 Act (transitional provisions and savings), paragraphs 1 to 4 and 6 are hereby repealed and the following provisions shall cease to have effect, namely—

 (a) paragraph 5(2);
 (b) paragraphs 8, 9(1) and 10(1);
 (c) in paragraph 11, sub-paragraph (1), in sub-paragraph (2)(c), the words 'or Part III of the 1997 Act' and, in sub-paragraph (3), the words from the beginning to '1995; and'; and
 (d) in paragraph 12, sub-paragraph (1) and, in sub-paragraph (2)(c), the words 'or Part III of the 1997 Act'.

(2) In paragraph 11(2) of that Schedule—

 (a) in paragraph (a)—
  (i)   for the words from 'sections 15' to '1997 Act' there shall be substituted the words 'sections 1, 1A, 3, 3A, 5, 6(1)(a), 7, 9, 11 to 13, 15 to 21, 26A and 27 of, and Schedules 2 and 6 to, the Prisoners and Criminal Proceedings (Scotland) Act 1993 ("the 1993 Act")'; and
  (ii) for the words 'the 1989 Act' there shall be substituted the words 'the Prisons (Scotland) Act 1989 ('the 1989 Act'); and
 (b) in paragraph (b), for the words from 'sections 15' to '1997 Act' there shall be substituted the words 'sections 1A, 2(4), 3A, 11 to 13, 15 to 21, 26A and 27 of, and Schedules 2 and 6 to, the 1993 Act'.

(3) In paragraph 12(2) of that Schedule—

 (a) in paragraph (a)—
  (i)   for the words from 'sections 15' to '1997 Act' there shall be substituted the words 'sections 1, 1A, 3, 3A, 5, 6(1)(a), 7, 9, 11 to 13, 15 to 21, 26A and 27 of, and Schedules 2 and 6 to, the Prisoners and Criminal Proceedings (Scotland) Act ("the 1993 Act")'; and
  (ii) for the words 'the 1989 Act' there shall be substituted the words 'the Prisons (Scotland) Act 1989 ("the 1989 Act")'; and
 (b) in paragraph (b), for the words from 'sections 15' to '1997 Act' there shall be substituted the words 'sections 1A, 2(4), 3A, 11 to 13, 15 to 21, 26A and 27 of, and Schedules 2 and 6 to, the 1993 Act'.

139 In Schedule 6 to the 1997 Act (repeals), the entries relating to sections 33 to 51 and 65 of the 1991 Act are hereby repealed.

Crime and Punishment (Scotland) Act 1997 (c.48)

140 to **143** [*Applies to Scotland only.*]

Sex Offenders Act 1997 (c.51)

144 In subsection (1)(a) of section 4 of the Sex Offenders Act 1997 (young sex offenders), after the word 'under' there shall be inserted the words 'a detention and training order or'.

Section 120(1) SCHEDULE 9

TRANSITIONAL PROVISIONS AND SAVINGS

Presumption of incapacity

1 Nothing in section 34 of this Act shall apply in relation to anything done before the commencement of that section.

Effect of child's silence at trial

2 Nothing in section 35 of this Act shall apply where the offence was committed before the commencement of that section.

Sexual or violent offenders: extended sentences

3 Section 58 of this Act does not apply where the sexual or violent offence was committed before the commencement of that section.

Drug treatment and testing orders

4 Section 61 of this Act does not apply in relation to an offence committed before the commencement of that section.

Young offenders: cautions

5—(1) Any caution given to a child or young person before the commencement of section 65 of this Act shall be treated for the purposes of subsections (2) and (4) of that section as a reprimand.

(2) Any second or subsequent caution so given shall be treated for the purposes of paragraphs (a) and (b) of subsection (3) of that section as a warning.

Abolition of secure training orders

6 In relation to any time before the commencement of subsection (7) of section 73 of this Act, section 9A of the 1997 Act shall have effect as if after subsection (1) there were inserted the following subsection—

'(1A) Section 9 above applies to periods of detention which offenders are liable to serve under secure training orders as it applies to sentences of imprisonment.'

Sentencing guidelines

7—(1) Section 80 of this Act does not apply by virtue of subsection (1)(a) of that section in any case where the Court is seised of the appeal before the commencement of that section.

(2) In this paragraph 'the Court' and 'seised' have the same meanings as in that section.

Confiscation orders on committal for sentence

8 Section 83 of this Act does not apply where the offence was committed before the commencement of that section.

Football spectators: failure to comply with reporting duty

9 Section 84 of this Act does not apply where the offence was committed before the commencement of that section.

Power to release short-term prisoners on licence

10—(1) Section 99 of this Act does not apply in relation to a prisoner who, immediately before the commencement of that section, has served one or more days more than the requisite period for the term of his sentence.

(2) In this paragraph 'the requisite period' has the same meaning as in section 34A of the 1991 Act (which is inserted by section 99 of this Act).

Early release: two or more sentences

11—(1) Where the terms of two or more sentences passed before the commencement of section 101 of this Act have been treated, by virtue of section 51(2) of the 1991 Act, as a single term for the purposes of Part II of that Act, they shall continue to be so treated after that commencement.

(2) Subject to sub-paragraph (1) above, section 101 of this Act applies where one or more of the sentences concerned were passed after that commencement.

Recall to prison of short-term prisoners

12—(1) Sub-paragraphs (2) to (7) below have effect in relation to any prisoner whose sentence, or any part of whose sentence, was imposed for an offence committed before the commencement of section 103 of this Act.

(2) The following provisions of this Act do not apply, namely—

    (a) section 103;
    (b) paragraphs 83(1)(b) and 88(3)(a) of Schedule 8 to this Act and section 119 so far as relating to those paragraphs; and
    (c) section 120(2) and Schedule 10 so far as relating to the repeal of section 38 of the 1991 Act and the repeals in sections 37(1) and 45(4) of that Act.

(3) Section 33 of the 1991 Act has effect as if, in subsection (3)(b) (as amended by paragraph 80(1) of Schedule 8 to this Act), for the words 'section 39(1) or (2)' there were substituted the words 'section 38(2) or 39(1) or (2)'.

(4) Section 33A of the 1991 Act (as inserted by paragraph 81 of Schedule 8 to this Act) has effect as if—

    (a) in subsection (1), for the words 'section 38A(1) or 39(1) or (2)' there were substituted the words 'section 38(2) or 38A(1)'; and

(b) in subsection (3), for the words 'section 39(1) or (2)', in both places where they occur, there were substituted the words 'section 38(2)'.

(5) Section 34A of the 1991 Act (as inserted by section 99 of this Act) has effect as if, in subsection (2)(g), for the words 'section 39(1) or (2)' there were substituted the words 'section 38(2)'.

(6) Section 40A of the 1991 Act (as inserted by section 105 of this Act) has effect as if, in subsection (1), for the word '39' there were substituted the word '38'.

(7) Section 44 of the 1991 Act (as substituted by section 59 of this Act) has effect as if—

(a) in subsections (3) and (4), after the words 'subject to' there were inserted the words 'any suspension under section 38(2) above or, as the case may be,'; and
(b) in subsection (7), for the words 'sections 37(5) and 39(1) and (2)' there were substituted the words 'section 37(5), 38(2) and 39(1) and (2)'.

(8) Section 45 of the 1991 Act has effect as if, in subsection (3) (as amended by paragraph 88(2) of Schedule 8 to this Act), for the words 'section 39(1) or (2)' there were substituted the words 'section 38(2) or 39(1) or (2)'.

(9) For the purposes of this paragraph and paragraph 13 below, consecutive sentences, or sentences that are wholly or partly concurrent, shall be treated as parts of a single sentence.

Release on licence following recall to prison

13 Section 104 of this Act does not apply in relation to a prisoner whose sentence, or any part of whose sentence, was imposed for an offence committed before the commencement of that section.

Release on licence following return to prison

14—(1) Section 105 of this Act does not apply where the new offence was committed before the commencement of that section.

(2) In this paragraph 'the new offence' has the same meaning as in section 40 of the 1991 Act.

Remand time: two or more sentences

15—(1) Where the terms of two or more sentences passed before the commencement of paragraph 11 of Schedule 8 to this Act have been treated, by virtue of section 104(2) of the Criminal Justice Act 1967, as a single term for the purposes of section 67 of that Act, they shall continue to be so treated after that commencement.

(2) Subject to sub-paragraph (1) above, paragraph 11 of Schedule 8 to this Act applies where one or more of the sentences concerned were passed after that commencement.

SCHEDULE 10

REPEALS

Chapter	Short title	Extent of repeal
30 Geo 3 c.48.	Treason Act 1790.	The whole Act.
36 Geo 3 c.7.	Treason Act 1795.	The whole Act.
36 Geo 3 c.31.	Treason by Women Act (Ireland) 1796.	The whole Act.
57 Geo 3 c.6.	Treason Act 1817.	The whole Act.
11 & 12 Vict c.12.	Treason Felony Act 1848.	Section 2.
21 & 22 Geo 5 c.24.	Sentence of Death (Expectant Mothers) Act 1931.	The whole Act.
23 Geo 5 c.12.	Children and Young Persons Act 1933.	In section 47(2), the words from the beginning to 'court; and'. In Schedule 2, in paragraph 15(a), the word 'shall', in the second place where it occurs, and, in paragraph 17, the words 'or, if a metropolitan stipendiary magistrate, may sit alone'.
1945 c.15 (N.I.).	Criminal Justice Act (Northern Ireland) 1945.	Sections 32 and 33.
1967 c.80.	Criminal Justice Act 1967.	In section 56, subsections (3), (6) and (13). Section 67(5)(c).
1968 c.19.	Criminal Appeal Act 1968.	In section 10(2), the words '(other than a supervision order within the meaning of that Part)'.
1969 c.54.	Children and Young Persons Act 1969.	Section 12D. Section 13(2). In section 16, subsection (10) and, in subsection (11), the words 'seventeen or'. Section 23(14)(a). In section 34, in subsection (1), paragraph (a) and, in paragraph (c), the words 7(7), 7(8),'. Section 69(5). In Schedule 6, the entries relating to sections 55, 56(1) and 59(1) of the Children and Young Persons Act 1933.

Chapter	Short title	Extent of repeal
1972 c.71.	Criminal Justice Act 1972.	Section 49.
1973 c.62.	Powers of Criminal Courts Act 1973	In section 1, in subsections (8)(b) and (8A) the words '37 or'.
		Section 1B(10).
		In section 1C(1), paragraph (b) and the word 'and' immediately preceding it.
		In section 2(1), the words 'by a probation officer' and the words from 'For the purposes' to 'available evidence'.
		Section 11.
		Section 14(8).
		In section 31, in subsection (3A), the words 'Subject to subsections (3B) and (3C) below,', subsections (3B) and (3C), in subsection (4), the words '4 or' and, in subsection (6), the words 'about committal by a magistrates' court to the Crown Court'.
		Section 32(5).
		Section 42(2).
		In Schedule 1A, paragraph 6(7).
		In Schedule 5, paragraph 35.
1976 c.63.	Bail Act 1976.	In section 3(5), the words 'If it appears that he is unlikely to remain in Great Britain until the time appointed for him to surrender to custody'.
1980 c.43.	Magistrates' Courts Act 1980.	Section 37.
		In sections 38(2) and 38A(2), the words ', in accordance with section 56 of the Criminal Justice Act 1967,'.
		In section 108(2), the words 'a probation order or'.
		In section 125(4)(c), the word 'and' at the end of sub-paragraph (ii).
		In section 126, the word 'and' at the end of paragraph (c).
		In Schedule 7, paragraph 120(b).

Chapter	Short title	Extent of repeal
1982 c.48.	Criminal Justice Act 1982.	Section 1A(4A). Section 1B. In section 1C(2), the words 'but if he is under 18 at the time of the direction, only for a temporary purpose'. In section 3(1)(a), the words 'under section 1A above'. Section 18(7). In section 19, in subsection (3)(a), the words 'revoke it and' and, in subsection (5), the words 'revoke the attendance centre order and'. Section 66(3). In Schedule 14, paragraph 28.
1987 c.42.	Family Law Reform Act 1987.	Section 8(1). In Schedule 2, paragraph 26.
1988 c.33.	Criminal Justice Act 1988.	Section 69(2). In Schedule 15, paragraph 40.
1989 c.45.	Prisons (Scotland) Act 1989.	In section 39(7), the words from 'and the foregoing' to the end.
1991 c.53.	Criminal Justice Act 1991.	In section 6(4), the word 'and' immediately following paragraph (e). In section 31(1), in the definition of 'custodial sentence', in paragraph (b), the words 'or a secure training order under section 1 of the Criminal Justice and Public Order Act 1994'. Section 33(4). In section 37, in subsection (1), the words 'any suspension under section 38(2) below or, as the case may be,' and, in subsection (4), the words '(which shall include on his release conditions as to his supervision by a probation officer)'.

Chapter	Short title	Extent of repeal
		Section 38.
		In section 45(4), the words 'any suspension under section 38(2) below; or'.
		In section 61(1), paragraph (b) and the word 'or' immediately preceding that paragraph.
		Section 62.
		In Schedule 2, in paragraphs 3(1)(d) and 4(1)(d), the words 'revoke the order and' and, in paragraph 17(1), the words from 'and the court' to the end.
		In Schedule 11, paragraphs 10, 11 and 14.
		In Schedule 12, paragraph 17(3).
1993 c.9.	Prisoners and Criminal Proceedings (Scotland) Act 1993.	Section 11(3)(b) and (4). Section 14(2) and (3). Section 16(7)(b). In paragraph 6B(1) of Schedule 6, the word 'and' after head (a).
1993 c.47.	Probation Service Act 1993.	Section 17(5A).
1994 c.33.	Criminal Justice and Public Order Act 1994.	Sections 1 to 4. Section 20. In section 35, in subsection (1), the words 'who has attained the age of fourteen years' and subsection (6). Section 130(4). In Schedule 10, paragraph 42.
1994 c.37.	Drug Trafficking Act 1994.	Section 2(7)(a).
1995 c.46.	Criminal Procedure (Scotland) Act 1995.	Section 118(4A)(c)(iii). In section 175(5C), the words 'paragraph (a) of'. In section 209(1), the words 'not less than twelve months but'.
1997 c.43.	Crime (Sentences) Act 1997.	Section 1. Section 8.

Chapter	Short title	Extent of repeal
		Sections 10 to 27.
		In section 31(2), the words '(which shall include on his release conditions as to his supervision by a probation officer)'.
		In section 35, in subsection (5), paragraph (c) and the word 'and' at the end of paragraph (d), and in subsection (8), in paragraph (a), the words 'to revoke the order and deal with an offender for the offence in respect of which the order was made' and the word 'and' at the end of that paragraph.
		Section 43(4).
		Section 54(2).
		In Schedule 1, in paragraph 9(1), paragraph (a) and, in paragraph (b), the words 'to that and', paragraph 9(5), paragraph 10(4), in paragraph 11(6), the words 'or Part III of the 1997 Act', in paragraph 12(5), in the Table, the entry relating to the expression 'prison rules' and, in paragraph 13(5), in the Table, the entry relating to the expression 'prison rules'.
		In Schedule 2, paragraphs 4 and 8.
		In Schedule 4, paragraph 6(1)(b), paragraphs 9 and 11 and paragraph 12(4).

Chapter	Short title	Extent of repeal
		In Schedule 5, paragraphs 1 to 4, paragraph 5(2), paragraph 6, paragraph 8, paragraph 9(1), paragraph 10(1), in paragraph 11, sub-paragraph (1), in sub-paragraph (2)(c), the words 'or Part III of the 1997 Act' and, in sub-paragraph (3), the words from the beginning to '1995; and', and in paragraph 12, sub-paragraph (1) and, in sub-paragraph (2)(c), the words 'or Part III of the 1997 Act'. In Schedule 6, the entries relating to sections 33 to 51 and 65 of the Criminal Justice Act 1991.
1997 c.48.	Crime and Punishment (Scotland) Act 1997.	Section 4. Chapter I of Part III. In Schedule 1, paragraph 1, paragraph 9(7), paragraph 10(2)(a), paragraph 13(3), in paragraph 14, sub-paragraphs (2)(a), (3)(e), (4) to (7), (9), (10)(a), (11)(b), (12), (13) to (15) and (17), and paragraph 21(3). Schedule 2.

Chapter	Short title	Extent of repeal
		In Schedule 3, in the entry relating to the Prisons (Scotland) Act 1989, the words 'In section 39, subsection (7)', in the entry relating to the Prisoners and Criminal Proceedings (Scotland) Act 1993, the words relating to sections 1, 3(2), 5, 6(1), 7, 9, 12(3), 16, 17(1), 20, 24, 27(2), (3), (5) and (6) and Schedule 1, in the words relating to section 14, the words 'and, in subsection (4), the words "short-term", in the words relating to section 27(1), the words 'the definitions of "short term prisoner" and "long-term prisoner" and' and 'and the words from "but" to the end' and, in the entry relating to the Criminal Procedure (Scotland) Act 1995, the words relating to section 44.
1997 c.50.	Police Act 1997.	In section 94(4), the word 'and' immediately preceding paragraph (c).

APPENDIX II

Crime and Disorder Act 1998 (Commencement No 2 and Transitional Provisions) Order 1998

SI 1998/2327

In exercise of the powers conferred upon him by section 121 of the Crime and Disorder Act 1998, the Secretary of State hereby makes the following Order:

1—(1) This Order may be cited as the Crime and Disorder Act 1998 (Commencement No 2 and Transitional Provisions) Order 1998.

(2) In this Order, 'the 1998 Act' means the Crime and Disorder Act 1998.

2—(1) The following provisions of the 1998 Act shall, subject to articles 5 to 8 below, come into force on 30 September 1998—

(a)   sections 5 to 9 (crime and disorder strategies; parenting orders);

(b)   section 10(1) to (5) (appeals against parenting orders);

(c)   sections 11 and 12 (child safety orders);

(d)   section 13(1) and (2) (appeals against child safety orders);

(e)   sections 14 and 15 (local child curfew schemes);

(f)   sections 17 and 18 (duty to consider crime and disorder implications; interpretation);

(g)   sections 28 to 37 (racially aggravated offences; abolition of doli incapax; effect of child's evidence at trial; abolition of death penalty for treason and piracy; aim of youth justice system);

(h)   section 38(4) (definition of youth justice services);

(i)   sections 41 and 42 and Schedule 2 (Youth Justice Board), to the extent that they are not already in force;

(j)   section 43(1) (time limits);

(k)   sections 47 and 48 (powers of youth courts; and of stipendiary magistrates to sit alone);

(l)   section 50 (early administrative hearings);

(m)   section 52(6) (indictable-only offences) and Schedule 3, for the purpose of making both regulations under paragraph 1 of that Schedule and rules which make such provision as is mentioned in paragraph 2(7) of that Schedule;

(n)   sections 53 to 64 and Schedule 4 (criminal justice system; miscellaneous; dealing with sexual or violent offenders; and those dependent on drugs);

(o)   sections 67 to 70 and Schedule 5 (reparation orders; action plan orders);

(p)   section 71(5) (selection of supervisor for supervision order);

(q)   section 72 (breach of requirements in supervision orders);

(r)   sections 82 and 83 (increase in sentences for racial aggravation; power to make confiscation orders on committal for sentence);

(s)   section 85 (interpretation) [*and other provisions applying to Scotland only*];

(t)   section 97, for the purpose of making an order under section 23 of the 1969 Act (prescribed description of children and young persons who may be remanded or committed to local authority secure accommodation);

(u)   section 100(1), for the purpose of making orders under section 37A of the 1991 Act (responsible officers for offenders released on licence with curfew conditions);

(v)   sections 101 and 102 (early release; two or more sentences; restriction on consecutive sentences for released prisoners);

(w)   sections 104 to 107 and Schedule 7 (release on licence following recall or return to prison; pre-consolidation amendments; amendments to Chapter I of Part II of the 1997 Act) [*and other section applying to Scotland only*];

(x)   sections 113 and 115 (deputy authorising officer under Part III of Police Act 1997; disclosure of information) [*and other sections applying to Scotland only*];

(y)   section 119 and the provisions of Schedule 8 mentioned in paragraph (2) below (minor and consequential amendments) [*and other section applying to Northern Ireland only*];

(z)   section 120(1) and paragraphs 1 to 4, 6, 8, 11, 12(1) and (3) to (9), and 13 to 15 of Schedule 9 (transitional provisions and savings); and

(aa)   section 120(2) and Schedule 10 so far as they repeal the provisions mentioned in paragraph (3) below (repeals).

(2) The provisions of Schedule 8 referred to in paragraph (1)(y) above are –

(a)   paragraph 2;

(b)   paragraph 4;

(c)   paragraph 9(1)(b);

(d)   paragraph 10(a);

(e)   paragraph 11;

(f)   paragraph 13;

(g)   paragraph 16;

(h)   paragraph 18;

(i)   paragraphs 20 and 21;

(j)   paragraph 24;

(k)   paragraph 30;

(l)   paragraph 34(1) and (2);

(m)   paragraph 38

(n)   paragraph 40(1);

(o)   paragraphs 42 and 43;

(p)   paragraphs 46 and 47;

(q)   paragraph 50(5);

(r)   paragraphs 53 and 54;

(s)   paragraphs 56 to 60;

(t)   paragraph 62;

(u)   paragraphs 68 and 69 [*and others applying to Scotland only*];

(v)   paragraphs 74 and 75;

(w)   paragraph 77(b);

(x)   paragraph 78(a) and (c);

(y)   paragraphs 79 to 82;

(z)   paragraph 83(1)(a) and (4) to (6);

(aa)   paragraphs 84 and 85;

(bb)   paragraph 87;

(cc)   paragraph 88(1), (2) and (3)(b);

(dd)   paragraph 89;

(ee)   paragraphs 91 and 92;

(ff)   paragraphs 96(1) to (5) and (7);

(gg)   paragraph 97 [*and other applying to Scotland only*];

(hh)   [*applies to Scotland only*];

(ii)   paragraph 113;

(jj) and (kk) [*apply to Scotland only*];

(ll)   paragraph 130;

(mm) paragraph 131(3);

(nn)   paragraphs 132 to 134;

(oo)   paragraph 135(1), (2)(b) and (3) to (8); and

(pp)   paragraphs 136 to 140 [*and others applying to Scotland only*].

(3) The provisions which are referred to in paragraph (1)(aa) above are the entries in Schedule 10 to the 1998 Act relating to-

(a) the Treason Act 1790;

(b) the Treason Act 1795;

(c) [*applies to Northern Ireland only*];

(d) the Treason Act 1817;

(e) the Treason Felony Act 1848;

(f) the Sentence of Death (Expectant Mothers) Act 1931;

(g) the 1933 Act [Children and Young Persons Act 1933];

(h) [*applies to Northern Ireland only*];

(i) section 56(3) and (13) of the Criminal Justice Act 1967;

(j) the Criminal Appeal Act 1968;

(k) the 1969 Act [Children and Young Persons Act 1969];

(l) the Criminal Justice Act 1972;

(m) sections 1B, 1C, 11, 14, 31 and 32 of, and Schedules 1A and 5 to, the 1973 Act [Powers of Criminal Courts Act 1973], and the words from 'For the purposes' to 'available evidence' in section 2(1) of that Act;

(n) the Bail Act 1976;

(o) sections 38, 38A and 108 of, and Schedule 7 to, the 1980 Act [Magistrates' Courts Act 1980];

(p) sections 3, 18, 19 and 66 of, and Schedule 14 to, the 1982 Act [Criminal Justice Act 1982];

(q) the Family Law Reform Act 1987;

(r) the Criminal Justice Act 1988;

(s) [*applies to Scotland only*];

(t) sections 6, 33 and 37(4) of, and Schedules 2 and 11 to, the 1991 Act [Criminal Justice Act 1991];

(u) [*applies to Scotland only*];

(v) sections 35 and 130(4) of the 1994 Act [Criminal Justice and Public Order Act 1994];

(w) [*applies to Scotland only*];

(x) sections 1, 8, 10 to 27, 35, 43 and 54 of, and Schedules 1, 2, 4, 5 and 6 to, the 1997 Act [Crime (Sentences) Act 1997];

(y) [*applies to Scotland only*]; and

(z) the Police Act 1997.

3—(1) The following provisions of the 1998 Act shall, subject to article 9 below, come into force on 30 September 1998 in the areas specified in Schedule 1 to this Order—

(a) sections 38(1) to (3) and (5), 39 and 40 (youth justice services; youth offending teams; and youth justice plans);

(b) paragraphs 17, 19, 23, 26, 27, 32, 33, 34(3), 73, 76, 77(a), 94, 95, 96(6) and 131(1) and (2) of Schedule 8; and

(c) the entries in Schedule 10 relating to the words 'by a probation officer' in section 2(1) of the 1973 Act and to section 31(2) of the 1997 Act.

(2) Section 46 (date of first court appearance in bail cases) and, to the extent that. it is not already in force, section 49 (powers of magistrates' courts exercisable by single justice etc.) of the 1998 Act shall come into force on 30 September 1998 in the areas specified in Schedule 2 to this Order.

(3) Sections 65 and 66 of, and paragraphs 25 and 61 of Schedule 8 and paragraph 5 of Schedule 9 to, the 1998 Act (reprimands and warnings) shall come into force on 30 September 1998 for the purpose of warning a person under section 65 in any area specified in Schedule 3 to this Order.

4—(1) The following provisions of the 1998 Act shall come into force on 1 December 1998–

(a) sections 2 and 3 (sex offender orders);
(b) section 4 (appeals against orders), so far as relating to a sex offender order;
(c) section 16 (removal of truants to designated places etc.);
(d) [*applies to Scotland only*];
(e) to (h) [*apply to Scotland only*];
(i) sections 25 to 27 (powers to require removal of masks etc.; retention and disposal of things seized; power of arrest for failure to comply with requirement);
(j) [*applies to Scotland only*]; and
(k) paragraph 36 of Schedule 8.

(2) The following provisions of the 1998 Act shall come into force on 4 January 1999 for the purpose of sending any person for trial under section 51 of that Act from any area specified in Schedule 2 to this Order—

(a) section 51 and, to the extent that it is not already in force, section 52 (no committal proceedings for indictable-only offences etc.);
(b) Schedule 3, to the extent that it is not already in force;
(c) paragraphs 3, 5(1)(a) and (2), 8, 12, 28, 29, 37, 40(2), 44, 45, 48, 49, 52(2), 63 to 67, 93 and 125(a), 126, 127(a), 128 and 129 of Schedule 8; and
(d) in Schedule 10, the entries relating to sections 125 and 126 of the 1980 Act.

5—(1) In relation to any time before the commencement of sections 38 to 40 of the 1998 Act in an area not specified in Schedule 1 to this Order—

(a) subsection (4A) of section 37 of the 1991 Act (as inserted by paragraph 83(5) of Schedule 8 to the 1998 Act) shall have effect as if paragraph (b) of that subsection and the word 'or' immediately preceding it were omitted; and
(b) section 31(6) of the 1997 Act (as amended by paragraph 131(3) of Schedule 8 to the 1998 Act) shall have effect as if the words 'and for the words "the words in parentheses" there shall be substituted the words "subsection (2A) above" ' were omitted.

(2) In relation to any time before the commencement of sections 75 to 77 of the 1998 Act –

(a) section 55(1A)(d) of the 1933 Act (as inserted by paragraph 2 of Schedule 8 to the 1998 Act) shall have effect as if the words 'section 77(3)of the Crime and Disorder Act 1998 (breach of requirements of supervision under detention and training order) or' were omitted;

(b) section 31(1) of the 1991 Act (as amended by paragraph 78(a) and (c) of Schedule 8 to the 1998 Act) shall have effect as if the definition of a detention and training order were omitted;

(c) paragraphs 8(2) and 9(2) of Schedule 1 to the 1997 Act (as amended by paragraph 135(3)(a) and (4)(b) of Schedule 8 to the 1998 Act) shall have effect as if the words 'and sections 75 to 77 of the Crime and Disorder Act 1998' were omitted; and

(d) paragraphs 8(4) and 9(4) of Schedule 1 to the 1997 Act (as amended by paragraphs 135(3)(b) and (4)(c) of Schedule 8 to the 1998 Act) shall have effect as if the words 'and sections 76 and 77 of the Crime and Disorder Act 1998' were omitted.

(3) In relation to any time before the commencement of sections 99 and 100 of the 1998 Act –

(a) section 2(4)(b)(i) of the Repatriation of Prisoners Act 1984(b) (as substituted by paragraph 56 of Schedule 8 to the 1998 Act) shall have effect as if the words ', 33A(2), 34A(3)' were omitted;

(b) paragraph 2(4) of Schedule 2 to the Repatriation of Prisoners Act 1984 (as substituted by paragraphs 58(2) and 59(3) of Schedule 8 to the 1998 Act) shall have effect as if the words '33A(2), 34A(3),' were omitted;

(c) section 33A of the 1991 Act (as inserted by paragraph 81 of Schedule 8 to the 1998 Act) shall have effect as if—

   (i) in subsection (1)(b), the words '34A(3) or' were omitted;

   (ii) in subsection (1)(b), the words '38A(1) or' or as that subsection has effect by virtue of paragraph 12(4) of Schedule 9 to the 1998 Act, 'or 38A(1)' were omitted; and

   (iii) subsection (2) were omitted;

(d) section 37 of the 1991 Act (as amended by paragraph 83(1)(a) and (4) to (6) of Schedule 8 to the 1998 Act) shall have effect as if –

   (i) in subsection (1), the words ', (1B)' were omitted; and

   (ii) in subsection (4A), the words 'may in the case of a person released on licence under section 34A above whose sentence is for a term of less than twelve months, and' and 'in any other case,' were omitted; and

(e) section 45 of the 1991 Act (as amended by paragraph 88(1), (2) and (3)(b) of Schedule 8 to the 1998 Act) shall have effect as if, in subsection (1), the words '34A,' were omitted.

6—(1) Paragraphs 2(4) and 30(2) of Schedule 7 to the 1998 Act shall not apply in relation to an offender committed to (but not sentenced by) the Crown Court before 30 September 1998.

(2) Neither paragraph 17 of Schedule 7, nor the repeal of section 11 of the 1973 Act by Schedule 10, to the 1998 Act shall affect the operation of an order made under that section before 30 September 1998.

(3) Paragraphs 37(2) and (3)and 38(3) of Schedule 7 to the 1998 Act shall not apply in relation to attendance centre orders made before 30 September 1998.

(4) In paragraph 46 of Schedule 7 to the 1998 Act –

(a) sub-paragraph (1) shall not apply in relation to any proceedings under Schedule 2 to the 1991 Act which have been begun before 30 September 1998; and

(b) sub-paragraphs (2) and (8). shall not apply where the breach of the relevant order occurred before 30 September 1998.

7 [*Applies to Scotland only.*]

8—(1) Where a person is sentenced for a sexual offence within the meaning of Part I of the 1991 Act which was committed before 30 September 1998, the substitution of section 44 of that Act by section 59 of the 1998 Act shall not have effect and, in relation to such a person, neither paragraph 103 of Schedule 8, nor the repeal of section 14(2) and (3) of the 1993 Act by Schedule 10, to the 1998 Act shall have effect.

(2) [*Applies to Scotland only.*]

9 Nothing in article 3(1) above shall require the local authority in an area specified in Schedule 1 to this Order, acting under section 38(1) of the 1998 Act, to secure that the youth justice service mentioned in subsection (4)(c) of that section (support for children and young persons remanded or committed on bail while awaiting trial or sentence) is available in their area.

SCHEDULE 1   Article 3(1)

AREAS IN WHICH THE PROVISIONS OF THE 1998 ACT SET OUT IN ARTICLE 3(1) SHALL COME INTO FORCE ON 3O SEPTEMBER 1998

1. The counties of Bedfordshire, Devon and Hampshire.

2. The Isle of Wight.

3. The cities of Portsmouth, Sheffield, Southampton and Westminster.

4. The Royal borough of Kensington and Chelsea.

5. The London boroughs of Hammersmith and Fulham, and Lewisham.

6. The Metropolitan boroughs of St Helens and Wolverhampton.

7. The boroughs of Blackburn with Darwen, and Luton.

SCHEDULE 2   Articles 3(2) and 4(2)

AREAS IN WHICH THE PROVISIONS OF THE 1998 ACT SET OUT IN ARTICLES 3(2) AND 4(2) SHALL COME INTO FORCE ON 30 SEPTEMBER 1998 AND 4 JANUARY 1999, RESPECTIVELY

1. The petty sessions areas of Bromley; Croydon; and Sutton.

2. The petty sessional divisions of Aberconwy; Arfon; Blackburn, Darwen and Ribble Valley; Burnley and Pendle; Colwyn; Corby; Daventry; Dyffryn Clwyd; Eifionydd and Pwllheli; Gateshead; Kettering; Meirionnydd; Newcastle-under-Lyme and Pirehill North; Newcastle-upon-Tyne; Northampton; Rhuddlan; Staffordshire Moorlands; Stoke-on-Trent; Towcester; Wellingborough; and Ynys Mon/Anglesey.

SCHEDULE 3

Article 3(3)

AREAS IN WHICH THE PROVISIONS OF THE 1998 ACT SET OUT IN ARTICLE 3(3) SHALL COME INTO FORCE ON 30 SEPTEMBER 1998

1. The county of Hampshire.

2. The Isle of Wight.

3. The cities of Portsmouth, Sheffield, Southampton and Westminster.

4. The Royal borough of Kensington and Chelsea.

5. The London borough of Hammersmith and Fulham.

6. The Metropolitan borough of Wolverhampton.

7. The borough of Blackburn with Darwen.

INDEX

References are to paragraph numbers.